REAL WORLD

MICRO

EDITED BY ARMAĞAN GEZICI, ROB LARSON,

BRYAN SNYDER, CHRIS STURR,

AND THE *DOLLARS & SENSE* COLLECTIVE

REAL WORLD MICRO, TWENTY-NINTH EDITION

Published by:
Economic Affairs Bureau, Inc. d/b/a *Dollars & Sense*
Mailing address: P.O. Box 209, Portsmouth, NH 03802
617-447-2177; dollars@dollarsandsense.org.
For order information, contact Economic Affairs Bureau or visit: www.dollarsandsense.org.

Real World Micro is edited by the *Dollars & Sense* Collective, which also publishes *Dollars & Sense* magazine and the classroom books *Real World Macro, Current Economic Issues, The Coronavirus Crisis Reader, Real World Globalization, Labor and the Global Economy, Real World Latin America, Real World Labor, Real World Banking and Finance, The Wealth Inequality Reader, The Economics of the Environment, Introduction to Political Economy, Unlevel Playing Fields: Understanding Wage Inequality and Discrimination,* and *Our Economic Well-Being.*

The 2022 *Dollars & Sense* Collective:
Betsy Aron, Elizabeth H. Henderson, Tom Louie, John Miller, Jawied Nawabi, Zoe Sherman, Bryan Snyder, Abhilasha Srivastava, Chris Sturr, and Jeanne Winner.

Co-editors of this volume: Armağan Gezici, Rob Larson, Bryan Snyder, and Chris Sturr
Design and layout: Chris Sturr.
Cover image: Volkswagen's first new-generation electric car being built with Siemens automation technology, at the Volkswagen Zwickau-Mosel Plant, Zwickau, Germany, February 19, 2020. Credit: JuliaRoesler, via Wikimedia Commons (CC BY-SA 4.0 license).

Printed in U.S.A

CONTENTS

CHAPTER 5 • MARKET FAILURE I: MARKET POWER

CHAPTER 6 • MARKET FAILURE II: EXTERNALITIES

CHAPTER 7 • LABOR MARKETS

CHAPTER 8 • THE DISTRIBUTION OF INCOME AND WEALTH

CHAPTER 9 • TAXATION

CHAPTER 10 • TRADE AND DEVELOPMENT

INTRODUCTION

It sometimes seems that the United States has not one, but two economies. The first economy exists in economics textbooks and in the minds of many elected officials. It is a free-market economy, a system of promise and plenty, a cornucopia of consumer goods. In this economy, people are free and roughly equal, and each individual carefully looks after him- or herself, making uncoerced choices to advance his or her economic interests. Government is but an afterthought in this world, since almost everything that people need can be provided by the free market, itself guided by the reassuring "invisible hand."

The second economy is described in the writings of progressives, environmentalists, union supporters, and consumer advocates as well as honest business writers who recognize that real-world markets do not always conform to textbook models. This second economy features vast disparities of income, wealth, and power manifested in a system of class. It is an economy where employers have power over employees, where large firms have the power to shape markets, and where large corporate lobbies have the power to shape public policies. In this second economy, government sometimes adopts policies that ameliorate the abuses of capitalism and other times does just the opposite, but it is always an active and essential participant in economic life.

If you are reading this introduction, you are probably a student in an introductory college course in microeconomics. Your textbook will introduce you to the first economy, the harmonious world of free markets. *Real World Micro* will introduce you to the second.

Why "Real World" Micro?

A standard economics textbook is full of powerful concepts. It is also, by its nature, a limited window on the economy. What is taught in most introductory economics courses today is in fact just one strand of economic thought—neoclassical economics. Fifty years ago, many more strands were part of the introductory economics curriculum, and the contraction of the field has imposed limits on the study of economics that can confuse and frustrate students. This is particularly true in the study of microeconomics, which looks at markets for individual goods or services.

Real World Micro is designed as a supplement to a standard neoclassical textbook. Its articles provide vivid, real-world illustrations of economic concepts. But beyond that, our mission is to address two major sources of confusion in the study of economics at the introductory level.

The first source of confusion is the striking simplification of the world found in orthodox microeconomics. Standard textbooks describe stylized economic interactions

1

between idealized buyers and sellers that bear scant resemblance to the messy realities of the actual economic activity that we see around us. There is nothing wrong with simplifying. In fact, every social science must develop simplified models; precisely because reality is so complex, we must look at it a little bit at a time in order to understand it. Still, these simplifications mystify and misrepresent actual capitalist social relations and excise questions of race, gender, and class from the analysis.

Mainstream economic analysis calls to mind the story of the tipsy partygoer whose friend finds him on his hands and knees under a streetlight. "What are you doing?" asks the friend. "I dropped my car keys across the street, and I'm looking for them," the man replies. "But if you lost them across the street, how come you're looking over here?" "Well, the light's better here." In the interest of greater clarity, economics often imposes similar limits on its areas of inquiry.

As the title *Real World Micro* implies, one of our goals is to confront mainstream microeconomic theory with a more complex reality to direct attention to the areas not illuminated by the streetlight, and particularly to examine how inequality, power, and environmental imbalance change the picture. The idea is not to prove the standard theory "wrong," but to challenge you to think about where the theory is more and less useful, and why markets may not operate as expected.

This focus on real-world counterpoints to mainstream economic theory connects to the second issue we aim to clarify. Most economics texts uncritically present key assumptions and propositions that form the core of standard economic theory. They offer much less exploration of a set of related questions: What are alternative propositions about the economy? Under what circumstances will these alternatives more accurately describe the economy? What differences do such propositions make? Our approach is not to spell out an alternative theory in detail, but to raise questions and present real-life examples that bring these questions to life. For example, textbooks carefully lay out "consumer sovereignty," the notion that consumers' wishes ultimately determine what the economy will produce. But can we reconcile consumer sovereignty with an economy where one of the main products in industries such as soft drinks, cars, and music is consumer desire itself? We think it is valuable to see ideas like consumer sovereignty as debatable propositions and that requires hearing other views in the debate.

In short, our goal in this book is to use real-world examples from today's economy to raise questions, stimulate debate, and dare you to fthink critically about the models in your textbook.

Here is a quick overview:

Chapter 1, Perspectives on Microeconomic Theory, starts off the volume by taking a hard look at the strengths and weaknesses of actual markets, with special attention to weaknesses that standard textbooks tend to underemphasize.

Chapter 2, Supply and Demand, presents real-world examples of supply and demand in action. *Dollars & Sense* authors question the conventional wisdom on topics such as price volatility, affordability of essential goods like housing, size of global market for drugs, volatility in cryptocurrency markets, and price regulations like the minimum wage and rent control.

Chapter 3, Consumers, raises provocative questions about utility theory and individual consumer choice. What happens when marketers shape buyers' tastes? What happens when important information is hidden from consumers or choices are far too limited? How can consumer decisions include broader considerations like environmental sustainability or labor conditions? What roles should government play in consumer protection?

Chapter 4, Firms, Production, and Profit Maximization, illustrates how business strategies to maximize profits may come at the expense of the social good, and challenges students to think about different ways of organizing firms. The chapter considers issues such as how different types of tech companies regard "net neutrality," how managers at Boeing profits to increase stock price instead of investments, and the relation between the profit motive and essential goods like healthcare.

Chapter 5, Market Failure I: Market Power, explores market power and monopoly, just one example of the unequal power relationships that pervade our economic system. The chapter critiques market power in such industries as big tech, retail, and shipping, but also questions whether small business prevalence would be an improvement.

Chapter 6, Market Failure II: Externalities, addresses cases where processes of production, exchange, and consumption affect not only the parties to those transactions, but also third parties (especially negatively). It considers how public policy should address cases where such spillover effects create a divergence between private and social costs and benefits.

Chapter 7, Labor Markets, examines the ways in which labor-market outcomes can be affected by unionization, globalization, and a host of other factors largely left out of the standard supply-and-demand models. Among the issues discussed are the reasons for union decline, the labor shortage in the wake of the Covid-19 economic shock, and restrictions on freedom of speech in the workplace.

Chapter 8, The Distribution of Income and Wealth, discusses the causes and consequences of inequality, countering the mainstream view that inequality is good for growth. The chapter examines the contours of inequality, with particular attention to race and gender. It questions conventional views attributing rising inequality to technological change and globalization, and considers the impact of a changing balance of power between workers and employers. And it deals with issues of wealth and poverty, both domestic and global.

Chapter 9, Taxation, explores issues of incomes, wealth, and taxation, including who actually pays taxes and at what rates. It also explores whether changes in taxes lead to changes in economic behavior and outcomes. This proposition is explored in the areas of taxes on high-income individuals and their effects on savings and investment, as well as taxes on financial transactions and effects on speculative activity. Finally, it discusses the idea of taxing unrealized capital gains.

Chapter 10, Trade and Development, covers key issues in trade policy and the world economy. The chapter's articles explain the notion of "comparative advantage," question the value of free trade and foreign investment for development, address the impacts of globalization on workers (in both high-income and low-income countries), and address whether U.S. prosperity *depends* on exploitation of developing countries. ❑

Chapter 1

PERPECTIVES ON MICROECONOMIC THEORY

INTRODUCTION

Economics is all about tradeoffs. The concept of "opportunity cost" reminds us that in order to make a purchase, or even to make use of a resource that you control (such as your time), you must give up other possible purchases or other possible uses of that resource. Markets broaden the range of possible tradeoffs by facilitating exchange between people who do not know each other, and in many cases never meet at all. Think of buying a pair of athletic shoes in Atlanta from a company based in Los Angeles that manufactures shoes in Malaysia and has stockholders all over the world. As the idea of gains from trade suggests, markets allow many exchanges that make both parties better off.

But markets have severe limitations as well. The economic crisis that began in 2008 has made those limitations all too clear. Even lifelong free-marketeers such as former Federal Reserve Chair Alan Greenspan have been forced to question their belief in the "invisible hand."

In this chapter's first article, "The Unreal Basis of Neoclassical Economics," members of the steering committee of the Union for Radical Political Economics take issue with the "Ten Principles of Economics" set out in Gregory Mankiw's best-selling textbook, which the authors say "should more accurately be titled 'Ten Principles of Unrealistic Neoclassical Theory.'" The authors conclude: "It is hard to imagine a less useful set of ideas to guide modern societies in designing a good economic system. Unfortunately, almost all other mainstream principles of economics textbooks parrot these same principles." This textbook offers alternatives to this perspective.

Next, economist Tim Koechlin describes his experience when he took Economics 100, encountering an orthodoxy where certain subjects, like poverty and power, were treated with silence. Worse, his story (in Article 1.2) includes teachers who resist questioning and condescend to critics, including students, which Koechlin suggests is sadly typical of the field.

Markets and price determination, in neoclassical economics, have been idealized into elegant, utility-maximizing perfection. Chris Tilly, in "Shaking the Invisible Hand" (Article 1.3), uncovers the curious assumptions necessary to allow for the market mechanism to be the most efficient allocator of scarce resources. He provides us with eight "Tilly Assumptions" underlying perfectly functioning markets. If any of these assumptions is violated, then there is a possibility of "market failure," or less-than-optimal economic results.

In "Pursuing Profits—Or Power?" (Article 1.4), James K. Boyce questions the assumption that the firm seeks to maximize profits alone. In Boyce's view, a great deal of business behavior (especially political behavior) suggests that corporate decision-makers often put the pursuit of power above profits.

Alejandro Reuss provides us with a clear discussion of the idealized neoclassical view of exchange, with a particular focus on labor markets, in "Freedom, Equity, and Efficiency" (Article 1.5). Ideal neoclassical markets offer the promise of freedom of choice, equity (fairness), and efficiency, but often fail to deliver on all three counts. Reuss walks us through these neoclassical standards and contrasts them to the not-so-rosy reality of unrestrained labor-market competition.

In "Sharing the Wealth of the Commons" (Article 1.6), Peter Barnes focuses our attention on the oft-ignored forms of wealth that we do not own privately, but are held in various "commons." He challenges the way that conventional economists view the environment and other goods that are shared by many people.

The chapter's final article, an interview with economist Juliet Schor (Article 1.7), explores the causes behind U.S. consumerism. Schor looks beyond some of the "usual suspects"—like advertising—by linking the rise of consumerism to labor-market forces that have prevented the reduction of work time. She argues that future changes in U.S. consumption behavior, and therefore long-term environmental sustainability, depend on reducing hours of work.

Discussion Questions

1. (General) What things should not be for sale? Beyond everyday goods and services, think about human bodies, votes, small countries, and other things that might be bought and sold. How do you draw the line between what should be bought and sold and what should not?

2. (General) Several articles in this chapter list core assumptions or ideas that economists use to organize their thinking about markets. Many of these assumptions, besides simplifying markets so they can be easily modeled, also remove unsavory aspects of our society (for example, assuming no "externalities" such as pollution). Can models that sanitize a system be used to really understand it?

3. (Article 1.1) The authors point to flaws in the various key ideas that prominent economists (like Gregory Mankiw) consider to be important in economic theorizing. Of the assumptions they list, which ones seem most reasonable and unreasonable to you? Which objections do you think succeed and which do not?

4. (Article 1.2) Tim Koechlin describes his experience in Econ 100, which is considered more rigorous and scientific than other social studies. Does his story suggest an academic field that is scientific, or one that resists questioning?

5. (Article 1.3) Write out the eight "Tilly Assumptions" and corresponding realities using Tilly's exact terms for the assumptions. Are these assumptions reasonable?

6. (Article 1.3) For each of the eight "Tilly Assumptions," explain how the market mechanism would fail if the assumption were violated.

7. (Article 1.4) Boyce argues that firms frequently put power before profits. If greater power goes hand in hand with higher profits, how can we tell what aim firms are actually pursuing?

8. (Article 1.5) According to neoclassical theory, how do markets deliver "efficient" results if all "barriers" to exchange are removed? In what sense are these results "efficient"?

9. (Article 1.5) How is the word "freedom" defined by neoclassical economists? What freedoms do they argue workers lose under regulated labor markets? How does this compare to your view of what kinds of freedoms are valuable?

10. (Article 1.5) Does the unfettered operation of the market mechanism deliver "equity" to society? In your view, what would fair labor-market processes or outcomes look like?

11. (Article 1.6) Barnes says that we take for granted not only an enormous number of resources, including the natural environment, but also the laws and institutions that make economic activity possible. Is his point the same as saying that there are market failures, such as pollution externalities, that prevent markets from taking into account the full value of the environment?

12. (Article 1.7) Schor argues that, far from being the consequence of human beings' inherently insatiable wants, consumerism is the result of various social and institutional factors. What does she see as the key factors pushing people to consume more and more? What are the main reasons, in her view, that consumer behavior in the United States has differed from that in other countries?

Article 1.1

THE UNREAL BASIS OF NEOCLASSICAL ECONOMICS

**BY AL CAMPBELL, ANN DAVIS, DAVID FIELDS,
PADDY QUICK, JARED RAGUSETT, AND GEOFFREY SCHNEIDER**
December, 2018, Annual Review of Political Economy

Ten years after the financial crisis, we still find mainstream economists engaging in overly simplistic analysis that does not accurately capture the dynamics of the real world. People studying economics need to know that the principles of mainstream economics are hopelessly unrealistic. In this short article, we demonstrate that the 10 principles of economics in Gregory Mankiw's best-selling textbook are divorced from reality and reflect an extreme and unwarranted bias towards unregulated markets. Mankiw's "Ten Principles of Economics" should more accurately be titled "Ten Principles of Unrealistic Neoclassical Theory."

Mankiw's Principle #1: People Face Tradeoffs/ There is no such thing as a free lunch.

Mankiw ignores the historical determination of the distribution of resources and the crucial distinction between those whose income comes almost entirely from the performance of labor and those whose income comes from their ownership of capital. As a result he is unable to recognize the political power that results from the concentration of wealth in the capitalist class, and to analyze the distributional impact of decisions in which those who gain are often significantly different from those who lose. In addition, history is full of accounts of forcible appropriation of resources that appeared to be "free" to those who acquired them.

Mankiw's Principle #2: The Cost of Something Is What You Give Up to Get It/Opportunity Cost

Insofar as individuals are able to make decisions, their choices can be described as "giving up" one opportunity in order to take up another. This tells us nothing about the determination of the choices that are available to them. The "choice" of a worker as to whether to take on a dangerous job or face eviction from a home requires a very different analysis than one suitable for a discussion of the choice between apples and oranges. On a different level, an analysis of the "trade-off" between income now and increased income in the future requires an understanding of ecological limits to the growth of material production.

Mankiw's Principle #3: Rational People Think at the Margin.

Neither consumers nor producers, nor humans in many other social roles, generally act on the margin. The assertion of marginal analysis that decisions must be such as to equate marginal benefit with marginal cost is simply a restatement of the first derivative condition resulting from maximization subject to a constraint, rather than a reflection of real human choice. Mainstream theory then defines behavior according to this mathematical construction even though it does not govern actual choice in the real world. But more important is the presumption that all decision-making is guided by the well-being of isolated individuals, and thus that "rationality" consists of behavior that maximizes the benefit of the individual decision-maker. This dismisses the fact that people are social animals whose decision-making recognizes the interaction between individuals, and it ignores how in the real world people make decisions considering their whole situation under possible alternatives, material restraints, imperfect information, their cognitive abilities, the existing power structures, and culture.

Mankiw's Principle #4: People Respond to Incentives.

This is tautological. Furthermore, models based on monetary incentives by selfish, isolated individuals and firms in perfectly competitive markets are unrealistic and ignore crucial real-world issues. Monetary incentives are not all that matters. In the real world, people make many decisions on the basis of their evaluation of the resulting well-being of many people beyond themselves, or on social and cultural norms.

Mankiw's Principle #5: Trade Can Make Everyone Better Off.

Trade can increase total production, but trade has distributional impacts, with winners and losers. Trade in modern capitalism tends to foster inequality while undermining wages and working conditions for many laborers. This principle promotes unregulated trade, but unregulated trade has not proven to be the best route to economic development, nor is it good for all people. In the real world, infant industries, immiserating growth, terms of trade shocks, and increasing inequality render this principle useless as a policy guide.

Mankiw's Principle #6: Markets Are Usually a Good Way to Organize Economic Activity.

As there are no measurable units by which one can classify all specific economic activities in the real world as "good" or not, principle #6 is nothing more than a neoclassical ideological declaration of faith. Markets are human creations that operate differently in various economic systems, and the various existing and potential economic systems themselves are human creations. The first real question then is if under an existing system private capitalist markets driven by the profit motive do better than possible alternative human creations for providing the good or service, potentially driven directly by the desire to meet specific human needs. Important examples providing evidence of the inferior performance (efficiency and effectivity) of private capitalist market-driven systems are well run social security systems and single-payer health care systems. Avoiding the error of accepting the system as given, a deeper question would be if under some different economic system, which was not built to favor capitalist accumulation, alternatives could outperform profit-driven markets operating in capitalist systems.

Mankiw's Principle #7: Governments Can Sometimes Improve Market Outcomes.

Behind this assertion is the idea that markets are natural and could run without any government intervention, and that such natural markets tend to be efficient but sometimes are not quite optimal. In those cases the efficiency of markets could be improved by government tweaks. To the contrary, in the real world, all markets are created by governments, which both establish the rules of the game and enforce them, and thereby determine market outcomes. If the government passes laws requiring that food be safe, that changes the market for food, and yields different market outcomes than if those laws did not exist. With this understanding, principle #7 is reduced to the not very profound statement that because governments create markets, they have the ability to create them with better or worse outcomes. Further, the issue always ignored by neoclassical economics of social divisions is particularly important for considering "better market outcomes": better for whom? Market rules are shaped by power structures to benefit some classes and other social groups more than others (for example capitalists at the expense of workers, First World countries at the expense of Third World countries, etc.).

Mankiw's Principle #8: A Country's Standard of Living Depends on Its Ability to Produce Goods and Services.

Higher GDP per capita does not necessarily result in a higher material standard of living for all people within, as well as between, countries. Furthermore, neoclassical economics operates with a definition of "standard of living" as the amount of goods and services consumed, so this principle reduces to the not quite tautological, but not very insightful, claim that the amount of goods and services consumed in a country depends on its ability to produce them. In the real world, what people are concerned with is their quality of life, which includes social respect, power to act on one's desires, conditions of work (and not just pay), social relations, and much more. Neoclassical economics does not address the extension of principle #8 to what people in the real world are actually concerned with, their quality of life, for which the goods and services produced are just one among many determinants.

Mankiw's Principle #9: Prices Rise When the Government Prints Too Much Money.

Since the neoclassical definition of "too much money" is the amount that makes prices rise, this is a tautology. In the real world, the relationship between prices and the money supply is complex: expanding money might cause a jump in prices or it might cause no price increases at all, depending on many other things in the economy. The applied policy transformation of this into the incorrect claim that "prices rise when the government prints more money" is an ideological artifice, used today to justify austerity policies and keeping wages low.

Mankiw's Principle #10: Society Faces a Short-Run Tradeoff between Inflation & Unemployment.

The relationship between inflation and unemployment is complex and does not follow a systematic pattern. By the 1970s data from the real world had caused textbooks to go from Phillips Curves to Shifting Phillips Curves to abandoning them entirely. In view of that experience, principle #10 of a short-term trade-off between inflation and unemployment has become a neoclassical ideological justification for challenging those who advocate policies that would reduce the rate of unemployment, by fostering fears of inflation that may never materialize.

In conclusion, Mankiw's so-called "Ten Principles of Economics" ignore crucial realities of the economic world. In particular, Mankiw excludes power imbalances, inequality, social forces, development experiences, the realities of market behaviors, laws and outcomes, realistic measures of quality of life, and recent macroeconomic data from his principles. It is hard to imagine a less useful set of ideas to guide modern societies in designing a good economic system. Unfortunately, almost all other mainstream principles of economics textbooks parrot these same principles. Students of economics will have to look elsewhere for useful analysis of the economy and how to build a democratic economy and society that works for all. ❏

Source: Gregory Mankiw, *Principles of Economics*, 7th Edition. (Cengage, 2015).

Article 1.2

WHAT I LEARNED (AND DIDN'T LEARN) IN ECON 100

BY TIM KOECHLIN
July/August 2019

In my first semester in college I enrolled in Economics 100: "Economic Principles." I was interested in understanding poverty, inequality, and other forms of injustice. Why did some of us live in abundance, while most others had so little? Why did my neighbors and I, in Montclair, N.J., enjoy what seemed like effortless prosperity while residents of Newark, N.J.—just a few miles from my home—endured poverty, unemployment, lousy schools, and profoundly limited opportunities?

When I described my interests to a family friend, she said: "Who is rich, who is poor, and why? That's economics." So I took an economics course.

Econ 100 was a large class, with 100 or more students. We met in a small auditorium. Professor Richard von Bargan (not his real name), the chair of the economics department, was a portly white guy in in his 50s. He wore a checkered sport coat, a loud tie, and longish sideburns. (In the mid-1970s, for a brief moment, "conservative" characters were invited to take on some slightly wild affectations—sideburns, longish hair, striped and/or colorful dress shirts with oversized collars, and wide, colorful ties. Professor von Bargan brought a few flashes of "the modern look" to class, but no one was fooled.) During his lectures, Professor von Bargan paced back and forth, from one end of the black board to the other, with a piece of chalk in his right hand. He would occasionally pause for a moment and look out at us to emphasize a point. In profile, he looked a little bit like Alfred Hitchcock.

I was struck by two things on the first day of class, and throughout the semester. First, the premise of Professor von Bargan's course was that capitalism—which he called the "market system"—was magnificent. The focus of the course was to explain the logic and mechanisms by which this system achieved its magic; how it served "consumers" and "households." In the parlance of economics—and Professor von Bargan—the unfettered market reliably delivered an economy that was "optimal." This, to say the least, was baffling to me. I'd assumed that the failure of American capitalism was self-evident. To the contrary, Professor von Bargan's starting point was that it was a smashing success.

Second, I was struck by Professor von Bargan's smugness. He regularly reported that most people (i.e., non-economists) simply "don't seem to get it." His lectures were full of stories about the abundant misunderstandings and misconceptions that "most people" had about the economy. The stories typically started with a foolish pronouncement by a colleague (not an economist), a columnist, or someone he had encountered at a cocktail party. After laying out the economic misperception of the day, Professor von Bargan would pause for dramatic effect and then, the reveal: "What my colleague (or neighbor) fails to understand is … ." Each story was delivered with a tone of mild exasperation. "They" didn't get it, and they didn't seem to get that they didn't get it. Rent control? Bad for tenants. The minimum wage? Bad for workers. Protecting workers from import competition? It's inefficient—and, in fact, "protectionism" makes the country and its workers poorer. Welfare and other anti-poverty programs? They provide the wrong incentives and, ultimately, undermine the well-being of the poor. Isn't the market system racist? No! Actually, the market is color blind, and it punishes racist employers! Why are the "world's poor" so poor? It's not colonialism, that's for sure. To the contrary, "we" have done our best to help. They ought to emulate us, rather than blame us for their backward economic policies, and their sadly stagnant economies. But, alas, they fail to understand.

Forty years later, I remain perplexed by the project of the discipline of economics. I understand Professor von Bargan's story much better now, and I learned some useful things in that class—things that still remain fundamental to my understanding of the economy. But the piece of information that made the biggest impression was the message that the professor hammered home on day one—the "Market System" is undoubtedly the best that we can do. Economic "failures" generally come from the failure of policymakers to recognize this truth. And it turns out that lots of economists—not just Professor von Bargan—are smug and, by default, exasperated by the ignorance and imprecision of non-economists. For goodness sake, leave policy to the experts. (More than this—leave policy of all kinds to the economists! An outbreak of violence? Call a game theorist! Failing schools? Rising crime rates? Get the incentives right! Economists have a powerful impulse to colonize other disciplines.) And, if you want to get economics, don't rely on your instincts. Your instincts are often wrong and so, too, are the instincts of your political science professors. Take economics and learn how to actually think.

I also learned a lot of other stuff—some of it nonsense, and some of it vaguely useful, but far from essential. But more importantly, lots of stuff didn't come up. Lots of important questions were dismissed, obscured, and/or delegitimized: Aren't unrestrained multinational corporations dangerous? Doesn't trade hurt workers? Isn't colonialism foundational to 20th-century capitalism, or, at least, worth a moment's attention? Isn't capitalism rooted in exploitation? Isn't the wealth of the world's rich countries somehow related to the poverty of poor countries? Isn't capitalism racist? Sexist? Isn't foreign policy influenced by the agenda of capital? Aren't people sometimes "irrational"? Aren't people unselfish sometimes? Why do we evaluate our society by its "efficiency"—rather than equality, sustainability, the quality of our relationships and/or communities, or fun? Is more really better? In what ways might the pursuit of profit, efficiency, and/or economic growth undermine, contradict, and erase projects, values, and concerns that might make us, and our lives, better? Doesn't coming of age and living in a system that rewards selfishness constrain, contort, and diminish what we can be? These and other potentially deep questions were dismissed—or, again, they never came up. If you got it—if you thought like an economist—you'd get that we didn't need to address that question. The list of important questions from which economics averts our eyes is very long. And thus lots of talented, creative thinkers—interested in social justice, fairness, racial, gender, and environmental inequality, and the ways in which work might make our lives meaningful (or not)—were turned off, and swore they'd never take another economics class. No wonder.

Professor von Bargan didn't get most of this. He didn't think about the silences and evasions and erasures in economics. He couldn't see them. And he treated questions that began to get at the profound limits of economics as if they were evidence of ignorance or "intellectual laziness." When he was asked: "Are people simply selfish? Is that really a comprehensive theory of human behavior?" He could have said: "Interesting question. Maybe not! Probably not. But for now, this assumption makes it easier to grasp the mechanics of our model." But instead he rolled his eyes and said, "What you fail to understand ... ." A smug, exasperated dismissal.

A third message—which I got only a bit later—is this: Economics is serious. Economics is a science. Other social sciences are soft and unscientific—armchair theorizing. Economics is about modeling. It's about data. It's about math. Indeed, if there is no math, it isn't really economics. So, if you want a seat at the table, calculus, geometry, linear algebra, and econometrics are prerequisites. Arguments that are not "rigorous" (that is, not expressed as a mathematical model) are dismissed as "hand-waving," or—worse, perhaps—sociology.

My students often tell me that they haven't taken economics because they aren't good at math. Given the way economics is done—the way it is taught—I'm not surprised. But this is a ridiculous and appalling state of affairs—and a loss. Lots of students are interested in a critical understanding of inequality, poverty, trade, globalization, racial inequality, and environmental degradation. But, apparently, nothing meaningful can be said about any of these matters until you do some math. Economics can't be taught without problem sets.

Professor von Bargan was an extreme character, perhaps. And mainstream economics has changed in some important (and encouraging) ways over the 40 years since I took Econ 100. But I am sure that many (too many) current intro to economics students can relate to my experience of Econ 100.

There is, of course, a long, rich, and magnificent history of alternatives to this story. And many scholars, teachers, and students of economics have criticized and pushed back against this mainstream narrative and curriculum. Indeed, *Dollars & Sense*—to cite just one of many important examples—has provided a powerful and effective counter-narrative to the hegemonic mainstream story for years, an effort that has validated the legitimate skepticism of countless students. But, alas, 40 years after I took Econ 100, the narrative presented in mainstream textbooks is not very different from the story I heard from Professor von Bargan. It celebrates the "efficiency" of the "market system," its focus is absurdly narrow, and its smug dismissal of important questions continues.

As a consequence, too many students leave Econ 100 believing that capitalism is demonstrably the best we can hope for. Many potentially great multidisciplinary economists flee the field, or never consider it, and economics disproportionately attracts (and is reproduced by) people who like to model things, and don't find the deafening silences in the discipline all that problematic. And too many intro to economics students don't hear lots of important stories about economic democracy, the limits of growth, the legacy of colonialism, or the relationships among capitalism, racism, and sexism. And when these silences are noted by students, too often, they aren't taken seriously by their Econ 100 professors. Those silences speak very loudly. ❑

Article 1.3

SHAKING THE INVISIBLE HAND
The Uncertain Foundations of Free-Market Economics

BY CHRIS TILLY
November 1989; updated March 2011

> It is not from the benevolence of the butcher, the brewer or the baker that we
> expect our dinner, but from their regard to their own interest ... [No individ-
> ual] intends to promote the public interest ... [rather, he is] led by an invisible
> hand to promote an end which was no part of his intention.
>
> *—Adam Smith,* The Wealth of Nations, *1776*

Seen the Invisible Hand lately? It's all around us these days, propping up conservative arguments in favor of free trade, deregulation, and tax-cutting.

Today's advocates for "free," competitive markets echo Adam Smith's claim
that unfettered markets translate the selfish pursuit of individual gain into the greatest benefit for all. They trumpet the superiority of capitalist free enterprise over
socialist efforts to supplant the market with a planned economy, and even decry liberal attempts to moderate the market. Anything short of competitive markets, they
proclaim, yields economic inefficiency, making society worse off.

But the economic principle underlying this fanfare is shaky indeed. Since the
late 19th century, mainstream economists have struggled to prove that Smith was
right—that the chaos of free markets leads to a blissful economic order. In the
1950s, U.S. economists Kenneth Arrow and Gerard Debreu finally came up with a
theoretical proof, which many orthodox economists view as the centerpiece of modern economic theory.

Although this proof is the product of the best minds of mainstream economics,
it ends up saying surprisingly little in defense of free markets. The modern theory
of the Invisible Hand shows that given certain assumptions, free markets reduce the
wasteful use of economic resources—but perpetuate unequal income distribution.

To prove free markets cut waste, economists must make a number of far-fetched
assumptions: there are no concentrations of economic power; buyers and sellers know
every detail about the present and future economy; and all costs of production are
borne by producers while all benefits from consumption are paid for by consumers (see
box for a complete list). Take away any one of these assumptions and markets can lead
to stagnation, recession, and other forms of waste—as in fact they do.

In short, the economic theory invoked by conservatives to justify free markets
instead starkly reveals their limitations.

The Fruits of Free Markets

The basic idea behind the Invisible Hand can be illustrated with a story. Suppose
that I grow apples and you grow oranges. We both grow tired of eating the same
fruit all the time and decide to trade. Perhaps we start by trading one apple for one

orange. This exchange satisfies both of us, because in fact I would gladly give up more than one apple to get an orange, and you would readily pay more than one orange for an apple. And as long as swapping one more apple for one more orange makes us both better off, we will continue to trade.

Eventually, the trading will come to a stop. I begin to notice that the novelty of oranges wears old as I accumulate a larger pile of them and the apples I once had a surplus of become more precious to me as they grow scarcer. At some point, I draw the line: in order to obtain one more apple from me, you must give me more than one orange. But your remaining oranges have also become more valuable to you. Up to now, each successive trade has made both of us better off. Now there is no further exchange that benefits us both, so we agree to stop trading until the next crop comes in.

Note several features of this parable. Both you and I end up happier by trading freely. If the government stepped in and limited fruit trading, neither of us would be as well off. In fact, the government cannot do anything in the apple/orange market that will make both of us better off than does the free market.

Adding more economic actors, products, money, and costly production processes complicates the picture, but we reach the same conclusions. Most of us sell our labor time in the market rather than fruit; we sell it for money that we then use to buy apples, oranges, and whatever else we need. The theory of the Invisible Hand tells us a trip to the fruit stand improves the lot of both consumer and seller; likewise, the sale of labor time benefits both employer and employee. What's more, according to the theory, competition between apple farmers insures that consumers will get apples produced at the lowest possible cost. Government intervention still can only make things worse.

This fable provides a ready-made policy guide. Substitute "Japanese autos" and "U.S. agricultural products" for apples and oranges, and the fable tells you that import quotas or tariffs only make the people of both countries worse off. Change the industries to airlines or telephone services, and the fable calls for deregulation. Or re-tell the tale in the labor market: minimum wages and unions (which prevent workers from individually bargaining over their wages) hurt employers and workers.

Fruit Salad

Unfortunately for free-market boosters, two major short-comings make a fruit salad out of this story. First, even if free markets perform as advertised, they deliver only one benefit—the prevention of certain economically wasteful practices—while preserving inequality. According to the theory, competitive markets wipe out two kinds of waste: unrealized trades and inefficient production. Given the right assumptions, markets ensure that when two parties both stand to gain from a trade, they make that trade, as in the apples-and-oranges story. Competition compels producers to search for the most efficient, lowest-cost production methods—again, given the right preconditions.

Though eliminating waste is a worthy goal, it leaves economic inequality untouched. Returning once more to the orchard, if I start out with all of the apples and oranges and you start out with none, that situation is free of waste: no swap can make us both better off since you have nothing to trade! Orthodox economists acknowledge that even in the ideal competitive market, those who start out rich stay rich, while the poor remain poor. Many of them argue that attempts at redistributing income will most certainly create economic inefficiencies, justifying the preservation of current inequities.

But in real-life economics, competition does lead to waste. Companies wastefully duplicate each other's research and build excess productive capacity. Cost-cutting often leads to shoddy products, worker speedup, and unsafe working conditions. People and factories stand idle while houses go unbuilt and people go unfed. That's because of the second major problem: real economies don't match the assumptions of the Invisible Hand theory.

Of course, all economic theories build their arguments on a set of simplifying assumptions about the world. These assumptions often sacrifice some less important aspects of reality in order to focus on the economic mechanisms of interest.

Assumptions and Reality

The claim that free markets lead to efficiency and reduced waste rests on eight main assumptions. However, these assumptions differ sharply from economic reality. (Assumptions 1, 3, 4, and 5 are discussed in more detail in the article.)

ASSUMPTION ONE: *No market power.* No individual buyer or seller, nor any group of buyers or sellers, has the power to affect the market-wide level of prices, wages, or profits.
REALITY ONE: Our economy is dotted with centers of market power, from large corporations to unions. Furthermore, employers have an edge in bargaining with workers because of the threat of unemployment.

ASSUMPTION TWO: *No economies of scale.* Small plants can produce as cheaply as large ones.
REALITY TWO: In fields such as mass-production industry, transportation, communications, and agriculture, large producers enjoy a cost advantage, limiting competition.

ASSUMPTION THREE: *Perfect information about the present.* Buyers and sellers know everything there is to know about the goods being exchanged. Also, each is aware of the wishes of every other potential buyer and seller in the market.
REALITY THREE: The world is full of lemons—goods about which the buyer is inadequately informed. Also, people are not mind-readers, so sellers get stuck with surpluses and willing buyers are unable to find the products they want.

ASSUMPTION FOUR: *Perfect information about the future.* Contracts between buyers and sellers cover every possible future eventuality.
REALITY FOUR: Uncertainty clouds the future of any economy. Futures markets are limited.

But in the case of the Invisible Hand, the theoretical preconditions contradict several central features of the economy.

For one thing, markets are only guaranteed to prevent waste if the economy runs on "perfect competition": individual sellers compete by cutting prices, individual buyers compete by raising price offers, and nobody holds concentrated economic power. But today's giant corporations hardly match this description. Coke and Pepsi compete with advertising rather than price cuts. The oil companies keep prices high enough to register massive profits every year. Employers coordinate the pay and benefits they offer to avoid bidding up compensation. Workers, in turn, marshal their own forces via unionization—another departure from perfect competition.

Indeed, the jargon of "perfect competition" overlooks the fact that property ownership itself confers disproportionate economic power. "In the competitive model," orthodox economist Paul Samuelson commented, "it makes no difference whether capital hires labor or the other way around." He argued that given perfect

ASSUMPTION FIVE: *You only get what you pay for.* Nobody can impose a cost on somebody else, nor obtain a benefit from them, without paying.
REALITY FIVE: Externalities, both positive and negative, are pervasive. In a free market, polluters can impose costs on the rest of us without paying. And when a public good like a park is built or roads are maintained, everyone benefits whether or not they helped to pay for it.

ASSUMPTION SIX: *Price is a proxy for pleasure.* The price of a given commodity will represent the quality and desirability and or utility derived from the consumption of the commodity.
REALITY SIX: "Conspicuous Consumption" (Veblen) and or "snob effects" will often distort prices from underlying utility and marketers will try to position commodities accordingly.

ASSUMPTION SEVEN: Self-interest only. In economic matters, each person cares only about his or her own level of well-being.
REALITY SEVEN: Solidarity, jealousy, and even love for one's family violate this assumption.

ASSUMPTION EIGHT: No joint production. Each production process has only one product.
REALITY EIGHT: Even in an age of specialization, there are plenty of exceptions to this rule. For example, large service firms such as hospitals or universities produce a variety of different services using the same resources.

—*Chris Tilly and Bryan Snyder*

competition among workers and among capitalists, wages and profits would remain the same regardless of who does the hiring. But unemployment—a persistent feature of market-driven economies—makes job loss very costly to workers. The sting my boss feels when I "fire" him by quitting my job hardly equals the setback I experience when he fires me.

Perfect Information?

In addition, the grip of the Invisible Hand is only sure if all buyers and sellers have "perfect information" about the present and future state of markets. In the present, this implies consumers know exactly what they are buying—an assumption hard to swallow in these days of leaky breast implants and chicken à la salmonella. Employers must know exactly what skills workers have and how hard they will work—suppositions any real-life manager would laugh at.

Perfect information also means sellers can always sniff out unsatisfied demands, and buyers can detect any excess supplies of goods. Orthodox economists rely on the metaphor of an omnipresent "auctioneer" who is always calling out prices so all buyers and sellers can find mutually agreeable prices and consummate every possible sale. But in the actual economy, the auctioneer is nowhere to be found, and markets are plagued by surpluses and shortages.

Perfect information about the future is even harder to come by. For example, a company decides whether or not to build a new plant based on whether it expects sales to rise. But predicting future demand is a tricky matter. One reason is that people may save money today in order to buy (demand) goods and services in the future. The problem comes in predicting when. As economist John Maynard Keynes observed in 1934, "An act of individual saving means—so to speak—a decision not to have dinner today. But it does not necessitate a decision to have dinner or to buy a pair of boots a week hence ... or to consume any specified thing at any specified date. Thus it depresses the business of preparing today's dinner without stimulating the business of making ready for some future act of consumption." Keynes concluded that far from curtailing waste, free markets gave rise to the colossal waste of human and economic resources that was the Great Depression—in part because of this type of uncertainty about the future.

Free Lunch

The dexterity of the Invisible Hand also depends on the principle that "You only get what you pay for." This "no free lunch" principle seems at first glance a reasonable description of the economy. But major exceptions arise. One is what economists call "externalities"—economic transactions that take place outside the market. Consider a hospital that dumps syringes at sea. In effect, the hospital gets a free lunch by passing the costs of waste disposal on to the rest of us. Because no market exists where the right to dump is bought and sold, free markets do nothing to compel the hospital to bear the costs of dumping—which is why the government must step in.

Public goods such as sewer systems also violate the "no free lunch" rule. Once the sewer system is in place, everyone shares in the benefits of the waste disposal, regardless of whether or not they helped pay for it. Suppose sewer systems were sold in a free market, in which each person had the opportunity to buy an individual share. Then any sensible, self-interested consumer would hold back from buying his or her fair share—and wait for others to provide the service. This irrational situation would persist unless consumers could somehow collectively agree on how extensive a sewer system to produce—once more bringing government into the picture.

Most orthodox economists claim that the list of externalities and public goods in the economy is short and easily addressed. Liberals and radicals, on the other hand, offer a long list: for example, public goods include education, healthcare, and decent public transportation—all in short supply in our society.

Because real markets deviate from the ideal markets envisioned in the theory of the Invisible Hand, they give us both inequality and waste. But if the theory is so far off the mark, why do mainstream economists and policymakers place so much stock in it? They fundamentally believe the profit motive is the best guide for the economy. If you believe that "What's good for General Motors is good for the country," the Invisible Hand theory can seem quite reasonable. Business interests, government, and the media constantly reinforce this belief, and reward those who can dress it up in theoretical terms. As long as capital remains the dominant force in society, the Invisible Hand will maintain its grip on the hearts and minds of us all. ❑

Article 1.4

PURSUING PROFITS—OR POWER?

BY JAMES K. BOYCE
July/August 2013

D o corporations seek to maximize profits? Or do they seek to maximize power? The two may be complementary—wealth begets power, power begets wealth—but they're not the same. One important difference is that profits can come from an expanding economic "pie," whereas the size of the power pie is fixed. Power is a zero-sum game: more for me means less for you. And for corporations, the pursuit of power sometimes trumps the pursuit of profits.

Take public education, for example. Greater investment in education from preschool through college could increase the overall pie of well-being. But it would narrow the educational advantage of the corporate oligarchs and their privately schooled children—and diminish the power that comes with it. Although corporations could benefit from the bigger pie produced by a better-educated labor force, there's a tension between what's good for business and what's good for the business elite.

Similarly, the business elite today supports economic austerity instead of full-employment policies that would increase growth and profits. This may have something to do with the fact that austerity widens inequality, while full employment would narrow it (by empowering workers). If we peel away the layers of the onion, at the core again we find that those at the top of the corporate pyramid put power before profits.

As one more example, consider the politics of government regulation. Corporations routinely pass along to consumers whatever costs they incur as a result of regulation. In the auto industry, for instance, the regulations that mandated seat belts, catalytic converters, and better fuel efficiency added a few hundred dollars to car prices. They didn't cut automaker profit margins. If the costs of regulation are ultimately borne by the consumer, why do they face such stiff resistance from the corporations? The answer may have less to do with profits than with power. Corporate chieftains are touchy about their "management prerogatives." They simply don't like other folks telling them what to do.

In a famous 1971 memorandum to the U.S. Chamber of Commerce, future Supreme Court Justice Lewis Powell wrote, "The day is long past when the chief executive office of a major corporation discharges his responsibility by maintaining a satisfactory growth of profits." To counter what he described as an attack on the American free-enterprise system by labor unions, students, and consumer advocates, Powell urged CEOs to act on "the lesson that political power is necessary; that power must be assiduously cultivated; and that when necessary, it must be used aggressively and with determination." He was preaching to a receptive choir.

The idea that firms single-mindedly maximize profits is an axiom of faith of neoclassical Econ 101, but alternative theories have a long history in the broader profession. Thorstein Veblen, John Maynard Keynes, and Fred Hirsch all saw an individual's position relative to others as a key motivation in economic behavior.

Today a sound-bite version of this idea is encountered on bumper stickers: "He Who Dies with the Most Toys Wins."

In his 1972 presidential address to the American Economics Association, titled "Power and the Useful Economist," John Kenneth Galbraith juxtaposed the role of power in the real-world economy to its neglect in orthodox economics: "In eliding power—in making economics a nonpolitical subject—neoclassical theory ... destroys its relation with the real world."

On the free-marketeer side of the ideological spectrum, the pursuit of power is depicted as a pathology distinctive to the State. "Chicago school" economist William Niskanen theorized that public-sector bureaucrats seek to maximize the size of their budgets, taking this as a proxy for "salary, perquisites of the office, public reputation, power, patronage, ease of managing the bureau, and ease of making changes." He called this "the peculiar economics of bureaucracy."

But the pursuit of power isn't unique to government bureaucracies. It's commonplace in corporate bureaucracies, too. In his presidential address, Galbraith made the connection: "Between public and private bureaucracies—between General Motors and the Department of Transportation, between General Dynamics and the Pentagon—there is a deeply symbiotic relationship."

Recognizing the real-world pursuit of power not only helps us understand behavior that otherwise may seem peculiar. It also redirects our attention from the dichotomy between the market and the state toward a more fundamental one: the divide between oligarchy and democracy. ❏

Sources: Sarah O'Connor, "OECD warns of rising inequality as austerity intensifies," *Financial Times*, May 15, 2013 (ft.com); Lewis F. Powell, Jr., "Confidential Memorandum: Attack on American Free Enterprise System," Aug. 23, 1971 (law.wlu.edu); John Kenneth Galbraith, "Power and the Useful Economist," *American Economic Review*, March 1973; William A. Niskanen, "The Peculiar Economics of Bureaucracy," *American Economic Review*, May 1968.

Article 1.5

FREEDOM, EQUITY, AND EFFICIENCY
Contrasting Views of Labor Market Competition

BY ALEJANDRO REUSS
April 2012

The basic world-view of neoclassical economists is that, in markets, people engage voluntarily in exchanges with each other, and that this means market exchanges leave both parties better off. If someone cannot be forced to make a trade, they will only do so if it leaves them at least a little better off than they would have been otherwise. Left to their own devices, people will find and exhaust all the possibilities for trades that boost the overall social well-being. Policies that interfere with people's ability to make voluntary trades, then, can only subtract from the well-being of society as a whole.

The neoclassical narrative depends on many (often unspoken) *assumptions*. Individuals must be rational and self-interested. The assumption of "rationality" means they must act in ways that further their objectives, whatever these objectives may be. The assumption of "self-interest" means that, in making decisions, they must only take into account benefits and costs to themselves. They must have perfect information about all factors (past, present, and future) that could affect their decisions. Their actions must not affect any "third parties" (anyone other than those directly involved in the exchange and agreeing to its terms). There must be many buyers and sellers, so that no single buyer or seller (and no group of buyers or sellers colluding together) can impose the prices they want. Several other assumptions may also be important.

The Neoclassical View

Implicitly, the neoclassical story appeals to ideas about freedom, equity (fairness), and efficiency. Very few people would say they are against any of these virtues, but different people embrace different definitions. Different people, for example, have different ideas about what people should have the freedom to do, and what "freedoms" would impinge on the freedoms, rights, or well-being of others. So really the issue is, when neoclassical economists say that unregulated market competition is desirable, for example, as a matter, of "freedom," what view of freedom are they basing this on?

Freedom

By "freedom," neoclassical economists mean freedom from force or threat of force. They would recognize that someone making an exchange when threatened with violence—when confronted with "an offer they can't refuse," in the *Godfather* sense of that phrase—is not really engaging in a voluntary transaction. That person could very well make an exchange leaving them worse off than they would have been otherwise (except that they may have saved their own neck). On the other hand, suppose a person is faced only with very undesirable alternatives to engaging in a trade. Suppose they have "no choice" but to accept a job, because the alternative is to starve. Neoclassical economists would point out that these circumstances are not of the potential employer's making. It is quite unlike, in their view, conditions that are directly imposed by the other party (like having a gun held to one's head). If the impoverished worker accepts a job offer, even at a very low wage or under very bad working conditions, the neoclassical economist would argue that this is evidence that he or she really is made better off by the exchange. Restricting his or her freedom to engage in this exchange, in the neoclassical view, only makes him or her worse off.

Equity

Neoclassical economists argue that restrictions on market competition can unfairly benefit some market participants (buyers or sellers) or potential market participants at the expense of others. This kind of equity concern enters into neoclassical theory in several ways:

First, restrictions on competition may affect the ability of different people (or firms) to participate in a market—to offer what they have for sale or to bid on what others offer for sale. Suppose that the government issues special licenses to some people or firms that permit them to engage in a certain trade, like driving a taxi, while denying such licenses to others. (Such policies create "barriers to entry," in the language of neoclassical economics.) Such restrictions are, in the neoclassical view, unfair to the unlucky (or less-influential) individuals or firms who do not receive licenses and so are locked out of the market.

Second, restrictions may affect the ability of different people to use whatever advantage they may have, to compete in a market. A price floor, for example, prevents lower-cost sellers from using their cost advantage (their willingness to accept a lower price) to compete in the market. In the neoclassical view, this favors higher-cost sellers at the expense of their lower-cost competitors.

Third, restrictions may affect the ability of sellers to fetch the highest price they can, constrained only by competition from other sellers, and of buyers to pay the lowest price they can, constrained only by bidding from other buyers. A price floor, by restricting producers from competing on price (preventing any from offering prices below the floor), may favor producers in general at the expense of consumers. By the same token, a price ceiling (a maximum legal price) may favor consumers at the expense of producers.

Efficiency

In the neoclassical view, a resource is used "efficiently" as long as the benefit from using that resource is greater than the cost. Let's think about a company—say, an auto company—that has to decide how many machines to rent or how many workers to hire for its operations. It will consider how many extra cars it can produce if it rents one additional machine, or hires one additional worker. The company will figure out how much income it will get from the sale of those additional cars. That is, it will multiply the number of additional cars by the price it will get per car. Ultimately, it will compare this extra income against the rental cost paid for the machine, or the wage paid to the worker. The company will rent a machine, or hire a worker, as long as the extra income it gets is more than the additional cost it has to pay.

In the neoclassical view, this is "efficient" not only from the standpoint of the company, but from the standpoint of society as a whole. If the cost of using an extra machine or hiring an extra worker is less than value of the extra cars produced, the use of the machine or worker is also "efficient" from the standpoint of society as a whole.

There's just one more problem. In the neoclassical view, for private actors to make decisions that are also "efficient" form the standpoint of society as a whole, the prices they base their decisions on have to be the *right* prices. That is, each price has to reflect the true cost of a good to society as a whole. So how do we know, in this view, what is the "right price"?

The "Right" Wage

Let's look at an example using, in the language of neoclassical economics, the "price of labor" (or wage). Suppose that the going wage in a certain place is $20 per hour. According to neoclassical economists, a company will hire a worker as long as the extra benefit it gets from each extra hour of labor (the extra units produced times the price the company gets per unit) is at least as much as the additional cost it pays for that extra hour of labor ($20). Suppose, however, that the wage was only this high because there were barriers to competition in the labor market. If the wage without barriers would have only been, say, $10, then a company would hire an extra worker as long as the extra benefit it got from each extra hour of labor was at least $10 per hour.

How do we know whether the "right" wage is $20 or $10? In the view of neo-classical economists, the right wage—like any other right price—reflects the true cost to society of the good involved (here, an hour of labor). The cost of labor is whatever pains the worker endures as a result of that hour of work. This includes having to show up for work, when one might prefer to be someone else, having to follow the employer's orders, when one would rather be "doing one's own thing," putting up with the conditions at work, which could be dangerous, unhealthy, or unpleasant, and so on. It is competition in the labor market that makes workers reveal what they really require to compensate them for the burdens of labor.

If the price of labor, due to barriers to labor-market competition, is "too high," then employers will use "too little" labor. If the wage is $20, due to barriers, then employers will not hire an extra hour of labor unless it results in the production of at least $20 of additional goods. As a result of the inflated price of labor, society will have turned its back on who-knows-how-many opportunities to get between $10 and $20 of goods at a true cost of $10 worth of labor. In other words, wages that are inflated by barriers to competition result in an "inefficient" use of resources.

Critiques of the Neoclassical View

Economists associated with different schools of thought may use normative concepts like "freedom," "equity," or "efficiency," but mean something very different by these ideas than what neoclassical economists mean. (Some may choose not to use these terms, and instead invoke other normative concepts, like "justice," "equality," "the good life," and so on.) Here, however, we will focus on contrasts with the neoclassical views of freedom, equity, and efficiency described above.

Freedom

Neoclassical economists emphasize workers' freedom of choice to accept low wages, long hours, bad working conditions, and so on. Workers would not accept those conditions, they argue, unless doing so would leave them better off than they would be otherwise. In this view, institutions like unions or policies like minimum-wage laws interfere with workers' freedom to make a deal that would leave them better off.

Many liberal and almost all radical economists, on the other hand, emphasize how the conditions that an individual will "freely" accept depend on the alternatives available to them. If the only alternative is to starve in the street, most people would work even very long hours, under very bad conditions, for very low pay. Instead of seeing these workers as having "freely" accepted such agreements, however, one could view them as lacking any real freedom to *refuse* these conditions.

Union contracts, minimum-wage laws, and other restraints on competition between workers do, indeed, restrict each individual worker's "freedom" to accept lower wages, worse conditions, and so on, just as neoclassical economists argue. However, this view ignores the benefit to each worker—that these institutions also *protect* each worker from other workers undercutting him or her. Instead of seeing restraints on labor competition as robbing workers of the freedom to accept lower wages or worse conditions, one can instead see them as giving workers the freedom to demand higher wages or better conditions.

Equity

Barriers to labor-market competition, neoclassical economists argue, favor some workers at the expense of others and workers at the expense of consumers. An alternative view is that restraints on labor-market competition allow workers to get a better deal (higher pay, better conditions, etc.) from employers. The absence of these restraints, on the other hand, may result in higher profits for employers while relegating workers to lower pay and worse conditions. Which outcome one prefers depends on how one values benefits to one group of people (workers) compared to benefits to another (employers).

There are several reasons that someone might favor the interests of workers over those of employers, and therefore approve of changes that benefit workers even if these benefits come at the expense of employers:

1. **Ideas of "fairness" based on social "custom" or "convention."** In most societies where people work for wages, there are evolving ideas about what is a "fair" wage or "decent" living. Partly, such ideas may be based on what people have become accustomed to in the past. Partly, they may reflect expectations that conditions of life will improve over time, and especially from one generation to the next.

2. **Commitment to greater economic and social equality.** People who get most of their income from property (ownership of businesses, land or buildings, or financial wealth) are likely to be at the top of the income ladder. Most of the people at the bottom or in the middle, on the other hand, get most of their income from work. Therefore, changes that benefit workers as a group (at the expense of employers) tend to bring about a more equal distribution of income in society.

3. **Ideas about who creates and deserves to keep society's wealth.** Some "radical" economists argue that labor is the source of all new wealth produced in society.

Owners of property take a piece of this wealth by controlling things (like farms, mines, factories, etc.) that everyone else needs in order to work and live. In this view, there is no such thing as a "fair" distribution of income between workers and employers, since the employing class exists only by virtue of taking part of what workers produce.

Much of the history of labor movements around the world centers on attempts to *restrain* competition between workers, to keep workers from undercutting each other on the wages or conditions they will accept, and therefore to benefit workers as a group. Unions, for example, are compacts by which each member agrees *not* to accept a lower wage or worse conditions than the other members. Unions also set conditions on hours, benefits, and conditions of work. No individual can bargain a lower wage or worse conditions, in order to get a job, and thereby force other workers to do the same. Labor legislation like the minimum-wage laws, maximum hours (or overtime) laws, and laws regulating labor conditions, likewise, all restrain competition between workers.

Efficiency

We have already described one concept of efficiency used by neoclassical economists: The key idea is that resources are used if (and only if) the benefit to society is greater than the cost. Neoclassical economists also use another concept of efficiency: An efficient condition is one in which nobody can be made better off without making someone worse off. This definition, pioneered by the Italian neoclassical economist Vilfredo Pareto, is known as "Pareto efficiency." The two definitions are connected: If resources were being wasted (used inefficiently), they could be used to make someone better off without making anyone worse off.

Neoclassical economists call a *change* that makes some people better off without making anyone worse off a "Pareto improvement." There are very few changes in public policies, however, that make some people better off while literally making nobody worse off. Most policy changes, potentially affecting millions of people, make some people better off and others worse off. In these cases, neoclassical economists apply what they call the "compensation test." They compare the benefits to the "winners" from some change in public policy to the losses to the "losers." If the total gains are greater than the total losses, neoclassical economists argue, the winners could compensate the losers—and leave everyone at least a little better off.

In most cases where there are both winners and losers due to a change in public policy, however, the winners do not actually compensate the losers. These are not, then, actual efficiency improvements in the sense that some people are made better off while nobody is made worse off. Restraints on labor-market competition, for example, may benefit workers at the expense of their employers. (Eliminating such policies, meanwhile, may have the opposite effect.)

Judging whether these changes are for the better, then, involves weighing the benefits to some people against the losses to others. How one resolves such an issue depends on one's normative ideas, or values, about whose interests should take precedence. In other words—which side are you on? ❑

Article 1.6

SHARING THE WEALTH OF THE COMMONS

BY PETER BARNES
November/December 2004

We're all familiar with private wealth, even if we don't have much. Economists and the media celebrate it every day. But there's another trove of wealth we barely notice: our common wealth.

Each of us is the beneficiary of a vast inheritance. This common wealth includes our air and water, habitats and ecosystems, languages and cultures, science and technologies, political and monetary systems, and quite a bit more. To say we share this inheritance doesn't mean we can call a broker and sell our shares tomorrow. It does mean we're responsible for the commons and entitled to any income it generates. Both the responsibility and the entitlement are ours by birth. They're part of the obligation each generation owes to the next, and each living human owes to other beings.

At present, however, our economic system scarcely recognizes the commons. This omission causes two major tragedies: ceaseless destruction of nature and widening inequality among humans. Nature gets destroyed because no one's unequivocally responsible for protecting it. Inequality widens because private wealth concentrates while common wealth shrinks.

The great challenges for the 21st century are, first of all, to make the commons visible; second, to give it proper reverence; and third, to translate that reverence into property rights and legal institutions that are on a par with those supporting private property. If we do this, we can avert the twin tragedies currently built into our market-driven system.

Defining the Commons

What exactly is the commons? Here is a workable definition: The commons includes all the assets we inherit together and are morally obligated to pass on, undiminished, to future generations.

This definition is a practical one. It designates a set of assets that have three specific characteristics: they're 1) inherited, 2) shared, and 3) worthy of long-term preservation. Usually it's obvious whether an asset has these characteristics or not.

At the same time, the definition is broad. It encompasses assets that are natural as well as social, intangible as well as tangible, small as well as large. It also introduces a moral factor that is absent from other economic definitions: it requires us to consider whether an asset is worthy of long-term preservation. At present, capitalism has no interest in this question. If an asset is likely to yield a competitive return to capital, it's kept alive; if not, it's destroyed or allowed to run down. Assets in the commons, by contrast, are meant to be preserved regardless of their return.

This definition sorts all economic assets into two baskets, the market and the commons. In the market basket are those assets we want to own privately and manage for profit. In the commons basket are the assets we want to hold in common and manage for long-term preservation. These baskets then are, or ought to be, the yin and yang of economic activity; each should enhance and contain the other. The role of the state should be to maintain a healthy balance between them.

The Value of the Commons

For most of human existence, the commons supplied everyone's food, water, fuel, and medicines. People hunted, fished, gathered fruits and herbs, collected firewood and building materials, and grazed their animals in common lands and waters. In other words, the commons was the source of basic sustenance. This is still true today in many parts of the world, and even in San Francisco, where I live, cash-poor people fish in the bay not for sport, but for food.

Though sustenance in the industrialized world now flows mostly through markets, the commons remains hugely valuable. It's the source of all natural resources and nature's many replenishing services. Water, air, DNA, seeds, topsoil, minerals, the protective ozone layer, the atmosphere's climate regulation, and much more, are gifts of nature to us all.

Just as crucially, the commons is our ultimate waste sink. It recycles water, oxygen, carbon, and everything else we excrete, exhale, or throw away. It's the place we store, or try to store, the residues of our industrial system.

The commons also holds humanity's vast accumulation of knowledge, art, and thought. As Isaac Newton said, "If I have seen further it is by standing on the shoulders of giants." So, too, the legal, political, and economic institutions we inherit—even the market itself—were built by the efforts of millions. Without these gifts we'd be hugely poorer than we are today.

To be sure, thinking of these natural and social inheritances primarily as economic assets is a limited way of viewing them. I deeply believe they are much more than that. But if treating portions of the commons as economic assets can help us conserve them, it's surely worth doing so.

How much might the commons be worth in monetary terms? It's relatively easy to put a dollar value on private assets. Accountants and appraisers do it every day, aided by the fact that private assets are regularly traded for money.

This isn't the case with most shared assets. How much is clean air, an intact wetlands, or

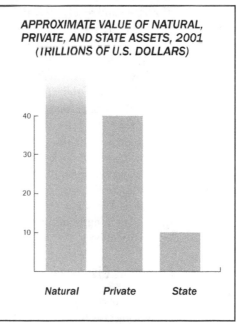

APPROXIMATE VALUE OF NATURAL, PRIVATE, AND STATE ASSETS, 2001 (TRILLIONS OF U.S. DOLLARS)

Darwin's theory of evolution worth in dollar terms? Clearly, many shared inheritances are simply priceless. Others are potentially quantifiable, but there's no current market for them. Fortunately, economists have developed methods to quantify the value of things that aren't traded, so it's possible to estimate the value of the "priceable" part of the commons within an order of magnitude. The surprising conclusion that emerges from numerous studies is that the wealth we share is worth more than the wealth we own privately.

This fact bears repeating. Even though much of the commons can't be valued in monetary terms, the parts that can be valued are worth more than all private assets combined.

It's worth noting that these estimates understate the gap between common and private assets because a significant portion of the value attributed to private wealth is in fact an appropriation of common wealth. If this mislabeled portion was subtracted from private wealth and added to common wealth, the gap between the two would widen further.

Two examples will make this point clear. Suppose you buy a house for $200,000 and, without improving it, sell it a few years later for $300,000. You pay off the mortgage and walk away with a pile of cash. But what caused the house to rise in value? It wasn't anything you did. Rather, it was the fact that your neighborhood became more popular, likely a result of the efforts of community members, improvements in public services, and similar factors.

Or consider another fount of private wealth, the social invention and public expansion of the stock market. Suppose you start a business that goes "public" through an offering of stock. Within a few years, you're able to sell your stock for a spectacular capital gain.

Much of this gain is a social creation, the result of centuries of monetary-system evolution, laws and regulations, and whole industries devoted to accounting, sharing information, and trading stocks. What's more, there's a direct correlation between the scale and quality of the stock market as an institution and the size of the private gain. You'll fetch a higher price if you sell into a market of millions than into a market of two. Similarly, you'll gain more if transaction costs are low and trust in public information is high. Thus, stock that's traded on a regulated exchange sells for a higher multiple of earnings than unlisted stock. This socially created premium can account for 30% of the stock's value. If you're the lucky seller, you'll reap that extra cash—in no way thanks to anything you did as an individual.

Real estate gains and the stock market's social premium are just two instances of common assets contributing to private gain. Still, most rich people would like us to think it's their extraordinary talent, hard work, and risk-taking that create their well-deserved wealth. That's like saying a flower's beauty is due solely to its own efforts, owing nothing to nutrients in the soil, energy from the sun, water from the aquifer, or the activity of bees.

The Great Commons Giveaway

That we inherit a trove of common wealth is the good news. The bad news, alas, is that our inheritance is being grossly mismanaged. As a recent report by the advocacy group

Friends of the Commons concludes, "Maintenance of the commons is terrible, theft is rampant, and rents often aren't collected. To put it bluntly, our common wealth—and our children's—is being squandered. We are all poorer as a result."

Examples of commons mismanagement include the handout of broadcast spectrum to media conglomerates, the giveaway of pollution rights to polluters, the extension of copyrights to entertainment companies, the patenting of seeds and genes, the privatization of water, and the relentless destruction of habitat, wildlife, and ecosystems.

This mismanagement, though currently extreme, is not new. For over 200 years, the market has been devouring the commons in two ways. With one hand, the market takes valuable stuff from the commons and privatizes it. This is called "enclosure." With the other hand, the market dumps bad stuff into the commons and says, "It's your problem." This is called "externalizing." Much that is called economic growth today is actually a form of cannibalization in which the market diminishes the commons that ultimately sustains it.

Enclosure—the taking of good stuff from the commons—at first meant privatization of land by the gentry. Today it means privatization of many common assets by corporations. Either way, it means that what once belonged to everyone now belongs to a few.

Enclosure is usually justified in the name of efficiency. And sometimes, though not always, it does result in efficiency gains. But what also results from enclosure is the impoverishment of those who lose access to the commons, and the enrichment of those who take title to it. In other words, enclosure widens the gap between those with income-producing property and those without.

Externalizing—the dumping of bad stuff into the commons—is an automatic behavior pattern of profit-maximizing corporations: if they can avoid any out-of-pocket costs, they will. If workers, taxpayers, anyone downwind, future generations, or nature have to absorb added costs, so be it.

For decades, economists have agreed we'd be better served if businesses "internalized" their externalities—that is, paid in real time the costs they now shift to the commons. The reason this doesn't happen is that there's no one to set prices and collect them. Unlike private wealth, the commons lacks property rights and institutions to represent it in the marketplace.

The seeds of such institutions, however, are starting to emerge. Consider one of the environmental protection tools the United States currently uses, pollution trading. So-called cap-and-trade programs put a cap on total pollution, then grant portions of the total, via permits, to each polluting firm. Companies may buy other firms' permits if they want to pollute more than their allotment allows, or sell unused permits if they manage to pollute less. Such programs are generally supported by business because they allow polluters to find the cheapest ways to reduce pollution.

Public discussion of cap-and-trade programs has focused exclusively on their trading features. What's been overlooked is how they give away common wealth to polluters.

To date, all cap-and-trade programs have begun by giving pollution rights to existing polluters for free. This treats polluters as if they own our sky and rivers. It means that future polluters will have to pay old polluters for the scarce—hence valuable—right to dump wastes into nature. Imagine that: because a corporation polluted in the past, it gets free income forever! And, because ultimately we'll all pay for limited pollution via higher prices, this amounts to an enormous transfer of wealth—trillions of dollars—to shareholders of historically polluting corporations.

In theory, though, there is no reason that the initial pollution rights should not reside with the public. Clean air and the atmosphere's capacity to absorb pollutants are "wealth" that belongs to everyone. Hence, when polluters use up these parts of the commons, they should pay the public—not the other way around.

Taking the Commons Back

How can we correct the system omission that permits, and indeed promotes, destruction of nature and ever-widening inequality among humans? The answer lies in building a new sector of the economy whose clear legal mission is to preserve shared inheritances for everyone. Just as the market is populated by profit-maximizing corporations, so this new sector would be populated by asset-preserving trusts.

Here a brief description of trusts may be helpful. The trust is a private institution that's even older than the corporation. The essence of a trust is a fiduciary relationship. A trust holds and manages property for another person or for many other people. A simple example is a trust set up by a grandparent to pay for a grandchild's education. Other trusts include pension funds, charitable foundations, and university endowments. There are also hundreds of trusts in America, like the Nature Conservancy and the Trust for Public Land, that own land or conservation easements in perpetuity.

If we were to design an institution to protect pieces of the commons, we couldn't do much better than a trust. The goal of commons management, after all, is to preserve assets and deliver benefits to broad classes of beneficiaries. That's what trusts do, and it's not rocket science.

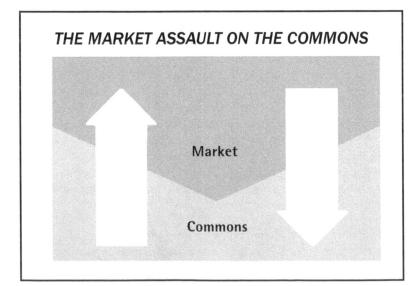

THE MARKET ASSAULT ON THE COMMONS

Market

Commons

Over centuries, several principles of trust management have evolved. These include:

- Trustees have a fiduciary responsibility to beneficiaries. If a trustee fails in this obligation, he or she can be removed and penalized.
- Trustees must preserve the original asset. It's okay to spend income, but don't invade the principal.
- Trustees must assure transparency. Information about money flows should be readily available to beneficiaries.

Trusts in the new commons sector would be endowed with rights comparable to those of corporations. Their trustees would take binding oaths of office and, like judges, serve long terms. Though protecting common assets would be their primary job, they would also distribute income from those assets to beneficiaries. These beneficiaries would include all citizens within a jurisdiction, large classes of citizens (children, the elderly), and/or agencies serving common purposes such as public transit or ecological restoration. When distributing income to individuals, the allocation formula would be one person, one share. The right to receive commons income would be a nontransferable birthright, not a property right that could be traded.

Fortuitously, a working model of such a trust already exists: the Alaska Permanent Fund. When oil drilling on the North Slope began in the 1970s, Gov. Jay Hammond, a Republican, proposed that 25% of the state's royalties be placed in a mutual fund to be invested on behalf of Alaska's citizens. Voters approved in a referendum. Since then, the Alaska Permanent Fund has grown to over $28 billion, and Alaskans have received roughly $22,000 apiece in dividends. In 2003 the per capita dividend was $1,107; a family of four received $4,428.

What Alaska did with its oil can be replicated for other gifts of nature. For example, we could create a nationwide Sky Trust to stabilize the climate for future generations. The trust would restrict emissions of heat-trapping gases and sell a declining number of emission permits to polluters. The income would be returned to U.S. residents in equal yearly dividends, thus reversing the wealth transfer built into current cap-and-trade programs. Instead of everyone paying historic polluters, polluters would pay all of us.

Just as a Sky Trust could represent our equity in the natural commons, a Public Stock Trust could embody our equity in the social commons. Such a trust would capture some of the socially created stock-market premium that currently flows only to shareholders and their investment bankers. As noted earlier, this premium is sizeable—roughly 30% of the value of publicly traded stock. A simple way to share it would be to create a giant mutual fund—call it the American Permanent Fund—that would hold, say, 10% of the shares of publicly traded companies. This mutual fund, in turn, would be owned by all Americans on a one share per person basis (perhaps linked to their Social Security accounts).

To build up the fund without precipitating a fall in share prices, companies would contribute shares at the rate of, say, 1% per year. The contributions would be the price companies pay for the benefits they derive from a commons asset, the large, trusted market for stock—a small price, indeed, for the hefty benefits. Over time, the mutual fund would assure that when the economy grows, everyone benefits. The top 5% would still own more than the bottom 90%, but at least every American would have some property income, and a slightly larger slice of our economic pie.

Sharing the Wealth

The perpetuation of inequality is built into the current design of capitalism. Because of the skewed distribution of private wealth, a small self-perpetuating minority receives a disproportionate share of America's nonlabor income.

Thomas Paine had something to say about this. In his essay "Agrarian Justice," written in 1790, he argued that, because enclosure of the commons had separated so many people from their primary source of sustenance, it was necessary to create a functional equivalent of the commons in the form of a National Fund. Here is how he put it:

> There are two kinds of property. Firstly, natural property, or that which comes to us from the Creator of the universe—such as the earth, air, water. Secondly, artificial or acquired property—the invention of men. In the latter, equality is impossible; for to distribute it equally, it would be necessary that all should have contributed in the same proportion, which can never be the case .... Equality of natural property is different. Every individual in the world is born with legitimate claims on this property, or its equivalent.

Enclosure of the commons, he went on, was necessary to improve the efficiency of cultivation. But:

> The landed monopoly that began with [enclosure] has produced the greatest evil. It has dispossessed more than half the inhabitants of every nation of their natural inheritance, without providing for them, as ought to have been done, an indemnification for that loss, and has thereby created a species of poverty and wretchedness that did not exist before.

The appropriate compensation for loss of the commons, Paine said, was a national fund financed by rents paid by land owners. Out of this fund, every person reaching age 21 would get 15 pounds a year, and every person over 50 would receive an additional 10 pounds. (Think of Social Security, financed by commons rents instead of payroll taxes.)

A Progressive Offensive

Paine's vision, allowing for inflation and new forms of enclosure, could not be more timely today. Surely from our vast common inheritance—not just the land, but the atmosphere, the broadcast spectrum, our mineral resources, our threatened habitats and water supplies—enough rent can be collected to pay every American over age 21 a modest annual dividend, and every person reaching 21 a small start-up inheritance.

Such a proposal may seem utopian. In today's political climate, perhaps it is. But consider this. About 20 years ago, right-wing think tanks laid out a bold agenda. They called for lowering taxes on private wealth, privatizing much of government, and deregulating industry. Amazingly, this radical agenda has largely been achieved.

It's time for progressives to mount an equally bold offensive. The old shibboleths—let's gin up the economy, create jobs, and expand government programs—no longer excite. We need to talk about fixing the economy, not just growing it; about income for everyone, not just jobs; about nurturing ecosystems, cultures, and communities, not just our individual selves. More broadly, we need to celebrate the commons as an essential counterpoise to the market.

Unfortunately, many progressives have viewed the state as the only possible counterpoise to the market. The trouble is, the state has been captured by corporations. This capture isn't accidental or temporary; it's structural and long-term.

This doesn't mean progressives can't occasionally recapture the state. We've done so before and will do so again. It does mean that progressive control of the state is the exception, not the norm; in due course, corporate capture will resume. It follows that if we want lasting fixes to capitalism's tragic flaws, we must use our brief moments of political ascendancy to build institutions that endure.

Programs that rely on taxes, appropriations, or regulations are inherently transitory; they get weakened or repealed when political power shifts. By contrast, institutions that are self-perpetuating and have broad constituencies are likely to last. (It also helps if they mail out checks periodically.) This was the genius of Social Security, which has survived—indeed grown—through numerous Republican administrations.

If progressives are smart, we'll use our next New Deal to create common property trusts that include all Americans as beneficiaries. These trusts will then be to the 21st century what social insurance was to the 20th: sturdy pillars of shared responsibility and entitlement. Through them, the commons will be a source of sustenance for all, as it was before enclosure. Life-long income will be linked to generations-long ecological health. Isn't that a future most Americans would welcome? ❑

Article 1.7

THE FUTURE OF WORK, LEISURE, AND CONSUMPTION

AN INTERVIEW with JULIET SCHOR
May/June 2014

Economist Juliet Schor is known worldwide for her research on the interrelated issues of work, leisure, and consumption. Her books on these themes include The Overworked American: The Unexpected Decline of Leisure, The Overspent American: Upscaling, Downshifting, and the New Consumer, *and* Plenitude: The New Economics of True Wealth *(retitled* True Wealth *for its paperback edition). She is also a professor of sociology at Boston College.* —Eds.

Dollars & Sense: We wouldn't expect patterns of work, leisure, and consumption to change overnight, but we're now more than half a decade into a profound crisis. Obviously it's had a big impact on employment, incomes, and so forth, but do you see any lasting changes emerging?

Juliet Schor: Some of the trends that were pretty significant before the crash have abated. I'm thinking most particularly about what I've called the "fast fashion model" of consumption—cheap imports of manufactured goods that people were acquiring at accelerating rates, the acceleration of the fashion cycle, and the cycle of acquisition and discard. The trend was people buying things, holding them for shorter and shorter periods of time and then discarding them either into some kind of household storage, into a waste stream, or into secondary markets. You had an amazing period of acquisition of consumer goods. I first started looking at this in the realm of apparel, but it was also in consumer electronics, ordinary household appliances, and pretty much across the board in consumer goods.

Of course, a lot of it was financed by debt or longer working hours, but manufactured goods just became so cheap. The idea that you could buy a DVD player for $19—and yes, people were trampling each other in the stores on Black Friday to get them—but that's just an extraordinary period. So that has changed, because the economics of that have changed. Going forward, I don't think we're going to see that level of availability of cheap goods that we saw before. So I think that cycle has slowed down.

The other big thing has been the bifurcation of the consumer market. That's something that's been going on for a long time—the falling out of the middle as a result of the decline of the middle class, the growth of a really low-end in the consumer market with dollar stores and a retail sector where even Walmart is considered expensive. The other side was the expansion of the hyper-luxury market.

Trends in income and wealth are reflected in the consumer sphere. There's more reluctance to take on debt, so debt-fueled consumer buying is lessened. There's also less availability of consumer credit for households now. The other big thing that I've been looking at is the rise of "alternative cultures" of consumption; that is, people moving out of the branded, advertised goods and the mass-produced lifestyles that dominated in the last couple of decades into more ecologically aware lifestyles with more artisanal- and self-production.

D&S: Stepping back and looking more broadly at the emergence of this mass consumer culture in the United States after World War II, what do you see that are the key factors that are at the root of consumer capitalism in the United States? It seems a little facile to focus too narrowly on just advertising. Some scholars point to mass media images and what kinds of lifestyles people aspire to. John Kenneth Galbraith pointed more generally to the relentless stream of new products fueling new desires—the so-called "dependence effect." How do you see those influences, as well as others, sorting out?

JS: I don't want to completely dismiss factors like the old monopoly capital idea or the advertising and marketing story, which is that shortfalls of demand led to a big effort to get people to buy things, but I don't buy that story, for the most part. If you think about the postwar period, you had a labor market in which firms were unwilling to use productivity growth to reduce hours of work, and I wrote a book about that, *The Overworked American*. Part of that was about firms and why they don't want to do that. So in the postwar period, you have, from the labor market side, a situation where all productivity growth is getting channeled into income—into expansion of output—so it goes to wages and profits.

Now, of course, workers aren't getting the benefits of productivity growth, but in the postwar era, they did. There were contracts that were explicitly tied—3% productivity, 3% real wage growth. So that creates consumer demand, because that income is getting into people's pockets. Now you can ask the question: Why don't they save it? I don't think it's advertising, primarily, that determines why people didn't save more. There, I think, you have to look at social competition, and the fact that you have an unequal society in which how you live, what you buy, and what you have are important determinants of social position. Rising income gives you a constantly rising norm, and people consume to keep up with that norm. I think it would have played out more or less similarly if there weren't any advertising. The products might have been different but this sort of "consumer escalator," the fact that you have growing levels of consumption, is really coming much more from the production side. So in that way, I'm much more Marxian than Keynesian, I would say.

D&S: Turning to the contrast between the United States and other high-income capitalist countries, especially in terms of the shape of the labor movement and the role of the state: How did working hours get reduced in other countries? In France or Germany, for example, the average employed person works about 300 hours less per year than in the United States. So that strikes me as quite central, in your analysis, in terms of understanding consumption patterns in different countries.

JS: In the United States in the postwar period, the state devoted a lot of energy to the promotion of consumption, whether it was the highway system or suburbanization. That was in part out of a fear of the "Keynesian problem" of inadequate demand after World War II. In Europe, I guess I would point to two things. First, after the war, they had a supply-side problem, which was that they had to rebuild productive capacity rather than what we had, which was the demand-side problem. So our state was much more oriented to promoting consumption than European states, which were more oriented towards rebuilding their societies. In Europe, working hours continued to fall and they didn't in the United States.

That's the way you need to think about it—everybody was on a common trajectory of work-hours decline from about 1870. Of course, the United States was the leader in all of that. We had the shortest working hours and we were the first ones to put in reforms of working hours: The United States was the leader on no Sunday work, no Saturday work, etc. I think the factors are the role of trade unions—both that trade unions were much stronger in Europe and also that in the United States, trade unions turned against the reduction of working hours after World War II. That has to do mostly with the Cold War, and with the conservative nature of U.S. trade unions. So in the 1950s, the AFL-CIO became—"hostile" may be too strong a word—became extremely disinterested in the idea of shorter hours of work. That's something that did not happen in Europe.

The other thing is that the incentives facing firms in the United States were really different, in terms of U.S. employers having much higher per worker fixed costs, because of health insurance. There are some European countries where health insurance is provided at the firm level, but mostly not. In the United States that turns out to be a powerful disincentive to reduce working hours, and it becomes a powerful incentive for raising working hours. The growth in inequality, which is more pronounced in the United States, also raised working hours. I think those are the key factors which lead the United States and Europe to diverge quite rapidly on the issue of work time. That divergence turns out to have all sorts of very important consequences.

One of the things you have seen in the patterns of leisure time activities in the United States is you've got time-stressed households doing really money-intensive things like going to the Caribbean for three days, or spending a lot of money to "de-stress," or spending money to reward themselves for working so hard. So we definitely have quite a bit of that in the United States because work is so demanding and stressful and that shapes the leisure patterns. You get what economists call goods- or income-intensive leisure.

D&S: If we think of consumption behavior as social—as aiming to enhance a person's social status—can we think of any important social constraints on the amounts or patterns of consumption? If many people disapprove of polluting or wasteful forms of consumption, like the Hummer, can we observe a social constraint on that? Or, in what are very difficult economic times for a lot of people, is there any effect on people reining in unseemly levels of luxury consumption?

JS: Well, I'll start with the latter. I was reading about and experiencing people's reluctance to engage in ostentatious displays at the time of the crash, and in its early aftermath. I think, by now, that didn't last very long. One of the things about the most ostentatious stuff is that we're increasingly a gated society, so the wealthy are consuming lavishly outside of the view of the ordinary and the poor. There is certainly less celebration of it, and you see it less in the culture now than before the crash, for sure. The Hummers are a very interesting case. I have a friend who did research on the war between Hummer drivers and the Prius drivers, the Prius drivers being referred to as "pious" drivers by the Hummer folks. Now the Hummer vehicle has collapsed as a consumer product. Hummer drivers were subjected to a lot of social disapproval. It also became economically less-desirable when the price of gas went up.

There is definitely a rising ecological consciousness that is attempting to moralize consumption in ways that yield social approval or disapproval of low-carbon versus high-carbon lifestyles. It isn't mainstream yet. It's much more prevalent in highly educated groups, it tends to be more bicoastal, it's a kind of "forward trend" in the consumer culture. You do see more and more, as you move into the mainstream, people attempting to do more ecologically. I think there's widespread sentiment about that. Then, of course, you also have so many people who are just trying to make ends meet that they feel it is not possible for them to think about ecological impact. Of course, the irony is that the people who are just trying to make ends meet are the ones with the low carbon footprints, but the discourse of environmental impact is permeating through consumer culture.

D&S: Going back to something about advertising: It seems to have become more pervasive, both in terms of physical spaces that are filled with advertising and products advertised to users. In the last couple of decades, we've seen the advent of direct marketing of prescription pharmaceuticals, for example, directly to the people who will end up using them. There's a pushback, such as criticism of advertising to children, but it seems largely that there's widespread tolerance of this pervasiveness of advertising in daily life.

JS: This is a little counterintuitive, but part of why advertising has become so pervasive is that the core of advertising, which is television spots, have become so unimportant. People don't have to watch them anymore, and that's huge for advertisers. I think the 30- or 60-second TV spots are much more powerful than the kinds of things that advertisers have moved towards in terms of the spatial expansion of advertising. I think that advertising on the web is much less powerful. So, that's one of the paradoxes of advertising in the contemporary moment: The moment when advertising is much more pervasive in terms of space and place, is a moment when it's much less powerful. Advertisers have been able to move in a few directions that have been productive for them, like word of mouth advertising, and so forth, but those forms are also being delegitimized. People know the person sitting next to them in a bar telling them to drink this vodka might be paid by the company.

Prescription drugs are a big exception, because that came about as a regulatory change. Drug companies weren't allowed to advertise directly to consumers before. If it weren't for pharmaceuticals and ads directed at kids, the advertising industry would be in big trouble. Now the kid story is, I think, a little bit different than the adult story, in the sense that you have a much more powerful approach to children now than you did in the past. The approach to children, I think, is a lot more effective than the approach to adults, which I think is declining in effectiveness. So, you can see a theme in what I'm saying about advertising. Today, I would say I feel less worried about advertising than I did before I started studying it. I think people tune it out. I don't want to go too far on this, but to me it's not where the main action is in terms of what's driving consumer patterns.

D&S: We see some examples of people, in their purchasing decisions, transcending a kind of narrow consumer mentality: They're thinking about environmental impacts, say, in buying a hybrid or electric car. In terms of other products they may be thinking about labor conditions, such as buying fair trade goods or no sweatshop apparel or footwear. On the other hand, one might look at this as reinforcing a core aspect of consumerist capitalism: That whatever it is that you may want, it's for sale and you can buy it.

JS: There's a debate in sociology and the social sciences more generally—because there are other disciplines that have weighed in on this question—about the critique of ethical consumption, political consumption, green consumption. Some argue that it's actually detrimental because it leads people to think that this purchasing behavior can solve problems, and it leads them to be less likely to join in collective solutions to environmental problems, labor problems, poverty, and development in the global South.

I did a study of that, and I used two different data sets: One was a random sample survey of all Americans. The other was an intentional survey of people who are political or ethical consumers, or what we called "conscious consumers," with about 2,000 participants. What we found is that there are actually very high levels of correlation between people engaging in this kind of purchasing and being socially and politically involved in trying to solve these problems in collective ways. And we also looked at the time sequencing and found a group of people who are politically involved already and then you add on this "walk the talk" aspect—if you're going to be fighting sweatshops, then don't buy sweatshop clothing, and if you're concerned about environmental impacts then you don't want to be buying things that are at odds with your values.

So you have people who were political first, then extended to their purchasing behavior, and you have people who got into both at around the same time, and you have people who moved in the other direction—who first did the conscious consuming and then became politically active. Certainly the idea that becoming a "green consumer" undermines your likelihood of engaging in collective action around this is not at all supported by the data in the United States, and there have also been some studies in Europe that show the same thing.

I think the fact of the matter is that changing marketplace behavior in the kind of society we have today is an important component in a broad-based campaign, whether it's on the environment or labor conditions or whatever. We see a lot of the NGOs involved in campaigns that have a market-based dimension—and those have been some of the most successful campaigns in recent years—because it's so hard to get the state to act to do these things, because it is captured by business. People have turned to the market in part because it's an arena where it looks like you can have some results, at least in the short term.

Ultimately, can you stop climate change through consumer behavior and through just market behavior? Definitely not. Can you ensure good working conditions merely by market-oriented activity? Definitely not. To think that it's sufficient is the real mistake, but I don't think that most people who work in this field, who try to work on transforming consumer behavior, have such a naive view.

D&S: We've already talked about ways in which consumption is connected to people's lives at work, and the availability of leisure time, as well as some changes in patterns of consumption related to broader social objectives. What kinds of changes in consumption—and in the forces shaping consumption—do you envision?

JS: Well, I have a hard time thinking about the future without orienting all of my thinking about climate, because I just don't see much of a positive future unless we can address climate change very significantly. And that means, for wealthy countries, pretty radical emissions cuts in a pretty short period of time. It actually means that for most countries. So, as I think about the future, I think about what we could do both to address climate change through radical emissions reductions and also increase social justice, reduce inequality, and start solving the enormous problems that we have in this country. My most recent book, *True Wealth*, is about how to do that. Obviously, we need to get onto a renewable energy system, there's no question about that. We need a carbon tax or carbon regulation, and that's stuff that is very well known. What is not understood, I don't think, is that we can't successfully address climate change with a model in which we continue to try to expand the size of the economy.

We're going to have to deal with working hours, because that's the only way to stop expanding the size of the economy in any sensible way. So the core of what we need to do is to get back on the trajectory of using productivity growth to reduce hours of work. And that then opens up incredible possibilities in terms of rebalancing the labor market, integrating the unemployed, and having a fairer distribution of hours. We're talking about the distribution of income, but not about the distribution of hours, which is one of the things that drives the distribution of income. So, fair access to the work that exists, giving people more time off from work, and doing much more as a society—and probably a lot on the local and community level—to ensure basic needs for people.

With declining work hours, people's incomes are pretty much stabilized, so you need to bring the incomes of the bottom up, and you need to bring the incomes of the top down. Part of that has to be a redistribution of work opportunity and creating community provisioning of basic needs, like publicly owned utilities which provide power and heat for people at reasonable prices, enhanced public transportation, more public provisioning of food. There are really interesting things going on in global-South countries bringing farmers and consumers together in local food economies that are not just about high-priced organic food, which is what we have here, but low-priced food that ensures food security for people. So, shorter hours, basic needs being met—including housing, education, healthcare—that's the direction I would like to see us go, and I think that really it all flows out from a kind of commitment to climate protection. It could all flow out from a commitment to basic needs, too. They really integrate.

Time use is central, and I think you get a totally different culture of consumption if people's incomes are on a basically stabilized trajectory and what they're getting is more and more free time. So, you have a new culture of consumption that is not about the acquisition of the new, it's not the "work and spend" pattern as I've called it, it's not "throw away" or media driven, it's more "true materialist," where you really pay attention to the things you have, and it's a kind of earthier consumption. ❑

Chapter 2

SUPPLY AND DEMAND

INTRODUCTION

Textbooks tell us that supply and demand work like a well-oiled machine. The Law of Supply tells us that as the price of an item goes up, businesses will supply more of that good or service. The Law of Demand adds that as the price rises, consumers will choose to buy less of the item and seek available substitutes. Only one equilibrium price can bring businesses' and consumers' intentions into balance. Away from this equilibrium point, surpluses or shortages tend to drive the price back toward the equilibrium. Of course, government actions such as taxation or setting a price ceiling or floor can move the economy away from its market equilibrium, and create what economists call "deadweight losses" and chronic surpluses (gluts) and shortages. The articles in this chapter challenge this orthodoxy.

Marc Breslow argues that supply and demand do not always produce the best outcomes for society. He notes that the "price gouging" that we suffer during shortages or feared shortages—especially for hard-to-substitute goods like gasoline—is simply supply and demand at work (Article 2.1).

The next two articles take on the mainstream textbook criticisms of price ceilings and price floors. Economist Stephen Barton questions the textbook models' conclusion that residential rent control leads to permanent shortages. He discusses various ways housing is not like other commodities, and as a result, there is a disconnect between supply and demand in rental housing (Article 2.2).

John Miller writes about the controversy surrounding minimum wage increases in "Getting Up to Speed on the Minimum Wage" (Article 2.3), noting that while conservative opposition has remained steady, recent research has eroded the consensus that raising the wage floor eliminates jobs. Miller notes that employers and consumers tend to absorb wage increases since they reduce employee turnover costs, increase productivity, and lead to limited price increases.

In "Drugs and Global Capitalism" (Article 2.4), Sasha Breger-Bush takes the simple approach of rationally tallying up the total size of the drug market, including not only the gigantic pharmaceutical industry, but also highly popular drugs taken by billions of people, including tobacco, alcohol, coffee and tea, as well as the usual "street drugs" like marijuana and cocaine. This grouping allows us to see fascinating patterns, like the use of stimulants such as coffee to wring more productivity out of workers.

In "Are Governments Economically Stupid in Failing to Suspend Patent Protection for Vaccines?" (Article 2.5), Arthur MacEwan evaluates the argument that the developed countries (like the United States and the EU) are hurting their own interest by protecting pharmaceutical patent protection for coronavirus vaccines, since doing so will lead to a wider spread of the disease in the developing world which will in turn hurt developed countries' own economies. MacEwan observes that the decision is rational from the point of view of the drug companies, who often write the intellectual property protections found in trade deals and the World Trade Organization. The U.S. decision to support temporary exemptions to intellectual property laws around the vaccine won't be enough without agreement from the EU and broader support for vaccine manufacture in poor countries.

In "Leaky Governance" (Article 2.6) Francisco J. Aldape argues that government should not just facilitate private markets for personal goods, but also create the broad frameworks for production of public goods—those made available to everyone who needs them, like parks and schools. He uses the Mexican government's recent successes in suppressing fuel theft as an example of shifting how a major market works, to the benefit of development and safety.

Finally, in "Crypto Will Not Liberate Us" (Article 2.7), Hadas Thier takes issues with the view that cryptocurrency is a feasible egalitarian alternative that anyone with an internet connection can participate globally. Against the arguments endorsing crypto for developing countries, Thier discusses the cases of El Salvador and Venezuela to argue how volatile and speculative crypto currencies can only amplify social inequalities. Far from translating into less hierarchy or greater democracy, decentralized blockchain technology is intrinsically rooted in market mechanisms that do not always produce the best outcomes for society.

Taken together, these articles call into question the claims that markets always operate efficiently and lead to the best social allocation of resources. The articles also imply a constructive role for the "visible hand" of government.

Discussion Questions

1. (General) Several of these articles call for a larger government role in regulating supply and demand. What are some possible results of expanded government involvement, positive and negative? On balance, do you agree that government should play a larger role?

2. (Article 2.1) Breslow says that shortages have different effects on prices in the short run and the long run. Explain the difference. How is this difference related to the concepts of elasticity of demand and elasticity of supply?

3. (Article 2.2) Explain some of the ways in which housing is different from other commodities.

4. (Article 2.2) How do modern rent control systems differ from the rent control of 50 or 60 years ago? How does this bear on economists' criticisms of rent control?

5. (Article 2.3) Miller suggests that minimum wage increases lead to offsetting benefits for firms, which lower some costs even as wages go up. What are some of these effects?

6. (Article 2.3) Have more conservative economic commentators, like the *Wall Street Journal* editorial page, changed their views as more economic research is published on the minimum wage? Have economists always been opposed to wage floors?

7. (Article 2.4) How does the Covid-19 pandemic demonstrate that the global economy depends on drugs? What evidence does Sasha Breger Bush provide for thinking that even before the pandemic, drugs were indispensable to the global economic system?

8. (Article 2.5) Why does the pharmaceutical industry insist on protection of its patents, or "intellectual property"? Describe the effect of IP on the ability of the companies to make money.

9. (Article 2.5) The pharmaceutical industry representatives say its patents (and resulting high profits) are needed to support further research. What examples does MacEwan give of drug research (including vaccines) being developed instead through extensive public funding?

10. (Article 2.6) Aldape argues that governments should encourage the availability of public goods. What are public goods, and why does Aldape suggest they are a "pro-poor" development tool?

11. (Article 2.7) What are some of the counterarguments Thier presents against the suggestion that many developing countries can benefit from the adoption of cryptocurrencies? Do you agree with these?

12. (Article 2.7) What is an "NFT"? What is the main criticism Thier presents against the use of NFTs?

Article 2.1

PRICE GOUGING: IT'S JUST SUPPLY AND DEMAND

BY MARC BRESLOW
October 2000, updated May 2015

Critics of the oil industry charge that the companies conspire to raise prices during shortages, ripping off consumers and gaining huge profits through illegal behavior. The industries respond that there is no conspiracy, prices rise due to the simple functioning of supply and demand in the market. The media debate the question: can evidence be found of a conspiracy? Or are rising prices simply due to increased costs as supplies are short? Politicians ask whether companies are guilty of illegal activity, and demand that investigations be opened.

What's going on? In reality, critics of the industries are missing the point of how a capitalist "free market" operates during times of shortages. The industry spokespersons are more on target in their explanations—but that doesn't mean what the companies are doing is okay. In fact, they *are* profiting at the expense of everyone who is forced to pay outrageous prices.

Both the media and public officials want to know whether rising costs of operation are causing the high prices, and therefore the companies are justified. Why? Because simple textbook economics says that in a competitive market we should get charged according to costs, with companies only making a "normal" profit. But a careful reading of the texts shows that this is only in the "long run" when new supplies can come into the market. In the short run, when a shortage develops, "supply and demand" can force prices up to unbelievable levels, especially for any product or service that is really a necessity. It doesn't have any relationship to the cost of supplying the item, nor does it take a conspiracy. The industry spokespeople are right that market pressures are the cause.

What confuses consumers is why a relatively small shortage can cause such a huge price jump, as it did for gasoline and electricity. Why, if OPEC (the Organization of the Petroleum Exporting Countries) reduces world oil supplies by only 1% or 2%, can the price of gasoline rise by perhaps 50%? Why shouldn't prices rise by the 1% or 2%? The answer lies in a common-sense understanding of what happens during a shortage. Everyone who owns a car, and still needs to get to work, drop the kids off at childcare, and buy groceries, still needs to drive. In the short run, you can't sell your car for a more energy-efficient one, nor move someplace where public transit is more available, nor find a new day care center closer to home. Even if there are subways or buses available where you live, tight work and family time schedules probably make it difficult for you to leave the car at home.

So, as prices rise, everyone continues trying to buy as much gasoline as they did before (in technical terms, the "short-run price elasticity of demand" is very low). But there is 2% less gas available, so not everyone can get as much as they want. Prices will continue rising until some people drop out of the market, cutting back on their purchases because they simply can't afford to pay the higher prices. For something as essential to modern life as gasoline, this can take quite a price jump. If the price goes from $3.00 to $3.50 will you buy less? How about $4.00? Or $4.50? You can see the problem. Prices can easily rise by 50% before demand falls by the 2% needed for supply and demand to equalize.

Note that this situation has nothing to do with the costs of supplying gasoline, nor do oil companies in the United States have to conspire together to raise prices. All they have to do is let consumers bid for the available gasoline. Nothing illegal has taken place—OPEC is acting as a cartel, "conspiring," but the United States has no legal power over other countries. Profits can go up enormously, and they may be shared between OPEC, oil companies such as Exxon/Mobil and Royal Dutch Shell, and firms lower on the supply chain such as wholesalers and retail gas stations.

Housing is perhaps the worst of these situations, as no one should be forced to leave their home. But the "invisible hand" of the market will raise prices, and allocate housing, according to who has the greatest purchasing power, not who needs the housing. A highly-skilled computer programmer, moving into San Francisco from elsewhere, will get an apartment that some lesser-paid worker, maybe a public school teacher or a bus driver, has been living in, perhaps for many years.

In all these cases, the market has done what it does well—allocate sales to those who can afford to buy, without regard to need; and allocate profits to those who have a product in short supply, without regard to costs of production. The human costs to people of moderate- and low-incomes, who are priced out of the market, can be severe. But they can be prevented—by price controls that prevent price-gouging due to shortages. Such controls have been used many times in the United States—for rent in high-demand cities, for oil and gas during the "crises" of the 1970s, and for most products during World War II. Maybe it's time we made them a staple of sensible economic policy. ❏

Sources: "In Gas Prices, Misery and Mystery," Pam Belluck, *New York Times*, June 14, 2000; "Federal action sought to cut power prices from May," Peter J. Howe, *Boston Globe*, Aug. 24, 2000; "Industry Blames Chemical Additives for High Gas Prices," Matthew L. Wald, *New York Times*, June 26, 2000.

Article 2.2

THE ECONOMICS OF RESIDENTIAL RENT CONTROL
A Not-So-Simple Matter of Supply and Demand

BY STEPHEN BARTON
January/February 2019

As the United States emerged from the financial crisis and recession of 2007–2009, rents in many areas increased rapidly, reaching previously unheard-of levels. This resulted in a massive and continuing transfer of wealth from tenants to real estate investors, displacement of hundreds of thousands of tenants, and a major increase in homelessness. In response, several cities in California and New York passed the first new rent control ordinances in over 30 years and there are serious efforts to eliminate state-level prohibitions on rent controls in Illinois, Oregon, and Washington. In California, a broad coalition of community and tenant organizations put an initiative measure on the November 2018 ballot to repeal statewide restrictions on local rent controls. The ballot measure lost, but the effort received national publicity and brought renewed attention to the case for rent control.

Much of the economic literature critical of rent control is based on analyses of the stringent controls established during World War II, which lasted into the 1970s in New York City and parts of Europe. This generation of rent controls sometimes held rents below the level necessary to operate and maintain the controlled buildings, delivering short-term benefits to tenants at the cost of long-run deterioration. These findings simply do not apply to modern "second generation" rent control systems. Throughout the United States the courts have established that landlords have a constitutional right to a fair return on their investment, which typically requires annual increases in rent ceilings sufficient to cover increases in operating and maintenance costs and an increase in normal cash flow (profit) so that the value of that cash flow is not reduced by inflation. Economist Richard Arnott suggested that in light of this, "economists should reconsider their blanket opposition to current rent control systems and evaluate them on a case-by-case basis." Research on the practical effects of second generation rent controls has come up with mixed results, largely because to be effective rent controls must be part of a broader set of programs. You will not learn about that from the public policy discourse found in the news media or, indeed, from most economists.

Rent control can provide tenants with stability and fair rents in cities where the rental housing market is unable to stabilize rents on its own. It can protect millions of tenants very quickly and at low cost, with its administration paid for by fees charged to the landlords benefitting from increased rents. The opponents of rent control claim the "science" of economics has shown that rent control is not only ineffective but harms the low and moderate-income people it is intended to help and endangers needed housing development. When closely examined, however, these claims prove to be based on simplistic, misleading models of the rental housing market and to ignore important non-monetary human values in favor of a utopian idealization of "the market."

A Choice of Values

Rent control provides tenants with stability and predictable rents. The real estate industry has long told us that homeownership is good because it increases community stability, while renters are "transient." Then when tenants demand the stability that can be provided by rent control, the real estate industry switches from the civic language in which stability is a virtue to the economic language of efficiency so that harmful "transience" becomes beneficial "mobility." In the economics literature, it is said that rent control results in "reduced mobility" and that this causes an "inefficient allocation" of rental units. This is typically illustrated with stories about a few high-income tenants who choose to remain in a rent controlled apartment rather than move into a higher-rent apartment closer to a new job or of a size more suited to their current needs. It is never illustrated with the stories of the low-income seniors, childcare workers, and others who are able to stay in their community rather than being pushed out entirely because they could not afford the current market rent for any size of apartment. Nor do the analyses focused on mobility distinguish between moves that people make voluntarily to improve their lives and moves forced by increasing rents (displacement). There is a substantial medical and sociological literature documenting that the displacement of low-income people creates severe stress, with long-term health and mental health impacts—costs that receive no attention from the economics literature.

When there is a shortage of any good, rising prices ration the existing supply, allocating the scarce good to those willing and able to pay the most. If we let prices ration scarce housing, we are saying that high-income people are more deserving of access to the neighborhood or city of their choice than low-income people, and that the time people have lived in an area and the presence of family and friends is important only to the extent that it is backed up by an ability to pay higher rents.

Housing Is Not a Simple Commodity

Mainstream economists and the real estate industry typically argue that affordable housing crises are a simple matter of supply and demand. In a typical statement, the National Multifamily Housing Council, a major industry association, assures us that rents "provide the economic incentives needed to attract new investment in rental housing, as well as to maintain existing housing stock. In this respect, housing is no different from other commodities, such as food and clothing—the amount producers supply is directly related to the prevailing market price." In this model, rental housing is a simple commodity and the rental housing market is self-correcting, so that rising rents will quickly generate additional supply and restore affordability, while rent controls will necessarily result in reduced maintenance and less construction of new housing.

In the real world, rental housing is a far more complex commodity than tomatoes or shirts, and those complexities create serious problems in matching supply with demand. Among the barriers to perfect competition is the fact that demand for housing is dependent on its location. Apartment modules can be built in a factory in Idaho and shipped for hundreds of miles to California, but unlike smart phones, their value when assembled depends on where they are ultimately located.

Housing Prices Include Land Value and Land Rent

Housing necessarily sits on land, whose value as a location is created by the larger society rather than by the building owner. Much of the value of rental housing in California comes from competition for access to coastal locations with growing job markets and high levels of natural and cultural amenities. In *The Wealth of Nations*, generally considered the founding work of market economics, Adam Smith pointed out that the "rent of houses" can be divided into the "building rent," the rent actually necessary to operate and maintain the building, and the "ground rent," which reflects demand for a desirable location. Smith went on to say that ground rent is a "species of revenue which the owner, in many cases, enjoys without any care or attention of his own." The real estate industry knows this quite well. It is virtually impossible to attend a real estate conference without hearing, multiple times, that the three most important determinants of whether an investment in real estate will be profitable are "location, location, and location."

What the industry loves about increases in land value is that they require little, if any, investment on the part of the property owner. Instead they result from

---

Paul Krugman Gets It Wrong Twice in One Column

Opponents frequently point to "liberal economist Paul Krugman," winner of a Nobel Prize in economics, to show that liberals and conservatives alike oppose rent control. On June 7, 2000, Krugman wrote a column in the *New York Times* about a story published on the previous day describing how dozens of applicants for apartments offered for rent in San Francisco were trying to impress prospective landlords with résumés, credit reports, and personal enthusiasm. Krugman knew this must be caused by rent control, even though he stated that he "didn't know a thing about" the San Francisco housing market. "Landlords don't want groveling—they would rather have money. In uncontrolled markets the question of who gets an apartment is settled quickly by the question of who is able and willing to pay the most."

But under San Francisco's rent-stabilization system, rents for new tenancies are set by the landlord without restriction and then controlled again based on the new initial rent. These landlords could easily have raised their asking prices or had prospective tenants bid against each other, so what was really going on?

San Francisco was in the midst of the first dot-com boom. Thousands of newly hired, highly paid tech workers were moving into the city and rents were skyrocketing. Some landlords had not realized how high they could raise the rents, and were learning this when so many prospective tenants showed up. Other landlords were unsure whether the dot-com boom would last and wanted to get stable tenants rather than risk having tenants move out a few months later and have to re-rent the apartment at a lower rent. And in fact, when the dot-com boom collapsed in 2002, thousands of tech workers lost their jobs and rents went part of the way back down for a few years before turning upward again. So the story Krugman read the day before reflected the effects of incomplete knowledge and economic uncertainty rather than the effects of rent control.

Krugman followed this error with yet another. He claimed San Francisco had "an absence of new apartment construction, despite those high rents, because landlords fear that controls will be extended." In fact, rising rents had already resulted in a substantial increase in apartment construction that continues to this day. The fact that Paul Krugman could produce a column of such breathtaking inaccuracy demonstrates the hold that simplistic models of the rental-housing market have on even top-level economists.

the private and public actions of the residents in making their community a good place to live, typically some combination of government services and investment in infrastructure, neighborhood amenities, and private investment that increases employment. The real estate industry argues that rent control forces the landlord to "subsidize" tenants, when in fact the landlords are extracting unearned land rent from their tenants, taking publicly created value for private profit.

Adam Smith argued further that "though a part of this revenue should be taken from (the owner) in order to defray the expenses of the state, no discouragement will thereby be given to any sort of industry. ... A tax upon ground-rents would not raise the rents of houses." He was one of the first in a long line of economists, the most notable American being Henry George, who recognize that land-value taxation is "efficient" because it taxes value created by the larger society, not the value created by the property owner or the property owner's employees. This analysis of land rent also applies to rent control, which can be used to limit increases in land rent without reducing the rent below what is actually necessary to operate and maintain the building.

When it is possible to sufficiently increase the supply of housing at a desirable residential location, then the location will not be scarce and market competition will eliminate the land rent. Some inland locations are surrounded by flat, easily buildable land in all directions. But especially in coastal cities, geographic constraints limit the potential to increase the supply of housing. Since these limited urban areas are largely built out, they can only increase housing supply through increases in density, and this increases the per-unit construction cost. Geographic constraints are exacerbated by the real estate industry's successful century-long campaign to identify the single-family home as the "American Dream" and to create land-use regulations that exclude higher-density housing from single-family neighborhoods.

The opponents of rent control invariably claim that high housing costs are entirely the result of government interference with the market through exclusionary land-use regulations and that eliminating them will allow the market to become fully competitive and solve the supply problem. This ignores the other limitations of geography and increasing costs of production with increasing density. A recent study from the Federal Home Loan Mortgage Corporation estimates that two-thirds of San Francisco's excessive housing cost is the result of its geography, since 75% of the area within 50 miles of its downtown is under water or on steep hills, and another third of the excess housing cost is the result of restrictive zoning. It also ignores the disconnect between supply and demand that results from two other factors that distinguish rental housing from other commodities: its high development cost and its long life.

There Is a Disconnect between Supply and Demand in Rental Housing

The real estate industry endlessly repeats the claim that the rental housing affordability crisis is a "simple matter of supply and demand" and that increased supply is the only legitimate response. This is quite understandable, since this approach preserves the current massive transfer of income from tenants to real estate investors indefinitely. A very long period of time is required to substantially increase supply when adding 2% to the housing stock in a given year is a high rate of production. Currently, California is adding less than 1% per year and there is already a statewide and nationwide shortage of skilled construction workers that will take years to overcome before production can substantially increase. In areas with growing economies, it is hard for housing production to keep up. Nor is there any certainty that increased production of new housing will be sustained long enough to reduce rent burdens on most tenants.

Rising demand for rental housing increases rents throughout the rental-housing stock but does not generate additional housing supply at all price levels. Supply can only be added through new construction, and the expected rent for a newly constructed building must be enough to profitably pay off the costs of its construction as well as meet the ongoing costs to operate and maintain it. Then, once much of the cost of construction is paid off, after the first decade or so of operation, the property can be profitably operated and maintained at a substantially lower rent. If continued new housing construction pulls higher-income tenants away from buildings as they age, then owners of the older buildings will compete to attract tenants and will bring rents down closer to the minimum necessary to profitably operate and maintain the building. This process is called "filtering down." Most tenants live in older rental housing because they cannot afford the rents necessary to pay off the costs of construction but can afford to pay enough for a landlord to profitably operate and maintain the building once the construction costs are paid off.

However, there is no market mechanism to ensure "filtering" will happen or that the amount of housing that filters down will match the need for it. The Joint Center for Housing Studies at Harvard University reports that multifamily housing production increased for several years, but as vacancy rates have risen at the high

---

Three Mainstream Economists Hide Their Own Findings

Economists Rebecca Diamond, Timothy McQuade, and Franklin Qian recently conducted a sophisticated study of the effects of the 1994 expansion of rent stabilization to two- to four-unit properties in San Francisco. Their study found that thousands of renters were able to remain in San Francisco due to rent controls. It also found that the owners of the newly regulated small buildings shifted 15% of the units out of the rental market, mostly by converting them to condominiums, and that this loss of rental units increased market rents. Having found effects that both reduced and increased gentrification, the authors proceeded to make the much-publicized claim that "rent control has actually fueled the gentrification of San Francisco, the exact opposite of the policy's intended goal." What they really found was that allowing condominium conversion had fueled gentrification and undercut the positive effects of rent stabilization.

They also found that the overall financial benefits to tenants were still higher than the costs that resulted from allowing condominium conversions. But they hid this finding by explicitly omitting from their calculations the "benefits for renters who moved into the impacted units in later years (after 1994) which presumably were also quite large" and by closing the study in 2012, just after the end of the recession and before the rapid rent increases of the last six years. As a result, opponents of rent control routinely make the false claim that this study showed that the benefits of rent control to one group of tenants were entirely offset by its costs to other tenants. The authors conclude that a massive program of rent subsidies would work better than rent control, but make no suggestions for where the money might come from. It appears that three mainstream economists were so deeply attached to market solutions that they were unable to accept their own findings.

end of the rental market, multifamily housing production has declined, even though vacancies remain low in the rest of the rental market. The only way to directly respond to the growing need for housing with lower rents is for government to subsidize the costs of new construction, thus creating what is commonly referred to as "affordable housing" where rents only need to cover the costs of operation, maintenance, and a renovation reserve.

Increases in the rents charged for older housing cannot result in the production of additional older housing. They simply inflict hardship on tenants and transfer income from non-owners to owners. Their only "purpose" is to ration access to scarce rental housing based on who can pay the most money. These are the increases that are limited by rent controls.

Rent control, in its various forms, reduces the hardships caused by rent increases that result from a scarcity of older housing. It provides an alternative method of rationing access, giving priority to security of tenure and stability rather than to whoever has the most money. Modern rent-control systems in the United States exempt new construction, which makes sense because that is the sector of the rental housing market in which price increases will generate additional supply. This in turn explains why the empirical literature finds that modern rent control systems have no discernable effect on new construction.

Tenants Lack Bargaining Power Under Conditions of Scarcity

Since rent control simply limits the level of land rent, and owners receive at least as much rent as they would in a perfectly competitive market, they will have the revenue necessary to profitably operate and maintain their property. To evade this conclusion, opponents of rent control typically make two self-contradictory arguments: that increased supply will stabilize and even lower rents without reducing maintenance, but that if rent controls stabilize rents somehow landlords will be unable to maintain their property.

When they are not simply hypocritical, arguments that rent controls will result in reduced maintenance and lower housing quality are based on a simplistic understanding of the rental housing market. Maintenance is not a direct response to the amount of rent paid but rather to the differential between the rent that can be obtained for well-maintained versus poorly maintained rental housing. In a tight rental housing market, reduced maintenance may not result in much of a reduction in rent, especially for those landlords with lower-income tenants who have few alternatives and little bargaining power. We see this routinely with low-income tenants in coastal California, who often live in substandard conditions yet pay rents that would be well above average in other parts of the United States.

Rent-control systems under which landlords can evict tenants only with good cause (i.e., for good reasons such as non-payment of rent or damaging the unit rather than for complaining about poor maintenance) can help re-establish the differential by empowering tenants to call for code enforcement and petition the rent control program for rent decreases for code violations. A study of Washington, D.C., found that code violations declined after rent control began and that the exempt housing stock had a higher rate of deficiencies than the housing under rent control. A recent review of the empirical literature sponsored by the National Multifamily Housing Council, which is hostile to rent controls, found that "rent-controlled buildings potentially can suffer from deterioration or lack of investment, but the risk is minimized when there are effective local requirements and/or incentives for building maintenance and improvements."

Rent Regulation Must be Part of a Broader Program to be Effective

Rent control needs companion policies because landlords will work to evade regulation by finding other more profitable ways to use the rental housing under their control. A frequent finding in studies of rent control is that some landlords will convert their rental properties to condominiums and sell them to owner-occupants, thus reducing the overall stock of rental housing. Local governments have control over condominium conversion and often ban this response by landlords. Alternatively, some cities treat this as a desirable effect and pass accompanying legislation to give tenants a right of first refusal to buy their apartment, provide them with down-payment assistance, and offer lifetime leases to those who don't want to buy. There are also a few landlords who have sufficient income from property in other cities that they can afford to hold buildings vacant in protest against rent control. Vacant building taxes provide one potential response. As the latter situation makes clear, what is involved here is a power struggle, not simply the impersonal forces of the market at work.

Rent control systems in New York City and in a few other cities have "vacancy control," meaning that rents are not allowed to increase to current market levels when a tenant moves out and a new tenant moves in. It is often claimed that landlords will select higher-income tenants over lower-income tenants to reduce non-payment of rent, so that rent control will not benefit the tenants who need it most. There is some evidence to the contrary from the experience of Berkeley under strong rent control, where it appeared that apartments continued to circulate within the same social circle as tenants moved out. In addition, Berkeley allowed landlords to obtain higher rents when they rented to tenants receiving federal Section 8 assistance, leading to high participation in that program. Nonetheless, the landlord maintains control over the selection of new tenants, so it could be useful to explore providing incentives to encourage landlords to rent lower-rent units to lower-income tenants.

Many rent control systems allow rent to jump to whatever the market will bear between the departure of an old tenant and the arrival of a new tenant, a policy called "vacancy decontrol." A cap on rent increases starts up again at the start of a new tenancy. (This type of system is often called "rent stabilization" in contrast with stronger "rent control.") Since these systems can be evaded by evicting long-term tenants, they are normally accompanied by a requirement that landlords show "good cause" for evictions. Landlords faced with a combination of rent control, vacancy decontrol, and good cause for eviction requirements may become less tolerant of minor lease violations and increase evictions for cause. Cities can deal with this by providing emergency rental assistance to renters who suffer short-term loss of income and by requiring that landlords provide tenants with sufficient opportunity to correct a lease violation. This portfolio of policies—vacancy decontrol, rent control, good cause, and emergency rental assistance—reduces displacement. Since rents rise to the market level as tenants move, such systems do not maintain affordability over the long run and other affordability programs are necessary.

The power of the real estate industry is such that sometimes policy moves the wrong way, as shown by the abolition of rent controls in Massachusetts in 1994, the abolition of vacancy controls in California in 1995, and the many statewide prohibitions on local rent controls. In any place where rent control is needed because the market does not supply sufficient housing affordable to lower-income tenants, the long-term goal should be to provide capital subsidies to build up the supply of permanently affordable housing owned by nonprofit housing corporations, limited-equity cooperatives, and community land trusts. Social ownership protects against political changes hostile to the presence of low-income residents. That is a very long-term and expensive solution, but taxes on land value or land rent would be one very fair way to raise the money. The California cities of Berkeley and East Palo Alto increased their taxes on the gross receipts of residential rental properties to fund affordable housing and homelessness prevention, as close to a tax on land rent as state law allows.

Finally, many people don't make enough money to afford even the minimum rent necessary to pay for the ongoing operation and maintenance of rental housing. Even when the rental housing market is working well, or if there is a substantial supply of socially owned housing rented at cost, the lowest-income people will need rent subsidies or, better yet, higher wages and a guarantee of a decent income for those unable to work.

Rent Control and Human Rights

Rent control is one of many efforts to uphold human dignity by expanding human rights, those rights which are held to be inherent in all people, and restraining forms of private property that give owners power over non-owners. Economist and historian Albert O. Hirschman described three rhetorical themes consistently used by opponents of human rights. These themes, which he called "the rhetoric of reaction," are: *perversity*—the argument that a reform will harm those it is intended to help; *futility*—the argument that a reform will do no good; and *jeopardy*—the argument that the reform will endanger progress already made. This is an accurate description of the arguments made against rent control and in defense of the power of real estate investors to exact unearned land rent from tenants. Opponents claim it will harm tenants by reducing the supply of rental housing through conversion to owner-occupancy, result in reduced maintenance to match lower rents, and endanger the new construction needed to house a growing population. But as we have seen, the rental housing market is not a simple matter of supply and demand. Instead, it is inherently prone to failure and persistent scarcity in urban areas with growing economies. When demand far outstrips supply, only rent regulation has sufficient scope and timeliness to stabilize tenants' lives, reduce forced displacement, and limit the hardships caused by unfair and unnecessary rent increases. ❏

Sources: Joshua D. Ambrosius, et al. "Forty years of rent control: Reexamining New Jersey's moderate local policies after the great recession," *Cities* (2015); Richard Arnott, "Time for Revisionism on Rent Control?," *Journal of Economic Perspectives*, Winter 1995; Stephen Barton, "Land Rent and Housing Policy: A Case Study of the San Francisco Bay Area Rental Housing

Market," *American Journal of Economics and Sociology* (fundaffordablehousing.org); Stephen Barton, "Land Value, Land Rent and Progressive Housing Policy," *Progressive Planning*, Fall 2010 (fundaffordablehousing.org); Sean Becketti & Elias Yannopoulos, "Is Geography Destiny," Freddie Mac, September 2017 (freddiemac.com); Rebecca Diamond, Timothy McQuade, and Franklin Qian, "The Effects of Rent Control Expansion on Tenants, Landlords and Inequality: Evidence from San Francisco," National Bureau of Economic Research, Working Paper 24181, January 2018 (nber.org); Lee S. Friedman, *Microeconomics of Public Policy Analysis*, Chapter 13, "The Control of Prices to Achieve Equity in Specific Markets" (Princeton University Press, 2002); Henry Grabar, "Rent Control is Back," Slate, Oct. 17, 2018 (slate.com); Michael Hiltzik, "Proposition 10," *Los Angeles Times*, Oct. 19, 2018 (latimes.com); W. Dennis Keating, Michael B. Teitz & Andrejs Skaburskis, *Rent Control: Regulation and the Rental Housing Market*, Center for Urban Policy Research, New Brunswick, 1998; Neil Mayer, "Rehabilitation decisions in rental housing: an empirical analysis," *Journal of Urban Economics*, 1981; Nicole Montojo, Stephen Barton and Eli Moore, *Opening the Door for Rent Control: Toward a Comprehensive Approach to Protecting California's Renters*, Haas Institute for a Fair and Inclusive Society, University of California, Berkeley, September 2018 (haasinstitute.berkeley.edu); E. O. Olsen, "What do economists know about the effect of rent control on housing maintenance?," *Journal of Finance and Economics*, 1988; Manuel Pastor, Vanessa Carter, and Maya Abood, *Rent Matters: What are the Impacts of Rent Stabilization Measures?*, Program for Environmental and Regional Equity, University of Southern California, October 2018 (dornsife.usc.edu); Lisa Sturtevant, *The Impacts of Rent Control: A Research Review and Synthesis*, Multifamily Housing Research Council, Washington D.C., May 2018; Miriam Zuk and Karen Chapple, "Housing Production, Filtering and Displacement: Untangling the Relationships," Research Brief, Institute of Governmental Studies, May 2016 (urbandisplacement.org).

Article 2.3

GETTING UP TO SPEED ON THE MINIMUM WAGE
The Wall Street Journal *editors need to do their homework.*

BY JOHN MILLER
May/June 2021

> "The Young and the Jobless: The minimum wage hike has driven the wages of teen employees to $0.00"
> —The Editorial Board, *Wall Street Journal*, Oct. 3, 2009

> "Reality check for a $15 Minimum Wage: How many jobs for the young and unskilled do Democrats want to lose?"
> —The Editorial Board, *Wall Street Journal*, Feb. 8, 2021

> "Raising the Minimum Wage Definitely Costs Jobs"
> —David Neumark, *Wall Street Journal*, March 18, 2021

In 2009, Congress raised the federal minimum wage to $7.25 per hour. In February of this year, the House of Representatives passed the Raise the Wage Act of 2021, which would double the $7.25 minimum wage to $15 by 2025. But the Senate declined to include raising the minimum wage in the American Rescue Plan it approved in March, although Senate Democrats are talking about adding the minimum wage increase to the Biden infrastructure proposal currently being considered by Congress.

Regardless of whether it is 2009 or 2021, the *Wall Street Journal* editors are still convinced that raising the minimum wage would mean unemployment for the very workers the legislation intends to help. The fact that it has been 12 years since Congress last increased the minimum wage, or that the current proposal would increase the minimum wage in gradual steps, isn't about to change their minds.

Why are the editors so cocksure that raising the minimum wage is a bad idea? That's easy. After all, anyone who has taken introductory economics was taught that imposing a wage floor in a low-wage labor market (above the equilibrium wage) would leave many workers without a job. And on top of that, for many years the consensus position of the economics profession was that minimum wage increases inevitably cause job losses, and the only question of interest was just how many jobs would be lost.

But just because the editors are wedded to their claim that the minimum wage is a jobs killer doesn't mean you should be, too. To begin with, the assumptions that underlie this simplistic introductory lesson about the minimum wage, which you saw illustrated on the chalkboard of old or on today's electronic whiteboard, are routinely violated. For one thing, labor markets are seldom competitive. Nor are all things held constant when the minimum wage increases, especially productivity and price levels. (More about that below.)

More importantly, the consensus among economists that the minimum wage inevitably destroys jobs has been steadily unraveling since the early 1990s. More and more evidence has piled up suggesting that the negative employment effect of increasing the minimum wage is negligible or even nonexistent.

But none of that has registered with the *Wall Street Journal* editors, who are content to recycle their editorials without a mention of this new minimum wage research. I doubt their recycling is good for the environment—and it is surely bad for honest discourse about the impact of increasing the minimum wage. Their ideological blindness contributes to, and, indeed, celebrates, the unwillingness of politicians to face up to the fact that the minimum wage is a poverty wage.

Outdated and in Need of Reconsideration

The "new literature" on the minimum wage is now nearly 30 years old. But it is still news to the *Wall Street Journal* editors.

At the beginning of this year, London School of Economics economist Alan Manning wrote honestly of the difficulty of discerning the "elusive employment effect" of the minimum wage, to use his words, in a leading economics journal. But instead of paying attention to the advances and limitations highlighted in Manning's article, the *Wall Street Journal* editors grabbed hold of the CBO's assessment of the budgetary effects of The Raise the Wage Act of 2021. The CBO report found that a $15 minimum wage would cost 1.4 million workers their jobs. For the editors, the report was a "Reality Check for a $15 Minimum Wage," which showed that "the gains would come at a high cost."

But nowhere do the editors mention the high degree of uncertainty around the CBO's employment loss estimates. For instance, the CBO's estimate of the median, or middle, estimate of the lost jobs from the increases in minimum wage in the studies they reviewed was 1.0 million. That was less than the average estimate of the number of lost jobs (which was pulled from a few studies that found extremely large job losses were likely). The report cautions that there is a one-third chance that the number of workers who lose their job from boosting the minimum wage would be between zero and 1.0 million workers.

Economist Michael Reich, a minimum wage expert at the University of California, Berkeley whose work is cited by the CBO, took issue with the report's pessimistic estimates. "A phased increase would likely be absorbed without detectable effects on employment," he said on a call to reporters.

Writing in the *Monitor Consult*, Reich explained that the CBO relied on state-level data on wages and employment. But in his research conducted with Anna Godoey, Reich used more detailed data from over 150 counties and metropolitan areas in 45 states to assess the likely effect of increasing the minimum wage to $15 by 2025. They found that higher minimum wages do not have adverse effects on employment.

Their study found that consumers and the economy absorb higher wage standards. Higher minimum wages reduce employee turnover costs, reducing recruiting and training costs for firms, and increase worker productivity. In addition, low-wage employers, such as restaurants, absorb minimum wage costs through small price increases.

Godoey and Reich's findings are consistent with the increasing number of studies that have found little or no job loss as a result of minimum wage increases. Economists David Card and Alan Krueger conducted the first and still most important of these studies in 1994. Card and Krueger found that after New Jersey increased its minimum wage there were no job losses among fast-food workers; indeed, their level of employment actually increased relative to that of nearby fast-food workers in Pennsylvania.

What Do We Know About the Minimum Wage?

A $7.25 minimum wage is indeed a poverty wage. A minimum wage worker working 40 hours a week earns at most $15,000 a year. That income falls below the poverty line for a family with two or more members. An income of $15,000 a year is far less than the typical expenditures of a family of three as calculated by the Joint Economic Committee, and not even enough to cover the average cost of rental housing.

At $15 an hour the minimum wage would alleviate poverty. It would exceed the poverty line for a family of four in 2021. A $15 minimum wage would lift 3.7 million people out of poverty, just over one-third of them children, according to the Economic Policy Institute. A recent Congressional Budget Office (CBO) study, even with its large estimates of job losses, still finds that a $15 minimum wage would lift 900,000 people out of poverty.

An increase in the federal minimum wage is long overdue. The purchasing power of the minimum wage reached its peak in 1968—52 years ago—and has been on the decline ever since. If the minimum wage had kept up with inflation, it would be $11.90 today. If the minimum wage had also kept up with productivity gains since 1968, the minimum wage would have reached $31.67, according to calculations by economist Robert Pollin, who has written extensively about the minimum wage. Today, some 29 states and Washington, D.C., along with several cities, already have a minimum wage that is higher than $7.25.

Raising the minimum wage to $15 would boost the income of about one-fifth of the labor force. Not only would minimum wage workers get a raise, but a higher minimum wage would also push up the wages of other low-income workers. The Economic Policy Institute estimates that by 2025, a $15 minimum wage would directly increase the wages of 22.1 million workers and push up the wages of another 10.1 million low-income workers—that's 32.2 million workers altogether. Even the recent CBO study, which the 2021 *Wall Street Journal* editorial relies upon, allows that a $15 minimum wage would raise the wages of 27 million workers.

The chief beneficiaries from increasing the minimum wage are adult workers, not teenagers. What's more, women and minority workers will especially benefit from a wage increase. The vast majority of minimum wage workers are adults—just 20% are 16 to 19 years of age, according to the Bureau of Labor Statistics. The Economic Policy Institute reports that a $15 minimum wage would benefit 25.8% of all women workers and 31.6% of single parents. Also, 31.3% of Black workers would benefit, as would 26.0% of Hispanic workers.

Low wage workers would benefit from raising the minimum wage to $15 even if it caused large job losses. No less than David Neumark, perhaps the preeminent defender of the traditional view of the minimum wage, allowed in his recent *Wall Street Journal* opinion piece that, "It's true that some workers would experience higher incomes and that, on net, incomes of low-wage workers would probably rise."

Beyond a $15 Minimum Wage

As you can imagine, the new research on the minimum wage did not go down easy in the economics profession. But economists would do well to remember their own history of supporting the original minimum wage and other labor reforms of the Progressive Era a century ago. Leading labor economists of the day employed some of the same arguments used to support the current push for a living wage to make the case for a minimum wage, such as higher wages enhancing economic efficiency.

Many Progressive Era reformers considered any employer who paid less than a living wage to be a "parasitic" employer. Their low wages undercut the market share and profits of firms that were paying their workers a living wage. At the same time, it fell to the community and taxpayers to provide the support necessary to sustain employees who could not survive on low wages.

Combatting parasitic wages is no less of a compelling reason for raising the minimum wage today than it was for enacting a minimum wage a century ago. But that alone will not be enough. A $15 minimum wage would fall short of a living wage for a single adult in much of the country, and far short of a living wage for an adult with children. (For more detailed estimates by geographic location, see MIT's living wage calculator at livingwage.mit.edu.) Yet more needs to be done to counteract the decades old wage stagnation that has eroded the living standard of so many workers.

We should not let the chalk dust of introductory economics, or the outdated opinions of the *Wall Street Journal* editors, stand in the way of enacting these reforms. ❑

Sources: David Neumark, "Raising the Minimum Wage Definitely Costs Jobs," *Wall Street Journal*, March 18, 2021; "The Federal Minimum Wage," Joint Economic Committee, July 1, 2019; Joint Economic Committee, "Criticisms of Minimum Wage Increases Lag Behind Latest Research," March 25, 2021; David Cooper, Zane Mokhiber, and Ben Zipperer, "Raising the federal minimum wage to $15 by 2025 would lift the pay of 32 million workers," Economic Policy Institute, March 9, 2021 (epi.org); "Hiking the Minimum Wage to $15 is Key—But is hardly a living wage," interview with Robert Pollin, *Truthout*, March 7, 2021 (truthout.org); David Card and Alan Krueger, "Minimum Wages and Employment: A Case Study of the Fast-Food Industry in New Jersey and Pennsylvania," *The American Economic Review*, Sept. 1994; Alan Manning, "The Elusive Employment Effect of the Minimum Wage," *Journal of Economic Perspectives*, Winter 2021; "The Budgetary Effects of the Raise the Wage Act of 2021," Congressional Budget Office, February 2021; Edward Lempinen, "A $15 minimum wage would costs jobs, right? Probably not, economists say," *Berkeley News*, March 18, 2021; Michael Reich, "65 Billion Reasons Why the Senate Can Pass a $15 minimum Wage by Reconciliation, *Morning Consult*, Feb. 4, 2021; Anna Godoey and Michael Reich, "The US can raise the minimum wage to $15 without hurting jobs," CNN Business Perspectives, July 11, 2019; Robert Prasch, "American Economist in the Progressive Era on the Minimum Wage," *Journal of Economic Perspectives*, Spring 1999; Marilyn Power, "Parasitic-Industries Analysis and Arguments for a Living Wage," *Feminist Economics*, Vol. 5, Issue 1, 1999.

Article 2.4

DRUGS AND GLOBAL CAPITALISM

The sheer size of the drug economy suggests its pervasive entanglement with global capitalism.

BY SASHA BREGER BUSH
September/October 2020

The idea that drugs are indispensable to the global capitalist economic system is more apparent today than it would been have less than a year ago. Much of the world's population today waits, scared and isolated, for the global drug economy to deliver us from the Covid-19 pandemic. Remdesivir, ivermectin, hydroxychloroquine, heparin, dexamethasone, azithromycin, lopinavir-ritonavir, ribavirin, and interferon-beta, among other drugs, are currently being touted in various quarters as effective treatments for the illness caused by the SARS-CoV-2 virus. The global race to produce an effective vaccine continues at a breathtaking pace, with Moderna, AstraZeneca, and many other companies and laboratories working to find one that works. At this particular moment it is a bit easier to see the tight relationships between drugs and global capitalism. Without effective vaccines and/or treatments for Covid-19, workers cannot work as they did before, consumers cannot consume as they did before, some factories cannot produce as much as they did before because of collapsed demand, while others cannot produce enough to meet surging demand, ships cannot dock and warehouses are either too empty or too full, and financial markets move up and down with the news about vaccine and other drug trials.

Yet the data suggest that even in times when the world is not wrestling with a global pandemic, drugs play central and critical roles in relation to global capitalism. Generally, the relationship between drugs and capitalism takes two major forms. First, drugs are a source of wealth and income. Drug revenues stem not only from direct drug production and sales, but also from other, more indirect pathways. Second, drugs act as a kind of insurance that help manage and mitigate the damage capitalist dynamics do to human and other beings, as well as social and ecological systems. Of course, these two points overlap, as this drug "insurance" works to allow continued profit making and accumulation. The discussion below is not a comprehensive one, for there are too many important connections between drugs and capitalism for one article to exhaust. Rather, I clarify and highlight a series of these relationships that I think are the most salient.

Direct Drug Revenues

The global drug market is absolutely enormous and represents a sizeable proportion of global economic activity. "Drugs" in modern societies have come to be understood largely as black-market products that are addictive and "personality destroying" (cocaine, heroin, amphetamines, and the like). The term—"drugs"—thus carries some legalistic and moralistic baggage that interferes with one's ability to observe drug markets clearly. One major consequence of categorizing drugs in the typical way is to minimize their apparent size and relative importance in the global economy, for when "drug" market figures are quoted they typically include only a handful of the great many substances that rightfully qualify as such. In fact, there is a really broad array of products that seem to be drugs even though we do not often call them by that name. The question "what is a drug?" is thus an important one for research purposes, and there is no clear answer to it. What is clear, though, is that toying with the category of "drugs" makes hidden features of the global drug economy more visible, opening up new avenues for research.

The drug-market figures typically quoted in the news are of two types: black-market drugs and prescription drugs. The last years for which figures are available indicates that global illegal drug markets were about $425 billion in 2014, while the global pharmaceutical and medicine market was roughly $1.2 trillion in 2018. Yet, by my rough accounting, this accounts for little more than half of the global drug market. If we add to this tally global markets in alcohol and tobacco products and in caffeinated beverages like coffee, tea, and soda, the sum grows very large indeed. I also added U.S. markets in other kinds of drugs like vitamin supplements, over-the-counter medications, and veterinary drugs, for which data are readily available (the U.S. market is the largest globally in these products). Of course, there are other substances that I do not provide figures for that could and probably should be included (e.g., khat and betel nut are widely consumed around the world, but the data is pretty spotty), and then still others that might be included with some controversy (e.g., sugar and corn syrup). These back-of-the-envelope calculations thus represent only a portion of the actual global drug economy, but even so, the figure is enormous—almost $3 trillion—as indicated in Table 1 below.

To put this figure into perspective, the World Bank estimates that in 2018, world GDP was about $80.7 trillion, meaning that the global drug economy accounted for, at a minimum, 3.5% of global GDP that year. This is more than six times the size of recent estimates of the illegal drug market, and almost double the market size that one might figure by simply summing together illegal and pharmaceutical drug markets.

Based on 2017 GDP data from the World Bank, the chunk of the global drug economy tallied in the table is about 15% of the size of the U.S. economy, more than twice the size of the economy of Australia, and more than four times the size of the economy of Saudi Arabia.

It was about five times larger than the semiconductor and electronics industry in 2018, according to IBIS World data (i.e., industry revenues for semiconductor and electronic parts manufacturers). It is more than $600 billion larger than the global revenues of commercial banks in 2018 (according to IBIS World). And the global drug economy is about 25% larger than total global revenues in 2018 from oil and gas exploration and production (according to IBIS World, in 2018 global oil and gas exploration and production revenues were roughly $2.28 trillion).

Moreover, market growth in one corner of the drug market can boost growth in other corners. In other words, individual drug products do not always substitute for one another, but rather complement each other such that the sales of one drug can help boost the sales of others. For example, one recent study finds that while alcohol consumption is often negatively related to crack-cocaine consumption, it is positively

Table 1: Size of the Global Drug Economy[1]

Market segment	Size	Measure
Global pharmaceutical and medicine manufacturing	$1.188 trillion	Industry revenues[2]
Global beer manufacturing	$208.3 billion	Industry revenues
Global cigarette and tobacco manufacturing	$684.3 billion	Industry revenues
Global spirits manufacturing	$78.8 billion	Industry revenues
Global wine manufacturing	$104.6 billion	Industry revenues
Global soft drink manufacturing (carbonated soft drinks and functional beverages only)[3]	$121.3 billion	Industry revenues
Illegal drugs (cannabis, cocaine and cocaine-based products, opiates, and amphetamine-type substances/ATS only)	$426 billion	Retail value[4]
Global coffee market	$18.033 billion	Global coffee trade multiplied by ICO indicator price
Global tea market	$15.25 billion	Gross production value (based on farmgate prices)
US vitamin and supplement manufacturing	$30.7 billion	Industry revenues
US OTC cough and cold medicine manufacturing (non-Rx)	$10.48 billion	Industry revenues
US animal health biotechnologies (vaccines and other drugs for use in animals)	$6.1 billion	Industry revenues
Minimum size of the global drug economy in 2018: $2.891 trillion (USD)		

Sources: All figures are from IBIS World Database (ibisworld.com) except for for illegal drugs (from Global Financial Integrity's 2017 report, gfintegrity.org), coffee (from the International Coffee Organization, Ico.org), and tea (from the U.N. Food and Agricultural Organization, fao.org/faostat). All units are current U.S. dollars; all figures are for 2018, except coffee, which is for 2015–2016, and tea, which is for 2016.

Notes:

[1]The market segments estimated here may overlap to some extent. For example the global coffee export market overlaps with the market for manufactured soft drinks in that this latter category includes some ready-to-drink coffee products. This imprecision is unavoidable given current categories for and modes of data collection and analysis. That said, it seems reasonable to assume that whatever "extra" market size is calculated as a consequence of such overlap, the final/total figures for the global drug market as a whole are still likely underestimated because most of the figures presented do not represent final retail values, which are considerably higher in most cases. Wherever possible, I err on the side of underestimating the size of the global drug market. For some market segments, only data for U.S. markets were available.

[2]IBIS World Database's definition of industry revenue: "The total sales of industry goods and services (exclusive of excise and sales tax); subsidies on production; all other operating income from outside the firm (such as commission income, repair and service income, and rent, leasing and hiring income); and capital work done by rental or lease. Receipts from interest royalties, dividends and the sale of fixed tangible assets are excluded" (IBIS World Database). While the inclusion of subsidies and rental income, for example, may result in an over-estimation of the size of this market segment, please bear in mind that these figures are for manufacturing revenues, and thus likely under-estimate the final value of consumer drug purchases globally.

[3]The category of carbonated soft drinks includes both caffeinated and non-caffeinated beverages. "Functional" beverages include energy drinks, sports drinks (including powdered ones), relaxation drinks, and ready-to-drink coffees and teas.

[4]The method used by Global Financial Integrity here was to take the most recent retail market estimates for four global illegal drug submarkets (cannabis, opiates, cocaine, and amphetamine-type substances) from the UNODC and to adjust them upward for inflation (to 2014). Of the two methods employed, this one produced the lowest size estimate. The other method—based on UNODC's most recent estimates of illegal drug markets as a % of GDP—arrived at a much larger figure: US$652 billion in 2014. I use the smaller of the two figures here, so as to consistently try to consistently underestimate the size of the global drug market wherever possible.

associated with powder cocaine use. When people consume cocaine, they also typically increase their consumption of alcohol, such that profits in one drug domain result in profits in another. As another example, many drugs cause side effects that make consumers uncomfortable or ill or may put them in danger. Other drugs are often prescribed by physicians to manage these side effects, for example, anti-nausea drugs used to mitigate the side effects of chemotherapy treatments or laxatives used to treat constipation among patients treated with opioids. In some cases, the very same company that produces and markets a drug that causes harm to consumers also produces other drugs that mitigate that harm. Purdue Pharma, the manufacturer of OxyContin, also produces and markets buprenorphine, the opioid drug used to treat opioid addiction in the context of medically assisted therapy.

Indirect Drug Profits

Activity in global drug markets also facilitates indirect profit making. One of the best examples of these indirect effects comes from drug-market regulation, and specifically how the War on Drugs in the United States and abroad allows for capital accumulation and concentration. Dawn Paley, in her book *Drug War Capitalism*, focuses on the imperial dimensions of the drug war, arguing that efforts to crack down on drug production in Latin America helps to clear people and agricultural production from the land, "freeing" it up to be used for other purposes, like mining and extraction by multinational conglomerates. And many volumes have been written, (for example, Michelle Alexander's *The New Jim Crow*) on the ways that the drug war in the United States enriches participants in the prison-industrial complex and other law enforcement arenas, to the detriment, especially, of people of color and the poor.

Profits also flow from patterns of drug consumption and the impacts of drug consumption on human physical and mental states. Occupational drug consumption is in many cases associated with more productive workers, for example with workers who partake of central nervous system (CNS) stimulants like caffeine and amphetamines. CNS stimulants are deeply intertwined with the history of capitalism, and especially with the lives of workers. The birth of factory work changed the way people labored and the conditions in which they labored, generating massive demand for drugs like coffee and tea—stimulants that traders readily exported from plantations across the Global South, worked by slaves and indentured servants, into imperial centers across the global North. Political economist Raj Patel deftly connects capitalist prerogatives in Britain during the early Industrial Revolution with the physiological effects of CNS stimulants on the bodies and minds of workers, contrasting the effects of stimulants with those of beer, a CNS depressant:

> The demise of beer's place in everyday life does, however, show how traders in tea and sugar were able to ride, and further cause, changes in centuries-old tastes, reduce levels of nutrition and get a more caffeinated workforce for the 'workshop of the world' as a result. This, then, is the genealogy of the can of Red Bull. Tea was the original Jolt. It was a drink high in basic stimulants and carbohydrates, sweet and perky.

Like other CNS stimulants, caffeinated beverages like coffee and tea and Red Bull work to improve productivity by improving energy, focus and concentration, and reducing appetite/hunger. The implicit subsidy to the employer conferred by rampant worker consumption of stimulants should be squarely noted. With CNS stimulates reducing worker appetites, workers' need for breaks is also minimized and the low wages paid to workers are made more tolerable by reducing worker food expenditures. On this point, Patel links the practice of female factory workers drinking tea with milk and sugar in early industrial Britain to slaves on plantations across the Global South chewing sugar cane—both provide much needed energy and calories to workers quickly and cheaply on the job site, with minimal interruption or cost to employers.

The central importance of stimulants for work under capitalism is partly indicated by the simple fact that employers often readily supply their employees with such drugs for the explicit purpose of improving their performance. One of the more well-known examples of this pattern is the widespread dispensation of amphetamines to troops during World War II, on both the Allied and Axis sides of the conflict. Nicolas Rasmussen's excellent history of this episode indicates that Germany was first to provide methamphetamines to its troops:

> Indeed, April through June 1940, the peak of the Blitz, corresponds to the wartime peak in the German military's consumption of amphetamines. According to Steinkamp, the Wehrmacht used 35 million 3mg methamphetamine tablets for these three months alone, and much less thereafter. In both the United States and Britain, top-level scientific advisory bodies devoted to the military problems of "fatigue" earnestly began studying the effects of the drugs and their military utility.

When American troops landed in North Africa in 1942, U.S. General Dwight D. Eisenhower ordered half a million doses of Benzedrine sulfate for soldiers on this front of the war. And British troops received 20 milligrams of Benzedrine daily prior to a battle in Egypt that same year.

As with certain kinds of military occupations, there are some jobs for which stimulant use is practically endemic to the occupation itself. Notably, workers in occupations that require long shifts and/or night work often consume CNS stimulants to complete their assigned tasks.

That human bodies do not perform optimally at night provides even more fuel for stimulant demand, with CNS stimulants often utilized by laborers who work night shifts to help them overcome the fatigue and confusion associated with interrupting their body's circadian rhythm. For example, a 2019 study of drug consumption among long-haul truckers around the world found that more than 20% of truckers use amphetamines at work, while 2.2% use cocaine (most of the studies reviewed for this meta-study were done about truckers working in the Americas, but all six inhabitable continents were represented, and were conducted via questionnaire). The study's authors note, "It appears that truck-drivers choose stimulant substances as a form of performance-enhancing drug, in order to increase productivity."

And, of course, when soldiers are injured or traumatized in battle, or when truckers have an accident on the road late at night, we partly turn to drugs to try to put their bodies and minds back together again, so they can work another day. Veterans of the

U.S. conflicts in Iraq and Afghanistan, for example, were often heavily dosed with zolpidem (Ambien), a powerful sedative/hypnotic, to help them with insomnia. In fact, the way drugs are used to enhance workforce productivity—variously used to boost productivity and then also to treat work-related trauma, illness, and injury—is not all that different from the way in which industrial meat producers utilize antibiotics and other drugs to ensure profitability in the context of concentrated animal feeding operations that can often make the animals sick.

Drugs as Insurance for Capitalism

As most critical observers of capitalism have noted, this is a volatile and often-brutal system that wreaks havoc on individuals and communities, on other species, and on the Earth itself. The damage that capitalism causes can to some extent be mitigated or covered up by drug consumption. A few examples help to illustrate this point.

For at least 200 years, observers have noted that capitalism is prone to economic and financial crisis. In the Marxist tradition, this is understood as a consequence of systematic overproduction and underconsumption that leads to imbalances. In the Keynesian tradition, this is understood as a consequence of poorly regulated financial markets that subject the economy to boom-bust cycles. Whatever the cause, economic crises have historically catalyzed massive upheavals and social unrest. Drugs figure in here as insurance in at least two ways. On the macroeconomic level, some drug markets appear to move countercyclically, with drug market revenues remaining stable or even increasing as general economic conditions deteriorate. This exerts a stabilizing force on the macroeconomy during times of crisis. For example, in the 1980s, Colombia was faced with an economic crisis in which they were short on the foreign exchange necessary to pay off dollar-denominated debts. But, unlike many other countries that defaulted on their debts during this period, Colombia did not default and did not require International Monetary Fund or World Bank structural-adjustment loans. Why? Cocaine exports generated a flow of dollars into Colombia that officials bought with local currency in black foreign exchange markets. Some of the dollars were then used to pay foreign debts and stave off default.

That individual consumers often increase drug consumption during times of economic crisis and hardship is also fairly well documented in the medical literature. Economic crises generate hardship and suffering, for example owing to loss of income, unemployment, and housing problems. Drug consumers, on average, consume more drugs under such conditions. For example, in a 2018 study, researchers surveyed 180 European drug consumers about their consumption during the previous economic crisis and found that almost 60% of those surveyed had increased drug consumption during the crisis, compared to only about 25% who reported decreased consumption. Researchers found that, "The main reason given for increasing drug use was greater amount of free time available. Other important reasons were greater substance availability during this period, more stress at work and seeking comfort in response to the loss of a stable source of income, social status and/or family." In another example here in the United States persistently high levels of unemployment among certain demographic groups have contributed to the opioid epidemic.

Not only did drugs thus help "dull the pain," so to speak, associated with stress and suffering during the Great Recession in Europe, but it also provided a way for unemployed people to use their free time. To the extent that drugs co-opt proletarian time and reduce perceptions of suffering among the populace, this works to maintain the status quo and preempt protest, opposition, and civil unrest. This dynamic is just as visible today as it was in the 19th century when the British "pacified" the population of China with opium, thereby mitigating the pushback against British imperialism. Indeed, in Denver, Colo., where I live and work, our mayor quickly and conspicuously reversed his decision to stop marijuana and liquor sales when we locked down for the coronavirus in March. As *The Independent* reported: "According to local reports, the administration had to change its course after residents flocked to the shops to panic buy alcohol and marijuana the night before the lockdown came into force."

Onward

Drugs are an integral feature of capitalist economies. They are a source of direct revenue and income, accounting for at least 4% of world GDP in recent years (and likely much more). Drugs are also a source of indirect revenue and income that stem not only from the regulation of the global drug economy, but also from the close integration of drugs into working life. Drugs also provide insurance services of a sort that help to insulate capitalism from the pushback and fallout that often results from its volatile and brutal operations. Put differently, in much the same way that debt permits consumption beyond the limits posed by income, so, too, do drugs permit labor and suffering beyond the limits posed by biology and mental health.

These insights open up a variety of avenues for future research and exploration. One key set of questions involves occupational drug consumption. How prolific is occupational drug consumption? In what kinds of occupations? What kinds of drugs are consumed? By whom? Why? How? Under what conditions? Do employers provide these drugs? And so on. My travels through the drug economy have left me with the suspicion that, in the United States at least, occupational drug use is rampant and occurs in a variety of settings that we would not necessarily expect. For example, I am a university professor, and what little data is available indicates that university faculty consume certain kinds of drugs at levels well above the national average, including anti-anxiety and anti-depressant drugs. What is it about this occupation that seemingly facilitates above-average consumption of these particular drugs? Is this relatively high level of consumption related to the nature of the work itself and the conditions in which professors labor? Or is it related to structural changes in the academic labor market?

Another key set of questions involves the insurance function that drugs play in relation to global capitalism. In a sense, drug consumption is perhaps usefully considered as a signal or a marker of risk in capitalist systems. In some contexts, economic risks partly cause drug consumption, as in the example above of consumption in response to economic shock, and then the drug consumption itself works to mitigate another set of risks that are largely political and social (e.g., unemployed people with lots of free time). Many empirical questions arise here, especially about the relationship between social structures and individual behavior. Do individual drug behaviors, and changes in those behaviors, relate in any way to broader structural and systemic economic conditions? How and why? Are there stable and predictable relationships between drug consumption on the one hand, and structural economic conditions on the other? In what contexts? In other words, to roughly paraphrase Hunter S. Thompson, is it true that the brutal reality of capitalism is intolerable without drugs? ❏

Sources: Michelle Alexander, *The New Jim Crow: Mass Incarceration in the Age of Colorblindness*, The New Press, 2020; Adam Dean and Simeon Kimmel, "Free trade and opioid overdose death in the United States." *Population Health*, August 2019; G. Dini, N.L. Bragazzi, A. Montecucco, A. Rahmani, and P. Durando, "Psychoactive drug consumption among truck-drivers: a systematic review of the literature with meta-analysis and meta-regression," *Journal of Preventive Medicine and Hygiene*, June 2019; Louise Hall, "Coronavirus: Denver mayor forced to reverse lockdown of alcohol and marijuana shops following panic buying." *The Independent*, March 24, 2020; M. Gossop, V. Manning, and G Ridge, "Concurrent use and order of use of cocaine and alcohol: behavioural differences between users of crack cocaine and cocaine powder, *Addiction*, August 2006; Mary J. Gilchrist, Christina Greko, David B. Wallinga, George W. Beran, David G. Riley, and Peter S. Thorne, "The Potential Role of Concentrated Animal Feeding Operations in Infectious Disease Epidemics and Antibiotic Resistance," *Environmental Health Perspectives*, February 2007; Dawn Paley, *Drug War Capitalism*, AK Press, 2014; Raj Patel, Stuffed and Starved, Melville House, 2008; Nicholas Rsmussen, "Medical Science and the Military: The Allies' Use of Amphetamine during World War II." *Journal of Interdisciplinary History* (Autumn 2011); Fernando Rojas, "The IMF and the Adjustment of the Colombian Economy to Recession." *Africa Development*, 1985; R. Shayegani, K. Song, M.E. Amuan, C.A. Jaramillo, B.C. Eapen, and M.J. Pugh, "Patterns of zolpidem use among Iraq and Afghanistan veterans: A retrospective cohort analysis," *PloS One*, January 2018; Mindy Weisberger, "Nazis Dosed Soldiers with Performance Enhancing 'Superdrug'." *Live Science*, June 25, 2019; Robert Gregory Williams, *States and Social Evolution*, University of North Carolina Press, 1994; Oriana Zill and Lowell Bergman, "The Black Peso Money Laundering System." Frontline (pbs.org) R. Porter and M. Hough, "The history of the 'drugs problem'," *Criminal Justice Matters* (Summer 1996).

Article 2.5

ARE GOVERNMENTS ECONOMICALLY STUPID IN FAILING TO SUSPEND PATENT PROTECTION FOR VACCINES?

BY ARTHUR MacEWAN
July/August 2021

Dear Dr. Dollar,

A recent study from the International Chamber of Commerce (ICC) showed that the rich countries' failure to support worldwide vaccinations against Covid-19 is likely to do severe harm to their own economies. Based on the study, Oxfam commented: "The U.S., U.K., Germany, France, Japan, and Italy together could lose as much as $2.3 trillion in GDP this year unless they stop fighting on behalf of a handful of big drug companies to retain the intellectual property of the vaccine." And, Oxfam continues, "The United States could lose up to $2,700 per person in household spending in 2021" due to the global economic impacts of highly unequal vaccine distribution. Moral issues aside, how can the governments of rich countries act in such a seemingly stupid manner, doing such harm to their own economies?
—Katharine Rylaarsdam, Baltimore, Md.

The immediate answer to this question is that a set of very powerful firms owe their monopolistic positions and thus high profits to the protection of their patents and copyrights. These include the pharmaceutical firms, information technology firms, and many others.

Not only have they been able to exercise their power to preserve patent and copyright laws—i.e., preserve their monopolies and profits—but they have been able to extend these laws internationally and increase the number of years that their patents and copyrights remain in force. Indeed, on the international level, the protection of trade-related aspects of international property rights (TRIPS) has been a major part of so-called "free trade" agreements —with representatives of the firms writing relevant parts of these agreements. (Don't miss the irony of "free trade" agreements being designed to protect monopolies.)

The close relationship between pharmaceuticals and government policy derives in part from their industry being one of the largest in terms of lobbying expenditures. Also, there is the revolving door between the industry and the government, illustrated by the activities of Sally Susman, a top officer at Pfizer. In the 1990s, Susman worked for the Senate Finance Committee and then the Department of Commerce, where she focused on international trade issues. In the more recent decades, she has been a major fundraiser for Barack Obama and Joe Biden, and for other Democratic candidates—and has become a leader of lobbying for her firm and the pharmaceutical industry.

Just as important as the power that the firms wield through money and connections, the protection of the firms' profits has long been enhanced by the widespread belief that patents and copyrights are an inducement to technological progress, which benefits society at large over the long run. (More on this below.) Raw power, buttressed by this widespread belief, has made government reluctant to act against these high-riding firms—even when the economy in general might suffer immediate damage. It may be wrong and venal, but it's not stupid.

Covid-19 and the Current Context

There is, however, good news—since the study from the ICC and the Oxfam press release were issued earlier this year, the U.S. government has agreed to a temporary suspension of patent restrictions that could make Covid-19 vaccinations more widely available in low-income countries. The bad news is that this step by the U.S. government, however welcome, is not nearly enough. The European Union and some other high-income countries are not going along with the suspension of patent restrictions, and, according to the rules of the World Trade Organization (WTO)—the enforcer of those "free trade" agreements—the suspension would require unanimous consent. Further, lifting patent restrictions would be effective only if the companies currently producing the vaccines share their technological know-how with producers in low-income countries.

Although the WTO director-general has expressed the hope of getting a favorable consensus by December, as the saying goes, justice delayed is justice denied: Even if a December consensus is obtained, millions will die due to the delay in getting the vaccines to people in low-income countries.

Yet, the delay involves more than deaths. While the humanitarian impact is severe, there is also the economic impact mentioned in the ICC study, and not just in the counties where Covid-19 continues to be rampant. Globalization has greatly increased the economic ties among countries—traditional exports, imports, and investments, often involving complex supply chains. Businesses in high-income countries have become increasingly dependent on the well-being of the entire global economy. The production of the vaccines provides an example. According to The Economist, "Pfizer's vaccine requires 280 inputs from suppliers in 19 countries."

The study from the ICC examines the network of economic ties among countries and estimates how the lack of vaccinations in many parts of the world will impact the entire system. The study is dependent on many assumptions, and the authors present several alternative scenarios, each based on different assumptions. It is clear, however, that major economic costs to the rich countries could be substantial, even when the virus is effectively limited within their own borders.

And, of course, the spread of the pandemic in countries with low levels of vaccination could lead to the generation of virus variants that are not readily controlled by existing vaccines. These variants would surely spread to the rich countries, causing a new surge with much more humanitarian and economic impacts. The ICC study does not consider this type of event.

Profits and Rationalizations

The protection of intellectual property rights through patents, whatever its impact on GDP in the United States, appears to work well for the pharmaceutical companies. On average, firms in the pharmaceutical industry have profit rates (return on invested capital) at least 50% higher than the average of (nonfinancial) publicly traded firms across the economy.

The suspension of patent protections, even a temporary suspension of a particular patent, is a threat to the pharmaceuticals' profits. The firms have operated under "rules of the game" that have been very favorable. A change of those rules opens the door to an undermining of their position. Suspension of a patent protection is, from their perspective, a "slippery slope," which can have major—for them, negative—consequences.

But, of course, the pharmaceutical companies and their supporters don't argue their position by making a direct appeal to maintain their monopolistic profits. Instead, they claim that the protection of intellectual property rights (their patents) is necessary to create an incentive for technological progress, a payment for the risks they take in developing new medicines. The firms, the argument goes, will not undertake the risks of developing new drugs (vaccines and others) unless they can count on substantial profits when they succeed. A spokesperson for the German government, which has been opposing the suspension of the vaccine patents, stated, "The protection of intellectual property is a source of innovation and must remain so in the future."

Government Direct Support for the Development of the Covid-19 Vaccine

Pfizer and **BioNTech** did not receive direct government support for vaccine research. They did, however, receive a U.S. government commitment of $1.95 billion for the large-scale manufacturing and delivery of 100 million doses of the Covid-19 vaccine. Also, Pfizer's German partner in the development of the vaccine, BioNTech, was given an additional $445 million by the German government to help accelerate vaccine production by building out manufacturing and development capacity in its home market.

Moderna got $955 million from the U.S. government to support clinical development programs and to scale up vaccine manufacture. Then, the government committed another $1.5 billion to help Moderna deliver the vaccine.

Johnson & Johnson received $456 million from the U.S. government for clinical trials and other vaccine development activities. Under a separate $1 billion agreement, the U.S. government committed to acquire 100 million doses of Johnson & Johnson's vaccine.

AstraZeneca has been provided with $1.6 billion from the U.S. government for development, manufacture, and delivery of the vaccine.

Novavax was awarded $1.6 billion for late-stage development of the vaccine, including Phase 3 clinical trials, large-scale manufacturing, and delivery of 100 million doses.

Sanofi and **GlaxoSmithKline** were provided $2.1 billion by the U.S. government for development, clinical trials, manufacturing, and delivery of 100 million doses of the vaccine.

Merck and **IAVI**: The U.S. government awarded Merck and IAVI $38 million for vaccine research.

Sources: Miriam Valverde, "How Pfizer's and Moderna's COVID-19 vaccines are tied to Operation Warp Speed," Politifact, November 12, 2020 (politifact.com); Riley Griffin and Drew Armstrong, "Pfizer Vaccine's Funding Came From Berlin, Not Washington," Bloomberg News, November 9, 2020 (bloomberg.com).

Reality

Reality, however, tends not to support this argument. First of all, the development of medicines has long depended on heavy expenditures by the government, providing billions of dollars over the years supporting basic research through the National Institute of Health, the National Science Foundation, and other government agencies. Years of government-funded research (mRNA research) led to the basis of the Covid-19 vaccine technology. The pharmaceuticals built on this research to create the vaccines and then claimed the patents.

Further, there was the several billion dollars that the U.S. government provided directly to pharmaceuticals for the development of Covid-19 vaccines, under Operation Warp Speed. A listing of what the companies received is provided in the sidebar. This support, along with the long-term government funding of basic research, greatly reduced (if it did not eliminate) the companies' risks.

Also, there is a basis to argue that the extension and protection of intellectual property rights actually inhibits innovation. New ideas are built on old ideas, but, if old ideas are patented and not shared, they cannot be built on. Microsoft's development, for example, depended on building on old ideas, but then it controlled its new ideas, limiting further innovation. There are many historical cases of innovation without patents. The economic historian David Landes relates how medieval Europe was "one of the most inventive societies that history has known," without patents—providing, as examples, the water wheel, eyeglasses, and the mechanical clock.

Perhaps the best argument against the sorts of protection we now have for intellectual property and for patent suspension in the current pandemic is provided by the following two quotations.

When asked who held the patent for the polio vaccine that he had developed, Jonas Salk replied: "Well, the people, I would say. There is no patent. Could you patent the sun?"

The most famous inventor in U.S. history, Benjamin Franklin, declined to obtain patents for his various devices, offering this explanation in his autobiography: "That as we enjoy great Advantages from the Inventions of Others, we should be glad of an Opportunity to serve others by any Invention of ours, and this we should do freely and generously." ❑

Sources: Cem Cakmakli et al., "The Economic Case for Global Vaccinations," National Bureau for Economic Research working paper, April 2021 (nber.org); "Failure to vaccinate globally could cost up to $2,000 per person this year in rich nations," Oxfam America, April 5, 2021 (oxfamamerica); Peter S. Goodman et al., "What Would It Take to Vaccinate the World Against Covid?" *New York Times*, May 15, 2021 (nytimes.com); Jomo Kwame Sundaram, "US Support for Vaccine Waiver Welcome, but More Needed," IDEAS Network (networkideas.org); "Ten million reasons to vaccinate the world," *The Economist*, May 15th, 2021 (economist.com); Dean Baker, "Patents and the Pandemic: Can We Learn Anything?" Center for Economic and Policy Research, April 12, 2020 (cepr.net); Aswath Damodaran, data on return on capital, with lease and R&D adjustments, January 5, 2021 (www.stern.nyu.edu/~adamodar/); Arthur MacEwan, "Property: Who has a right to what, and why?" *The Wealth Inequality Reader*, 4th edition, 2012; KEI staff, "Who is Sally Susman, and why does she want poor people to pay higher prices for medicines?," *Knowledge Ecology International*, March 15, 2012 (keionline.org); Center for Responsive Politics, OpenSecrets (opensecrets.org).

Article 2.6

LEAKY GOVERNANCE
The Politics and Economics of Gasoline Theft in Mexico

BY FRANCISCO J. ALDAPE
September/October 2019

This past January, a gasoline pipeline explosion in the town of Tlahuelilpan in Mexico's Hidalgo state made headlines across the globe when the blast killed more than 130 people, one of the highest death tolls yet that has been caused by fuel theft. The illegal tapping of gasoline pipelines has been on the rise in Mexico since the start of the millennium—the number of reported illegal tappings increased from 213 in 2006 to 12,581 in 2018, and tappings increased 528% between 2012 and 2017.

The upward trend of crude oil prices at the beginning of this decade made the theft of fuel a very lucrative business for local gangs and cartels, and they were able to provide gasoline at lower prices to impoverished consumers through selling it on the black market, according to a 2018 study by Citizens' Observatory, a think tank in Mexico. In 2018, illegal taps siphoned around 56,000 barrels of fuel a day—totaling $3 billion in profits (even though the total amount of stolen hydrocarbon fuel represents a small percentage of the country's total oil production).

Mexico is the world's 11th biggest oil producer, and the 10,560-mile-long network of pipes that are used to transport the fuel stretch across mostly rural sections of the country. The majority of the pipes are just a few feet underground, making it easy to access and puncture fuel lines. Once a fuel line is punctured, the fuel can then be accessed by attaching a valve or a hose. However, fuel theft, known as huachicoleo, has also become increasingly dangerous. Local cartels and gangs routinely perform illegal drilling on pipelines and use violence to assert control over their illegally accessed supply. Yet attempts to puncture gas lines often result in massive leaks, leading people in rural communities to gather around pipelines to collect the free fuel. In fact, before the explosion that took place last January, there were videos showing a small military contingent trying to prevent more than 500 men, women, and children carrying red jerrycans, buckets, and whatever else they could find from gathering the leaking fuel, but without much success.

Elected on a platform of rooting out corruption, Andrés Manuel López Obrador, who became president last December, has pledged to take decisive action to regulate the provision of gasoline. Soon after his swearing-in, President López Obrador temporarily shut down several of the nation's main pipelines, deployed more than 5,000 soldiers and marines to patrol the pipelines, and used tank trucks guarded by military vehicles to distribute gasoline and diesel. He also asked all Mexican citizens to help with the problem of fuel theft by not using or selling stolen fuel. In particular, he requested that members of the most affected communities call the police to report illegal activities, and he encouraged the heads of families to prohibit their children from becoming involved in the thefts. While this strategy—particularly the decision to shut down several pipelines—initially resulted in fuel shortages for several days and created long lines at gas stations in the capital and some central states, it seems to have reduced the number of thefts considerably. Three months after the plan to end fuel theft was introduced by the new government, gasoline theft dropped from 81,000 barrels a day in November 2018 to 4,000 barrels a day in April 2019—a reduction of 95%—according to Octavio Romero Oropeza, the CEO of Petróleos Mexicanos (PEMEX), the state-owned oil company. Moreover, President López Obrador's strategy has allowed PEMEX to increase their profits by $600 million, and Romero Oropeza is confident that PEMEX can now regulate an adequate supply of fuel to meet the total national demand.

The substantial increase in the number of illegal taps of gas pipelines in Mexico—as well as the López Obrador administration's successful intervention in curbing the thefts—highlight the crucial role that government plays in determining how markets work. (This is an especially challenging task given that an ideal market, which would be equitable and function smoothly, does not exist, least of all in Mexico.) Fuel theft in Mexico is just one of many examples of how a breakdown in government controls can cause markets to go off the rails: the 2008 financial crisis amply demonstrated that financial markets do not serve social ends when set loose from oversight; workers are at a greater risk when labor markets are ill-governed; and consumers are at a greater risk when consumer protection laws are not enforced.

Using the situation in Mexico as a jumping-off point, we can examine the importance of government regulation on how oil markets function. We can also use the fuel theft example to explore why some essential goods, such as fuel, are distributed through the market, whereas others, like air, are (typically) treated as a common good. What can this episode tell us about the dynamics between oil markets and government regulation? And how do President López Obrador's policies fit with growing international demands to diminish reliance on fossil fuels in light of the ecological risks posed by climate change?

Markets Need Governance

For markets to be governed toward socially positive ends, the governance needs to be carried out by those with democratic legitimacy who have an interest in using their position to carry out public-spirited purposes. But governance is easily corrupted, and taking on corruption is a tall order. More than half a century of government corruption and crony capitalism laid the groundwork for the rapid increase in the number of fuel thefts in Mexico. In the absence of legitimately and competently administered democratic governance, an unstable sort of governance asserted through violence—that is, organized crime—stepped into the void. In keeping with the rampant government corruption that has cropped up across many sectors, some government officials and PEMEX employees have been accused of collaborating with criminal organizations, contributing to the rise in the number of fuel thefts in recent years. In light of these problems, the strategy adopted by President López Obrador—the country's first progressive president in more than 70 years—to restore some type of governance of the oil industry involves reorganizing PEMEX and carrying out a moral campaign aimed at establishing PEMEX's legitimacy by combating corruption within the company and maintaining control of the country's energy resources, which are considered vital to fostering economic development.

Even the most libertarian economists recognize the need for governments to enforce contracts, and would applaud the suppression of theft. However, President López Obrador has also used policy to determine who can get access to fuel at what prices, a choice that most mainstream economists would argue against. Economic orthodoxy holds that markets are already sufficiently self-regulated in the sense that the unencumbered interaction between buyers and sellers will tend to produce an equilibrium (and ideal) price. At a theoretical level, the equilibrium price is considered to clear the demand and supply of goods, which usually implies that at this price buyers and sellers are satisfied with their transaction. But as we shall see, in the real world outside of economics textbooks, our social goals require more hands-on governance.

Public vs. Private Goods

Indeed, a significant part of governance consists of figuring out what is treated as private property that can be traded on the market in the first place. Some goods and services are made available to everyone free of charge. These are known as "public goods." Typical examples of public goods include water fountains in public parks, public roads, public schools, or public sanitation. Why then, does PEMEX sell their product, rather than provide it free of charge to all who need it, the way that, for example, public school education is supplied? Selling gas effectively imposes a significant burden on individuals who may lack the necessary means to access this essential good. Despite a general decrease in petroleum prices around the world in the last couple of years, gasoline prices in Mexico have averaged 20.51 Mexican pesos a liter for regular gasoline, which is equivalent to $3.95 a gallon in the United States, according to GlobalPetrolPrices.com (a website that tracks prices at gas stations). Faced with these prices, many of the poor families in Mexico that do not have enough purchasing power to cover the cost of their daily needs are forced to seek alternatives, such as consuming stolen gasoline, which, in turn, reinforces the rise of illicit activities performed by the huachicoleros (gas thieves).

So treating gas as a private good is problematic, but treating it as a public good would raise other concerns. Mexico does rely on fossil fuels, but the question of how to ensure adequate access for all to this (currently) essential good should be a short-term question. A better question is this: In what ways can the government, along with business and social organizations, help to reduce or eliminate the entrenched dependence on oil and gasoline around the world? Given the extensive historical reliance of many capitalist countries on fossil fuels to promote economic development, developing economies like Mexico could continue relying on these resources to catch up with more advanced countries. However, this is a dangerous approach, as less-developed countries may suffer more from ecological disasters. According to a recent U.N. report, titled "Poverty & Death: Disaster Mortality 1996–2015," approximately 90% of natural disaster deaths take place in low- and middle-income countries. We need emissions reductions in the wealthiest economies and emissions avoidance in developing economies. In the case of Mexico, the centrality of its oil industry and the policies pursued by President López Obrador to encourage the construction of a new oil refinery may, in the long-run, represent a serious detriment to his overall goal of a more prosperous Mexico.

Despite the environmental concerns and the potential barriers to access imposed by selling gas as a private good, PEMEX revenues can be, and at times have been, an important source of funding for other government activities that improve the lives of the most vulnerable. Though President López Obrador does not propose that gas be distributed as a public good, he does propose that the sale of gas should once again be used as a source of revenues for public, pro-poor programs.

Governments Can Choose Social Goals for the Market

PEMEX has managed the production and distribution of gasoline since 1938 when President Lázaro Cárdenas declared the nationalization of all petroleum reserves, including those used by foreign oil companies in Mexico. Since then, the production of oil has provided a significant source of government revenues, and it accounted for approximately 32% of total government revenues in 2017. In general, the profitability of the oil industry has closely followed the erratic movements of international crude oil prices, in particular during the late 2000s when the price of oil rose to over $140 per barrel. However, in more recent years, the country has been faced with a severe decline in domestic oil and gas production, and in 2014 the government implemented a series of reforms that privatized sections of the energy sector in an attempt to boost production with greater private investment. For a variety of reasons, which include the mismanagement of both PEMEX and the industry as a whole, there has been a steady decline in Mexican crude oil production over the last decade, which intensified after 2014. PEMEX was unable to benefit from the surge in oil prices at the beginning of this decade because the company lacked responsible leadership and adequate financial resources. President López Obrador fiercely opposed attempts at privatization before his presidency; it will be interesting to see whether such a push for privatization will be halted or at least restricted under his leadership.

Above all, President López Obrador and his administration aim to reorganize and rehabilitate PEMEX so that the company can start producing more oil and once again become profitable without charging prohibitively high prices. (For more, see James M. Cypher and Mateo Crossa's "Dancing on Quicksand: A Retrospective on NAFTA on the Eve of Its Replacement," *D&S*, March/April 2019.) One reason for the current rise in fuel prices is the increasing use of automobiles, and the resulting increase in the need for fuel. Despite this increased demand, no new refineries have been built since the 1970s, which means that Mexico relies on imported gasoline from the United States. Fuel that is imported from the United States goes through many firms, all of which try to push up the price in order to increase their bottom line. Corruption has also added unnecessary costs that are then reflected in the price at the pump. In this respect, one of the most important policies of the new administration includes a project to build a new oil refinery in the southern state of Tabasco, which aims to provide greater employment opportunities in the region (100,000 jobs according to PEMEX) and help the country become closer to achieving energy independence. Thus, in addition to combating corruption in PEMEX and other political institutions, President López Obrador anticipates that through greater economic self-sufficiency and much greater political democratization, it may be possible to reorient the economy around the objective of helping the poorest members of society instead of only serving the interests of Mexico's oligarchs and transnational capital. He vows that everyone will have a representative voice in his government, but also highlights that they will give "preference to the most impoverished and vulnerable," affirming when he took the oath of office that "for the good of all, the poor come first." This principle applies to oil industry policies as much as any other sector.

Nevertheless, the new ecological challenges presented by climate change cast a significant cloud over any plans to use oil revenue for pro-poor development. Historically, petroleum was central in Mexico's political and economic development. In keeping with this history, President López Obrador seems to be putting all of his cards on the expected success of a resurgence in oil production and an increase in the global price of crude oil to promote the country's economic development. Still, recent downward trends in the price of crude oil and the difficulties of creating new oil refineries can work against these expectations. By contrast, other developed countries are implementing taxes on fossil fuels (or at least trying to, as in France, though without much success—see Aarth Saraph, "Understanding France's Gilets Jaunes," *D&S*, January/February 2019) and advocating for greater investments on renewable energies. So far President López Obrador has deflected criticisms for not including more "green" alternatives and for his seemingly unbounded optimism in fossil fuels to provide the necessary economic base for a stronger economy.

What Gasoline Theft Teaches Us

The recent Mexican experience with gas pipelines, and the fossil fuel sector more broadly, reveals the importance of balancing public and private interests within an adequate regulatory framework. The escalation of fuel theft in Mexico and related accidents in many states have largely been a result of the lack of effective governance. The López Obrador administration understands that the government needs to provide a better regulatory framework to create more stable conditions in the distribution of gasoline, and has taken steps to do so.

However, the significant rise in gasoline prices across the nation—which has coincided with the privatization of sections of the energy industry—along with the push to reduce the use of fossil fuels in response to the climate change crisis, present several difficulties for the new administration. President López Obrador is working on the assumption that improving the administration of PEMEX and encouraging good social values (e.g., honesty) among its personnel and the broader citizenship will result in stronger governance of the oil industry. Whether or not these efforts will be enough remains to be seen. Furthermore, better governance of the oil industry can at best be a stopgap measure. To deal effectively with the new problems created by the ongoing climate crisis, it is essential to try to phase out fossil fuels, which also means challenging the vested interests of big oil companies and finding a different source of revenue for the Mexican government. Although President López Obrador's policies may be detrimental to the environment in the long term, this pragmatic approach remains the most promising option for achieving economic gains (such as increased employment opportunities and reduced gasoline costs) given the limited options available to his government in the present situation. This does not mean that Mexico should not do more to promote more environmentally friendly policies. Still, the tension between phasing out fossil fuels and adopting more renewable resources, which is faced by Mexico and other developing countries, requires a stronger commitment by more developed countries, such as the United States, to implement a set of policies to limit the overall emission of greenhouse gases and achieve a just transition to renewable energies.

Sources: Matthew Bremner, "A Gas Heist Gone Wrong, an Explosion, and 137 Deaths in Mexico," *Bloomberg Businessweek*, June 26, 2019 (bloomberg.com); PEMEX, "Annual Reports (2006– 2018)" (pemex.com); Citizens' Observatory, "The theft of oil in pipelines: An enemy of the environment," November 2018 (igavim.org); CIA, "The World Factbook: Country Comparison, Crude Oil Production" (cia.gov); PEMEX Press Release, "Theft of fuel in Mexico decreases 95 percent and increases crude oil production," April 23, 2019 (pemex.com); Kirk Semple, "Mexico Declares Victory Over Fuel Thieves. But Is It Lasting?," *New York Times*, May 5, 2019 (nytimes.com); OECD, "Mexico's effort to phase out and rationalize its fossil-fuel subsidies," Nov. 15, 2017 (oecd.org); U.S. Department of Commerce's International Trade Administration, "Mexico Country Commercial Guide," Oct. 12, 2018 (export.gov); Michael Hudson, "Global Warming and U.S. National Security Diplomacy," *Socialist Economist*, August 30, 2019 (socialisteconomist.com); Robert Brelsford, "PEMEX to proceed with Dos Bocas refinery project," *Oil & Gas Journal*, May 10, 2019 (ogj.com); Centre for Research on the Epidemiology of Disasters, "Poverty & Death: Disaster Mortality 1996–2015," U.N. Office for Disaster Risk Reduction, October 12, 2016 (cred.be).

Article 2.7

CRYPTOCURRENCY WILL NOT LIBERATE US
Deflating the egalitarian fantasies of digital currencies.

BY HADAS THIER
January/February 2022

"It's the ultimate egalitarian system...anyone can participate, you don't need a bank, you don't need anyone's permission." So explains Bitcoin billionaire Michael Saylor in a recent interview with Fox News host Tucker Carlson. The point of Bitcoin, Saylor goes on, is to "fix the money, and money is energy, and energy is life."

Cryptocurrencies, like Bitcoin, Ethereum, Dogecoin, and more than 10,000 others, are digital currencies that allow people to buy and sell things online. Cryptocurrencies (or "crypto," as they're known) come in the form of digital coins or "tokens," though they function as assets for investment more easily than as means of exchange. Over the last few years—and during this past year in particular—cryptocurrencies have gone from being a fringe investment made mostly by hardcore crypto adherents into a $2 trillion industry, including many mainstream investors getting in on the action.

Crypto uses a technology called "blockchain," and Bitcoin, by far the most widely held cryptocurrency, uses what's known as "proof of work" blockchain technology. A *blockchain* is a digital database that, rather than being owned by an individual and stored on a single computer, is distributed among computers on a shared network. A blockchain's database is secured through the cooperation of many computer "nodes" in the system. In the case of *proof of work*, this requires computers in the network to verify each transaction by creating and solving complex mathematical questions. In solving increasingly complex, random puzzles, the owners of these computers participate in building out a public, virtual ledger of all transactions, and are rewarded with new Bitcoins for their troubles (this is known as "Bitcoin mining").

An enormously wasteful computer arms race has taken off to facilitate this process. Millions of computers around the world work ceaselessly around the clock to solve riddles whose solutions mean nothing and whose actions produce nothing, at great environmental cost. It is estimated that Bitcoin processes annually exhaust the same amount of energy as the entire country of Argentina. A single transaction requires 707 kilowatt-hours of electricity, emitting half a ton of CO_2. According to Digiconomist's Bitcoin Energy Consumption Index, one Bitcoin transaction uses as much power as an average U.S. household uses over 73 days. A study published in *Nature* in 2018 estimated that the process of verifying and mining Bitcoin could *on its own* raise global temperatures above 2 degrees Celsius by 2048. (This was before the most explosive growth of Bitcoin trading took off; Bitcoin's energy consumption has almost tripled since that time.)

Yet with tens of millions of people around the world owning crypto assets, and with thousands of fervent believers, cryptocurrencies seem to have something for everyone. Conservatives like Carlson love Bitcoin's supposed anti-inflation mechanisms; millennial millionaires geek out on making money through disruptive technologies; handfuls of Redditors have gotten rich overnight; and techno-libertarians imagine a world governed by autonomous individuals unfettered by the state.

Crypto for the Left?

As crypto moves into mainstream financial circles, many of its proponents are trying to redirect attention from its disastrous climate implications and associations with money laundering by giving the technology a left-wing makeover. Cryptocurrency, left crypto devotees argue, is a leaderless movement to unseat the plutocrats who have benefitted hand over fist from our centralized banking system.

A recent article by Alex Gladstein in *Bitcoin Magazine*, "Check Your Financial Privilege," argues:

> Critics in the dollar bubble miss the bigger global picture: that anyone with access to the internet can now participate in Bitcoin, a new money system with equal rules for all participants, running on a network that does not censor or discriminate, used by individuals who do not need to show a passport or an ID and held by citizens in a way that is hard to confiscate and impossible to debase… Until now, governments and corporations have controlled the rules of money. That is changing… Anyone with internet access now has an escape from their unreliable and exploitative national monetary system.

Gladstein has penned a series of lengthy articles, each of which claim that Bitcoin will answer one or another variety of global inequality. Africans living in countries that had been colonized by France, and which, despite their independence,

---

How Do Blockchains Work?

A *blockchain* is a database, but unlike a traditional database, which is owned or secured by a single entity, a blockchain is "distributed," i.e., it is shared among a network of a computers (or "nodes"). Rather than storing data in tables, a blockchain holds information in groupings of data known as "blocks." Every time a new block of transactions is formed, it gets timestamped and given a code (known as a "hash") created by a mathematical function. Every new entry is validated through a "consensus mechanism" (an agreed upon method of validation), most commonly either "proof of work" (computer nodes must compete to solve complex mathematical equations in order to validate the block) or "proof of stake" (computer nodes are randomly assigned the power to validate a new transaction, based on how many "tokens," or digital coins, the node holds). All the other nodes in the system have some time to verify the winning computer's work. The block is then attached to the chain of previous blocks of data, creating an immutable and permanent record. A blockchain has been compared to a digital notary, since like a notary public, it functions to verify or certify information and prevent anyone from tampering with it.

still have their economic fates determined by French banks, could free themselves from the monetary domination of the French-backed currency (the C.F.A. franc). Palestinians in Gaza who are not only physically barred from free movement, but are also economically dependent on their oppressors, can now "buy the dip" and make money off Bitcoin investments (i.e., buy Bitcoin when its value has dropped, and make a profit when and if the value bounces back up).

Echoing this same sentiment, Jack Mallers, the founder of Strike, a digital wallet company (a "digital wallet" is an app that stores crypto tokens), gave an emotionally wrought speech at this summer's Bitcoin2021 conference in Miami, Fla. as he reported on his recent mission to El Salvador. Mallers spent three months in El Salvador and worked with the neoliberal, authoritarian administration of President Nayib Bukele to introduce Bitcoin as legal tender there (a law stipulating that businesses must accept Bitcoin as a form of payment was later passed by El Salvador's Congress in the middle of the night). Through tears, 27-year-old Mallers told attendees about El Salvador's dirt roads and broken ATMs, and the many unbanked Salvadorans that he met. "It was sad. There just wasn't a lot of hope. I gave talks, I talked to kids. I told them, 'Man, we've got this. Bitcoin's here, we've got this.'"

Mallers, whose father founded one of the largest futures brokerages in Chicago and whose net worth is unknown but is most certainly in the millions, told attendees that he's proud of everyone in the room. "I hope you find solace in knowing that you helped those that haven't been helped in 250 years." Forget the haters, Mallers assured the audience: "The kid I went to high school with is gonna lean over a bar in Manhattan and drink a $35 old-fashioned and tell me Bitcoin doesn't matter. Privileged fucking asshole."

A Question of Class Power, Not Technology

But there are a few glaring problems with this narrative. To begin with, the results thus far in El Salvador are underwhelming at best. Remittances—salary transfers from Salvadorian migrants in the United States to families back home—make up about a quarter of the nation's gross domestic product. So having a means of transferring money across borders without fees or intermediaries could be helpful. In fact, Bitcoin transactions do come with (often high) fees. More importantly, Bitcoin's value fluctuates wildly, and most Salvadorans have been hesitant to use it because of this volatility. Whatever they may gain from avoiding exploitative Western Union fees, they may lose much more from the fluctuating values of remittances that come in the form of Bitcoin.

The adoption of Bitcoin in fact triggered mass protests in El Salvador, where according to a recent poll conducted by El Salvador's chamber of commerce, 93% of Salvadoran people are opposed to its adoption. Nevertheless, the government created a "Chivo Wallet" app to send and receive Bitcoin transactions and gave $30 worth of Bitcoin to anyone who adopted the wallet. The *New York Times* reported that many ATMs ran out of dollars soon thereafter, as Salvadorans rushed to convert their Bitcoins to dollars and withdraw cash. The Chivo Wallets themselves have also been vulnerable to hackers who have stolen funds from hundreds of Salvadorans with no recourse. Now President Bukele has announced plans to build a Bitcoin city at the foot of a volcano, designed in the shape of a coin. The city will harness the volcano's geothermal energy to power Bitcoin mining.

These problems stem from the fact that Bitcoin and other digital tokens should more aptly be called "crypto assets" rather than "cryptocurrencies." Speculators have made (and lost) phenomenal amounts of money through trading crypto and crypto-based derivatives, but so far cryptocurrencies have gained very little traction as a practical medium of exchange, due to the volatility of their value and the logistical impracticalities associated with transactions. (The claim that cryptocurrency cannot be debased is also laid to waste by this volatility. The value of the dollar may erode because of inflation, but it has never seen its value cut in half in a single day.)

There's a deeper problem still: Even in a best-case yet unlikely scenario, where cryptocurrencies could play a stable and seamless role in facilitating monetary transactions in the developing world, it assumes that the main roadblock to global equality is that people don't have access to financial products, microloans, and property rights. But capitalism has created deep geopolitical and social problems that cannot be overcome with a monetary technofix. The key global challenge that we face is not one of technology, but of class power.

The profoundly unequal and U.S.-dependent economy in El Salvador, for instance, has its roots in a monocrop export economy first developed under Spanish colonization and later enforced by U.S.-driven free-trade agreements. And of course, a 12-year, U.S.-backed civil war devastated Salvadoran society and the economy. The country is now in a deep economic crisis, and the adoption of Bitcoin has only triggered further instability. On top of this, entangling El Salvador within CO_2-emitting Bitcoin mining schemes will diminish the country's limited energy supply and make the population more vulnerable to the ravages of climate change.

The proposition by Gladstein that Bitcoin could bring liberation to Palestine is an even greater stretch. Unironically opening an article about Bitcoin and Palestine with the observation that the Palestinian he interviewed only has access to electricity a few hours per day, Gladstein moves on to ask: "Why can't Palestinians easily order goods on Amazon or receive money from abroad?" as though Amazon orders are high on the list of Palestinian concerns. He rightly chronicles the kneecapping of the Palestinian economy by the Israeli occupation, but eventually concludes that "money lies at the very root of [Palestinian] struggles... They do not have control of their currency."

The systematic undermining of the Palestinian economy in fact reflects a much deeper colonial ill. Will Bitcoin overturn decades of ethnic cleansing, occupation, control of resources, and continued brutality and annexation? Or will it simply provide Palestinians, who already suffer from deep economic precarity, a means to speculate with meager funds (assuming they have access to the internet to do so)?

On the other hand, Venezuela, where the economy has been in a years-long hyperinflationary free fall, provides a good test case for Bitcoin and other digital tokens. Cryptocurrencies have become popular in Venezuela as a tool to receive remittances, a medium to exchange the floundering Venezuelan bolivar for foreign currencies, and a means to help businesses hedge against the inflation of the bolivar. Yet crypto use is mostly limited to Venezuelan businesses and the wealthy, while the majority of Venezuelans have neither stable internet connections nor enough money to dabble in crypto trading.

Even Bitcoin devotees know this. In an interview with *Bitcoin Magazine* entitled "Bitcoin can't fix everything," Peter McCormack explained with not-so-subtle disdain: "When I went to the slums, it became painfully clear that these people aren't going to download a Bitcoin wallet and back up their private keys, right?" Venezuelan crypto supporter Diana Aguilar similarly reported for CoinDesk:

> The fallacy that bitcoin could "save" a country's whole economy assumes the country meets all the requirements for mainstream adoption. Just to start, there would be needed widespread computer and financial literacy, reliable electricity infrastructure, stable internet service and an economy that not only allows the majority of citizens to count on a device to keep their digital wallets but also the safe migration from fiat money to digital money.

The crypto community desperately wants to prove that digital tokens like Bitcoin can be used as currency, and that they can save failing economic systems. But when given the exact perfect storm of hyperinflation, government support for cryptocurrencies, and growing popularity of digital tokens, the project still falls flat. Beyond the logistical impracticalities of making it work are the deeper geopolitical causes of Venezuela's failing economy, at the heart of which is a century-old dependence on oil. When oil prices collapsed in 2014, this brought about a spiraling economic crisis. Combined with ongoing U.S. interference and devastating economic sanctions, these factors have created a political and economic pressure cooker in Venezuela.

Persistent Plutocracy

Underlying the conviction that cryptocurrencies can level the global playing field—or the domestic one—is the assumption that the decentralized technology behind blockchains is inherently equalizing. It isn't.

To the contrary, researcher and writer Olivier Jutel has chronicled the ways in which American hegemony over the governing infrastructure of the internet and platforms on the network have only exacerbated global inequalities. Jutel notes that the Pacific Islands have become a tech-frontier for blockchain because of "regulatory openness based upon imperial power imbalances," allowing for tax shelters and tax-free economic development zones. "Tech experimentation in the developing world has the benefit of connecting companies to aid-funding streams and outsourcing risk to some of the most fragile environments in the world with value extracted for the benefit of stakeholders including private entrepreneurs and large companies."

There may be blockchain technology or future blockchain innovations that could be used for good. Not all cryptocurrencies use the climate-destroying proof-of-work process, for instance. And not all blockchain technology powers cryptocurrencies per se. There are some who argue that blockchain-powered *decentralized autonomous organizations* (DAOs) provide models to cooperatively run businesses, or that *nonfungible tokens* (NFTs) can help artists realize better compensation through royalties that are programmed into a digital art work's metadata. (See box, "What Is an NFT?") But the underlying logic of cryptocurrencies entrenches rather than subverts free-market capitalism in several ways.

First, the market determines which crypto assets and technologies are invested in. For instance, there are alternate blockchain processes, such as "proof of stake," that are less damaging to the environment (see box, "How Do Blockchains Work"?). In order to participate in verifying blockchain transactions, participants in those currencies prove their trustworthiness by locking away a certain amount of crypto coins rather than by solving mathematical problems. But Bitcoin's hegemony within the crypto industry incentivizes investment to flow to the energy-guzzling proof-of-work blockchains. Thus coins using proof-of-work algorithms currently make up over 65% of the crypto market. The dynamic isn't different from the one which forces the planet into an interminable wait for the market to properly incentivize a transition away from fossil fuels. And in fact, it's worse: Cryptocurrencies aren't regulated by the EPA or any other institution. Nor do they have a centralized headquarters to protest or tens of thousands of workers within the industry who have the potential to organize against it. The logic of the market rewards profitability above all else. The world of cryptocurrencies reflects this same logic, but with no government regulations to enforce any restraints.

Second, crypto assets have promoted the commodification of everything, from Twitter CEO Jack Dorsey's first tweet (the proof of "ownership" of this tweet sold for just under $3 million) to virtual land grabs on the "metaverse" (a digital plot of land in Decentraland—an open-source 3D virtual world platform—recently sold for $2.5 million), and the financialization of our daily interactions. As co-founder of the DAO software company Syndicate, Ian Lee, put it to the *Financial Times*, the goal is to turn internet "users and contributors into investors, and vice versa."

What Is an NFT?

NFTs ("non-fungible tokens") are digital assets such as media files (think digital images, audio files, or videos) that live on the Ethereum blockchain. They are not "fungible," i.e., replaceable, because each has its own unique identification code. Each NFT contains ownership details and can also include "metadata"—accompanying information describing the underlying data (for instance, digital art work can include a smart contract to pay out royalties to the artist every time the NFT trades hands). NFTs essentially assign a certificate of ownership to media files. The media file itself may still be completely public and downloadable. But the ownership tag on it (a "token") can only reside with one entity. As Jacob Silverman has described: "People who own [NFTs] don't technically own the media you interact with, they own a description of that media." Nevertheless, NFTs have functioned as digital collectibles, with the potential of being highly speculative assets. You might buy the NFT of Jack Dorsey's first tweet for $2.9 million one day, with the expectation that you'll be able to sell it to someone else for $4 million the next. While NFTs were supposed to help artists get fair compensation, they may end up being the Beanie Babies of the digital age.

An article in CoinDesk explained:

> Crypto can turn … passive efforts [on the internet]—scrolling, exploring,
> socializing—into financial transactions. What would it mean to live in a world
> where every single image, song, health record, Twitter "like" and blog post has
> a discrete token attached? … Things don't "go viral" without a massive network
> of individual interactions. In a tokenized future, an early "like" on a post that
> eventually becomes popular could be a kind of historical artifact; trading it
> on the secondary market might prove lucrative. Same goes for a highly rated
> comment in a comment section.

Whereas the internet created a vast and replicable abundance of digital content, crypto assets introduce enforced scarcity to the digital world in order to claim ownership. An NFT assigns a digital receipt to an item, which is verified on a blockchain. NFTs can thus commercialize any digital item, and bind it to a system of ownership, financial transactions, and speculation. Meanwhile DAOs set up organizational structures in which you must purchase tokens to participate in discussions.

Lastly, as media studies professor Nathan Schneider has put it, both proof-of-work and proof-of-stake technology entrench a "persistent plutocracy," whatever the libertarian aspirations of their creators. Both processes, he notes, "grant governance rights roughly in proportion to a given node's buy-in on the network—through computing power or token holdings, respectively." The more machines are put to work solving puzzles, the greater the chances of mining a Bitcoin. "As the complexity of the computations increases, it becomes harder for the average person to profit, since one must have thousands of machines to remain competitive," Schneider explains. "And so the system begins to resemble a traditional centralized capitalist system that remains profitable—to the very wealthy." The very unequal access to mining cryptocurrencies belies the argument made by Gladstein and others that "anyone with access to the internet" can equally participate in the system and be subject to the same rules.

Indeed, a recent paper by finance professors Antoinette Schoar and Igor Makarov found that as of the end of 2020, the top 1,000 investors controlled about three million Bitcoins, out of just under 19 million. The top 10,000 Bitcoin accounts hold five million Bitcoins. As the *Wall Street Journal* pointed out recently, this means that "approximately 0.01% of bitcoin holders control 27% of … bitcoin in circulation. By comparison, in the U.S., where wealth inequality is at its most extreme in decades, the top 1% of households hold about a third of all wealth." That's an almost 100-fold increase in inequality as it compares to the dollar economy.

This underscores an important point: Decentralized technology does not necessarily translate into less hierarchy or greater democracy. As Schoar points out: "Somebody who can easily spend a hundred million dollars' worth of Bitcoin and sell it or buy it can have a massive price impact in the market," while as "a regular retail investor, you might suddenly find yourself x percent down because of massive volatility, which might be created by a few large investors randomly deciding to sell some of their holdings." The *Financial Times* reported on exactly this phenomenon when cryptocurrency investments tanked at the beginning of December 2021, likely due to the actions of one or two big players unloading large amounts of bitcoin.

Investors who are powerful enough to influence the value of a coin through the movement of their assets are reverently referred to as "whales" in crypto circles. The financial clout held by whales is also magnified by the large social media presence many of them possess—such that a single tweet from Elon Musk, the billionaire founder of Telsa, can send the value of currencies skyrocketing or plummeting. Since speculative growth depends on people's perceptions of rising value, having the ability to hype up a large audience grants crypto influencers a lot of power.

Cyber-Libertarianism or Democratic Accountability?

In 2018 Phil Gramm and Hernando de Soto penned an op-ed entitled "How Blockchain Can End Poverty" for the *Wall Street Journal*. Gramm had previously been the chairman of the U.S. Senate Committee on Banking, Housing, and Urban Affairs and sponsored the Gramm-Leach-Bliley Act in 1999, which removed Depression-era laws regulating banking and finance. (Ending these regulations, especially Glass-Steagall, contributed greatly to the financial crisis of 2008.) De Soto is a Peruvian neoliberal economist, at the forefront of policies favoring deregulation and property rights. They argued:

> The great economic divide in the world today is between the 2.5 billion people who can register property rights and the five billion who are impoverished, in part because they can't… If Blockchain technology can empower public and private efforts to register property rights on a single computer platform, we can share the blessings of private-property registration with the whole world. Instead of destroying private property to promote a Marxist equality in poverty, perhaps we can bring property rights to all mankind. Where property rights are ensured, so are the prosperity, freedom and ownership of wealth that brings real stability and peace.

The technology that powers cryptocurrency is varied, and its underlying philosophy runs a spectrum. But at the heart of crypto culture lies a belief that financialized property is the key to human advancement, and that economic incentives lead to personal autonomy. In fact, that's not so different from mainstream capitalist ideology. Arguably it's worse: Crypto libertarians want to trade a world run by institutions that benefit the wealthy by design, but are somewhat regulated by democratic processes, for a world that is controlled completely by the ultra-wealthy, with no mechanism for democratic control.

The argument from crypto's left proponents is that a technocratic social order will free us from hierarchy and state domination. Ultimately this is a faux-left position that has no proven track record in the actual practice of trading in cryptocurrencies. Instead, the world that has been erected around blockchain technology is characterized by the increased concentration of wealth and power.

Insofar as there are anti-establishment goals within the crypto community, they stem from a cyber-libertarian ideology that distrusts states and public institutions.

That's an understandable position to arrive at—a reaction against decades of neoliberal states hollowing out government services, attacking the working class, and creating profound inequality. Trust in depleted and broken government institutions is abysmally low.

Yet the answer is not to toss out the entire edifice of the state and representative government, but to push for greater accountability and reforms, including public control of banks and redistributive fiscal policies. At minimum, there are simpler and less planet-warming solutions on hand to solve many of the problems that crypto purports to address. The state, if it's pushed by collective action, can play a positive, interventionist role: for instance, banking the unbanked through postal banking, or making money transfers accessible by regulating financial services companies and capping transfer fees. It's true that the government will not, on its own, implement reforms for the greater good. But utilizing the features of representative democracy offers us a better shot at making change than the shadowy world of cryptocurrencies.

Ultimately liberation doesn't come from atomized action and individual economic power. It flows through democratic movements for civil and economic rights for every human on the planet, whether they possess a digital token or not. ❏

Sources: Camilo Mora et al., "Bitcoin emissions alone could push global warming above 2°C, Nature Climate Change, August 2019 (nature.com); Alex Gladstein, "Check Your Financial Privilege," Bitcoin Magazine, May 12, 2021 (bitcoinmagazine.com); "El Salvador Becomes The First Country to Declare Bitcoin Legal Tender," Bitcoin Magazine YouTube channel, June 5, 2021 (youtube.com); Alex Gladstein, "Can Bitcoin Be Palestine's Currency of Freedom?" *Bitcoin Magazine*, July 22, 2021 (bitcoinmagazine.com); Olivier Jutel, "Blockchain Imperialism in the Pacific," *Big Data & Society*, February 18, 2021 (journals.sagepub.com); Nathan Schneider, "Cryptoeconomics as a Limitation on Governance," available at OSFHOME (osf.io); Igor Makarov and Antoinette Schoar, "Blockchain Analysis of the Bitcoin Market," SSRN, October 14, 2021 (ssrn.com); Julie Ryan Evans, "62% of Cryptocurrency Investors Believe They'll Get Rich Off Those Investments," Magnify Money, April 13, 2021 (magnifymoney.com); Phil Gramm and Hernando de Soto, "How Blockchain Can End Poverty," *Wall Street Journal*, January 25, 2018 (wsj.com); Anatoly Kurmanaev, Bryan Avelar, and Ephrat Livni, "Bitcoin Preaches Financial Liberty; A Strongman Is Testing That Promise," *New York Times*, October 7, 2021 (nytimes.com); Gary Silverman, "Crypto's wild ride raises new liquidity concerns," Financial Times, December 11, 2021 (ft.com); "Bitcoin Energy Consumption Index," Digiconomist (digiconomist.net/bitcoin-energy-consumption); Miles Kruppa and Hannah Murphy, "Crypto assets inspire new brand of collectivism beyond finance," *Financial Times*, December 27, 2021 (ft.com); David Hollerith, "Despite Utility, Bitcoin Cannot Fix Venezuela," Bitcoin Magazine, February 25, 2020 (bitcoinmagazine.com); Diana Aguilar, "Bitcoin Can't Fix Venezuela: I Should Know," CoinDesk, May 2, 2019 (coindesk.com); Andrés Engler, "After Identity Theft, Salvadorans Now Report Funds Disappearing From Chivo Wallets," CoinDesk, December 30, 2021 (coindesk.com); Jacob Silverman, "Bursting the NFT Bubble," Tech Won't Save Us with Paris Marx (podcast), April 8, 2021 (podcasts.apple.com).

Chapter 3

CONSUMERS

INTRODUCTION

The "two economies" described in the introduction to this book—the textbook economy and the economy portrayed by critics of the status quo—come into sharp contrast when we consider the theory of consumer choice. In the textbook model of consumer choice, rational individuals seek to maximize their well-being by choosing the right mix of goods to consume and allocating their "scarce" resources accordingly. They decide for themselves how much they would enjoy various things, and make their choices based on full information about their options. More of any good is always better, but diminishing marginal utility says that each additional unit of a good consumed brings less additional enjoyment than the one before. The theory attempts to assess the utility of each individual uniquely. Yet for most people, very limited budgets not only limit their set of choices but also distort their consumer preferences. What's more, full information about choices and opportunities is hardly freely available. In some cases, consumers are forced into "choices" that are determined by the powerful corporations.

The first article in this chapter contends that the idea of consumer sovereignty—that consumer wishes determine what gets produced—does not fit the facts. Helen Scharber notes, in "The 800-Pound Ronald McDonald in the Room" (Article 3.1), how the advertising that saturates our daily lives constantly creates new wants. In recent years, advertisers have been increasingly targeting children in order to convince them to nag their parents into buying products they suddenly "need."

Deborah M. Figart's "Underbanked and Overcharged" (Article 3.2) argues that low-income communities are ill-served by both conventional banks and "alternative financial service providers" (AFSPs), such as check-cashing outlets. Low-income areas may lack convenient nearby outlets for conducting financial transactions, and community members typically face high fees and interest rates from both banks and AFSPs. Figart points to a possible solution: recent proposals for the revival of "postal banks" operated by the U.S. Postal Service.

The next article, "Forced Arbitration Is Bad for Consumers" (Article 3.3) turns to another way banks win out over consumers: through forced arbitration. As Heidi Shierholz explains, banks win the vast majority of cases when they are able to force consumers into arbitration, and they win big. This is in contrast to class action lawsuits, which return hundreds of millions of dollars to consumers when banks break the law.

Next, in "The Limits of Ethical Consumerism" (Article 3.4), Marc Triller sets out reasons to believe that individual efforts by consumers aren't the best way to reduce societal and environmental harms caused by corporations.

Next, in "Campus Struggles Against Sweatshops Continue" (Article 3.5), Sarah Blaskey and Phil Gasper turn our attention to activism around global labor conditions. They show how people on the consumption side, in this case students and faculty at U.S. colleges and universities, have banded together with workers on the other side of the world to fight "sweatshop" conditions in apparel production.

In the chapter's final article, "Leveraging Financial Markets for Social Justice" (Article 3.6), Doug Orr focuses on consumer activism in financial markets and discusses various methods through which social activists can change corporate behavior. Orr argues that campaigns to get institutional investment funds to divest from fossil fuel companies are the least effective action to take against climate change. Highlighting the differences among divestment, defunding, and engagement by investors as possible forms of activism in financial markets, Orr suggests that the best way of bringing about social change is by direct intervention in the market mechanism though policies like a carbon tax.

The articles in this chapter challenge the idea of consumer sovereignty in a market economy, drawing attention to the cases where consumer choices are limited or influenced by corporations, delivering harmful outcomes for consumers. The limitations on consumer power also imply that consumer activism or boycotts cannot successfully substitute for effective government intervention in the market economy.

Discussion Questions

1. (Article 3.1) Standard consumer theory still applies if advertising is simply a way to inform consumers. But critics suggest that advertising shapes our tastes and desires. Think of some of your recent purchases. For which purchases was advertising primarily a source of information, and for which was it more of a taste-shaper?

2. (Article 3.1) According to Scharber, what are the negative impacts of advertising directed at children? Would you support a law banning advertising to young children? Why or why not?

3. (Article 3.2) Why might private for-profit enterprises not supply desired services at affordable prices, as in the case of financial services in low-income communities? Is the establishment of public service providers a good solution?

4. (Article 3.3) Why do Wells Fargo and other banks prefer forced arbitration to class action lawsuits? Why is this bad for consumers? What remedy does the Consumer Financial Protection Bureau propose to banks ability to force consumers into arbitration?

5. (Article 3.4) What is "ethical consumerism"? What reasons does Marc Triller give for thinking that ethical consumerism isn't an effective way of addressing

harms caused by corporations? What are the alternatives to ethical consumerism, in Triller's view?

6. (Articles 3.5) How can consumers overcome the problem of "asymmetric information" in making purchases? Consider cases when consumers are interested in something (like labor conditions) that they cannot directly observe from the product itself.

7. (Articles 3.5) Why might people on the consumption side of a market (like apparel buyers) consider factors other than product price and quality in their purchasing decisions? Do you think changes in consumer purchasing behavior are enough to bring about social change, in terms of things like labor conditions and environmental impacts of production methods?

8. (Article 3.6) How is "divestment" different from "defunding" a corporation? What reasons does Orr give to support his argument that divestment is the *least* effective tool of social activism? In his view, what are the better alternatives to achieve social change? Do you agree?

Article 3.1

THE 800-POUND RONALD McDONALD IN THE ROOM

BY HELEN SCHARBER

January 2007

When your child's doctor gives you advice, you're probably inclined to take it. And if 60,000 doctors gave you advice, ignoring it would be even more difficult to justify. Last month, the American Academy of Pediatrics (AAP) issued a policy statement advising us to limit advertising to children, citing its adverse effects on health. Yes, banning toy commercials might result in fewer headaches for parents ("Please, please, pleeeeeeease, can I have this new video game I just saw 10 commercials for????"), but the AAP is more concerned with other health issues, such as childhood obesity. Advertising in general—and to children specifically—has reached astonishingly high levels, and as a country, we'd be wise to take the doctors' orders.

Advertising to kids is not a new phenomenon, but the intensity of it is. According to Juliet Schor, author of *Born to Buy*, companies spent around $100 million in 1983 on television advertising to kids. A little more than 20 years later, the amount earmarked for child-targeted ads in a variety of media has jumped to at least $12 billion annually. That's over $150 per boy and girl in the United States. And it's not as though kids only see ads for action figures and sugary cereal; the other $240 billion spent on advertising each year ensures that they see ads for all kinds of products, everywhere they go. According to the AAP report, "the average young person views more than 3,000 ads per day on television, on the internet, on billboards, and in magazines." Ads are also creeping into schools, where marketers have cleverly placed them in "educational" posters, textbook covers, bathroom stalls, scoreboards, daily news programs, and bus radio programming.

If advertising to children is becoming increasingly ubiquitous, it's probably because it's becoming increasingly profitable. Once upon a time, kids didn't have as much market power as they do today. The AAP report estimates that kids under 12 now spend $25 billion of their own money annually, teenagers spend another $155 billion, and both groups probably influence around $200 billion in parental spending. Not too surprising, considering that 62% of parents say their children "actively participate" in car-buying decisions, according to a study by J.D. Power & Associates. Marketers are also becoming more aware of the long-term potential of advertising to children. While they may not be the primary market now, they will be someday. And since researchers have found that kids as young as two can express preferences for specific brands, it's practically never too early to begin instilling brand loyalty.

But while small children have an incredible memory for commercial messages, they may not have developed the cognitive skills necessary to be critical of them. In 2004, the American Psychological Association (APA) also called for setting limits on advertising to kids, citing research that "children under the age of eight are unable to critically comprehend televised advertising messages and are prone to accept advertiser messages as truthful, accurate and unbiased." Many people take offense at the idea that we might be manipulated by marketing. Aren't we, after all, intelligent enough to make up our own minds about what to buy? The research cited by the APA, however, shows that children are uniquely vulnerable to manipulation by advertising. Marketers therefore should not be allowed to prey on them in the name of free speech.

Such invasive advertising to children is not only an ethical problem. The AAP cited advertising's effects on health through the promotion of unhealthy eating, drinking, and smoking as the main motivation for setting limits. Children's health issues certainly merit attention. The Center for Disease Control, for example, has found that the prevalence of overweight children (ages 6 to 11) increased from 7% in 1980 to about 19% in 2004, while the rate among adolescents (ages 12 to 19) jumped from 5% to 17%. In addition to physical health problems, Schor argues that extensive marketing has negative effects on children's emotional well being. In her research for *Born to Buy*, Schor found links between immersion in consumer culture and depression, anxiety, low self esteem and conflicts with parents. The big push to consume can also lead to financial health problems, as many Americans know all too well, with credit card debt among 18 to 24-year-olds doubling over the past decade.

Not even the staunchest critics of marketing to children would argue that advertisements are completely at fault for these trends. Yet, the commercialization of nearly everything is negatively affecting children's well being in rather profound ways. Why, then, is hardly anyone paying attention to the 800-pound Ronald McDonald in the room? Perhaps it's because advertising appears to be a necessary evil or a fair tradeoff—maybe little Emma's school couldn't afford a soccer team without Coke on the scoreboard, for example. Or perhaps some would argue that parents who don't approve of the commercial culture should limit their kids' exposure to it. Increasingly invasive marketing techniques make it practically impossible to simply opt out of commercial culture, though. Thus, decisions to limit marketing to children must be made by the country as a whole. Sweden, Norway, Greece, Denmark, and Belgium have already passed laws curbing kid-targeted advertising, and according to 60,000 pediatricians, if we care about the health of our kids, we should too. ❑

Sources: American Association of Pediatrics, Policy Statement on Children, Adolescents, and Advertising, December 2006 (pediatrics.aappublications.org/cgi/content/full/118/6/2563); American Psychological Association, "Television Advertising Leads to Unhealthy Habits in Children" February 2004 (www.apa.org/news/press/releases/2004/02/children-ads); Jennifer Saranow, "Car makers direct more ads at kids," *Wall Street Journal*, November 9th, 2006 (www.commercialexploitation.org/news/carmakers.html); David Burke, "Two-year olds branded by TV advertising" (www.whitedot.org/issue/isssory.aps?slug=Valkenburg); Center for a New American Dream, *Kids and Commercialism* (www.newdream.org/kids/); Juliet Schor, *Born to Buy: The Commercialized Child and the New Consumer Culture* (New York: Scribner, 2004); "Facts about Childhood Overweight," Center for Disease Control (www.cdc.gov/Healthy Youth/overweight/index.html).

Article 3.2

UNDERBANKED AND OVERCHARGED
Creating alternatives to the "alternative financial service providers."

BY DEBORAH M. FIGART
July/August 2014

Driving down Atlantic Avenue, the main commercial thoroughfare in Atlantic City, N.J., one can easily count at least three times as many check-cashing outlets as banks. At these stores, you can cash your paycheck or government check (for a fee), send a wire transfer to a relative or friend overseas, or pay some bills.

Many traditionally African-American neighborhoods and poor census tracts, like this one, do not have a single bank nearby. The U.S. banking system is working for well-heeled customers. It isn't working for poor people.

Over 30 million households—more than one in four—are unbanked or underbanked. That means they have no access to traditional banking services or that they have a bank account but also rely on Alternative Financial Service Providers (AFSPs). According to the Federal Deposit Insurance Corporation's 2011 FDIC National Survey of Unbanked and Underbanked Households, the number of financially excluded households has increased since the publication of its first survey in 2009, with the number of unbanked alone increasing by over 800,000. The incidence of financial exclusion is highest among households that are African-American, Hispanic, lower-income, younger, or less-educated (see Figure 1).

The FDIC asked people why they had never had a bank account or why they had closed any prior account. Some reasons are listed in Figure 2. (Respondents were able to select more than one option.) Since the exact language of the FDIC's survey choices changed between 2009 and 2011, four reasons from the 2009 survey are included for further information.

FIGURE 1: PERCENTAGES OF HOUSEHOLDS, BY CHARACTERISTIC OF HOUSEHOLDER, UNBANKED OR UNDERBANKED, 2011

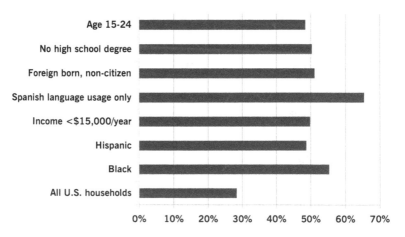

The responses suggest how difficult it is to survive at the lower end of the income distribution. Living paycheck to paycheck, the unbanked feel they do not have enough money to open and maintain a bank account, especially if there is a minimum balance requirement or the bank charges low-balance fees. The survey also reveals social barriers to being a bank customer. If your primary language is not spoken at the bank, for example, then you may feel banks are unwelcoming. This is one reason that over half of immigrant/non-citizen households, and that nearly two-thirds of households where only Spanish is spoken, are unbanked or underbanked

Logistical problems can be a major barrier. "Do I have the proper documents to open an account?" "Is there a bank near me that is convenient?" Banks and savings-and-loans ("thrifts") are under-represented in minority and low-income areas, and AFSPs cluster in those communities. (Scholars who study the issue call this the "spatial void hypothesis.") These spatial voids have only intensified since the 2008 financial crisis, as mainstream banks have ostensibly become more risk-averse—at least regarding low- and moderate-income households and communities.

Alternative financial services are big business in the United States, with an FDIC estimate of $320 billion in annual revenues. The sheer number of check-cashing outlets, payday lenders, auto-title lenders, and issuers of loans on anticipated tax refunds—over 13,000 according to the trade association Financial Service Centers of America—places them nearly on par numerically with banks and credit unions. (Combined, banks and credit unions number almost 15,000, according to the FDIC and National Credit Union Association.) AFSPs are not a "fringe" phenomenon in another sense—many are owned by large mainstream banks that have sought to profit in the market niches left unexploited by regular banking.

In states where check-cashing stores are regulated, fees are clearly posted in business locations, so it is fairly easy to determine the costs to customers. For example, cashing a

FIGURE 2: SOME REASONS HOUSEHOLDS DO NOT HAVE AN ACCOUNT OR CLOSED THEIR ACCOUNT, 2011 AND 2009

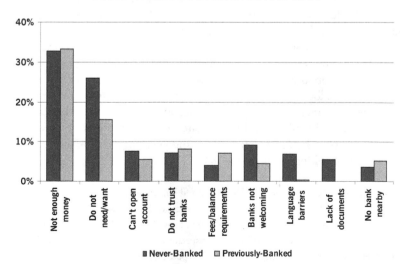

■ Never-Banked   ☐ Previously-Banked

Note: The last four categories appeared only in the 2009 survey.

government check (or direct deposit services for these checks) costs 1-3% of the face value of the check. Paychecks from businesses typically carry a 1-5% fee. Determining the typical fees for transaction services in mainstream banks is more difficult because of complicated fee structures that are dependent upon minimum balances. For people with limited needs for transaction services, and who would risk low balance penalties if they used a mainstream bank, AFSPs may in fact be a reasonable alternative.

Fees for transaction services, however, pale in comparison to the cost of credit. To make ends meet, 12 million Americans rely on short-term payday loans each year, at interest rates of about 300-750% (annual percentage rate, or APR). (Thirty-five states allow payday lending.) For the average borrower, a two-week payday loan stretches into five months of debt, with total interest payments greater than the amount of the loan. Wanting in on the action, big banks have issued payday loans to their own customers, terming them "deposit-advance loans," presumabaly to make them sound more legitimate.

With increased pressure from the new Consumer Financial Protection Bureau (CFPB) and the FDIC, the greedy practices of payday lenders, especially those operating on the internet, are gradually being investigated and curtailed. Now, banks are pulling back from deposit-advance loans. They are also beginning to cut off accounts for payday lenders and are allowing bank customers to halt automatic withdrawals to payday lending companies. What a difference the Dodd-Frank financial regulation law and the CFPB are beginning to make.

U.S. Senator Elizabeth Warren (D-MA) wants to take the solutions to financial exclusion one step further, beyond regulatory protections against harmful lending and transaction practices. In a recent Huffington Post opinion piece, she urges a serious consideration of postal banks, backing a new report from the U.S. Postal Service (USPS) Office of the Inspector General. The Postal Service, she argues, could partner with banks to offer basic services, including bill paying, check cashing, and small loans.

The idea has precedents. The United States had a postal savings system for accepting and insuring small deposits from 1911 to 1967. The government was thought to be a safe place to stash savings. Savers were paid interest on money that the postal service accepted and redeposited in local banks. After World War II, banks offered higher interest rates to compete for deposits and postal deposits fell. The convenience of the local post office faded in importance as Americans increasingly enjoyed access to cars.

But the idea of postal banks is once again garnering widespread support (44% in favor vs. 37% opposed in a recent YouGov/Huffington Post poll). For millions of Americans, the local post office is one of the geographically closest retail outlets. Unlike private financial-service providers subject to patchy state-by-state regulations, federal postal banks would be regulated in all U.S. states. They would help ease the spatial void in poorer communities and guard against exploitative practices by unregulated banking "alternatives." ❑

Sources: 2011 FDIC National Survey of Unbanked and Underbanked Households, September 2012; FDIC National Survey of Unbanked and Underbanked Households, December 2009; Sen. Elizabeth Warren, "Coming to a Post Office Near You: Loans You Can Trust?" Huffington Post Blog, Feb. 1, 2014 (huffingtonpost.com); Office of the Inspector General, U.S. Postal Service, "Providing Non-Bank Financial Services for the Underserved," Report Number RARC-WP-14-2007, Jan. 27, 2014; Pew Charitable Trusts reports on Payday Lending in America (pewstates.org).

Article 3.3

FORCED ARBITRATION IS BAD FOR CONSUMERS

BY HEIDI SHIERHOLZ
October 2017; Economic Policy Institute

Many financial institutions use forced arbitration clauses in their contracts to block consumers with disputes from banding together in court, instead requiring consumers to argue their cases separately in private arbitration proceedings. Embattled banking giant, Wells Fargo, made headlines by embracing the practice to avoid offering class-wide relief for its practices related to the fraudulent account scandal and another scandal involving alleged unfair overdraft practices.

New data helps illuminate why these banks—and Wells Fargo in particular—prefer forced arbitration to class action lawsuits. We already knew that consumers obtain relief regarding their claims in just 9% of disputes, while arbitrators grant companies relief in 93% of their claims. But not only do companies win the overwhelming majority of claims when consumers are forced into arbitration—they win big.

Some crucial background helps illustrate the stakes. In July 2017, the Consumer Financial Protection Bureau (CFPB) issued a final rule to restore consumers' ability to join together in class action lawsuits against financial institutions. Based on five years of careful study, the final rule stems from a congressional directive instructing the agency to study forced arbitration and restrict or ban the practice if it harms consumers.

In recent weeks, members of Congress have introduced legislation to repeal the CFPB rule and take away consumers' newly restored right to band together in court. Opponents of the rule have suggested that the bureau's own findings show consumers on average receive greater relief in arbitration ($5,389) than class action lawsuits ($32). As we have previously shown, this is enormously misleading. While the average consumer who wins a claim in arbitration recovers $5,389, this is not even close to a typical consumer outcome. Because consumers win so rarely, the average consumer ends up paying financial institutions in arbitration—a whopping $7,725.

A recent report released by the nonprofit Level Playing Field hones in on Wells Fargo's use of arbitration in consumer claims. Compiling publicly reported data from the American Arbitration Association (AAA) and JAMS (initially named Judicial Arbitration and Mediation Services, Inc.), the report found that just 250 consumers arbitrated claims with Wells Fargo between 2009 and the first half of 2017. This number is surprisingly small, since this period spans the prime years of the bank's fraudulent account scandal.

But we can take this data a step further by looking at Wells Fargo's overall gains and losses in arbitration. As one might suspect based on the CFPB data, Wells Fargo indeed won more money in arbitration between 2009 and the first half of 2017 than it paid out to consumers, despite creating 3.5 million fraudulent accounts during that same period.

What is even more troubling is that forced arbitration seems to be significantly more lucrative for Wells Fargo than for other financial institutions. In arbitration with Wells Fargo, the average consumer is ordered to pay the bank nearly $11,000. We calculated a mean of $10,826 awarded to the bank across all claims in the Level Playing Field report.

No wonder Wells Fargo prefers forced arbitration to class action lawsuits, which return at least $440 million, after deducting all attorneys' fees and court costs, to 6.8 million consumers in an average year. Banning consumer class actions lets financial institutions keep hundreds of millions of dollars that would otherwise go back to harmed consumers—and Wells Fargo seems to have harmed huge numbers of consumers.

Opponents of the CFPB's arbitration rule argue that allowing consumers to join together in court will increase consumer costs and decrease available credit. Most recently, the Office of the Comptroller of the Currency (OCC) claimed that restoring consumers' right to join together in court could cause interest rates on credit cards to rise as much as 25%.

However, examining the OCC's study, it appears the agency merely duplicated the conclusion reached by the CFPB and based its 25% estimate solely on results it admits are "statistically insignificant at the 95% (and 90%) confidence level." In its 2015 study, the CFPB considered this same data and accurately assessed that there was no "statistically significant evidence of an increase in prices among those companies that dropped their arbitration clauses."

Perhaps more importantly, claims that the arbitration rule will increase consumer and credit costs are also contradicted by real-life experience. Consumers saw no increase in prices after Bank of America, JPMorgan Chase, Capital One, and HSBC dropped their arbitration clauses as a result of court-approved settlements, and mortgage rates did not increase after Congress banned forced arbitration in the mortgage market. Of course, many would argue that banks like Wells Fargo should bear any increase in cost associated with making consumers whole for egregious misconduct.

Once again, the numbers are clear: Class actions return hundreds of millions in relief to consumers, while forced arbitration pays off big for lawbreakers like Wells Fargo. ❑

Sources: Michael Hiltzik, "No Surprise: Wells Fargo Is Leveraging Its Arbitration Clause to Win an Advantageous Scandal Settlement," *Los Angeles Times*, March 31, 2017; "Wells Fargo Wants Court to Toss Overdraft Lawsuits and Let It Use Arbitration," Associated Press, August 24, 2017; Heidi Shierholz, "Correcting the Record: Consumers Fare Better under Class Actions Than Arbitration," Economic Policy Institute, August 1, 2017; Consumer Financial Protection Bureau, "New Protections against Mandatory Arbitration," web page accessed July 31, 2017; Sylvan Lane, "GOP Lawmakers Introduce Measures to Repeal Consumer Bureau Arbitration Rule," *The Hill*, July 20, 2017; U.S. Senate Committee on Banking, Housing, and Urban Affairs, "Senators File Resolution Disapproving of CFPB Arbitration Rule" [majority press release], July 20, 2017; Level Playing Field, Wells Fargo and Forced Consumer Arbitration: September 2017 Update; Stacy Cowley, "Now Wells Fargo up to 3.5 Million Fraudulent Accounts," *San Francisco Chronicle*, August 31, 2017; Renae Merle, "U.S. Chamber of Commerce Suing to Block Rule Allowing Consumers to Sue Their Banks," *Washington Post*, September 29, 2017; Office of the Comptroller of the Currency (OCC), OCC Review: Probable Cost to Consumers Resulting from the Consumer Finance Protection Bureau's Final Rule on Arbitration Agreements, U.S. Department of the Treasury, September 20, 2017; Consumer Financial Protection Bureau, Arbitration Study: Report to Congress, pursuant to Dodd–Frank Wall Street Reform and Consumer Protection Act § 1028(a), March 2015; Adam J. Levitin, "Mandatory Arbitration Offers Bargain-Basement Justice," *American Banker* BankThink (blog), May 13, 2014.

Article 3.4

THE LIMITS OF ETHICAL CONSUMERISM
Can we save the world, one bamboo spork at a time?

BY MARC TRILLER
July/August 2021

Just before the coronavirus pandemic hit, my partner and I visited a pop-up exhibition in New York City called "Arcadia Earth." Billed as a climate change "museum," it features a series of immersive art installations that are designed to teach visitors "how small lifestyle changes will have a massive impact on the future of our planet." The exhibit leads guests through a maze of 15 rooms portraying the effects of various ecological crises. One room is a rainbow-hued cave constructed with 44,000 discarded plastic bags, representing the number of bags used in New York State every minute. In another space, discarded textile fabrics depict the hanging entrails of animals slaughtered in factory farms. Other installations illustrate the ravages of deforestation, overfishing, and global warming. Throughout the exhibit, display panels entreat visitors to take actions such as eating less meat, giving up single-use plastics, and purchasing more environmentally sustainable products. The overarching theme is that individuals can help save the Earth from ecological crisis by making better consumption decisions.

While the experience was certainly evocative, what I found most striking was the final stage of the exhibition: a home goods shop featuring a curated selection of "healthier" products "that benefit the planet, small businesses, and you," according to the exhibit's website. As I contemplated the shelves of bamboo sporks, nontoxic face lotions, and stainless-steel lunchboxes, it occurred to me that the entire immersive art experience had been ingeniously designed to emotionally prime me to purchase these goods at the end of the maze.

In fact, I later learned that Valentino Vettori, the creator of the art exhibit, is a professional designer for retail fashion storefronts. On his personal website, Vettori describes his conception of experiential retail:

> [Retail stores] are no longer asked merely to sell a product, we are called upon to tell a story. Brands that want to keep moving forward need to be bold and replace the archaic "dollar-per-square ft" formula with the dynamic "impression per square ft" approach. ... Our designs are made to invite consumers to step off the street and into a whole new world that engages, stimulates and inspires them with an unforgettable experience.

"Arcadia Earth" is the perfect manifestation of this experiential retail vision. Rather than merely hawking string tote bags and biodegradable toothbrushes, "Arcadia Earth" guides consumers through an awe-inspiring yet unsettling encounter with a planet in peril. Throughout the art exhibition, visitors are reminded at least a dozen times of how their individual consumption habits are endangering the environment. Yet, the end of the journey provides an opportunity for redemption. By purchasing a collapsible mug or a refillable bottle of shampoo, the consumer can experience relief from their guilt and possess a physical symbol of their commitment to saving the Earth.

Could it be that "Arcadia Earth" is a good-faith venture to inspire people to action? After all, "Arcadia Earth" must have to compensate the artists, pay its staff, and shell out some ridiculous amount of rent for its retail space in the fashionable NoHo neighborhood. What's the harm in having a gift shop to keep things afloat? More importantly, aren't they correct to point out that we are killing the planet with all the meat we eat, the crappy consumer goods we buy, and the mountains of waste we generate? It seems sensible that if we all made small changes in our consumption habits, it could have a major positive impact.

This line of thinking comprises the basic premise of the ethical consumerism movement. Ethical consumption (otherwise known as "conscious consumption") is the practice of purchasing goods and services that are produced in a manner that minimize social and environmental damage. By "voting" with their dollars and choosing products that align with their values, the thinking goes, ethical consumers can protect the environment and influence businesses to be more sustainable, ethical, and accountable. In this framework, individual purchases can be viewed as acts of political activism. "By buying products that don't contain palm oil, you're casting a vote to save orangutans and the Indonesian rainforest in which they live," the website for *Ethical Consumer* magazine tells us. The bottom line with this conscious consumption philosophy is that every individual can help save the world from ecological crisis by rejecting unsustainable products and choosing instead to buy green, organic, eco-friendly, socially responsible, zero-waste, ethically-sourced consumer goods. However, there are some questions that linger: Is this kind of consumerism actually feasible for most people? And does this approach actually help us save our rapidly warming planet?

The idea of ethical consumption has featured prominently in media outlets like the *New York Times*, which questions its readers, "Are you an ethical consumer?" and publishes articles such as "How to Be a More Conscious Consumer, Even If You're on a Budget." The *Times* also offers a carbon footprint quiz for readers to evaluate whether they are making "good climate choices." Not-for-profit organizations like the Ethical Consumer Research Association take the additional step of publishing ethical shopping guides, rating over 40,000 brands and products so consumers can purchase the most ethical goods. Ethical consumption has even been embraced by corporate associations stressing the importance of individual actions such as recycling, minimizing plastic waste, and reducing the size of one's carbon footprint.

Despite ethical consumption's widespread acceptance in liberal, well-to-do circles, a close examination reveals that ethical consumption cannot be relied upon as a stand-alone solution. While individual efforts to reduce societal and environmental harm are commendable, the ethical consumption framework has at least three major shortcomings that make it inadequate for addressing the ecological crises we currently face. These issues include the difficulty of determining the "most ethical" product, the exaggeration of consumer power relative to corporate power, and the distortion of responsibility for solving social and environmental issues.

The Calculation Problem

In many cases, it's incredibly difficult—if not downright impossible—to determine what the "most ethical" product is, or even which product is marginally "more ethical." For instance, if I want to buy a laptop computer, and I have five models from five different companies to choose from, how do I determine which model is the most ethical? For simplicity, let's say the only factor that's important to me is the total emissions generated by the product. If I want to be thorough, I need to account for all emissions expended in the manufacturing process, including: research and development; sales and marketing; sourcing raw materials; manufacturing, assembling, transporting, and warehousing the computer components; warehousing and distributing the finished product; shipping for returns, maintenance, and replacement parts; and finally, the lifetime power usage of the device.

To properly calculate this, one would have to map the entire global supply chain for each of the five laptops, which is no easy feat. As the coronavirus pandemic illustrated, many international corporations have supply chains that are so complex that the companies avoided mapping them due to the time and costs involved. Unless each company had already mapped its supply chain and was willing to make the data publicly available (both highly unlikely), a private individual mapping the supply chain for a single laptop computer would probably need years to complete the research. Moreover, even if one were able to map the entire supply chain, the information obtained would soon be irrelevant as the technology, processes, and suppliers would undoubtedly change. And unless one has the most up-to-date information about each laptop's supply chain, it will be nearly impossible to determine which product is the most "ethical" on an ongoing basis. This holds true for emissions, plastic waste, labor conditions, and any other criteria by which one might measure a product's "ethicalness." In short, it is nearly impossible for an individual to obtain this information about a single product, much less every one of the thousands of consumer goods that the average person buys over a lifetime.

Clearly very few people have this kind of time on their hands, so what if instead of trying to always purchase the most ethical product, people just made consumption decisions that were marginally more ethical? For instance, instead of driving six days per week, one could take public transportation or bike once per week, resulting in a weekly emissions reduction of about 17%. In theory, if everyone adopted this behavior, carbon emissions would drop.

The problem with this approach is that there is a risk that the individual changes in consumption would be so small that the overall environmental impact would be negligible. For instance, during the coronavirus pandemic, many Americans eliminated commuting and other kinds of travel altogether, and estimated daily vehicle miles plummeted by nearly 16%. However, greenhouse gas emissions only fell by about 10%. Although this decline in emissions exceeded the United Nation's 7.6% annual reduction target, if a global pandemic that brings much of the country to a standstill for months only reduces emissions by 10%, it's unreasonable to expect small, voluntary changes to make an impact of this magnitude year-over-year. Furthermore, as the United States recovers from the pandemic, the emissions reductions gained during the pandemic will likely be reversed unless immediate action is taken to invest in green energy infrastructure.

An additional complicating factor in the ethical consumption calculus is the difficulty comparing ethical attributes. How does one evaluate trade-offs among different products' ethical or unethical characteristics? For example, consider farmers' markets. In theory, buying blueberries at your local farmers' market is good because it supports community businesses, the farmers don't use genetically modified (GMO) seeds, and perhaps the berries are organic. Yet, from the standpoint of carbon emissions, farmers' markets are extremely inefficient because each farmer has to transport their own produce to the market, often multiple times per week. If you also have to drive 10 minutes to the farmers' market, but the supermarket is only a two-minute walk from your home, one could argue that it's actually more eco-friendly (if we're looking strictly at a consumer's car emissions) to shop for blueberries at the supermarket. But how does one weigh this against the pollution caused by the supermarket's unsustainable packaging and plastic grocery bags? To further complicate matters, what if the blueberries for sale at the farmers' market are picked by migrant workers being paid subminimum wages? In this case, there's no clear determinant for which blueberries are more or less ethical.

Even if one were able to objectively compare a product's ethical attributes, many people lack the ability to purchase the "more ethical" products simply because they can't afford them. Due to financial constraints, poor folks justifiably prioritize factors such as cost and functionality over other considerations because their daily survival depends on it. This raises the question, if someone chooses a less sustainable product over a more sustainable product, does this make them unethical? Furthermore, if someone doesn't "vote with their dollar" by buying more "sustainable" products, does that mean they're voting against sustainability? If every act of consumption carries moral weight, then one's ability to be good is ultimately constrained by one's wealth. Unless one accepts the premise that the poor can never be good, it's difficult to see how the ethical consumption framework can be universally applied.

Consumer Versus Corporate Power

Another key issue with the ethical consumption framework is that it is constructed on the shaky foundation of "consumer sovereignty." According to this conception of consumers and producers, every firm is like a dinghy adrift at sea, tossed about by the waves and rapidly shifting currents of consumer preference. Like Poseidon, the mythical consumer is a fickle deity with the power to either summon a tempest to wreck the boat, or clear the weather and allow it to pass safely. All the power rests in the hands the consumer, and if the firm fails to satisfy the consumer's every whim, the business is sunk.

Although consumer purchasing decisions certainly affect corporations, it's important to understand that a consumer's choice set (i.e., the number of consumption alternatives available to them) is heavily influenced by corporate interests. In other words, as a consumer, you may be able to order your meal à la carte, but big business picks what goes on the menu. This power to shape consumers' preferences and constrain their available consumption options is evident in two key areas: advertising and policymaking.

Marketing research has shown that advertising has a significant impact on consumer buying behavior. For instance, a recent study published in the *Business*

Studies Journal empirically demonstrated that factors such as an ad's familiarity, entertainment value, and social appeal, combined with the total expenditure on the campaign, all positively influence consumers to purchase the advertised product. Although a host of individual and social factors also influence consumer purchasing decisions, advertising is the most direct way for companies to vie for consumers' attention. As a result, U.S. corporations collectively spent $240 billion on advertising in 2019, with the 20 biggest U.S. advertisers spending upwards of $2 billion apiece. That same year, Amazon topped the list by spending an astonishing $6.9 billion on advertising—the equivalent of $21,000 per minute.

Corporate efforts to influence consumer behavior often begin before most people are aware it's happening. Many companies employ cradle-to-grave marketing strategies to shape children's tastes before they're old enough to purchase goods or understand marketing's persuasive intent. Even for adults, well-designed ads can create subconscious, emotional associations that frame consumer goods as the keys to realizing our instinctual needs for things like food and social connection. For instance, a 2013 study featured in the *Journal of Marketing* demonstrated that merely seeing images of someone eating pizza enhanced people's experiences during their own subsequent indulgence in a slice of pizza. The researchers also found that pizza ads provided a sense of social acceptability that justified the viewers' indulgence in unhealthy food.

Regardless of whether consumers are conscious of these effects, corporations deluge us with advertisements to influence our emotions, desires, and consumption behaviors. Considering that the average person is exposed to somewhere between 6,000 and 10,000 ads per day, it would be a mistake to believe that our tastes and preferences are free from corporate influence.

While advertising has the power to impact a consumer's preferences and consumption behavior, corporations can also shape a consumer's choice set by influencing policymaking. This can be accomplished by contributing to dark money groups (which can donate unlimited sums to political nonprofits and super PACs without disclosing their donors), sponsoring think tanks that support pro-corporate policies, as well as funding "grassroots" activist groups that pressure elected officials.

One of the most effective ways to shape policy is through lobbying, on which American corporations spent $2.99 billion in 2020. Lobbyists—many of whom are former government officials—have extensive ties to legislators and members of regulatory agencies. Thus, by hiring the right lobbying firm, corporations can gain an unprecedented level of access to government decision makers and a seat at the table to defend their interests.

Since 1998, U.S. oil and gas companies have spent over $2.4 billion on lobbying, and their investment has paid off handsomely. Despite the fact that fossil fuels are one of the biggest drivers of climate change, a recent report from Public Citizen revealed that over 65% of top U.S. Department of the Interior meetings with the private sector between 2017 and 2019 took place with oil, gas, and coal groups. In contrast, sessions with conservation and renewable energy interests comprised only 12% of the department's meetings.

The extent of the oil and gas industry's political influence is also evidenced by U.S. Climate Envoy John Kerry's recent remarks that half of the emissions cuts necessary to reach net-zero carbon emissions will be made by technologies that have not yet been invented. Kerry's statement reveals that the fossil fuel lobby has successfully convinced him that the solution to climate change is not achieved by cutting emissions and immediately transitioning to green energy. Rather, the optimal course of action is to basically cross our fingers and hope that new technologies will be invented so that oil and gas companies can continue business as usual.

This example illustrates that when it comes to public investment, the consumer's policy preferences and consumption choices are irrelevant. Consumers can't choose to address climate change immediately with current technology, because that option has been blocked by fossil fuel interests. In other cases, ethical consumers might want their local utilities to be powered by wind and solar energy, or they might prefer taking a train to work rather than driving. However, unless these public services already exist, there's no way to "vote" for them by paying an electric bill or buying a train ticket. One might argue that a consumer could "vote with their dollar" by donating to political candidates who support building green infrastructure. Yet, as is the case with lobbying, in a system in which our dollar is our vote, the people with the deepest pockets will always get the most votes.

Blame Consumers, Absolve Corporations

A third major problem with the ethical consumption framework is that it blames consumers and burdens them with fixing problems that have been caused by corporations. For instance, in the "Arcadia Earth" exhibit, their signage on plastic pollution merely states, "Plastic waste is entering our food chain." (As if microplastics have some sort of collective consciousness and are plotting to destroy the planet!) The implicit message is that individual consumers cause climate change and plastic pollution by making unethical consumption choices. Therefore, consumers bear the ultimate responsibility for solving the crisis.

This framing distorts the truth that a handful of corporations disproportionately drive the plastic crisis. Just 20 firms produce 55% of the world's plastic waste, and the recent fossil fuel boom has made production of "virgin" plastic much cheaper than using recycled plastic. With the plastics market worth hundreds of billions of dollars annually, these corporations have a significant economic incentive to ramp up their production.

In order to justify the expansion of the plastics industry, the industry has launched a massive campaign to suppress efforts to reduce plastic waste while emphasizing the significance of recycling. For instance, plastics industry lobbyists actively oppose efforts to restrict the production of new plastics by pushing for state laws that prohibit local bans on plastics. In addition, groups such as the American Beverage Association lobby against container deposit laws that have been shown to save energy, prevent pollution, and reduce the amount of plastic waste sent to landfills and incinerators.

While the plastics industry privately resists all attempts at regulation, it publicly feigns concern for the environment by stressing the importance of recycling. The United States only recycles about 9% of its plastic waste, and while some of the failure can be blamed on careless consumers, much of the plastic waste that arrives at recycling centers is either incinerated, sent to a landfill, or exported to countries that lack sufficient infrastructure to manage it. The root of the problem stems from the fact that the very notion of plastic recycling is largely a sustainability scam. A 2020 study by Greenpeace uncovered that regardless of what the label says, only two types of plastic bottles and jugs (PET No. 1 and HDPE No. 2) are legitimately recyclable in the United States. This means that over 60% of plastics manufactured globally are not even recyclable! In spite of the fact that recycling alone is insufficient to absorb the ever-increasing levels of single-use plastics being produced, the industry continues to peddle the narrative that consumers are to blame.

The concept of ethical consumption dovetails nicely with this corporate propaganda. Instead of illuminating how ecological crises are caused by corporations' willful shifting of costs onto consumers and the environment, the ethical consumption framework absolves corporations and holds consumers responsible for both causing and solving the problem.

Toward Collective Action

While the espoused goals of ethical consumption are laudable, ethical consumption alone is insufficient for solving the planetary crises we currently face. Our discussion of ethical consumption's implications reveals that it is nearly impossible to figure out which products are optimally ethical, and even if one could, this framework can't be universally applied because it requires a certain level of time and income. Furthermore, this approach presumes that isolated acts of consumption have the power to influence corporate behavior. While this may be true to a limited extent, ethical consumption downplays corporations' power to shape consumers' tastes and constrain their choice sets. Finally, ethical consumption shifts blame for social and ecological issues from corporations to consumers.

To be clear, my intent is not to criticize people's attempts to minimize the social and ecological harms caused by consumption. Individual efforts at minimizing social and environmental damage are important, but isolated acts of personal consumption won't make much of an impact. In fact, ethical consumption's singular focus on buying products forecloses alternatives to an economic system that depends on endless consumption and growth.

In the future, instead of agonizing over the "best" item to put in our shopping carts, perhaps we could tap into the anxiety we feel about our economic system and use it to motivate us to take action. For meaningful change to take place, we don't need ethical consumers as much as we need consumer activists. Community organizing, boycotts, rallies, and other forms of political activism are the only proven ways we have to successfully pressure corporations and governments to make the changes necessary to save the Earth from climate catastrophe. And, in the event you forget your stainless-steel water bottle in your rush to get to the local climate change protest, I know of a home goods shop in NoHo that has some great deals. ❏

Sources: Valentino Vettori, "Our Motivation," company website (valentinovettori.com/experiential-retail); Tim Hunt, "Why Shop Ethically?" *Ethical Consumer* website, April 6, 2021 (ethicalconsumer.org); Jeremy Engel, "Are You an Ethical Consumer?" *New York Times*, December 14, 2018 (nytimes.

com); Kristin Wong, "How to Be a More Conscious Consumer, Even If You're on a Budget," *New York Times*, October 1, 2019; Veronica Penney, "Think You're Making Good Climate Choices? Take This Mini-Quiz," *New York Times*, August 30, 2020; Jill Mislinski, "America's Driving Habits as of March 2021," *Advisor Perspectives*, May 24, 2021 (advisorperspectives.com); Kate Larsen, Hannah Pitt, and Alfredo Rivera, *Preliminary US Greenhouse Gas Emissions Estimates for 2020*, Rhodium Group, January 12, 2021 (rhg.com); Tashrifa Haider and Shadman Shakib, "A Study On The Influences of Advertisement On Consumer Buying Behavior," *Business Studies Journal*, 2017 (abacademies.org); Statista, "Media advertising spending in the United States from 2015 to 2022" (statista.com); "Leading National Advertisers 2020 Fact Pack," *Ad Age*, July 13, 2020 (adage.com); Katie Jones, "How Total Spending by U.S. Advertisers Has Changed, Over 20 Years," *Visual Capitalist*, Oct. 16, 2020 (visualcapitalist.com); Morgan Poor, Adam Duhachek, H. Shanker Krishnan, "How Images of Other Consumers Influence Subsequent Taste Perceptions," *Journal of Marketing*, Nov. 1, 2013; James McNeal, *The Kids Market: Myth and Realities* (Paramount Market Publishing, 1999); Sam Carr, "How Many Ads Do We See A Day In 2021?," *PPC Protect*, Feb. 15, 2020 (ppcprotect.com); Kim Barker and Marian Wang, "Super-PACs and Dark Money: ProPublica's Guide to the New World of Campaign Finance," ProPublica, July 11, 2011 (propublica.org); Nicholas Kusnetz, "Heartland Launches Website of Contrarian Climate Science Amid Struggles With Funding and Controversy," Inside Climate News, March 13, 2020 (insideclimatenews.org); "The Climate Denial Machine: How the Fossil Fuel Industry Blocks Climate Action," Climate Reality Project, September 5, 2019 (climaterealityproject.org); OpenSecrets, "Business, Labor & Ideological Split in Lobbying Data" (opensecrets.org); OpenSecrets, "Industries"; "Analysis Finds 65% of Top Interior Meetings Included Energy Groups, Lobbyists," Public Citizen, May 20, 2020 (citizen.org); Jessica Murray, "Half of emissions cuts will come from future tech, says John Kerry," *The Guardian*, May 16, 2021 (theguardian.com); Sandra Laville, "Twenty firms produce 55% of world's plastic waste, report reveals," *The Guardian*, May 17, 2021; Sharon Lerner, "Waste Only: How the Plastics Industry Is Fighting to Keep Polluting the World," The Intercept, July 20, 2019 (theintercept.com); Michele Nash-Hoff, "Why Are There So Few States with 'Bottle Bill' Laws?" *Industry Week*, Sept. 16, 2015 (industryweek.com); Laura Parker, "A whopping 91% of plastic isn't recycled," *National Geographic*, Dec. 20, 2018 (nationalgeographic.com); Jan Dell, "157,000 Shipping Containers of U.S. Plastic Waste Exported to Countries with Poor Waste Management in 2018," Plastic Pollution Coalition, March 6, 2019 (plasticpollutioncoalition.org); Nicole Javorsky, "'Recyclable' labels on plastic products are often misleading, says review," The Hill, Feb. 18, 2020 (thehill.com); Statista, "Production volume of high density polyethylene resin worldwide in 2016 and 2022" (statista.com); GAIA, "Discarded: Communities on the Frontlines of the Global Plastic Crisis," April 2019 (wastetradestories.org).

Article 3.5

CAMPUS STRUGGLES AGAINST SWEATSHOPS CONTINUE

Indonesian workers and U.S. students fight back against Adidas.

BY SARAH BLASKEY AND PHIL GASPER
September/October 2012

Abandoning his financially ailing factory in the Tangerang region of Indonesia, owner Jin Woo Kim fled the country for his home, South Korea, in January 2011 without leaving money to pay his workers. The factory, PT Kizone, stayed open for several months and then closed in financial ruin in April, leaving 2,700 workers with no jobs and owed $3.4 million of legally mandated severance pay.

In countries like Indonesia, with no unemployment insurance, severance pay is what keeps workers and their families from literal starvation. "The important thing is to be able to have rice. Maybe we add some chili pepper, some salt, if we can," explained an ex-PT-Kizone worker, Marlina, in a report released by the Worker Rights Consortium (WRC), a U.S.-based labor-rights monitoring group, in May 2012.

Marlina, widowed mother of two, worked at PT Kizone for 11 years before the factory closed. She needs the severance payment in order to pay her son's high school registration fee and monthly tuition, and to make important repairs to her house.

When the owner fled, the responsibility for severance payments to PT Kizone workers fell on the companies that sourced from the factory—Adidas, Nike, and the Dallas Cowboys. Within a year, both Nike and the Dallas Cowboys made severance payments that they claim are proportional to the size of their orders from the factory, around $1.5 million total. But Adidas has refused to pay any of the $1.8 million still owed to workers.

Workers in the PT Kizone factory mainly produced athletic clothing sold to hundreds of universities throughout the United States. All collegiate licensees like Adidas and Nike sign contracts with the universities that buy their apparel. At least 180 universities around the nation are affiliated with the WRC and have licensing contracts mandating that brands pay "all applicable back wages found due to workers who manufactured the licensed articles." If wages or severance pay are not paid to workers that produce university goods, then the school has the right to terminate the contract.

Using the language in these contracts, activists on these campuses coordinate nationwide divestment campaigns to pressure brands like Adidas to uphold previously unenforceable labor codes of conduct.

Unpaid back wages and benefits are a major problem in the garment industry. Apparel brands rarely own factories. Rather, they contract with independent manufacturers all over the world to produce their wares. When a factory closes for any reason, a brand can simply take its business somewhere else and wash its hands of any responsibilities to the fired workers.

Brands like Nike and Russell have lost millions of dollars when, pressed by United Students Against Sweatshops (USAS), universities haver terminated their contracts. According to the USAS website, campus activism has forced Nike to pay severance and Russell to rehire over 1,000 workers it had laid off, in order to avoid losing more collegiate contracts. Now many college activists have their sights set on Adidas.

At the University of Wisconsin (UW) in Madison, the USAS-affiliated Student Labor Action Coalition (SLAC) and sympathetic faculty are in the middle of a more than year-long campaign to pressure the school to terminate its contract with Adidas in solidarity with the PT Kizone workers.

The chair of UW's Labor Licensing Policy Committee (LLPC) says that Adidas is in violation of the code of conduct for the school's licensees. Even the university's senior counsel, Brian Vaughn, stated publicly at a June LLPC meeting that Adidas is "in breach of the contract based on its failure to adhere to the standards of the labor code." But despite the fact that Vaughn claimed at the time that the University's "two overriding goals are to get money back in the hands of the workers and to maintain the integrity of the labor code," the administration has dragged its feet in responding to Adidas.

Instead of putting the company on notice for potential contract termination and giving it a deadline to meet its obligations as recommended by the LLPC, UW entered into months of fruitless negotiations with Adidas in spring of 2012. In July, when these negotiations had led nowhere, UW's interim chancellor David Ward asked a state court to decide whether or not Adidas had violated the contract (despite the senior counsel's earlier public admission that it had). This process will delay a decision for many more months—perhaps years if there are appeals.

Since the Adidas campaign's inception in the fall of 2011, SLAC members have actively opposed the school's cautious approach, calling both the mediation process and the current court action a "stalling tactic" by the UW administration and Adidas to avoid responsibility to the PT Kizone workers. In response, student organizers planned everything from frequent letter deliveries to campus administrators, to petition drives, teach-ins, and even a banner drop from the administration building that over 300 people attended, all in hopes of pressuring the chancellor (who ultimately has the final say in the matter) to cut the contract with Adidas.

While the administration claims that it is moving slowly to avoid being sued by Adidas, it is also getting considerable pressure from its powerful athletics director, Barry Alvarez, to continue its contract with Adidas. As part of the deal, UW's sports programs receive royalties and sports gear worth about $2.5 million every year.

"Just look at the money—what we lose and what it would cost us," Alvarez told the *Wisconsin State Journal*, even though other major brands would certainly jump at the opportunity to replace Adidas. "We have four building projects going on. It could hurt recruiting. There's a trickle-down effect that would be devastating to our whole athletic program."

But Tina Treviño-Murphy, a student activist with SLAC, rejects this logic. "A strong athletics department shouldn't have to be built on a foundation of stolen labor," she told *Dollars & Sense*. "Our department and our students deserve better."

Adidas is now facing pressure from both campus activists in the United States and the workers in Indonesia—including sit-ins by the latter at the German and British embassies in Jakarta. (Adidas' world headquarters are in Germany, and the company sponsored the recent London Olympics.) This led to a meeting between their union and an Adidas representative, who refused to admit responsibility but instead offered food vouchers to some of the workers. The offer amounted to a tiny fraction of the owed severance and was rejected as insulting by former PT Kizone workers.

In the face of intransigence from university administrations and multinational companies prepared to shift production quickly from one location to another to stay one step ahead of labor-rights monitors, campus activism to fight sweatshops can seem like a labor of Sisyphus. After more than a decade of organizing, a recent fundraising appeal from USAS noted that "today sweatshop conditions are worse than ever."

Brands threaten to pull out of particular factories if labor costs rise, encouraging a work environment characterized by "forced overtime, physical and sexual harassment, and extreme anti-union intimidation, even death threats," says Natalie Yoon, a USAS member who recently participated in a delegation to factories in Honduras and El Salvador.

According to Snehal Shingavi, a professor at the University of Texas, Austin who was a USAS activist at Berkeley for many years, finding ways to build links with the struggles of the affected workers is key. "What I think would help the campaign the most is if there were actually more sustained and engaged connections between students here and workers who are in factories who are facing these conditions," Shingavi told *Dollars & Sense*. Ultimately, he said, only workers' self-activity can "make the kind of changes that I think we all want, which is an end to exploitative working conditions."

But in the meantime, even small victories are important. Anti-sweatshop activists around the country received a boost in September, when Cornell University President David Skorton announced that his school was ending its licensing contract with Adidas effective October 1, because of the company's failure to pay severance to PT Kizone workers. The announcement followed a sustained campaign by the Sweatfree Cornell Coalition, leading up to a "study in" at the president's office. While the contract itself was small, USAS described the decision as the "first domino," which may lead other campuses to follow suit. Shortly afterwards, Oberlin College in Ohio told Adidas that it would not renew its current four-year contract with the company if the workers in Indonesia are not paid severance.

Perhaps just as significant are the lessons that some activists are drawing from these campaigns. "The people who have a lot of power are going to want to keep that power and the only way to make people give some of that up is if we make them," Treviño-Murphy said. "So it's really pressure from below, grassroots organizing, that makes the difference. We see that every day in SLAC and I think it teaches us to be not just better students but better citizens who will stand up to fight injustice every time." ❑

Sources: Worker Rights Consortium, "Status Update Re: PT Kizone (Indonesia)," May 15, 2012 (workersrights.org); Andy Baggot, "Alvarez Anxiously Awaits Adidas Decision," *Wisconsin State Journal*, July 13, 2012 (host.madison.com); United Students Against Sweatshops (usas.org), PT Kizone update, June 15, 2012 (cleanclothes.org/urgent-actions/kizoneupdate).

Article 3.6

LEVERAGING FINANCIAL MARKETS FOR SOCIAL JUSTICE
Is divestment effective?

BY DOUG ORR
January/February 2022

Social justice avtivists often focus on changing the behavior of, or limiting the damage caused by, firms or industries that are hurting the well-being of groups of individuals or society as a whole. These "bad actors" could be entire industries, such as private prisons or tobacco, or individual firms, such as hedge funds or private equity firms that buy up non-financial firms and profit by running them into bankruptcy, leading to mass layoffs and destroyed communities. Some of the worst corporate bad actors are firms that are driving climate change.

Activist efforts to rein in bad actors include demonstrations to demand that states stop using private prisons and to limit the sales and advertising of tobacco products. Other efforts include lobbying for legislation to ban the use of fracking in the process of oil extraction and to limit the use of single-use plastic products. Other activists put their lives on the line to attempt to physically stop the completion of oil pipelines.

Still other activists see intervention in financial markets, as is the case with the push to get institutional investment funds to divest from fossil fuel companies, as a tool to effect change. Unfortunately, focusing on financial markets is often the *least* effective action to take. Climate change is an existential threat to life on the planet. To stop and reverse it, and halt other threats to our well-being, we need real change in personal and corporate behavior, and we will need to avoid diverting our time and energy on tactics that only produce superficial changes. Understanding *how and why* some tools and tactics are more effective than others in changing corporate behavior is, therefore, absolutely essential to success.

Financing a Corporation vs. Buying and Selling Existing Stock

To begin to understand why financial-market intervention is the least effective tactic for activists, we must examine some key concepts that are often confused. In public discussions of the world of finance, two completely different concepts are often incorrectly used interchangeably. Those concepts are: 1) buying or selling a share of stock on a stock exchange and 2) providing financing to a corporation.

Financing a corporation means providing money to cover the day-to-day operations of a firm or to allow it to expand. Several methods are used to finance a corporation. The first, which is usually used to quickly expand an up-and-coming corporation, is to purchase a share of stock directly from the firm when it is sold for the first time, at a firm's "initial public offering," or IPO. Lyft held its IPO on March 29, 2019, selling 32.5 million shares at $72 each. This brought in $2.34 billion of new cash that the firm could use to expand its operations, or to buy up its competitors. IPOs are extremely rare. IPO sales make up less than 0.2% of all stock sales in the United States each year.

A more common form of financing is for a firm to issue *bonds* (which are just IOUs), which allow them to borrow large sums of money. All large corporations borrow money in this way to cover long-term operations or to expand operations. The final, and most common, form of financing is *bank loans*. This bank financing affects the cash flow of the firm, and the ability to attract bank financing is critical to the functioning of a firm.

Buying or selling stock on a stock market does not finance a corporation. After the initial purchase of a stock share directly from the corporation, if the shareholder decides to sell their stock, they must find a buyer. This is the role of stock markets. Except in times of financial panic, finding a buyer is incredibly easy. When the share is sold, the buyer provides money to the seller, but the corporation itself is not affected in any way by this sale of stock. No money flows into or out of the corporation. The sale of the stock does not affect the corporation's cash flow or its ability to function.

Once a share of stock is sold at an IPO, the shareholder has partial ownership of the firm, which gives them the right to have a proportional say in the operation of the firm and to receive dividend payments. However, given the huge number of shares issued by large corporations, individual shareholders have very little voice in how the company is run. When workers own a limited number of shares in their individual retirement accounts, they own a small part of "labor's capital," but they have no voice in the operation of firms. This is one of the many reasons defined-benefit pension systems are critically important. By aggregating labor's capital, it gives labor a voice. Just as unions are necessary because individual workers have little power relative to their employer, labor's capital has little power unless it is aggregated in defined-benefit pension systems.

Pension funds that own a very large number of shares have much more power to affect the behavior of firms. The power of aggregating labor's capital is part of the reason corporations and right-wing politicians constantly push to convert defined-benefit pension plans into individual uninsured defined-contribution savings plans, such as 401(k) or 403(b) retirement plans. Individual owners of stock are essentially voiceless.

Divestment Is Not Defunding

Two other financial concepts that are also very different and are also incorrectly used interchangeably are "divestment" and "defunding," or ending direct financing. Selling a share of stock is called *divestment*. If an extremely large number of stockholders decide to divest at the same time, it has the potential to reduce the selling price of a firm's stock temporarily, but it has *almost no impact* on the functioning of the firm, and the stock price almost always rebounds quickly.

For example, in the third quarter of 2021, the California State Teachers Retirement System (CalSTRS) held 7.48 million shares of ExxonMobil, which seems like a lot. But the average daily trade volume of Exxon stock was 21.5 million shares. If CalSTRS sold all their shares in one day, that would be about one-third of the trades on that one day and would have no effect beyond that day. This would not affect the price of Exxon stock and Exxon would likely not even notice.

On the other hand, the decision to *end financing* of a corporation has the potential to have a *major* impact on the functioning of the corporation. If a firm is not able to issue bonds because no one will buy them, it will be difficult for the firm to expand its operations. If the firm cannot get access to bank loans, it cannot fund its day-to-day operations. Small, "mom-and-pop" firms have limited access to this type of financing, which is why the failure rate of small firms is so much higher than that of large corporations. If a large number of investors decide to refuse to buy bonds that a firm is trying to sell, the firm will not be able to gain access to the cash necessary to run the business. The same is true if banks refuse to lend to the firm. This lack of financing is the most common cause for bankruptcy filings.

Pension Funds and Divestment vs. Defunding "Bad Actors"

There is a growing movement in the United States calling on institutional investors to divest from some "bad actor" firms and industries. When several very large pension funds around the country, including CalSTRS, the largest teacher-only pension fund in the world, and the New York State Teachers Fund, decided to divest from two firms in the private prison industry, CoreCivic and GEO Group, the share prices of those firms did not decline. In fact, the divestment of these two very large pension funds had no impact on the behavior of these two firms.

However, when JPMorgan Chase decided to stop providing financing to these firms, by no longer underwriting bond issues or making loans, it brought about an immediate reaction from these firms. Pushing banks to end the financing of bad actors has a much bigger impact than pushing for divestment. The idea is to cut off the cash flow.

The distinction between divestment and defunding is an important issue with respect to CalSTRS. CalSTRS holds some of its assets directly, but it holds many assets through contracts with outside managers. Some of these are mutual fund managers, and some are private equity managers. In these contracts, CalSTRS provides direct financing to the managers, who then invest the funds. Some private equity managers serve both the corporate and social interest, but some behave as "vulture capitalists." The national research department of the American Federation of Teachers (AFT) provides periodic reports calling out these bad actors.

Bad-actor managers, such as Mitt Romney's Bain Capital, sometimes buy a controlling interest in a firm, drive down wages of workers, plunge the firm into debt, and transfer all this money to themselves. If these outside managers are engaged in bad-actor activities, their ability to function will be greatly reduced if CalSTRS pulls its direct funding and allocates it to other outside managers who behave in a more socially responsible way. If a large number of pension funds simultaneously pulled their money from one of these vulture funds, the fund manager would suffer a significant cash flow loss and might be put out of business.

Engagement vs. Divestment

Another method used to attempt to change corporate behavior through financial markets is through *engagement*. If a pension fund, or group of pension funds, owns sufficiently large blocks of shares, they can submit resolutions at annual shareholder meetings. These resolutions can change the behavior of firms, change the makeup of the board of directors, and in some cases, lead to replacing the CEO. The effect of this type of engagement, while limited, is more effective in changing firm behavior than divestment.

Why Do Some People Believe That Divestment is Effective?
The (Misunderstood) Case of Apartheid-Era South Africa

Many people look back at the movement to get colleges and universities to divest from Apartheid-era South Africa as an indication of the effectiveness of divestment. But this is a misreading of the anti-Apartheid movement.

The anti-Apartheid movement outside of South Africa, which started primarily in England and Europe, first focused on supporting the efforts of the South African people themselves in their struggles against Apartheid. These struggles took the form of work stoppages, mass demonstrations, civil disobedience, and, ultimately, armed struggle. It was these internal struggles that ultimately ended Apartheid, but international pressure did help.

The international anti-Apartheid movement focused first on developing boycotts of South African products and imposing sanctions on South African businesses and government officials. It also targeted major banks to stop lending to South African businesses. The goal was to restrict the flow of money to the South African economy. The movement was relatively successful, and the boycotts and sanctions expanded over time.

The movement in the United States for divestment from South Africa came later in the process. While the divestments had almost no direct effect on South African businesses, the consciousness-raising aspect of the movement greatly expanded the already existing boycotts of South African products in the United States. It led more U.S. companies, and popular performers, to stop doing business in South Africa. It forced some U.S. banks to defund South African businesses by refusing to make loans. It also increased pressure on the U.S. government to enforce already existing sanctions on South African businesses and members of the South African government. The increased social awareness ultimately led to the passage of the Comprehensive Anti-Apartheid Act in 1986, over President Ronald Reagan's veto, which banned new investments in South Africa. Because Reagan's enforcement of the act was lax, Representative Charles Rangel added an amendment to the 1987 Budget Reconciliation Bill that ended the ability of U.S. firms to claim tax credits in the United States for taxes paid in South Africa.

The boycotts, sanctions, and cancelation of business contracts had a direct and powerful effect on the cash flow of the South African economy, and it was this that put the most pressure on the government for change. Had these concrete sanctions and boycotts not already been in place, the consciousness-raising aspect of the divestment movement would likely not have had much impact.

Sources: Robert E. Edgar, ed., Sanctioning Apartheid (Africa World Press 1990); Richard Knight, "Sanctions, Disinvestment, and U.S. Corporations in South Africa," 1990 (richardknight.homestead.com).

CalSTRS engagement efforts have led to significant changes in the behavior of several firms. Coalitions of institutional investors have had success at several large corporations in getting more women and people of color appointed to corporate boards of directors. These changes in the board makeup have led to changes in the hiring and promotion practices at these firms.

A very significant recent example involves ExxonMobil. A coalition of large institutional investors, led by a fund called Engine 1 and including CalSTRS and CalPERS removed three members of the Exxon board who have a "drill baby drill" focus, and replaced them with three new board members who have a clear understanding of the role of fossil fuels in driving climate change and have a focus on moving Exxon to become an alternative fuel company. While this success is more likely to change the behavior of Exxon than divestment would have, it is still a very limited success in the face of the current climate crisis because the change will come too slowly.

Unfortunately, financial markets have so many actors that attempts to change corporate behavior through either divestment or directly ending funding often have limited impact. When "moral" investors pull out, "immoral" investors step in. Thus, it is often much more productive to focus efforts to effect social change outside the financial sector. This can be done through boycotts of products. It can also be done through passing legislation that directly sanctions the behavior of firms, such as imposing fuel efficiency standards for new vehicles, imposing a state or national tax on carbon emissions, or ending government use of private prisons.

Is Divestment an Effective Tool for Social Change?

The reason we need to understand the limited role of financial markets in efforts to effect positive social justice change is so that we can understand the best policy recommendations and demands.

Many progressive economists, including Robert Pollin at the University of Massachusetts–Amherst and the Political Economy Research Institute, do not

---

Pension Funds, Divestment, and "Stranded Assets"

Trustees of pension funds have the fiduciary responsibility to manage fund assets. If the climate justice movement is successful, the global economy will abandon the use of fossil fuels. The share price of fossil fuel companies' stock is determined, in part, by their assets, and much of their assets are reserves still in the ground. If these assets become "stranded" because they are no longer in demand, the share prices of the companies will decline. While we know that this will occur, the timing of this decline is still being debated. When it does become imminent, more investors will dump these stocks.

Two large New York pension funds recently announced they were divesting from fossil fuel companies. In their statements explaining their actions they did not claim divestment would change the behavior of these companies. But rather, they referred to the potential loss in value as a result of stranded assets. In this case, divestment is not the *cause* of the movement away from fossil fuels, but rather the *result*.

support the idea of divestment as a tool for social change. This is because research has shown that divestment, by itself, *has almost no impact in changing corporate behavior.* For a pension fund or college to divest from an industry, they have to sell the stock. They cannot sell unless someone else is buying the stock. Money goes from one shareholder to another, but there is no financial impact on the industry itself. Because there is no financial impact on the industry, corporations have no incentive to change their behavior. *Almost every pension fund in the United States divested from the tobacco industry and the behavior of that industry did not change.* The same is true for the gun industry. What has changed the behavior of the tobacco industry has been a significant increase in taxes on tobacco products and direct regulation of the sale and advertising of these products.

Historically, the main effect of divestment campaigns is consciousness-raising, i.e., making the broader public aware of an issue. That is a very important role, but by itself that is not enough unless there is a concrete focus for that new awareness (see sidebar, "Why Do Some People Believe that Divestment Is Effective?"). Unfortunately, many organizations that are trying to fight climate change focus on divestment as their only policy demand. Students are holding sit-ins and risking arrest trying to get their colleges to divest from fossil fuel companies. If the colleges do divest, many of those students, because they do not understand the effects of divestment, are going to declare victory and move on to something else. If that happens, the divestment campaign is *actually counterproductive* because it does not affect industry behavior and it *diverts the energy of activists.*

The policy debate between engagement vs. divestment is essentially the same as the economist Albert O. Hirschman's concepts of voice vs. exit. When people find themselves connected to a problematic or declining organization, they face a choice between *voice*—trying to improve the organization by criticizing it or proposing improvements—and *exit*—just withdrawing from the organization. Engagement, while often limited in its level of success, is the exercising of the voice of labor's capital. Divestment is a form of exit, which is justified only by considerations other than trying to change the behavior of the corporation (see sidebar, "Pension Funds, Divestment, and 'Stranded Assets'").

Bypassing the Market

It would be far more effective if these students were sitting in and risking arrest at state legislatures demanding the implementation of a state-wide carbon tax, or state-level regulations. They could also be picketing the headquarters of banks making loans to fossil fuel companies. These campaigns would serve a consciousness-raising role, but unlike calling for divestment, calling for direct intervention in the market, if successful, would actually have a significant impact on slowing the climate crisis.

Given that we live in an economy in which the market allocates almost all resources, changing the functioning of the market through direct intervention is an important policy goal. Many progressive economists support the idea of a "carbon tax." This fee would be charged on all forms of carbon, not just fossil fuel companies. If everyone in society had to pay for the full environmental cost of the carbon they use, they would have an incentive to find ways to reduce their carbon footprint.

They would find ways to buy less gasoline, use more efficient methods to heat their homes, and buy less plastic packaging.

When the price of gasoline spiked in 2008, people stopped buying Hummers and other huge trucks and started buying smaller, more fuel-efficient vehicles. Unfortunately, when the price of gas came back down, the sales of big pickup trucks went back up. A carbon fee would permanently raise the price of gas. From a social justice perspective, this creates a significant problem because low-income households would be hard pressed to pay the higher prices. This is why advocates of a carbon fee recommend rebating the revenue raised back to households, using a progressive formula in which lower-income households would receive a larger rebate. The same approach would be used to cover the increased cost of home heating.

More than 50 cities and counties in the United States have passed ordinances to eliminate the use of natural gas for heating and cooking in all new construction. The state of California will end the sale of fossil fuel powered automobiles by 2035. These are examples of bypassing the market completely and using direct regulation. When the downside risk of a market activity is very large and potentially irreversible, direct intervention to bypass or control the market is often the fastest and most effective method to change behavior.

A Policy Test: What Do Corporations Resist?

The best way to judge the potential effect of a policy recommendation is to *watch the industry response to a proposal*. The sugary drinks industry spent millions of dollars to fight a small tax on soda in San Francisco, but the tobacco and weapons industries spent very little money to fight divestment. Chevron is not spending much money to fight the divestment movement, but they are spending millions to fight a carbon tax and increased regulation.

Part of the climate justice movement, especially in Europe, has focused directly on getting banks to stop lending to fossil fuel companies. A good example is NatWest, the largest bank in Scotland and until recently the largest bank in the world, which has committed to ending loans to fossil fuel companies and moving their financing to firms and industries that are fighting climate change. Cutting off cash flow to fossil fuel firms has a direct effect on their ability to function and their response has been quick in coming.

The American Legislative Exchange Council (ALEC), an organization funded by climate change deniers and ultra-wealthy right-wing donors, creates policy language on many issues, and provides fully written legislative bills for their right-wing allies to introduce in state legislatures. ALEC has already developed policy language to make it illegal for banks to refuse lending to fossil fuel companies. The threat of cutting off the cash flow is what scares the industry.

Climate change presents an existential threat to the planet in the form of increased intensity of hurricanes and other storms, such as the extreme tornadoes that hit the Tennessee Valley on December 11, 2021, which was well beyond the normal tornado season. At the same time, climate change has increased the number and severity of droughts. Both storms and droughts threaten food systems. Climate change will lead to increased conflict over resources and the forced migration of millions of people. In addition to its effects on humans, it will also lead to ocean acidification and mass extinction of animal species.

There is no time to lose in the fight against climate change. So, the argument comes down to the question of which tactic is going to have the quickest and most significant impact. The climate crisis is real, and the damages are already occurring. The failure of the recent United Nations global climate summit in Glasgow drives home the need to focus efforts on those tactics that will have immediate and concrete impacts. Focusing activists' attention on financial markets and especially on divestment is not our best option. If we use the most effective tools available, such as direct regulation, taxation, and a Green New Deal, we can either change the behavior of some of these firms or put them out of business altogether. ❏

Sources: Robert Pollin and Tyler Hansen, "Economics and Climate Justice Activism: Assessing the Fossil Fuel Divestment Movement," Political Economy Research Institute, April 24, 2018 (peri.org); Robert Pollin, Jeannette Wicks-Lim, Shouvik Chakraborty, Caitlin Kline, and Gregor Semieniuk, "A Program for Economic Recovery and Clean Energy Transition in California," Political Economy Research Institute, June 10, 2021 (peri.org); "The Big Squeeze: How Asset Managers' Fees Crush State Budgets and Workers' Retirement Hopes," American Federation of Teachers, May 2017 (aft.org); Samir Sonti, "Lifting the Curtain on Private Equity," American Federation of Teachers, March 2021 (aft.org); Irina Ivanova, "Cities are Banning Natural Gas in New Homes Because of Climate Change," CBS News, December 6, 2019 (cbsnews.com); Eshe Nelson, "Britain Turns to Bankers to Blaze a Green Trail," *New York Times*, December 2, 2021 (nytimes.com); Alex Kotch, "ALEC Launches Attack on Banks That Divest From Fossil Fuels," Exposed by the Center for Media and Democracy, December 3, 2021 (exposedbycmd.org); Rebecca Leber, "Divestment Won't Hurt Big Oil, and That's OK," *The New Republic*, May 20, 2015 (newrepublic.com); Stacy Morford, "The Guardian's fossil fuel divestment campaign could do more harm than good," The Conversation, March 24, 2015 (theconversation.com); Sara Salinas, "Lyft IP Stock Starts Trading on Public Market," CNBC, March 29, 2019 (cnbc.com).

Chapter 4

FIRMS, PRODUCTION, AND PROFIT MAXIMIZATION

INTRODUCTION

How do producers make decisions? Textbooks describe a process that is ratio-nal, benign, and downright sensible. There is one best—least costly and most profitable—way to produce any given amount of goods or services. Given a particu-lar scale of operations, there is one most-profitable amount to produce. Businesses adjust their total output and the mix of inputs at the margin until they achieve these most profitable outcomes. They pay the going wage for labor, just as they pay the going price for any input. And when businesses have achieved the lowest possible costs, market competition ensures that they pass on savings to consumers.

This chapter describes a reality that is a bit more complicated, and in some ways uglier, than the textbook model. Very large companies are not the passive price-tak-ers of neoclassical lore but do in fact affect the market-wide levels of prices, profits, and wages, and manufacture their own demand. Thus, large corporations are the very embodiment of market power (violating Tilly Assumption #1, Article 1.2).

Alejandro Reuss starts things off with a primer on corporations (Article 4.1). He describes the ways that corporations are "special"—that is, different from other capitalist enterprises—and why they have become the dominant form of business organization in many countries. He concludes by discussing how corporations' eco-nomic power—their control over investment and employment—can translate into political power.

In "If Corporations Are People, What Kind of People Are They?" (Article 4.2), Geoff Schneider holds corporate America up to the World Health Organization's guidelines for psychopathic behavior. The recent record of multinational corporate behavior checks off every box the WHO uses to diagnose psychopathy.

In Article 4.3, "What's Good for Wal-Mart ...," John Miller provides a salient example of firms' market power. (Note: the retailer changed its name from "Wal-Mart" to "Walmart" in 2017.) He suggests that there may not be just "one best way" for retail businesses, but rather two: a "high road" based on high levels of service, skilled and decently paid employees, and higher prices, as exemplified by the business model at Costco; and a "low road" that offers low prices, no frills, and a low-paid, high-turnover workforce, which is Walmart's business model. Despite

Walmart's growth and its position as the world's largest retailer, the author questions whether the business model has in fact proven beneficial for the U.S. economy as a whole.

In "Neutralized" (Article 4.4) Rob Larson reviews the basics of the debate over net neutrality, providing an industrial analysis that explains the huge stakes and the lineup of powerful companies on either side. With more and more of our business and personal lives shifting online, the ability of telecom companies like Comcast and AT&T to control the flow of information through broadband "pipes" is only getting more pivotal.

Next, Bill Barclay performs an autopsy of the nursing home industry in "Caring by the Dollar" (Article 4.5). Today's skilled nursing homes operate on a "throughput" model where residents are meant to receive therapy and drugs that allow them to move on to less intensive care facilities and allowing fresh patients in. Companies have grown fast to achieve economies of scale underwritten by Medicaid's cost-plus model; corporate income in the sector has skyrocketed, but giant debt taken on to finance the expansion meant that when Medicaid's payment model changed, aggressive cost-cutting was required. The cuts included cuts to personal protective equipment for staff, making the Covid-19 pandemic far more devastating to nursing homes than it had to be.

Finally, in "Boeing Hijacked by Shareholders and Execs!" (Article 4.6), Marie Duggan gives an account of how Boeing executives have failed to invest in innovation and employees, and instead chose to use company profits to increase the stock price through stock buybacks. Duggan provides detailed evidence on how Boeing executives' efforts to make the share price impervious to bad news relied on cultivating government complicity and suppressing workers' voices.

Taken together, these articles suggest that corporate decision-making is rarely a rational process focused on a simple choice of output to maximize profits. Instead, the process is afflicted by conflicts of interest among stakeholders with wider adverse consequences for our lives in areas of health, access to information, and aviation safety, among others.

Discussion Questions

1. (General) The authors of the articles in this chapter present various firm strategies as a choice, rather than an imperative. How does this compare with the standard microeconomic analysis of business decision-making?

2. (General) Miller suggests that we should change the rules of the competitive game to steer businesses toward better treatment of workers. Present-day capitalism already has some such rules (such as those forbidding slavery). What rule changes do articles in this chapter propose? What do you think of these proposals?

3. (Article 4.1) How do corporations differ from other capitalist firms? How should the fact that corporations are chartered by the government, and shareholders given special protections by law (such as limited liability), affect our attitudes about government regulation of corporate operations?

4. (Article 4.2) Schneider describes an episode in which General Motors (GM) decided not to recall dangerously defective ignition switches in its vehicles due to the significant cost of doing so. Instead, the firm instructed dealerships to urge buyers to use lighter keychains. What sanction could a normal human expect if found guilty of this behavior? What sanction did GM receive?

5. (Article 4.3) John Miller implies that there is more than one "best" way to organize production. Do you agree? If other ways of organizing production are equally good, why are certain ways dominant, at least in particular industries?

6. (Article 4.4) Rob Larson reviews the lineup of big capital on either side of the net neutrality debate, with telecommunications companies like Comcast and Verizon against it and online platforms like Google and Facebook supporting it. Larson suggests, however, that the debate is shifting as the corporate lineup is changing—what changes in the tech platforms' business models are driving this?

7. (Article 4.5) The coronavirus is well-known to be more dangerous for the aged, who have greater health risks in general. How did market forces lead firms like Genesis to leave their residents more vulnerable? How did changes in payment rules for public programs like Medicaid and Medicare effect this?

8. (Article 4.6) In figures 2 and 3, Duggan describes a widening gap between free cash and capital expenditure flows of Boeing corporation since the late 1990s. What does this gap tell us about the company practices? Why did this happen? What are the consequences of this trend?

9. (Article 4.6) Duggan describes various practices through which Boeing suppressed employee dissent and gained government approval. Do you think these practices are in line with the profit-maximization assumption for corporate behavior? Why or why not?

Article 4.1

WHAT ARE CORPORATIONS?

BY ALEJANDRO REUSS
April 2012

When people use the word "corporation," they are usually referring to certain private, for-profit businesses, especially the largest businesses in the United States or other capitalist economies. When we think of corporations, we usually think of "big business." Besides size, people often picture other features of corporations when they hear the word. A corporation can have many shareholders—all part-owners of the company—instead of being owned by a single owner or a couple of partners. A corporation has a board of directors, elected by some or all of the shareholders, which may direct the overall way the corporation is managed. The board usually hires a few top executives, who then make decisions about how the corporation in managed on a day-to-day basis.

Corporations do not have to be large. There are corporations of all different sizes. Even a small company with a few employees could be a corporation. There are some large companies that are not corporations, but the very largest companies, which may have hundreds of thousands of employees and may sell billions of dollars of goods each year, are almost always corporations. Various different kinds of businesses can be corporations, including manufacturing companies (such as General Motors), retail companies (like Walmart), or financial companies (like Bank of America or Liberty Mutual).

Even though some not for-profit entities are also—legally speaking—corporations, people usually use the word "corporation" as shorthand for for-profit companies like General Motors or Wal-Mart. A corporation, in this sense, is a particular type of capitalist enterprise—a "capitalist corporation."

What Is a Capitalist Enterprise?

By "capitalist enterprise," we just mean a private, for-profit business whose owners employ other people in exchange for wages. By this definition, a private business where a "self-employed" owner works, but which does not hire other people for wages, is not a capitalist enterprise.

In the United States and other similar economies, relatively few people are business owners. Farm workers do not usually own the farms where the work. Miners do not usually own the mines. Factory workers usually do not own the factories. People who work in shops or offices usually do not own those businesses. Most workers do not own the buildings where they go to work, the materials or tools they use, or the products they produce. Instead, they work for pay at capitalist enterprises that are owned by others.

Workers get paid a wage or salary by the owner of the business, who in turn owns whatever the worker produces using the materials and tools provided. The owners of a business, of course, do not usually want the goods that employees produce, but want to sell these goods. If a capitalist enterprise cannot sell these goods for more than what it cost to produce them, it cannot make a profit.

Even a business that makes a profit may not stay in business for very long if the profit is less than "normal" (whatever that may be). The owners may decide that it is not worth investing in that business, if it is possible for them to make a larger profit in another business. In addition, businesses that make higher profits can reinvest these profits to expand and modernize, and may put the less profitable business at a competitive disadvantage in the future. Therefore, owners of capitalist enterprises are under competitive pressure to make the most profit they can.

How Are Corporations Special?

In many ways, capitalist corporations are like other capitalist enterprises. However, corporations are also defined by their special legal status, which makes them different from other capitalist enterprises. Corporations are granted a "charter" by the government, which means that the corporation exists as a legal entity. (In the United States, state governments grant corporate charters.)

All the things that make corporations different from other capitalist enterprises are determined by government policy. Corporate law creates certain special privileges for corporations that other businesses do not have. It also imposes special obligations on corporations (especially those whose shares are bought and sold on the stock market). The most important of these special characteristics are "limited liability," the "fiduciary responsibility" of management to the corporation's shareholders, "public disclosure" requirements, and the corporate "governance" structure.

Limited Liability

If a corporation cannot pay its debts, it can declare bankruptcy, and the people it owes can get paid off from the sale of its assets, like the buildings or machinery it owns. If the proceeds are not enough to pay off all the debts, however, the shareholders are not responsible (not "liable") to pay the rest. This is what we mean by the term "limited liability." Someone who buys stock in a corporation is risking whatever they paid for the stock, but cannot lose more than this amount. If the corporation goes bankrupt, the shareholders' stock becomes worthless, but the shareholders cannot be forced, legally, to pay whatever debts the corporation has left unpaid.

The justification usually given for the legal principle of limited liability is that it promotes economic growth and development. The idea is that, if companies were limited to what an individual or family, or perhaps a couple of partners, could scrape together to start a business, they would not be able to operate at the scale that modern corporations do. They would not have enough money to buy expensive machinery, let alone buy large factories or put together huge assembly lines.

Even if the reason given for limited liability is to fuel economic growth, however, we should remember that this is also a big favor from the government for the people who own shares in corporations. First, limited liability means that the government gives the shareholders of a corporation a certain kind a protection from other people's claims against it. Second, it means that corporations may take bigger risks in hopes of bigger profits, since the shareholders are not on the hook for all the corporation's liabilities if these risks do not pay off.

Fiduciary Responsibility

A single person who fully owns an entire company (known as a "privately held" company) can use the company's funds for whatever he or she likes, whether that is expanding the company's operations or buying luxury cars. In contrast, corporate executives receive a salary and other compensation (often lavish, in the case of large companies) decided by the board of directors or a committee of the board. They are legally free to spend this income as they wish.

Corporate executives also control how company funds are spent, but are not free to treat corporate funds as their own. This means that the chief executive of a company is not legally entitled to use company funds to remodel his or her house, buy fancy cars, take expensive vacations, and so on. Of course, executives still fly on private jets, take "business trips" to exotic locales, enjoy fancy "business dinners," and so on, but they have to justify these as necessary costs of doing business. If shareholders think that executives have failed in their fiduciary responsibility, they can actually sue the company.

Some legal scholars and economists have extended this idea to the logical extreme that corporate managers are legally obligated to the shareholders and only the shareholders. In this view, management decisions must be guided by the sole objective of enhancing "shareholder value" (in effect, the profitability of the corporation, and therefore the value of an ownership stake in it). This means that they cannot put other people's interests ahead of those of the shareholders. According to the "shareholder value" doctrine, if managers decide to pay workers more than they really have to, they are giving away the company's (that is, the shareholders') money. Likewise, they have no legal duty to the broader community, beyond abiding by the law. They do not have to "give back," say, by funding schools, libraries, or parks in the communities where they operate.

The shareholder value doctrine is not new, and it is not just something that pro-business comentators have made up. The doctrine was clearly articulated no later than 1919, in a Supreme Court opinion (*Dodge v. Ford Motor Company*) no less. However, in practice, the courts have been reluctant to intervene in disputes between shareholders and management (in effect, declining to open up the can of worms of deciding what the right business decisions would be).

Public Disclosure

Corporations that sell shares of stock on the stock market are called "publicly traded corporations." Each time a corporation sells a share of its stock to an individual or another company, it raises some money. This is one way the company can finance its operations. In actual fact, most stock sales do not involve a corporation selling stock to a member of the public, but one member of the public selling shares to another (that is, resale of shares that a corporation had previously issued). Therefore, most stock sales do not result in any money going to the corporation that originally issued it.

By law, publicly traded companies have to disclose certain business information. They have to file forms with the government listing their officers (board members and top executives), the officers' compensation (salaries and other benefits), the company's profits or losses, and other information. The idea behind disclosure requirements is to protect shareholders or people who might consider purchasing shares in a company, often referred to as the "investing public."

In practice, corporate "insiders" (board members, top executives, etc.) have much more information about the financial condition of a corporation than members of the public. This has led to well-publicized scandals in recent years, such as the Enron case. Corporate executives sold the stock they owned when the price was high, knowing that in reality the company was not as profitable as the public thought, and that the stock price would soon plummet.

Corporate Governance

When an individual buys a share (or many shares) of a corporation, he or she gets certain property rights. Shareholders are not legally entitled to receive a share of the company's profits each year. The company management decides how much of this money to pay out to shareholders (as "dividends") and how much to keep. A corporation might keep cash reserves, use profits to buy existing businesses, use them to expand its existing operations (for example, by buying or renting additional factory or office buildings, buying new machinery, hiring additional workers, etc.). It is not necessarily preferable for shareholders to receive all or most of the company's profit for a year in the form of dividends. By using "retained earnings" to expand, a corporation may increase in overall value. This increases the value of an ownership share in the company (the value of the stock that shareholders own).

Shareholders have the right to sell their shares if and when they wish. This gives them a stake in the profitability of the corporation, since the price of a share (on the stock exchange) is likely to go higher the more profitable the company is. A shareholder who does not want to be a part owner of the company anymore is not entitled to sell back the shares to the company, nor to take "their" piece of the company with them. The corporation is not required to give the shareholder any tangible asset—the shareholder cannot claim any particular thing owned by the corporation—nor is the corporation forced to sell off tangible assets in order to pay a shareholder who does not want his or her shares anymore. This way, shareholders come and go, but the corporation itself stays intact.

Shareholders also have a say in the governance structure of the corporation. You can think of a corporation as a political entity, like a small (or, in some cases, not so small) country. Shareholders are like the citizens. They are entitled to attend annual shareholder meetings, where they can address questions or comments to the corporation's directors (board members) and executives. Shareholders are entitled to vote in elections to the board of directors (except for those holding certain classes of "nonvoting" or "preferred" stock). They can even run for election to the board of directors, if they so wish.

Corporate elections are different from government elections. First, in corporate elections, only shareholders are allowed to vote. The decisions made by a corporation's management may affect many other people—workers, people in communities where the corporation has operations, etc. However, if they are not shareholders in the corporation, they are not entitled to vote. In addition, in corporate elections, different shareholders do not get the same number of votes. Rather, each shareholder gets a number of votes equal to the number of shares he or she owns (excluding nonvoting stock). Someone who owns one share gets one vote; 10 shares, 10 votes; 100 shares, 100 votes.

In practice, a large shareholder does not need to own anywhere near a majority of the shares to effectively control a company. People who own very few shares in a company, if disgruntled with the management, are more likely to just sell their shares than to devote a lot of time and energy to getting the management replaced. Relatively small shareholders, in fact, usually just sign away their voting rights to other, larger shareholders. This way, a very wealthy individual may have effective control of a company even though he or she "only" owns, say, 5% of the total shares. Keep in mind that 5% of the stock in the largest corporate giants could be worth billions of dollars.

Corporations, Economic Power, and Political Power

Large corporations are certainly among the most powerful entities in the U.S. economy and politics. We can start by classifying the power of large corporations into economic power, on the one hand, and political power, on the other. Economic power has to do with the ability of large corporations to dictate to others (other businesses, workers, etc.) the conditions under which they will do business. Political power has to do with their ability to get what they want from the government, including both favors they can get from the government and influence over the overall direction of government policy.

Mainstream or "neoclassical" economists do not talk about economic power very much. Mostly, they talk about "market" economies as if nobody exercised any power over anyone else—buyers and sellers engaging in voluntary exchanges, each free from any kind of coercion from other buyers or sellers. The main form of economic power neoclassical economists do talk about is "market power"—basically, the ability of a seller (or buyer) to dictate higher (or lower) prices to others, because of a lack of competition.

In the view of radical political economists, employers as a group have economic power in a different sense. Most of the economic activity in capitalist economies depends on the economic decisions made by capitalist enterprises, such as how much output to produce, how many people to hire, whether to buy new machines or new buildings (this is what economists mean by "investment"), and so on. If capitalist employers decide not to hire people to produce goods and services, many people will be unemployed. Tax collections will be low, and governments are likely to experience budget deficits, unless they dramatically cut spending. Moreover, if capitalist enterprises are not hiring, unemployment is high, and many people are afraid of losing their jobs, the party in power probably will not survive the next election.

If the owners and managers of capitalist enterprises do not like the kinds of economic policies the government is putting in place, they may decide not to hire or invest. In some cases, where capitalists feel very threatened by government policies, they may actually do this with the conscious political aim of bringing down the government. More often, a decline in employment and investment can arise from a simple decline in "business confidence." The owners and managers of capitalist enterprises become pessimistic about being able to sell their goods at a profit, and make a business decision to cut back on production, employment, and investment. The effect, however, can still be to force the government to bend over backwards to maintain profitable conditions for business, in order to avoid an economic downturn. This way, the economic power of capitalist enterprises over the whole economy can result in their getting the kinds of government policies that favor them. ❑

Article 4.2

IF CORPORATIONS ARE PEOPLE, WHAT KIND OF PEOPLE ARE THEY?

BY GEOFF SCHNEIDER
June 2016

In 1886, the U.S. Supreme Court ruled, in *Santa Clara County v. Southern Pacific Railroad*, that corporations have the same legal status as persons. The legal rights of corporations gradually have been expanded in the United States since that time to include the right to free speech and to contribute unlimited amounts to political campaigns (a product of the Supreme Court's 2010 *Citizens United* ruling). A key question that emerges from U.S. corporate personhood is: If corporations are people, what kind of people are they?

One of the key characteristics of a corporation is that, by its very legal structure, it is an amoral entity. It exists for the sole purpose of making profits, and it will do whatever is necessary to increase profits, without considering ethical issues except insofar as they impinge on the bottom line. A crucial reason for this behavior is that chief executive officers (CEOs) and other executives have a legal "fiduciary duty" to act in the best financial interests of stockholders. As conservative economist Milton Friedman stated in his book *Capitalism and Freedom*, "there is one and only one social responsibility of business—to use its resources and engage in activities designed to increase its profits so long as it stays within the rules of the game, which is to say, engages in open and free competition without deception or fraud." Thus, those who control corporations are obligated to do whatever they can within the law to make as much money as possible.

This can lead to behavior that some have called psychopathic. In the provocative 2003 film, "The Corporation," the filmmakers argue that corporations meet the diagnostic criteria used by psychiatrists to determine if a person is psychopathic. Those criteria are:

- Callous disregard for the feelings of others;
- Reckless disregard for the safety of others;
- Incapacity to maintain enduring relationships;
- Deceitfulness: repeated lying and conniving others for profit;
- Incapacity to experience guilt; and
- Failure to conform to social norms with respect to lawful behaviors.

Although at first blush the claim that corporations are psychopaths seems incredible, if we consider the worst behaviors of corporations over the last few decades, and the disturbing frequency with which such behaviors seem to recur, it is possible to see why so many people hold corporations in such low esteem. Below, we describe briefly some of the most horrific behaviors of large corporations in recent years.

Rana Plaza Building Collapse, 2013:

An Example of Corporate Abuses of Subcontracting and Sweatshops
For decades, U.S. and European clothing manufacturers have been moving their operations overseas to countries with extremely low wages and with few safety or environmental regulations. One of their favorite destinations in recent years has been Bangladesh, where wages for clothing workers are the lowest in the world (only $0.24 per hour until the minimum wage was raised to $0.40 per hour in 2014), and where few safety standards are enforced. Bangladesh now has more than 5,000 garment factories handling orders for most of the world's top brands and retailers, and is second in garment manufacturing output behind China.

In 2013, the Rana Plaza building that housed several clothing factories collapsed, killing 1,134 people in the worst disaster in garment-industry history. It was later discovered that the building was constructed with substandard materials in violation of building codes. Even more disturbing was the fact that the owners of the factories insisted that employees return to work even after an engineer inspected the building the day before the collapse and deemed it unsafe due to cracks in the walls and clear structural deficiencies. The factories were making clothes for Walmart, Benetton, and many other large, multinational companies.

Disasters like this one, along with the torture and killing of a Bangladeshi labor activist in 2012, are a product of the subcontracting system used by large clothing manufacturers. The corporations issue specifications for the garments that they want to have manufactured, and contractors around the world bid for the right to make the garments. The lowest bidder wins. But what kind of factory is likely to have the lowest bid? Given the regular occurrence of disasters and labor abuses in garment factories, it appears that the contractors who win bids are those who are the most likely to pay workers the least under the most unsafe conditions. Huge multinational clothing companies are only too eager to participate, while at the same time claiming that they are not responsible for the deaths and abuses because they themselves were not the factory owners. The factory owners in Bangladesh were charged with murder, but there were no major consequences for the clothing companies. The callous disregard for the feelings and safety of others and incapacity to experience guilt that many clothing manufacturers display is certainly consistent with the definition of a psychopath.

BP Oil Spill in the Gulf of Mexico, 2010:

Taking Chances with People's Lives and the Environment
The 2010 BP oil spill in the Gulf of Mexico was the worst in U.S. history. The Deepwater Horizon oil rig exploded on April 20, 2010, killing 11 people and spilling 210 million gallons of oil into the Gulf. Investigations into the causes of the spill indicated significant negligence.

- Deepwater drilling procedures were adapted from shallow-water techniques, without adequate consideration of the differences of the deep-water environment.
- Federal regulators relaxed requirements for environmental reviews, tests,

and safety plans at the request of BP, and encouraged but did not require key backup systems.

- BP used well casings, cement, and other equipment that violated company safety guidelines and industry best practices, despite concerns raised by BP engineers.
- Warning signs were ignored, and safety tests delayed despite the warning signs.

The human and environmental costs of the spill were devastating. In addition to the human deaths, millions of birds, turtles, dolphins, and fish were killed. The Gulf tourism industry was devastated for several years, costing businesses $23 billion in lost revenue. And the Gulf still has not recovered, with ongoing problems cropping up related to the environment and wildlife.

The primary culprit here was BP's relentless pursuit of lower costs. Poor quality materials plus skimping on safety measures created conditions for the explosion and meant that BP was unable to deal with the disaster once it happened. Although BP was found guilty of negligence and fined a record $18.7 billion, that amount was only about 8% of their annual revenue, and no BP official went to prison.

ExxonMobil and Climate Change Denial, 1981-2008:

Lying to People for Profit
In 1981, a team of researchers at Exxon conclusively established the connection between thew burning of fossil fuels, the spewing of greenhouse gases into the air (especially carbon), and climate change. Their research was supported by dozens of other studies by climate scientists. These studies have been so convincing that over 97% of climate scientists agree that climate change is occurring and that human activity is a significant cause. As anyone who studies scientific research will know, it is rare to have near-universal agreement on something as complex as climate change, which helps us to understand that the evidence for climate change is overwhelming.

Despite this evidence, Exxon, which merged with Mobil in 1999, spent millions of dollars on a public-relations effort to deny the existence of climate change so that they could continue to sell as much of their oil as possible. As documented in the book *Merchants of Doubt* (later adapted as a film of the same name), Exxon funded foundations who paid a small group of scientists and public-relations professionals to cast doubt on the idea of climate change in order to prevent action from being taken. And their impact in the United States was dramatic. While much of the world was taking climate change seriously and enacting policies to begin reducing greenhouse gas emissions, the United States was increasing its use of fossil fuels and its emissions.

ExxonMobil now states publicly that it accepts the idea that climate change is occurring, and the company has stopped formally funding climate change denialism. However, ExxonMobil's reduction in public funding of denialism has coincided with a dramatic increase in untraceable "dark money" being used to fund climate change denialism. One cannot help but wonder who is funding such efforts.

Thanks to ExxonMobil and others who have prevented progress on climate change, we are now faced with the prospect of dramatic climate events that will cost many people their lives. We are likely to see increasing droughts, food shortages, heat waves, sea-level rise, floods, and other disasters that threaten our very existence. All so that ExxonMobil and other giant companies could sell more barrels of oil. As is so often the case, there have been no criminal prosecutions related to these incidents.

Enron's Fraudulent Use of Derivatives and Shell Companies, 1990-2002:

Financial Deregulation Plus Executive Stock Options are a Toxic Mix

One of the arguments in favor of corporations is that, thanks to the profit motive, they tend to innovate in order to make money. But, what kind of innovations might result from the profit motive? Enron executives Kenneth Lay and Jeffrey Skilling used the deregulated environment in financial markets in the 1990s and early 2000s (the same environment that also produced the financial crisis) to create an innovative financial model build on fraud and subterfuge.

Enron was the world's largest energy trading company, with a market value of $68 billion. But its real innovation was in shady accounting practices. Enron would start by undertaking a legitimate investment, such as building a power plant. They would then immediately claim all of the expected profit from the power plant on their books, even though they had yet to make any money on the investment, making them appear to be an incredibly profitable company. If the power-plant profits ever came in below expectations, Enron would transfer the unprofitable assets to a shell company—a company that did not really exist formally, other than as a vehicle for Enron to dispose of losses—thereby hiding Enron's losses from its investors. Shell-company investors were given shares of Enron common stock to compensate them for the shell-company losses. Thus, Enron appeared to be incredibly profitable even while it was incurring losses, which caused its stock price to soar.

Much of the reason for this behavior was the incentive system created by financial markets. At the time, most CEOs and highly placed executives were paid most of their salaries in stock options. This meant that they could make more money if they could get the company's stock price to increase, which would allow them to cash in their stock options at a higher value. In theory, paying CEOs in stock options gave them an incentive to run the company in the most profitable way possible, which would then cause the stock price to go up. But stock options also gave executives an incentive to artificially prop up stock prices in order to cash in, which is what the Enron executives did. Meanwhile, the accounting auditors who were supposed to flag questionable and illegal financial transactions looked the other way in order to keep Enron's business.

As Enron's losses mounted, the executives cashed in all of their stock options and left the company bankrupt. More than 5,000 employees lost their jobs and millions of investors lost their savings. Lay, Skilling, and 15 other Enron executives were found guilty of fraud. But these sordid events didn't stop an even bigger financial market manipulation from dragging down the entire global economy less than a decade later.

Goldman Sachs, CMOs, and the Financial Crisis of 2007-2008:

Betting Against Your Own Clients

The global financial crisis of 2007–2008 was a product of a number of corporate misdeeds, fueled by greed and the deregulation of financial markets. To increase their profits in the early 2000s, banks started loaning money to extremely risky, subprime borrowers with very poor credit scores to purchase houses. The banks then bundled large groups of these subprime mortgage loans into securities called collateralized mortgage obligations (CMOs). The banks did not care about the creditworthiness of borrowers because they immediately sold these securities to investors.

As more and more subprime borrowers took out mortgage loans, the real-estate market boomed, forming a huge bubble. At the peak of the bubble in 2006-2007, default rates on mortgages started to increase rapidly. Realizing that subprime loans were likely to fail, Goldman Sachs and several other big investment banks began to do something highly unethical: They sold bundles of subprime mortgages (as CMOs) to investors, and they used financial instruments called credit default swaps to bet that the mortgages in the CMOs they sold were going to default and that the CMOs would become worthless. In other words, they sold investors CMO securities that they believed were going to fail, and they even made bets in financial markets that the CMOs they sold would fail. Goldman Sachs was not the only investment bank to do this. Deutsche Bank and Morgan Stanley also engaged in similar transactions to profit at the expense of their own investors.

As in so many other cases of corporate malfeasance, the consequences amounted to little more than a slap on the wrist. Goldman Sachs paid a $550 million fine in 2010 to settle the fraud case brought by the Securities and Exchange Commission (SEC), an amount that was just 4% of the $13.4 billion in profits Goldman Sachs made in the previous year. In 2016, Goldman Sachs agreed to an additional $5.1 billion fine for misleading investors about the quality of the CMOs they sold them. However, not a single Goldman Sachs official went to jail.

VW Programs Cars to Cheat on Emissions Tests, 2009-2015:

The Things a Company Will Do to Become #1

Martin Winterkorn, Volkswagen's chief executive officer from 2007 to 2015, established the goal of making VW the largest car company in the world, and he embarked on an ambitious plan to achieve that goal. Much of his plan hinged on developing fuel-efficient, clean diesel cars as an alternative to hybrids. But, when VW discovered that it could not develop an inexpensive technology to remove pollution without compromising the car's gas mileage and overall performance, they turned to a fraudulent approach. VW programmed 10.5 million cars so that the cars would detect when they were being tested for emissions, and during testing the cars' engines would run in a way that they would meet emissions standards. But when the cars were driven normally, they would spew pollutants at a rate much higher than allowed by law.

A nonprofit group, the International Council on Clean Transportation, discovered the problem when they tested numerous diesel cars in 2013. They alerted the Environmental Protection Agency (EPA), which launched an investigation in 2014. As is so often the case, VW responded to the investigation aggressively, accusing regulators and testers of being incompetent. But additional testing established conclusively that VW cars had been programmed to reduce emissions when tested, and to spew large amounts of pollutants when driven normally. The EPA told VW that it would no longer allow the company to sell diesel cars in the United States in 2015, and accused them of violating the Clean Air Act. Particularly problematic was the fact that VW diesels spewed large amounts of nitrogen oxide, in amounts up to 40 times the legal limit. Nitrogen oxide is a pollutant that causes emphysema, bronchitis, and contributes to many other respiratory diseases. The EPA estimates that the additional pollution from VW diesel cars will cause as many as 34 deaths and sicken thousands of people in the United States. Other studies predicted up to 200 premature deaths.

VW did briefly become the largest car company in the world in July of 2015 when they surpassed Toyota, but since the scandal became public the company has fallen back. On June 27, 2016, VW agreed to pay $14.7 billion in fines to the government and compensation for VW diesel car owners. A criminal inquiry is also underway.

General Motors' Faulty Ignition Switches, 2005-2007:

Why Would Anyone Sell a Product That They Knew Could Kill People?

Imagine yourself as a CEO or vice president of a major corporation. An engineering report comes across your desk, noting that a part in one of your products is faulty, and that the consequences of that part failing could be the injury or even deaths of some of your customers. Would you still sell the faulty product, even knowing that it might kill people? This is what General Motors (GM) did with its faulty ignition switch.

This particular sordid story starts in 2010, when a 29-year-old nurse named Brooke Melton died in a car crash after losing control of her car. Her parents, who knew that she was a safe driver and that her car had been behaving oddly, sued GM and hired engineering experts to try to determine the cause of the crash. They discovered that the problem was the ignition switch that had been installed on over 22 million GM cars manufactured from 2001 to 2007. The ignition switch could turn from "On" to "Acc" just by being bumped lightly or if the key was on a particularly heavy keychain. The shift from "On" to "Acc" could disable the power steering, anti-lock braking, and airbags and cause the car to stall.

As the investigation progressed, the full scale of GM's deceit became apparent. In 2001, GM engineers initially detected the defective part, labelling it the "switch from hell." Problems with the switch cropped up repeatedly over the next several years. In 2005, internal documents show that GM acknowledged the problem but chose not to fix it because it would be too costly. Instead, they sent a note to GM dealerships telling them to urge customers to use lighter key chains. Each year, people died as ignition switches failed and air bags failed to deploy, but GM continued to hide the problem and refused to recall cars and repair the problem.

Finally, thanks to the Melton lawsuit and government investigations that followed, GM recalled the vehicles and repaired the faulty switch. But not before at least 124 people died in crashes related to the faulty part. GM paid a $900 million fine in 2015, and other settlements with victims brought the total cost of the debacle to $2 billion. While this put a dent in the company's 2015 profits of $9.7 billion, no individuals faced criminal charges for their actions.

Are Corporations Psychopaths?

Above, we highlighted seven examples of horrific corporate behavior. In each case, corporations exhibited many of the behaviors characteristic of psychopaths, especially a callous disregard for the feelings and safety of others, deceitfulness, avoidance of admitting guilt and taking responsibility for their actions, and failure to respect social and ethical norms and the law. But, are these behaviors typical of powerful, profit-hungry corporations, or are they exceptions?

As we all know, many corporations behave ethically, and many invent useful and innovative products that improve our lives. Yet, every year a certain number of corporations cast ethics and morality to the side and engage in unscrupulous behavior, resulting in economic harm, injury, and even deaths. There appear to be aspects of the corporate structure that encourage such behavior, including the relentless quest for maximum profits, the lack of personal responsibility for any illegal actions taken by the corporation, and the power corporations have to manipulate the legal system and government regulators.

Regarding the last point, one of the elements to every story above was the inadequate efforts of government regulators. The push for deregulation by various politicians directly facilitated many of the above corporate misdeeds. And government regulators are often overmatched by corporate legal teams with almost unlimited resources, which allows many corporations to avoid serious consequences even in cases where they have done something horrible. Even when corporations have been caught red handed in clear violation of the law, the penalties are usually little more than a slap on the wrist and are often far less than the profits from the offense in question. Corporate wealth and power appear to allow them to avoid significant checks on their behavior. Thus, instead of engaging in "open and free competition without deception or fraud," as Milton Friedman hoped that they would, some corporations use deception and fraud with near impunity in order to outdo the competition.

Such problems could be fixed. We need a regulatory system with teeth, where corporate lobbyists don't have undue influence over how they are regulated. And we need real consequences for corporate crime. When corporations find out that their actions or products may harm people, if they refuse to take action and to inform the public and regulators of the problem, the people who make those decisions should go to prison.

Finally, like real people, corporations should face real consequences when they break the law. A corporation that engages in particularly egregious behavior, especially a corporation that does so repeatedly, should face sanctions that have a real impact on executives and stockholders. For cases in which a corporation causes deaths, the corporation should face the "death penalty": having its charter revoked and its assets seized by the public. If stockholders could potentially lose all of their investment in a company that behaved illegally, they would begin checking up on companies and we would see much less illegal and unethical behavior.

Of course, all of these solutions require us to get corporate money out of politics. As long as corporations can buy off politicians, they can continue to act as psychopaths and face very little in the way of consequences. ❑

Selected Sources: Julfikar Ali Manik and Nida Najar, "Bangladesh Police Charge 41 With Murder Over Rana Plaza Collapse," *New York Times*, June 1, 2015 (nytimes.com); Julfikar Ali Manik and Jim Yardley, "Building Collapse in Bangladesh Leaves Scores Dead," *New York Times*, April 24, 2013; "One Year After Rana Plaza" (editorial), *New York Times*, April 27, 2014; Lauren McCauley, "Workers Decry Multinationals' Greed Following Disaster in Bangladesh," Common Dreams, April 25, 2013 (commondreams.org); Ian Urbina, "In Gulf, It Was Unclear Who Was in Charge of Rig," *New York Times*, June 5, 2010; Ben Bryant, "Deepwater Horizon and the Gulf Oil Spill—the Key Questions Answered," *The Guardian*, April 20, 2011 (theguardian.com); Douglas Fischer, "'Dark Money' Funds Climate Change Denial Effort," *Scientific American*, Dec. 23, 2013 (scientificamerican.com); Oliver Milman, "Oil Industry Knew of 'Serious' Climate Concerns More Than 45 Years Ago," *The Guardian*, April 13, 2016; Suzanne Goldenberg, "Exxon Knew of Climate Change in 1981, Email Says—but it Funded Deniers for 27 More Years," *The Guardian*, July 8, 2015; Bill Keller, "Enron for Dummies," *New York Times*, Jan. 26, 2002; Gretchen Morgenson and Louise Story, "Banks Bundled Bad Debt, Bet Against It and Won," *New York Times*, Dec. 23, 2009; "Senate Panel Says Goldman Misled Clients, Lawmakers on CDOs," Bloomberg News, April 13, 2011 (bloomberg.com); Guilbert Gates, Jack Ewing, Karl Russell, and Derek Watkins, "How Volkswagen's 'Defeat Devices' Worked," *New York Times*, March 16, 2017.

Article 4.3

WHAT'S GOOD FOR WAL-MART . . .

BY JOHN MILLER
January/February 2006

"Is Wal-Mart Good for America?"

It is a testament to the public relations of the anti-Wal-Mart campaign that the question above is even being asked.

By any normal measure, Wal-Mart's business ought to be noncontroversial. It sells at low costs, albeit in mind-boggling quantities. ...

The company's success and size ... do not rest on monopoly profits or price-gouging behavior. It simply sells things people will buy at small markups and, as in the old saw, makes it up on volume. ... You may believe, as do service-workers unions and a clutch of coastal elites—many of whom, we'd wager, have never set foot in Wal-Mart—that Wal-Mart "exploits" workers who can't say no to low wages and poor benefits. You might accept the canard that it drives good local businesses into the ground, although both of these allegations are more myth than reality.

But even if you buy into the myths, there's no getting around the fact that somewhere out there, millions of people are spending billions of dollars on what Wal-Mart puts on its shelves. No one is making them do it. ... Wal-Mart can't make mom and pop shut down the shop anymore than it can make customers walk through the doors or pull out their wallets.

What about the workers? ... Wal-Mart's average starting wage is already nearly double the national minimum of $5.15 an hour. The company has also recently increased its health-care for employees on the bottom rungs of the corporate ladder.

—*Wall Street Journal* editorial, December 3, 2005

"Who's Number One? The Customer! Always!" The last line of Wal-Mart's company cheer just about sums up the *Wall Street Journal* editors' benign view of the behemoth corporation. But a more honest answer would be Wal-Mart itself: not the customer, and surely not the worker.

The first retail corporation to top the Fortune 500, Wal-Mart trailed only Exxon-Mobil in total revenues last year. With 1.6 million workers, 1.3 million in the United States and 300,000 offshore, Wal-Mart is the largest private employer in the nation and the world's largest retailer.

Being number one has paid off handsomely for the family of Wal-Mart founder Sam Walton. The family's combined fortune is now an estimated $90 billion, equal to the net worth of Bill Gates and Warren Buffett combined.

But is what's good for the Walton family good for America? Should we believe the editors that Wal-Mart's unprecedented size and market power have redounded not only to the Walton family's benefit but to ours as well?

Low Wages and Meager Benefits

Working for the world's largest employer sure hasn't paid off for Wal-Mart's employees. True, they have a job, and others without jobs line up to apply for theirs. But that says more about the sad state of today's labor market than the quality of Wal-Mart jobs. After all, less than half of Wal-Mart workers last a year, and turnover at the company is twice that at comparable retailers.

Why? Wal-Mart's oppressive working conditions surely have something to do with it. Wal-Mart has admitted to using minors to operate hazardous machinery, has been sued in six states for forcing employees to work off the books (i.e., unpaid) and without breaks, and is currently facing a suit brought by 1.6 million current and former female employees accusing Wal-Mart of gender discrimination. At the same time, Wal-Mart workers are paid less and receive fewer benefits than other retail workers.

Wal-Mart, according to its own reports, pays an average of $9.68 an hour. That is 12.4% below the average wage for retail workers even after adjusting for geography, according to a recent study by Arindrajit Dube and Steve Wertheim, economists at the University of California's Institute of Industrial Relations and long-time Wal-Mart researchers. Wal-Mart's wages are nearly 15% below the average wage of workers at large retailers and about 30% below the average wage of unionized grocery workers. The average U.S. wage is $17.80 an hour; Costco, a direct competitor of Wal-Mart's Sam's Club warehouse stores, pays an average wage of $16 an hour.

Wal-Mart may be improving its benefits, as the *Journal*'s editors report, but it needs to. Other retailers provide healthcare coverage to over 53% of their workers, while Wal-Mart covers just 48% of its workers. Costco, once again, does far better, covering 82% of its employees. Moreover, Wal-Mart's coverage is far less comprehensive than the plans offered by other large retailers. Dube reports that according to 2003 IRS data, Wal-Mart paid 59% of the healthcare costs of its workers and dependents, compared to the 77% of healthcare costs for individuals and 68% for families the average retailer picks up.

A recent internal Wal-Mart memo leaked to the *New York Times* confirmed the large gaps in Wal-Mart's healthcare coverage and exposed the high costs those gaps impose on government programs. According to the memo, "Five percent of our Associates are on Medicaid compared to an average for national employees of 4 percent. Twenty-seven percent of Associates' children are on such programs, compared to a national average of 22 percent. In total, 46 percent of Associates' children are either on Medicaid or are uninsured."

A considerably lower 29% of children of all large-retail workers are on Medicaid or are uninsured. Some 7% of the children of employees of large retailers go uninsured, compared to the 19% reported by Wal-Mart.

Wal-Mart's low wages drag down the wages of other retail workers and shutter downtown retail businesses. A 2005 study by David Neumark, Junfu Zhang, and Stephen Ciccarella, economists at the University of California at Irvine, found that Wal-Mart adversely affects employment and wages. Retail workers in a community with a Wal-Mart earned 3.5% less because Wal-Mart's low prices force other businesses to lower prices, and hence their wages, according to the Neumark study. The same study also found that Wal-Mart's presence reduces retail employment by 2% to 4%. While other studies have not found this negative employment effect, Dube's research also reports fewer retail jobs and lower wages for retail workers in metropolitan counties with a Wal-Mart. (Fully 85% of Wal-Mart stores are in metropolitan counties.) Dube figures that Wal-Mart's presence costs retail workers, at Wal-Mart and elsewhere, $4.7 billion a year in lost earnings.

In short, Wal-Mart's "everyday low prices" come at the expense of the compensation of Wal-Mart's own employees and lower wages and fewer jobs for retail workers in the surrounding area. That much remains true no matter what weight we assign to each of the measures that Wal-Mart uses to keep its costs down: a just-in-time inventory strategy, its ability to use its size to pressure suppliers for large discounts, a routinized work environment that requires minimal training, and meager wages and benefits.

How Low Are Wal-Mart's Everyday Low Prices?

Even if one doesn't subscribe to the editors' position that it is consumers, not Wal-Mart, who cause job losses at downtown retailers, it is possible to argue that the benefit of Wal-Mart's low prices to consumers, especially low-income consumers, outweighs the cost endured by workers at Wal-Mart and other retailers. Jason Furman, New York University economist and director of economic policy for the 2004 Kerry-Edwards campaign, makes just such an argument. Wal-Mart's "staggering" low prices are 8% to 40% lower than people would pay elsewhere, according to Furman. He calculates that those low prices on average boost low-income families' buying power by 3% and more than offset the loss of earnings to retail workers. For Furman, that makes Wal-Mart "a progressive success story."

But exactly how much savings Wal-Mart affords consumers is far from clear. Estimates vary widely. At one extreme is a study Wal-Mart itself commissioned by Global Insight, an economic forecasting firm. Global Insight estimates Wal-Mart created a stunning savings of $263 billion, or $2,329 per household, in 2004 alone.

At the other extreme, statisticians at the U.S. Bureau of Labor Statistics (BLS) found no price savings at Wal-Mart. Relying on Consumer Price Index data, the BLS found that Wal-Mart's prices largely matched those of its rivals, and that instances of lower prices at Wal-Mart could be attributed to lower quality products.

Both studies, which rely on the Consumer Price Index and aggregate data, have their critics. Furman himself allows that the Global Insight study is "overly simplistic" and says he "doesn't place as much weight on that one." Jerry Hausman, the MIT economist who has looked closely at Wal-Mart's grocery stores, maintains that the CPI data that the Bureau of Labor Statistics relies on systematically miss the savings offered by "supercenters" such as Wal-Mart. To show the difference between prices at Wal-Mart and at other grocers, Hausman, along with Ephraim Leibtag, USDA Economic Research Service economist, used supermarket scanner data to examine the purchasing patterns of a national sample of 61,500 consumers from 1988 to 2001. Hausman and Leibtag found that Wal-Mart offers many identical food items at an average price about 15-25% lower than traditional supermarkets.

While Hausman and Leibtag report substantial savings from shopping at Wal-Mart, they fall far short of the savings alleged in the Global Insight study. The Hausman and Leibtag study suggests a savings of around $550 per household per year, or about $56 billion in 2004, not $263 billion. Still, that is considerably more than the $4.7 billion a year in lost earnings to retail workers that Dube attributes to Wal-Mart.

But if "Wal-Mart hurts wages, not so much in retail, but across the whole country," as economist Neumark told *BusinessWeek*, then the savings to consumers from Wal-Mart's everyday low prices might not outweigh the lost wages to all workers. (Retail workers make up just 11.6% of U.S. employment.)

Nor do these findings say anything about the sweatshop conditions and wages in Wal-Mart's overseas subcontractors. One example: A recent Canadian Broadcasting Corporation investigative report found that workers in Bangladesh were being paid less than $50 a month (below even the United Nation's $2 a day measure of poverty) to make clothes for the Wal-Mart private label, Simply Basic. Those workers included 10- to 13-year-old children forced to work long hours in dimly lit and dirty conditions sewing "I Love My Wal-Mart" T-shirts.

Making Wal-Mart Do Better

Nonetheless, as Arindrajit Dube points out, the relevant question is not whether Wal-Mart creates more savings for consumers than losses for workers, but whether the corporation can afford to pay better wages and benefits.

Dube reasons that if the true price gap between Wal-Mart and its retail competitors is small, then Wal-Mart might not be in a position to do better—to make

---

The Costco Alternative? Wall Street Prefers Wal-Mart

In an April 2004 online commentary, *BusinessWeek* praised Costco's business model but pointed out that Costco's wages cause Wall Street to worry that the company's "operating expenses could get out of hand." How does Costco compare to low-wage Wal-Mart on overhead expenses? At Costco, overhead is 9.8% of revenue; at Wal-Mart, it is 17%. Part of Costco's secret is that its better paid workers are also more efficient: Costco's operating profit per hourly employee is $13,647; each Wal-Mart employee only nets the company $11,039. Wal-Mart also spends more than Costco on hiring and training new employees: each one, according to Rutgers economist Eileen Appelbaum, costs the company $2,500 to $3,500. Appelbaum estimates that Wal-Mart's relatively high turnover costs the company $1.5 to $2 million per year.

Despite Costco's higher efficiency, Wall Street analysts like Deutsche Bank's Bill Dreher complain that "Costco's corporate philosophy is to put its customers first, then its employees, then its vendors, and finally its shareholders. Shareholders get the short end of the stick." Wall Street prefers Wal-Mart's philosopy: executives first, then shareholders, then customers, then vendors, and finally employees.

In 2004, Wal-Mart paid CEO Lee Scott $5.3 million, while a full-time employee making the average wage would have received $20,134. Costco's CEO Jim Senegal received $350,000, while a full-time average employee got $33,280. And *BusinessWeek* intimates

up its wage and benefit gap and still maintain its price advantage. But if Wal-Mart offers consumers only minor price savings, then its lower wages and benefits hardly constitute a progressive success story that's good for the nation.

If Wal-Mart's true price gap is large (say, the 25% price advantage estimated by Hausman), then Wal-Mart surely is in a position to do better. For instance, Dube calculates that closing Wal-Mart's 16% overall compensation gap with other large retailers would cost the company less than 2% of sales. Raising prices by two cents on the dollar to cover those increased compensation costs would be "eminently absorbable," according to Dube, without eating away much of the company's mind-boggling $10 billion profit (2004).

Measures that set standards to force Wal-Mart and all big-box retailers to pay decent wages and provide benefits are beginning to catch on. Chicago, New York City, and the state of Maryland have considered or passed laws that would require big-box retailers to pay a "living wage" or to spend a minimum amount per worker-hour for health benefits. The Republican board of Nassau County on Long Island passed an ordinance requiring that all big-box retailers pay $3 per hour toward healthcare. Wal-Mart's stake in making sure that such proposals don't become law or spread nationwide goes a long way toward explaining why 80% of Wal-Mart's $2 million in political contributions in 2004 went to Republicans.

Henry Ford sought to pay his workers enough so they could buy the cars they produced. Sam Walton sought to pay his workers so little that they could afford to shop nowhere else. And while what was good for the big automakers was probably never good for the nation, what is good for Wal-Mart, today's largest employer, is undoubtedly bad for economic justice. ❏

---

that the top job at Costco may be tougher than at Wal-Mart. "Management has to hustle to make the high-wage strategy work. It's constantly looking for ways to repackage goods into bulk items, which reduces labor, speeds up Costco's just-in-time inventory, and boosts sales per square foot. Costco is also savvier ... about catering to small shop owners and more affluent customers, who are more likely to buy in bulk and purchase higher-margin goods."

Costco's allegedly more affluent clientele may be another reason that its profit per employee is higher than Wal-Mart's and its overhead costs a lower percentage of revenue. However, Costco pays its employees enough that they could afford to shop there. As the *BusinessWeek* commentary noted, "the low-wage approach cuts into consumer spending and, potentially, economic growth." —*Esther Cervantes*

Average Hourly Wage		Percentage of U.S. Workforce in Unions		Employees Covered by Company Health Insurance		Employees Who Leave After One Year	
Wal-Mart	Costco	Wal-Mart	Costco	Wal-Mart	Costco	Sam's Club*	Costco
$9.68	$16.00	0.0%	17.9%	48%	82%	21%	6%
* Sam's Club is the Wal-Mart unit that competes directly with Costco.							

Sources: "Is Wal-Mart Good for America?" *Wall Street Journal*, December 3, 2005; "Gauging the Wal-Mart Effect," *Wall Street Journal*, December 3, 2005; Arindrajit Dube & Steve Wertheim, "Wal-Mart and Job Quality—What Do We Know, and Should We Care?" October 2005; Jason Furman, "Wal-Mart: A Progressive Success Story," October 2005; Leo Hindery Jr., "Wal-Mart's Giant Sucking Sound," October 2005; A. Bernstein, "Some Uncomfortable Findings for Wal-Mart," *BusinessWeek* online, October 26, 2005, and "Wal-Mart: A Case for the Defense, Sort of," *BusinessWeek* online, November 7, 2005; Arindrajit Dube, Barry Eidlin, and Bill Lester, "The Impact of Wal-Mart Growth on Earnings Throughout the Retail Sector in Urban and Rural Counties," *Institute of Industrial Relations Working Paper*, UC Berkeley, October 2005; Arindrajit Dube, Ken Jacobs, and Steve Wertheim, "Internal Wal-Mart Memo Validates Findings of UC Berkeley Study," November 26, 2005; Jerry Hausman and Ephraim Leibtag, "Consumer Benefits from Increased Competition in Shopping Outlets: Measuring the Effect of Wal-Mart," October 2005; Hausman and Leibtag, "CPI Bias from Supercenters: Does the BLS Know that Wal-Mart Exists?" *NBER Working Paper No. 10712*, August 2004; David Neumark, Junfu Zhang, and Stephen Ciccarella, "The Effects of Wal-Mart on Local Labor Markets," *NBER Working Paper No. 11782*, November 2005; Erin Johansson, "Wal-Mart: Rolling Back Workers' Wages, Rights, and the American Dream," American Rights at Work, November 2005; Wal-Mart Watch, "Spin Cycle"; CBC News, "Wal-Mart to cut ties with Bangladesh factories using child labour," November 30, 2005; National Labor Committee, "10 to 13-year-olds Sewing 'I Love My Wal-Mart' Shirts," December 2005; Global Insight, "The Economic Impact of Wal-Mart," 2005.

Article 4.4

NEUTRALIZED
Big Tech's Retreat from Net Neutrality

BY ROB LARSON
July/August 2018

When the Federal Communications Commission (FCC) decided in 2015 to regulate internet providers through "net neutrality" principles, the conservative *Wall Street Journal* predicted a "Telecom Backlash." The great regional cable monopolies like Comcast and AT&T, as well as the wireless carriers like Verizon and Sprint, opposed the net neutrality orders because they would prevent them from further monetizing their control over the "pipes" that online data takes to reach end users. With the advent of the Trump administration, they ultimately got their way, as the FCC reversed itself on December 14, 2017 and undid the crucial "Title II" classification, which made broadband a telecommunication service rather than an information service, and therefore allowed the FCC to impose net neutrality-based regulations.

Meanwhile, the giant tech companies, like Facebook and Google's subsidiary YouTube, are usually viewed as supportive of Title II, and they had meaningfully opposed the telecoms earlier this decade in support of neutrality. However, Silicon Valley's growing dominance is drawing it into the telecommunication industry itself, diminishing its support for the popular neutrality principles. This change has the potential to reshape internet access, a pivotal development with ramifications for the entire U.S. economy.

Neutering Net Neutrality

The basic argument for net neutrality is relatively easy to understand. The main principle is that information traveling over a network shouldn't be subject to discrimination or favor, like speeding up the data flow for companies that can afford to pay the network operator, or slowing down (or even blocking) information from entities the operator doesn't care for. This basic principle has long applied to many familiar networks, like the traditional phone system. When you make a phone call for pizza delivery, for example, the mobile carriers can't steer your call to another pizzeria that paid for the privilege. They have to connect you to the one you dialed, and maintain a common standard of call quality. With the internet's rapid growth over the last 20 years and its deep integration into our social, political, and economic lives, the stakes for abandonment of these principles online are very high. Net neutrality activists have argued that leaving the cable monopolists and the cell carrier oligopolists a free hand allows them to consider collecting unearned "rent" income by charging popular, cash-flush sites higher rates for faster or more consistent content delivery, while slowing down (or "throttling") content from poorer or unfavored sites. It gives the telecom industry enormous discretionary power.

The issue came to real national attention in 2014, when rising media giant Netflix refused to pay telecom colossus Comcast for the rising proportion of its traffic coming from users streaming its library of TV shows and movies. In retaliation, Comcast throttled Netflix data, causing users of its service to experience prolonged wait times with downgraded quality. This became popularly associated with the "spinning wheel of death" displayed as Netflix's content streamed through relatively tiny network connections. This was a risky move for Comcast, as it came between America and its TV shows—about as smart as stepping between a bear and her cubs.

Historically, the FCC had been unable to impose neutrality standards on the industry since internet access was technically classified as an information service, rather than a telecommunication service. If it were reclassified as a telecom service, the cable and wireless firms' data plans could be designated "common carriers" like the traditional phone lines, considered to be too important to the economy to be unregulated. This reclassification would subject internet service to Title II of the Telecommunications Act, which would effectively impose net neutrality norms on the industry. The FCC did this in 2015, and undid it in 2017.

The first of three rounds of battle over neutrality in the United States began before the Netflix debacle, in December 2010, and was indicative of the FCC's long-standing reputation as a "captured" regulator. The FCC's then-chairman, Tom Wheeler, was a former cable industry lobbyist, and unsurprisingly, the FCC's first attempt at a neutrality policy was literally written by people from the industry.

This FCC order was prepared by lobbyists and attorneys for AT&T, Verizon, and Google, and actually did ban the net neutrality violations of blocking and discrimination among data transmission. But a gigantic omission pointed toward the reason for the phone corporations' participation: The rule confined itself to the "wired" internet, completely exempting service via a wireless signal. Liberal legal scholar Tim Wu, coiner of the term "net neutrality," observed the significance of this exemption in his fine book *The Master Switch*: "That enormous exception— AT&T and Verizon's condition for support of the rule—is no mere technicality, but arguably the masterstroke on the part of [the cell carriers]. It puts the cable industry at a disadvantage, while leaving the markets on which both AT&T and Verizon have bet their future without federal oversight."

Wireless was correctly understood at the time to be the growth center of the industry, so this exemption gave the cell service oligopoly a free hand to charge for prioritization and block content they didn't care for. Still, the telecom companies saw even the limited rules about wired internet to be an infringement on their corporate liberty, and their major trade associations, the United States Telecom Association and the National Cable & Telecommunications Association, filed lawsuits immediately after the decision. The regulation, the Open Internet Order 2010, was ultimately struck down in court in 2014, leading to the next round of the struggle.

Title II: The Quickening

To understand the second round of net neutrality confrontation, we need to look at the corporate forces on either side of the issue. On one side were the great telecom giants, with AT&T, Comcast, and Verizon opposing net neutrality so they

---

A Net Neutrality Glossary

Broadband: High-speed internet access, via wired cable or fiber connection, a cell phone tower network, satellite service, or a local wireless hotspot.

Captured regulator: A government body created to regulate certain market practices in an industry, but which has become largely taken over by the industry itself, through lobbying or political action.

Common carrier: A provider of network services that obeys net neutrality rules, like the phone system under Title II classification.

ISP: Internet service provider. Usually a private company (although a few embattled municipal networks exist) that runs a broadband network to consumers' computers and phones, transmitting data from content providers like websites.

Market power: The ability of a market actor (or combination of them) to influence prices or market conditions.

Net neutrality: The principle that all data traveling through information networks to consumers should be treated equally. Practices that violate the principle include the throttling of data to collect payment, discrimination among users or types of data, or paid promotion to ensure faster delivery.

Network effect: A service used in a network gains value as more users join. (If everyone you need to contact regularly has a telephone, telephone service is worth more to you than if they did not.) This feature tends to create market concentration and monopoly.

---

could charge more for choice access to their "bandwidth," or data flow capacity. Household-name tech platforms like Google, Facebook, and Amazon were on the opposing side, eager to continue their rapid online growth without increased costs for access to the telecom networks.

In November 2014, President Barack Obama recorded a video statement calling for Title II reclassification, largely in response to a groundswell of public comments on the FCC's online submissions facility, reaching over four million and largely supporting net neutrality. This was the result of a major activist campaign, combining online and offline action (see Rob Larson, "The Economics of Net Neutrality," *D&S*, July/August 2015). Unprecedented numbers of public comments poured into the FCC thanks to efforts by prominent media figures, but above all through the efforts of a new movement of activists engaged in consciousness-raising and organizing with others to formally recognize the new importance of the internet and the need for broadband providers to be held to the same standards as the traditional phone system. These activists were up against the usual barriers of apathy and distraction, as well as the somewhat technical nature of the issue and the vague feeling that the free-flowing internet somehow cannot be leashed. Their success in moving first President Obama and then the FCC's senior staff shows the quite real power of organized activism, power that will be needed on this issue and others for years to come.

Despite conservative claims of "regulatory overreach" by these bold activists, the FCC's 2015 neutrality order specifically elected to "forbear" using several of the regulatory tools of Title II, including price limits, and left several important issues unresolved. But it confirmed the main net neutrality provisions, and the FCC in its short-lived rules explicitly drew attention to the tsunami of public comments in justifying its decision: "Because the record overwhelmingly supports adopting rules and demonstrates that three specific practices invariably harm the open internet—blocking, throttling, and paid prioritization—this order bans each of them, applying the same rules to both fixed and mobile broadband internet access service."

A predictable chorus of conservative and neoliberal opposition quickly arose, led by Republican FCC commissioner Ajit Pai. Among the usual cant about overreach, Pai claimed no action was needed since "The internet is not broken." Netflix subscribers watching the spinning wheel while Comcast and other cable firms were throttling its data capacity might disagree. For their part, the cable and cellular internet service providers (ISPs) claimed that the threat of FCC interference will limit their infrastructure investments—meaning the networks would lay less cable and delay upgrading cell towers because of rising expenses or lower revenues. This oft-repeated claim was countered by reporting from the *MIT Technology Review*, which found that the telecom networks have a hilarious 97% profit margin on bandwidth investments. They're unlikely to walk away in the face of mild regulation—indeed, they haven't deserted European markets, where some network neutral provisions are in effect.

The Empires Strike Back

The Trump administration has amounted to a major setback for net neutrality, as it did for so many other important economic, social, and environmental policies. Trump appointed the leading Republican on the FCC, Pai, to head the agency, and he soon announced that the agency was reevaluating the Title II classification. Pai's main justification for doing so was his repeated claim that net neutrality was depressing investment in the telecommunications network, despite the industry's absurd profit rates. In fact, Comcast and other large broadband providers had continued to increase their capital investments in years since the FCC's neutrality rules were issued. On December 14, 2017, the commission voted to formally overturn the Title II ruling, despite continued telecom investment, and the lack of major competition among the cable companies that supply the wired broadband for Wi-Fi service.

Activism to save neutrality this time around was somewhat less dramatic than in the previous round, perhaps owing in part to the diminishing support of the influential tech titans. However, public comments poured in at the FCC once again, forcing them to "rate limit" submissions, ensuring tranches of comments were gradually submitted so as not to overwhelm their docket facility yet again. Twenty-three million comments were submitted by the time of the repeal vote, but many were clearly being generated by computer software programmed to churn them out. Many falsely alleged to have been submitted by public figures; others were posted under the names of dead or fictional people. Some of the fake comments supported net neutrality and Title II, but the *Wall Street Journal* reported that one anti-neutrality e-mail was posted at "a near-constant rate—1,000 every 10 minutes—punctuated by periods of zero comments, as if web robots were turning on and off ... The Comment has been posted on the FCC website more than 818,000 times." A report by telecom firms found many of the comments were attributable to "FakeMailGenerator.com." It's a pity that the public comment process at the FCC and other regulatory agency websites have been so heavily gamed.

So as of June 2018, net neutrality requirements are no longer in effect nationally in the United States. Exactly what this major reversal for freedom means as far as market conditions will take time to materialize. There are clues in coffee shops and with in-flight airline-sponsored internet access, which are exempt from neutrality rules since the companies are not telecom firms and provide web access as a perk. There, tech giants like Amazon prominently sponsor the service, and users are steered toward certain sites, although differences in bandwidth access aren't yet common. On mobile, the telecoms have been experimenting for some time with "zero rating," a practice of not counting use of certain partner websites or services against a data plan. These modest neutrality violations can be expected to expand over time, likely leading to poorer service and restricted access for those less able to pay.

From Platforms to Pipes

The dramatically waxing and waning fortunes of net neutrality owe a lot to the shifting stances of the giant tech platforms over neutrality. In the proposed 2010 rule written by industry, Google had agreed with Verizon that neutrality rules weren't even necessary on wireless systems. When Obama made his famous November 2014 video calling for Title II reclassification, Google founder Eric Schmidt told an administration official that the position was a mistake. Despite its alleged idealism, Google was among the first tech platforms to waver; as the *Wall Street Journal* put it, "Google and Net Neutrality: It's Complicated."

While in 2010 the tech giants directly signed on to the effort to support net neutrality, in 2014 they mostly left neutrality policy to their lower-profile internet Association, their trade group. The *National Journal* found "big web companies like Facebook and Google mostly stayed on the sidelines of the debate." Several prominent online companies did stage an "internet slowdown," replacing their normal home pages with a graphic of the spinning "loading" wheel, dramatizing the risks posed by fast- and slow-lanes. Participating firms included web mid-weights like Mozilla, Kickstarter, WordPress, and of course Netflix. Notably absent were the heavyweights like Google, Facebook, or Apple.

In 2017, their support was thinner still, and some tech figures argued that the reclassification wasn't necessary for effective neutrality. The business coverage ran headlines like "Web Firms Protest Efforts to Roll Back Net Neutrality," but the fine print reveals the companies involved are led by second-tier firms like Netflix, Reddit, and GoDaddy. And Netflix itself, the very poster child for net neutrality, was "less vocal" on the subject after it worked out satisfactory commercial deals with the telecom giants to route its data. The *Wall Street Journal* bluntly reported that the company "says it is less at risk now that it is big enough to strike favorable deals with telecom companies. The company did just that, reaching several deals in recent years to pay broadband providers for ample bandwidth into their networks." And "some big players," including Google and Amazon, "were content with relatively low-key efforts."

While the smaller firms were purposely displaying the annoying pinwheel, Google couldn't be bothered to include the image on the front of its incredibly prominent search engine page. Instead, the firm ran a post on its relatively obscure policy blog, while Amazon deployed a noncommittal button linking to the FCC comment facility, and Facebook CEO Mark Zuckerberg posted that he supported Title II but was "open to working with members of Congress." Hardly an aggressive stance. In 2017, the smaller online firms did reprise the deliberate display of the slow-loading pinwheel, but they were increasingly lonely among the towering tech colossi in doing so.

So why the reluctance to stick up for net neutrality again? After all, these firms do rely on open access to the telecom industry's "pipes" of the internet to deliver their oceans of free user content to their platforms globally. The answer is clear economics: The companies are themselves becoming ISPs like the telecom companies, investing heavily in new cables and other infrastructure to bring content and their platforms' services to users. They are losing their previously stark opposing interest to the telecom giants, and indeed their interests increasingly overlap.

Big Tech has moved further in this direction since the 2014–15 struggle. The business media frequently report on these changes. In early 2016, the *Wall Street Journal* reported that Microsoft and Facebook were jointly investing in a transatlantic data cable to add redundancy to the networks their platforms rely on. Because the project cost hundreds of millions of dollars, "only the very largest internet companies have made the plunge" into digital infrastructure on this scale. The deal indicated that "the biggest U.S. tech companies are seeking more control over the internet's plumbing."

Amazon has also invested in another undersea bundle of fiber optic cables, and in late 2016, Facebook and Google announced major investments in a high-speed line between Los Angeles and Hong Kong. Google is also laying an incredible 6,200-mile-long fully private cable from L.A. to its data center in Chile, part of an effort to catch up to Amazon and Microsoft in cloud computing. Fascinatingly, a Google cloud computing exec is reported to claim the company's telecommunications infrastructure "adds up the world's biggest private network, handling roughly 25% of the world's internet traffic ... without relying on telecom companies." Except that now, Google is a telecom company.

Indeed, all the tech giants have invested in their own high-speed data lines between major world cities for years. These investments are intended to ensure enough capacity to route information among the giants' enormous data centers. The business press suggests, amazingly, that "the investments have pushed aside the telephone companies that dominated the capital-intensive market for more than a century." The process is strikingly reminiscent of Rockefeller's money-gushing Standard Oil empire, which first conquered energy, and then began taking over the rail lines carrying that energy. These market developments make it easy to understand why the big tech firms are less and less interested in confronting the telecom industry: They are increasingly members of that industry, and they are gaining an economic interest in the possibility of prioritizing or penalizing different data. They are gaining control. This is a major long-term trend that will see the future blurring of the lines between tech and telecom.

Let this be a lesson to social and political movements: Capitalists are only social-change allies as long as it suits the bottom line.

Despite the blow to leftist and liberal morale from the Trump FCC's reversal and the spreading desertion of the mega-cap tech giants from the neutrality struggle, positive signs persist. Notably, in May 2018, Senate Democrats successful voted with a handful of Republicans to restore the Title II classification, a surprising victory but one doomed to die in the GOP-run House of Representatives. But the vote speaks to the enduring popularity of the idea. Net neutrality has a future in legislatures and administrations less devoted to the unfettered freedom of enormous cable monopolists to steer public attention away from war and economic inequality and toward pleasant corporate propaganda and pop songs. ❑

Sources: Tim Wu, *The Master Switch* (Vintage, 2011); David Talbot, "When Will the Rest of Us Get Google Fiber?" *MIT Technology Review*, February 4, 2013; Mark Scott, "Dutch Offer Preview of Net Neutrality," *New York Times*, Feb. 26, 2015; Miriam Gottfried, "Don't Get Too Excited About the FCC's New Rules," *Wall Street Journal*, April 16 2017; Cecilia Kang, "F.C.C. Repeals Net Neutrality Rules," *New York Times*, Dec. 14, 2017; "Net Neutrality breaks records," Fight for the Future, July 13, 2007; James Grimaldi and Paul Overberg, "Lawmakers Seek Checks on Phony comments before 'Net Neutrality' Vote, *Wall Street Journal*, Dec. 13, 2017; James Grimaldi and Paul Overberg, "Millions of People Post Comments on Federal Regulations. Many Are Fake," *Wall Street Journal*, December 12, 2017; John McKinnon and Ryan Knutson, "Want to See a World Without Net Neutrality? Look at These Old Cellphone Plans," *Wall Street Journal*, December 11, 2017; Alistair Barr, "Google and Net Neutrality: It's Complicated," *Wall Street Journal*, February 4, 2015; Brendan Sasso, "Despite fierce opposition from the major Internet providers, the FCC is poised to seize expansive new regulatory powers," *National Journal*, February 5, 2015; John McKinnon, "Web Firms Defend Net Neutrality As GOP Takes Aim," *Wall Street Journal*, April 13, 2017; Drew FitzGerald, "Netflix backs away From Fight Over Internet Rules Now That Traffic is Flowing," *Wall Street Journal*, Dec. 13, 2017; John McKinnon and Douglas MacMillan, "Web Firms Protest Efforts to Roll Back Net Neutrality," *Wall Street Journal*, July 12, 2017; Drew FitzGerald, "Facebook and Microsoft to Build Fiber Optic Cable Across Atlantic," *Wall Street Journal*, May 27, 2016; Drew FitzGerald, "Google, Facebook to Invest in U.S.-China Data Link," *Wall Street Journal*, Oct. 12, 2016; Drew FitzGerald, "Google Plans to Expand Huge Undersea Cables to Boost Cloud Business," *Wall Street Journal*, Jan. 16, 2018.

Article 4.5

CARING BY THE DOLLAR
Nursing Homes, Private Equity, and Covid-19

BY BILL BARCLAY
March/April 2021

The numbers are bleak. about 0.5% of the U.S. population lives in nursing homes (1.5 million people). This small group of people account for 40% (probably more) of the almost 400,000 U.S. Covid-19 deaths. By December 2020, residents of Genesis Health Care nursing homes were almost 3,000 of those deaths.

Why?

A common answer is, well, residents of nursing homes are older and, generally, in less good health than the population at large. But this "explanation" obscures more than it reveals about the actual story behind this slaughter. The bigger story is the nursing home industry itself, the way it is organized, the nature and limits of industry regulation and, of course, the financial incentives that structure this industry today and have done so for more than a half century. The story of Genesis Health Care—the largest operator of skilled nursing facilities in the United States—has much to teach us about this industry and the disaster of Covid-19. The firm both shaped and was shaped by the financial dynamics of caring by the dollar, seeking profits through providing health care for the elderly.

Genesis: A Story of Biblical Proportions

In the beginning—1985—the creators of Genesis Health Ventures, who came from within the skilled nursing facility industry, envisioned a new model of care for the elderly, an Edenic world that would build, according to the International Directory of Company Histories, "a comprehensive network of managed care facilities and services designed to help senior citizens maintain their independence and mobility." The new Eden "would be good for its patients, and for its bottom line."

Before Genesis came on the scene, most skilled nursing facilities were similar to traditional nursing homes and typically focused on providing patients with long-term stays. But these kinds of facilities were costly, and their profit margins were low. And as Genesis CEO and co-founder Michael Walker once said: "No one wants to end up in a nursing home."

Genesis pioneered a new model of care that they claimed would be better for patients, as well as the company's bottom line: get patients in the door, use medications from the firm's pharmacy subsidiary, get them into rehabilitation services provided by another subsidiary of the firm, get them out and home or to a less intensive care facility, often again a subsidiary, and get the next group of patients in. This was a continuous-flow model of health care provision, based on the demographics of aging that ensured new (and growing) demand for the services that a re-envisioned skilled nursing facility could provide. It was also one that sought scale in order to maximize profits.

Building the New Eden: Horizontal and Vertical Integration

Genesis had a relatively humble beginning. It began in 1985 with a company valuation of $32 million and just nine skilled nursing facilities, a far cry from the value and scale of the major chains at the time.

However, in the short span of 1985–1988, Walker built this new model, starting with acquiring the related businesses to create the new Eden. Genesis expanded both horizontally and vertically, buying other skilled nursing facilities and adding rehabilitation and pharmacy operations as profit centers to its available services. These additional services are usually more profitable than actual in-patient care.

Genesis also acquired a company called Physician Services. This addition allowed Genesis to become the first company in the industry to employ its own primary care physicians for its patients. The continuous-flow model was thus extended into the diagnostic and prescription functions of the company.

In 1991, Walker took the company public through an Initial Public Offering (IPO). At that point, Genesis owned more than 40 skilled nursing facilities and 13 life-care communities scattered across multiple states, mostly in the Northeast. The IPO price valued Genesis at almost $2.5 billion, or more than 75 times its starting value of $32 million in 1985.

This rapid expansion did not, of course, come cheaply. Genesis, like the other newly emerging chains, needed to borrow money to finance new acquisitions in

---

A Brief History of the Nursing Home Industry

Unlike hospitals, where the for-profit model is relatively recent (the majority of hospitals were still nonprofit in the 1980s), the bulk of nursing homes, or skilled nursing facilities, have been organized on a for-profit basis for many decades. The provision of medical services; the manufacture, distribution and utilization of medical supplies; and the logistics of caring for the elderly are primarily driven by the search for profitable investment.

The widely reported failure of the industry to protect patients from Covid-19 is one more chapter in the continued saga of inadequate care, patient neglect, and regulatory violations in the pursuit of profit. Congressional investigations in the late 1990s (patient abuse complaints doubled between 1996–2000) and again in 2007 found skilled nursing home facilities deficient in a variety of quality-of-care measures, most importantly infection control, as well as frequently inadequate staffing levels, which often resulted in serious patient illness or even death. The General Accounting Office (GAO) 2020 report, "Infection Control Deficiencies were Widespread and Persistent in Nursing Homes Prior to Covid-19 Pandemic," again documented widespread failures of patient care beginning prior to the pandemic and continuing into 2020.

How Did We Get Here: The Begats

The passage of the Social Security Act in 1935 begat the first wave of skilled nursing home growth, and proprietary facilities began to replace the older model of not-for-profit nursing homes. Money in the hands of older people defined a potential market for health care and supervision rather than the pre-existing simple provision of room and board.

The market was slow to develop, however, until the 1946 Hill-Burton Act provided low-cost federal financing for the construction of new nursing homes. From 1939 to 1950, the number of skilled nursing facilities increased tenfold. More importantly for the industry's profits, occupancy rates—the all-important ratio of skilled nursing facility

order to achieve economic scale quickly. Banks (and investors) were happy to lend. The cost-plus payment model that was part of Medicaid legislation assured Genesis and its investors a steady stream of profits. As a 1969 article in *Barron's* had made plain: "Nobody can lose money in this industry."

By 1996, five years after Genesis's IPO, the company brought in $650 million in revenue a year and employed more than 25,000 people. In that same year, Genesis's new CFO, George Hager, won the Cain Brothers award for "creative financial solutions." Among Hager's creative solutions was the decision to establish a real estate investment trust for some 37,000 of Genesis's beds. This off-balance-sheet financing gave a significant boost to the company's revenues.

Just two years later, Genesis's annual profits reached $1 billion, and the company acquired MultiCare, another skilled nursing home chain, in a deal valued at $1.4 billion. The acquisition doubled the number of facilities and beds owned or operated by Genesis. But more than expanding their market share, Genesis was also looking for a change in their mix of customers. At the time, about 60% of the company's patients were Medicaid recipients. Of MultiCare's patients, in contrast, only 32% were Medicaid recipients, and the remaining 68% were either Medicare or private-pay patients. Both Medicare and private payers (non-Medicare insurers) reimbursed at twice the Medicaid rate for in-patient care, making it possible for Genesis to further boost their profits.

---

residents to beds—had more than doubled from the 1939 level of only 35%. The link between federal health policy and the for-profit care of the elderly had been established.

As late as the 1950s and 1960s, however, the nursing home industry was significantly different from that of today. Although, as noted above, largely organized along for-profit lines, nursing homes were primarily a family business. Medical supplies were purchased from outside vendors and medical services were provided by non-affiliated physicians. The business model was based on owning the land and buildings and overseeing the operations of the skilled nursing facility as a stand-alone business.

The passage of the Medicare and Medicaid Act in 1965 begat a fundamental reorganization of the nursing home industry. The first, most obvious impact was simply the growth in the number of skilled nursing facility beds. At the time Medicaid and Medicare were established, there were 460,000 skilled nursing facility beds in the United States. In 1973, only eight years after he Act, the number of skilled nursing facility beds more than doubled to 1.1 million. Gross revenues for skilled nursing facilities increased 14 times over, with more than half of these monies coming from the federal government.

But the changes in the political economy of the industry were much more than simply a matter of size. The industry was reorganized. Chains that owned 20, 50, 100, or more skilled nursing facilities sprouted up like mushrooms after the Spring rain of federal money, replacing small, family-owned outfits. Medicaid's cost-plus reimbursement system, under which skilled nursing facilities were reimbursed at a profitable rate for care with no ceiling on the total cost per patient, assured a steady stream of profits to participants in the industry. In addition, the Centers for Medicare and Medicaid Services (CMS) "relaxed" the compliance standards for skilled nursing facilities to be eligible for reimbursements. The result was a rapid growth in beds and facilities.

In fact, the late 1960s and early 1970s saw a stock market boom—in nursing home stocks! Wall Street soon saw Medicare and Medicaid as a risk-free source of revenue. In 1966 there were less than a dozen publicly-traded nursing home chains, by 1969 there

The Snake in the Garden

How did a company with $1 billion in revenue pull off a $1.4 billion acquisition? Another creative financial solution. Genesis turned to private equity firms Cypress Group and Texas Pacific Group for financing, and in exchange these firms took effective control of the company. Cypress had been founded by former Lehman Brothers bankers, and Texas Pacific Group was already an active private equity investor in the health care industry. The deal valued MultiCare at 10.5 times earnings before interest, taxes, depreciation, and amortization (EBITDA). This acquisition price was significantly above the usual 6–8 times EBITDA that was common in skilled nursing home mergers. In addition, Genesis paid the partnership an additional $50 million for MultiCare's pharmacy business and another $24 million for its rehabilitation business. Both the costs of the acquisition and the additional payments resulted in additional debt, raising Genesis's total debt load to over $1 billion.

Two years later, Genesis filed for bankruptcy.

Wandering in the Wilderness

The official company history says it was the reduction of payment rates under Medicaid and Medicare that triggered the bankruptcy in 2000. However, this narrative ignores the reality of more than $1 billion in debt carried by Genesis. The

---

were 58, and by 1970 there were 90. The best known, the so-called "Fevered Fifty," promised investors returns of 20-25% a year.

But this federal largesse begat another change in the industry. In the late 1990s, Congressional Republicans and the Clinton administration, concerned about the impact of rising Medicaid payments on the federal budget, significantly revised the cost-plus payment system to reduce Medicaid outlays to skilled nursing facilities. Most of the reductions came from limiting federal matching payments to states. However, the new reimbursement structure did not extend to ancillary services.

The short-term result was the use of strategic bankruptcy filings by five of the largest skilled nursing facility chains from 1998–2000, the three years immediately following the new reimbursement system. A second, long-term result was the penetration of the skilled nursing industry by private equity (PE): by 2004, four of the 10 largest skilled nursing facility chains had been bought by private equity firms.

Private Equity Enters the Skilled Nursing Facility World
Private equity (PE) can best be understood as an *extractive* industry—the extraction of cash by acquiring and reorganizing the operations of other businesses. The skilled nursing home industry's apparently guaranteed cash flow, coupled with a growing population of potential customers and significant real estate assets, was too good an opportunity for PE firms to pass up. The CEOs and management teams of skilled nursing facility chains made the usual argument: PE ownership and management would bring efficiencies to the industry that were beyond the scope of existing skilled nursing facilities and would, at the same time, improve the quality of care for residents.

What do we know about the validity of these claims?

In the early 2000s some studies provided limited support for the chain model of skilled nursing home ownership, including chains owned by PE firms, and showed higher financial returns in terms of the number of occupied beds and the number of

company was not alone in bankruptcy court: It appeared that the entire skilled nursing industry—or at least what had been called "the fevered fifty" portion, the hot skilled nursing home stocks of the late 1960s and early 1970s—was going under. Genesis was joined in bankruptcy filings by MultiCare, and preceded by Vencor Inc. of Kentucky, Sun Healthcare Group of New Mexico, and Integrated Health Services of Maryland, among others.

What had actually happened was the collapse of the then-dominant skilled nursing business model. That model was based on the cost-plus payments received under Medicaid that allowed skilled nursing facilities to receive a steady flow of government payments that covered any procedures, medications, ancillary services, etc. that were provided to a patient. With the new Medicaid payment system, the very feature that attracted private equity to the industry—reliable cash flow from taxpayers that assured profitable per resident returns and thus rewarded rapid growth—was called into question.

However, despite the claims of Genesis and others, the revenues it generated remained sufficient to cover costs—but at a lower rate of profitability. The Government Accountability Office's analysis of the revised reimbursement system's impact highlighted the fact that providing more ancillary services would allow Genesis (and others) to continue to enjoy a steady flow of profits:

Routine [inpatient] services (which include general nursing, room and board, and administrative overhead) were subject to cost limits, but payments for ancillary services and capital-related costs were virtually unlimited. Because higher ancillary

---

years without detriment to patient care. At one point, Florida's Agency for Health Care Administration even claimed that "There is no evidence to support that the quality of nursing home care suffers when a facility is owned by a private equity firm or an investment company."

However, by 2012 the benefits of PE-owned skilled nursing facilities were being called into question. The most extensive and longer-term analysis, whose results were published in *Health Care Management Review*, looked at data from 18,000 nursing homes from 2000–2007, and found declining and inferior care quality in PE-owned skilled nursing facility chains. These findings are particularly persuasive because of the inclusion of larger and longer established PE chains, and the inclusion of the scores that these facilities received through the Centers for Medicare and Medicaid Services' five-star rating system (CMS rates all individual skilled nursing facilities on this scale, ranging from a low of one star to a high of five stars).

Acquisition by PE firms did increase skilled nursing home facility efficiency as measured by volume (the rate of new admissions), which is an important driver of profitability. But acquisition by PE firms also resulted in a lower five-star ranking compared to the facility's pre-acquisition score. This ratings drop was driven by a decline in frontline nursing staff, certified nursing assistants, and licensed practical nurses. There was also an increased rate of readmissions to hospitals from PE-owned skilled nursing facilities compared to both non-PE owned chains and not-for profit skilled nursing facilities.

But private equity still ended up on top: The net result was increased annual revenue of almost $800,000 per facility.

Sources: Rohit Pradhan et al., "Private Equity Ownership and Nursing Home Financial Performance," *Health Care Management Review*, May 2012; Atul Gupta et al., "Does Private Equity Investment in Healthcare Benefit Patients? Evidence from Nursing Homes," NYU Stern School of Business, Nov. 12, 2020 (available at ssrn.com).

service costs triggered higher payments, facilities had no financial incentive to furnish only clinically necessary services and little incentive to deliver them efficiently.

Genesis illustrates the case nicely: In 2000–2002, total company revenue grew 12.7%. Their in-patient services revenue grew only 8.4%, while revenue from Genesis's pharmacy services grew almost 20%.

Although the financial problems for Genesis's business model and that of the other four largest skilled nursing bankruptcy filers were real, the bankruptcy path was a strategic choice. It was a course of action designed to restructure debts or avoid debt payments and/or to gain leverage in debt renegotiations. It also opened up the skilled nursing industry to further penetration by private equity firms.

Seeking Canaan

In 2003 Genesis emerged from bankruptcy, and returned to its long-time business strategy of growing by both vertical and horizontal integration. They quickly acquired skilled nursing facilities, assisted and independent living facilities, and that old reliable revenue generator, rehabilitation clinics.

Genesis grew rapidly for the next few years. Private equity firms as well as Genesis management took notice—and sought to extract cash and spin off assets. In 2006, Genesis management, led by now CEO George Hager, approached the Genesis board with a proposed leveraged buyout (LBO) that valued the company at about $1.5 billion. The board, however, sought outside advice from Goldman Sachs. The result was a bidding war in which a syndicate of Formation Capital and JER Partners outbid both management and a competing private equity firm, Fillmore Capital Partners. Less than 10 years after the company relied on private equity to finance its acquisition of MultiCare, Genesis returned to private equity control in a deal valued at about $2 billion in 2007.

As noted earlier, what attracts private equity, as well as Genesis's management, to the skilled nursing facility industry is cash flow. The fact that Genesis raked in $10,000 for each of its occupied beds made it an attractive acquisition. In addition, the company's concentration in the Northeast was a plus, since Medicaid pay rates were above the U.S. average in that region.

The private equity firms had considerable experience with the health care industry and proceeded to reorganize Genesis to squeeze as much value as possible out of the company's existing assets. From the perspective of private equity, Genesis was a bundle of different assets, the most valuable of which was real estate. After all, land can be put to many uses beyond that of housing a skilled nursing facility. And Genesis had a lot of real estate: the company owned 65% of its facilities, often in prime locations.

In 2011, Genesis, under the aegis of their private equity owners, sold their real estate assets for $2.4 billion. The buyer was a real estate investment trust (REIT) known as Health Care Real Estate Investment Trust. The REIT then leased the facilities back to Genesis. First-year lease payments were set at $198 million and would increase at an annual rate of 3.5%. Stripping out real estate was sort of like selling your furniture to pay your mortgage: money up front but an empty shell going forward.

Genesis was not the only, or even the first, in the skilled nursing industry to make use of the REIT structure to divide operations from property. This Operating Company/Property Company structure has several advantages, from the perspective of the owners if not the patients. First, it becomes very difficult for patients, or their families, to sue the operating company for significant damages because it does not have substantial assets and residents cannot reach through to the assets held by the property company. Second, in the Genesis/Health Care REIT deal (as in others) much of the profits of the operating company are effectively transferred to the property company, via lease payments and a range of management services agreements, further insulating them from litigation. This structure benefits the private equity firm owners as they extract value from what in essence becomes an operating shell that functions as a flow-through financial structure. An additional benefit of the Operating Company/Property Company structure is the reduction of corporate income taxes that would otherwise be owed by a combined company, because REITs are subject to a lower corporate tax rate. Finally, this structure allows the operating company to take on additional debt, which is often necessary because of the cash drain into the property company owned by the private equity firms. So, on top of its other advantages, this structure is a sophisticated form of asset stripping.

In 2014, Genesis was sold to investors as an operating company by the private equity syndicate (Formation Capital and JER Partners) and, after a merger in 2015 with Skilled Healthcare Group, the company again emerged from private equity, becoming a listed company on the New York Stock Exchange. As a result of the merger, by 2015 Genesis was the largest health care chain in the United States with over 50,000 beds, which was 30% more beds than the next largest chain, Manor Care. The firm had also expanded beyond its market in the Northeast into California and elsewhere.

Hager continued to expand Genesis, and for a while this strategy seemed to work. By the end of 2017, Genesis had 70,000 employees and a company valuation of over $5 billion. And Hager was doing well. In 2017 he was paid 45 times the median salary of those 70,000 employees, and more than three times the average CEO compensation in the skilled nursing industry.

(It's worth noting that women of color comprise about half of the employees in the skilled nursing industry, and they're typically paid $25,000–$30,000 a year.)

However, all of this growth often came at the expense of quality of care. In 2017, Genesis was fined $53.6 million by the U.S. Department of Justice (DOJ) for "upcoding" Medicare patients' treatments. Upcoding means assigning an inaccurate billing code to a medical service to increase the reimbursement amount. In short, fraud.

Nonetheless, growth continued. In 2018 Genesis warned of possible bankruptcy, but this appears to have been another effort to avoid upcoming debt payments and/or persuade creditors to restructure the debt. At that time, Genesis leased over three-quarters of the facilities they operated and was carrying over $1.5 billion in debt. And Hager's salary continued to climb, reaching a CEO/median employee salary ratio of 72:1 with $2.5 million compensation in 2018.

In 2019 the Genesis board of directors rewarded Hager with yet another raise, bringing his annual salary to $3 million, resulting in a CEO/median employee compensation ratio of 95:1.

In contrast, the other four executives at Genesis saw their salaries decrease by 15% from 2018 to 2019. Each of the eight Board members received more than $250,000 for making these difficult decisions. Of course, Hager, as CEOs generally do, had the balance of power in choosing board members.

Plague

Genesis and Hager were doing well, so what could go wrong?

A lot, as it turns out.

Beginning in March 2020, Covid-19 began spreading rapidly in Genesis's Burlington, Vt. Health and Rehab Center. This outbreak occurred shortly after the state, under the leadership of Attorney General T. J. Donovan, reached a $740,143 settlement with Genesis to resolve "allegations of neglect that resulted in serious injury to three residents and the death of a fourth," according to the attorney general's website. (Donovan had received $8,000 in political donations from Genesis, a significant contribution to his $49,000 reelection campaign expenditures.) Although the impetus for the investigation had been inadequate staffing, particularly of registered nurses, the staffing level only increased from 0.5 registered nurse hours per patient per day to 0.6 hours after the settlement. Both numbers are well below the Center for Medicare and Medicaid Service's (CMS) minimum of 0.75 registered nurse hours per patient per day.

During the course of 2020, one in six Covid-19 deaths in Vermont came from Genesis's Burlington facility. (According to the *New York Times*, the Burlington center was "known as the nursing home of last resort," even before the pandemic hit.) But it was not the only Genesis facility that contributed to Vermont deaths; their Rutland and Berlin facilities also reported high numbers of Covid-19 cases and deaths. Relatives of a patient at the Burlington facility who later died from Covid-19 reported that, when they were finally allowed to visit, there was a lack of personal protective equipment for staff, and some staffers failed to wear masks. Genesis claimed that there was never a shortage of PPE at the facility.

But Vermont, sadly, was not alone among the victims of Genesis. New Hampshire found that one in five Covid-19 deaths occurred in three Genesis facilities, and Connecticut reported that 235 of the state's 286 Covid-19 deaths were in nursing homes. Again, Genesis facilities were heavily involved. A New Jersey analysis of Covid-19 deaths found that facilities owned by private equity firms, including those owned by Genesis, had a higher rate of both deaths and cases than facilities that were not owned by private equity.

Nationally, Genesis had reported more than 1,500 Covid-19 deaths by mid-2020 when total U.S. Covid-19 deaths were still below 100,000; and by mid-December Genesis reported over 2,800 Covid-19 deaths. This latter number was undoubtedly an undercount because several of Genesis's facilities had a policy of not reporting a Covid-19 death if a facility resident was sent to a hospital because of Covid-19 and subsequently died there rather than in the Genesis facility.

Genesis, like the rest of the skilled nursing industry, responded to the pandemic and the ensuing crisis by urging Congress to grant both financial relief and legal insulation from possible Covid-19 lawsuits. The company hired a friend of former President Donald Trump to lobby for additional Covid-19 funds and joined the push—led by a lobbyist who was the former chief of staff for Senator Mitch McConnell—to get a federal liability shield law enacted.

Exodus

By mid-2020, the failure of Genesis was marked enough that the firm was one of five nursing home chains to receive a Congressional inquiry letter from the House's Select Subcommittee on the Coronavirus Crisis as part of their investigation into Covid-19 and nursing homes. The inquiry asked the company to provide a large range of information, covering staffing (noting the high frequency of understaffing in for-profit skilled nursing facilities such as Genesis), protective measures to stem the spread of Covid-19, revenue received from Medicaid and Medicare, compensation for senior officers, and more.

As the pandemic worsened, Genesis's new admissions declined, causing its all-important occupancy rate to drop and revenues to plunge. Relatives of residents began to demand accountability. Genesis's finances continued to deteriorate throughout 2020. In the second quarter of 2020, Genesis reported negative earnings, and although the company received at least $300 million in Covid-19 support from the federal government, by the third quarter of 2020 Genesis was warning of possible bankruptcy.

By September 2020, Genesis was seeking to sell several of its Vermont facilities in a desperate effort to raise cash. Nonetheless, in October 2020, only one month before Genesis reported a 2020 third quarter loss of over $60 million, the board handed CEO Hager a $5 million "retention bonus." With that added to his regular CEO compensation, Hager had now achieved the S&P 500 "respectable" CEO/median employee compensation ratio of 251:1. All of this was soon reflected in Genesis's stock price, which dropped sharply during 2020. Late in the year, with the stock price falling below $1, Genesis was warned by the NYSE that failure to get the price back above the $1 mark would result in delisting.

Genesis was delisted from the NYSE on January 1, 2021. Five days later, Hager was out as CEO.

The Industrialization of Housework

In the 18th and 19th centuries, feminists, socialists, and others interested in the gender division of labor talked and wrote extensively on the "emancipation of women." Much of this analysis focused on the potential for industrializing housework and allowing women to move beyond the confines of the house and seek waged employment.

This line of thinking has helped develop the idea of a care economy, which has rapidly grown in the last few decades, due to the movement of care work out of the house and into waged work. Much of the theoretical and practical work has been focused on early childhood. Some countries, for example the Nordic countries, have socialized much of both early childhood care work and its financing. Others, the United States and the United Kingdom being prime examples, have commodified the care work of childhood. In these countries, a use value—the necessity of caring for the next generation—has become an exchange value, with families purchasing day care services in the marketplace, if they can afford it.

To date, there has been less focus on care labor at the other end of life. But here, too, we have walked down the path of making high-quality elder care an exchange value to be purchased, rather than a use value to receive as a citizen.

Revelations: Nursing Homes and the Care Economy

This article has said little about the actual work that occurs in skilled nursing facilities, the care of older people who, at least in our current health care system, are not able to remain in their homes without significant assistance from others. This work, carried out primarily by women, especially women of color, is part of what economists have labeled "the care economy."

It is the care economy that has been the locale of much of women's waged labor, whether caring and educating the young, or tending to the ill or the elderly. This work is often underpaid and unrecognized by policymakers. The story of Genesis, and the failure of the for-profit skilled nursing home industry in the face of Covid-19, offers an opportunity to overcome that neglect.

If we are to learn from the story of Genesis and the lethal impact of Covid-19 on our system of caring for the elderly, we must think carefully and clearly about the failings of our current system of caring for those aged members of our society who are not able to fully take care of themselves.

As a first, immediate step, CMS should render skilled nursing facilities with repeated violations ineligible to receive additional hospital-discharged patients or receive any payments under Medicaid until they correct these violations. Medicaid is the primary payer for more than 60% of skilled nursing home residents, and most of these residents are discharged from hospitals. This step alone would go a significant way toward remedying the disaster of skilled nursing facilities and Covid-19.

But we need to go much further.

The for-profit and fragmented nature of the U.S. health care system leaves the poor, and especially the elderly poor, who are dependent on Medicaid, at risk. As in many other policy areas, we discriminate between the elderly eligible for Medicare and/or able to draw on other resources and the elderly poor. In contrast, several other countries, particularly the Nordic countries, have universal, tax-based long-term care systems. In the United States, on the other hand, long-term care insurance is yet another commodity that can, for a price, be purchased in the market.

All of us reading this article should remember the statement by the founder of Genesis that "No one wants to end up in a nursing home." Taking this seriously means that we need to explore how we can create more options for elderly people who—almost always—want to stay in their own home. In the United States today, the care work that allows many older people to stay outside of a nursing home falls disproportionately on women. This pattern has been exacerbated during the Covid-19 pandemic as more women have left the labor force to care for both the young and the old. Many of the jobs these women have left may not be there on the other side of the pandemic. And the impact will be harshest on low wage and women of color workers.

Even in good times, this care labor is treated as a free good. Many of the long-term care social policies in other rich, industrialized countries illustrate other, more human and humane approaches to caring for the elderly. For example, Denmark, with 20% of the population over 65, (compared to 15.5% in the United States) has a national policy of keeping people in their own homes for as long as possible. This policy is implemented through a visiting nurse system and the use of technologies such as digital medicine boxes.

There is much to explore in how to organize this facet of care work in a manner that is humane for clients and caregivers alike. The lethal impact of for-profit skilled nursing facilities, often in the hands of private equity, should impel us to think and act now. ❑

Sources: John E. Dicken, "Infection Control Deficiencies Were Widespread and Persistent in Nursing Homes Prior to COVID-19 Pandemic," U.S. Government Accountability Office, May 20, 2020 (gao.gov); Institute of Medicine Committee on Implications of For-Profit Enterprise in Health Care, For-Profit Enterprise in Health Care, (National Academy of Sciences, 1986); Health Resources and Services Administration, "Hill-Burton Free and Reduced-Cost Health Care," April 2019 (hrsa.gov); Nicole Aschoff, "Vultures in the E.R.," *Dollars & Sense*, January/February 2013 (dollarsandsense.org); Duke University Fuqua School of Business, #COVID19CapitalRelief Database (centers.fuqua.duke.edu); Florida Agency for Health Care Administration, "Long Term Care Review: Florida Nursing Homes Regulation, Quality, Ownership, and Reimbursement," Oct. 2007 (fmda.org); Atul Gupta, Sabrina T. Howell, Constantine Yannelis, and Abhinav Gupta, "Does Private Equity Investment in Healthcare Benefit Patients? Evidence from Nursing Homes," University of Chicago Booth School of Business, Nov. 2019 (chicagobooth.edu); Reference for Business, "Genesis Health Ventures, Inc.—Company Profile, Information, Business Description, History, Background Information on Genesis Health Ventures, Inc.," (referenceforbusiness.com); Statement of Laura A. Dummit before the Special Committee on Aging, United States Senate, "Nursing Homes: Aggregate Medicare Payments Are Adequate Despite Bankruptcies," Government Accountability Office, Sept. 5, 2000 (gao.gov); John George, "Genesis Healthcare gets some debt relief," *Philadelphia Business Journal*, Feb. 22, 2018 (bizjournals.com); ExecPay News, "Genesis Healthcare CEO George Hager's 2019 pay rises 8% to $3M," April 24, 2020 (execpay.org); Kim Barker, "A Nursing Home's 64-Day Covid Siege: 'They're All Going to Die,'" *New York Times*, June 8, 2020 (nytimes.com); Elizabeth Anderson, "Vermont Settles Allegations of Neglect and False Claims with Three Genesis Healthcare Nursing Homes," Office of the Vermont Attorney General, Feb. 20, 2020 (ago.vermont.gov); Select Subcommittee on the Coronavirus Crisis, "Clyburn Launches Sweeping Investigation Into Widespread Coronavirus Deaths In Nursing Homes," June 16, 2020 (coronavirus.house.gov); Janet Weiner, Norma B. Coe, Allison K. Hoffman, and Rachel M. Werner, "Issue Brief: Policy Options for Financing Long-Term Care in the U.S.," University of Pennsylvania Leonard Davis Institute of Health Economics, April 2020 (ldi.upenn.edu).

Article 4.6

BOEING HIJACKED BY SHAREHOLDERS AND EXECS!

How Boeing workers are battling against perverse corporate incentives, and what their story tells us about our financialized economy.

BY MARIE CHRISTINE DUGGAN
July/August 2021

" It felt as if boeing had been hijacked by corporate thugs," Kevin Sanders, a 30-year employee of the company, told Al Jazeera reporter Will Jordan in a documentary that aired in 2014. Sanders was not alone. For the last 20 years, Boeing employees have fought a bitter, losing battle to defend the technological integrity of the planes they build. The many employees who have put their jobs on the line include quality inspectors Gerald Eastman (in 2002) and John Woods (in 2010), and Curtis Ewbank, a specialist in flight-deck systems (in 2020). Yet the company management has repeatedly failed to invest in innovation and employees, instead siphoning cash from manufacturing in order to make the company's stock price rise. Two decades of executives taking money out of manufacturing has had the predictable and tragic consequence of undermining the quality of Boeing planes, despite the long hours put in by its workforce. Hundreds of passengers died in crashes in 2018 and 2019. Then, on February 22, 2021, the engine of a Boeing 777 flying from Denver to Honolulu disintegrated in midair. While there weren't any fatalities, the FAA and Japan's civil aviation bureau grounded over a hundred 777s worldwide.

Boeing has no competitor in the United States and only one major competitor abroad. This level of monopoly makes it possible for Boeing executives to forego making better, safer planes and instead put money into manipulating its share price. In 2020, after nearly 800 orders were cancelled, Boeing simply slashed prices on its 737 Max in order to sell them to discount airline Ryanair. The failure of Boeing management to fund innovation and quality control has had repercussions for the tens of thousands of workers at Boeing. The company's supply chain even reaches into my town in rural New Hampshire, where a firm that supplies parts to commercial airplanes trains high school students as machinists and pays employees to get computer science degrees. One of the reasons Boeing is "too big to fail" is that those independent, well-managed suppliers hold up what is left of the social fabric in a multitude of small towns across the country.

The mismanagement of Boeing—and the struggle of its employees to stem the decline—is not simply the story of one company gone terribly wrong. It is the story of incentives for all publicly held corporations in the United States gone horribly wrong. And it is also the story of many in lower levels of the hierarchy inside the firm putting their jobs on the line in a struggle to retain a focus on quality. These corporations with a ticker symbol are getting signals from the particular market economy in which we live to siphon profits away from new equipment and away from the experienced workforce—which means away from innovation. The result across the economy as a whole is a decline in U.S. productivity and innovation. Figure 1 shows the growth rate of U.S. manufacturing productivity between one year and the next—or in this case, the rate of decline, since output per hour of U.S. manufacturing actually dropped into negative territory from 2015 to 2019, meaning U.S. manufacturing workers produced less per hour in 2019 than they did in 2015. Productivity depends largely on the quality of equipment that workers are given to work with, as well as on the level of worker education and experience. The graph shows the five-year moving average, a way

FIGURE 1. LABOR PRODUCTIVITY IN U.S. MANUFACTURING, PERCENTAGE CHANGE FROM ONE YEAR AGO (FIVE-YEAR MOVING AVERAGE)

Source: St. Louis Federal Reserve (fred.stlouisfed.org).

FIGURE 2: FREE CASH FROM OPERATIONS VS. FREE CASH SPENT ON NEW CAPITAL (BOTH AS A % OF TOTAL)

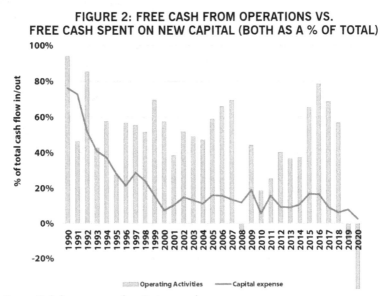

Source: Cash flow statements from Boeing annual reports.

to smooth out annual ups and downs and see the general direction in which we are headed—which is down. Sure, our small start-ups are innovative—but large, publicly-held corporations dominate our industrial base, and they have the incentive to stop upgrading production in order to free up funds to prop up share price. In this "new normal," management undermines the skills and dedication of the workforce while maximizing insiders' incomes (even when the firm is losing money) and making less innovative—and in this case deadly—products.

What Happened to Capital Accumulation?

Most Americans believe that U.S. manufacturing is in decline because wages are lower in China or because robots are taking over. But China does not yet manufacture commercial jets, and if robots were taking over, then U.S. manufacturing productivity would be rising. Boeing's management chose to remove design and production of the Boeing 787 Dreamliner from the United States to high-wage nations such as Italy (fuselages), Japan (wings), and Korea (raked wing tips and flap supports) as early as 2005. Why did executives at Boeing outsource crucial technological innovation and manufacturing? Since innovation is expensive, Boeing executives wanted to make Italian, Japanese, and Korean firms pay for it. Executives at U.S. headquarters would thereby free up funds to make stock price rise. Upper management cares about stock price because, since 1998, executive pay has included stock options—the right to purchase shares at a set price. If they can purchase the shares at, say, $50, and then make the share price rise to, say, $80, then executives can purchase quite a few shares at the lower price, and sell them the next day at the higher price, thereby transforming themselves personally into millionaires (as opposed to enriching the company). Such compensation gives them the incentive

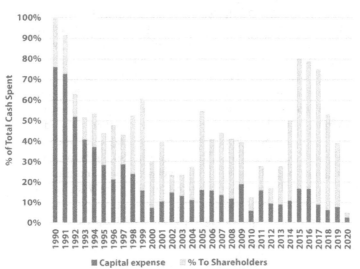

FIGURE 3. SHAREHOLDERS VS. PRODUCTION: HOW BOEING SPENDS "FREE CASH" FLOW

Source: Cash flow statements, Boeing annual reports.

to loot the firm. The Boeing CEO from 2005 to 2015 who oversaw development of the 737 Max was Jim McNerney, and according to economists Bill Lazonick and Matt Hopkins, he earned no less than $239 million by the time he retired. Dennis Muilenburg, who was CEO at the time of the plane crashes, received $72 million in 2018–2019, before he resigned under pressure. Muilenburg collected an additional $81 million in stock-based pay on his way out the door. Although current CEO David Calhoun technically was paid "only" $559,000 in 2020, he stands to earn stock options with an expected value of $20 million dollars and a $7 million reward for returning the 737 Max to service.

The process of taking money out of the company is evident in Figure 2 and Figure 3. "Free cash" is the term for the resources a company has available to spend after it has covered operations costs and the costs of maintaining existing equipment. The gray bars in Figure 2 show the percentage of "free cash" that Boeing obtained from operations (i.e., selling planes created by the workers in the production process), which typically provided 40% to 80% of the cash Boeing was free to spend annually. (Boeing obtained the remaining percentage of "free cash" largely from new loans—like a lot of American households, Boeing borrows every year, though at a lower rate of interest than the typical consumer.)

In many years up until 2018, the corporation obtained the bulk of its "free cash" flow from operations, yet the falling blue line in Figure 2 indicates that Boeing only puts between 10% and 20% of its cash back into new equipment for production operations—known as "capital expenditures." With roughly 60% coming from operations, and only 15% going back into operations, Boeing's cash flow statements reveal a slow erosion of manufacturing capacity, as the company spends less and less on capital equipment of any kind. If this is how the U.S. capitalist class accumulates capital, then it's no wonder capitalism in the United States isn't doing well.

So, how does Boeing actually spend its "free cash"? The yellow bars in Figure 3 show the combined spending on dividends to shareholders and stock buybacks. Both types of spending wind up in shareholders' pockets, and both raise share price. In 2017, the year before the first deadly plane crash, Boeing's spending on dividends and stock buybacks was 66% of total spending, while only 9% of Boeing's cash went into new equipment to manufacture planes. In other words, payouts to shareholders were seven times larger than spending on new equipment for manufacturing. This is a shocking reversal from how Boeing spent its cash in 1990, when 76% of total spending went to new equipment for production, and only 23% went to shareholders. The results of more than a decade of such mismanagement of the corporation's resources were tragic, to such an extent that hundreds of people lost their lives. The result was also, sadly, predictable, because spending cash on shareholders instead of new equipment and the workforce inevitably leads to a shoddier product. (Not shown in Figure 3 is what Boeing spends on debt service and acquisitions; since the firm is no longer innovative, it either buys out competitors or acquires start-ups that have innovated.)

A Share Price Impervious to Disaster

The dramatic increase in spending on dividends and stock buybacks in 2014 (see Figure 3) was perhaps designed to compensate for the terrible news in 2013 that the lithium-ion batteries in Boeing's 787 Dreamliner had exploded and burst into flames on a runway in Boston, and mid-air in Japan. These disasters occurred on brand-new planes. Some electrical engineers argue that Boeing never fixed the problem—if an individual cell inside the battery overheats, the flammable electrolytes around it catch fire, and the battery may start to emit smoke. Because of the oxidizers in the electrolytes, fire suppressant won't work on putting out the fire. After the Boeing 787 incidents in 2013, Airbus switched from lithium-ion to nickel-cadmium batteries for its A350 plane, a rival to the 787. Boeing instead added insulation to the box containing the lithium-ion batteries, and built a vent so that when (not if, but when) the batteries explode, the smoke will not spread to the rest of the plane, but will rather flow outside.

Awkward workarounds like this one for potentially fatal aspects of plane design became the new normal at Boeing. The GE LEAP engine is state-of-the art and energy-efficient. For that reason, Boeing wanted to put two of them in each 737 Max, which debuted in 2017. But the 737 was designed in the 1960s, and there is not enough space between the wing and the ground to put the GE LEAP engine, which is larger than anybody in the 1960s ever imagined a plane engine would be. One workaround is that the housing for the rotary fan of the engine is not itself a cylinder—the side on the bottom is square, which gave Boeing another inch of room between the plane and the ground. Even so, the placement of the engines tends to force the plane's nose up (called a "stall") which could make it fall from the sky. So Boeing added a hidden computer system that would push the nose of the plane down, counteracting the natural tendency of the plane with such a heavy engine under its wings. That workaround proved fatal on October 19, 2018, when a faulty sensor triggered the computer to push Lion Air Flight 610 into a nosedive despite the pilots' desperate efforts to regain manual control. Figure 4 shows that Boeing's share price went down slightly after the crash, only to rally and head for the stratosphere in the months afterwards. Then on March 10, 2019, Ethiopian Airlines Flight 302 crashed for exactly the same reason: A faulty sensor on the brand-new Boeing plane triggered the computer to put the plane into a nosedive from which the pilots could not wrest manual control. Hundreds of people died in both crashes. Many aid workers were on the Ethiopian Airlines flight, including Ralph Nader's grandniece.

What is surprising is that Boeing's share price increased eightfold between the time its faulty plane design first hit the evening news in 2013 with battery fires on runways, through the computer seizing the controls and forcing a plane to crash in Indonesia in 2018. Even the crash of the second plane in March 2019 barely dented the company's share price. One reason Boeing's share price stayed high was the fact that U.S. interest rates have been rock bottom since 2008. All share prices rise in a low-interest rate environment. Furthermore, Boeing increased its stock buybacks every year between 2013 and 2018, from $2 billion per year to $9 billion per year. What's more, after the first 737 Max crash, Boeing increased its dividend by 20%.

Figure 3 indicates the increased stock buybacks and increased dividends, both of which inflate share price.

Indeed, only the Covid-19 disruption of travel actually caused a serious decline in the share price of Boeing planes (see Figure 4), from which it has since recovered. Compare that to a famous story in aviation history: After World War II, the British aviation company de Havilland built the first passenger plane, the Comet. Three Comets blew up in midair, one after the other. It turned out that fuselage engineering appropriate for fighter jets during World War II would not hold up to the years of repetitive use that a passenger plane had to endure. De Havilland's reputation was ruined, and plane innovation passed from Britain to the United States.

Boeing Corrupts Government

Boeing executives' efforts to make the share price impervious to bad news relied on cultivating government complicity and suppressing workers' voices. To see this clearly, we have to go all the way back to the beginning of the 2000s. That's because there is at least a 10-year lag between the time when a new plane is conceived and when the finished product is delivered to the customer. Since the Boeing 737 Max first crashed in 2018, we need to travel back 10 years, to 2008, to understand why the plane was not redesigned from the ground up to accommodate the larger LEAP engines. We would find in 2008 that Boeing's management was in conflict with its own machinists after a 90-day strike. Since the 787 Dreamliner's batteries first caught fire on runways in 2013, we would need to go back to 2003 to see why the plane was developed with flawed lithium-ion batteries. We would find in 2003 that the *Seattle Times* had just started publishing a multi-year series of articles on Boeing, detailing how passenger safety was becoming compromised in development, and the Federal Aviation Administration (FAA) did not call them on it. It is unsurprising that the FAA did nothing. A revolving door between the private sector and regulatory agencies provides an incentive for regulators to please private companies. For example, from 1989 to 2013, Ali Bahrami was head of the FAA, after which he moved on to a more lucrative career as a Boeing lobbyist (from 2013 to 2017), before returning to the FAA in 2017.

By 2003, Boeing was not competing for defense contracts by means of the quality of its planes. Instead, Boeing was convicted of bribing the Air Force in order to obtain a contract for planes to refuel tanker aircraft in midair. In particular, Boeing CFO Michael Sears offered Air Force acquisitions officer Darleen Druyun a job at Boeing with a fat salary. It turned out that this was not the first time Boeing had relied on Druyun to tip the scales in its favor. However, this time Boeing executives were caught in the act. Sears went to prison for four months for offering a job to Druyun while she was employed by the Air Force to negotiate a multibillion-dollar contract with Boeing. Druyun herself got nine months and CEO Philip J. Condit resigned. However, the culture at Boeing of cheating to get ahead may not really have changed: In 2005, the new CEO, Harry Stonecipher, was pushed out for promoting his lover to a senior management position. These two scandals suggest that in the 2003 to 2005 period, Boeing did not see the quality of its planes as the source of the company's success.

Boeing Workforce Fights Back

While Boeing executives have focused on creating a high share price impervious to bad news, workers at all levels have been pushing for product quality and passenger safety. To see this clearly, we have to go all the way back to 2002, when quality-control inspector Gerald Eastman discovered fraud in quality control. When neither Boeing nor the FAA acted, Eastman passed internal Boeing documents to *Seattle Times* reporter Dominic Gates, kicking off the series of investigative articles that the paper began publishing in 2003. In 2008, Boeing fired Eastman, who struggled to convince investigators that he was acting in the public interest. The police asked him why, if quality control at Boeing was so lax, planes weren't falling out of the sky. Boeing worked closely with state prosecutors to convict him, hoping to sentence him to four-and-a-half years in prison. However, no conviction emerged because one juror viewed Eastman as a hero, and a total of two jurors refused to convict, resulting in a hung jury. Boeing settled with Eastman on lesser charges.

In 2008, 25,000 machinists in the heart of Boeing's production process at four plants around Puget Sound in Washington State, plus 2,250 more in Oregon and Kansas, went on strike for 90 days (see Josh Eidelson, "Conflicting Dreams: The strikes that made Boeing a national flashpoint," *D&S*, September/October 2011). Some striking machinists came from families who had worked at Boeing for three generations. They were building the 787 Dreamliner, and protested not only health care cost increases, but also the company's outsourcing of key parts of production, such as the fuselage and wings, to other high-wage countries. Shipping these large parts into Washington State from around the globe for final assembly had already proved to be a cumbersome, delay-inducing process. The machinists' union strike put another significant dent into Boeing's profits. As the world economy plunged into recession, Boeing's share price tumbled extra hard. Boeing had been making the 787 Dreamliner in Everett, Wash. CEO McNerney declared war on Boeing's union machinists by deciding to open a second, non-union plant to produce the Dreamliner in North Charleston, S.C.

In 2011 the South Carolina plant opened, which gave Boeing leverage to cut into the standard of living of its Washington State machinists. In 2013, Boeing eliminated the defined-benefit pension plan and shifted considerable health care costs onto workers in Washington State. The union voted to accept that contract, but it was a bitter, split vote. Machinist Shannon Ryker told Will Jordan, a reporter with Al Jazeera, "For [CEO] Jim McNerney to be earning a pension at approximately a quarter of a million dollars a month, and to think that it is ok to take my $2,200-a-month pension is outrageous."

At least one major customer was aware that building planes with non-union machinists at a brand-new plant would cut into quality. Qatar Airways refused to accept airplanes unless they were produced in Washington State rather than South Carolina. In 2014, Al Jazeera, which is based in Qatar, aired its devastating documentary, in which a worker wearing a wire documented the lack of discipline inside the South Carolina plant: cocaine and painkillers sold on site; workers with no training as machinists who did not understand that using brute force to get a fastener into an ill-fitting hole could lead to catastrophic troubles at 30,000 feet 100 flights later. Several employees stated that they did not consider the planes they were making to be safe enough for them to personally fly on. The contrast between the quality at the Everett and North Charleston plants suggests that even with the divisions, empowering workers through unions serves to protect the integrity of production.

In 2017, the International Association of Machinists (IAM) tried to organize 3,000 Boeing employees in South Carolina. The effort failed in part because then-Governor Nikki Haley urged workers to reject what she described as a "union power grab," even appearing in a Boeing radio ad opposing the unionization—for which she was rewarded with a nomination to Boeing's board in 2019.

Even so, in May 2018, a courageous group of 200 flight-line workers—the mechanics that inspect the planes before they're delivered to customers—voted to join the IAM. In a video produced by the machinists' union about this fight, technician Michael Voirin explains that while he resented being paid $14 per hour less than his counterparts in Washington State, pay wasn't his main concern. He worked the second shift, from 5 p.m. to 1 a.m. At a previous union job, he had been able to spend time with his children, but for the three years he worked at Boeing, mandatory overtime cut into that. He was at work doing mandatory overtime for Boeing on the day his 15-year-old daughter died. As he states in the video from the machinists' union:

> I know the union can't stop overtime, but I also know there's processes for the overtime. And that [with] the union, it's black and white, it's no more at the last minute telling you on Friday, "Oh you're all up Saturday and Sunday," or at 9 o'clock at night saying, "mandatory two hours over…" It's really affected my life because I've lost a lot of family time. I'm getting up to that age where I have a certain number of weekends left and I don't really want to spend them at work.

As these workers organized for a union, the fact that they lived in a state where it was legal to "fire at will" gave the company the opportunity to eliminate the employees who were pro-union and committed to quality and loyal to each other, such as Joseph Delmarco, a licensed mechanic who did a last post-flight check on a plane before it went out to the customer. In the IAM video, Delmarco states:

> I had been the lead for probably three years or so prior to the incident. … I was pro-union, but at the same time I was a company guy. I showed up to work, I worked my butt off, I did everything I could do to make us look good as a company, and, you know, I got the best performance reviews you can get from the company from the past two years, accolades with extra bonusses and stuff for staying late, helping them out, doing this, that, and the other. This is the only thing that I can think of that would've put myself in a category to get myself into trouble so to speak by them, which was being pro-union, that is the only thing really that I could think of. … I loved to work on the airplane, I loved the 787, so I was always going above and beyond, and a lot of people knew that of me, so when they saw that I got fired for something so minuscule, everybody was like, "Man, am I next on the chopping block? I could get fired for anything if those guys would fire you."

A major reason the South Carolina flight-line workers wanted a union was because it would have given them the ability to say "no" to the forced overtime. It turns out that relentless overtime not only put families in South Carolina at risk, but also caused the kind of employee fatigue in Renton, Wash. that made errors inevitable. In the fall of 2018, the Renton, Wash. Boeing factory produced the two 737 Max planes that crashed months later even though they were brand new. Ed Pierson, a Boeing senior manager, testified to the House Transportation and Infrastructure Committee in late 2019 as part of an investigation into the October 2018 and May 2019 plane crashes that the plant was under intense pressure to get planes completed. In early 2018, the delayed delivery of critical parts had slowed down the production of new planes, so Boeing promised shareholders to increase the output of planes at the Renton factory from 47 to 57 per month. But the plant did not have enough electricians and mechanics to keep up with this pace. Pierson stated in his testimony:

> The planned factory overtime rate more than doubled. ... I knew that employee fatigue from excessive overtime inevitably produces process breakdowns—e.g., workmanship mistakes, missed inspection items, incomplete paperwork, or failure to follow established functional test procedures—all of which add considerable risk to the safety of airplanes.

He jumped over two levels of his chain of command in June 2018 to email the general manager, Scott Campbell, the following, which he read to the committee in 2019:

> I fully appreciate the importance of doing our best to meet ... delivery schedules. But there is a much, much higher risk [of] ... inadvertently imbedding [sic] safety hazard(s) into our airplanes. As a retired Naval Officer and former Squadron Commanding Officer, I know how dangerous even the smallest of defects can be to the safety of an airplane. Frankly right now all my internal warning bells are going off.

Pierson testified that he had "recommended that Boeing '[s]hut down the production line to allow our team time to regroup so we can safely finish the planes.'" Management ignored his concerns and increased the pressure on workers at the factory to speed up production in fall 2018. The immediate cause of the 737 Max disasters in 2018 and 2019 was that sensors on each plane gave faulty information to the flight deck that the 737 Max was going nose-up, which triggered the hidden software to push the plane nose down, causing them to crash. In a follow-up document which Pierson published in May 2021, he asks why brand-new sensors would fail, and answers by explaining how flight deck electronics are installed:

The proper installation of an airplane's electrical infrastructure is challenging work necessitating significant attention to detail. Factory workers are frequently required to perform intricate, physically demanding tasks in tight spaces while in awkward physical positions (overhead, bending, reaching, etc.).

Nine weeks of overtime had exhausted the staff. Furthermore, management got rid of the face-to-face meetings where the outgoing shift would inform the incoming shift which tasks were left unfinished. Pierson met personally with Campbell on July 18, 2018:

> I ... reiterated my recommendation that Boeing shut down the line to address product and worker-safety risks. In response, Mr. Campbell told me, "We can't do that. I can't do that." I pushed back, explaining that I had seen operations in the military shut down over less substantial safety issues, and those organizations had national security responsibilities. Mr. Campbell responded tersely, "The military isn't a profit-making organization."

When Lion Air Flight 610 crashed in October, Pierson retired. In every public appearance, he expressed his heartfelt condolences to the families for their loss. It is clear this tragedy hit the plant staff hard.

The Danger of Monopoly and a Financial Market Bubble

Many observers have attributed the decline in Boeing's production quality to its merger with McDonnell Douglas back in 1997. But it seems likely that the bubble in the stock market between 1997 and 2000 was the real cause of the change. That bubble was facilitated by ultra-low interest rates, similar to the ones we have now. Anytime a bubble emerges in financial markets, that is going to stimulate people to take money out of production and gamble it on bets in the stock market—especially if insiders are permitted to use company profits to rig the outcome of the bets.

The importance of the merger with McDonnell Douglas is that it meant Boeing had monopoly control of airline production in the United States. Other commentators have attributed Boeing's decline to fierce competition from Airbus, but that logic is faulty. When firms compete for market share, they are forced to produce better-quality products at lower cost—or they lose to the competition. When Airbus produced the extraordinarily fuel-efficient A320Neo, Boeing responded by adding larger, more efficient engines to its existing line of planes without modifying the design of the body. According to Bill Lazonick and Mustafa Erdem Sakinç, it would have cost Boeing $7 billion to redesign the plane from the ground up to accommodate the larger engines, but Boeing thought that was too expensive—which is ironic, since Boeing was spending about $7 billion per year on stock buybacks by 2015. Boeing's 737 Max did get plenty of orders, but that is because there wasn't much competition. Even now, Boeing is not planning to design a better plane in the near future. Yet Southwest and United are buying the flawed 737 Max with the too-big engines anyway. With only one other major airplane manufacturer in the world, and no other commercial jet manufacturer in the United States, Boeing has little financial incentive to create a better product, and instead spends massive amounts of money on manipulating political figures to pressure others to purchase its planes. Former presidents Barack Obama and Donald Trump both fought for the brand, and Boeing donated to President Joe Biden's inauguration. At this time, pressuring U.S. allies to purchase U.S. planes means pressuring them to purchase Boeing planes. And Boeing has lowered its price, too. The low price has resulted in Boeing hemorrhaging profits—the company lost millions in 2019 and billions in 2020 (see Figure 2). But nobody seems to care. Profits are falling, but the share price still rises (see Figure 4).

A share price that is impervious to the declining quality of the new products that the firm introduces is dangerous because it means that U.S. corporate executives will be rewarded even if they spend company profits in a way that destroys product quality. And that is in fact why this story is worth telling. Executives have a clear incentive to siphon cash from the large publicly held corporations they run in order to push up share price because that is how to make their stock options pay off. And they do.

FIGURE 4. BOEING SHARE PRICE, 2011 TO 2021

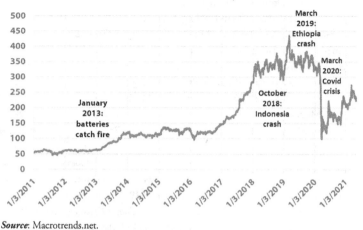

Source: Macrotrends.net.

Holding Boeing Accountable

The Puget Sound area has been the heart of Boeing production for so many decades that the community's level of aerospace machining skills is unparalleled. In a sign that the plane disasters of 2018 and 2019 did not cause Boeing's management to gain a new respect for the importance of employee dedication and skill, Boeing announced in October 2020 that it would no longer make the 787 Dreamliner in its Everett, Wash. plant, instead shifting all 787 production to the non-union North Charleston, S.C. plant.

In June 2021, after years of pressure from the families that lost loved ones in the two 737 Max crashes of 2018 and 2019, Bahrami finally retired from the FAA due in part to criticisms over safety and his close relationship with Boeing. President Biden would not have to look far to replace FAA leadership, because we know who has had the courage and integrity to speak out: Ed Pierson, the plant manager who spoke out about conditions at the 737 Max plant in Renton, Wash.; or perhaps Curtis Ewbank, a flight deck system specialist who was suspended by Boeing because he wrote to Congress in 2019 stating that Boeing knew there were flaws in the flight control systems of the 737 Max and the 777.

Until 1982 it was not legal for companies to purchase shares of their own stocks, and Senator Tammy Baldwin (D-Wisc.) introduced a bill in 2018 that would restore that common sense. Her Reward Work Act also calls for representatives of workers' unions to sit on company boards. Her bill was reintroduced in 2019, and it is currently stuck in committee. The Biden administration is currently lobbying to pass an infrastructure bill that will provide funds to a range of industries, and aviation companies are lobbying for their share. We learned in 2009 that bailing out banks without conditions was unwise. It would be wise to pass Senator Baldwin's bill prior to providing U.S. corporate executives with billions. Such a change would free engineers and machinists at U.S. corporations from corporate thuggery so that these new funds will finally be invested in people and production. ❑

Sources: Marc Anderson, "Dreamliner Okayed for Flight in US, but Battery Faces Scrutiny" in IEEE Spectrum, Institute of Electrical and Electronics Engineers, April 26, 2013 (spectrum.ieee.org); Will Jordan, "The Boeing 787: Broken Dreams," Al Jazeera Investigations, September 10, 2014 (available on YouTube); Dominic Gates, "Flawed analysis, failed oversight: How Boeing, FAA certified the suspect 737 MAX flight control system," *Seattle Times*, March 17, 2019 (seattletimes.com); Dominic Gates and Mike Baker, "Engineers say Boeing pushed to limit safety testing in race to certify planes, including 737 MAX," *Seattle Times*, March 5, 2019; Dominic Gates and Mike Baker, "The inside story of MCAS: How Boeing's 737 MAX system gained power and lost safeguards," *Seattle Times*, June 22, 2019; Dominic Gates, Steve Miletich, and Lewis Kamb, "Boeing rejected 737 MAX safety upgrades before fatal crashes, whistleblower says, *Seattle Times*, October 3, 2019; Mike Baker and Dominic Gates, "Lack of redundancies on Boeing 737 MAX system baffles some involved in developing the jet," *Seattle Times*, March 26, 2019; Dominic Gates, "Newly stringent FAA tests spur a fundamental software redesign of Boeing's 737 MAX flight controls," *Seattle Times*, August 1, 2019; Dominic Gates, "Boeing's 737 MAX crisis leaves it badly behind in 'arms race' for next decade's jets," *Seattle Times*, December 29, 2019; Dominic Gates, "Boeing has lost more than 800 orders for the 737 Max this year," *Seattle Times*, July 14, 2020; William Lazonick and Mustafa Erdem Sakinç, "Make Passengers Safer? Boeing Just Made Shareholders Richer," *American Prospect*, May 31, 2019 (prospect.org); Bill Lazonick and Eric Hopkins, "The Mismeasure of Mammon: Uses and Abuses of Executive Pay." Working Paper 49, Institute for New Economic Thinking, 2016 (ineteconomics.org); Philip E. Ross, "Boeing's Battery Blues" IEEE Spectrum, February 26, 2018; Kevin Hirten and Al Jazeera Investigative Unit, "The 'Fake' Boeing 787 Rollout," Al Jazeera, September 10, 2014 (aljazeera.com); Michael Lynn, *Birds of Prey: Boeing vs. Airbus*, Basic Books, 1997; Eamonn Fingleton, "Boeing Goes to Pieces" *The American Conservative*, January 8, 2014 (theamericanconservative.com); Michael Oneal, "Boeing CEO Fired Over Relationship," *Chicago Tribune*, March 7, 2005 (chicagotribune.com); "Making a Change," International Association of Machinists, May 2, 2019 (goiam.org); Robert G. Pushkar, "Comet's Tale," *Smithsonian Magazine*, June 2002 (smithsonianmag.com); Ali Bahrami employment history, Open Secrets Revolving Door project, accessed June 23, 2021 (opensecrets.org); Michael Sainato, "'It's Because We Were Union Members': Boeing Fires Workers Who Organized," *The Guardian*, May 3, 2019 (guardian.com); Peter Pae, "Ex-Boeing CFO gets jail for tanker scandal," *Chicago Tribune*, February 18, 2005 (chicagotribune.com); Leslie Wayne, "Ex-Pentagon Official Gets 9 Months for Conspiring to Favor Boeing," *New York Times*, October 2, 2004 (nytimes.com); Ed Pierson, "Boeing 737 Max--Still Not Fixed," Ed Pierson's website, January 20, 2021 (edpierson.com); Sen. Tammy Baldwin, sponsor, S.915 - Reward Work Act, 116th Congress, introduced March 27, 2019 (congress.gov); Ed Pierson, "Statement of Ed Pierson Before the House Transportation and Infrastructure Committee," December 19, 2019 (whistleblowers.org); David Koenig, "Boeing CEO David Calhoun waived pay but still collected $21 million in stock benefits," *Chicago Tribune*, March 8, 2021; Dominic Gates, "787 Battery Blew Up in '06 Lab Test, Burned Down Building," *Seattle Times*, January 29, 2013; David Koenig, "FAA Safety Official Retires; Was Criticized over Boeing Jet," Associated Press, June 2, 2021 (apnews.com); "Global aviation industry seeks share of U.S. infrastructure package," Reuters, March 31, 2021 (reuters.com); Gillian Rich, "United Airlines Buying Boeing 737 Max Jets, Airbus 321neo Planes In Biggest Aircraft Order In Decade," Investor's Business Daily, June 29, 2021 (investors.com).

Chapter 5

MARKET FAILURE I:
MARKET POWER

INTRODUCTION

With monopoly, we finally encounter a situation in which most economists, orthodox and otherwise, agree that unfettered markets lead to an undesirable outcome. If a firm is able to create a monopoly, it faces a downward-sloping demand curve—that is to say, if it reduces output, it can charge a higher price. Economists argue that competitive forces tend to undermine any monopoly, but failing this, they support antitrust policy as a backstop. The concept of monopoly not only points to an important failing of markets, but it opens the door to thinking about many possible market structures other than perfect competition, including oligopoly, in which a small group of producers dominates the market. Monopoly and oligopoly are examples of market structures in which firms wield "market power" (violating Tilly Assumption #1—see Article 1.2). That is, individual firms can affect the market-wide level of prices, profits, and wages. Market power alters how markets function from the ideal of perfect competition and delivers significantly less optimal results.

We begin this chapter with another seminal article by Chris Tilly, "Is Small Beautiful? Is Bigger Better? Small and Big Businesses Both Have Their Drawbacks" (Article 5.1). This article walks through the pluses and minuses of large and small businesses, and finds both wanting.

The financial crisis of 2007–2008 provided particularly egregious examples of what happens when we institute *laissez-faire* ("hands-off") regulatory regimes, especially in the area of finance, and the rise of Big Tech in recent decades, which is the focus of several articles in this chapter, provides another example. In "A Brief History of Mergers and Antitrust Policy" (Article 5.2), Edward Herman provides a long-term context for the discussion of monopoly, reviewing the history of U.S. antitrust law over the last century. He also criticizes economists for justifying a hands-off policy toward big business mergers over the last few decades.

Non-economists can be forgiven for being confused when economists of all stripes use the term "monopoly" beyond its narrow, technical definition (a market with only one seller) to refer more broadly to the kind of market power and reduced competition that comes with market concentration and reduction to just a few sellers or a few buyers. So the 2020 approval of a merger between telecom companies Sprint and T-Mobile will reduce the already monopolistic industry from four major wireless providers to just three—technically an "oligopoly," but still considered an example of a monopolized market. In "Monopoly Everywhere" (Article 5.3), Armağan Gezici shows how monopoly pervades more than just Big Tech in the U.S. and global economies, with extreme market concentration in industries ranging from pharmacy chains and home improvement stores to chemicals, seeds, and beer.

Next, in "Monopoly So Fragile" (Article 5.4), Cory Doctorow discusses hubris and monopoly. From an ill-fated cargo ship being stuck in the Suez Canal, to Charles Koch demonstrating the "visible hand" of market power, we find examples of our Masters of the Universe engaging in economic decision-making that is far less than "efficient."

Article 5.5 takes a much-needed break for drinks with "Hopsopoly," a review of the beer industry. Years of corporate consolidation at the top of the industry have led to a few gigantic firms dominating global beer brewing. These enormous brewers are also buying the distribution networks through which beer reaches consumers, giving them a powerful new lever of control over the market to fight the popularity of craft labels.

In "The Bankruptcy Games" (Article 5.6), Bill Barclay provides ample examples of the destructive nature of private equity. Emerging from the Great Lockdown of the Covid-19 pandemic, we find that during the time of crisis, private equity firms were profiteering from the crisis, destabilizing the economy, and stunting the recovery.

Next, in "How 'Big Oil' Works the System and Keeps Winning" (Article 5.7), Naomi Orsekes and Jeff Nesbit review the oil and gas industry's shifting strategies for maintaining their position as the center of the U.S. energy industry. From Rockefeller's strategizing prior to the breakup of Standard Oil to the industry's heavy ad spends to denying climate science and then shaping it, the history of the industry shows that strategic planning will be needed to out-game Big Oil.

Finally, in "Power, Wages, and Inequality" (Article 5.8), Arthur MacEwan reviews an uncharacteristically blunt Treasury Department report finding that employers have used a variety of means to lower compensation for their employees, by up to 20% in some markets. Tools like the threat of outsourcing, the concentration of industry leaving fewer employers to work for, automation, and requirements that workers not work for competitors or even discuss their pay have distorted labor markets enough that even the most pro-business arms of the government have to comment.

Discussion Questions

1. (Article 5.1) List the pros and cons of large and small businesses that Tilly discusses. How does this compare with the problems associated with market structure that your textbook mentions? Be sure to compare Tilly's list of small-business flaws with what your textbook has to say about small business.

2. (Articles 5.1 and 5.2) In what ways do these articles show that corporations control "the marketplace of ideas"? What are the possible consequences? What, if anything, should be done about it?

3. (Article 5.3) What are some examples of industries with enough market concentration to count as "monopolized"? What are the causes of market concentration in different industries? What are some of the negative consequences of market concentration?

4. (Article 5.4) What makes a monopoly "brittle"? What effect does hubris have on efficiency?

5. (Article 5.5) Describe the multiple layers of the beer industry, from production to wholesaling to retail. What limits has the Justice Department placed on Anheuser-Busch InBev's ability to buy and control distributors? Do you feel this will be enough to preserve consumer access to smaller craft labels?

6. (Article 5.6) What are "leveraged buyouts"? How do they relate to market power and market concentration?

7. (Article 5.6) Explain how the use of leverage can elevate the returns on an acquisition from "respectable" to "outstanding."

8. (Article 5.7) Describe how the energy industry has shaped the debate about energy products and climate policy, including through marketing and its role in climate science.

9. (Article 5.8) Summarize the various means by which employers are able to lower compensation for their workforce, according to the U.S. Treasury Department.

Article 5.1

IS SMALL BEAUTIFUL? IS BIG BETTER?
Small and big businesses both have their drawbacks.

BY CHRIS TILLY
July/August 1989, revised April 2002

Beginning in the late 1980s, the United States has experienced a small, but significant boom in small business. While big businesses have downsized, small enterprises have proliferated. Should we be glad? Absolutely, declare the advocates of small business. Competition makes small businesses entrepreneurial, innovative, and responsive to customers.

Not so fast, reply big business's boosters. Big corporations grew big because they were efficient, and tend to stay efficient because they are big—and thus able to invest in research and upgrading of technology and workforce skills.

But each side in this debate omits crucial drawbacks. Small may be beautiful for consumers, but it's often oppressive for workers. And while big businesses wield the power to advance technology, they also often wield the market power to bash competitors and soak consumers. In the end, the choices are quite limited.

Big and Small

Is the United States a nation of big businesses, or of small ones? There are two conventional ways to measure business size. One is simply to count the number of employees per firm. By this measure, small businesses (say, business establishments with less than 20 employees) make up the vast majority of businesses (Table 1). But they provide only a small fraction of the total number of jobs.

The other approach gauges market share—each firm's share of total sales in a given industry. Industries range between two extremes: what economists call "perfect competition" (many firms selling a standardized product, each too tiny to affect the market price) and monopoly (one business controls all sales in an industry). Economy-wide, as with employment, small businesses are most numerous, but control only a small slice of total sales. Sole proprietorships account for 73% of established businesses, far outnumbering corporations, which are 20% of the total (the remainder are partnerships). But corporations ring up a hefty 90% of all sales, leaving sole proprietors with only 6%. It takes a lot of mom-and-pop stores to equal General Motors' 1999 total of $177 billion in sales.

Industry by industry, the degree of competition varies widely. Economists consider an industry concentrated when its top four companies account for more than 40% of total sales in the industry (Table 2). At the high end of the spectrum are the cigarette, beer, and aircraft industries, where four firms account for the bulk of U.S. production.

No market comes close to meeting the textbook specifications for perfect competition, but one can still find industries in which a large number of producers compete for sales. The clothing and restaurant industries, for example, remain relatively competitive. Overall, about one-third of U.S. goods are manufactured in concentrated industries, about one-fifth are made in competitive industries, and the rest fall somewhere in between.

Beating the Competition

Those who tout the benefits of small, competitive business make a broad range of claims on its behalf. In addition to keeping prices low, they say the quality of the product is constantly improving, as companies seek a competitive edge. The same desire, they claim, drives firms toward technological innovations, leading to productivity increases.

The real story is not so simple. Competition does indeed keep prices low. Believe it or not, clothing costs us less—in real terms—than it cost our parents. Between 1960 and 1999, while the overall price level and hourly wages both increased nearly sixfold, apparel prices didn't even triple. And small businesses excel at offering variety, whether it is the ethnic restaurants that dot cities or the custom machine-tool work offered by small shops. Furthermore, however powerful small business lobbies may be in Washington, they do not influence the legislative process as blatantly as do corporate giants.

But those low prices often have an ugly underside. Our sportswear is cheap in part because the garment industry increasingly subcontracts work to sweatshops—whether they be export assembly plants in Haiti paying dollar-a-day wages, or the "underground" Los Angeles stitcheries that employ immigrant women in virtual slavery. Struggling to maintain razor-thin profit margins, small businesses cut costs any way they can—which usually translates into low wages and onerous working conditions.

"There is a rule of survival for small business," Bill Ryan, president of Ryan Transfer Corporation, commented some years ago. "There are certain things you want to have [in paying workers] and certain things you can afford. You had better go with what you can afford." Bottom line, workers in companies employing 500 or more people enjoy average wages 30% higher than their counterparts in small businesses.

Part of this wage gap results from differences other than size—unionization, the education of the workforce, the particular jobs and industries involved. But University of Michigan economist Charles Brown and his colleagues

TABLE 1: SMALL BUSINESS NATION?

Most businesses are small, but most employees work for big businesses

Company size (number of employees)	Percent of all firms	Percent of all workers
1–4	54%	6%
5–9	20%	8%
10–19	13%	11%
20–49	8%	16%
50–99	3%	13%
100–249	2%	16%
250–499	0.4%	10%
500–999	0.2%	7%
1,000 or more	0.1%	13%

Note: "Businesses" refers to establishments, meaning business locations.

Source: County Business Patterns, 1998.

controlled for all these differences and more, and still found a 10% premium for big business's employees. A note of caution, however: Other recent research indicates that this wage bonus is linked to long-term employment and job ladders. To the extent that corporations dissolve these long-term ties—as they seem to be rapidly doing—the pay advantage may dissolve as well.

Small business gurus make extravagant claims about small businesses' job-generation capacity. An oft-quoted 1987 report by consultant David Birch claimed that businesses with fewer than 20 employees create 88% of new jobs. The reality is more mundane: over the long run, businesses with 19 or fewer workers account for about one-quarter of net new jobs. One reason why Birch's statistics are misleading is that new small businesses are created in great numbers, but they also fail at a high rate. The result is that the *net* gain in jobs is much smaller than the number created in business start-ups.

For companies in very competitive markets, the same "whip of competition" that keeps prices down undermines many of competition's other supposed benefits. The flurry of competition in the airline industry following deregulation, for example, hardly resulted in a higher quality product. Flying became temporarily cheaper, but also less comfortable, reliable, and safe.

Technological innovation from competition is also more myth than reality. Small firms in competitive industries do very little research and development. They lack both the cash needed to make long-term investments and the market power to guarantee a return on that investment. In fact, many of them can't even count on surviving to reap the rewards: only one-third to one-half of small business start-ups survive for five years, and only about one in five makes it to 10 years. A 1988 Census Bureau survey concluded that in manufacturing, "technology use is positively correlated with plant size." Agriculture may be the exception that proves the rule. That highly competitive industry has made marked productivity gains, but its research is supported by the taxpayer, and its risks are reduced by government price supports.

Of course, the biggest myth about competition is that it is in any way a "natural state" for capitalism. In fact, in most markets the very process of competing for high profits or a bigger market share tends to create a concentrated, rather than a competitive, market structure.

TABLE 2: WHO COMPETES, WHO DOESN'T	
Industry	*Percent of sales by top four firms*
Light truck and utility vehicle manufacturing	96%
Breweries	91%
Home center stores	91%
Breakfast cereal manufacturing	78%
General book stores	77%
Credit card issuing	77%
Lawn equipment manufacturing	62%
Cable providers	63%
Computer and software stores	51%
Sock manufacturing	30%
Hotels and motels (excl. casinos)	22%
Gas stations	9%
Real estate	4%
Bars	2%

Source: 2002 Economic Census.

This process occurs in several ways. Big firms sometimes drive their smaller competitors out of business by selectively cutting prices to the bone. The smaller firms may lack the financial resources to last out the low prices. In the 1960s, several of IBM's smaller competitors sued it for cutting prices in a pattern that was designed to drive the smaller firms out of the market. Large corporations can also gain a lock on scarce resources: for example, large airlines like United and American operate the comprehensive, computerized information and reservation systems that travel agents tap into—and you can bet that each airline's system lists their own flights first. Or businesses may exploit an advantage in one market to dominate another, as Microsoft used its control of the computer operating system market to seize market share for its internet browser.

Other firms eliminate competitors by buying them out—either in a hostile takeover or a friendly merger. Either way, a former competitor is neutralized. This strategy used to be severely limited by strict antitrust guidelines that prohibited most horizontal mergers—those between two firms that formerly competed in the same market. The Reagan administration's team at the Justice Department, however, loosened the merger guidelines significantly in the early 1980s. Since that time, many large mergers between former competitors have been allowed to go through, most notably in the airline industry.

The Power of Concentration

Concentration, then, is as natural to market economies as competition. And bigness, like smallness, is a mixed bag for us as consumers and workers. For workers, bigness is on the whole a plus. Whereas competition forces small businesses to be stingy, big firms are on average more generous, offering employees higher wages, greater job security, and more extensive fringe benefits. In 1993, 97% of businesses with 500 or more workers provided health insurance; only 43% of businesses with 25 or fewer employees did so. Large firms also provide much more employee training. The strongest unions, as well, have historically been in industries where a few firms control large shares of their markets, and can pass along increased costs to consumers—auto, steel, and tires, for example. When profits are threatened, though, firms in concentrated markets also have more resources with which to fight labor. They are better able to weather a strike, oppose unionization, and make agreements with rivals not to take advantage of each other's labor troubles. In addition, large companies, not surprisingly, score low on workplace autonomy.

What about consumers? Corporations in industries where there are few competitors may compete, but the competitive clash is seldom channeled into prolonged price wars. The soft drink industry is a classic example. David McFarland, a University of North Carolina economist, likens soft drink competition to professional wrestling. "They make a lot of sounds and groans and bounce on the mat, but they know who is going to win," he remarked.

Coke and Pepsi introduce new drinks and mount massive ad campaigns to win market share, but the net result is not lower prices. In fact, because competition between industry giants relies more on product differentiation than price, companies pass on their inflated advertising expenses to consumers. In the highly concentrated breakfast cereal market, the package frequently costs more than the contents. And of every dollar you pay for a box, nearly 20 cents goes for advertising.

It takes resources to develop and market a new idea, which gives large corporations distinct advantages in innovation. The original idea for the photocopier may have come from a patent lawyer who worked nights in his basement, but Xerox spent $16 million before it had a product it could sell. RCA invested $65 million developing the color television. RCA could take this gamble because its dominance in the television market ensured that it would not be immediately undercut by some other firm.

But market dominance can also translate into complacency. The steel industry illustrates the point. A few major producers earned steady profits through the 1950s and 1960s but were caught off-guard when new technologies vaulted foreign steel-makers to the top of the industry in the 1970s. Similarly, when IBM dominated the computer industry in the 1960s and early 1970s, innovation proceeded quite slowly, particularly compared to the frantic scramble in that industry today. With no competitors to worry about, it was more profitable for IBM to sit tight, since innovation would only have made its own machines obsolete.

And large corporations can also put their deep pockets and technical expertise to work to short-circuit public policy. In the 1980s, when Congress changed corporate liability laws to make corporate executives criminally liable for some kinds of offenses, General Electric's lobbyists and legal staff volunteered to help draft the final regulations, in order to minimize the damage.

Big businesses sometimes hide their lobbying behind a "citizen" smokescreen. The largest-spending lobby in Washington, D.C. in 1986 was Citizens for the Control of Acid Rain. These good citizens had been organized by coal and electric utility companies to oppose tighter pollution controls. Along the same lines, the Coalition for Vehicle Choice (now, who could be against that?) was set up by Ford and General Motors in 1990 to fight higher fuel efficiency standards.

Concentration or Conglomeration

Over the last couple of decades, the mix of big and small businesses has changed, but the changes are small and—at first glance—contradictory. Over time, employment has shifted toward smaller firms, though the shift has been subtle, not revolutionary. Meanwhile, the overall level of industry-by-industry sales concentration in the economy has increased, but only slightly. As older industries become more concentrated, newer, more competitive ones crop up, leaving overall concentration relatively steady. In his book *Lean and Mean*, economist Bennett Harrison points out that there is actually no contradiction between the small business employment boomlet and big firms' continued grip on markets. Big businesses, it turns out, are orchestrating much of the flowering of small business, through a variety of outsourcing and subcontracting arrangements.

But if industry-by-industry concentration has changed little over the decades, conglomeration is a different matter. Corporate ownership of assets has become much more concentrated over time, reflecting the rise in conglomerates—corporations doing business in a variety of industries. Five decades ago, the top 200 manufacturing firms accounted for 48% of all sales in the U.S. economy. By 1993, the 200 biggest industrial businesses controlled 65% of sales.

Most mainstream economists see these groupings as irrelevant for the competitive structure of the economy. Antitrust laws place no restrictions on firms from different industries banding together under one corporate roof. But sheer size can easily affect competition in the markets of the individual firms involved. A parent company can use one especially profitable subsidiary to subsidize start-up costs for a new venture, giving it a competitive edge. And if one board of directors controls major interests in related industries, it can obviously influence any of those markets more forcefully.

A case in point is the mega-merger of Time Inc. and Warner, which will soon be joining with America Online. The resulting conglomerate will control massive sections of the home entertainment business, bringing together *Time*'s journalists, film and television producers, and authors, Warner's entertainment machine, which includes Home Box Office, the nation's largest pay television channel, and AOL's huge share of the internet access market. The conglomerate can influence the entertainment business from the initial point—the actors, writers, and directors—up to the point where the finished products appear on people's televisions or computers. Conglomeration also multiplies the political clout of large corportions. No wonder Disney and other entertainment giants have also hopped on the conglomeration bandwagon.

Choose Your Poison

Competition, concentration, or conglomeration: The choice is an unsavory one indeed. Opting for lots of tiny, competing firms leaves labor squeezed and sacrifices the potential technological advantages that come with concentrated resources. Yet the big monopolies tend to dominate their markets, charge high prices, and waste countless resources on glitzy ad campaigns and trivial product differentiation. And the big conglomerate firms, while not necessarily dominant in any single market, wield a frightening amount of political and economic power, with budgets larger than those of most countries.

Of course, we don't have much to say about the choice, no matter how much "shopping for a better world" we engage in. Market competition rolls on—sometimes cutthroat, other times genteel. Industries often start out as monopolies (based on new inventions), go through a competitive phase, but end up concentrating as they mature. As long as bigness remains profitable and the government maintains a hands-off attitude, companies in both competitive and concentrated industries will tend to merge with firms in other industries. This will feed a continuing trend toward conglomeration. Since bigness and smallness both have their drawbacks, the best we can do is to use public policies to minimize the disadvantages of each. ❏

Sources: Bennett Harrison, *Lean and Mean: The Changing Landscape of Corporate Power in the Age of Flexibility* (University of Michigan, 1994); Charles Brown, James Hamilton, and James Medoff, *Employers Large and Small* (Harvard University Press, 1990).

Article 5.2

A BRIEF HISTORY OF MERGERS AND ANTITRUST POLICY

BY EDWARD HERMAN
May/June 1998

Government efforts to prevent or break up monopolies are called antitrust policy. They assume that when a few companies dominate an industry, this weakens competition and hurts the public by reducing production, raising prices, and slowing technical advance. Antitrust has gone through cycles during this century. In some years, strongly pro-business presidencies (usually Republican) have allowed businesses to merge at will. These have often been followed by "reform" administrations, which tend to restrain, but not to reverse, concentrations of corporate power.

The federal government first took on a strong antitrust role with the Sherman Act of 1890, which outlawed monopoly and efforts to obtain it. In 1914 the Clayton Act also put restrictions on stock purchases and interlocking directorates that would reduce competition. This legislation responded to public anger and fears about "trusts," which brought separate firms under common control. Most notorious were Rockefeller's Standard Oil Trust and James Duke's American Tobacco Company, which employed ruthless tactics to drive their competitors out of business.

Early on the antitrust laws also treated organized labor as a "monopoly," and were used in breaking the Pullman strike in 1892. In 1908, the Supreme Court awarded damages to an employer against whom unions had organized a secondary boycott. This led to the Clayton Act exempting unions from its restrictions.

Otherwise, the federal government only minimally enforced the Sherman Act until President Theodore Roosevelt was elected in 1900. Then in 1911 the Supreme Court decided that both the Standard Oil and American Tobacco trusts were "bad trusts," and ordered their dismantling. But in 1920 the Court refused to condemn the U.S. Steel consolidation, because it was a "good trust" that didn't attack its smaller rivals. This began a long period when the Antitrust Division and the courts approved mergers that produced industries with a few dominant firms, but which were "well-behaved." And in the 1920s, Republicans virtually ended antitrust enforcement.

The Golden Age

President Franklin D. Roosevelt revived antitrust during 1938 to 1941, and antitrust law had its golden age from 1945 to 1974, fueled by a liberal Supreme Court, anti-merger legislation passed in 1950, and mildly progressive enforcement (though less so in the Republican years). During this period Alcoa's monopoly over aluminum production was broken (1945), and the Court found the tobacco industry guilty of "group monopoly" (1946), although the companies were only assessed a modest fine.

During the 1960s, when antitrust law blocked mergers among companies in the same industry, businesses adapted by acquiring firms in unrelated industries. Many such "conglomerate" mergers took place during 1964-68, when Lyndon Johnson was president. Companies like International Telephone and Telegraph, Ling-Temco-Vought, Gulf & Western, Tenneco, and Litton Industries grew rapidly.

The Reagan-Bush Collapse

Antitrust policy went into recession around 1974, then plunged during the presidencies of Ronald Reagan and George H. W. Bush. They aggressively dismantled antitrust, imposing drastic cuts in budgets and manpower, installing officials hostile to the antitrust mission, and failing to enforce the laws. During 1981-89, the Antitrust Division of the Justice Deptartment challenged only 16 of over 16,000 pre-merger notices filed with them.

Despite his high-profile contest with Microsoft, President Bill Clinton largely accepted the conservative view that most mergers are harmless. During his two terms, federal authorities approved or ignored many giant mergers. These included Westinghouse's buyout of CBS, the joining of "Baby Bells" Bell Atlantic and Nynex, and the combination of Chemical Bank and Manufacturers Hanover. During 1997 alone, 156 mergers of $1 billion or more, and merger transactions totalling more than *$1 trillion*, passed antitrust muster.

Clinton's failure to attack giant mergers rests nominally on the alleged efficiency of large firms and the belief that globalized markets make for competition. Federal Trade Commission head Robert Pitofsky said, "this is an astonishing merger wave," but not to worry because these deals "should be judged on a global market scale, not just on national and local markets."

But the efficiency of large size—as opposed to the profit-making advantages that corporations gain from market power and cross-selling (pushing products through other divisions of the same company)—is eminently debatable. And many markets are not global—hospitals, for example, operate in local markets, yet only some 20 of 3,000 hospital mergers have been subjected to antitrust challenge. Even in global markets a few firms are often dominant, and a vast array of linkages such as joint ventures and licensing agreements increasingly mute global competition.

The Clinton administration's failure to contest many giant mergers did not rest only on intellectual arguments. It also reflected political weakness and an unwillingness to oppose powerful people who fund elections and own or dominate the media. This was conspicuously true of the great media combinations—Disney and Cap-Cities/ABC, and TimeWarner and Turner—and the merger of Boeing and McDonnell-Douglas, which involved institutions of enormous power, whose mergers the stock market greeted enthusiastically.

The Economists Sell Out

Since the early 1970s, powerful people and corporations have funded not only elections but conservative economists, who are frequently housed in think tanks such as the American Enterprise, Hoover, and Cato Institutes, and serve as corporate consultants in regulatory and antitrust cases. Most notable in hiring economic consultants have been AT&T and IBM, which together spent hundreds of millions of dollars on their antitrust defenses. AT&T hired some 30 economists from five leading economics departments during the 1970s and early 1980s.

Out of these investments came models and theories downgrading the "populist" idea that numerous sellers and decentralization were important for effective competition (and essential to a democratic society). They claimed instead that the market can do it all, and that regulation and antitrust actions are misconceived. First, theorists showed that efficiency gains from mergers might reduce prices even more than monopoly power would cause them to rise. Economists also stressed "entry," claiming that if mergers did not improve efficiency any price increases would be wiped out eventually by new companies entering the industry. Entry is also the heart of the theory of "contestable markets," developed by economic consultants to AT&T, who argued that the ease of entry in cases where resources (trucks, aircraft) can be shifted quickly at low cost, makes for effective competition.

Then there is the theory of a "market for corporate control," in which mergers allow better managers to displace the less efficient. In this view, poorly-managed firms have low stock prices, making them easy to buy. Finally, many economists justified conglomerate mergers on three grounds: that they function as "mini capital markets," with top managers allocating capital between divisions of a single firm so as to maximize efficiency; that they reduce transaction costs; and that they are a means of diversifying risk.

These theories, many coming out of the "Chicago School" (the economics department at the University of Chicago), suffer from over-simplification, a strong infusion of ideology, and lack of empirical support. Mergers often are motivated by factors other than enhancing efficiency—such as the desire for monopoly power, empire building, cutting taxes, improving stock values, and even as a cover for poor management (such as when the badly-run U.S. Steel bought control of Marathon Oil).

Several researchers have questioned the supposed benefits of mergers. In theory, a merger that improves efficiency should increase profits. But one study by Dennis Mueller, and another by F. W. Scherer and David Ravenscraft, showed that mergers more often than not have reduced returns to stockholders. A study by Michael Porter of Harvard University demonstrated that a staggering 74% of the conglomerate acquisitions of the 1960s were eventually sold off (divested)—a good indication that they were never based on improving efficiency. William Shepherd of the University of Massachusetts investigated the "contestable markets" model, finding that it is a hypothetical case with minimal applicability to the real world.

Despite their inadequacies, the new apologetic theories have profoundly affected policy, because they provide an intellectual rationale for the agenda of the powerful. ❏

Sources: "Competition Policy in America: The Anti-Antitrust Paradox," James Brock, *Antitrust Bulletin*, Summer 1997; "The Promotional-Financial Dynamic of Merger Movements: A Historical Perspective," Richard DuBoff and Edward Herman, *Journal of Economic Issues*, March 1989; "Antimerger Policy in the United States: History and Lessons," Dennis C. Mueller, *Empirica*, 1996; "Dim Prospects: effective competition in telecommunications, railroads and electricity," William Shepherd, *Antitrust Bulletin*, 1997.

Article 5.3

MONOPOLY EVERYWHERE
Extreme market concentration goes beyond Big Tech.

BY ARMAĞAN GEZICI
January/February 2020

In October 2019, 47 attorneys general joined a New York-led antitrust investigation of Facebook with the concern that, according to New York's attorney general, "Facebook may have put consumer data at risk, reduced the quality of consumers' choices, and increased the price of advertising." Earlier the same year, a similar state investigation was launched into Google's advertising practices. At the federal level, the Justice Department is now investigating Facebook and Google, while the Federal Trade Commission is reported to have started an investigation of Facebook and Amazon.

However, concerns about tech companies' market power go beyond issues of data privacy and the way they handle disinformation and hate speech. The increased market power of tech companies and corporations in many other industries have also recently received great attention.

Many U.S. markets and industries are dominated by large corporations. According to data released in 2019 by the Open Markets Institute, Amazon dominates e-commerce, which was a $525.9 billion market in 2018 (around 10% of all retail sales in the U.S.). Google's Android and Apple's iOS hold a 99% share of the market for smart phone operating systems. In retail, Walmart controls 72% of all warehouse clubs and supercenters in the United States. The market shares of Home Depot and Lowe's in home improvement stores add up to a whopping 81%. Combined, Walgreens and CVS comprise 67% of all pharmacy sales.

Many large corporations have international operations and sizeable global market shares. In a world of high mobility for capital, large corporations are multinational. The locations of their headquarters seem irrelevant to their activities, except for regulatory and tax purposes. Global markets for agricultural seeds and chemicals, for instance, have long been dominated by three companies: Germany's Bayer, which bought U.S. giant Monsanto in 2018; DowDupont, which was the biggest chemical conglomerate in the world until 2019; and Syngenta, a Swiss-based company, which bought agricultural branches of two other global companies, Novartis and Zeneca, in the last decade, and is currently owned by a Chinese state-owned enterprise. Even in industries with a large variety of brands that seem to offer consumers a choice of many companies, many of those brands can be owned by just one company. For example, Anheuser-Busch Inbev, a holding company that was created in 2008 through the mergers of various American, Brazilian, British, and Belgian beer companies, holds a 41% share of the beer market in the United States and owns 55 different brands.

That capitalism would be dominated by monopolies has long been viewed as inevitable. But the process of monopolization has accelerated in the last couple of decades. Recent research shows that more than 75% of U.S. industries have become more concentrated and the average size of publicly traded firms has tripled since the mid-1990s. Studies also find that, during this period, profitability has risen for firms in industries that have experienced increases in concentration levels. Many of these larger and more profitable firms, such as those mentioned above, are found to be in the retail, information, transportation, and warehousing sectors of the economy. Thanks to their dominant positions in their respective markets, these companies can easily increase the prices of products or reduce the cost of production. Before giving examples of how they achieve higher price-cost margins and profitability, let us first take a look at one big change that allowed the current monopolization in the U.S. economy to occur.

Drivers Behind the Recent Wave of Monopolization

An increased number of mergers and acquisitions are visible in almost all industries. The lax enforcement of antitrust laws has much to do with the uptick in mergers and acquisitions. The Sherman Antitrust Act of 1890 and other legislation in the decades that followed outlawed any "restraints of trade" that reduce competition and any concentrations of market power that restrict interstate commerce. The Clayton Antitrust Act of 1914, for instance, explicitly blocked mergers that would result in more consolidated industries, and it also forbade interlocking directorates (membership on the board of directors of two or more firms by the same individual). Until the 1980s, these two acts and other industry-specific regulatory laws continued to keep the monopolization of U.S. industries in relative control.

However, after the 1980s, the Department of Justice adopted an entirely new framework for evaluating mergers and acquisitions: instead of considering the effects

---

Monopolies, Monopsonies, Oligopolies, Oligopsonies: A Note on Terminology

In a **perfectly competitive** marketplace, no single participant can influence prices because there are so many buyers and sellers, each of which represents only a very small portion of the total marketplace.

By contrast, a **monopoly** is a type of uncompetitive market in which there is only one seller. The classic textbook example is the post-WWII diamond monopoly held by the DeBeers company.

A **monopsony** is a type of uncompetitive market in which there is only one buyer. The classic example is a labor market in a one-factory town; the relationship Walmart has with many of its suppliers is another good example.

An **oligopoly** is an uncompetitive market with only a few sellers (like the U.S. markets for airline tickets), while an **oligopsony** is an uncompetitive market with only a few buyers (like the U.S. market for published books which is dominated by Amazon and Barnes & Noble, or the global market for unroasted coffee beans).

As a shorthand, I refer to all of types of uncompetitive markets as "monopolies," and those companies that enjoy market power as "monopolists." Some economics textbooks technically define an "oligopoly" as a market in which the 50% of the market is controlled by four or fewer firms, while others employ the looser definition noted above.

Note: This sidebar is excerpted from Sasha Breger Bush's "No Friendship in Trade," from the March/April 2015 issue of *Dollars & Sense*, which also appears in the 18th edition of *Real World Globalization*.

on smaller businesses and entrepreneurship, the focus solely shifted to whether a deal would promote "efficiency" and "consumer welfare," with a promise of lower prices. Yet, as seen in the figure below, it was not until the "new economy" boom" of the mid-1990s that the current spate of mergers and acquisitions took off. Over the last two decades, the number of mergers and acquisitions nearly tripled, surpassing the merger wave of the late 1960s and early 1970s. Rising pressures from shareholders in a rapidly financializing economy, coupled with low interest rates and high stock market valuations for mergers and acquisitions, were also responsible for creating the conditions for this expansion. Over the same period, the lack of intervention from regulatory agencies created incentives for firms to engage in mergers and acquisitions, which further reduced competition. A Supreme Court case in 2004 on Verizon's refusal to share its telephone network with its competitor, AT&T, was the perfect example of this paradigm shift. The court unanimously ruled in favor of Verizon, holding that the telecommunications company's "monopoly power" was "an important element of the free-market system," a display of "business acumen," and resulted in "the incentive to innovate."

NUMBER AND VALUE OF MERGERS AND ACQUISITIONS IN NORTH AMERICA, 1985 TO 2018

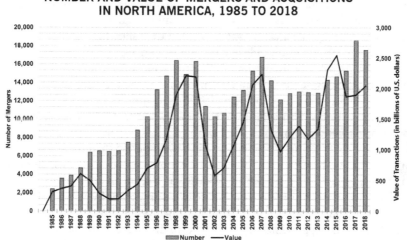

Dire Consequences of Monopsony and Monopoly Power

As antitrust legislation became more focused on pricing and consumer welfare, the regulatory control over monopolies has become further irrelevant for certain industries due to globalization. For the last two decades, the availability of cheap imports and the opportunity to produce globally in low-cost locations has allowed large companies to keep consumer prices relatively low. In particular, retail giants like Walmart have been able to dictate their own terms and prices with suppliers, acting as monopsonies (as one of few buyers) as well as monopolies (one of few sellers).

The dire consequences of monopsony power (see sidebar for a definition of "monopsony") have been particularly noticeable in labor markets. Since Walmart stores and Amazon warehouses are typically the largest employers in local labor markets for low-skilled labor, employees in these areas can be forced into low-paying jobs or precarious working conditions because they don't have any alternatives. In high-tech industries that rely on relatively high-skilled labor, non-compete agreements, where employers contractually constrain employees from joining competing companies for some period of time after they leave, are an important component of the U.S. labor market. It is true that monopsony cannot always be equated with monopoly power. Yet, especially in industries with low consumer prices, the monopsony power of these large companies in the labor market is as important as the use of cheap foreign inputs in keeping their prices low. While specific monopsonistic practices in the labor market vary greatly across industries, recent studies find that industries with a growing concentration of large firms are also those that pay a lower share of industry incomes to their employees.

A stronger case can be made for antitrust regulation in industries with monopolies that can charge extraordinarily high prices. The U.S. pharmaceutical industry is a case in point. Americans spend more on prescription drugs—average costs are about $1,200 per person per year—than anyone else in the world. What really sets the United States apart from most other countries is high prices. Unlike other nations, the United States doesn't directly regulate medicine prices. In Europe, the second-largest pharmaceutical market after the United States, governments negotiate directly with drug manufacturers to limit what their state-funded health systems pay. The U.S. pharmaceutical industry's response to demands for price regulation has been that it will kill innovation. U.S. drug companies claim that they need higher prices than those that prevail elsewhere so that the extra profits can be used to augment research and development (R&D) spending to continue to innovate and patent new drugs. This is far from the reality. A recent academic study shows 18 big pharmaceutical companies listed in the S&P 500 spent more on share buybacks and dividends ($516 billion) in a recent 10-year period than they did on R&D ($465 billion). As these companies spend their profits on boosting their stock performance, there has been a prominent productivity decline in drug discovery in the U.S. pharmaceutical industry. According to a working paper by William Lazonick for the Institute for New Economic Thinking, the overall clinical approval success rate declined from approximately one-in-five to approximately one-in-eight during the 2000s. In addition to allocating their profits to activities that maximize shareholder value, pharmaceutical companies also contribute to the decline in the diversity of ideas and research potential through mergers and acquisitions, since there are increasingly fewer companies to carry out research.

With Verizon, AT&T, T-Mobile, and Sprint as the only operators, the industry of wireless carriers in the United States is another distinctly high-price industry. U.S. mobile data pricing has been found to be four times more expensive than prices in many European Union countries, which have four wireless carriers instead of three. Economics textbooks tell us about how utilities, such as telecommunications, are "natural monopolies," yet the striking difference between the United States and the European Union can only be understood by differences in regulatory policy. While E.U. governments have forced companies to lease their networks to competitors at cost, U.S. regulators have not done so, allowing a formidable barrier against competitors. In October 2019, the U.S. Federal Communications Commission approved a merger between Sprint (owned by the Japanese conglomerate Softbank) and T-Mobile (owned by Germany's Deutsche Telekom), suggesting that the merger would "enhance competition." Those in opposition to this move estimate that the merger will result in the loss of potentially thousands of jobs in the short term and in the long term, according FCC commissioner Geoffrey Starks, "it will establish a market of three giant wireless carriers with every incentive to divide up the market, increase prices, and compete only for the most lucrative customers." When it comes to shopping for internet services, most Americans typically have just two choices. The first choice is internet providers, many of which—including CenturyLink, Frontier, and AT&T—started out as, or bought, phone companies, giving them control of one of the only physical lines that serve each household. Typically, the second is cable TV providers who, in turn, own the cables that enter almost every home. It appears that the telecommunications companies carve up territory to avoid competing with more than one other provider, effectively creating local monopolies.

Companies gaining market power through mergers and acquisitions claim they benefit consumers by providing better technologies and higher quality products at lower prices thanks to the synergies expected of mergers and acquisitions. This argument fits perfectly within the paradigm of neoliberal economics, which tends to see rising market power as the inevitable result of top firms gaining market share by adopting new technologies that increase their efficiency. In this view, monopolistic companies are "super-star firms" competing either on the merits of their innovations or superior efficiency; the important driver of the monopolization is technological change, not anticompetitive practices. These claims are hard to reconcile with the aggregate economic trends of the last two decades. Since the beginning of the 2000s, despite relatively high corporate profits, the U.S. economy has been in a period of slower capital accumulation marked by weak investment, declining labor share of income, and lower aggregate productivity growth, signaling a slowing down in technological progress and dynamism. This is the same period where a considerable rise of market concentration has occurred in most U.S. industries.

While the causes of increasing concentration and monopolization might be different across industries, there is good reason to doubt the claims of corporations and their advocates, and to look deeper into the negative consequences of increasing monopoly power for workers, suppliers, and consumers in the United States and across the globe. ❑

Sources: New York State Office of the Attorney General, "Attorney General James Gives Update On Facebook Antitrust Investigation," Oct. 22, 2019 (ag.ny.gov); Gustavo Grullon, Yelena Larkin, and Roni Michaely, "Are U.S. Industries Becoming More Concentrated?," *Review of Finance*, July 2019; William Lazonick et al., "U.S. Pharma's Financialized Business Model," Institute for New Economic Thinking Working Paper, July 13, 2017; Standish Fleming, "Pharma's Innovation Crisis, Part 2: How to Fix It," *Forbes*, Sept. 11, 2018 (forbes.com); Richard Gonzales, "FCC Clears T-Mobile/Sprint Merger Deal," NPR, Nov. 5, 2019 (npr.org); Chris Zubak-Skees and Allan Holmes, "How Broadband Providers Seem to Avoid Competition," The Center for Public Integrity, April 1, 2015 (publicintegrity.org).

Article 5.4

MONOPOLY SO FRAGILE

With industry consolidation, container ships have gotten too big to sail.

BY CORY DOCTOROW
July/August 2021

A big boat, the Ever Given, stuck in the Suez Canal, catastrophically disrupting global logistics—it wasn't just predictable, it was inevitable. For decades, the shipping industry has consolidated into just a few companies, and ships got bigger—too big to sail.

As economist and antitrust expert Matthew Stoller points out in a recent article, in 2000 the 10 biggest shippers controlled 12% of the market; today, it's more than 82%, and even that number is misleadingly rosy because of alliances among the megashippers that effectively turn them into one company.

The Suez crisis illustrates one of the less-appreciated harms of monopoly: All of us are dunderheads at least some of the time. When a single person wields a lot of unchecked power, their follies, errors, and blind spots take on global consequence.

The "efficiencies" of the new class of megaships—the Ever Given weighs 220 kilotons and is as long as the Empire State Building—were always offset by risks, such as the risk of getting stuck in a canal or harbor.

Despite this, a handful of executives were able to green-light their deployment. Either these execs didn't believe the experts, or they didn't care (maybe they thought they'd retire before the crisis), or they thought they could externalize the costs onto the rest of us.

Running a complex system is a game of risk mitigation: not just making a system that *works* as well as possible, but also making one that *fails* as well as possible. Build the Titanic if you must, but for the love of God, make sure it has enough lifeboats.

Monopolies are brittle. The ideology that underpins them is fundamentally eugenic: that there exist among us superbeings, genetic sports who were born with the extraordinary insights and genius that entitle them to rule over the rest of us. If we let nature run its course, according to this ideology, these benevolent dictators will usher in an era of global prosperity.

This is catastrophically, idiotically, manifestly wrong. First, even people who are very smart about some things are very stupid about other things.

Charles Koch took over his father's hydrocarbon empire in the late 1960s and correctly concluded that the industry was being held back by a focus on short-term profits. He made a series of long-term bets on new production technologies and grew the business a thousandfold.

Being patient and farsighted made Koch one of the richest people in world history—and one of the most influential. He pioneered a kind of slow, patient policy entrepreneurship, investing in a network of think tanks that mainstreamed his extremist ideology over several decades.

And yet, this man who became a billionaire and changed the character of global politics with his foresight, has managed to convince himself that there is no climate emergency. That patience, foresight, and cool weighing of probabilities have gone out the window completely.

Smart people are often fools (so are regular people). History is full of them. Take William Shockley, the Nobel Prize-winning inventor of silicon transistors who failed in industry because he became obsessed with eugenics and devoted his life to a racist sterilization campaign.

Moreover, fools sometimes succeed. Take Mark Zuckerberg, who justified his self-serving "real names" policy for Facebook users (which makes it easier to target ads by banning pseudonyms) by claiming that any attempt to present yourself in different ways to different people is "two-faced."

That is a genuinely idiotic thing to believe: Presenting yourself differently to your lover, your parents, your toddler, your boss, and your friends isn't "two-faced," it's human. To do otherwise would be monstrous.

But even when monopolists aren't idiots, they are still dangerous. The problem with Zuckerberg isn't merely that he's uniquely unsuited to being the unaccountable czar of 2.6 billion peoples' social lives—it's that *no one* should have that job.

Monopolists all have their own cherished idiocies (as do the rest of us), but they share a common pathology: the ideology, popularized by Thomas Friedman and others, that "efficiency" is the highest virtue.

The whole basis for 40 years of tolerating (even encouraging) monopolies is the efficiencies of scale that come from consolidating power into a few hands, and the shared interests that arise from a brittle interdependence.

Who would go to war with the trading partner that controls the world's supply of some essential item?

This was always, predictably, a system that would work well but fail badly. Clustering the world's semiconductor production in Taiwan made chips cheap and plentiful, sure. But then the 1999 Taiwan earthquake shut down all of the world's computer sales. There are plenty of examples like this that Stoller lists in his article, for instance, a single vaccine factory in England shuts down in 2004 and the United States loses half of its flu vaccines.

Despite the increasing tempo of supply-chain crises that ripple out across the world, we have allowed monopolists to "take the fat out of the system at every joint," as Thomas Friedman advocated in a 2005 interview about his book *The World Is Flat*, setting up a thousand crises among us and yet to come.

Bed makers can't make mattresses for want of foam. RV manufacturers can't get enough "fridges, air conditioners, and furniture" to meet orders, according to Stoller. Often, the pivotal items are obscure and utterly critical, like the $1 flat-steel form ties, without which home construction halts.

"For the want of a nail, the shoe was lost," starts the centuries-old proverb. We've understood that tightly coupled systems have cascading failures since the 13th century. "Resiliency" is inefficient—but only if you ignore what happens when brittle systems fail.

Every monopolist necessarily shares an ideology that elevates brittleness to a virtue. They must, because monopolies are brittle. One foolish mistake, one ship wedged in a canal, one delusive denial of climate change, and we all suffer.

Every monopolist believes in their own infallibility. They must, because to have someone as fallible as me or you in charge of the world's social media or shipping or flat steel form ties is otherwise a recipe for disaster.

Of all the dangerous things monopolists are wrong about, this belief in their own inability to be wrong is the most dangerous. ❑

Sources: Matt Stoller, "What We Can Learn from a Big Boat," BIG Newsletter, March 28, 2021 (mattstoller.substack.com); Daniel H. Pink, "Why the World Is Flat: The playing field is being leveled, says globalization guru Thomas Friedman—from Shanghai to Silicon Valley, from al Qaeda to Wal-Mart," *Wired*, May 1, 2005 (wired.com); Amanda Anderson, "'Never experienced a shortage like this': RV industry warns trailers could be hard to find this summer," CTV News Edmonton, March 27, 2021 (edmonton.ctvnews.ca); "Shortage in Form Ties Could Create Temporary Shutdown in Residential Construction, says CFA," press release, Concrete Foundations Association, March 15, 2021 (forconstructionpros.com).

Article 5.5

HOPSOPOLY
Global beer mergers reach a new level.

BY ROB LARSON
January/February 2017

When major beer label Budweiser announced that they would rename their product "America" through the 2016 U.S. election, it raised droll hackles from a variety of observers. George Will suggested in the conservative *National Review* that the beer was less than fully American because it was produced by a foreign-owned firm, an irony also observed in the more liberal *Washington Post*. John Oliver's HBO staff did what most U.S. media did in 2016, and took the opportunity to give more TV time to the Trump campaign, in this case to mock Trump's taking credit for the name change. Most commenters counted themselves clever for being aware the Bud label is foreign-owned, but all of them missed the real point: It's not that "America" is foreign-owned, but that it's owned by a brand-new global semi-monopoly that perfectly represents the power-mongering of neoliberal capitalism.

Macrobrew

There are indeed American men and women who will tell you it broke their hearts when in 2008 Anheuser-Busch was bought by the InBev transnational. InBev is itself a product of the merged Belgian InterBrew giant and the Brazilian conglomerate AmBev, as Barry Lynn reviews in his book on market concentration, *Cornered*. Lynn observes that this merger, along with 2007's union of Miller and Coors under South African Breweries' control, meant that beer-loving America was subject to corporate decisions made further and further away, and thus "basically reduced to reliance on a world-bestriding beer duopoly, run not out of Milwaukee or St. Louis but out of Leuven, Belgium, and Johannesburg, South Africa."

And now, just Belgium! Unmentioned in any of the recent rash of commentary was that "America's" owner AB InBev itself announced this year a $108 billion purchase of SAB Miller, which together would sell about 30% of the world's beer, including 45% of total beer sales in the United States. The merger would create a "New World of Beer" in which AB InBev will have "operations across multiple continents and a host of countries," as the business press described it. The *Financial Times* projected that the combined global giant is expected "to control almost half the industry's total profits." SAB Miller will also benefit from bringing its operations under AB InBev's umbrella, since the latter pays an incredibly low effective tax rate in its Belgian corporate home, paying well under 1% on its nearly $2 billion profit in 2015.

Of course, regulators have to approve large-scale mergers in each of the many, many countries in which the merged empires do business. The European Union's competition laws, and antitrust law in the United States, are meant to bring legal action against monopolists, or firms planning to merge into something close to one. But in the neoliberal era, a capital fact is the steep drop-off of anti-monopoly suits—the business press has reported that, from President Ronald Reagan to President Barack Obama, the repeated promise to aggressively enforce limits to market concentration "hasn't worked out that way." And indeed, for the proposed hopsopoly the news is so far, so good. In addition to Australia and South Africa, the European Union is set to allow the consolidation, China's Ministry of Commerce okayed the plan and the U.S. Justice Department approved the $100 billion deal, with reservations (see below).

These approvals require certain divestments—sales of pieces of the corporate empires before, or just after, they merge. Such sales can keep market concentration numbers just low enough for regulators to sign off. Yet these deals are so big that the divestments are *themselves* concentrating the market—Molson Coors is buying AB InBev's share of their currently joint-owned MillerCoors for $12 billion. These spun-off assets mean Molson Coors will itself have a 25% share of the U.S. beer market, second only to the new SAB-AB InBev combination. In the same way, Constellation Brands became the third-largest American brewer by buying several beer labels from the Mexican firm Grupo Modelo back in 2013, when InBev was buying it and needed to divest a few brands to appease regulators.

Tapping the Craft Keg

Smaller-batch craft beers produced by independent microbrewers provides limited escape from monopolized beer. Constellation paid a full $1 billion for the California craft brewer Ballast Point, in a move the *Wall Street Journal* suggested "signals that the craft-beer industry, which has a roughly 10% market share in the United States, has crossed a threshold and become a big business that large brewers expect to continue to grow in the years to come." The growth potential of microbrews is a valuable opportunity for the majors, especially considering that beer's share of total U.S. alcoholic-beverage spending fell in 2015 for the sixth straight year, and not just to its perennial foe—wine—but also to liquor as the craft cocktail trend flourishes. And this is in spite of the industry spending over a billion (yes, billion) dollars annually just on TV ads.

This all means that the future growth center of microbrews is increasingly essential to the industry majors, as are export markets. But the growth hopes for microbrews are dimming. The industry must look fearfully at the slowing growth of craft labels, with a mid-single digit growth rate in 2015–16, down from double digits in previous years. What growth there is, is concentrated in the labels held by the industry giants. Market observers notice that while niche labels are still taking market share from the majors, albeit more slowly, "AB InBev's own U.S. craft portfolio … increased sales 36% in the first half [of 2016]. After a spate of acquisitions, most notably that of Goose Island, AB InBev is the third-largest craft brewer in the country," although that reflects the fragmented, unconcentrated contours of that market segment. The *Journal* notes, "Craft beer accounts for just 1% of the company's total volume," still an important future growth center for what they call "big beer."

That slowing craft growth is having big effects on the markets for beer ingredients, especially hops, the flowering body of the *Humulus lupulus* plant used to give beers their bitter or sweet flavors. Hops suppliers haven't been able to keep up with spiking demand from craft brews for a wide array of obscure varieties, despite a growing proportion of U.S. hops growers producing for small labels since the global brands' hops are now mostly grown in Germany. The slow-growing plant, and the fast-changing demand for particular varieties have limited the ability of hops growers to keep pace, and with the market's own growth now slowing, the fear is rising of an oversupply in the industry if crops are only harvested as demand fades. The very small size of the many craft labels, and their uncertain prospects, means farmers are often resistant to committing their production to obscure microbrewers.

Growth-seeking is also driving the major brewers toward foreign markets, as the *New York Times*' DealBook feature observes that "in China, Anheuser-Busch InBev and SABMiller are betting on premium products," with "the two beer behemoths" buying up large stakes in China's top-selling brands. "Together, the international brewers account for about one-third of the overall beer market in China. As they pursue a merger, given their dominance, Anheuser-Busch InBev and SABMiller are expected to prune their portfolio in China to keep regulators happy," and indeed the popular Snow brand was ultimately sold off to a Chinese state-owned company.

These different growth prospects are all threatened by a gradual worldwide reconsideration of the health benefits of modest alcohol consumption. While public health agencies had for years considered small amounts of alcohol to have some health upsides (mostly heart-related), the emerging view is that these benefits are outweighed by health risks, leading to a growing number of health agencies amending their guidance to recommend lower levels of consumption.

Economies of Ale

Scale economies occur when a firm's per-unit costs decrease as the scale of production increases. Typically observed in industries, like manufacturing, that have high upfront costs, economies of scale arise from "spreading" a large starting investment over a growing amount of output. A brewery that cost $10 million to build, and which produces one million cans or bottles in a year, would have a per-unit fixed cost of $10. Producing 10 million cans, the per-unit fixed cost is just a dollar per can. The big costs of brewing tanks, sturdy equipment for mixing the ground grains and the flavorful hops, the cost of the actual brewery structure itself—all add to a brewery's starting investment and create the potential for scale economies.

Economies of scale are usually observed at the plant or factory level, but can also arise at higher levels of operation, including in administration. For example, two large companies may merge and then lay off one of their human resources departments, if one computerized HR office can handle all the employees at the new, merged firm. But these returns to scale, associated with a higher level of market concentration, are often counterbalanced by increasing layers of corporate bureaucracy and the challenges of managing large commercial empires.

So returns to scale constitute strong incentives for firms to grow, both in dollar terms and in market share, gaining scale and profitability. They do have limits, but once firms have reached large and cost-efficient sizes they are often happy to go on growing or merging, in order to gain more market power. The result is that in many industries, from the manufacturing sector to telecommunications to financial services, rich competitive markets give way over time to other market structures, including the few large companies of an oligopoly or the single colossal monopolist.

As with other industries, from tobacco to chemicals, the industry is pushing back in significant part by getting directly involved in the research process. A former cigarette-industry executive now working for booze giant Diageo claimed in the press that a study critical of alcohol advertising was "junk science" and said, "We push back when there are dumb studies." This raises again the prospect of "science capture," the growing phenomenon of private entities with a material interest attempting to influence the scientific process. Indeed, some are funding their own research, the findings of which unsurprisingly support the economic activity of the industry doing the funding.

High-Proof Political Economy

The corporate beer empires aren't shy about using their newly enlarged market power, either. *Cornered* author Barry Lynn recounts a classic episode in which Anheuser-Busch targeted Boston Beer, the owner of Sam Adams:

> For reasons still not entirely clear, the giant firm unleashed a devastating, multifront assault by armies of lawyers, lobbyists, and marketers who accused Boston Beer (to the government and to the public through the media) of deceptive packaging. Anheuser-Busch then followed up with an even more devastating second assault, in which it locked Boston Beer products out of the immensely powerful distribution networks that it controls. Ultimately, an arbitrator rejected all of the megafirm's contentions, and Boston Beer survived to brew another day, but the company, less than 1% the size of Anheuser-Busch, was left on the verge of bankruptcy.

Boston Beer remains the second-largest U.S. craft brewer, but the industry has not forgotten this power play.

And today's even-bigger corporations are brewing up new retail-level strategies. The *Journal* reports that AB InBev had planned to "offer some independent distributors in the U.S. annual reimbursements of as much as $1.5 million if 98% of the beers they sell are AB InBev brands." The money would come in the form of the conglomerate footing the bill for distributors' share of marketing costs, like displays at the retail level. The move has craft brewers crying foul, and understandably, since it leaves independents with a pitifully small fraction of store display space and promotion dollars left for them to fight over. The incentive plan also requires that distributors only carry craft brewers that operate below certain low thresholds of annual production, which most do.

The importance of this corporate proposal lies in the middle-man layer of the industry, created by state laws at the end of Prohibition. Beer brewers must sell their output to distributors, who then sell it on to the retailers where you pick up a six-pack. While there are hundreds of distributors in the United States, most are under agreement to sell exclusively either product from AB InBev or MillerCoors. But in addition to deals like these, the beer manufacturers are also able to buy and operate their own distributors—the state of California is investigating AB InBev after it bought two distributors in the state, with concerns about the giant declining to carry independent micros. The company presently owns 21 distributors in the United States and has further used its gigantic revenues to continue buying up independent brewers like Goose Island—now part of the global company and thus available to AB InBev's distributors—on its terms.

Raise a Glass

Popular opposition to the megamerger has been scattered, in a year punctuated by billion-dollar mergers in agriculture, chemicals, insurance, and drugs. In South Africa, a market important enough to require merger clearance as a condition of the deal (and the "SA" in "SABMiller"), a labor union objected to the deal's terms. Among those terms are rules covering a 2010 issue of SAB shares to workers and retailers, which would have matured in 2020. The union membership prefers to "cash out" earlier, or be granted an up-front payment in addition to the existing shares. Labor opposition to market concentration is always notable, although this case revolves more around the treatment of the workforce on a quite specific compensation issue, rather than an objection to capital accumulation in general.

The ultimate approval of the merger by the South Africa's Competition Tribunal was significantly a foregone conclusion. As *Bloomberg* observes, South Africa's bond rating has been downgraded, reflecting world investor fear of policy changes not to their advantage. This meant that the country's leader, President Jacob Zuma of the African National Congress (ANC), was especially eager to approve the megadeal, all the more after recent poor showings for the ANC in local races. This led to unusually prompt action by Zuma—*Bloomberg* noted in March 2016 that "SABMiller itself is still waiting for approval to merge its African soft-drink bottling assets, 15 months after it filed the request."

A number of other unions represent organized brewery workers in the United States, including the Machinists, the Operating Engineers, the Auto Workers, and the International Brotherhood of Teamsters (IBT). The IBT lodged an objection to a particular feature of the deal, writing a letter to the Attorney General requesting antitrust scrutiny of the related closure of the "megabrewery" operated by MillerCoors in Eden, N.C. While MillerCoors is to be sold to Molson as part of the deal, the closure does affect the market significantly, particularly since the huge facility produces 4% of all U.S. beer output, making the reduction more than can be compensated for at other facilities. This significant tightening of supply raised the question of antitrust violation to the IBT, due both to the further concentration of the market but also to the fact that the facility was essential for rival brewer Pabst, which for years has not brewed its own hipster swill but has had it produced by Miller under contract at the Eden brewery. Miller had previously indicated it has no interest in maintaining the deal past its expiration. The U.S. legal settlement appears to make no mention of this issue, but Pabst is now suing Miller over the terms of their brewing agreement, and the IBT lawsuit against Miller continues. For their part, unions from the acquiring company have also been skeptical, noting that the giant corporation has cut its Belgian workforce in half, to just 2,700 over 10 years. The *Times* reports, "They also predict that the company will load up on debt to buy SABMiller, leading to pressure for further cutbacks."

Beyond labor, the large and still-growing craft sector of the marketplace has looked with suspicion on industry consolidation for some time and had a clear eye of the stakes, if not typically engaging in action beyond contacting legislators or regulators. The press in brewery-heavy St. Louis describes how craft independents view the deal "warily," as "smaller breweries remain worried a larger A-B InBev will have more influence on what beers retailers stock on their shelves and hamper access to supplies such as hops." They also see influence-building intent behind legislation the corporations have supported, like a bill passed by the Missouri state legislature allowing brewers to lease large commercial coolers to retailers. Craft brewers oppose the governor signing the bill, "arguing only large brewers such as A-B InBev can afford to buy the coolers, which will likely be filled by retailers with A-B brands."

Likewise, industry rag *All About Beer Magazine* has expressed enormous skepticism of not just the new megadeal but the whole history of consolidation in the industry, in the United States and the United Kingdom. In a beautiful expression of widespread market-skepticism, Lisa Brown wrote, "This is about a company that has historically used the strategy of controlling and purchasing the wholesale tier of the industry now getting much more influence and potential control of that sector, while also gaining a lot more spending money for lawyers and lobbying."

Reflecting these popular sentiments, the Brewers Association—the industry group representing the many small craft brewers and independent labels—requested significant safeguards from the Department of Justice should the deal clear. It wanted an end to AB InBev's preferential distribution and limits to its "self

---

Opiate of the Masses

Fittingly, the first great scholar of capital concentration, Karl Marx, was a product of the beer-loving German people. Marx pioneered the study of capitalism's near-universal gravitational tendency, and for today's economy we have an analytical vocabulary to help understand the growth of capital.

- Concentration of capital, the growth of market share by a few big firms within a market.
- Consolidation, the growth of corporate capital by buying firms in separate industries.
- Capital accumulation, the overall growth in the capital stock of an economy.

Marx wrote in his giant classic study, *Capital*, that "the laws of this centralization of capitals, or of the attraction of capital by capital," depended ultimately on "the scale of production. Therefore, the larger capitals beat the smaller. It will further be remembered that, with the development of the capitalist mode of production, there is an increase in the minimum amount of individual capital necessary to carry on a business under its normal conditions." In other words, fancier technology and more expensive investments make it harder for small brewers to operate at the low costs of established firms.

Many more conservative economists have resisted this conclusion, and insisted that free markets have an enduringly competitive character, even in older industries. Friedrich Hayek, the Austrian economist and one of the conservative world's most revered thinkers, derided the argument that "technological changes have made competition impossible in a constantly increasing number of fields ... This belief derives mainly from the Marxist doctrine of the 'concentration of industry.'"

Marx might reply by raising a glass in toast, filled with amber-hued global corporate beer.

distribution" plans, since influence over distributors gives big brewers an additional potential lever of power over retailers. Evidently the DOJ heard the complaints, because happily for today's craft drinkers the department's allowance of the merger came with numerous conditions on top of the planned divestments, with some directed at these kinds of maneuvers. The department limited AB InBev from enforcing distributor incentive deals (like the one above), and crucially imposed a cap of 10% on the proportion of AB InBev's sales that can be sold through wholly-owned distributors. This is intended to limit the giant's influence over distribution and hopefully reserve shelf space for independent labels.

The agency further put the Big Beer giant under a new requirement to submit for approval all acquisitions of craft beers for the next 10 years, benefiting consumers desiring a wider range of brews, and preserving more successful independents from corporate concentration. These requirements, resulting from demands for redress from retailers and craft brewers, do sound satisfyingly stringent. However, the firm retains enormous market power, is strategically positioned to grow in developing markets (especially in Africa), and can be expected to work to undermine or evade these rules in the future. As always, antitrust rules keep oligopoly form maturing into full monopoly, and impose meaningful limits on anticompetitive practices, at least when enforced aggressively. That enforcement tends to ebb and flow however, and it's unclear how the Trump administration will prioritize breaking up giant mergers with its emerging neoliberal shape.

With the worldwide trend for tighter corporate ownership and global oligopoly, it's the investor class that's getting fat off our beer. A more aggressive labor movement of organized malters and brewers, reinforced by irate craft consumers, could resist further job cuts and demand bolder regulatory roadblocks to this consolidation. Or better yet, rather than choosing your poison between super-concentrated markets or moderately concentrated ones, an incensed and tipsy anticapitalist movement could take over these global giants' facilities and brew the beers themselves.

There are few consumers who enjoy shop-talk about their personal favorites more than beer drinkers, providing a natural opportunity for sharing this and other episodes of capitalist globalization. Raising consciousness about capitalism's predations, even in beer, could encourage a movement to socialize brewing. In a democratically managed economic system, the freewheeling ethos of the microbrew movement would be free to flourish without being blackballed out of the market by the majors, or bought out if they manage to succeed.

Now *that* would be a happy hour! ❑

Sources: Tripp Mickle, "Budweiser to Rebrand Beer to America Through Elections," *Wall Street Journal*, May 11, 2016 (wsj.com); George Will, "This Bud's for You, America," *National Review*, May 18, 2016; Travis M. Andrews, "Budweiser seeks approval to be called 'America' this summer," *Washington Post*, May 10, 2015 (washingtonpost.com); Tripp Mickle and Saabira Chaudhuriab, "InBev's SABMiller Deal Still Faces Hurdles," *Wall Street Journal*, Nov. 11, 2015; Barry Lynn, *Cornered: The New Monopoly Capitalism and the Economics of Destruction* (John Wiley & Sons, 2009); James Fontanella-Khan and Patti Waldmeir, "China brewer sale clears path to AB InBev's £71bn SABMiller deal," *Financial Times*, March 2, 2016 (ft.com); James Kanter, "Anheuser-Musch InBev Aims Its Tax-Trimming Skills at SABMiller," *New York Times*, Oct. 19, 2015 (nytimes.com);

Leonard Silk, "Economic Scene; Antitrust Issues Facing Reagan," *New York Times*, Feb. 13, 1981; Brent Kendall, "Justice Department Doesn't Deliver on Promise to Attack Monopolies," *Wall Street Journal*, Nov. 7, 2015; Foo Yun Chee and Martinne Geller, "EU regulators to conditionally clear AB Inbev, SABMiller deal," Reuters, May 20, 2016; Tripp Mickle and Saabira Chaudhuriab, "SABMiller Board Backs AB InBev's Higher Offer," *Wall Street Journal*, July 29, 2016; Tripp Mickle and Brent Kendall, "Justice Department Clears AB InBev's Takeover of SABMiller," *Wall Street Journal*, July 20, 2016; Gina Chon and Scheherazade Daneshkhu, "AB InBev-SABMiller merger critics in US seek concessions," *Financial Times*, Dec. 8, 2015; Tripp Mickle, "Constellation Brands to Buy Craft-Beer Maker for $1 Billion," *Wall Street Journal*, Nov. 16, 2015; Tripp Mickle, "Cocktails Sip Away at Beer's Market Share," *Wall Street Journal*, Feb. 15, 2016; Nathalie Tadena, "Bud Light is a Heavier TV Ad Spender than its Peers," *Wall Street Journal* CMO TOday blog, May 22, 2014; Trefis Team, "Does The Declining U.S. Beer Trend Spell Doom For Brewers?," *Forbes*, June 29, 2015 (forbes.com); Stephen Wilmot, "Why Craft Brewing Slowdown Won't Benefit Big Beer," *Wall Street Journal*, Aug. 26, 2016; Tripp Mickle, "Trouble Brewing in the Craft Beer Industry," *Wall Street Journal*, Sept. 27, 2016; Amie Tsang and Cao Li, "China embraces Craft Beers, and Brewing Giants Take Notice," Dealbook, *New York Times*, Jan. 15, 2016; Justin Scheck and Tripp Mickle, "With Moderate Drinking Under Fire, Alcohol Companies Go on Offensive," *Wall Street Journal*, Aug. 22, 2016; Tripp Mickle, "Craft Brewers Take Issue With AB InBev Distribution Plan," *Wall Street Journal*, Dec. 7, 2015; Tripp Mickle, "Anheuser Says Regulators Have Questioned Pending Distributor Buyouts," *Wall Street Journal*, Oct. 12, 2015; Tripp Mickle, "AB InBev Defends SABMiller Buy to Senate," *Wall Street Journal*, Dec. 8, 2015; Tripp Mickle, "AB InBev Facing Union Opposition to SABMiller Acquisition," *Wall Street Journal*, June 3, 2016; Janice Kew, "Zuma Appeal to Business Bodes Well for AB InBev-SAB Beer Merger," Bloomberg News, March 15, 2016; James P. Hoffa, president, International Brotherhood of Teamsters, letter to U.S. Attorney General Loretta Lynch, June 6, 2016 (teamster.org); Bruce Vielmetti, "Historic brewing names Pabst, MillerCoors locked in legal battle," (Milwaukee) *Journal Sentinel*, May 5, 2016 (jsonline.com); Lisa Brown, "Craft brewers eye merger of A-B InBev and SABMiller warily," *St. Louis Post-Dispatch*, June 26, 2016 (stltoday.com); Lew Bryson, "Mega-Merger? How About No?," *All About Beer Magazine*, May 17, 2016; Brewers Association press release, "Brewers Association Statement on AB InBev Acquisition of SABMiller," July 20, 2016; U.S. District Court for the District of Columbia, United States of America v. Anheuser-Busch InBev SA/NV, and SABMiller plc, July 20, 2016; Karl Marx, *Capital*, vol. 1, ch. 25 (1867); Friedrich Hayek, *The Road to Serfdom* (1944).

Article 5.6

THE BANKRUPTCY GAMES

Private equity cashes in on the Covid-19 slump.

BY BILL BARCLAY
November/December 2020

In the first six months of the Covid-19 slump, unemployment levels in the retail trade and oil and gas extraction were some of the highest among all U.S. industries, eclipsed only by leisure and hospitality. Certainly, this was bad news for these two industries and their employees—but not for all of them. Despite what we have been repeatedly told, we are not all in this together. The strategic use of Chapter 11 bankruptcy filings has actually been good for some, especially executives, in these two industries (and elsewhere), as well as in the private equity firms that have invested in these industries. These two groups—executives and private equity firms—have been largely responsible for driving companies like fracking pioneer Chesapeake Energy and century-plus-old luxury retailer Nieman Marcus, owner of Bergdorf Goodman and MyTheresa, into a financial ditch.

To understand why executives and private equity investors become richer destroying companies than by making investments to ensure that these businesses are financially sound, it is essential to understand the difference between personal bankruptcy and corporate bankruptcy. While personal bankruptcy can be devastating for individuals, businesses using Chapter 11 of the bankruptcy code can enjoy a number of benefits.

Bankruptcy: Personal and Corporate

The difference between personal and corporate bankruptcy is most clear in terms of what happens upon a declaration of bankruptcy. A person declaring bankruptcy immediately loses control of their assets under most declarations and a bankruptcy court appoints a trustee to handle the assets of the bankrupt individual. The trustee acts whether the filing is under Chapter 7 or Chapter 13 of the bankruptcy code. Generally, the trustee has the power to dispose of any assets owned by the individual bankrupt filer. (Under Chapter 13, the individual retains some control over their assets during the bankruptcy proceedings.)

In contrast, most corporate bankruptcies, including those triggered by Covid-19, are filed under Chapter 11. In this case, the bankrupt company retains possession of the assets of the company (referred to as "debtor-in-possession" or "DIP"). Thus, the same management will usually continue to run the business and will seek to reduce the pre-existing debt. The bankruptcy court will automatically issue a stay that prevents most creditors from attempting to collect any debts owed by the filing company. Very importantly, a DIP may raise new money by issuing new debt.

Now, you may ask, why would anyone lend to a bankrupt company? Because, in the event of the actual liquidation of the business, DIP financing will be paid before any other outstanding debt or equity that the bankrupt company may have.

Corporate debt is ranked in terms of seniority. Senior debt will be repaid first. Junior debt is repaid only if there are sufficient funds left over after covering all senior debt. Vulture capital funds are attracted to this kind of debt, precisely because it jumps the queue in seniority and also will pay a higher rate of interest. (I am not recommending that you buy such debt!)

With this understanding in mind, let's consider two companies in the retail industry (primarily clothing) and two in the oil and gas industry (both extraction and processing). Together, these two industries that, at least on the surface, are very different starkly illuminate some of the political economic dynamics that have become even more pronounced during the Covid-19 slump.

Retail: Reaping the Whirlwind of PE

Private equity (aka "PE") firms have been attracted to retail stores, especially clothing, for more than a decade. Between 2002 and 2019, private equity firms took over a range of clothing retailers, including household names like Nieman Marcus, J.Crew, Belk, Nine West, and Claire's, among others. But what attracted private equity to retail in the first place?

Retailers had traditionally carried only small amounts of debt but generated significant cash flows. Although the profit margins in retail, especially clothing, are often small, many retail stores, such as Sears and J.C. Penney, own the land on which a number of their stores are located. This real estate is an asset that can be used to secure the debt that private equity issues to finance the takeover. Following an acquisition, private equity firms—the new management—authorize the acquired firm to pay out a "special dividend" to the new owners, i.e., the private equity firm itself. This debt is then carried on the books of the acquired firm. Thus, when a private equity firm takes over a business, it behaves like a virus invading a healthy cell. The virus takes over the healthy function of the cell and forces the cell to deplete itself for the benefit of the virus or, in the financial world, the private equity firm.

In addition, until 2017, the tax code allowed private equity firms to write off the interest on debt incurred in the process of a leveraged buyout (LBO) against profits. A leveraged buyout is the acquisition of one company by another in which the acquiring company uses large amounts of borrowed money to pay for the acquisition (see box). Thus, the acquirer commits a relatively small amount of their own capital, leaving them free to repeat the process. In essence, the private equity firm has an interest-free loan to undertake an LBO.

LBO targets are the prey; private equity firms are the predator.

J.Crew
In 2011 J.Crew was taken private in a $3 billion LBO led by TPG Capital and Leonard Green and Partners. When a firm is taken private, it is no longer listed on a stock exchange and thus not available for other investors to purchase shares. The debt raised to carry out the LBO became a part of J.Crew's balance sheet, and J.Crew was responsible for interest on, and eventually principle repayment of, this debt. But the burden imposed by the private equity firms did not stop there. The two

acquiring firms required J.Crew to borrow another $787 million for dividend payments to—you guessed it—TPG Capital and Leonard Green and Partners.

Even though cost-cutting moves, including layoffs, had reduced J.Crew's workforce by 10%, by 2020 J.Crew was floundering under a debt load of $1.7 billion. J.Crew then filed for Chapter 11 in early May, the first major clothing retailer to do so in the midst of the Covid-19 pandemic. This was a major comedown for a brand that Vogue called "a significant voice in the conversation on American style," in 2011.

Bankruptcy is bad news for many of the firm's 14,000 employees—but not for the private equity firms. In 2016, as the company was struggling under its debt load and declining revenues, the possibility of bankruptcy loomed on the horizon. The new management transferred J.Crew's intellectual property rights—its brands—to a Cayman Islands shell corporation, where they are now out of the reach of J.Crew's creditors but securely under the control of the private equity firms. Pioneered with J.Crew, this approach to asset stripping is now referred to as the "J.Crew trapdoor" (sometimes also called "J.Screwed"). The show continues on stage, but the valuable assets have fallen through the floor into a shell corporation.

Meanwhile, some J.Crew stores are reopening, allowing an undetermined number of employees (or new hires) to come back to work. The firm had over 500 stores before the Covid-19 crisis; as of mid-August, the firm's website lists just 170 open stores. J.Crew is also seeking to cancel leases for at least 67 stores.

The "L" in LBOs: Leverage

The large returns to a private equity firm in a successful leveraged buyout (LBO) and subsequent resale are the result of the use of leverage in the initial acquisition. It is leverage that produces the high return on investment that private equity firms use as a marketing pitch for investors. The leverage in a leveraged buyout is the result of borrowing the bulk of the money needed to take over the target firm while committing a limited amount of capital on the part of the acquirer.

Until the 2007 LBO of TXU Energy, KKR's 1988 LBO of RJR Nabisco, the saga that was the basis for the 1993 film "Barbarians at the Gate," was the largest LBO. KKR was also involved in the TXU LBO, along with Goldman Sachs and Texas Pacific Group.

Although the details of financing any specific LBO can be complex, the basic math involved is simple. Consider these two different approaches to acquiring an imaginary company, Acme Industries, which demonstrate the importance of leverage in LBOs.

In both cases, Acme Industries is taken over at the price of $80 million, and Acme's earnings are $10 million prior to any payments of interest and taxes, depreciation, and any amortization (aka "EBITA").

The "Respectable" Approach

Stodgy, LLC pays $80 million of its own capital to acquire Acme Industries.

After one year, Stodgy sells Acme for $100 million. Stodgy's profit is $20 million, for a return on investment of 25%.

This is a *respectable* return on investment.

(By comparison, the average annual return on investment for bonds from 1926 to 2018 was about 5.3%; the average annual return on investment for stocks over the same period was about 10.1%.)

Of course, TPG Capital and Leonard Green and Partners walk away with control of the J.Crew brand, which they can now market to other retailers—after unloading the LBO debt onto J.Crew's books.

Neiman Marcus

J.Crew may have been a mass-market retailer, but Neiman Marcus never saw itself that way, nor did its customers. Founded in 1907 in Dallas, Texas, the stores sold Chanel handbags and Loro Piana cashmere. In the 1980s, the White Plains, N.Y., store offered smoked salmon and herring from Murray's Sturgeon Shop in Manhattan. One year the company's Christmas catalogue even offered a $20 million personal submarine.

Not for nothing did the store have the nickname "Needless Markup."

The store's philosophy was summed up by long-time CEO Burt Tansky when he said: "We work very hard to create a luxurious experience for our customers—whether it's the amazing merchandise, the fresh flowers, or the artwork."

The first time Neiman Marcus came (likely unwillingly) in the sights of private equity was in the 2005 LBO of the store by TPG Capital and Warburg Pincus. They took the firm private at a price of over $5 billion. At the time, Neiman Marcus was at the top of the retail pack. These two firms held onto Neiman Marcus for eight years, then sold it in 2013 to the private equity firm Ares Management, along with

---

The "Outstanding" Approach

TurboCharged, LLC commits just $20 million of its own capital and borrows the remaining $60 million at an interest rate of 10%.

The $60 million becomes part of Acme's balance sheet. The result is a 6:1 ratio of debt to earnings, the guideline that was issued by the Fed in 2013—and then retracted.

After one year, TurboCharged sells Acme for $100 million. Similar to the "respectable" approach, TurboCharged has a profit of $20 million. But unlike Stodgy, TurboCharged has only committed $20 million of its own capital in the acquisition.

Once TurboCharged pays one year's interest ($6 million) and repays the loan ($60 million), TurboCharged now has $34 million in capital ($100 million – $60 million – $6 million = $34 million).

After TurboCharged subtracts their original investment of $20 million from their $34 million in capital, TurboCharged's profit is $14 million, for a return on investment of 70%.

This is an *outstanding* return on investment—leverage is the difference.

Summing Up

Leveraged buyouts are a core tool used in private equity deals. And, as the hypothetical example illustrates, the one that most of all accounts for the outsized profits claimed by private equity firms in their marketing pitch to your and my pension funds. As the new owners of companies they take over, the buyout firms have other strategies to boost their haul, as the cases of Neiman Marcus and J.Crew illustrate. These include additional borrowing by the acquired company to pay out a large dividend to the private equity acquirer, mass layoffs in the name of "efficiency," assets stripping, raiding pensions, etc. But the use of leverage—using other people's money for the buyout itself—is the underlying strategy for these other looting tactics.

the Canada Pension Investment Board, for $6 billion. The new acquirers planned an initial public offering (IPO) in 2015, but that never happened. Despite carrying a debt load that exceeded its revenue, the company continued to expand. The high-water mark of this continued expansion occurred in March 2019, when Neiman Marcus opened its first store in Manhattan, a 188,000-square-foot Hudson Yards anchor store that occupied three floors. This came after a 2018 financial performance that produced profits smaller than their required interest payments.

Within a week of J.Crew's bankruptcy filing, Neiman Marcus also filed for Chapter 11 protection, threatening the livelihood and jobs of its more than 13,000 employees. There were a few in the company, however, who reaped millions. In February, Neiman Marcus paid a bonus of $4 million to its CEO, and a week before filing for Chapter 11, paid another $25 million to other executives. For a little perspective, the average apparel associate, the highest paid employee category at the store, would have to work for almost 70 years to earn $4 million.

But, as in the case with J.Crew, that is not the end of the story. In 2014 Neiman Marcus had acquired German-based MyTheresa, "an online shopping destination for children, men, and women's luxury clothing, bags, shoes, and accessories," where, for $450, you can buy a pink leather AirPods case from Bottega Veneta. In 2016, Neiman Marcus Group LTD LLC transferred ownership of MyTheresa to its parent company, the Neiman Marcus Group, Inc. at the direction of Neiman's private equity acquirers. This insulated MyTheresa from creditors in the recent bankruptcy proceedings because it is the LLC, not The Neiman Marcus Group, Inc. that filed Chapter 11. And, of course, the private equity firms retain control of the parent and the assets of the parent.

Neiman Marcus told the bankruptcy court that 21 locations, some full stores, and others the firm calls "Last Call" facilities, will close permanently. As in the case with J.Crew, the bankruptcy road is just beginning.

The Fracking Revolution

In 2006 the United States imported 60% of the oil we consumed. By late 2019, the United States became a net exporter of petroleum products, exporting 772,000 barrels per day, including both crude and refined petroleum. The United States also became the world's leading producer of oil, as domestic production almost tripled in those 14 years. Of course, the source of this huge increase in production and the much-lauded "energy independence" was the new technology for extracting oil or gas from shale: hydraulic fracturing, or fracking. But, as I have argued elsewhere (see "A Rolling Loan Gathers No Loss: Fracking, Covid-19, and Zombie Finance," Chicago Political Economy Group, April 18, 2020, accessible via cpegonline.org), the Covid-19 slump has revealed that the foundation of that "energy independence" is nothing more than a financial house of cards.

Chesapeake Energy

If there is one company that embodied the fracking revolution in fossil fuels, it was Chesapeake Energy, often considered the poster child for that new extractive technology. Chesapeake was the brainchild of Aubrey McClendon who made it to

#134 on Forbes magazine's richest 500 list in 2008. This was only 19 years after he co-founded Chesapeake, 15 years after Chesapeake's IPO, and only a decade after he adopted the hydraulic fracturing technology developed by George Mitchell. McClendon was not a technology pioneer, he simply believed—very strongly—that fracking would be the path to energy independence for the United States and riches for himself and his company. Under his leadership, Chesapeake bid aggressively for leases on land that gave it the rights to extract gas and oil from below the surface—as much as a mile or more underground.

At the apex of its success, Chesapeake had 175 operating rigs sprawling across the country, from Texas and Louisiana to Pennsylvania and Ohio. The company focused on natural gas more than petroleum. At one point, Chesapeake was the second largest producer of natural gas in the United States, eclipsed only by ExxonMobil. McClendon even surreptitiously financed a "Coal is Filthy" campaign and approached some environmental groups to argue for a joint effort to position natural gas as the clean energy bridge from coal and oil to green energy.

McClendon was betting that the price of natural gas would not fall below the $8–9/thousand cubic feet range; in fact, he believed it would only go up. President Vladimir Putin and a Goldman Sachs/KKR LBO of utility company TXU were making the same bet. That did not turn out to be the case.

McClendon was ousted from Chesapeake in 2013. He had already driven Chesapeake into a precarious financial position: from 2010 to 2012, Chesapeake spent $30 billion more on drilling and leasing than it took in as revenue.

While McClendon was profligate in both his corporate and personal life, that was not the basic problem for Chesapeake and other companies who built their business model around fracking. The fundamental problem is financial: The companies have never been able to achieve consistent profitability. Chesapeake's stock hit an all-time high in July 2018 at $1,080 per share, but by mid-2019 the company was reporting negative earnings per share.

Fracking wells have a relatively short life. Therefore, companies must constantly drill new ones. Drilling to depths of a mile or more doesn't come cheap, so Chesapeake borrowed billions over the last decade to continue drilling. Like other frackers, Chesapeake kept promising investors that they would get repaid out of future profits. Investors, including pension funds, bought Chesapeake's BBB-rated debt because it paid higher interest rates than better-quality debt. The ready market for its debt allowed Chesapeake (and others) to roll over old debt—as the saying goes, "a rolling loan gathers no loss." But the future of profitability never came.

The Covid-19 slump upended—or maybe just awakened investors to—these calculations. Plunging prices and a glut of oil and natural gas have illuminated the reality: Fracking companies are a prime example of what the Bank for International Settlements calls "zombies," companies that cannot meet interest payments on their debt, much less pay off the principal.

On June 28, 2020, Chesapeake filed for bankruptcy, just after awarding $25 million to executives and other senior employees in May. Paying out bonuses while under Chapter 11 supervision would require a bankruptcy court's okay; paying them out a few days earlier got them around that obstacle.

From the early 2000s, the United States chased the Holy Grail of energy independence. But, instead of taking the renewable energy route, we chose the path of fossil capital, betting on a technology—fracking—that is environmentally destructive and financially unviable. Thus, we lost two decades of opportunity to begin the transition to an economy based on renewable energy.

California Resources Corporation (CRC): Occidental Death and Dismemberment?

In 2014 Occidental Petroleum (Oxy) decided to exit California fossil fuel production. Oxy had made very little investment in California for several years, and oil and gas production in the state had declined steadily since the 1980s. California, which had vied with Oklahoma for the number one spot in U.S. oil production during the 1920s and 1930s, was moving toward an energy future in which the role of oil and gas would be significantly reduced. So, Oxy created a new company called the California Resources Corporation (CRC). And Oxy gifted this new company with debt—a lot of debt, over $6 billion.

With oil at $100/barrel or more at the time, this debt may have seemed manageable, although there were doubters. Some thought that Oxy was simply dumping some assets in a political jurisdiction where they no longer wanted to play, an impression reinforced by Oxy's move of the company's headquarters from Los Angeles to Houston that same year.

CRC acquired all the production assets of Oxy in California and became the state's largest producer of natural gas and second-largest oil producer. Unlike Chesapeake or Whiting, the two largest fracking bankruptcies, CRC is a conventional driller. However, the company was dependent on the same debt roll-over financing to continue operating. CRC's share price initially reflected an optimistic outlook, achieving an all-time high of $51.50 in 2015 and almost matching that in 2018 at over $50 when crude prices topped $75/barrel.

But the Covid-19 pandemic drove crude below $60, $50, and even $40/barrel, not viable levels for CRC. The company's interest coverage in 2019 was already below 1.0. (Interest coverage refers to the ratio between a firm's revenue before interest and taxes are paid out and the required interest payments on the firm's debt.) A ratio of less than 1.0 means the firm is not generating enough revenue to meet required interest payments, much less any repayment of principal. In short, by 2019 CRC was an example of a zombie company—but not yet recognized by all. By mid-2020, in debt to JPMorgan Chase, Bank of America, and others, CRC filed for bankruptcy on June 14. The company immediately went into the DIP mode, raising about $1 billion in financing.

But now interesting issues and problems are emerging. These include idle wells, the status of CRC's drilling permits, and potential cleanup costs. Importantly, the latter issue raises the question of who will pay them if CRC doesn't have the resources—and it looks like it doesn't.

Let's take each issue in turn.

CRC has more than 11,000 wells in California. But almost half of them, about 5,000, are idle. And many of these idle wells have been inactive for a long time—on average, about two decades—strongly suggesting that they will never again be brought into production. And, of course, many thus date back to Oxy's time in California, a point to which I'll return.

Many of these idle wells—as well as many of the active wells—are less than 1,000 feet from residences, frequently near communities of color. (Full disclosure: In 2018 I worked on a Ventura City Council campaign for a candidate from the Latino West Side of Ventura, Calif., an area adjacent to both active and idle wells. One of the candidate's big issues was the need to expand the buffer zone between drilling sites and residences. In 2020, the Ventura County Board of Supervisors adopted the strongest buffer zone requirement in the United States—2,500 feet between an oil/gas well and any residences or schools. CRC is not happy.)

A large number of CRC's drilling permits are old, dating back to the 1940s–1970s. And many were granted with few if any restrictions on the number of wells that could be drilled in the defined area and without any sunset clauses. This largesse is now being called into question. In the recent Ventura County Board of Supervisors election, CRC spent over $800,000 to defeat a candidate committed to re-examining these permits and to protect an incumbent who has been a reliable pro-fossil fuel vote. At the time of this political expenditure, the largest ever for this kind of election, CRC had only about $22 million in free cash.

Environmentalists have known for decades that the impact of fossil fuel extraction does not end when the drilling stops: wells have to be plugged and the damage to the surrounding environment mitigated. This cleanup is costly, perhaps running up to as much as $50,000 per idle well. CRC calculates that its potential cleanup liability is at least $500 million; the actual figure is likely much higher. While CRC has paid into California's fund for plugging idle wells, run by CalGEM, the fund contains only about $112 million. The most recent estimate for cleanup costs for all drilling sites across the state is more than $9 billion.

If CRC cannot cover the costs of cleanup, or manages to discharge this debt during Chapter 11 negotiations with creditors, there is one possible solution. Under California law, the state can seek restitution from the "immediate preceding owner"—that is, of course, Occidental Petroleum. In CRC's bankruptcy, as in too many other cases in the flood of bankruptcies that are now occurring, the corporate decision makers are not suffering. In late March 2020, only three months prior to the Chapter 11 filing, CRC management revised their bonus system. Under the amended plan, CEO Todd A. Stevens will get a payout double his annual compensation if he is forced out. That would equal $21 million. Not bad work, if you can get it.

What Should Be Done?

Economic downturns reveal structural problems in the political economy. And in sudden crises, such as the Covid-19 slump or the Great Financial Crisis, these problems are starkly highlighted. But a crisis is also an opportunity and, unlike the Obama administration's handling of the financial crisis, we should not let this one go to waste.

Many changes to our financial markets and their regulation are needed, including those specific to the bankruptcy game as it is playing out in retail, fossil fuels, and other industries. The plan that Senator Elizabeth Warren released during her presidential campaign had some useful proposals for fixing the bankruptcy system. Much of what she proposed was to give individuals a better chance of coming out of bankruptcy in a financially secure position, but she did include some measures, such as reforms to the fraudulent transfer law, that could apply to corporate bankruptcies as well.

Separate from Warren's proposals and with a focus on the issues around Chapter 11 bankruptcy, here are a few interventions that would change both the bankruptcy game and the LBO practice. First, the Office of the United States Trustee (OUST), which is the division of the Department of Justice tasked with overseeing bankruptcy cases, should be charged with doing a one-year look back on all payouts to insiders. For example, in the year prior to J.Crew's Chapter 11 filing, the firm paid out over $17 million to various insiders. Some of these were probably reasonable, but others could be called into question, and the OUST could bring questionable payments to the attention of the bankruptcy court for potential reversal. The one-year look-back period for insider payments is identical to that applied to preferences in bankruptcy filings (actions that benefit one creditor to the detriment of another), but seeking to reverse questionable payments made to insiders during the lead-up to bankruptcy is not presently part of the OUST's mandate.

The enhanced ability to claw back payments to insiders would itself sharply curtail the widespread pattern of shoveling money to the very executives that guided a firm into bankruptcy in the first place. Now, the counter argument is that these payouts are needed or the executives may leave the firm in its hour of need. But that seems very doubtful; who is eager to hire a CEO, CFO, etc. of a firm that just filed Chapter 11?

In a slightly more reasonable world, we would probably prohibit LBOs because they are primarily predatory and because they often destroy value and jobs as they did to J.Crew and Neiman Marcus. If we can't yet prohibit LBOs, we can and should restrain the LBO market. The Federal Reserve made some small and inadequate steps in that direction when it issued "guidelines" on LBO financing in 2013. At that time the guidelines suggested—and it turns out it was only a suggestion—that leverage, which is debt assumed by the target company in an LBO compared to the company's earnings before interest, tax, depreciation, and amortization (EBITA), should not exceed 6.0. If this guideline (or preferably a lower ratio) had been made mandatory, it would have required acquiring firms to put up some additional equity, because the guideline would have limited the debt that could be loaded onto the target company. However, in 2018 the Fed backed down, clarifying that the 6.0 ratio was a not-to-be enforced guideline. In the same year, the ratio exceeded 7.0 for the first time since—you guessed it—the onset of the Great Financial Crisis in late 2007.

So, we have been going in the wrong direction. A new administration should require the Federal Reserve to revisit this guideline and exert pressure for a lower leverage ratio.

Or, perhaps even more useful: prohibit banks from financing any LBO where the private equity buyers are not willing to pony up at least 50% of the purchase price. Now there would be squeals of outrage from Wall Street that fewer deals will get done—but would that be bad? It is worth reminding ourselves that in 2009, in the midst of the Great Financial Crisis when credit markets were tight, private equity firms dug deeper into their pockets and provided an average of over 50% of their own capital in LBOs. Under this restriction, banks would have an incentive to make more loans to firms that are planning to expand business and create, rather than destroy, jobs.

As noted previously, it is common for the target in an LBO, once the takeover has occurred, to issue a large dividend to the acquiring firms. This usually piles additional debt on the acquired firm, above and beyond the debt used to leverage the takeover. A further restriction that should be imposed is a prohibition on any dividend payout for some period after the acquisition. The result might be investment in improving the operations of the acquired firm, which is the alleged reason for most LBOs.

As to fracking, as I have argued elsewhere (see "Empty shelves and zombie fracking firms," *Democratic Left*, Summer 2020, accessible via democraticleft.dsausa. org), I believe the market is going to take care of that line of business. But that does not mean that "the market" will solve the cleanup problem. What is needed immediately is more funding for the cleanup costs of fossil fuel extraction. A small first step would be to hire the more than 100,000 laid-off oil and gas workers to clean up abandoned wells, a proposal for which Joe Biden has indicated support.

Of course, the overall and hardest-to-tackle problem is the financialization of the U.S. economy that allows LBOs, rolling BBB-rated debt, and the huge build-up of corporate debt. While the Great Financial Crisis of 2007–2008 offered a chance to reverse the ravages of financialization, it was a wasted crisis, and the financial sector has come back stronger than before. The largest banks now control a greater share of assets, financial sector profits have recaptured the 25–30% share of total profits they claimed prior to the crisis, and the ratio of corporate debt to GDP is now even greater than before the crisis. There is much to be done, but that is a topic for another time. ❑

Note: An earlier version of this article was published by the Chicago Political Economy Group (CPEG) at cpegonline.org.

Sources: Center for Popular Democracy, Pirate Equity: How Wall Street Firms are Pillaging American Retail, July 2019 (populardemocracy.org); Emily Holt, "And at Long Last, It's Showtime: J.Crew's Runway Debut at NYFW," *Vogue*, Sept. 13, 2011 (vogue.com); Americans for Financial Reform, "Fact Sheet: J. Crew Succumbs to Bankruptcy after Private Equity Debt, Financial Looting," May 4, 2020 (ourfinancialsecurity.org); J.Crew Group, Inc., "J.Crew Group, Inc. Provides Update on Store Re-Opening Plans," PR Newswire, June 12, 2020 (prnewswire. com); Julie Dunn, "Responsible Party: Karen Katz; Submarines for Sale. One Size Fits All," *New York Times*, Oct. 29, 2000 (nytimes.com); Sapna Maheshwari and Vanessa Friedman, "The Pandemic Helped Topple Two Retailers. So Did Private Equity," *New York Times*, May 14, 2020 (nytimes.com); mytheresa.com/en-us/; Bethany Biron, "Neiman Marcus is closing another department store, bringing its total closings to 22 locations. Here is the full list," *Business Insider*, August 24, 2020 (businessinsider.com); U.S. Energy Information and Administration, "Despite the U.S. becoming a net petroleum exporter, most regions are still net importers," February 6, 2020 (eia.gov); Bill Barclay, "A Rolling Loan Gathers No Loss: Fracking, COIVD 19, and Zombie Finance," Chicago Political Economy Group, April 18, 2020 (cpegonline.org); U.S. Energy

Information Administration, "Natural Gas," August 31, 2020 (eia.gov); Spin Doctor, "California Resources Corporation Faces Bankruptcy: Is It Occidental Death & Dismemberment?," Stock Spinoffs, June 29, 2020 (stockspinoffs.com); Dan Brekke, "Major California Oil Producer Falls Victim to Collapse in Crude Prices Amid Pandemic," KQED, July 16, 2020 (kqed.org); Mark Olalde, "Why is big oil pumping money into Ventura County's board of supervisor elections?," *The Desert Sun*, Feb. 19, 2020 (desertsun.com); Janet Wilson and Mark Olalde, "California Resources Corp., leading oil and gas producer, files for Chapter 11 bankruptcy," *The Desert Sun*, July 16, 2020 (desertsun.com); Kevin Crowley, Rachel Adams-Heard and David Wethe, "Bankruptcy Is a Jackpot for CEOs Helming Failed Oil Companies," Bloomberg News, June 4, 2020 (bloomberg. com); Elizabeth Warren, "Fixing Our Bankruptcy System to Give People a Second Chance," (elizabethwarren.com); United States Bankruptcy Court, Eastern District of Virginia Richmond Division, "Statement of Financial Affairs for J.Crew Operating Corp," Case No. 20-32186, June 12, 2020; Kristen Haunss, "US federal agencies open door to more aggressive buyout loans," Reuters, Sept. 6, 2018 (reuters.com); Jonathan Schwarzberg, Leela Parker Deo, "LPC: Private equity firms put more capital, less debt into LBOs," Reuters, August 26, 2020 (reuters. com); Bill Barclay, "Empty shelves and zombie fracking firms," *Democratic Left*, Summer 2020 (democraticleft.dsausa.org); Michael R. Bloomberg, "Let's Hire Laid-Off Oil and Gas Workers to Fight Climate Change," Bloomberg News, August 3, 2020 (bloomberg.com).

Article 5.7

HOW "BIG OIL" WORKS THE SYSTEM AND KEEPS WINNING

Oil and gas interests have refined their techniques to stay a step ahead over decades.

BY NAOMI ORESKES AND JEFF NESBIT

Despite countless investigations, lawsuits, social shaming, and regulations dating back decades, the oil and gas industry remains formidable. After all, it has made consuming its products seem like a human necessity. It has confused the public about climate science, bought the eternal gratitude of one of America's two main political parties, and repeatedly out-maneuvered regulatory efforts. And it has done all this in part by thinking ahead and then acting ruthlessly. While the rest of us were playing checkers, its executives were playing three-dimensional chess.

Take this brief tour of the industry's history, and then ask yourself: Is there any doubt that these companies are now working to keep the profits rolling in, even as mega-hurricanes and roaring wildfires scream the dangers of the climate emergency?

The John D. Rockefeller Myth

Ida Tarbell is one of the most celebrated investigative journalists in American history. Long before Bob Woodward and Carl Bernstein exposed the Watergate scandal, Tarbell's reporting broke up the Standard Oil monopoly. In 19 articles that became a widely read book, *History of the Standard Oil Company*, published in 1904, she exposed its unsavory practices. In 1911, federal regulators used Tarbell's findings to break Standard Oil into 33 much smaller companies.

David had slayed Goliath. The U.S. government had set a monopoly-busting standard for future generations. John D. Rockefeller, Standard Oil's owner, lost. The good guys won—or so it seemed.

In fact, Rockefeller saw what was coming and ended up profiting—massively—from the breakup of his company. Rockefeller made sure to retain significant stock holdings in each of Standard Oil's 33 offspring companies and position them in different parts of the United States where they wouldn't compete against one another. Collectively, the 33 offspring companies went on to make Rockefeller very, very rich. Indeed, it was the breakup of Standard Oil that tripled his wealth and made him the wealthiest man in the world. In 1916, five years after Standard Oil was broken up, Rockefeller became the world's first billionaire.

Say It Ain't So, Dr. Seuss!

One of the offspring of Standard Oil was Esso (S-O, spelled out), which later launched one of the most successful advertising campaigns in history. It did so by relying on the talents of a young cartoonist who millions would later adore under his pen name, Dr. Seuss. Decades before authoring the pro-environment parable *The Lorax*, Theodore Geisel helped Esso market "Flit," a household spray gun that killed mosquitoes. What Americans weren't told was that the pesticide DDT made up 5% of each blast of Flit.

When Esso put considerable creative resources behind the Flit campaign, it was looking years ahead to a time when it would also successfully market oil-based products. The campaign ran for 17 years in the 1940s and 1950s, at the time an unheard of run for an ad campaign. It taught Esso and other Standard Oil companies how to sell derivative products (like plastics and pesticides) that made the company and the brand a household name in the minds of the public. In its day, "Quick, Henry, the Flit!" was as ubiquitous as "Got Milk?" is today.

At the time, the public (and even many scientists) didn't appreciate the deadly nature of DDT. That didn't come until the 1962 publication of Rachel Carson's book *Silent Spring*. But accepting that DDT was deadly was hard, in part because of the genius of Geisel, whose wacky characters—strikingly similar to the figures who would later populate Dr. Seuss books—energetically extolled Flit's alleged benefits.

Geisel later said the experience "taught me conciseness and how to marry pictures with words." The Flit ad campaign was incredibly smart and clever marketing. It taught the industry how to sell a dangerous and unnecessary product as if it were something useful and even fun. Years later, ExxonMobil would take that cleverness to new heights in its advertorials. They weren't about clever characters. But they were awfully clever, containing few, if any, outright lies, but a whole lot of half-truths and misrepresentations. It was clever enough to convince the *New York Times* to run them without labeling them as the advertisements that they, in fact, were. Their climate "advertorials" appeared in the op-ed page of the *New York Times* and were part of what scholars have called "the longest, regular (weekly) use of media to influence public and elite opinion in contemporary America."

Controlling Climate Science

Big Oil also saw climate change coming. As abundant investigative reporting and academic studies have documented, the companies' own scientists were telling their executives in the 1970s that burning more oil and other fossil fuels would overheat the planet. (Other scientists had been saying so since the 1960s.) The companies responded by lying about the danger of their products, blunting public awareness, and lobbying against government action. The result is today's climate emergency.

Less well-known is how oil and gas companies didn't just lie about their own research. They also mounted a stealth campaign to monitor and influence what the rest of the scientific community learned and said about climate change.

The companies worked with scientists in universities and made sure they were present at important conferences. They nominated them to be contributors to the Intergovernmental Panel on Climate Change (IPCC), the United Nations body whose assessments from 1990 onward defined what the press, public, and policymakers thought was true about climate science. While the IPCC reports, which rely on consensus science, were sound, Big Oil's scientific participation gave them an insider's view of the road ahead. More ominously, they introduced the art of questioning the consensus science in forums where every word is parsed.

The industry was employing a strategy pioneered by tobacco companies, but with a twist. Beginning in the 1950s, the tobacco industry cultivated a sotto voce network of scientists at scores of American universities and medical schools, whose work it funded. Some of these scientists were actively engaged in research to discredit the idea that cigarette smoking was a health risk, but most of it was more subtle; the industry supported research on causes of cancer and heart disease other than tobacco, such as radon, asbestos, and diet. It was a form of misdirection, designed to deflect our attention away from the harms of tobacco and onto other things. The scheme worked for a while, but when it was exposed in the 1990s, in part through lawsuits, the bad publicity largely killed it. What self-respecting scientist would take tobacco industry money after that?

The oil and gas industry learned from that mistake and decided that, instead of working surreptitiously, it would work in the open. And rather than work primarily with individual scientists whose work might be of use, it would seek to influence the direction of the scientific community as a whole. The industry's internal scientists continued to do research and publish peer-reviewed articles, but the industry also openly funded university collaborations and other researchers. From the late 1970s through the 1980s, Exxon was known both as a climate research pioneer, and as a generous patron of university science, supporting student research and fellowships at many major universities. Its scientists also worked alongside senior colleagues at NASA, the Department of Energy, and other key institutions, and funded breakfasts, luncheons, and other activities at scientific meetings. Those efforts had the net effect of creating goodwill and bonds of loyalty. It's been effective.

The industry's scientists may have been operating in good faith, but their work helped delay public recognition of the scientific consensus that climate change was unequivocally man-made, happening now, and very dangerous. The industry's extensive presence in the field also gave it early access to the cutting-edge research it used to its advantage. Exxon, for example, designed oil platforms to accommodate more rapid sea level rise, even as the company publicly denied that climate change was occurring.

Don't Call It Methane, It's "Natural" Gas

Methane is an even more powerful greenhouse gas than carbon dioxide, yet it has received far less attention. One reason is that the oil and gas industry has positioned methane—which marketing experts cleverly labeled "natural gas"—as the future of the energy economy. The industry promotes methane gas as a "clean" fuel that's needed to bridge the transition from today's carbon economy to tomorrow's renewable energy era. Some go further and see gas as a permanent part of the energy landscape: BP's plan is renewables plus gas for the foreseeable future, and the company and other oil majors frequently invoke "low carbon" instead of "no carbon."

Except that methane gas isn't clean. It's about 80 times more potent at trapping heat in the atmosphere than carbon dioxide is.

As recently as a decade ago, many scientists and environmentalists viewed "natural gas" as a climate hero. The oil and gas industry's ad guys encouraged this view by portraying gas as a coal killer. The American Petroleum Institute (API) paid millions to run its first-ever Super Bowl ad in 2017, portraying gas as an engine of innovation that powers the American way of life. Between 2008 and 2019, API spent more than $750 million on public relations, advertising, and communications (for both oil and gas interests), an analysis by the Climate Investigations Center found. Today, most Americans view gas as clean, even though science shows that we can't meet our climate goals without quickly transitioning away from it. The bottom line is that we can't solve a problem caused by fossil fuels with more fossil fuels. But the industry has made a lot of us think otherwise.

There's little chance the oil and gas industry can defeat renewable energy in the long term. Wind, solar, and geothermal, which are clean and cost-competitive, will eventually dominate energy markets. Researchers at the University of California, Berkeley, GridLab, and Energy Innovation have found that the United States can achieve 90% clean electricity by the year 2035 with no new gas and at no additional cost to consumers. But the oil and gas industry doesn't need to win the fight in the long term. It just needs to win *right now* so it can keep developing oil and gas fields that will be in use for decades to come. To do that, it just has to keep doing what it has done for the past 25 years: win today, fight again tomorrow.

A Spider's Web of Pipelines

Here's a final example of how the oil and gas industry plans for the next war even as its adversaries are still fighting the last one. Almost no one outside of a few law firms, trade groups, and congressional staff in Washington, D.C., knows what the Federal Energy Regulatory Commission (FERC) is or does. But the oil and gas industry knows, and it moved quickly after Donald Trump became president to lay the groundwork for decades of future fossil fuel dependency.

FERC has long been seen as a rubber stamp for the oil and gas industry: The industry proposes gas pipelines, and FERC approves them. When FERC approves a pipeline, that approval grants the pipeline eminent domain, which in effect makes the pipeline all but impossible to stop.

Oil and gas industry executives seized upon Trump's arrival in the White House. In the opening days of his administration, independent researchers listened in on public trade gatherings of industry executives, who talked about "flooding the zone" at FERC. The industry planned to submit not just one or two but nearly a dozen interstate gas pipeline requests. Plotted on a map, the projected pipelines covered so much of the United States that they resembled a spider's web.

Once pipelines are in the system, companies can start to build them, and utility commissioners in every corner of America see this gas "infrastructure" as a fait accompli. And pipelines are built to last decades. In fact, if properly maintained, a pipeline can last forever in principle. This strategy could allow the oil and gas industry to lock in fossil fuel dependency for the rest of the century.

In hindsight, it's clear that oil and gas industry leaders used outright climate change denial when it suited their corporate and political interests throughout the 1990s. But now that outright denial is no longer credible, they've pivoted from denial to delay. Industry PR and marketing efforts have shifted massive resources to a central message that, yes, climate change is real, but that the necessary changes will require more research and decades to implement, and above all, more fossil fuels. Climate delay is the new climate denial.

Nearly every major oil and gas company now claims that it accepts the science and supports sensible climate policies. But their actions speak louder than words. It's clear that the future they want is one that still uses fossil fuels abundantly—regardless of what the science says. Whether it is selling deadly pesticides or deadly fossil fuels, they will do what it takes to keep their products on the market. Now that we're in a race to a clean energy future, it's time to recognize that they simply can't be trusted as partners in that race. We've been fooled too many times. ❑

Note: This article was originally published on Yale Climate Connections as part of Covering Climate Now, a global collaboration of news outlets strengthening coverage of the climate story. To read the original article, go to yaleclimateconnections.org/2021/12/how-big-oil-works-the-system-and-keeps-winning. To learn more about Yale Climate Connections, visit yaleclimateconnections.org.

Sources: Inside Climate News, "Exxon: The Road Not Taken" (insideclimatenews.org); Brian Kahn, "Shell Just Got Wrecked in Dutch Court," Gizmodo, May 26, 2021 (gizmodo.com); Brian Kahn, "Big Oil's Lies Are Finally Getting the Public Scrutiny They Deserve on Social Media," Gizmodo, Jan. 29, 2021 (gizmodo.com); Brian Khan and Dharna Noor, "The IPCC Warns This Is a Make-or-Break Decade for Humanity," Gizmodo, August 9, 2021 (gizmodo.com); Encyclopedia Britannica, "The History of the Standard Oil Company" (britannica.com); World History Project, "Theodor Seuss Geisel (Dr. Seuss) Creates Artwork for the 'Flit' Ad Campaign" (worldhistoryproject.org); Rachel Carson, *Silent Spring* (Mariner Books, 2022); Geoffrey Supran and Naomi Oreskes, "The forgotten oil ads that told us climate change was nothing," *The Guardian*, Nov. 18, 2021 (theguardian.com); Sidney Fussell, "Exxon Acknowledged Climate Change Internally But Still Spread Denialist Propaganda," Gizmodo, August 23, 2017 (gizmodo.com); Emily Atkin and Molly Taft, "Misleading climate ads from Big Oil explode ahead of Big Oil climate hearing," Heated, Oct. 27, 2021 (heated.world); BP, "Gas & low carbon energy" (bp.com); Michael Tadeo, "API launches Power Past Impossible campaign during Super Bowl showing natural gas and oil benefit to consumers in everyday life," American Petroleum Institute, Feb. 5, 2017 (api.org); Climate Investigations Institute, "American Petroleum Institute" (climateinvestigations.org); Expert Panel on Harnessing Science and Technology to Understand the Environmental Impacts of Shale Gas Extraction, "Environmental Impacts of Shale Gas Extraction in Canada," Council of Canadian Academies, 2014 (cca-reports.ca); Molly Taft, "What It's Like to Hunt Methane," Gizmodo, Nov. 8, 2021 (gizmodo.com); Tom Engelhardt, "Naomi Oreskes, A 'Green' Bridge to Hell," TomDispatch, July 27, 2014 (tomdispatch.com); Joel Rosenberg, "Electrify Everything in Your Home," Rewiring America, December 2021 (rewiringamerica.org); Amol Phadke, Sonia Aggarwal, Mike O'Boyle, Eric Gimon, Nikit Abhyankar, "Illustrative Pathways to 100 Percent Zero Carbon Power by 2035 Without Increasing Consumer Costs," Energy Innovation, September 2020 (energyinnovation.org); Federal Energy Regulatory Commission, "Shaping the Grid of the Future" (ferc.gov); Amy Westervelt, "Big oil's 'wokewashing' is the new climate science denialism," *The Guardian*, Sept. 9, 2021 (theguardian.com).

Article 5.8

POWER, WAGES, AND INEQUALITY

A recent government report has an unexpected focus—power in the workplace.

BY ARTHUR MacEWAN

On March 7, 2022, the U.S. Department of the Treasury issued a report titled, "The State of Labor Market Competition." It is not what one might expect from the U.S. government. It is apparent that something is unusual when the first chapter is "Theories of Labor Market Power," and the word "power" appears 15 times in the executive summary, 12 times in the introduction, and too many times to count in the body of the report. Power, after all, is generally absent from mainstream myths of how labor markets work.

The basic message of the report is that: "...The American labor market is characterized by high levels of employer power." And:

> ...A careful review of credible academic studies places the decrease in wages at roughly 20% relative to the level in a fully competitive market. In some industries and occupations, like manufacturing, estimates of wage losses are even higher.

At the center of employers' power is that many firms operate as *monopsonies* in the labor market. A pure monopsony is the only buyer in a market, but a very large employer, or a few very large employers, in a market can operate in a monopsonistic manner. Like monopolies that can largely set the prices of what they sell, monopsonists can largely set the prices—wages in the context of the report—of what they buy.

Good examples would be a Walmart store or an Amazon warehouse in a comparatively rural area, where employment options are relatively limited. Indeed, the message of the report is illustrated by a 2018 report in *The Economist*:

In the years since Amazon opened its doors in Lexington County [South Carolina], annual earnings for warehouse workers in the area have fallen from $47,000 to $32,000, a decline of over 30%." Employers' power, however, is exhibited in several ways beyond the direct setting of wages.

Power in the Labor Market

Power in the labor market (and other economic and political realms as well) is often a matter of what alternatives are available. For example, workers' power is limited in relation to their employer when they have very few employment alternatives or when they lack information about alternatives. On the other hand, employers' power is enhanced when they have alternative ways of organizing production or when they can limit the alternatives available to their workers.

Examples from the report of how power exists or is created in U.S. labor markets include the following:

- Employers can outsource (sometimes internationally) parts of their operations. Creating separations among various production activities in this way is called "fissuring." A common example in recent decades has been firms' outsourcing of janitorial work.

- Employers can demand that their employees sign "noncompete" agreements, which prevent them from working for a competitor firm if they leave their current job. Examples of other such agreements demanded by employers are training repayment agreements, non-solicitation agreements, and nondisclosure agreements. All of these sorts of agreements limit employees' ability to change jobs—i.e., limit their alternatives.

- Employers can establish mandatory arbitration agreements, preventing workers from legal recourse to rectify violations of labor laws, antitrust laws, or employment terms.

- Employers can often adopt "skill-based technical changes"—that is, substituting machines for workers. Because particular skills are often the basis of workers' bargaining power, their power can be undermined by such employer action, or even by the threat, explicit or implicit, of such action.

- Employers can discourage or even formally prohibit workers from exchanging information about their wages, restricting workers' knowledge of their alternatives within or outside the firms.

Hospital Mergers: Tough on Skilled Health Workers... But an Irony

According to "The State of Labor Market Competition," through consolidation, the number of hospitals in the United States declined by 16% in the last quarter of the 20th century, but with no evidence of improved quality. Yet, there is evidence of a rise in the monopsonistic power of the remaining hospitals. According to the Treasury Department report, consolidations of large hospitals, "cause wage growth among skilled workers and nursing and pharmacy workers to slow." With the reduced alternatives for skilled workers after such mergers, one study found that a 10% decline in the wages of nurses would tend to lead to only a 1% employment decline in the short run. The report points out that this is "a much smaller change in employment than one would expect in a perfectly competitive market where hospitals had little market power." Ironically, however, low-wage hospital workers (e.g., those in the hospitals' food services) in jobs that require little training tended not to experience a slowdown in wage growth. Their opportunities were not confined to the increasingly monoponistic hospital market. (While factors other than mergers are involved, the median wage of registered nurses adjusted for inflation declined by 6% between 2010 and 2020. This trend might be altered by the rising shortage of nurses in the pandemic—resulting from the need for more medical services and the departure of many nurses from the profession because of burnout.)

Source: American Nurses Association, "Employment and Earnings of Registered Nurses in 2010" (nursingworld.org); Bureau of Labor Statistics, Occupational Outlook Handbook, 2021 (bls.gov).

- Mergers, either by reducing the number of firms and jobs in an area or simply by increasing the dominance of the one resulting firm, can alter the labor market in favor of the employers. (See box.)

The high cost for workers of moving to take advantage of better job markets elsewhere also reduces their power, without any direct action by employers. All of these factors limit workers' alternatives or are possible because workers' alternatives are already limited, leaving them with little power to resist employers' actions. Each adds to the asymmetry of power between employers and workers.

Labor Markets and Economic Inequality

As compared to the textbook fantasy of "free markets," including labor markets where employers and employees enter on equal footing, the reality described in the Treasury Department's report makes one of the foundations of economic inequality very clear. Keeping workers' wages down—by 20%—means keeping employers' incomes (and their wealth) up.

It appears, then, that labor markets operate in tandem with other, more frequently cited sources of rising inequality—the form that globalization has taken, the decline of labor unions (which employers actively pursue), new technology, rising monopoly power (along with rising monopsony power), and lack of government enforcement of economic regulations.

Economic inequality is the result of a combined set of factors and cannot be fully understood in terms of a single cause. The operation of labor markets, however, is an important one of those factors. ❏

Sources: U.S. Department of the Treasury, "The State of Labor Market Competition," March 7, 2022 (treasury.gov); "What Amazon does to wages," *The Economist*, January 20, 2018 (economist.com); Eduardo Porter, "Employer Practices Limit Workers' Choices and Wages, U.S. Study Argues," *New York Times*, March 7, 2022 (nytimes.com); Marshall Steinbaum, "How Widespread Is Labor Monopsony? Some New Result Suggest It's Pervasive," Roosevelt Institute, Dec. 18, 2017 (rooseveltinstitute.org); Noam Scheiber and Ben Casselman, "Why Is Pay Lagging? Maybe Too Many Mergers in the Heartland," *New York Times*, Jan. 25, 2018 (nytimes.com).

Chapter 6

MARKET FAILURE II: EXTERNALITIES

INTRODUCTION

Markets sometimes fail. Mainstream economists typically focus on cases in which existing markets fail to facilitate exchanges that would make both parties better off. When a factory pollutes the air, people downwind suffer a cost. They might be willing to pay the polluter to curb emissions, but there is no market for clean air. In cases like this, one solution is for the government to step in with regulations that ban industries from imposing pollution costs on others. The same goes when private markets do not provide sufficient amounts of public goods, such as vaccines, from which everyone benefits whether they contribute to paying for them or not. Again, government may step in to correct the market failure. But what percentage of pollution should industries be required to eliminate? How much should be spent on public health? To decide how much government should step in, economists propose cost-benefit analysis, suggesting that the government weigh costs against benefits, in much the same way a firm decides how many cars to produce.

Orthodox economists typically see market failures as fairly limited in scope. In fact, they deny that many negative consequences of markets are market failures at all. When workers are paid wages too low to meet their basic needs, economists do not usually call their poverty and overwork market failures, but "incentives" to get a higher-paying job. When economists do recognize market failures, most argue that the problems are best solved by markets themselves. So pollution, for example, should be reduced by allowing firms to trade for the right to pollute. Finally, orthodox economists worry about government failure—the possibility that government responses to market failures may cause more problems than they solve. They conclude that the "invisible hand" of the market works pretty well, and that the alternatives, especially the "visible hand" of the state, will only make matters worse.

The chapter starts off with an article ("Why the Climate Change Is Also the Crisis of Capitalism," Article 6.1) whose authors, Ying Chen and Güney Işikara, suggest that the enormous challenge of climate change results from the use of the great world economic surplus for purposes of profit. The marketplace has seen a pathetically small degree of carbon reduction, due to the lack of money to be made from it, compared to burning more fossil fuels, so Chen and Işikara suggest a state-led Green New Deal-inspired use of the surplus to deliver us from climate's worst wrath.

In "Pricing the Priceless: Inside the Strange World of Cost-Benefit Analysis" (Article 6.2), Lisa Heinzerling and Frank Ackerman point out key flaws in the use of cost-benefit analysis to guide government action. While weighing the costs of a course of action (like pollution limits) against the benefits has a superficial plausibility, cost-benefit analysis fails to clarify the nature of public choices. It fails, for example, to account for all relevant costs or benefits, it downgrades the importance of the future, and it does not deal with the problem of how costs and benefits are distributed.

In "Can We Afford a Stable Climate?" (Article 6.3) and "Inequality, Sunk Costs, and Climate Justice" (Article 6.4), environmental economist Frank Ackerman emphasizes the failings of a cost-benefit analysis approach to climate policy. Instead, he proposes that we think about climate policy as a matter of insurance. The risks of doing nothing are incalculable and the costs of doing something are real but manageable. The task is not to decide how much action is worthwhile, but to muster our resources to do everything we can as quickly as possible.

In their article "Mapping Environmental Injustice" (Article 6.5), authors Klara Zwickl, Michael Ash, and James K. Boyce remind us that issues of race, class, and the distribution of power in society are never far off, including on environmental issues. They describe how the impacts of toxic air pollution fall along the contours of the American social hierarchy. Poor people tend to have higher exposure than rich people, and people of color tend to have higher exposure than white people.

Finally, in "Climate Change, Social Justice, and the Green New Deal" (Article 6.6), Arthur MacEwan returns to discuss the sometimes-thorny intersection of action to stabilize the climate and efforts to address major issue of social justice. While both can be served by a jobs program to employ in renewable energy the former workers from the retired coal mining and gas fracking industries, they can be in more direct conflict, as in the need to access rare minerals in indigenous lands. MacEwan explores these opportunities for synergy and potentials for conflict.

Discussion Questions

1. (Article 6.1) Chen and Işikara argue that capitalism is systematically unable to address the great challenge of climate change. What do they propose as a broad means of addressing this looming disaster?

2. (Article 6.2) Heinzerling and Ackerman point out a number of flaws in cost-benefit analysis. These weaknesses suggest that the cost-benefit approach will work better in some situations, worse in others. Describe when you would expect it to work better or worse, and explain.

3. (Article 6.2) Make a list of types of goods that are harder to put a price on (valuate) than others. Why is it so hard to price these types of goods?

4. (Article 6.3) Explain Ackerman's initial analogy between ambitious climate policy and fire insurance. The overwhelmingly likely outcome is that your house will not burn down this year. Why might you buy a home insurance policy that covers fire damage anyway? What features of the fire insurance example match up well with the way we should think about climate policy? What features of the fire insurance example do not match up so well?

5. (Article 6.4) Ackerman emphasizes that an ambitious policy to de-carbonize the economy and lessen the extent of climate change is necessary, but he acknowledges that there will be some financial losses that come from making such a large transition and these are not evenly distributed. Furthermore, the harms that come from the changes in climate and sea level that we do not avoid are also unevenly distributed. Who is likely to suffer the greatest harms from the climate change we do not avoid? Who is likely to experience the greatest financial losses from the transition away from fossil fuel use? How do we decide which losses to compensate, and to what degree?

6. (Article 6.5) Two possible explanations for disparities in environmental conditions along lines of income or race are "selection" and "move-in." "Selection" means that polluting industries make decisions to locate in predominantly low-income or non-white areas. "Move-in" means that people with fewer resources are more likely to move into areas where environmental quality is lower. What do you think of these two explanations? Would your views of "environmental injustice" differ depending on which factor is more important?

7. (Article 6.6) MacEwan suggests that social justice goals and action to stop climate change can be in conflict, but can also be improved together. Give an example of conflicting justice and climate goals from the article, and explain how policy frameworks like the Green New Deal can potentially address both constructively.

Article 6.1

WHY THE CLIMATE CRISIS IS ALSO THE CRISIS OF CAPITALISM

BY YING CHEN AND GÜNEY IŞIKARA
July/August 2019

Many people are wary of bringing a critique of capitalism into the discussion of climate change, even if they are genuinely concerned about the crisis and actively looking for effective solutions. All it takes is the mention of any word ending with "-ism," and skeptics will conclude that the discussion is unnecessarily ideological.

However, looking at the climate crisis through a Marxist lens can give us greater insight into the political inertia that has stalled the implementation of any kind of coordinated national response to climate change. The way capitalism operates in the United States, with its all-encompassing forces that have played a major role in creating today's environmental disaster, is also standing in the way of the implementation of a comprehensive solution. We can only understand the impact of capitalism on the current crisis by viewing capitalism as a specific economic system and assessing its historical impact—as well as its limits and contradictions.

Capitalism and Economic Surplus

From a Marxist perspective, the key defining feature of an economic system is its ownership structure. It is those who own the means of production (the raw materials, such as land and machines, that are used to produce goods) who also have the right to claim the surplus. Surplus, also known as surplus product or surplus value, is the difference between the final product that emerges from the production process and the total amount of input involved in creating that product. In feudalist societies, the surplus mostly took the form of the extra crops appropriated by the landlord after providing the serfs with just enough food to survive. In capitalism, roughly speaking, surplus takes the form of the profit that the capitalist claims after paying for inputs such as raw materials and workers' wages.

The term "economic surplus," coined by the political economist Paul A. Baran, measures surplus at a societal level. It is the difference between the total output of the society and the level of consumption that is needed for the reproduction of society at its current standard of living. Depending on how it is being used, economic surplus can take the concrete form of grand architecture such as the pyramids in Egypt or China's Great Wall, or less explicitly in the form of developing individual and social capacities, such as mass education.

Today, the economic surplus of the United States ranges from $8.4 to $10.8 trillion. However, having an economic surplus does not necessarily mean it will be used effectively or for the right purposes. The issue lies in who controls the economic surplus and whether they are motivated by the desire to turn a profit. When the surplus is under public control, profit motives can be largely averted and the use of surplus for social purposes is more straightforward: the Morrill Land-Grant College Act of 1862 made it possible to use the proceeds from federal land sales to establish colleges nationwide. The Rural Electrification Act of 1936, part of President Franklin D. Roosevelt's New Deal, provided federal loans for the installation of electrical distribution systems in previously ignored rural areas. However, when the surplus is in private hands, policies to encourage investment for social purposes are more likely to be influenced by the profit motive. For example, when it comes to carbon reduction, the results of various market-based attempts are far from satisfactory within national boundaries, and are often entirely offset on a global scale as a result of offshoring.

Capitalism Is Approaching Its Historical Limit

Capitalism once stood for a progressive stage of historical development. Even Karl Marx and Frederick Engels, capitalism's most radical critics, agreed that the "massive and colossal productive forces" created under capitalism—manifested by material abundance, advanced technology, and enhanced productivity—was unprecedented compared to all previous economic systems. It was precisely the development of productive forces, previously hindered by the class of the "indolent" and "ignorant" landlords, as described by Adam Smith, now unleashed under capitalism, that granted capitalism its political legitimacy to replace feudalism as an alternative economic system. As a result, capitalism manages to generate abundant economic surplus, which provides the material base for the improvement of people's living standards.

Today, however, the global capitalist regime is mired in economic stagnation, with extreme income inequality on the one hand, and the massive waste of human resources through unemployment and underemployment on the other. And on top of these issues is the ecological crisis, which, with its global scope, is the most dire challenge of all. Each of the failed, mostly market-based, attempts to mitigate the climate crisis thus far have made it more apparent than ever that the root cause of the crisis is the endless accumulation of capital, which is nothing more than the very definition of capitalism itself.

Many say that capitalism has always been resilient in the aftermath of crises. However, most of the capitalist crises were only postponed rather than resolved. The impact of the Great Depression was mitigated by the creation of a 75% tax on the rich so that some economic surplus could be used to address urgent public needs. Up until the 1900s, such compromise from the capitalist class was unprecedented in the United States. Instead of leading to a head-on collision between capitalism and public interests, the recession in the 1970s was temporarily relieved by the widespread implementation of neoliberal policies beginning in the 1980s. These policies not only brought a substantial loss in well-being to the working class, but also planted the seeds of the 2008 crisis, in which we are still deeply entrapped.

Today, when those who claim a significant portion of the economic surplus have the least to lose from climate destabilization, it is hardly surprising that they have a different perception of the urgency of the issue. One example is the recent announcement from Jeff Bezos, Amazon's founder and the richest person in the world, that he will invest in the development of space technologies as a solution to climate change. Turning a blind eye toward the poor in Bangladesh—who would be among the first to suffer the loss of their homes when sea levels rise as a result of climate change—Bezos prefers to use his money to divert attention away from the Earth and toward a new planet that people, mostly likely those in his class, can relocate to in the indefinite future.

The Green New Deal and Capitalism's Legitimacy

The uniqueness of climate change is that it threatens the reproduction of the inhabitable ecosystem that we live in today. The ecosystem is as essential as food, clothing, shelter, and transportation, if not more so. Hence the expenditure on its preservation, through the Green New Deal, falls within the cost of the necessary reproduction of human society.

Yet the surplus-owning class is reluctant to consider spending on climate change mitigation. Economists who are sympathetic to the Green New Deal have cautiously proposed public debt as a solution, in an attempt to circumvent any implications of transferring private wealth into the hands of the government, as occurred under the New Deal.

Such reluctance from the surplus-owning class to preserve human beings' only habitat demonstrates the irrationality of the capitalist economic system; and their hesitancy raises the larger question of whether capitalism itself has come to its own historical limit. This kind of crisis of confidence in our political and economic institutions is not new to capitalism. During the Great Depression in the 1930s—when one-quarter of the labor force was unemployed and radical left organizations were in their heyday—was the last time capitalism faced such a life-or-death challenge. The current planetary disaster is posing a threat no less severe than what occurred nearly 90 years ago.

There are only two possible trajectories. The capitalist class will either allocate part of the surplus it owns to a more comprehensive solution to the ecological crisis, such as the Green New Deal (which would most likely happen as a result of pressure from the broader public, i.e., the working classes). Or, it will continue to deploy its surplus for purposes other than climate action. At stake is both the political legitimacy of our current global economic system and the fate of a livable environment for human beings. Given the amount of hostility on the part of capitalists to the Green New Deal, capitalism itself is in overt conflict with the future of humanity. ❏

Sources: Paul A. Baran, The Political Economy of Growth (Monthly Review Press, 1957); Zhun Xu, "Economic Surplus, the Baran Ratio, and Capital Accumulation," *Monthly Review*, March 1, 2019; Baki Guney Isikara, "The Weight of Essentials in Economic Activity," Working Paper, 2019; Anders Fremstad and Mark Paul, "Overcoming the Ideology of Climate Inaction," Project Syndicate, Feb. 25, 2019 (project-syndicate.org); Enno Schröder and Servaas Storm, "Economic Growth and Carbon Emissions: The Road to 'Hothouse Earth' is Paved with Good Intentions," Institute for New Economic Thinking, November 2018; Catherine Clifford, "Jeff Bezos: I spend my billions on space because we're destroying Earth," CNBC, July 17, 2019 (cnbc.com); Mark Paul, "The Economic Case for the Green New Deal," Forbes, Feb. 20, 2019 (forbes.com).

Article 6.2

PRICING THE PRICELESS
Inside the Strange World of Cost-Benefit Analysis

BY LISA HEINZERLING AND FRANK ACKERMAN
March/April 2003

How strictly should we regulate arsenic in drinking water? Or carbon dioxide in the atmosphere? Or pesticides in our food? Or oil drilling in scenic places? The list of environmental harms and potential regulatory remedies often appears to be endless. In evaluating a proposed new initiative, how do we know if it is worth doing or not? Is there an objective way to decide how to proceed? Cost-benefit analysis promises to provide the solution—to add up the benefits of a public policy and compare them to the costs.

The costs of protecting health and the environment through pollution control devices and other approaches are, by their very nature, measured in dollars. The other side of the balance—calculating the benefits of life, health, and nature in dollars and cents—is far more problematic. Since there are no natural prices for a healthy environment, cost-benefit analysis creates artificial ones. Researchers, for example, may ask a cross-section of the affected population how much they would pay to preserve or protect something that can't be bought in a store. The average American household is supposedly willing to pay $257 to prevent the extinction of bald eagles, $208 to protect humpback whales, and $80 to protect gray wolves.

Costs and benefits of a policy, however, frequently fall at different times. When the analysis spans a number of years, future costs and benefits are discounted, or treated as equivalent to smaller amounts of money in today's dollars. The case for discounting begins with the observation that money received today is worth a little more than money received in the future. (For example, if the interest rate is 3%, you only need to deposit about $97 today to get $100 next year. Economists would say that, at a 3% discount rate, $100 next year has a present value of $97.) For longer periods of time, or higher discount rates, the effect is magnified. The important issue for environmental policy is whether this logic also applies to outcomes far in the future, and to opportunities—like long life and good health—that are not naturally stated in dollar terms.

Why Cost-Benefit Analysis Doesn't Work

The case for cost-benefit analysis of environmental protection is, at best, wildly optimistic and, at worst, demonstrably wrong. The method simply does not offer the policy-making panacea its adherents promise. In practice, cost-benefit analysis frequently produces false and misleading results. Moreover, there is no quick fix, because these failures are intrinsic to the methodology, appearing whenever it is applied to any complex environmental problem.

It puts dollar figures on values that are not commodities, and have no price.

Artificial prices have been estimated for many benefits of environmental regulation. Preventing retardation due to childhood lead poisoning comes in at about $9,000 per lost IQ point. Saving a life is ostensibly worth $6.3 million. But what can it mean to say that one life is worth $6.3 million? You cannot buy the right to kill someone for $6.3 million, nor for any other price. If analysts calculated the value of life itself by asking people what it is worth to them (the most common method of valuation of other environmental benefits), the answer would be infinite. The standard response is that a value like $6.3 million is not actually a price on an individual's life or death. Rather, it is a way of expressing the value of small risks of death. If people are willing to pay $6.30 to avoid a one in a million increase in the risk of death, then the "value of a statistical life" is $6.3 million.

It ignores the collective choice presented to society by most public health and environmental problems.

Under the cost-benefit approach, valuation of environmental benefits is based on individuals' private decisions as consumers or workers, not on their public values as citizens. However, policies that protect the environment are often public goods, and are not available for purchase in individual portions. In a classic example of this distinction, the philosopher Mark Sagoff found that his students, in their role as citizens, opposed commercial ski development in a nearby wilderness area, but, in their role as consumers, would plan to go skiing there if the development was built. There is no contradiction between these two views: as individual consumers, the students would have no way to express their collective preference for wilderness preservation. Their individual willingness to pay for skiing would send a misleading signal about their views as citizens.

It is often impossible to arrive at a meaningful social valuation by adding up the willingness to pay expressed by individuals. What could it mean to ask how much you personally are willing to pay to clean up a major oil spill? If no one else contributes, the clean-up won't happen regardless of your decision. As the Nobel Prize-winning economist Amartya Sen has pointed out, if your willingness to pay for a large-scale public initiative is independent of what others are paying, then you probably have not understood the nature of the problem.

It systematically downgrades the importance of the future.

One of the great triumphs of environmental law is that it seeks to avert harms to people and to natural resources in the future, and not only within this generation, but in future generations as well. Indeed, one of the primary objectives of the National Environmental Policy Act, which has been called our basic charter of environmental protection, is to nudge the nation into "fulfill[ing] the responsibilities of each generation as trustee of the environment for succeeding generations."

The time periods involved in protecting the environment are often enormous—even many centuries, in such cases as climate change, radioactive waste, etc. With time spans this long, any discounting will make even global catastrophes seem trivial. At a discount rate of 5%, for example, the deaths of a billion people 500 years from now become less serious than the death of one person today. Seen in this way, discounting looks like a fancy justification for foisting our problems off onto the people who come after us.

It ignores considerations of distribution and fairness.

Cost-benefit analysis adds up all the costs of a policy, adds up all the benefits, and compares the totals. Implicit in this innocuous-sounding procedure is the assumption that it doesn't matter who gets the benefits and who pays the costs. Yet isn't there an important difference between spending state tax revenues, say, to improve the parks in rich communities, and spending the same revenues to clean up pollution in poor communities?

The problem of equity runs even deeper. Benefits are typically measured by willingness to pay for environmental improvement, and the rich are able and willing to pay for more than the poor. Imagine a cost-benefit analysis of locating an undesirable facility, such as a landfill or incinerator. Wealthy communities are willing to pay more for the benefit of not having the facility in their backyards; thus, under the logic of cost-benefit analysis, the net benefits to society will be maximized by putting the facility in a low-income area. In reality, pollution is typically dumped on the poor without waiting for formal analysis. Still, cost-benefit analysis rationalizes and reinforces the problem, allowing environmental burdens to flow downhill along the income slopes of an unequal society.

Conclusion

There is nothing objective about the basic premises of cost-benefit analysis. Treating individuals solely as consumers, rather than as citizens with a sense of moral responsibility, represents a distinct and highly questionable worldview. Likewise, discounting reflects judgments about the nature of environmental risks and citizens' responsibilities toward future generations.

These assumptions beg fundamental questions about ethics and equity, and one cannot decide whether to embrace them without thinking through the whole range of moral issues they raise. Yet once one has thought through these issues, there is no need then to collapse the complex moral inquiry into a series of numbers. Pricing the priceless just translates our inquiry into a different language, one with a painfully impoverished vocabulary. ❑

This article is a condensed version of the report Pricing the Priceless, *published by the Georgetown Environmental Law and Policy Institute at Georgetown University Law Center. The full report is available on-line at www. ase.tufts.edu/gdae. See also Ackerman and Heinzerling's book on these and related issues,* Priceless: Human Health, the Environment, and the Limits of the Market, *The New Press, January 2004.*

Article 6.3

CAN WE AFFORD A STABLE CLIMATE?
Worst-Case Risks vs. Least-Cost Solutions

BY FRANK ACKERMAN
March/April 2019

The damages expected from climate change seem to get worse with each new study. Reports from the Intergovernmental Panel on Climate Change (IPCC) and the U.S. Global Change Research Program, and a multi-author review article in *Science*, all published in late 2018, are among the recent bearers of bad news. Even more signs of danger continue to arrive in a swarm of research articles, too numerous to list here. And most of these reports are now talking about not-so-long-term damages. Dramatic climate disruption and massive economic losses are coming in just a few decades, not centuries, if we continue along our present path of inaction.

It's almost enough to make you support an emergency program to reduce emissions and switch to a path of abrupt decarbonization: Something like the Green New Deal, the emerging proposal that would rapidly replace fossil fuels with massive investment in energy efficiency and clean energy, combined with high wages and standards, and fairness in the distribution of jobs and opportunities. (See Article 6.3, "Inequality, Sunk Costs, and Climate Justice.")

But wait: Isn't there something about economics we need to figure out first? Would drastic emission reductions pass a cost-benefit test? How do we know that the Green New Deal wouldn't require spending too much on climate policy?

In fact, a crash program to decarbonize the economy is obviously the right answer. There are just a few things you need to know about the economics of climate policy in order to confirm that Adam Smith and his intellectual heirs have not overturned common sense on this issue.

Worst-Case Risks: Why We Need Insurance

For uncertain, extreme risks, policy should be based on the credible worst-case outcome, not the expected or most likely value. This is the way people think about insurance against disasters. The odds that your house won't burn down next year are better than 99%—but if you own a home, you probably have fire insurance anyway. Likewise, young parents have more than a 99% chance of surviving the coming year, but often buy life insurance to protect their children if the worst should occur.

Real uncertainty, of course, has nothing to do with the fake uncertainty of climate denial. In insurance terms, real uncertainty consists of not knowing when a house fire might occur; fake uncertainty is the (obviously wrong) claim that houses never catch fire. See my book *Worst-Case Economics* for a more detailed exploration of worst cases and (real) uncertainty, in both climate and finance.

For climate risks, worst cases are much too dreadful to ignore. What we know is that climate change could be very bad for us; but no one knows exactly how bad it will be or when it will arrive. How likely are we to reach tipping points into an irreversibly worse climate, and when will these tipping points occur? As the careful qualifications in the IPCC and other reports remind us, climate change could be very bad surprisingly soon, but almost no one is willing to put a precise number or date on the expected losses.

One group does rush in where scientists fear to tread, guessing about the precise magnitude and timing of future climate damages: economists engaged in cost-benefit analysis (CBA). Rarely used before the 1990s, CBA has become the default, "common sense" approach to policy evaluation, particularly in environmental policy. In CBA-world, you begin by measuring and monetizing the benefits and the costs of a policy—and then "buy" the policy if, and only if, the monetary value of the benefits exceeds the costs.

There are numerous problems with CBA, such as the need to (literally) make up monetary prices for priceless values of human life, health, and the natural environment. In practice, CBA often trivializes the value of life and nature. Climate policy raises yet another problem: CBA requires a single number, such as a most likely outcome, best guess, or weighted average, for every element of costs (e.g., future costs of clean energy) and benefits (e.g., monetary value of future damages avoided by clean energy expenditures). There is no simple way to incorporate a wide range of uncertainty about such values into CBA.

Costs of Emission Reduction Are Dropping Fast

The insurance analogy is suggestive, but not a perfect fit for climate policy. There is no intergalactic insurance agency that can offer us a loaner planet to use while ours is towed back to the shop for repairs. Instead, we will have to "self-insure" against climate risks—the equivalent of spending money on fireproofing your house rather than relying on an insurance policy.

Climate self-insurance consists largely of reducing carbon emissions, in order to reduce future losses. (Adaptation, or expenditure to reduce vulnerability to climate damages, is also important but may not be effective beyond the early stages of warming. And some adaptation costs are required to cope with warming that can no longer be avoided—that is, they have become sunk costs, not present or future policy choices.) The one piece of unalloyed good news in climate policy today is the plummeting cost of clean energy. In the windiest and sunniest parts of the world (and the United States), new wind and solar power installations now produce electricity at costs equal to or lower than fossil fuel-burning plants.

A 2017 report from the International Renewable Energy Agency (IRENA) projects that this will soon be true worldwide: global average renewable energy costs will be within the range of fossil fuel-fired costs by 2020, with on-shore wind and solar photovoltaic panels at the low end of the range. Despite low costs for clean energy, many utilities will still propose to build fossil fuel plants, reflecting the inertia of traditional energy planning and the once-prudent wisdom of the cheap-fuel, pre-climate change era.

Super-low costs for renewables, which would have seemed like fantasies 10 years ago, are now driving the economics and the feasibility of plans for decarbonization. The Green New Deal may not be free, but it's not nearly as expensive today as it would have been just a little while ago.

Robert Pollin, an economist who has studied Green New Deal options, estimates that annual investment of about 1.5% of GDP would be needed. That's about $300 billion a year for the United States, and four times as much, $1.2 trillion a year, for the world economy. Those numbers may sound large, but so are the fossil fuel subsidies and investments that the Green New Deal would eliminate.

In a 2015 study, my colleagues and I calculated that 80% of U.S. greenhouse gas emissions could be eliminated by 2050, with no net increase in energy or transportation costs. Since that time, renewables have only gotten cheaper. (Our result does not necessarily contradict Pollin's estimate, since the last 20% of emissions will be the hardest and most expensive to eliminate.)

These projections of future costs are inevitably uncertain, because the future has not happened yet. The risks, however, do not appear dangerous or burdensome. So far, the surprises on the cost side have been unexpectedly rapid decreases in renewable energy prices. These are not the risks that require rethinking our approach to climate policy.

The disastrous worst-case risks are all on the benefits, or avoided climate damages, side of the ledger. The scientific uncertainties about climate change concern the timing and extent of damages. Therefore, the urgency of avoiding these damages, or conversely the cost of not avoiding them, is intrinsically uncertain, and could be disastrously large.

Climate Damages: Uncertain but Ominous, or $51 per Ton?

It has become common, among economists, to estimate the "social cost of carbon" (SCC), defined as the monetary value of the present and future climate damages per ton of carbon dioxide or equivalent. This is where the pick-a-number imperative of cost-benefit analysis introduces the greatest distortion: huge uncertainties in damages should naturally translate into huge uncertainties in the SCC, not a single point estimate.

According to scientists, climate damages are deeply uncertain, but could be ominously large. Alternatively, according to the best-known economic calculation, lifetime damages caused by emissions in 2020 will be worth $51 per metric ton of carbon dioxide, in 2018 prices.

These two rival views can't both be right. In fact, the $51 estimate comes from an awkward and oversimplified calculation; while it yields a better estimate than zero, it still threatens to obscure the meaning of deep uncertainty about the true value of climate damages.

The federal government's calculation of the SCC began under the Obama administration, which assembled an Interagency Working Group to address the question. In the Working Group's final (August 2016) revision of the numbers, the most widely used variant of the SCC was $42 per metric ton of carbon dioxide emitted in 2020, expressed in 2007 dollars—equivalent to $51 in 2018 dollars. Numbers like this were used in Obama-era cost-benefit analyses of new regulations, placing a dollar value on the reduction in carbon emissions from, say, vehicle fuel-efficiency standards.

To create these numbers, the Working Group averaged the results from three well-known models. These do not provide more detailed or in-depth analysis than other models. On the contrary, two of them stand out for being simpler and easier to use than other models. They are, however, the most frequently cited models in climate economics. They are famous for being famous, the Kardashians of climate models.

The Dynamic Integrated Climate-Economy (DICE) model, developed by William Nordhaus at Yale University, offers a skeletal simplicity: it represents the dynamics of the world economy, the climate, and the interactions between the two with only 19 equations. This (plus Nordhaus' free distribution of the software) has made it by far the most widely used model, valuable for classroom teaching, initial sketches of climate impacts, and researchers (at times including myself) who lack the funding to acquire and use more complicated models. Yet no one thinks that DICE represents the frontier of knowledge about the world economy or the environment. DICE estimates aggregate global climate damages as a quadratic function of temperature increases (i.e., damages as a percentage of world output are assumed to depend on the square of temperature increases), rising only gradually as the world warms.

The Policy Analysis of the Greenhouse Effect (PAGE) model, developed by Chris Hope at Cambridge University, resembles DICE in its level of complexity, and has been used in many European analyses. It is the only one of the three models to include any explicit treatment of uncertain climate risks, assuming the threat of an abrupt, mid-size economic loss (beyond the "predictable" damages) that becomes both more likely and more severe as temperatures rise. Perhaps for this reason, PAGE consistently produces the highest SCC estimates among the three models.

And, finally, the Framework for Uncertainty, Negotiation, and Distribution (FUND) model, developed by Richard Tol and David Anthoff, is more detailed than DICE or PAGE, with separate treatment of more than a dozen damage categories. Yet the development of these damages estimates has been idiosyncratic, in some cases (such as agriculture) relying on relatively optimistic research from 20 years ago rather than more troubling, recent findings on climate impacts. Even in later versions, after many small updates, FUND still estimates that many of its damage categories are too small to matter; in some FUND scenarios, the largest cost of warming is the increased expenditure on air conditioning.

Much has been written about what's wrong with relying on these three models. The definitive critique is the National Academy of Sciences study, which reviews the shortcomings of the three models in detail and suggests ways to build a better model for estimating the SCC. (Released just days before the Trump inauguration, the study was doomed to be ignored.)

Embracing Uncertainty

Expected climate damages are uncertain over a wide range, including the possibility of disastrously large impacts. The SCC is a monetary valuation of expected damages per ton of carbon dioxide. Therefore, SCC values should be uncertain over a wide range, including the possibility of disastrously high values. Yet the Working Group's methodology all but obscures the role of uncertainty in climate science.

A broader review of climate economics yields results consistent with the expected pattern. Look beyond the three-model calculation, and the range of possible SCC values is extremely wide, including very high upper bounds. Many studies have adopted DICE or another model as a base, then demonstrated that minor, reasonable changes in assumptions lead to huge changes in the SCC.

To cite a few examples: A meta-analysis of SCC values found that, in order to reflect major climate risks, the SCC needs to be at least $125.

A study by Simon Dietz and Nicholas Stern found a range of optimal carbon prices (i.e., SCC values), depending on key climate uncertainties, ranging from $45 to $160 for emissions in 2025, and from $111 to $394 for emissions in 2055 (in 2018 dollars per ton of carbon dioxide).

In my own research, co-authored with Liz Stanton, we found that a few major uncertainties lead to an extremely wide range of possible SCC values, from $34 to $1,079 for emissions in 2010, and from $77 to $1,875 for 2050 emissions (again converted to 2018 dollars).

Martin Weitzman has written several articles emphasizing that the SCC depends heavily on the unknown shape of the damage function—that is, the details of the assumed relationship between rising temperatures and rising damages. His "Dismal Theorem" article argues that the marginal value of reducing emissions—the SCC—is literally infinite, since catastrophes that would cause human extinction remain too plausible to ignore (although they are not the most likely outcomes).

Whether or not the SCC is infinite, many researchers have found that it is uncertain, with the broad range of plausible values including dangerously high estimates. This is the appropriate economic reflection of scientific uncertainty about the timing and extent of climate damages.

The Low Price of Self-Insurance

As explained above, deep uncertainty about the magnitude and timing of risks stymies the use of cost-benefit analysis for climate policy. Rather, policy should be set in an insurance-like framework, focused on credible worst-case losses rather than most likely outcomes. Given the magnitude of the global problem, this means "self-insurance"—investing in measures that make worst cases less likely.

How much does climate "self-insurance"—greenhouse gas emission reduction—cost? Several early (2008 to 2010) studies of deep decarbonization, pushing the envelope of what was technically feasible at the time, came up with mid-century carbon prices of roughly $150 to $500 per ton of carbon dioxide abated. (Prices were reported in 2005 dollars; multiply by 1.29 to convert to 2018 dollars.) Since then, renewable energy has experienced rapid progress and declining prices, undoubtedly lowering the cost of a maximum feasible reduction scenario.

Even a decade ago, at $150 to $500 per ton, the cost of abatement was comparable to or lower than many of the worst-case estimates of the SCC, or climate damages per ton. In short, we already know, and have known for a while, that doing everything on the least-cost emission reduction path will cost less, per ton of carbon dioxide, than worst-case climate damages.

That's it: the end of the economic story about evaluating climate policy. We don't need more exact, accurate SCC estimates; they will not be forthcoming in time to shape policy, due to the uncertainties involved. Since estimated worst-case damages are rising over time, while abatement costs (such as the costs of renewables) are falling, the balance is tipping farther and farther toward "do everything you can to reduce emissions, now." That was already the correct answer some years ago, and only becomes more correct over time. ❑

Sources: U.S. Global Change Research Project, *Fourth National Climate Assessment, Volume II: Impacts, Risks and Adaptation in the United States,* 2018; Intergovernmental Panel on Climate Change (IPCC), *Special Report: Global Warming of 1.5°C,* 2018; Philip Duffy et al., "Strengthened scientific support for the Endangerment Finding for atmospheric greenhouse gases," *Science,* Dec. 13, 2018; Frank Ackerman, *Worst-Case Economics: Extreme Events in Climate and Finance,* Anthem Press, 2017; Frank Ackerman and Lisa Heinzerling, *Priceless: On Knowing the Price of Everything and the Value of Nothing,* The New Press, 2004; Frank Ackerman, *Poisoned for Pennies: The Economics of Toxics and Precaution,* Island Press, 2008; International Renewable Energy Agency, *Renewable Power Generation Costs in 2017: Key Findings and Executive Summary,* 2018; David Roberts, "The Green New Deal, explained", Vox, 2018 (vox.com); Robert Pollin, "De-Growth vs. a Green New Deal," *New Left Review,* July-August 2018 (newleftreview.org); Frank Ackerman et al., "The Clean Energy Future: Protecting the Climate, Creating Jobs, Saving Money," Synapse Energy Economics, 2015 (frankackerman.com); U.S. Environmental Protection Agency, "The Social Cost of Carbon," 2017 (epa.gov); Interagency Working Group, "Technical Support Document: Technical Update of the Social Cost of Carbon for Regulatory Impact Analysis Under Executive Order 12866," August 2016 (epa.gov); Frank Ackerman and Charles Munitz, "Climate damages in the FUND model: A disaggregated analysis," *Ecological Economics* 77, 2012; Frank Ackerman and Charles Munitz, "A critique of climate damage modeling: Carbon fertilization, adaptation, and the limits of FUND," *Energy Research & Social Science,* 2016; National Academies of Science, Engineering and Medicine, *Valuing Climate Damages: Updating Estimation of the Social Cost of Carbon Dioxide,* National Academies Press, 2017; J.C.J.M. van den Bergh and W.J.W. Botzen, "A lower bound to the social cost of CO2 emissions," *Nature Climate Change,* 2014; Simon Dietz and Nicholas Stern, "Endogenous growth, convexity of damage and climate risk: How Nordhaus' framework supports deep cuts in carbon emissions," *The Economic Journal,* 2015; Frank Ackerman and Elizabeth A. Stanton, "Climate risks and carbon prices: Revising the social cost of carbon," Economics E-journal, 2012; Martin Weitzman, "On modeling and interpreting the economics of catastrophic climate change," *Review of Economics and Statistics,* 2009.

Article 6.4

INEQUALITY, SUNK COSTS, AND CLIMATE JUSTICE

BY FRANK ACKERMAN
March/April 2019

Climate change is at once a common problem that threatens us all, and a source of differential harms based on location and resources. We are all on the same boat, in perilous waters—but some of us have much nicer cabins than others. What is the relationship of inequality to climate policy?

The ultimate economic obstacle to climate policy is the long life of so many investments. Housing can last for a century or more, locking residents into locations that made sense long ago. Business investments often survive for decades. These investments, in the not-so-distant past, assumed continuation of cheap oil and minimally regulated coal—thereby building in a commitment to high carbon emissions. Now, in a climate-aware world, we need to treat all fossil fuels as expensive and maintain stringent regulation of coal. And it is impossible to repurpose many past investments for the new era: they are sunk costs, valuable only in their original location or industry.

If we could wave a magic wand and have a complete do-over on urban planning, we could create a new, more comfortable, and more sustainable way of life. Transit-centered housing complexes, surrounded by green spaces and by local amenities and services, could offer convenient car-free links to major employment sites. Absent a magic wand, the challenge is how to get there from here, in a short enough time frame to matter for climate policy.

Space is the final frontier in energy use. Instead of shared public spaces for all, an ever-more-unequal society allows the rich to enjoy immense private spaces, such as McMansions situated on huge exurban lots. This leads to higher heating and cooling costs for oversized housing, and to higher infrastructure costs in general: longer pipes, wires, and travel distances between houses. And it locks in a commitment to low population density and long individual commutes. Outside of the biggest cities, much of the United States is too sparsely settled for mass transit.

Pushing Toward Clean Energy

Carbon prices and other incentives are designed to push people and businesses out of the most emissions-intensive locations and activities. Along with the wealthy exurbs, cold rural states, with high heating and transportation requirements per person, will become more expensive. So, too, will investment in emissions-intensive production processes, whether in electricity generation, heavy industry, or agriculture.

The art of policymaking requires a delicate balance. Too much pressure to make fuel expensive can produce a backlash, as in the Yellow Vests protests in France, which successfully blocked an increase in the price of gasoline. Too little pressure leads to complacency, and to the false belief that enough is already being done. Subsidies to support the transition may be useful but must be time-limited to avoid becoming a permanent entitlement.

The Green New Deal, the hopeful, if still vague, political vision that is now drawing widespread attention, calls for a transition to clean energy, investment in low-carbon infrastructure, and a focus on equality and workers' rights. A massive jobs program is inseparable from this proposal: Clean energy requires huge amounts of work in construction, steelmaking (all those wind turbines), many branches of electronics, new technologies for motor vehicles, and more. It would create substantial net benefits for the country and the economy.

A more fine-grained analysis is needed, however, to identify those who might lose from a Green New Deal. Their losses will loom large in the policy debate, regardless of the benefits to the rest of society. For example, as Robert Pollin and his colleagues have pointed out, after years of seniority-based cutbacks, many of the remaining workers in legacy energy industries (coal mines, oil wells, fossil-fueled power plants) are nearing retirement age. Pension guarantees, combined with additional funding to allow early retirement, may be more important to these workers. New green jobs will be more important to their children, to the small number of younger workers in at-risk jobs, and to those who have historically been excluded or under-represented in industrial employment.

Older residents who have spent their lives and invested their savings in a rural community, or have no assets except a farm, should be welcome to remain in those communities. But the lingering mystique of an almost-vanished rural America should not lead to new initiatives to attract younger residents back to an energy-intensive, emissions-intensive lifestyle.

Responding to Inequality

Energy use and carbon emissions are quite unequally distributed within, as well as between, countries. In all but the poorest countries, the rich spend more on energy in absolute dollar terms, but less than others as a percentage of income. As a result, any carbon price introduced in the United States or other high-income countries will be regressive, taking a greater percentage of income from lower-income households.

To address this problem, economist James Boyce proposes refunding carbon revenues to households on an equal per capita basis, in a cap-and-dividend system. Boyce's calculations show that most people could come out ahead on a cap-and-dividend plan: only the richest 20% of U.S. households would lose from paying a relatively high carbon price, if the revenues were refunded via equal per capita dividends.

Other authors have proposed that some of the revenues could go to basic research or to infrastructure development, accelerating the arrival of sustainable energy use. Any use of the revenues, except distribution in proportion to individual fuel use or emissions, preserves the incentive effect of a carbon price. The question of cap-and-dividend versus investment in sustainable energy is largely a debate about what will make a regressive carbon price politically acceptable.

Stranded Assets

It is not only households that have invested too heavily in now-obsolete patterns of energy use. The same pattern arises in a different context, in the energy sector itself. Electric utilities have often invested in fossil-fuel-burning plants, expecting to recover their investment over 20 to 30 years of use. Now, as changing prices and priorities shut down some of those plants before the end of their planned lifetimes, the unrecovered investment is a stranded asset, no longer useful for producers or customers.

The problem is further complicated by the regulatory bargains made in many states. Depending on utility regulations (which differ from state to state), a utility may have formally agreed to allow state regulators to set its rates, in exchange for an opportunity to recover its entire investment over a long period of years. What happens to that regulatory bargain when a regulated plant becomes uneconomic to operate?

Businesses whose investments have gone badly do not elicit the same degree of sympathy as individuals stuck in energy-intensive homes and careers. Indeed, Milton Friedman, the godfather of modern conservative economics, used to emphasize that private enterprise is a profit and loss system, where losses are even more important than profits in forcing companies to use their resources effectively.

Despite Friedman's praise of losses, demanding that a utility absorb the entire loss on its stranded assets could provoke political obstacles to clean energy and climate policy. Neither zero recovery nor full recovery of a utility's stranded assets may be appropriate in theory. Once again, it is the political art of the deal, not any fixed economic formula, that determines what should be done. Offering utilities too little provokes opposition and delay; offering them too much is unfair to everyone else and could encourage similar mistaken investments in the future.

What Does Global Sustainability Look Like?

Climate change is a global problem that can only be solved by cooperation among all major countries. The challenge for American policy is not only to reduce our own emissions, but to also play a constructive role in global climate cooperation. U.S. leadership, in cooperation with China and Europe, is crucial to the global effort to control the climate. Reviving that leadership, which had barely surfaced under President Barack Obama before being abandoned by President Donald Trump, is among the most important things we can do for the world today.

In the longer run, questions of climate justice and international obligations are among the most difficult aspects of climate policy. High-income countries such as the United States and northern Europe bear substantial responsibility for the climate crisis worldwide. Among other approaches, the Greenhouse Development Rights framework combines historical responsibility for emissions and current ability to pay for mitigation in assigning shares of the global cost of climate stabilization.

In the current political climate there is no hope of achieving complete consensus about international burden-sharing before beginning to address the climate crisis. The urgency of climate protection requires major initiatives as soon as possible, in parallel with (not waiting for the conclusion of) discussions of international equity. U.S. actions on both fronts are essential for global progress toward climate stabilization. Significant steps toward equity and burden-sharing may be required to win the support of emerging economies such as India, Indonesia, and Brazil.

Assuming it succeeds, what would global sustainable development look like? In view of the rapid urbanization of emerging economies, the key question is, what kind of low-carbon urban life can the world afford? The sprawling, car-intensive and carbon-intensive expanse of Los Angeles, Phoenix, or Houston seems like an amazingly expensive mistake. The compact, energy-efficient, transit-based urbanism of Tokyo or Hong Kong is at least a contender, a high-income life with much lower resource use per person.

The American example matters around the world: if our vision of the good life remains one of extravagant sprawl, others will try to imitate it. If we develop a more sustainable vision of our own future, the whole world will be watching. ❑

Sources: James Boyce, "Carbon Pricing: Effectiveness and Equity," *Ecological Economics*, 2018; Milton Friedman, "Chrysler: Are Jobs the Issue?," *Newsweek*, Sept. 10, 1979; P. Simshauser, "Monopoly regulation, discontinuity and stranded assets," *Energy Economics*, 2017; Paul Baer et al., "The greenhouse development rights framework: Drawing attention to inequality within nations in the global climate policy debate," *Development and Change*, 2009; Robert Pollin et al., "Green New Deal for U.S. States," Political Economy Research Institute, University of Massachusetts–Amherst, 2017 (perri.umass.edu).

Article 6.5

MAPPING ENVIRONMENTAL INJUSTICE
Race, Class, and Industrial Air Pollution

BY KLARA ZWICKL, MICHAEL ASH, AND JAMES K. BOYCE
November/December 2015

E ast St. Louis, Ill., just across the Mississippi River from St. Louis, Mo., is not your typical American town. It has a hazardous waste incinerator, numerous chemical plants, and multiple "national priority" toxic waste sites. It's also home to 26,000 residents, 98% of them African-American. The median household income is about $21,000—meaning that half the households in the city have annual incomes even lower. The rate of childhood asthma is among the highest in the nation.

America's polluters are not color-blind. Nor are they oblivious to distinctions of class. Studies of environmental inequality have found that minorities and low-income communities often bear disproportionate pollution burdens. One of the reasons was revealed in a consultant report to the California Waste Management Board that surfaced in the 1980s: "A great deal of time, resources, and planning could be saved and political problems avoided if people who are resentful and people who are amenable to Waste-to-Energy projects [a.k.a. incinerators] could be identified before selecting a site," the report observed. It recommended that "middle and higher-socioeconomic strata neighborhoods should not fall at least within the one-mile and five-mile radii of the proposed site."

Rather than being distributed randomly across the U.S. population, pollution mirrors the distribution of power and wealth. Pollution disparities reflect conscious

FIGURE 1: INDUSTRIAL AIR TOXICS EXPOSURE BY EPA REGION

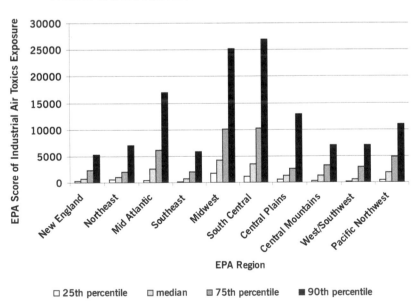

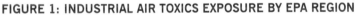

□ 25th percentile   ▨ median   ▦ 75th percentile   ■ 90th percentile

decisions—decisions by companies to locate hazardous facilities in vulnerable communities, and decisions by government regulators to give less priority to environmental enforcement in these communities. They can also reflect neighborhood changes driven by environmental degradation: pollution pushes out the affluent and lowers property values, while poorer people seeking low-cost housing move in, either unaware of the health risks or unable to afford alternatives. Even after accounting for differences related to income, however, studies find that racial and ethnic minorities often face higher pollution burdens—implying that disparities are the result of differences in political power as well as purchasing power.

The United States is a big, heterogeneous country. Electoral politics, social movements, industrial structure, residential segregation, and environmental policies differ across regions. So patterns of pollution may vary, too. Our recent study "Regional variation in environmental inequality: Industrial air toxics exposure in U.S. cities" examines these patterns to ask two key questions. First, is minority status or income more important in explaining environmental disparities? Second, does income protect minorities from pollution as much as it protects whites?

To tackle these questions, we used data on industrial air pollution from the U.S. Environmental Protection Agency (EPA). In the 1980s, in the wake of the deadly toxic gas release at a plant owned by the U.S.-based company Union Carbide in Bhopal, India, in which thousands of nearby residents were killed, environmental advocates in the United States demanded disclosure of information on hazards faced by communities near industrial facilities. In response, Congress passed the Emergency Planning and Community Right-to-Know Act of 1986, requiring corporations to disclose their releases of dangerous chemicals into our air, water, and lands. These are reported annually in the EPA's Toxics Release Inventory. The EPA

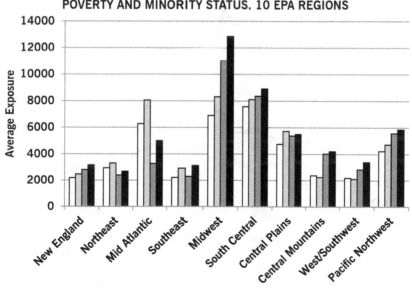

FIGURE 2: AVERAGE INDUSTRIAL AIR TOXICS EXPOSURE (EPA SCORE) BY POVERTY AND MINORITY STATUS, 10 EPA REGIONS

□ Non-poor white □ Poor white ▨ Non-poor minorities ■ Poor minorities has combined these data with information on the toxicity and dispersion of hazard-ous chemical releases to create the Risk-Screening Environmental Indicators (RSEI), the database we use, that estimates the total human health risks in neighborhoods across the country from multiple industrial pollution sources and chemicals.

Industrial air pollution varies greatly across regions of the country. Figure 1 shows the level of health risk faced by the median resident (in the middle of the region's exposure distribution) as well as by more highly impacted residents (in the 75th and 90th percentiles of exposure). The Midwest and South Central regions have the highest levels, reflecting historical patterns of both industrial and residen-tial development.

Figure 2 shows average pollution exposure by region for four groups: non-poor whites, poor whites, non-poor minorities and poor minorities. Poor minorities con-sistently face higher average exposure than non-poor minorities, and in most regions poor whites face higher average exposure than non-poor whites. In general, poor minorities also face higher exposure than poor whites, and non-poor minorities face higher exposure than non-poor whites. But in mapping environmental injustice we do find some noteworthy inter-regional differences—for example, in the contrast between racial disparities in the Midwest and Mid-Atlantic regions—that point to the need for location-specific analyses.

Finally, Figure 3 depicts the average pollution exposure for four racial/eth-nic groups across income strata at the national level. The most striking finding here is that racial disparities in exposure are much wider among people who live in lower-income neighborhoods. At the lower-income end of the scale, the aver-age exposures of African Americans are substantially greater than those of whites. The lower average exposures for Hispanics in low-income neighborhoods are largely explained by their concentration in western and southwestern cities with

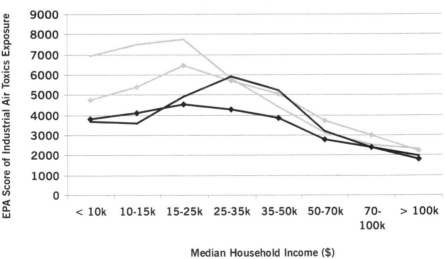

FIGURE 3: AVERAGE INDUSTRIAL AIR TOXICS EXPOSURE BY INCOME AND RACE/ETHNICITY, NATIONAL LEVEL

EPA Score of Industrial Air Toxics Exposure

Median Household Income ($)

——— African American   —◆— White   ——— Hispanic   —◆— Other Minority below-average pollution. Statistical analysis shows, however, that within these cities Hispanics also tend to live in the more polluted neighborhoods.

Pollution risk increases with average neighborhood income for all groups up to a turning point at around $25,000 per year. This can be explained by the positive association between industrialization and economic development. After that point, however, income becomes protective, and rising neighborhood income is associated with lower pollution exposure. Among these higher-income neighborhoods, racial and ethnic disparities in exposure are almost non-existent. But because of the correlation between minority status and income, minorities are more concentrated in lower-income communities whereas whites are more concentrated in upper-income communities. Based on where they live, whites may be more likely to see income as the main factor explaining disparities in pollution exposure, whereas African Americans are more likely to see the racial composition of neighborhoods as what matters most.

Environmental protection is not just about protecting nature from people: it's also about protecting people from other people. Those who benefit from industrial air pollution are the corporations that reap higher profits and their consumers, insofar as avoided pollution-control costs are passed on in the form of lower prices. Those who bear the greatest harm are the residents of nearby communities. Safeguarding the environment requires remedying this injustice and the imbalances of power that lie behind it. ❑

Sources: Michael Ash and T. Robert Fetter, "Who Lives on the Wrong Side of the Environmental Tracks?" *Social Science Quarterly*, 85(2), 2004; H. Spencer Banzhaf and Randall B. Walsh, "Do People Vote with Their Feet?" *American Economic Review*, 98(3), 2008; Vicki Been and Francis Gupta, "Coming to the nuisance or going to the barrios?" *Ecology Law Quarterly*, 24(1), 1997; James K. Boyce, "Inequality and Environmental Protection," in Jean-Marie Baland, Pranab K. Bardhan, and Samuel Bowles, eds., *Inequality, Cooperation, and Environmental Sustainability* (Princeton University Press, 2007); James K. Boyce, *The Political Economy of the Environment* (Edward Elgar, 2002); Paul Mohai and Robin Saha, "Reassessing Racial and Socioeconomic Disparities in Environmental Justice Research," *Demography*, 43(2), 2006; Rachel Morello-Frosch, et al., "Environmental Justice and Regional Inequality in Southern California: Implications for Future Research," *Environmental Health Perspectives*, 110(S2), 2002; Manuel Pastor, Jim Sadd, and John Hipp, "Which Came First? Toxic Facilities, Minority Move-In, and Environmental Justice," *Journal of Urban Affairs*, 23(1), 2001; Evan J. Ringquist, "Assessing Evidence of Environmental Inequities: A Meta-Analysis," *Journal of Policy Analysis and Management*, 24(2), 2005; Klara Zwickl, Michael Ash, and James K. Boyce, "Regional Variation in Environmental Inequality: Industrial Air Toxics exposure in U.S. Cities," *Ecological Economics*, (107), 2014.

Article 6.6

CLIMATE CHANGE, SOCIAL JUSTICE, AND THE GREEN NEW DEAL

BY ARTHUR MacEWAN
November/December 2021; updated May 2022

> *Dear Dr. Dollar:*
> The Green New Deal combines proposals to combat climate change with social justice proposals. I care about and work for social justice, but doesn't combating climate change need to be given top priority regardless of the impact on social justice? After all, if climate change isn't stopped, there will be no social justice! —*Anonymous, via e-mail*

This question seems to be based on the assumption that efforts to combat climate change and efforts to advance social justice are in conflict with each other. This need not be the case. In fact, social justice can advance efforts to combat climate change.

The Carbon Tax Example

Consider a carbon tax, a tax that would effectively raise the price of fossil fuels, reducing the purchase of those fuels and leading to innovations that would provide other ways of producing energy. A carbon tax could be one small part of combating climate change. But one of the problems with a carbon tax is that it would fall heavily on low-income people—as, for example, low-income people tend to drive, and need gasoline, as much as the rich. So the tax, which would raise the price of gasoline, would take a higher share of the incomes of the poor than of the rich (making it a "regressive" tax).

Yet, there is another way. As in British Columbia, the revenue from the tax could be redistributed in equal shares to everyone, regardless of their income. (See Arthur MacEwan, "Reducing Green House Gases," *D&S*, March/April 2016.) Thus this "rebate" would be a higher share of the incomes of the poor than of the rich (a "progressive" redistribution). Done in this way, the carbon tax could advance both social justice and the abatement of climate change.

Moreover, the imposition of a carbon tax without social justice considerations is likely to raise widespread opposition, as was the case in France. In late 2018, the French government raised the tax on fuel, which would have been a small step toward curtailing climate change. The government's action led to massive demonstrations across the country that sparked the yellow vest movement (named for the yellow vests that protesters wore). (See Aarth Saraph, "Understanding France's Gilets Jaunes," *D&S*, January/February 2019.) While the fuel tax was the catalyst for the yellow vest movement, these demonstrations were also directed against the broad social injustices caused by economic inequality and instability. As a result of the protests, the government was forced to rescind the fuel tax.

Inequality, Workers, and the Green New Deal

The Green New Deal emphasizes that workers who are displaced in the effort to halt climate change should be provided with secure jobs, pay, and benefits that leave them in good conditions.

For example, social justice—simply fairness—demands that workers in the fossil fuel industry not be forced to bear the burden of those efforts from which we all benefit.

There is no need for these provisions of the Green New Deal to place social justice in conflict with environmental protection. Quite the opposite.

As the experience with the Keystone XL pipeline demonstrated, workers and their unions will often oppose initiatives to halt climate change when their jobs are at risk. The pipeline into the United States would have facilitated the development of the Canadian tar sands oil deposits, the burning of which emits high levels of carbon dioxide. After years of struggles by groups opposed to the pipeline, the Biden administration finally stopped the construction of the pipeline earlier this year. The struggles to halt the pipeline took longer and might have been lost because the unions of the workers who would have been employed to build the pipeline, along with some allies in the labor movement, supported its construction.

In an economy with a high degree of economic inequality, job insecurity, and weakened labor unions, some workers will oppose programs that would curtail climate change but threaten their jobs. Efforts to reduce inequality, create job security, and strengthen unions—all social justice efforts included in the Green New Deal—are, then, good foundations for combating climate change.

Impact of the Green New Deal

The Green New Deal is not a piece of legislation, and it does not provide a blueprint for how government actions can halt climate change. It sets out principles to guide what must be done, and at the center of those principles is that success on climate change must be combined with social justice. It is a very practical matter. Big change—and actions to halt climate change will be a big change—will always generate resistance from people who fear that their livelihoods will be negatively affected. If, however, those actions are combined with social justice actions, such as good jobs, good wages, and a good health care system, resistance will be greatly reduced—and often embraced by a wide spectrum of society.

Unfortunately, however, the Green New Deal has not led to the enactment of any legislation in Washington. Efforts to include climate-related provisions in the infrastructure bill enacted in 2021 were blocked by Republicans and one or two Democrats in the Senate. And the Build Back Better legislation, which would include aspects advancing both climate and social justice principles of the Green New Deal, has faced the same opposition and has not been enacted. Of course, behind this opposition in Congress has been the pressure—money and lobbying—of the large fossil fuel corporations, firms that have profited and would continue to profit from moving climate change right along.

Nonetheless, the Green New Deal provides an important inspiration, and also a guide for the growing social movement attempting to halt climate change. Halting climate change will ultimately depend on the strength of this movement, made up of numerous organizations around the country. Regardless of its immediate success generating legislation in Washington, the Green New Deal has already attained the very important success of driving this movement forward.

The Ethical Issue

It is easy to see the concern for social justice expressed in the Green New Deal as solely an ethical issue. It is an ethical issue: as with all economic programs, efforts to halt climate change should take into account the way they have different impacts on different social groups. Workers, the poor, and people of color have suffered disproportionately from air and water pollution and from the initial impacts of climate change; every effort should be made to prevent them from bearing new burdens from actions to halt climate change. This seems only fair.

The social justice provisions called for in the Green New Deal, however, are not solely an ethical issue. Advancing social justice can be an important foundation for the fight against climate change.

Further Thoughts on Social Justice and Climate Change

In my "Ask Dr. Dollar" column in the November/December 2021 issue of *Dollars & Sense*, titled "Climate Change, Social Justice, and the Green New Deal," I wrote: "It need not be the case" that "efforts to combat climate change and efforts to advance social justice are in conflict with each other." And further: "Advancing social justice can be an important foundation for the fight against climate change."

I think these statements were correct, and I provided examples to support my argument. At the same time, however, I think what I wrote is misleading, implying that there are never conflicts between social justice and combating climate change. But there are. Here's a prime example: Mining for cobalt, an ingredient in lithium batteries, takes place under horrid conditions in the Congo, conditions that the *Washington Post* notes take a high human toll.

In buying these minerals or buying the batteries which depend on these minerals, we are supporting a nefarious system of labor exploitation. In not buying these products, however, we would be undermining some aspects of the efforts to inhibit climate change.

Another example is that some of the rare earth minerals needed in electronic equipment to reduce/replace fossil fuel use are located on the lands of indigenous peoples. The mining of these minerals can disrupt the cultures of indigenous peoples and severely damage their environments. Understandably, indigenous people often oppose this mining activity. Do we abandon the mining and hold back climate change, or do we violate social justice by ignoring the interests and objections of indigenous peoples?

I see no easy solution to the conundrum presented by these cases, and there are certainly other, similar cases. Yet, these conundrums cannot be ignored. I do not want my article to lead people to avoid dealing with the real conflicts between halting climate change and working for social justice.☐

Sources: Alexandria Ocasio-Cortez, "Recognizing the duty of the Federal Government to create a Green New Deal," House Resolution 109, February 2019 (congress.gov); Jolanda Jetten, Frank Mols, and Hema Preya Selvanathan, "How Economic Inequality Fuels the Rise and Persistence of the Yellow Vest Movement," International Review of Social Psychology, January 14, 2020; Jake Cigainero, "Who Are France's Yellow Vest Protesters, And What Do They Want?," NPR, December 3, 2018 (npr.org); Matthew Brown, "Keystone XL pipeline nixed after Biden stands firm on permit," AP News, June 9, 2021 (apnews.com); James Rosen, "Labor unions criticize Biden action against Keystone XL pipeline, KOMO News, January 21, 2021 (komonews.com); Robinson Meyer, "The Green New Deal Does Not, Strictly Speaking, Exist," *The Atlantic*, July 13, 2021 (theatlantic.com).

Chapter 7

LABOR MARKETS

INTRODUCTION

Mainstream economics textbooks emphasize the ways that labor markets are similar to other markets. In the standard model, labor suppliers (workers) decide how much to work in the same way that producers decide how much to supply, by weighing the revenues against the costs—in this case, the opportunity costs of foregone leisure, and other potential costs of having a job, like physical injury. Workers are paid their marginal product, the extra output the firm gets from employing one extra unit (e.g., hour) of labor. Workers earn different wages because they contribute different marginal products to output. Of course, economists of every stripe acknowledge that, in reality, many non-market factors, such as government assistance programs, unionization, and discrimination, affect labor markets. But in most economics textbooks, these produce only limited deviations from the basic laws of supply and demand. The articles here address the complexities of labor markets and unemployment, with special attention to the impact of non-market factors.

In the first article, "The Great Resignation and the Labor Shortage" (Article 7.1), John Miller carefully describes the numerous reasons for the "Great Resignation," meaning the tight labor markets following the Covid-19 economic crisis. The evidence suggests that rather than a higher level of "quits," the issues in U.S. labor markets are about workers shifting jobs within the same industries, and the differential impact of the pandemic on some parts of the labor market—far more Covid-19 infections and deaths among lower-income workers, a dearth of child-care options that tends to keep mothers from returning to the workforce, a loss of former flows of migrant labor, and more.

Journalist Eoin Higgins, in "Covid Destroyed the Illusions of the Restaurant Industry" (Article 7.2), recounts the stories of some workers who have been able to leave jobs in an industry that many find doesn't pay enough or provide safe and dignified working conditions. The Great Lockdown has hit the restaurant industry and its workers particularly hard and the forced lockdown has led many workers to reevaluate their former jobs and future employment.

In "Can the Decline of Unions Be Reversed?" (Article 7.3), Arthur MacEwan provides an up-to-date analysis of the current status of organized labor as well as to the hurdles that await unions going forward in the United States. MacEwan's focus is on the recent organizing drive at Amazon's fulfillment center in Bessemer, Alabama.

An interview with economist Nancy Folbre, "Household Labor, Caring Labor, Unpaid Labor" (Article 7.4), reveals that women's labor is often "invisible"—in this case to official government economic accounts—as unpaid household labor. As Folbre argues, the exclusion of this labor from government estimates of employment and output (GDP) is "pretty crazy, since we know that these services contribute to our living standards and also to the development of human capabilities."

Next, we have an article about some of the most vulnerable workers during the Covid-19 epidemic, "Essential—and Expendable—Mexican Workers" (Article 7.5). Mateo Crossa and James M. Cypher explore the effects of the Covid-19 pandemic on Mexican workers on both sides of the border, including the forced reopening of the maquiladoras in Mexico and of meat packing plants in the United States.

In "Credible Strike Threats" (Article 7.6), Robert Ovetz explains the relevance of not just strikes but also strike threats, which if done with credibility can be as effective as actual work stoppages. Ovetz also reviews the inadequate data on the subject and efforts to improve the data, which is important to help keep track of union activity and labor market developments.

Next, in "The Fight for $20 and a Union" (Article 7.7), Martin J. Bennett extensively summarizes the recent history of minimum wage laws in the United States. This includes repeated successes at winning wage-floor increases through various genres of labor movement-building, most prominently the Fight for $15. While nearly all the action has been at the state and city levels, the issue looms large over the 2022 midterm elections.

Finally, in "'Free' Labor and Unequal Freedom of Expression" (Article 7.8), Zoe Sherman tells a fascinating history of what "free speech" means in the workplace—workers in private workplaces have no speech rights, while employers have full authority to limit speech in the private setting. This has meant piles of workplace propaganda and captive meetings smearing unions, while workers who speak up are subject to retaliatory firings.

Labor markets are still in churn after the shock of Covid-19, a common event after epidemics. But wages have even now failed to keep up with the fast inflation brought about by Covid-19 supply disruptions and unusually large state aid, leaving women and other providers of unpaid and caring labor disproportionately out of the workforce. But workers looking to take advantage of these tight labor market conditions are still subject to employer-dominated speech laws, the riskiness of strikes under U.S. labor regulations, and weak national wage laws. Time will tell what results from this unusual landscape.

Discussion Questions

1. (Article 7.1) What does Miller suggest are the causes of the "Great Resignation"? How reasonable is this term?

2. (Article 7.2) Why have so many restaurant workers re-evaluated their jobs? Does the fact that they have done so suggest that enhanced unemployment benefits have been good for the economy, or that they have been bad for the economy?

3. (Article 7.3) Why has there been a recent upsurge in union organizing activity? Why are unions important for the economy as a whole?

4. (Article 7.4) In Folbre's view, how has the "invisibility" of household labor and production from official economic data had negative consequences, both on our economic understanding and economic policies?

5. (Article 7.5) What is the "precariat"? How is Mexican labor on this side of the border similar to that of a precariat? How have Mexican workers been treated in the American meat-packing industry during the Covid-19 pandemic? What groups of people determine how Mexican workers are treated on both sides of the border?

6. (Article 7.6) Ovetz outlines how strike threats can be effective in gaining concessions of employers. How did the case of the University of California lecturers demonstrate this potential?

7. (Article 7.7) Bennett describes the recent history of state and city minimum wage laws. What special steps have been taken in some jurisdictions to adjust the wage floor for tipped workers, and the tendency of the minimum wage to lag behind inflation?

6. (Article 7.8) Sherman's article explains how the First Amendment limits government action to restrict speech, but not employers'. How does this create an unequal playing field in efforts to unionize workplaces? What tactics have employers historically used to stymie organizing drives? How have workers recently attempted to circumvent these rules?

Article 7.1

THE GREAT RESIGNATION AND THE LABOR SHORTAGE
What makes 2022 a great year for a job makeover?

BY JOHN MILLER
May/June 2022

For those truly motivated to land a new role, ascend to the next level, boost their salary—or all three—conditions have rarely been better. Job listings are plentiful, wages are rising and unemployment is low.

Career coaches and compensation consultants agree that workers need to seize this advantageous moment.

Make a list of the aspects of your job that you hate, said Michele Woodward, a Washington, D.C.-based career coach who guides executives through their job changes. The exercise will help spotlight what's bothering you. Get specific and remember that hating "everything" isn't a clarifying answer, she added.

—"Why 2022 Is the Year You Get Your Dream Job," Kathryn Dill, *Wall Street Journal*, Jan. 3, 2022.

> *Take this job and shove it*
> *I ain't working here no more*
> *My woman done left and took all the reason*
> *I was working for*
> *You better not try to stand in my way*
> *As I'm a-walkin' out the door*
> *Take this job and shove it*
> *I ain't working here no more*

—*"Take This Job and shove it," lyrics by David Allan Coe, song by Johnny Paycheck, 1977.*

The folks over at the *Wall Street Journal* have an important announcement: 2022 is the perfect year to finally land your dream job. Career coaches and compensation consultants are urging enterprising job hunters to start by making a list of the aspects of your job that you hate.

But you don't need an overpriced career coach or a fancy consultant to get that advice. Just break into your vinyl vault and give Johnny Paycheck's pro- test ballad, "Take This Job and Shove it," a spin. His lyrics are nothing other than a list of the aspects of his job that he hates. But unlike in 1977, when Paycheck's hit topped the country and western charts, 2022 is in fact an advantageous moment for getting rid of your nightmare job and finding a better one.

But we'll need to take a closer look at the Great Resignation and the labor shortage that has fueled it to tease out just what conditions have contributed to workers acquiring the bargaining power needed to ditch their jobs and get a better one.

Sizing up the Great Resignation

To begin with, "resignations" is not a term economists use. What economists track is quits, employees who leave their jobs voluntarily. Quits increased rapidly with the economic recovery from the pandemic recession, reaching 4.51 million in November 2021, the highest level on record up to that point. And 4.54 million quits in March 2022 topped that record.

Economists do use the term "great," as in the Great Recession of 2008–2009, and the Great Depression of the 1930s. Calling today's record level of quits the "Great Resignation," however, is most likely an exaggeration. Historical evidence suggests that quit rates were higher in 1945 at the close of World War II and likely higher in the late 1990s during the dot-com bubble as well.

That quits are rising is hardly surprising. Workers hold on to their jobs for dear life in an economic downturn. When the pandemic struck, the number of workers quitting their jobs fell by more than two-fifths (43%) from January 2020 to April 2022. Quits rise when the economy expands, creating more jobs and making it easier for workers to find another job. Nor is it surprising that quits would reach record highs in the current recovery, which has already replaced almost all of the jobs that were lost to the pandemic shutdown.

More low-wage workers than better-paid workers have quit their jobs. In December 2021, the quit rate (the percentage of workers who quit their job) for workers in the well-paid finance sector was less than a third of the quit rate for retail workers, and less than a quarter of the rate for those working in hotel and restaurants, where average wages were less than half of those in finance. Also, workers' compensation (wages and benefits) in low-paid sectors, with their elevated quit rates, is rising rap- idly. Workers in the leisure and hospitality sector, which pays rock-bottom wages, quit twice as often as the aver- age rate for all workers. Their compensation rose 6.9% during 2021, well above the 4.1% average for all private-sector workers. Better pay for low-wage workers is good news, especially for the U.S. economy. Low- wage workers (workers who make less than two-thirds of median earnings) are nearly a quarter of the U.S. workforce (23.8%), a much larger share than the 13.9% average for advanced economies.

We also know that job-switchers have been getting bigger raises than workers who stayed put. As of March of this year, the annual wage in- crease of the typical job-switcher was 7.1%, while the wages of those who stayed in their job increased 5.3%, according to the Federal Reserve Bank of Atlanta. And a survey conducted by ZipRecruiter for the *Wall Street Journal* found that a little under one half of job-switchers (45%) got a raise of 11% or more, and a bit more than one-fifth of them (22%) got a signing bonus.

Finally, there is good evidence that, by and large, workers are quitting their jobs, not work. For instance, economist Elise Gould at the Economic Policy Institute found that in January 2022, the rate of hires was greater than the quit rate in all 14 major sectors of the economy. So, it seems likely that workers who quit their jobs are taking jobs in the same sector.

For that reason, Minneapolis Federal Reserve President Neel Kashkari doesn't "really buy the Great Resignation" story. Instead, he calls what's going on in the labor market "a churn away from the toughest jobs," such as long-haul trucking, with its debilitating working conditions. And in his *New York Times* blog, economist Paul Krugman asked if the Great Resignation is actually "a great rethink." As he sees it, the large number of lay- offs during the pandemic shutdown gave workers time to reflect on their work life. And the rising number of job openings provided them with an opportunity to switch jobs if that's what their gut told them to do.

What's Behind the Labor Shortage?

But if workers who quit their jobs for the most part remain in the labor force, then what explains the ability of workers to find better jobs and to command higher salaries? A hesitancy to return to unfulfilling jobs, or a preference for attractive jobs over the toughest jobs, might fuel their desire for better work. But are the desires of today's workers for a better job really any greater than those of yesterday's workers? Johnny Paycheck would surely dispute that claim.

What is different is the current labor shortage. Today the number of job openings is far greater than the number of unemployed people looking for work. Job openings have exceeded the number of unemployed in only two periods since the U.S. Bureau of Labor Statistics began tracking job openings in 2000. The first was from January 2018 to February 2020, the last two years of the decade-long expansion that was ended by the pan- demic shutdown. The other began in June 2021 during the current eco- nomic recovery and continues today. During the first period, the number of job openings for each unemployed worker peaked at 1.24. But in March 2022, that ratio reached 1.94, the highest level on record.

What accounts for the tightest labor market in the last two decades? Part of the answer is that the current recovery is on pace to add back jobs lost during the downturn in about half the time it took the long, sluggish recovery from the Great Recession to replace a smaller number of lost jobs. The average number of jobs created each month from April 2020 to April 2022 was four times the monthly average from January 2010 to January 2020.

While the number of job openings has gone up at a record pace, what explains the fact that the number of unemployed people looking for work has not matched the increasing number of job openings? Several factors are at work:

Increased obstacles for workers, especially mothers, to return to the labor force. While steadily increasing, the U.S. labor force participation rate (the percentage of the adult population employed or looking for work) in April 2022 was still below its peak level in February 2020, before the pandemic. In the eurozone and Canadian economies, both hard-hit during the pandemic downturn, labor force participation returned to its pre-pandemic levels by the end of 2021. The failure of U.S. labor force participation to bounce back in the same way can be attributed to a couple of factors. The first is that U.S. Covid-19 relief policies directly supported laid-off workers, while European policies subsidized employers so that they could continue to pay furloughed workers, keeping workers more closely tied to their employers. The second is infection and death rates from Covid-19. In Canada, for instance, infections and death rates per capita were but a third of those in the United States. U.S. Covid-19 death rates, in contrast, remain the highest of the 10 richest large countries. By mid-May 2022, Covid-19 deaths in the United States had topped one million, the most of any country, and second only to Brazil in the number of deaths per capita among major countries.

Also, unlike in other economic downturns, women lost their jobs more often than men in the pandemic recession. Employment losses were greatest in the service sector, where women hold most of the jobs. Childcare services, where four-fifths of the workers are women, were especially hard-hit, and as of March 2022 the number of childcare jobs was still 11.1% below their pre- pandemic level. The labor force participation rate for parents fell precipitously in the pandemic, but the most for women with children—3.18 percentage points from January to September 2020— as reported by economist Kathryn Edwards of the RAND Corporation. The labor force participation rates of women of prime working age (25 to 54 years old) remain below their pre-pandemic levels, although they have reached the same level as 2019. But without the increased childcare services that had supported the steady rise of women's labor force participation rates from 2015 to 2020, those rates are likely to remain depressed.

Those gender differences are also apparent in the quit rates of women who have returned to or remained in the labor force. Gusto, the payroll and benefits company, found that women's quit rate in January 2022 was 4.1%, considerably higher than the 3.4% quit rate for men. And the gender difference in quit rates was largest in the states with the highest incidence of daycare and school closings.

More retired people. Following the pandemic shutdown the number of retired workers increased by 3.6 mil- lion from February 20020 to June 2021. That was more than twice the average rate from 2010 to 2020. The uptick, however, was due to fewer retirees rejoining the labor force rather than more new retirees, as a study by Kansas City Federal Reserve Bank economists Jun Nei and Shu Kuei X. Yang documents. They point to "pan- demic health concerns," as the likely reason for the decline in the number of people transitioning from retirement back to employment. The percentage of the population over 55 years old in the labor force (employed or looking for work) in April 2022 is not only below its level at the onset of the pan- demic, but also no greater than it had been in 2008.

More self-employed workers. At the same time, the number of self-employed workers is well above the 2019 level, as Center for Policy Research economist Dean Baker has emphasized. Some of the self-employed are workers whose employers classify them as independent contractors to avoid regulation. But whether they're self-employed out of necessity or choice, their larger number reduces the number of unemployed people looking for work.

Fewer immigrant workers. Krugman points to another factor that is contributing to the labor shortage—the de- cline of international migration into the United States since 2016. From 2020 to 2021, net international immigration (entries less exits of immigrants) added 247,000 people to the U.S. population. But that number was less than a quarter of the 1,049,000 people net international immigration added to the U.S. population from 2015 to 2016. A far smaller net inflow of immigrants reduces the number of workers in the U.S. labor force.

Moving on Up

All told, from the low point of the pan- demic recession in April 2020 to March 2022, the number of job openings in- creased from one for every five unemployed workers to nearly two job openings for every unemployed work- er. That surely has brightened job prospects for workers, at least until the Fed's inflation fighting policies slow how quickly the economy grows and adds jobs.

So, you better start making your list of what you hate about your job and checking it twice, just as the career coaches and compensation consultants recommend. If you move quickly, this just might be the year you get a better job, and even, like Johnny Paycheck, let your boss know what they can do with your old job. ❑

Sources: Martin Sandbu, "On Wages and productivity," *Financial Times*, Aug. 19, 2021 (ft.com); Kathryn A. Edwards, "Women Are Leaving the Labor Force in Record Numbers," *Dallas Morning News*, Nov. 24, 2020 (dallasnews.com); Paul Krugman, "Wonking Out: Is the Great Resignation a Great Rethink?" *New York Times*, Nov. 5, 2021 (nytimes.com); Paul Krugman, "Whatever Happened to the Great Resignation," *New York Times*, April 5, 2022 (nytimes.com); Dean Baker, "Preview: Unemployment Likely to Hit 50 Year Low," Center for Economic and Policy Research, May 4, 2022 (cepr.net); Gregory Ip, "An American Labor Market Mystery," *Wall Street Journal*, Feb. 4, 2022 (wsj.com); Jun Nie and Shu-Kuei X. Yang, "What Has Driven the Recent Increase in Retirements," kcFED Economic Bulletin, Federal Reserve Bank of Kansas City, August 11, 2021 (kansascityfed.org); Neel Kashkari, Q&A with University of Minnesota Carlson School Alumni, University of Minnesota Carlson College of Administration, May 6, 2022; Luke Pardue, "A Real-Time Look at the 'Great Resignation'" (gusto.com); Gwynn Guilford and Sarah Chaney Cambon, "Workers are Changing Jobs, Raking In Big Raises – and Keeping Inflation High," *Wall Street Journal*, April 24, 2022 (wsj.com); Peter Coy, "Is the Great Resignation Overblown?" *New York Times*, Jan. 26, 2022 (nytimes.com).

Article 7.2

COVID DESTROYED THE ILLUSIONS OF THE RESTAURANT INDUSTRY

BY EOIN HIGGINS
July/August 2021

Restaurant owners are complaining that, because of generous unemployment benefits, their workers won't return to the industry now that restrictions imposed to deal with the coronavirus pandemic are loosening. These complaints are reported widely in the media.

But reporters are seldom talking to workers about their side of the story.

I spoke recently with people who have left or are leaving the industry in the wake of the pandemic. Here's what they said.

"The pandemic kind of stripped away the illusion of fairness and equity in the industry."

The restaurant industry is a hard business. Staff are expected to make the most of their shifts, whether the place is slammed or dead. And with hours likely to be cut at a moment's notice and low pay, the insecurity of the work can be stressful and exhausting.

Sarah, a restaurant professional who is leaving the business, once enjoyed the fast pace and camaraderie that service work can inspire in staff. Covid-19 was a wakeup call.

"I think like with everything else in society, the pandemic kind of stripped away the illusion of fairness and equity in the industry, or that it operated differently than other industries," she said.

The return of in-person dining has brought with it the nastier side of the customer experience, she said.

"Serving during a pandemic was truly awful, and during my bouts of unemployment this year I applied to grad school," said Sarah.

Jennifer, another industry professional who has returned to work, told me that at first after reopening, people were friendly and understanding—but around the holiday season, things got bad.

"People started getting really angry and nasty," Jennifer said. "They hate the lines and the waiting and that we are often out of something."

Unrealistic demands are being made on workers to sanitize and ensure public safety, said Jennifer. And this is all happening while management demands a level of service and customer attention at or beyond pre-Covid-19 levels.

"A lot of folks I know in the fine dining world are struggling because many places closed during the pandemic and some are re-opening but instead of hiring back their old staff they are trying to hire new staff for less money or less front-of-house staff," said Sean, a 10-year industry vet who organizes with the Restaurant

Organizing Project, a campaign launched by the Democratic Socialists of America in April 2020. Sean told me that all of this "means more front-of-house [staff] will do more work for the same or less money."

"I've got a wide variety of reasons why I don't want to come back."

Jeremy, a former Applebee's host, said he's not returning to the floor for a range of reasons.

"I worked as a host at Applebee's and I've got a wide variety of reasons why I don't want to come back," said Jeremy.

Chief among them, he told me, were the "brutal" shifts, the poor pay, and his fear that he could kill himself or the elders in his family if he went back.

Expanded government benefits helped make the decision to change careers an easy one, Jeremy said.

"It's enabled me to protect myself and pursue creative projects," Jeremy told me. "It's the perfect example of what happens when you don't have to work a brutal grind in some job that doesn't need to exist because you actually have a cushion of some kind, you can actually live."

Alan, a former dishwasher, said he's finished with the business—and that pandemic unemployment insurance is a big part of the reason.

"I was a dishwasher until we had to shut down because of restrictions," he told me. "The stimulus and unemployment benefits have definitely helped me be more picky about what jobs I'll take since I don't have to take anything I can get in order to cover rent and groceries."

I asked Alan if he'd go back to the industry. He said no, citing the security provided by the government aid.

"I have a degree in forestry and since I'm currently relatively financially secure, I can take more time to find a job in the field that I actually want to work in," Alan said.

"I made more money on unemployment than I did working at the bar."

Many service industry workers came out of pandemic lockdowns with a clear view of just how underpaid they really are after making far more from boosted unemployment insurance than they had made at their jobs.

Mark was laid off at the beginning of the pandemic. Once he went on unemployment, he said, things changed—for the better.

"I made more money on unemployment than I did working at the bar because they only gave me lunch shifts and I was part time," Mark told me. "They also overstaffed so there were fewer tips per person, I went from making $250-ish a week to a solid $600 a week from unemployment."

Lucas, a former Uber Eats driver, had a similar story.

"On a good week I could make about $200–$250 a week," Lucas told me. "When the CARES Act passed, I got $600 dollars a week [in] unemployment."

He returned to work briefly after the unemployment extension expired, but it wasn't worth it between poor pay, bad tips, and wear on his car. Plus, he already has respiratory issues.

Now he makes $450 a week on unemployment, still double an average week pre-Covid-19.

"Because of the stimulus checks and the unemployment, we've been able to stash away some money for the first time in a while," Lucas said.

"Having some time off to think and plan helped focus my desire to be paid better and treated better."

The people I talked to who aren't returning to the industry said the help from the government was a major motivator in getting time and space to make those decisions.

The break in work that the pandemic forced on Owen, a former line cook in Philadelphia, Penn., allowed for a reassessment of his life.

"I left because having some time off to think and plan helped focus my desire to be paid better and treated better," Owen explained, ticking off a number of familiar complaints about wages, hours, and a lack of respect from management.

Owen wasn't able to rely on unemployment, but support from friends and his partner, plus the stimulus payments, allowed him to focus on finishing school and getting a job where he's treated better. The search is on.

"I expect to make at least double and finally have nights and weekends off," Owen told me. "Hopefully I'll be treated with a little more dignity, but I know that's not always the case. Nowhere to go but up." ❑

Article 7.3

CAN THE DECLINE OF UNIONS BE REVERSED?

BY ARTHUR MacEWAN
May/June 2021

> Dear Dr. Dollar:
> *It seems pretty clear that strong labor unions have been important in reducing economic inequality. But as labor unions have represented a declining share of workers, inequality has gotten worse and worse. Insofar as the decline of unions has been a result of globalization and technological change, the picture is pretty bleak. So am I right to be pessimistic about significant reductions of inequality, at least through the impact of unions?*
> —Taya Abbott, Brookville, Ind.

Yes, strong labor unions have been a force for reducing economic inequality. While various factors are involved in the relationship between unions and equality, both unions' ability to raise workers' wages and their impact on government are involved. And, yes, things have gotten worse over the last several decades, both in terms of union membership numbers and inequality.

But, no, pessimism is not necessarily justified, both because much more is involved than globalization and technology and because of some recent potentially positive developments.

Some Potential Progress?

The recent defeat of the union drive by Amazon at its huge Bessemer, Ala., warehouse was, of course, a significant blow against union organizing. The size and importance of Amazon and its history of strongly resisting the unionization of its facilities drew a great deal of attention. Moreover, Alabama has long been an environment quite hostile to unions. Nonetheless, the union drive at Bessemer had raised the hopes of unions and union supporter across the county. So it would be easy to draw pessimistic lessons from this experience.

Yet the defeat should not have come as a surprise, and understanding that defeat could lead to positive responses. The experience in Alabama highlights the challenges facing unions and could force unions to find ways to respond more effectively to those challenges.

One of those challenges is the ability of a powerful firm, Amazon in this case, to frame the debate around a union drive. For example, according to a spokesperson, not surprisingly, Amazon claimed, "Our employees choose to work at Amazon because we offer some of the best jobs available everywhere we hire, and we encourage anyone to compare our overall pay, benefits, and workplace environment to any other company with similar jobs." Actually, various analysts have made the comparison, and have found that when Amazon builds a distribution center in an area, wages in the area tend to fall. An example is provided by a 2018 report in the

Economist magazine: "In the years since Amazon opened its doors in Lexington County [South Carolina], annual earnings for warehouse workers in the area have fallen from $47,000 to $32,000, a decline of over 30%." It seems that because of its size, Amazon's role in local labor markets is to push wages down generally.

More particularly, at Bessemer, while Amazon's presence may not have pushed area wages down, according to a March *New York Times* article: "The most recent figure for the median wage in Greater Birmingham, a metropolitan area of roughly one million people that includes Bessemer, was near $3 [an hour] above Amazon's pay there according to the Bureau of Labor Statistics."

Be that as it may, at Amazon's Bessemer operation, according to a February 7 report by National Public Radio, workers expressed concerns over "grueling productivity quotas and had wanted more input in shaping the workplace including how people get disciplined or fired." In the era of Covid-19, workers in many plants have turned their attention to job safety and layoffs, and have found union protection an important benefit. Nonetheless, Amazon appears to have been able to convince a majority of workers at the Bessemer warehouse that they were well-paid and that pay and benefits outweighed these sorts of problems.

Beyond Amazon, in the decade leading up to 2020, union victories in elections resulting from union petitions rose from an average of 65.7% in the 2010–2012 period to an average of 71.4% in the 2017–2019 period—not huge, but nonetheless notable. Moreover, in January and February of 2020, before the pandemic came to dominance, unions won 78% and 94%, respectively, of elections brought about by their petitions. Covid-19 appears to have thrown a monkey wrench in union organizing efforts, as the number of union recognition elections resulting from union petitions fell sharply in the rest of the year.

The experience of the last decade does not signal a dramatic turnaround for the unionization of the U.S. workforce and does not negate what happened at Amazon, but it does temper pessimism.

Political Factors

There remain, of course, the forces of globalization and technological change. While there is dispute over the relative impact of these two factors on unionization, it is clear that both jeopardize jobs and provide employers with a means to undercut unions. There are, however, two other factors that have been important in weakening unions over recent decades: political decisions and the increasingly aggressive anti-union activity of employers. Understanding these factors is a first step in figuring out how to conduct more effective organizing.

One way that political decisions, at various levels of government, undermine unions is the way in which globalization has been structured. If we take globalization to mean an increasing engagement with the international economy, there are different ways that this engagement can be accomplished. The U.S. government has implemented this engagement in ways that favor large firms, making it easy for them to move operations abroad without requiring them to bear the social costs of the dislocation they leave behind, or the environmental costs of the long-distance transportation of goods. Also, the U.S. government has been miserly in providing training and other means of support for workers displaced through globalization—or through technological change, environmental regulation, or anything else.

And then there are the direct anti-union actions of government. For example, the actions of the National Labor Relations Board (NLRB) have been especially unfriendly to unionization, as exhibited in its failure to stop workers engaged in union organizing from being fired. During Republican administrations, the NRLB has been much worse on this issue than during Democratic administrations. Yet, since the early 1950s, there has been an upward trend in the risk of being fired for people engaged in union drives.

As to Congressional action, after the National Labor Relations Act of 1935 gave a major boost to unionization, in 1947, in a very different political climate, the Taft-Hartley Act created a legislative context unfavorable to labor that has lasted for decades. The Employee Free Choice Act (EFCA), introduced in 2007, 2009, and 2016, was an example of an effort to shift the ground in favor of labor, but it was repeatedly rejected by Congress. The EFCA would have allowed a union to be certified as the official union to bargain with an employer if the union collected the signatures of a majority of workers; and the existing right of an employer to demand an additional, separate ballot would have been eliminated.

Currently, the Protecting the Right to Organize Act (the PRO Act), passed by the House of Representatives in 2020 and again in 2021, would give workers more power during disputes at work and add penalties for companies that retaliate against workers who organize. The passage of the PRO Act in the House was a sign of progress for unions. However, it has little chance of getting through a Republican filibuster in the Senate.

The political context of union-management relations has both set the stage for and been encouraged by the efforts of management to combat unionization. And a political change has also taken place in operations at the firm level. Labor historian John Logan (writing in 2006) describes the burgeoning of the "union-avoidance industry" over the

---

Not Only at the Federal Level

At the state level, direct actions to weaken unions and prevent wage increases have been widespread. Several southern states have had "right to work" laws in place for decades, and recently, other states have enacted such laws. In 2011, the attacks on unions in Wisconsin highlighted this trend. A "right to work" law prohibits a union from establishing a contract with an employer that requires all workers in the establishment to join the union. The result is that, even when a majority of workers have voted the union into existence and voted for the contract, a worker can decline to join, not pay union dues, and still get the benefits bargained for by the union. The PRO Act, if enacted (see main article), would override state "right to work" laws.

In many cases, as authorities in cities and towns have enacted pro-labor regulations, state governments have overridden ("pre-empted") those local regulations. On issues ranging from raising minimum wages to mandating paid leave to establishing fair scheduling, from 1997 to 2017, 26 state governments overrode local actions a total of 67 times, with 55 of these pre-emptions coming since 2011.

Based on the Economic Policy Institute's "Worker Rights Preemption in the U.S.: A Map of the Campaign to Suppress Worker Rights in the States," November 2017, (epi.org).

last several decades of the 20th century as involving consultants, law firms, industry psychologists, and strike management firms. He points out not only their success, but also that they have prospered in an atmosphere where he notes, quoting *Fortune* magazine, most U.S. employers "greet the prospect of unionization with the enthusiasm that medieval Europeans reserved for an outbreak of the Black Death." Logan concludes:

> Union avoidance experts have not been the major cause of union decline in the United States in the past half-century; nor have they been the sole source of the intensification of employer opposition to unionization since the 1970s…But they have contributed to the transformation of organizing campaigns into all-out struggles to the death.

What's the Point?

The point here is that the decline of unions and the difficulties that unions face in 2021 are not simply a result of some sort of inexorable forces, which is often how globalization and technological change are presented. The decline and difficulties have also been brought about by forces of political change, both through government and by the actions of employers and their allies in the union-avoidance industry.

What has been brought about by the force of political change can be reversed by political action, by more effective union organizing, including new approaches to organizing, and by greater pressure on the government by unions and their allies. This reality does not, perhaps, create a basis for optimism, but, along with some recent developments, leads to a rejection of pessimism.

In its efforts to prevent unionization at its Bessemer warehouse, Amazon hired the head of the consulting firm RWP Labor, one Russell Brown, who touts himself as "one of the nation's leading labor experts where he has worked with companies in maintaining a union-free workplace." As it turned out, the "expert" and the company were successful in this case, but that result was not automatic and can be reversed elsewhere. ❏

Sources: Celine McNicholas, Heidi Shierholz, and Margaret Poydock, "Union workers had more job security during the pandemic, but unionization remains historically low," Economic Policy Institute, Jan. 22, 2021 (epi.org); Jason Slotkin, "In Alabama, Workers At Amazon Warehouse Are Poised For Union Vote," NPR, Feb. 7, 2021 (npr.org); National Labor Relations Board, Election Reports, various years (nlrb.gov); "What Amazon does to Wages," *The Economist*, Jan. 20, 2018 (economist.com); Marshall Steinbaum, Eric Harris Bernstein, and John Strum, "Powerless: How Lax Antitrust and Concentrated Market Power Rig the Economy Against American Workers, Consumers, and Communities," Roosevelt Institute, Feb. 2018 (rooseveltinstitute.org); John Schmitt and Ben Zipperer, "Dropping the Ax: Illegal Firings During Union Election Campaigns, 1951–2007," Center for Economic and Policy Research, March 2009 (cepr.net); John Logan, "The Union Avoidance Industry in the United States, *British Journal of Industrial Relations*, December 2006 (jwj.org); Lee Fang, "Amazon hired Koch-backed anti-union consultant to fight Alabama warehouse organizing," The Intercept, Feb. 10, 2021 (theintercept.com); RWP Labor, rwplabor.com; Noam Scheiber, "Amazon Pay Isn't Highest," *New York Times*, March 19, 2021 (nytimes.com).

Article 7.4

HOUSEHOLD LABOR, CARING LABOR, UNPAID LABOR

AN INTERVIEW with NANCY FOLBRE

September/October 2015

Nancy Folbre *is a professor emerita of economics at the University of Massachusetts-Amherst. She is the author of numerous books, including* Who Pays for the Kids? Gender and the Structures of Constraint *(1994),* The Invisible Heart: Economics and Family Values *(2001), and* Valuing Children: Rethinking the Economics of the Family *(2008), related to household and caring labor.*

Dollars & Sense: You've written about the tendency in economics to view household labor (and especially women's labor) as "unproductive." Can you explain how this is reflected in conventional macroeconomic measures?

Nancy Folbre: Non-market household services such as meal preparation and childcare are not considered part of what we call "the economy." This means they literally don't count as part of Gross Domestic Product, household income, or household consumption.

This is pretty crazy, since we know that these services contribute to our living standards and also to the development of human capabilities. They are all at least partially fungible: time and money may not be perfect substitutes, but there is clearly a tradeoff. You can, in principle, pay someone to prepare your meals (as you do in a restaurant), or to look after your kids.

If you or someone else in your household provides these services for no charge (even if they expect something in return, such as a share of household earnings) that leaves more earnings available to buy other things. In fact, you could think of household income after taxes and after needs for domestic services have been met as a more meaningful definition of "disposable income" than the conventional definition, which is simply market income after taxes.

D&S: What is the practical consequence of not measuring household labor and production? Are economic policies and institutions different, especially in their impact on women, than what they would be if household labor were fully reflected in statistics on total employment or output?

NF: One macroeconomic consequence is a tendency to overstate economic growth when activities shift from an arena in which they are unpaid to one in which they are paid (all else equal). When mothers of young children enter paid employment, for instance, they reduce the amount of time they engage in unpaid work, but that reduction goes unmeasured. All that is counted is the increase in earnings that results, along with the increase in expenditures on services such as paid childcare.

As a result, rapid increases in women's labor force participation, such as those typical in the United States between about 1960 and the mid-1990s, tend to boost the rate of growth of GDP. When women's labor force participation levels out, as it has in the United States since the mid 1990s, the rate of growth of GDP slows down. At least some part of the difference in growth rates over these two periods simply reflects the increased "countability" of women's work.

Consideration of the microeconomic consequences helps explain this phenomenon. When households collectively supply more labor hours to the market, their market incomes go up. But they have to use a substantial portion of those incomes to purchase substitutes for services they once provided on their own—spending more money on meals away from home (or pre-prepared foods), and childcare. So, the increase in their money incomes overstates the improvement in their genuinely disposable income.

A disturbing example of policy relevance emerges from consideration of the changes in public assistance to single mothers implemented in the United States in 1996, which put increased pressure on these mothers to engage in paid employment. Many studies proclaimed the success because market income in many of these families went up. But much of that market income had to be spent paying for services such as childcare, because public provision and subsidies fell short.

D&S: You've also written extensively about "caring labor"? What is caring labor? To what extent is this labor (and the output of services associated with it) directly or indirectly captured by conventional measures like GDP?

NF: Everything I've discussed above is about quantity. But quality is also important. I define caring labor as labor where the quality of the services provided is likely to be affected by concern for the well-being of the care recipient. Love, affection, and commitment almost always enhance the care of dependents, and this is a big reason why market-provided services are not always perfect substitutes for those provided by family members and friends.

On the other hand, many people—especially women—work in occupations like childcare, eldercare, education, medicine, or social services where they genuinely care about their clients or "consumers." The market value of this work is counted as part of Gross Domestic Product and household income. But in many cases, the wage paid is considerably less than the value of the services provided. Workers in these jobs often give more in the way of quality than they are actually paid for.

D&S: As a practical matter, how could one go about measuring the value of services currently provided by unpaid household labor? In your estimation, how would our picture of economic life change if we did?

NF: It is pretty easy to estimate a lower-bound for the value of unpaid work by counting the number of hours that people spend engaging in it (which in the United States adds up to almost exactly the same total as hours of market work), and multiplying those hours times the hourly wage one would pay for a replacement.

Measures of hours worked in different activities such as meal preparation, childcare, cleaning, shopping, and so on are typically based on a nationally representative survey of individuals who report all of their activities on the preceding day. The American Time Use Survey, administered since 2003 on an annual basis as a supplement to the Current Population Survey, provides reliable, high-quality data on time use.

Several studies have used these data to assign a dollar value to non-market work in what is called a "satellite" national income account (because it revolves around, rather than replacing the conventional account). Obviously, including this value in a measure of "extended GDP" makes the economy look bigger. More importantly, it revises estimates of how the economy has grown over time—in the downward direction.

Counting the value of non-market work has an equalizing effect on measures of household income, not because low-income households do a lot more of it, but because most households of similar size and composition do about the same amount. Here again, the trends are more interesting than the levels: since the relative importance of non-market work has declined over time, its equalizing effect has probably also declined. ❏

Article 7.5

ESSENTIAL—AND EXPENDABLE—MEXICAN LABOR

On both sides of the border, Mexican workers are now essential—to U.S. corporations.

BY MATEO CROSSA AND JAMES M. CYPHER

July/August 2020

Lear Corporation—one of the world's largest auto parts manufacturers—rose to position 148 on *Fortune* magazine's famous list of the 500 largest firms in 2018. It operates with roughly 148,000 workers spread across 261 locations. Its largest presence is in Mexico, where approximately 40,000 low-paid workers make seats and labor-intensive electronic wiring systems to be used, primarily, by the U.S. auto giants in auto-assembly plants on both sides of the border. The largest share of these workers slog away in three huge Lear plants located in the notoriously dangerous border town of Ciudad Juárez in Mexico.

On April 10, 2020 a worker named Rigoberto Tafoya Maqueda died from Covid-19, which had swept in from the north. He had been diagnosed in Lear's clinic with a mild allergy and was forced to continue working without a face mask, gloves, or hand sanitizer. A short time later, he went to the government's Social Security hospital, on foot, where he died. Four days later, according to Lear, 13 more workers at the plant had died—but the workers' labor union claimed that the actual number of work-related deaths from the pandemic was 30. Lear claimed it was not responsible in the least, while offering hollow condolences to surviving family members.

As of late May, no investigation of the workplace had been conducted and no legal charges of negligence had been raised against Lear or any of the other 320 *maquiladoras*—also known as *maquilas*, or more recently, by outraged workers, as "*makilladoras*"—that employ approximately 230,000 in Juárez where workers have been sickened. By early May, 104 of these workers had perished, by early June the estimated number of worker deaths was above 200. In all of Mexico, this city, with the largest concentration of low-wage assembly plants, had the highest incidence of pandemic deaths—a mortality rate 2.5 times the national average.

Tijuana is the city with the second largest number of *maquilas* in Mexico. There, one in four "formal" sector workers (workers with registered jobs and certain rights to health care) work as low-wage laborers producing components for automobiles and many other industries. Tijuana is located in the state of Baja California in Mexico, where the highest number of pandemic deaths—519—had been recorded as of May 15. Of those deceased, 432 were *maquila* workers. By June 4, Tijuana had the highest number of Covid-19 deaths, 671, of any city in Mexico.

U.S. Business, U.S. State Department Demand: The *Maquilas* Must Open

Ciudad Juárez and Tijuana are tangible symbols of the imposed power structures under which transnational corporations operate throughout the Global South, most particularly in Mexico. In these two border cities, 1,000 miles apart, we find nearly one-fifth of the *maquila* workforce—500,000 out of a total of 2.6 million workers. Here, in response to corporations' treatment of workers during the pandemic, the scene has included bitter strikes, social outrage, and numerous well-attended protests all aimed at imposing plant closures and paid leave. The plant owners have refused to assume any responsibility whatsoever for their negligence, insisting that the work must go on. Instead, they have pressured local and federal governmental agencies to ensure that, in spite of an unsanitary environment, no new safety and health regulations of the workplace will be imposed. After reopening in late May, the plants have taken some measures to reduce health risks among the workers, including the use of masks and plastic dividers at workstations and in company lunchrooms.

At the same time, plants have increased the pace of production exponentially. Even with the measures taken, there have continued to be outbreaks of Covid-19 at the assembly plants. Indeed, the long-powerful U.S. National Association of Manufacturers (NAM) has used every opportunity to ensure that no sustained period of plant closures be implemented—including sending an unprecedented letter to Mexico's president on April 22, signed by 327 corporate titans who enjoy the lucrative benefits of sweating Mexican workers. Signatories included the heads of 3M Corporation ($32 billion in sales in 2019), Arcelor/Mittal USA ($15 billion in sales 2019), and Caterpillar ($54 billion in sales 2019). Using a lot of imagination, and no small amount of chutzpah, these captains of industry demanded that President Andrés Manual López Obrador (or AMLO, as he is known)—who had declared at the start of his presidency that the neoliberal era that had defined Mexico's economy since 1986 was over—declare that Mexican autoworkers were engaged in an "essential activity." The letter demanded that the president assure that "all interruptions in the North American manufacturing supply chain would be minimized in these critical moments." AMLO responded immediately by stating that Mexico and the United States would come to an agreement and that "there were exceptional questions" to resolve with the United States.

Has there ever been an occasion when a president of a sovereign nation has been told that its populace—beset by a vicious pandemic—would have to march into poisoned plants in order to maintain the profit margins of foreign-owned corporations?

If that was not enough, Christopher Landau, the U.S. ambassador to Mexico, gave himself a pat on the back in late April by declaring via Twitter, "I'm doing all I can to save supply chains between Mexico, the United States, and Canada." Immediately joining the fray, the employers' and manufacturers' "peak business organizations"—long the real rulers of Mexico—began to lobby and orchestrate political pressure to guarantee that *maquila* output would not be interrupted. The large owners associations included the *Consejo Coordinador Empresarial* (CCE), which is comprised of the largest Mexican firms, and the arch-conservative Mexican Employers Association (COPARMEX), which was formed in 1929 by the anti-union oligarchy based in industrial Monterrey, echoed the arguments presented by the NAM. Also joining in was the Association of the Mexican Auto Industry (which was founded in 1951 by Chrysler, Ford, General Motors, Nissan, and Volkswagen, and lists *no* Mexican-owned companies as members).

A National Security Issue?

At this point, an unexpected actor entered the scene: The Undersecretary of Defense of the United States, Ellen Lord, declared to reporters in late April, "I think one of the key things we have found out are some international dependencies..." adding that "Mexico right now is somewhat problematic for us." In her remarks, Lord said nothing about the Mexican workers who toil in the *maquilas* becoming ill or dying. (*Maquilas* are now located throughout the country, not just along the U.S.-Mexican border.) She also added the "national security" argument to her framing of the pandemic's impact on U.S.-Mexico supply chains: "these companies are especially important for our U.S. airframe production." And, indeed, over the past 20 years the United States has outsourced a modest amount of aerospace production: in Mexico this consists of labor-intensive components that are used by the U.S. civilian aviation firms, along with some Pentagon military contractors, and are typically manufactured in *maquilas*. One example of this minor sideline of *maquila* manufacturing—and the conditions that workers face at these factories—is a Honeywell plant in Juárez where, on April 22, workers engaged in a three-day wildcat strike after learning that Covid-19 had spread into the plant, killing at least one worker.

One protesting worker summarized the situation:

> They do not want to give us [sick] days, we are worried because of the pandemic, management does not listen to us, they only tell us [to keep working] and they will give us a bonus of $18-$31.50 [dollars per week] but they will not respond to our demands, we have been on strike three days but the truth is that they are paying no attention to us.

Inaugurating the USMCA

The U.S. pressure game got quick results: on May 12 the Mexican government declared that the aerospace *maquilas* (which, as of 2020, had only 57,000 direct employees) and the very large auto parts and auto assembly industry—which employs nearly 960,000 workers and is a mainstay of the "export-at-all-costs" neoliberal model—were "essential" industries. With this decree, the alarm bells ceased in the United States. Further, the Mexican government set June 1, 2020 as the date to return to full operation in the auto industry, which ensured that the beginning of the NAFTA-II agreement (officially the United States-Mexico-Canada Agreement, or the USMCA) was still on track for July 1, 2020. President Donald Trump will undoubtedly use the official launch of the USMCA to maximum effect as he hones his electoral strategy. AMLO supports this new agreement to "help stop the fall of the economy" and promote new foreign investments.

The list of transnational firms that are already in production—or will shortly resume—where Covid-19 has spread is a long one, and includes such companies as: Lear Corporation, Honeywell, Syncreon Borderland, Foxconn, Plantronics, Leoni, Rockwell, Mahle, Electrocomponentes de México, Electrolux, Hubbell, Commscope, Toro Company, Ethicon, Cordis, Syncreon, Flex, Keytronic, Optron, TPI, and APTIV. In April, shutdowns affected approximately 60% of all *maquiladora* workers in Juárez—a situation that was probably representative for the entire industry—suggesting that as many as 3,000 of the 5,162 *maquiladora* firms operating in April temporarily closed. The companies that are reopening are doing so without regard for the deaths of hundreds of their plant workers (some registered, some not). These firms have been the most enthusiastic advocates of restarting production as they have sought to drown out the resistance of their workers. On May 10, the *maquila* association (Index) reported that 55% of the *maquilas* were in operation. On May 19, as a great number of plants reopened, *maquila* workers in Jauréz and Matamoros marched to demand the closure of many plants, including those operated by Foxconn in Santa Teresa (where there were six Covid-19-related deaths, according to the workers), Electrocomponentes de México (10 deaths), Lear (30 deaths), Electrolux (seven deaths), Toro (two deaths), and Regal (13 deaths). The workers asserted that none of these operations—which make a range of products, from snow removal equipment to home appliances—were essential and that none of them had met the sanitation requirements as mandated two months earlier. In Juárez, 66 *maquilas* that make neither auto parts nor aviation parts (i.e., those never categorized as "essential") have remained in operation throughout the health crisis.

All across the borderland, from Tijuana (with an estimated 1,000 *maquilas*) through Mexicali in Baja California to Nogales, Sonora (with 70% of *maquilas* in operation on May 18), and on to Juárez, Chihuahua, and then to Ciudad Acuña, Cohauila (where 23,000 workers returned to their plants on May 20) and to the other end of the border in Matamoros, Tamaulipas (where the hospitals were full of dying workers), these states, and 269 municipal governments, had capitulated to the pressure from the United States to reopen. Meanwhile, the Mexican federal government refused to impose its own hygienic measures.

NAFTA: Myth of Development, Reality of Deindustrialization

The destructive impact of the pandemic on Mexico reveals further the direct consequences of 26 years of neoliberalism under NAFTA, which exacerbated inequality and largely destroyed the nation's public health system, while imposing a new regime of food precarity as once nationally produced grains sold at controlled prices are now imported. This shift away from producing staple foods in Mexico has resulted in the displacement of millions of peasant cultivators—many of whom eventually migrated to the United States to work in the dirtiest, hardest, most unstable, and unrewarded jobs available.

What's more, despite the increased prosperity that NAFTA promised, throughout the NAFTA era average workers' wages—measured in terms of their purchasing power of basic goods—have generally declined. Over the past nearly three decades, exports have surged (especially in auto and auto parts manufacturing), and Mexico has been forced to de-industrialize as the domestic market has drowned in a sea of cheap imports. As a result, the industrial share of the GDP fell from 36.2% in 1993 (the last year before NAFTA took effect) to only 29.6% in 2017 as manufacturing ceased to be the driving force of the economy. In the period from 2003 to 2016, national content (with value originating in Mexico) across Mexico's broad manufacturing export sector averaged only 41%, while 59% of the value of manufacturing exports does not originate in Mexico. Using cheap labor to process imported inputs into goods that are largely exported to the United States now defines Mexico's ever-plodding economy. A large portion of the millions of manufacturing sector jobs that were lost in the United States after 1993 were transferred to Mexico where an enormous army of impoverished wage workers crowded into the *maquiladora* firms—which, as mentioned, now directly employ 2.6 million throughout Mexico.

As was the case in 1992–1993, when the business and political elites of Mexico opened the road to NAFTA—portraying the agreement as a much-needed lever to promote development—these same forces are now eagerly awaiting the USMCA. This delusionary enthusiasm found its way into an essay written by AMLO and published by the office of the president on May 16, 2020:

> To be the neighbor of the most powerful economy in the world under the current circumstances of global recession will help us to drive forward our productive activities and create new jobs. It is a fact that the agreement will attract more foreign investment to our industrial export sector.

But the rage of the *maquila* workers has further unmasked this myth of economic development, despite the fact that, after some attention received in April, the media has largely ceased coverage of labor strife on the border. On the first of May, International Workers Day, the streets of Ciudad Juárez woke up to graffiti proclaiming "STOP MAKILLAS." In this manner a diverse collective of workers began a campaign to raise awareness about perilous workplace conditions—announcing that "*el virus es la makilla*" (the virus is the *ma*KILL*a*) and that "*la makilla te aniquila*" (the *ma*KILL*a* will annihilate you)—and to demand new protections centered on *Salud, Trabajo y Dignidad* (Health, Work, and Dignity). Through these protests, they were able to communicate to the nation the completely arbitrary and unaccountable manner in which the transnational firms were operating along the border and throughout the country. The current policy is for these firms to force workers into the plants (lest they literally starve) on the pretext that they are involved in "essential" activities. Firms expect workers to continue doing their jobs without sanitary protections, given that distancing in these factories is impossible. Indignant workers have drawn attention to those who have been summarily fired, without justification as required by the labor law, when they resisted being forced into the deadly plants. These workers were then denied their indemnification for losing their jobs. (The labor law requires that employers pay workers fired without cause three months of salary plus 20 days of pay for every year of service, and a number of other smaller payments.)

"STOP MAKILLAS!" was also the cry heard on May 12, when the Mexican government declared that *maquila* workers in the aerospace and auto industries were "essential" (essential to the United States) and had to be forced to work, regardless of the utter absence of health and safety protections for workers. The workers responded by demanding they be put on leave at full pay (as well as that all necessary sanitary measures be taken).

But workers' concerns and their demands are clearly unimportant to the U.S. government and hundreds of U.S. companies operating in Mexico. U.S. Ambassador Landau was blunt in his advocacy of reopening in his widely circulated statement:

> We have to protect [people's] health without destroying the economy. It's not impossible. … I'm here to look for win-win solutions. On both sides of the border, investment = employment = prosperity.

And so, only four weeks after shutting their doors, the *maquilas* were open without any clear information as to which, if any, measures had been taken to protect the returning workers. Most workers were forced back onto the shop floor (although some large export firms delayed until June 1). The agencies of the Mexican government (at all levels) and the company-controlled unions had fallen over backwards to ensure that the profits would soon again be flowing, primarily to the United States. In the border state of Chihuahua, for example, 93% of the 122 "essential" workplaces inspected were approved for operation by June 1. However, two weeks later, additional plant inspections resulted in the closure of 44 out of 208 *maquiladoras* for lack of compliance with sanitation requirements.

Drafted to Serve: Mexican Workers under the Defense Production Act

In March, the nationwide cries for more medical equipment evoked calls from Washington, D.C. to essentially conscript medical supply firms under the Defense Production Act. This Act was implemented in 1950 to force and enable the private sector to prioritize production and delivery of strategic supplies in a time of national emergency. The president then demurred, while stating that such a policy would amount to "nationalizing our businesses," then suggested that applying the act would be similar to steps taken in Venezuela under President Hugo Chávez (1999–2013).

According to President Trump, running out of crucial medical supplies during an unprecedented pandemic was not a sufficient reason to invoke the production authority of the state—failing market forces all along the medical supply chain could not be tampered with lest the United States slip into Venezuelan-style economic paralysis.

On the other hand, as the pandemic predictably arrived at the nation's cramped and fetid slaughterhouses, discomforting the Big Four meatpackers (JBS, with $39 billion in sales in 2017; Tyson, with $38 billion in sales; Cargill, the largest privately-owned firm in the United States, with $20 billion in sales; and Smithfield, with $15 billion in sales) and disrupting shoppers, these meatpacking behemoths did nothing. At their plants, the meatpackers could not be bothered to protect workers; and the spike of Covid-19 cases among meatpacking employees led to a slowdown in the slaughtering of animals, which led to shortages of meat. The president quickly swung 180° to apply the Act in late April. This mobilized a "critical infrastructure," especially the Big Four's infrastructure that very comfortably controls approximately 80% of the beef industry. (The top four in pork slaughterers controlled 64% of the market in 2011, while the top four in poultry producers controlled 56% of the market in 2019.) Unlike meeting the demand for medical supplies during a pandemic, slaughtering animals was, apparently, too "critical" to be left to the "free" market.

In 2017 the United States exported 13% of the cattle slaughtered, along with 27% of pigs, and 17% of chickens to other countries. While the Defense Production Act's powers could control foreign markets (exports and/or imports), U.S. slaughterhouses were left free to sell to the highest bidder.

In effect, U.S. slaughterhouse workers and all others involved in the meatpacking supply chain had been drafted to ensure that the flow of profits for the Big Four continued. Implementing the Act meant that workers could no longer receive unemployment benefits. They were now "free to choose" between zero income and near-zero job prospects outside the meatpacking plants or work in one of the three most impacted job sectors (the other two being nursing homes, which mass deaths from Covid-19 have turned into veritable death camps, and prisons and jails, where infections have run rampant).

There's No Business Like Agribusiness

Right behind the arms-contracting corporations and aerospace firms that swarm the Pentagon stands the mollycoddled U.S. agribusiness interests. Just as the Pentagon was long ago "captured" by the arms contractors who weave in and out of top positions in the Department of Defense in order to return to the contracting firms through Washington's "revolving door," so, too, do the corporate chieftains of agribusiness rotate through the Department of Agriculture and the many other federal and state agencies that work hard to ensure that profits stay high in the agricultural sector.

In this sector government assistance at the local, state, and federal level has long been readily forthcoming to control the labor force and manage the surges in demand for seasonal tasks. Meatpacking, of course, can be undertaken without too much regard to the seasons. It is therefore rightly considered a manufacturing process that long ago adopted "continuous" production processes—often on a 24-hour basis. Like the seasonal-crop farm labor force, slaughterhouses long ago found that the best labor force is an immigrant labor force, documented or not. And, predictably enough, nearly 50% of this labor force consists of "Hispanics." Since nearly two-thirds of all Hispanics (according to the U.S. Census) are Mexican-born, we find that the use of the Defense Production Act to keep the slaughterhouses open is part of the larger process now taking place in both Mexico and the United States to force poor Mexicans to risk pandemic death, or long-term decrepitude, in order to make vehicles and auto parts for the U.S. populace and to ensure that its meat-centric diet is maintained. Embodied Mexican labor—workers who were expelled from Mexico during the long night of neoliberalism (1986–2018)—is the key component of the meatpacking supply chain in the United States. *Disembodied* Mexican labor is the key labor-intensive input of the U.S. auto/auto parts supply chain, as we have explained above.

Werner Sombart's "Free Lunch"

Famously, in *Why Is There No Socialism in the United States?*, Werner Sombart claimed (in 1906) that U.S. workers, unlike their counterparts in Europe, were loyal to "the promised land of capitalism" because it provided them with "reefs of roast beef." Indeed, before Prohibition (1920–1933) a typical saloon in the United States provided an overflowing sideboard "free lunch" for the "thirsty" patrons—roast beef being a mainstay. Sated, workers could then proceed to "bring home the bacon."

So, what would happen if "reefs" of roast beef disappeared from the food system, along with that defining metric, bacon? We have seen that exhausted health care workers have been made to wait for protective equipment until the "free market" got good and ready to sell them such equipment at whatever prices the market will bear. But could the general populace be made to wait for meat at prohibitive prices? Oh, no.

In a society where well-being has largely been defined by the ability to consume, it has long been taken as a given that meat, or any other food item, would be immediately available in any quantity desired, provided that the buyer had sufficient funds. When that turned out to not be the case, the Defense Production Act was immediately deployed to force an overwhelmingly immigrant labor force to make an ugly decision—go to the front and hope to dodge the pandemic's bullets or face deportation, hunger, or both. Suddenly, from the long valleys of California to the largely Midwest slaughterhouses, Mexican workers who had risked arrest and deportation to get to the United States were carrying letters or cards showing that they were "essential." The farmworkers were, as usual, forced to face a daily diet of poisonous pesticides and the risk of infection from the deadly pandemic. But slaughterhouse workers must spend their work shift in tight quarters, in a closed structure among hundreds of workers, usually with circulating air that will bring all possible viral pathogens right to them.

The Pandemic Behind the Pandemic: Neoliberalism

Behind the pandemic of 2020, which has left Latinos with nearly a six times higher infection rate than the average Iowan, lies a deeper pandemic which has spread despair across the United States for four decades. This pandemic—known well outside the United States as neoliberalism—transformed the once heavily unionized labor force in the meatpacking industry into low-wage, disposable drudges. Wages that were 15% above the national manufacturing average in the 1970s had, by the 1990s, fallen 20% *below* the median. Once subject to industry-wide bargaining agreements, plant unions now bargain weakly: in 2019 only 19% of the 292,000 meat processing workers were union members. In the 1980s and 1990s slaughterhouses were mostly shifted to "right-to-work" rural states to break the legacy of the large-city unions. These states allow workers a "free ride"—they can have the benefits of a union contract without paying dues—and this feature makes it almost impossible to maintain a union shop. Doubling up, employers began recruiting immigrants, particularly from Mexico. Today, the labor force has a turnover rate ranging from 60–100%, and the meatpackers union has been largely silent as the pandemic has spread.

Just prior to the decision to impose a military-style command system in the slaughterhouses, the Big Four dominating the supply chain (and the many small operations), facing massive pandemic outbreaks, demanded that the federal government impose labor rules that would exempt them from any workplace liability for death or illness arising from the pandemic. Corporations are maneuvering to use the Defense Production Act as a "liability shield" in order to stave off an expected wave of lawsuits alleging workplace negligence—such a wave would raise their liability insurance rates. Under the new arrangement, proven "negligence" may not trigger a court award—workers would have to prove "gross negligence, recklessness, or willful misconduct."

Operating under the Defense Production Act, the meatpacking plants have become the spearhead of big U.S. capital—if they can weaken workers' rights to a demand a safe workplace, such new legal arrangements will be used by all sectors to weaken labor safety standards and drive down their operating costs.

Meanwhile, across the Midwest, the South, and the Rockies, where most plants are located, right-wing governors are working hand-in-glove with the meat barons, county health departments, and the Occupational Safety and Health Administration to hide any and all information with regard to infection rates and deaths from the pandemic. Only days after Trump invoked the Defense Production Act, data releases on the pandemic's spread at the slaughterhouses all but ceased. Still, county-wide data showed that in Finney County, Kan., home to a Tyson slaughterhouse, the infection rate on May 25, 2020 was one in every 26 people. This is nearly eight times the very high national average. The same results, as recorded by the *New York Times* map "Coronavirus in the United States," could be found over and over again: Cargill's plant in Ford County, Kan. produced an infection rate of one in every 21 people and Tyson's giant plant in Dakota City—operating with 4,300 workers—left nearby Woodbury County, Iowa with an infection rate of one in 39.

In Mexico and the United States, millions of "essential" Mexican workers—essential to the profits of U.S. super-corporations—are pressed to toil on: they must ensure that the U.S. populace face an even larger oversupply of motor vehicles and whatever "reefs of roast beef" remain after the lucrative export market has been supplied. ❏

Sources: De la Redacción, "Industriales de EU piden a México reabrir fábricas" *La Jornada*, April 23, (jornada.com.mx); Manuel Fuentes, "Maquiladoras, a laborar por órdenes del Norte," *La Silla Rota*, May 20, 2020 (lasillarota.com); Joe Gould, "COVID closed Mexican factories that supply US defense industry. The Pentagon wants them opened" *Defense News*, April 21, 2020 (defensenews.com); Paola Gamboa, "Un bono de 700 pesos no vale más que mi vida" *El Heraldo de Juárez*, April 20 2020 (elheralddeJuárez. com.mx); Patricia Mayorga, "Indiferencia gubernamental y empresarial expone a obreros de maquilas al COVID-19," *La Verdad*, June 19, 2020 (laverdadJuárez.com); "Iztapalapa y Tijuana, cerca de los 700 muertos por COVID-19; ¿qué municipios registran más contagios?," *Medio Tiempo*, June 6, 2020 (mediotiemp.com); "Piden cerrar maquiladoras en frontera mexicana por la pandemia de COVID" *INFOBE: México* , May 19, 2020 (infobae.com); Marco Antonio López, "Empleados acusan que los obligan a trabajar pese a muertes por COVID en maquiladoras de Chihuahua" *Animal Político*, May 18, 2020 (animalpolitico.com); René Villareal, "Comercio exterior y el desarrollo de capacidades" *Comercio Exterior*, Oct.-Dec. 2018; Andrés Manual Lopéz Obrador, "The New Political Economy in the time of the Corona Virus," Office of the President, May 16, 2020 (lopezobrador.org.mx); Alberto Morales, "AMLO comparte ensayo la nueva política económica en los tiempos del coronavirus" *El Universal*, May 16, 2020 (eluniversal.com.mx); Shawn Fremstad, Hye Jin Rho and Hayley Brown, "Meatpacking Workers are a Diverse Group," Center for Economic Policy Research, April 29, 2020 (cepr.net); Roger Horowitz, "The decline of unionism in America's meatpacking industry," *Social Policy* (32: 3, 2002); Union Stats, 2019 "Union Membership by Occupation: Standard Occupational Classification 7810—Butchers and Meat Processors," 2019 (unionstats.com); Michael Corkery, David Yaffe-Bellany and Drek Kravitz, "Meat Workers Left in the Dark Under Pressure" *New York Times*, May 25, 2020 (nytimes.com); "Coronavirus Map: Tracking the Global Outbreak" *New York Times*, May 25, 2020.

Article 7.6

CREDIBLE STRIKE THREATS

The predicted wave of strikes didn't materialize last fall, but strike threats have proved to be effective.

BY ROBERT OVETZ
March/April 2022

Abundant attention was given to the increase in strikes during "Striketober" and "Strikevember" last fall, catchy terms for months when many strikes were expected to occur. They not only turned out less than impressive but were matched by the fact that at least as many workers were also involved in making credible strike threats.

What, exactly, makes a strike threat credible? First, it has to be credible to the boss. The boss needs to know that the workers will take escalating actions leading to a strike, and that a supermajority of members have publicly committed to strike, have a strike fund, and have widespread public support. This tells the boss that meeting the workers' demands now is less costly than dealing with a strike in the future.

Second, the strike threat has to also be credible to the workers. If not enough union members publicly commit to striking, the leadership is not committed, or the strike end-date is announced before the strike has even begun, few workers will find it credible and they will not be willing to strike. Labor organizers Helena Worthen and Joe Berry define strike threats as follows: "It is essentially a display of power. It can also expose the union to a serious risk, because if it has to be carried out and doesn't get what was desired, it becomes a public record of weakness."

Despite the hype, during these two months, credible strike threats by University of California (UC) lecturers, Hollywood and TV workers, and an alliance of 22 nurse and staff unions at Kaiser Permanente in California and Oregon demonstrated that workers are quietly organizing strike threats that may be as or more effective than striking to get the goods.

UC Lecturers Teach Us About Credible Strike Threats

In 2020, after bargaining for one-and-a-half years, much of the time during an expired contract, the UC-AFT, which represents 6,500 non-senate faculty members and librarians, began an organizing campaign for lecturers, who are non-tenured and teach one-third of UC undergraduate classes. The lecturers initially issued a threat for a two-day strike against unfair labor practices in October, which led the UC to begin to move on the union's demands. To provide more time for bargaining, the two-day strike was then postponed to November, but was called off when the UC and the union reached a settlement in the middle of the night before the date of the strike. As a result, an historic settlement was reached, which dramatically improved the pay and job security of untenured lecturers, who are low paid and often not rehired after one year. This was the UC-AFT's first credible strike threat since it last struck in 2002. For

UC-AFT Vice President Trevor Griffey, speaking in an interview, "this is a really big deal for our union that we even did strike organizing at all."

As part of the strike threat, UC-AFT members crashed bargaining sessions, which are typically closed, forcing them to be opened to the public. Informational pickets and two nearly unanimous votes for an unfair labor practices strike made the strike threat credible to the UC. Just as UC-AFT members were about to escalate their tactics, the UC conceded to their demands and even increased their settlement offer. The lecturers' strike threat was credible to both the university system and UC-AFT members.

Counting Strike Threats

The tracking of strikes is limited and research on strike threats is almost nonexistent. While the U.S. Bureau of Labor Statistics (BLS) does track strikes, the bureau is significantly underreporting strike activity in the United States by only reporting strikes involving 1,000 or more workers, even though only 0.3% of U.S. business have 500 workers or more. Because the BLS only counts a tiny minority of all employers, it significantly undercounts the number of strikes that happen each year.

Using public news sources and government reports, my research assistant and I found 134 reported strike threats between 2012 and 2016 (see Table 1). Of these, 97 strike threats were settled without a strike in firms of any size workforce, involving a total of 701,700 workers. Of the 134 strike threats, 73 occurred in workplaces with fewer than 1,000 workers. Of these 73 strike threats, 20 resulted in strikes involving 8,573 workers, six had an unknown outcome at the time of the study, and the remainder resulted in no strike. We did not assess whether the strike threat was "credible," which would be useful to do at some point in the future.

For the same 2012–2016 period, the BLS reported 72 strikes in firms with 1,000 or more employees involving 352,000 workers (see Table 2). In addition to the number of workers threatening to strike being nearly twice the number that actually did strike, the number of threats was 134.7% higher than the number of strikes during this time.

In May 2018, the BLS published my letter to the editor of its newsletter, Monthly Labor Review, in which I made the case for counting strike threats. Still, the BLS declines to count strike threats. For this reason, I launched strikethreats.org, a website where rank-and-file union members and union officers can report their strike threats.

Striketober and Strikevember?

Comparing strike reports by the BLS with Cornell University's School of Industrial and Labor Relations' Labor Action Tracker for the months of October and November 2021 give starkly different results. The BLS shows only three strikes occurring during these two months, involving a total of 5,400 workers. In contrast, the Labor Action Tracker reports 60 strikes just in October involving 18,700 workers, and an additional 47 strikes in November involving 62,000 workers for a total of 85,830 workers—15 times the number of workers reported by the BLS. However, it is important to note that the Labor Action Tracker reported only three strikes in October involving more than 500 workers, which accounted for two-thirds of the strikers during that month, and 75% of the strikers in November were involved in just three strikes involving more than 330 workers.

While the Labor Action Tracker shows a substantially higher number of workers on strike than the BLS, its estimate of workers engaged in strike-related activity is still too low. While the Labor Action Tracker counts, respectively, 58 and 42 other "labor protests" for October and November (which the Labor Action Tracker project coordinators tell me may include strike threats) it doesn't tell us how many resulted in settlements.

By comparison, a minimum of about 78,500 workers (as many as 60,000 to 80,000 additional nurses and staffers joined this group when they ratified a contract with their employer in December 2021) were involved in the three largest known settled strike threats by UC lecturers, Hollywood and TV workers, and an alliance of nurse and staff unions at Kaiser Permanente during these two months. This means that there were at least twice as many workers engaged in strike-related organizing as the number reported by the Labor Action Tracker, and 30 times the number reported by the BLS. While the Labor Action Tracker is a far more reliable source than the BLS, neither captures an accurate level of strike-related organizing activity.

The strikes during these two months were extremely small and localized and, as a result, had a limited strategic impact. They were unlikely to have contributed to more workers striking because they did not occur at choke points in transport or logistics or spread along the supply chain. Strikes are not only prohibited by contracts but also constrained by labor law for unionized workers. Just announcing that more workers will strike will not result in more workers actually joining them. Larger strikes take a long-term organizing effort to overcome strike hesitancy among union leadership and members, build majority participation, and use escalating tactics in order to strategically spur strikes in other related workplaces and industries.

The focus on any strike is a narrow strategy. We certainly want to see more strikes, but we also want to see more that have a systemic strategic impact. But we still need to pay attention to the many workers engaged in strike organizing campaigns that win some or all of their demands by mounting a credible threat to strike.

Why Strike Threats Matter

The severe undercounting of workers organizing for strikes continues to skew the facts about the level of worker organizing throughout the United States by giving the misperception that workers are not interested in or even attempting to strike. Labor law, employer repression, automation, and unions' abandonment of organizing has clearly resulted in a continuing decline in the number of strikes. But strikes are not being correctly measured, or they are viewed as the only measurement that matters.

By counting strike threats, especially those that are credible enough to be settled on favorable terms to the workers before the strike occurs, we can see how more workers are increasingly restless and engaging in more potentially disruptive struggles than we have been led to believe by the government, academia, union leadership, and the media. ❑

Sources: Andy Kiersz, "The Impact of Small Business on the US Economy in 2 Extreme Charts," Business Insider, June 16, 2015 (businessinsider.in); Helena Worthen and Joe Berry, *Power Despite Precarity* (Pluto, 2021); Cornell School of Industrial and Labor Relations Labor Action Tracker (striketracker.ilr.cornell.edu); International Alliance of Theatrical Stage Employees, "Landmark tentative agreement reached for IATSE West Coast Film and Television Workers before Strike Deadline," Oct. 16, 2021 (iatse.net); Myung J. Chun, "Hollywood Crews Set Date for Strike if Talks Stall," *Los Angeles Times*, Nov. 13, 2021 (latimes.com); Robert Ovetz, *Workers' Inquiry and Global Class Struggle: Strategies, Tactics, Objectives* (Pluto, 2020); U.S. Bureau of Labor Statistics, "Work Stoppages," (bls.gov); Robert Ovetz, "Counting Strike Threats," letter to the editor, *Monthly Labor Review*, U.S. Bureau of Labor Statistics, May 2018, (bls.gov); Mikhail Zinshteyn, "UC Lecturers Win Raises, Other Concessions in Deal That Averts Planned 2-Day Strike," KQED, Nov. 17, 2021 (kqed.org); CBS News, "Kaiser Health Care Worker Strike Averted as Tentative Deal is Reached, Company Says," November 13, 2021 (cbsnews.com); Chris Isidore, "Strike Averted at West Coast Hospitals," CNN Business, November 13, 2021(cnn.com); Samantha Liss, "Kaiser Permanente Workers Ratify Contract Agreement After Narrowly Avoiding Strike," Healthcare Dive, Dec. 10, 2021 (healthcaredive.com).

Article 7.7

THE FIGHT FOR $20 AND A UNION
Another California Minimum Wage Earthquake?

BY MARTIN J. BENNETT
May/June 2022

California is the epicenter for a nationwide grassroots movement to raise the wage floor for U.S. workers. As of January 1, 2022, $15 an hour is the minimum wage for large employers in the state and $14 an hour for small ones (rising to $15 for all employers in 2023). Meanwhile, 39 California cities and counties have established rates that are higher than $15 an hour, with Emeryville, Calif., offering the highest hourly rate at $17.13.

The Fight for $15 movement has reshaped public opinion, pushing local and state officials around the country to approve a $15-per-hour minimum wage. Eleven states and 54 cities and counties have $15 minimum wage floors, according to the National Employment Law Project, and four in 10 workers live in states that are on the pathway to a $15 minimum wage.

At the national level, the Raise the Wage Act, approved by the House, would boost the federal minimum wage from $7.25 an hour to $15 an hour by 2025; but it is blocked in the Senate. In the 2022 midterm elections, this impasse could well impact the outcomes of competitive Senate and House races.

In California, an initiative to hike California's minimum wage to $18 an hour funded by tech entrepreneur Joe Sanberg appears to be a lock for the November 2022 ballot. California House races that Democrats must win could hinge on the state's minimum wage.

So, why has the higher wages movement exploded in California? How might the fight for higher minimum wages impact the 2022 midterms? And what's next for the movement?

Inequality and the California Higher Wages Movement

Soaring inequality in the Golden State, rising costs of living, and a large low-wage service sector are the story behind the higher wage movement. According to the California Budget and Policy Center, average real income for the top 1% skyrocketed by 134% while the incomes of the bottom 40% fell by 16% between 1987 and 2017.

The bottom has dropped out for California workers because of stagnating wages. In 2018 the median wage of $21.79, adjusted for inflation, was just 1% higher than in 1979. For the bottom 10%, hourly wages rose by a meager 4%. The California Future of Work Commission reported in 2021 that one in three California workers earned less than $15 per hour. The majority of those are essential workers who cannot work from home and experience high rates of Covid-19 workplace infections.

The United Ways of California estimate that in 2019 one-third of California households were working poor, i.e., with at least one household member working but without enough income to meet basic needs including food, shelter, health care, transportation, childcare, and taxes.

Rents have far outpaced wages for decades, further squeezing California workers. According to the California Housing Partnership, between 2000 and 2019, annual median rents increased by a whopping 35%, while renters' incomes grew by just 6%. As a result, California renters face increased overcrowding, eviction, displacement, and homelessness.

Origins of the Movement and the Fight for $15

The California higher-wages movement began in 1997 when the Los Angeles City Council approved the state's first living wage law. It required the city, large city contractors, and firms receiving economic development assistance to pay more than the state minimum wage. Proponents argued that contracting out city services to private employers had created poverty-wage jobs that forced workers to rely on government assistance.

Throughout California and nationwide, 120 cities and counties soon followed suit. In these campaigns, coalitions of labor, faith, immigrant rights, and environmental organizations educated the public about what it cost for working families to make ends meet and what local governments can do to address inequality. In 2003, San Francisco went a step farther, becoming the first California city to approve a citywide minimum wage higher than the state's—which, unlike living wage laws, covered virtually all local workers.

Such efforts multiplied after the 2008 financial collapse and the Great Recession. Occupy Wall Street exploded in 2011–2012, with more than 600 tent encampments in cities across the nation, including 143 in California. While Occupy protests ended, the movement energized new campaigns to halt foreclosures and evictions, promote financial regulation, end student debt, and raise the wage floor.

In 2012, New York City fast-food workers—among the lowest paid in the service sector—held a one-day strike demanding $15 and a union, which seemed like a pipe dream at the time. Yet, fast-food strikes supported by SEIU, the nation's second-largest union, spread to 190 cities by 2014, while low-wage workers organized sit-ins and civil disobedience demonstrations at McDonald's and Walmart stores in coastal California cities.

The Fight for $15 movement was born, and campaigns were launched across the country to pass citywide minimum wage laws. In 2012, there were just four U.S. municipalities with such laws, but Fight for $15 coalitions in SeaTac and Seattle, Wash., won the nation's first $15 citywide minimum wage laws in 2013 and 2014, respectively. Over the next two years, San Francisco, Los Angeles, San Jose, and San Diego followed suit. Since that time, 51 cities and counties nationwide have approved $15 minimum wage laws.

In 2015–2016, California higher-wage advocates collected enough signatures to approve a state $15 minimum wage ballot initiative. Polling indicated that the voters would overwhelmingly approve such a proposition, so the California legislature jumped in to enact the first $15 state minimum wage in 2016, followed by New

York, Massachusetts, Connecticut, New Jersey, Illinois, and Maryland over the next three years.

In November 2020, the dominos continued to fall when Florida voters approved a $15 minimum wage, and in 2021 when the Rhode Island, Virginia, and Delaware legislatures did the same. In addition, since 2016, nine states have adopted lesser minimum wage increases ranging from $11 an hour to $14.75.

Notably, most of these state and local minimum wage increases include an annual automatic cost-of-living adjustment to prevent the erosion of the purchasing power of the minimum wage over time.

Moreover, eight states that set their minimum wage above the $7.25 federal minimum have eliminated the unjust subminimum wage for tipped workers. The subminimum allows restaurants and other employers to pay tipped workers as little as $2.13 an hour as a base wage. After the Civil War, this practice was part of a legacy of racial segregation when railways, restaurants, and hotels–whose workforce was predominantly Black–did not want to pay wages to freed slaves. The One Fair Wage Coalition is currently leading a nationwide campaign to abolish the subminimum wage.

Business Gets on Board

The writing is on the wall for U.S. companies to get on board the moving train of higher minimum wages, and the pandemic has driven the message home. A growing number of large employers have raised entry-level pay in response to tightening labor markets, a record number of workers quitting low-wage jobs, and state and local minimum-wage mandates.

Bank of America leads all employers by setting its minimum pay at $21 an hour, committing to reach $25 by 2025. Amazon recently announced a boost of entry-level wages to $18 an hour. Costco and IKEA have hiked minimum pay to $16 an hour. Retailers like Target, Whole Foods, Best Buy, CVS, and Walgreens; insurers including Allstate, Aetna, and Nationwide; banks such as Wells Fargo and JPMorgan Chase; and tech companies including Google and Facebook have established a $15 entry-level wage.

A milestone in the Fight for $15 was McDonald's 2019 announcement that it would no longer oppose minimum wage increases at the federal, state, or local level. Now, a 2021 executive order by President Joe Biden has boosted starting pay to $15 an hour as of January 30, 2022 for hundreds of thousands of workers employed by federal contractors who receive new, renewed, or extended contracts.

The Wage Movement's Electoral Impact

The higher-wages movement has profoundly altered public opinion. In 2016, Senator Bernie Sanders was the only Democratic Party candidate to champion the $15 minimum wage, but after Sanders won 22 Democratic primaries that year, the party incorporated the $15 minimum wage into its platform. When the Democratic primaries kicked off in 2019, every Democratic presidential hopeful supported it.

Voters are solidly in favor of higher minimum wages. In 2021 the Pew Research Center reported that 62% of voters supported the federal Raise the Wage Act

($15 phased in by 2025). Public support spans states with both Republican and Democratic Party majorities, as demonstrated by Florida voters approving their ballot measure to increase the minimum wage to $15 an hour by a stunning 60% margin, despite President Donald Trump's narrow win in that state. But the political elites are not on board, as shown by how Florida's Republican governor, both senators, and party leadership all denounced the popular $15 minimum ballot initiative and by seven Democrats joining the Republicans in the U.S. Senate to defeat the federal bill.

With California now poised to raise its minimum wage to $18, it could ignite another round of increases among the states—especially given the record profits of large employers during the Covid-19 pandemic, spiraling inflation, and growing worker demands. The Congressional Research Service reports that, since 1996, minimum wage initiatives have passed in 26 states, and none have failed.

The 2022 Midterms and the Minimum Wage

The minimum wage looms over the 2022 midterms. A 2019 poll by Hart Research Associates found that two-thirds of voters in 57 Congressional districts that Democrats won in 2018 favored raising the federal minimum wage to $15. The poll also indicated that, by a large margin, voters are likely to support candidates who favor the Raise the Wage Act.

California has as many as nine House seats up for grabs, particularly in the Central Valley and Southern California. Redistricting has placed five incumbent Republicans in vulnerable positions, and experts rate three of these races as toss-ups. California Republicans are skating on thin ice if they oppose an $18 an hour state minimum wage.

Many swing states with competitive Senate races, such as Pennsylvania, North Carolina, Georgia, Wisconsin, and New Hampshire still set their minimum wage at the rock-bottom federal level of $7.25 an hour. Recent Progressive Change Institute polling shows that 53% of the voters in three of these states support a $15 minimum wage phased in by 2025. A candidate's support for the Raise the Wage Act could influence voters' choices in these battleground states. In Arizona and Nevada, where 2022 Senate races are a toss-up, voters have previously approved state minimum wage increases by lopsided majorities. In Nevada, voters will consider another state ballot initiative to raise the minimum wage to $12 an hour by 2024.

A candidate's position on the minimum wage could make a difference in 2022. This should favor Democrats since they have championed the higher-wage movement while Republicans have blocked raising the federal minimum wage for over a decade. The minimum wage is especially important for the Democrats' base constituency. The Economic Policy Institute reports that the federal Raise the Wage Act would boost pay for one in three Black workers and one in four Latino workers. Under the bill, nearly 60% of workers receiving a pay raise are women.

The Next Phase of the Movement

The United Ways of California calculate that a California living wage is no less than $21 per hour for each of two parents, employed full-time to support two children. The cost of living is much higher on the coast compared to the Central Valley, but $20 an hour is an aspirational goal for the entire state, if not the nation.

Allynn Umel, campaign director for the Fight for $15 and a Union, recently told CNBC, "Now, $15 is widely understood to be the bare minimum workers anywhere need to get by. $15 has always been the floor, not the ceiling, for wages—and working people will continue to demand lawmakers and employers increase pay to keep up with the rising cost of living and ensure that every community can thrive."

Ultimately, low-wage workers must unionize to win and maintain a living wage, comprehensive benefits, and protections for health and safety. Unionized workers in low-wage industries are already pushing for a wage floor higher than $18. In 2018, Oakland, Calif., voters overwhelmingly approved a Hotel Employee Minimum Wage ballot initiative proposed by UNITE HERE Local 2850 and the East Bay Alliance for a Sustainable Economy, which mandated that large hotels pay their workers $20 an hour (or $15 if health benefits are provided).

In 2021, 20,000 California janitors represented by SEIU United Service Workers West ratified a new contract that will lift wages to $20 an hour for most and enhance their medical and retirement benefits. Union home care or IHSS (in-home support services) workers in San Francisco won a wage increase to $18.75 an hour last year. SEIU 2015, the union representing home care and nursing home workers statewide, has launched a campaign to make $20 per hour the starting wage for all long-term care workers.

California was the first state to implement a $15 minimum wage, and the Golden State provided a model for the grassroots campaign that got it done. Once again, California is at the forefront of the movement to raise the wage floor—now the Fight for *$20* and a Union. The difference is that now the minimum wage issue could affect the outcome of the 2022 midterms in California and across the nation. ❑

Note: A version of this article was originally published on Beyond Chron (beyondchron.org/the-fight-for-20-and-a-union-another-california-minimum-wage-earthquake).

Sources: UC Berkeley Labor Center, "Inventory of U.S. City and County Minimum Wage Ordinances," January 31, 2022 (laborcenter.berkeley.edu); Yannet Lathrop, "Raises from Coast-to-Coast 2022," National Employment Law Project, December 20, 2021 (nelp.org); House Committee on Education and Labor, "Raise the Wage Act 2021 Factsheet," January 26, 2021 (edlabor.house.gov); Samantha Mansunga, "Should California have a $18 minimum wage? Voters may get to decide," *Los Angeles Times*, December 6, 2021 (latimes.com); Alissa Anderson et al., "Many Californians Are Struggling to Live in Our Communities," California Budget and Policy Center, January 2020 (calbudgetcenter.org); Alissa Anderson et al., "California Workers Are Increasingly Locked Out of the State's Prosperity," California Budget and Policy Center, December 2019 (calbudgetcenter.org); California Future of Work Commission, "The Future of Work in California: A New Social Compact for Work and Workers," March 2021 (labor.

ca.gov); United Ways of California, "The Real Cost Measurement in California 2021," July 2021 (unitedwaysca.org/realcost); California Housing Partnership, "California Affordable Housing Needs Report 2021," March 2021(chpc.net); Michaela Curran, Elizabeth A. G. Schwarz, and Christopher Chase-Dunn, "The Occupy Movement in California," Institute for Research on World Systems, University of California-Riverside, June 2014 (irows.ucr.edu); Martin J. Bennett, "California's $15 Minimum Wage Earthquake!" Beyond Chron, August 16, 2016 (beyondcrhon. org); U.S. Department of Labor, "U.S. Department of Labor Announces Proposed Rulemaking to Implement Executive Order, Increase Wages for Workers on Government Contracts," July 20, 2021 (dol.gov); Amina Dunn, "Most Americans support A $15 minimum wage" Pew Research Center, April 22, 2021 (pew.research.org); Emily Stewart, "The lesson Democrats should take from Florida's $15 minimum wage vote," Vox, November 5, 2020 (vox.com); Ameila Lucas, "More than half of U.S. states will raise their minimum wage in 2022, but employers are hiking pay faster," CNBC, December 29, 2021 (cnbc.com).

Article 7.8

SHUT UP AND WORK!
"Free" Labor and Unequal Freedom of Expression

BY ZOE SHERMAN
May/June 2022

U nionization drives at Amazon warehouses and Starbucks locations have attracted months of national media attention. During 2021 workers and union organizers at the Bessemer, Ala. Amazon warehouse and at several Starbucks stores in Buffalo, N.Y. described—and decried—management's suppression of pro-union speech through intensified surveillance of workers and threats of retaliation. Starbucks workers were suddenly accompanied on their shifts by managers chatting them up about the risks of unionization while they cleaned the espresso machines and bagged up the trash. A mailbox installed outside the Amazon warehouse was sheltered by an Amazon tent and within view of Amazon security cameras, causing workers to doubt whether their mail-in ballots were really secret. (The U.S. Postal Service said only USPS mail carriers had access to the mail; some workers said they saw Amazon security officers opening the box. The National Labor Relations Board had explicitly told Amazon not to request a new mailbox in that location.) Both Amazon and Starbucks workers were told that if they unionized their worksite, the location would close, and their jobs would disappear. Despite the threats, many workers persevered. In winter and spring of 2022, workers at several Starbucks locations unionized and workers at dozens more filed petitions to hold union elections. The newly organized Amazon Labor Union won an election to represent workers at a warehouse in Staten Island, N.Y. Regardless of the specific outcome of each unionization drive, these, and many other similar stories, raise the question of whether workers have real free speech rights and what it would take to strengthen workers' speech rights.

Free labor, Karl Marx noted, is free in two ways. Unlike slaves or serfs, wage workers are free to sell their labor time to any employer willing to hire them or withhold their labor from any employer they do not wish to serve. But also, workers are free to starve since they are "free" from ownership of the means of production. The rhetoric of personal liberty was prominent in the revolutions that fought to harness the state to the legitimation, promotion, and enforcement of the capital-wage labor relation. ("Certain inalienable rights," as Thomas Jefferson phrased it in England's soon-to-be-lost North American colonies. "*Les droits de l'homme*," as the French revolutionary *Declaration of the Rights of Man* put it.) The language of individual liberty obscured then—and continues to obscure now—the language of class. Looking through the lens of class reveals that, in lived practice, seemingly neutral liberties mean something very different for those on opposite sides of the capitalist class relation.

In the 21st-century United States, the "speech" that is granted Constitutional protection from constraint is frequently identified by the state as an activity of capital, enacted through market transactions. In market transactions, sellers relinquish ownership rights over what is sold; buyers gain them. There is an extensive market for the buying and selling of speech and access to audiences—the public relations and advertising industries, for example. One consequence of having a large speech-for-hire market is that capital commands an outsize share of voice. Even if you didn't work at the Bessemer Amazon warehouse, you probably saw the anti-union messaging in the lead-up to the (failed but later ruled invalid) union election in spring of 2021. Conversely, under a "free" labor regime, workers sell themselves piecemeal, by the hour, by the day. A life cannot be segmented into component parts so neatly. We find that when labor power is sold, free speech rights enter into the package—labor cedes them, and capital gains them.

Authoritarian Governments at Work

Philosopher Elizabeth Anderson calls workplaces sites of "private government." It is not just the state that governs. Any time decisions are made that subjects must follow, we have government. By this definition, workplaces are most definitely

---

Theories of Free Speech, Capitalist vs. Democratic

Jack Balkin, in his 2004 article, "Digital Speech and Democratic Culture," argued that capital's preferred interpretation of the First Amendment gained extra traction in the U.S. courts in the 1990s and early 2000s. Lawyers working for capital developed a capitalist theory of free speech. This interpretation of free speech accepts a capitalist organization of economic affairs as given. No surprise there. But democracies often respond to social movements by softening inequalities to make capitalism more palatable. Instead, the capitalist theory of free speech exaggerates class inequalities; It sees free speech as a tool to promote profitability for companies that control communications networks (e.g., internet providers) or content (e.g., movie studios). Under this theory, Balkin wrote, the ruling interpretation of the First Amendment "ties the right to speak ever more closely to ownership of capital." In this view, what matters is that Disney and Comcast can make a profit, not that you can tell your own stories.

Balkin emphasizes the different degrees of freedom for, on one side, the copyright owners and owners of the fiber optic cables and, on the other side, the rest of us. The current free speech regime also affords very different speech rights to those who sell their labor power than it does to those who purchase labor power. Employers have extraordinarily expansive speech rights. Employees have excruciatingly constrained speech rights. The wage-labor system feeds into a system of unequal speech rights and, reciprocally, the system of unequal speech rights feeds into the maintenance of the wage-labor system.

The capitalist theory of free speech didn't always dominate. For much of the 20th century, the dominant theory of free speech was that the purpose of free speech is to foster full debate and lead to successful participatory, democratic governance. Variations of this view were articulated by scholars and jurists like Oliver Wendell Holmes, Jr., Louis Brandeis, Zechariah Chafee, John Dewey, and Alexander Meiklejohn. Despite some differences, the variants of this theory of free speech all accept the premise that the legitimacy of the government depends on the openness of political debate. Repression of dissent, in this view, delegitimizes the policies chosen and the political system as a whole. Along with the enabler-of-democracy theory of free speech, 20th-century First Amendment interpretation established a hierarchy of speech categories, some of which merit greater protection from restraint than others. Speech that bears on political issues—that is, speech that contributes to the project of democratic self-government—traditionally is held in highest regard by the courts. In some contexts, the hierarchy of speech categories still shows up in legal reasoning.

governed: Bosses make decisions that workers must follow. The reason she calls this form of government "private" is that the people who must follow the rules (workers) have no say in setting the rules. Whether the governing authority is a state or non-state actor is a different question. By Anderson's definition, despotic rule at any site, whether state or non-state, is private government. Nationwide struggles for political democracy are an effort to make the government a public thing, elected by and accountable to the citizens. A standard-issue capitalist workplace is a site of private government not because the governing authority isn't the state, but because the governance is despotic.

Some people try to deny that employers really have substantive authority over workers by pointing to the core freedom that "free" labor does have—the right to quit. Anderson finds the denial absurd—"This is like saying that Mussolini was not a dictator, because Italians could emigrate"—but the denial does work as a diversionary tactic. Many people who are skeptical of state power or resistant to state power nevertheless accept employers' power. But we shouldn't trust any employer's power, even if they are not obviously abusing it right now. Even benevolent dictators are still dictators. If a "nice" employer is so inclined, they *may* offer a generous pay and benefits package and a pleasant work environment; they *may* even invite employee input into decisions and forbear to penalize employees who dissent. But that forbearance is at the employer's discretion. The employer may just as readily rescind employment perks, refuse employee input, and suppress dissent.

U.S. law only protects speech from constraints on freedom when it is the state that imposes the constraint. This is known as the "state action doctrine." The wording of the First Amendment does not say that all people may speak freely in all circumstances; it says that *Congress* may not pass laws restricting speech, press, assembly, or exercise of religion. Current legal thinking applies the same First Amendment constraints to state governments as to the federal government. However, the First Amendment places no limits on what private citizens might do to restrain others' speech. Employers regularly restrain workers' speech and this is generally considered legal.

Speaking About Unions

Outside the workplace, speech about (municipal, state, or federal) government generally carries the highest level of First Amendment protection. Within the workplace, speech about (private) government is probably the most vulnerable. Worker speech advocating for greater worker voice in governance—i.e., union organizing in not-yet-organized workplaces—is especially aggressively suppressed, despite provisions of the National Labor Relations Act (NLRA) that are meant to protect talk of unionization.

Employers use their property rights to amplify their own speech and suppress opposing speech. They can do so by purchasing copious amounts of anti-union speech and purchasing access to communications networks (or deploying internal communications networks they already own) to ensure that employees, government representatives, and the general public see and hear their message. The

U.S. speech-for-hire industry features an extensive sector devoted to anti-union speech. Union-avoidance specialists work to suppress union organizing and to prevent state intervention that might facilitate union organizing. Sociologist Ruth Milkman writes, "[T]he rules defining labor relations under the [National Labor Relations Act]… have been captured by the union-avoidance industry and by the employers who rely on it." Already in the mid-1950s, employer-affiliated industrial relations expert and self-described "union buster" Albert Beeson was named to the National Labor Relations Board (NLRB). In the hearing leading to his confirmation, he boasted of having weaponized the First Amendment against labor; he said that he had "free speeched" employees into voting against unionization.

At the same time that employers can purchase the services of union busters, employers also own the time of their employees. (If a worker uses paid work time to do something other than their assigned work duties, it is called "theft of time.") Paying a wage gives employers the authority to say how workers will use their days. Putting these two purchases together, employers faced with the possibility of unionization often hold captive-audience meetings—meetings that workers are required to attend during their work hours. Employers and their hired consultants fully air their arguments against the union. Employees can be penalized for skipping, leaving early, speaking, or asking "disruptive" questions. The mildest whiff of dissent counts as "disruption" from a worker, but employers' statements have to be staggeringly extreme before the NLRB will judge their speech to be inappropriately coercive, rather than acceptably persuasive. For example, a statement such as, "If you workers vote to unionize, I will be so angry I will fire you all," is an illegal coercive

---

Unfree Worker Speech Beyond the Workplace

If we accept that the workplace is an anomalous democracy-free zone, then maybe free speech at work doesn't matter. Workers weren't going to participate in making business decisions anyway, so it hardly matters what they would say. A zone of voicelessness within the workplace, however, is hard to contain. Lack of voice in the frankly undemocratic workplace radiates outward to erode voice in the purportedly democratic political realm. In his recent book *Politics at Work*, Alexander Hertel-Fernandez shows that in the past decade, an increasing share of U.S. employers are making increasing demands on employees to engage in political behavior beyond the firm. Having purchased their labor power, many employers—particularly those in heavily regulated industries—see their employees' time as a resource to be deployed for political ends, in pursuit of electoral and policy outcomes that they believe will favor their business interests. Examples include pressuring their employees to attend rallies, donate to, or volunteer for the employers' favored candidates, or to contact their representatives to urge policy actions that would benefit their employer.

Employers are politically empowered when unemployment is high. This happens in two ways: 1) The workers who most fear job loss are also most likely to accede to employers' political pressures, even though they are no more likely to have started out in agreement with their employer's political positions than are workers with better employment prospects. 2) Members of Congress and their staffers are more responsive to employer-mobilized workers when the unemployment rate in their district is higher.

threat, but statements like, "If you workers vote to unionize, I predict that I will have to cut jobs," often pass muster with the NLRB. The persuasion-versus-coercion distinction is absurd when the "persuader" signs the paycheck. Compare industries covered by the NLRA to those covered by the Railway Labor Act (RLA): The National Mediation Board, which has jurisdiction over transportation industries covered by the RLA (which also includes airlines), considers captive-audience meetings to be inherently coercive and disallows them. Union density is roughly 10 times higher in the railroad and airline industries than in other industries. Coincidence? It seems unlikely.

Perversely, a popular argument made by those in favor of employers' unlimited access to workers as audiences for their anti-union speech says that workers need access to all relevant viewpoints and information before they settle on their choice of political action. It would be a disservice to workers who will be voting in a representation election, this argument goes, to enforce employer silence and thus keep the employees ignorant of their employer's perspective. This right to be informed of the employer's viewpoint is so powerful that it cannot be waived; workers are not deemed able to determine for themselves when they have heard enough to know as much as they need to know. If an informed electorate is desirable, surely information as relevant as the employer's full financial statement should also be available to workers, yet the people making the informed electorate argument as a justification for captive-audience meetings don't insist on open books. Nor has the informed electorate argument been extended to require that workers be exposed to pro-union perspectives.

When workers *do* overcome the barriers to their speech and criticize the governance of their workplace, whether specifically on the topic of unionization or any other area of management activity, they are vulnerable to retaliation. Accounts of such retaliation are legion. Bias is baked into employers' meting out of consequences. There is a racialized skew in what kinds of behaviors are viewed as "disruptive" in a captive audience member. Any worker could be penalized or fired for speaking up, but workers of color are at even higher risk than white workers. (In the precedent-setting 1968 case Litton Systems, Inc., a Black employee's dismissal as a result of a question asked in a captive-audience meeting was upheld by the NLRB—he had asked if he could return to his assigned work duties since he had already heard the presentation at an earlier meeting and his attendance left his post unstaffed.) John-Paul Ferguson, a scholar of organizational behavior, finds evidence that employers facing interracial union organizing efforts become especially aggressive, even lawless, in their attempts to prevent union formation. The number of unfair labor practices complaints registered with the NLRB arising from employer suppression of interracial organizing campaigns is greater (in proportion to the number of such campaigns) than the number of complaints arising in less diverse workplaces. Diverse workplaces are slightly more likely to vote for a union if they get to hold an election, but employers' aggression in diverse workplaces often causes the unionization effort to stall before the election ever happens.

Knowing the severity of the potential consequences for speaking, workers often, sensibly, restrain themselves. Capital, of course, is freer.

Loosening Labor's Tongue

One person's exercise of free speech often interferes with another's. Attention is limited; one speaker can simply drown out another by consuming attention. Also, a speaker's reception is shaped by the context of past communications; if denigrating speech gets aired first, the target of the insults will have a harder time communicating effectively. As in so many other cases, we cannot all enjoy complete liberty at once; some individuals and groups can only gain freedom of speech when others are restrained. We face social choices about who may be restrained, to what extent, by what mechanism, and on what grounds. If we don't act collectively to coordinate constraints, the most powerful people are free to suppress the speech of the least powerful. The state action doctrine

---

The Shifting Meanings of Free Speech

Late 19th century "Gilded Age" through the 1920s: Advocates for political action to reduce inequality ran into a judiciary that sided with capital by upholding legislated restrictions on strikes, pickets, and boycotts, or imposing restrictions through court-issued injunctions. Labor partisans promoted an interpretation of free speech that would protect strikes, pickets, and boycotts, but state and federal legislatures and courts did not take up this view.

1930s: Franklin D. Roosevelt was elected as president in 1932 and many "New Deal" legislators were elected to Congress. Initially, the courts threw up roadblocks to implementation of New Deal legislation, but decisions issued in the 1930s began to distinguish property rights from personal rights. In a sudden reversal, judges started ruling that New Deal legislation was constitutional even when imposing contract constraints that would have been disallowed under earlier standards. At the same time, personal liberties that had less to do with property and contracts got greater constitutional protection than before.

1935: The National Labor Relations Act (NLRA) passed. The law protected unionization efforts in the covered industries by, among other provisions, requiring employer neutrality during unionization drives. The law improved conditions for a large share of white workers while reinforcing racial division among workers. Industries in which Black workers were a significant segment of the workforce were excluded from coverage.

1935 to 1947: Workers in the broad swath of industries prioritized in the New Deal, which were generally those with workforces that were primarily male and at least at the periphery of the umbrella of whiteness, had new protections for their speech. Private-sector unionization surged by a factor of more than four, from 3.8 million unionized workers to 14.6 million, reaching 31.8% of the non-farm labor force. Alarmed, employers complained that enforced neutrality during unionization drives violated their First Amendment free speech rights.

1947: The Taft-Hartley amendment to the NLRA eliminated the requirement of employer neutrality in union organizing drives and explicitly granted employers protection for almost all of what they wanted to say on the topic; matters have tilted ever farther in employers' favor since. Employers have become adept at wielding the First Amendment as a tool to maintain minority rule.

makes a distinction between actions the government takes to restrict speech (which may violate the First Amendment) and actions that private actors take to restrict speech (which do not violate the First Amendment). But the distinction dissolves into illogic when we think about everything the state does to give employers governing authority in their workplaces.

As things stand, the allocation of First Amendment free speech rights is wildly unequal. The prevailing interpretation of personal liberty (including speech) often conflates personal actions with uses of property. In practice, this amounts to a prioritization of property over people: The degree of liberty you enjoy is proportional to the amount of property you can command. The capitalist theory of free speech gives capital super-citizen status, with speech rights that are more expansive than those of ordinary citizens. Workers, meanwhile, are demoted to something less than full citizens, without substantive speech rights. For anyone not rich enough to live on their savings and income from investments, unemployment is a misery. The price of escaping the misery of unemployment is the need to labor for others *plus* the loss of democratic voice. When the hours of our lives can be sold to become the property of an employer, free speech, too, becomes alienable.

We hold these truths to be self-evident (under 21st century U.S. social relations): That all people of equal property are (roughly) equal (though the social-power-bestowing value of property may be discounted on the basis of race, gender, geography, etc.) and are endowed with certain alienable rights, among these life (which may be sold to capital by the hour), liberty (which is implicitly included in the labor-power sale), and the pursuit of happiness (as capital may direct the pursuits of those whose hours it purchases without deigning to consult workers on what those purposes should be). But what is self-evidently true for now need not always be.

Starbucks baristas spoke despite the pressure managers applied in captive-audience meetings, and some sites unionized. The union wins in Buffalo inspired more organizing drives at Starbucks locations across the country. Warehouse workers in Bessemer spoke despite Amazon's efforts to "free speech" them into compliance; the union lost the vote the first time, but in retrospect the NLRB ruled that Amazon's aggression constituted "unfair labor practices." (In addition to the issue of the mailbox, the NLRB cited the distribution of "Vote No" buttons and flyers while managers watched to see who picked them up and displayed them.) Months later, organizers for the Amazon Labor Union at the Staten Island warehouse crashed captive-audience meetings while they were off the clock to tell those who had been ordered to attend about the union. They assured their startled coworkers that the NLRA made it illegal for Amazon to fire them for speaking in favor of the union as long as they did so on their own time— and more were inspired to join the effort. Remarkably, Amazon, recently chided by the NLRB for their bad behavior in Bessemer, *did* refrain from firing the meeting crashers. The union won the Staten Island representation election. More locations are bound to follow. Perhaps sensing a change in the national mood, the NLRB's general counsel Jennifer Abruzzo circulated a memo on April 7 instructing field offices to consider captive-audience meetings to be a violation of the NLRA, despite the years of precedent to the contrary. Each time workers talk union, union talk becomes less unspeakable and the workplace gains more space for democratic voice. ❏

Sources: Elizabeth Anderson, *Private Government: How Employers Rule Our Lives (and Why We Don't Talk about It)* (Princeton University Press, 2017); Jack M. Balkin, "Digital Speech and Democratic Culture: A Theory of Freedom of Expression for the Information Age," *New York University Law Review*, 2004; John-Paul Ferguson, "Racial Diversity and Union Organizing in the United States, 1999-2008," *ILR* Review, January 2016; Douglas M. Fraleigh and Joseph S. Tuman, *Freedom of Speech in the Marketplace of Ideas* (Bedford/St. Martin's Press, 1997); Alexander Hertel-Fernandez, *Politics at Work: How Companies Turn Their Workers into Lobbyists* (Oxford University Press, 2018); Ruth Milkman, "The Double Game of Unions and the Labor Movement" in *Players and Arenas: The Interactive Dynamics of Protest*, edited by James M. Jasper and Jan Willem Duyvendak (Amsterdam University Press, 2015); More Perfect Union, "Starbucks Spreads Anti-Union Lies in Forced Employee Meetings," October 29, 2021 (perfectunion.us); Charles J. Morris, "Freeing the Captives: How Captive-Audience Meetings Under the NLRB Can Be Controlled," *Administrative Law Review*, 2017; Alina Selyukh, "Amazon Warehouse Workers Get to Re-Do Union Vote in Alabama," NPR, November 29, 2021 (npr.org); Associated Press, "Amazon Unionization Efforts Get a Boost Under a Settlement with U.S. Labor Board," NPR, December 23, 2021 (npr.org); Alan Story, "Employer Speech, Union Representation Elections, and the First Amendment," *Berkeley Journal of Employment and Labor Law*, 1995; Laura Weinrib, *The Taming of Free Speech: America's Civil Liberties Compromise* (Harvard University Press, 2016); An interview with Angelika Maldonado, "Here's How We Beat Amazon," *Jacobin*, April 2, 2022 (jacobinmag.com); National Labor Relations Board, "NLRB General Counsel Jennifer Abruzzo Issues Memo on Captive Audience and Other Mandatory Meetings," April 7, 2022 (nlrb.gov); Jay Greene, Jay Greene, "Labor board calls for re-vote at Amazon warehouse in Alabama in major victory for union," *Washington Post*, November 29, 2021 (wasingtonpost.com).

Chapter 8

THE DISTRIBUTION OF INCOME AND WEALTH

INTRODUCTION

For many mainstream economists, inequality in the distribution of income is a natural outcome of the functioning of markets. If workers get paid based on productivity, wage differences simply reflect underlying differences in productivity.

People who supply other inputs—investors or lenders supplying capital, land-owners supplying land—are similarly rewarded according to the marginal products of those inputs. Even poverty is largely seen as a result of low productivity, which can be interpreted more compassionately as the consequence of a lack of education and training, or, at an extreme, as a result of shirking and a whole host of moral failings. President Ronald Reagan's deliberate use of the term "welfare queen" during the 1980s to cast poor, Black women as undeserving of society's support is perhaps the most famous example of the latter. Indeed, in this view, a high degree of equality (or measures aimed at reducing inequality) would reduce the incentives for increasing productivity, slowing overall growth. Economists also argue that because the rich tend to save more (thus swelling the pool of resources available for investment), the larger the share of the economic pie that goes to them, the better the entire economy does. Trickle on down!

Chris Tilly, in his remarkable essay "Geese, Golden Eggs, and Traps" (Article 8.1), lays out the arguments for and against income equality and then takes down the rosy view of the economic benefits of inequality. His analysis shows how economies such as the United States' can end up in an "inequality trap" where high inequality leads to low growth, which in turn can lead to even higher inequality.

Next, in "The Rise in Inequality in the United States" (Article 8.2), Alejandro Reuss takes a data-driven approach to explaining the dizzying rise of inequality in the US, to the point that the richest 1% of households owns as much wealth as the bottom 40% of the country. He then reviews two major correlating factors to this concentration of wealth—worker membership in labor unions and the level of taxation directed at rich households, finding clear statistical tendencies for these to lower the share of total income going to the rich.

The next two articles look at patterns of inequality along lines of gender and race. In "'Equal Pay' Is Not So Equal" (Article 8.3), John Miller discusses unequal pay between men and women and responds to skeptics' claims that the pay gap is a statistical illusion. Meanwhile, "Undervaluation Is a Certainty," (Article 8.4), an interview with economist Michelle Holder, explores the background behind the often-cited statistic that Black women earn 61 cents for every dollar earned by a white man. Many counter that the number represents the different occupational distributions of these works—women are over-represented in low-wage industries while men are over-represented in higher-paying jobs and senior positions within them. However, the racial and gender pay gaps persist even after correcting for these issues.

For anyone who wants to explore questions of inequality and fairness, Gar Alperovitz and Lew Daly's article "The Undeserving Rich" (Article 8.5) provides some fascinating grist for the mill. They argue that growth is built on a base of collectively produced knowledge that each generation inherits—not merely on the efforts of individuals. Therefore, they argue, those who appropriate a disproportionate share are "undeserving" of their fortunes.

Next, in "Do People Care About Extreme Inequality" (Article 8.6), Arthur MacEwan explores whether people care about extreme inequality. MacEwan addresses the myths about opportunity, fair markets, and social mobility that lead many people to accept or ignore extreme inequality.

In "Concentration of Stock Ownership" (Article 8.7), Ed Ford vividly illustrates the point made by Thomas Piketty's *Capital in the Twenty-First Century* that wealth through ownership of financial assets (profits, interest, and dividends) increases significantly faster than returns on the sale of one's labor (wages). In this era of financialization, this tendency accelerates an already unsustainable level of inequality.

Finally, in "Financialization and Inequality" (Article 8.8), Arthur MacEwan returns to deliver a brief primer on financialization and how the growth of the financial sector has worked with other factors to generate massive inequality.

Discussion Questions

1. (Article 8.1) According to Tilly, many of the mechanisms linking equality and growth are political. Should economic models incorporate political behavior as well as economic behavior? What are some ways they could do that?

2. (Article 8.1) Explain Tilly's metaphor about the "Goose That Laid the Golden Eggs." How is equality the goose?

3. (Article 8.2) According to Alejandro Reuss's analysis of growing inequality in the United States, what is the relationship between organized labor and rising inequality? How does that relate to labor-based political parties in other advanced industrialized countries? What are the main reasons that inequality has grown so much more in the United States?

4. (Article 8.3) Why might someone think that the different industries and occupations men and women typically work in help explain away the gender pay gap? Why might someone think those differences can't explain it away?

5.   (Article 8.3) What policies might make the pay gap disappear, according to Miller?

6.   (Article 8.4) Can the difference between the incomes of white men and Black women be explained fully by their tendency to hold different positions in different industries? What other factors shape the "double pay gap"?

7.   (Article 8.5) Consider the following quotation:

> I think we've been through a period where too many people have been given to understand that if they have a problem, it's the government's job to cope with it. ... They're casting their problem on society. And, you know, there is no such thing as society. There are individual men and women, and there are families.
>   —British Prime Minister Margaret Thatcher, talking to *Woman's Own* magazine, October 31, 1987

After reading Alperovitz and Daly's article "The Undeserving Rich," how do you think the authors would respond to Thatcher? How would you respond?

8.   (Article 8.6) What are the "Two Myths" that MacEwan refers to in his article? What are the "Realities" as to these Myths?

9.   (Article 8.7) In his review of Thomas Piketty's *Capital in the Twenty-First Century* (*D&S*, July/August 2014), Steven Pressman summarized one of Piketty's central conclusions thus:

> Piketty, like Malthus, draws his dismal conclusion from the relationship between two growth rates. In Piketty's case, they are the rate of return to wealth or capital (r) and the growth rate of the economy (g). When r exceeds g, more money flows to those at the top and inequality increases; when r is less than g, more benefits of economic growth flow to workers, making income and wealth distribution more equal.

How do Ford's charts on inequality of stock ownership relate to this analysis from Piketty?

10.   (Article 8.8) What is "financialization"? Is financialization parasitic on "enterprise"? Is this a problem?

Article 8.1

GEESE, GOLDEN EGGS, AND TRAPS
Why inequality is bad for the economy.

BY CHRIS TILLY
July/August 2004

Whenever progressives propose ways to redistribute wealth from the rich to those with low and moderate incomes, conservative politicians and economists accuse them of trying to kill the goose that lays the golden egg. The advocates of unfettered capitalism proclaim that inequality is good for the economy because it promotes economic growth. Unequal incomes, they say, provide the incentives necessary to guide productive economic decisions by businesses and individuals. Try to reduce inequality, and you'll sap growth. Furthermore, the conservatives argue, growth actually promotes equality by boosting the have-nots more than the haves. So instead of fiddling with who gets how much, the best way to help those at the bottom is to pump up growth.

But these conservative prescriptions are absolutely, dangerously wrong. Instead of the goose-killer, equality turns out to be the goose. Inequality stifles growth; equality gooses it up. Moreover, economic expansion does not necessarily promote equality—instead, it is the types of jobs and the rules of the economic game that matter most.

Inequality: Goose or Goose-Killer?

The conservative argument may be wrong, but it's straightforward. Inequality is good for the economy, conservatives say, because it provides the right incentives for innovation and economic growth. First of all, people will only have the motivation to work hard, innovate, and invest wisely if the economic system rewards them for good economic choices and penalizes bad ones. Robin Hood-style policies that collect from the wealthy and help those who are worse off violate this principle. They reduce the payoff to smart decisions and lessen the sting of dumb ones. The result: people and companies are bound to make less efficient decisions. "We must allow [individuals] to fail, as well as succeed, and we must replace the nanny state with a regime of self-reliance and self-respect," writes conservative lawyer Stephen Kinsella in *The Freeman: Ideas on Liberty* (not clear how the free woman fits in). To prove their point, conservatives point to the former state socialist countries, whose economies had become stagnant and inefficient by the time they fell at the end of the 1980s.

If you don't buy this incentive story, there's always the well-worn trickle-down theory. To grow, the economy needs productive investments: new offices, factories, computers, and machines. To finance such investments takes a pool of savings. The rich save a larger fraction of their incomes than those less well-off. So to spur growth, give more to the well-heeled (or at least take less away from them in the form of taxes), and give less to the down-and-out. The rich will save their money and then invest it, promoting growth that's good for everyone.

Unfortunately for trickle-down, the brilliant economist John Maynard Keynes debunked the theory in his *General Theory of Employment, Interest, and*

Money in 1936. Keynes, whose precepts guided liberal U.S. economic policy from the 1940s through the 1970s, agreed that investments must be financed out of savings. But he showed that most often it's changes in investment that drive savings, rather than the other way around. When businesses are optimistic about the future and invest in building and retooling, the economy booms, all of us make more money, and we put some of it in banks, 401(k)s, stocks, and so on. That is, saving grows to match investment. When companies are glum, the process runs in reverse, and savings shrink to equal investment. This leads to the "paradox of thrift": if people try to save too much, businesses will see less consumer spending, will invest less, and total savings will end up diminishing rather than growing as the economy spirals downward. A number of Keynes' followers added the next logical step: shifting money from the high-saving rich to the high-spending rest of us, and not the other way around, will spur investment and growth.

Of the two conservative arguments in favor of inequality, the incentive argument is a little weightier. Keynes himself agreed that people needed financial consequences to steer their actions, but questioned whether the differences in payoffs needed to be so huge. Certainly state socialist countries' attempts to replace material incentives with moral exhortation have often fallen short. In 1970, the Cuban government launched the Gran Zafra (Great Harvest), an attempt to reap 10 million tons of sugar cane with (strongly encouraged) volunteer labor. Originally inspired by Che Guevara's ideal of the New Socialist Man (not clear how the New Socialist Woman fit in), the effort ended with Fidel Castro tearfully apologizing to the Cuban people in a nationally broadcast speech for letting wishful thinking guide economic policy.

But before conceding this point to the conservatives, let's look at the evidence about the connection between equality and growth. Economists William Easterly of New York University and Gary Fields of Cornell University have recently summarized this evidence:

- Countries, and regions within countries, with more equal incomes grow faster. (These growth figures do not include environmental destruction or improvement. If they knocked off points for environmental destruction and added points for environmental improvement, the correlation between equality and growth would be even stronger, since desperation drives poor people to adopt environmentally destructive practices such as rapid deforestation.)
- Countries with more equally distributed land grow faster.
- Somewhat disturbingly, more ethnically homogeneous countries and regions grow faster—presumably because there are fewer ethnically based inequalities.
- In addition, more worker rights are associated with higher rates of economic growth, according to Josh Bivens and Christian Weller, economists at two Washington, D.C., think tanks, the Economic Policy Institute and the Center for American Progress.

These patterns recommend a second look at the incentive question. In fact, more equality can actually strengthen incentives and opportunities to produce.

Equality as the Goose

Equality can boost growth in several ways. Perhaps the simplest is that study after study has shown that farmland is more productive when cultivated in small plots. So organizations promoting more equal distribution of land, like Brazil's Landless Workers' Movement, are not just helping the landless poor—they're contributing to agricultural productivity!

Another reason for the link between equality and growth is what Easterly calls "match effects," which have been highlighted in research by Stanford's Paul Roemer and others in recent years. One example of a match effect is the fact that well-educated people are most productive when working with others who have lots of schooling. Likewise, people working with computers are more productive when many others have computers (so that, for example, e-mail communication is widespread, and know-how about computer repair and software is easy to come by). In very unequal societies, highly educated, computer-using elites are surrounded by majorities with little education and no computer access, dragging down their productivity. This decreases young people's incentive to get more education and businesses' incentive to invest in computers, since the payoff will be smaller.

Match effects can even matter at the level of a metropolitan area. Urban economist Larry Ledebur looked at income and employment growth in 85 U.S. cities and their neighboring suburbs. He found that where the income gap between those in the suburbs and those in the city was largest, income and job growth was slower for everyone.

"Pressure effects" also help explain why equality sparks growth. Policies that close off the low-road strategy of exploiting poor and working people create pressure effects, driving economic elites to search for investment opportunities that pay off by boosting productivity rather than squeezing the have-nots harder. For example, where workers have more rights, they will place greater demands on businesses. Business owners will respond by trying to increase productivity, both to remain profitable even after paying higher wages, and to find ways to produce with fewer workers. The Congress of Industrial Organizations (CIO) union drives in U.S. mass production industries in the 1930s and 1940s provide much of the explanation for the superb productivity growth of the 1950s and 1960s. (The absence of pressure effects may help explain why many past and present state socialist countries have seen slow growth, since they tend to offer numerous protections for workers but no right to organize independent unions.) Similarly, if a government buys out large landholdings in order to break them up, wealthy families who simply kept their fortunes tied up in land for generations will look for new, productive investments. Industrialization in Asian "tigers" South Korea and Taiwan took off in the 1950s on the wings of funds freed up in exactly this way.

Inequality, Conflict, and Growth

Inequality hinders growth in another important way: it fuels social conflict. Stark inequality in countries such as Bolivia and Haiti has led to chronic conflict that hobbles economic growth. Moreover, inequality ties up resources in unproductive uses such as paying for large numbers of police and security guards—attempts to prevent individuals from redistributing resources through theft.

Ethnic variety is connected to slower growth because, on the average, more ethnically diverse countries are also more likely to be ethnically divided. In other words, the problem isn't ethnic variety itself, but racism and ethnic conflict that can exist among diverse populations. In nations like Guatemala, Congo, and Nigeria, ethnic strife has crippled growth—a problem alien to ethnically uniform Japan and South Korea. The reasons are similar to some of the reasons that large class divides hurt growth. Where ethnic divisions (which can take tribal, language, religious, racial, or regional forms) loom large, dominant ethnic groups seek to use government power to better themselves at the expense of other groups, rather than making broad-based investments in education and infrastructure. This can involve keeping down the underdogs—slower growth in the U.S. South for much of the country's history was linked to the Southern system of white supremacy. Or it can involve seizing the surplus of ethnic groups perceived as better off—in the extreme, Nazi Germany's expropriation and genocide of the Jews, who often held professional and commercial jobs.

Of course, the solution to such divisions is not "ethnic cleansing" so that each country has only one ethnic group—in addition to being morally abhorrent, this is simply impossible in a world with 191 countries and 5,000 ethnic groups. Rather, the solution is to diminish ethnic inequalities. Once the 1964 Civil Rights Act forced the South to drop racist laws, the New South's economic growth spurt began. Easterly reports that in countries with strong rule of law, professional bureaucracies, protection of contracts, and freedom from expropriation—all rules that make it harder for one ethnic group to economically oppress another—ethnic diversity has no negative impact on growth.

If more equality leads to faster growth so everybody benefits, why do the rich typically resist redistribution? Looking at the ways that equity seeds growth helps us understand why. The importance of pressure effects tells us that the wealthy often don't think about more productive ways to invest or reorganize their businesses until they are forced to. But also, if a country becomes very unequal, it can get stuck in an "inequality trap." Any redistribution involves a tradeoff for the rich. They lose by giving up part of their wealth, but they gain a share in increased economic growth. The bigger the disparity between the rich and the rest, the more the rich have to lose, and the less likely that the equal share of boosted growth they'll get will make up for their loss. Once the gap goes beyond a certain point, the wealthy have a strong incentive to restrict democracy, and to block spending on education which might lead the poor to challenge economic injustice—making reform that much harder.

Does Economic Growth Reduce Inequality?

If inequality isn't actually good for the economy, what about the second part of the conservatives' argument—that growth itself promotes equality? According to the conservatives, those who care about equality should simply pursue growth and wait for equality to follow.

"A rising tide lifts all boats," President John F. Kennedy famously declared. But he said nothing about which boats will rise fastest when the economic tide comes in. Growth does typically reduce poverty, according to studies reviewed by economist Gary Fields, though some "boats"—especially families with strong barriers to participating in the labor force—stay "stuck in the mud." But inequality can increase at the same time that poverty falls, if the rich gain even faster than the poor do. True, sustained periods of low unemployment, like that in the late 1990s United States, do tend to raise wages at the bottom even faster than salaries at the top. But growth after the recessions of 1991 and 2001 began with years of "jobless recoveries"—growth with inequality.

For decades the prevailing view about growth and inequality within countries was that expressed by Simon Kuznets in his 1955 presidential address to the American Economic Association. Kuznets argued that as countries grew, inequality would first increase, then decrease. The reason is that people will gradually move from the low-income agricultural sector to higher-income industrial jobs—with inequality peaking when the workforce is equally divided between low- and high-income sectors. For mature industrial economies, Kuznets' proposition counsels focusing on growth, assuming that it will bring equity. In developing countries, it calls for enduring current inequality for the sake of future equity and prosperity.

But economic growth doesn't automatically fuel equality. In 1998, economists Klaus Deininger and Lyn Squire traced inequality and growth over time in 48 countries. Five followed the Kuznets pattern, four followed the reverse pattern (decreasing inequality followed by an increase), and the rest showed no systematic pattern. In the United States, for example:

- Incomes became more equal during the 1930s through 1940s New Deal period (a time that included economic decline followed by growth);
- From the 1950s through the 1970s, income gaps lessened during booms and expanded during slumps;
- From the late 1970s forward, income inequality worsened fairly consistently, whether the economy was stagnating or growing.

The reasons are not hard to guess. The New Deal introduced widespread unionization, a minimum wage, social security, unemployment insurance, and welfare. Since the late 1970s, unions have declined, the inflation-adjusted value of the minimum wage has fallen, and the social safety net has been shredded. In the United States, as elsewhere, growth only promotes equality if policies and institutions to support equity are in place.

Trapped?

Let's revisit the idea of an inequality trap. The notion is that as the gap between the rich and everybody else grows wider, the wealthy become more willing to give up overall growth in return for the larger share they're getting for themselves. The "haves" back policies to control the "have-nots," instead of devoting social resources to educating the poor so they'll be more productive.

Sound familiar? It should. After two decades of widening inequality, the last few years have brought us massive tax cuts that primarily benefit the wealthiest, at the expense of investment in infrastructure and the education, childcare, and income supports that would help raise less well-off kids to be productive adults. Federal and state governments have cranked up expenditures on prisons, police, and "homeland security," and Republican campaign organizations have devoted major resources to keeping blacks and the poor away from the polls. If the economic patterns of the past are any indication, we're going to pay for these policies in slower growth and stagnation unless we can find our way out of this inequality trap. ❑

Article 8.2

THE RISE IN INCOME INEQUALITY IN THE UNITED STATES

BY ALEJANDRO REUSS
March 2020

Part 1: The Name of the Game Is Class Struggle

It's no secret that, over the last forty years, income inequality has soared in the United States. In the late 1970s, the top 10% of the U.S. population, ranked by income, received about one third of total U.S. income, or more than three times an equal share. They now receive about half of total income, or five times an equal share. Over the same period, the income share going to the top 1% has increased from about 10% of total income (ten times an equal share) to about 20% today (twenty times). The share going to the top 0.1% has increased from almost 3% (30 times an equal share) to over 10% (more than 100 times an equal share). This top one-thousandth of the income ranking gets about the same total income as the entire bottom forty percent of the U.S. population.

The compensation of nonsupervisory workers, who make up over 80% of the U.S. labor force, has stagnated since the 1970s. Most of the growth in incomes has been captured, instead, by business owners, executives, and others at the top of the income ranking. This shift in the income distribution is largely a product of changes in the balance of power—at the workplace level and at the political level—between different economic classes in U.S. society. Over the last forty years, owners and managers of large corporations have waged a relentless and highly successful campaign against the collective power of workers. Employers' efforts to break unions where they did exist and to oppose unionization where they did not, more often than not with the connivance of government officials, has borne bitter fruit: Union membership in the private sector has plummeted to less than one out of every 15 workers.

While especially pronounced in the United States, similar attacks have afflicted workers in many high-income or "advanced" economies. Weaker labor movements have meant higher degrees of income inequality. Comparing 20 different high-income countries over the period between 1980 and 2010, economists Florence Jaumotte and Carolina Ororio Buitron found that differences in unionization rates—across different countries and different years—accounted for more than 40% of the variation in the income shares of the top 10%. When the unionization rate is higher, the income share of the top 10% is lower; when the unionization rate is lower, the income share of the top 10% is higher. It is unlikely that the picture would change much if we looked instead at the top 1% or the top 0.1%, as the growth of their income shares are main drivers of the growth in the income share of the top 10%.

There are at least three major ways, described in previous research by economists and other social scientists, in which unions tend to narrow income inequalities:

UNION DENSITY AND TOP 10% INCOME SHARE, HIGH-INCOME CAPITALIST COUNTRIES, 1970 TO 2011

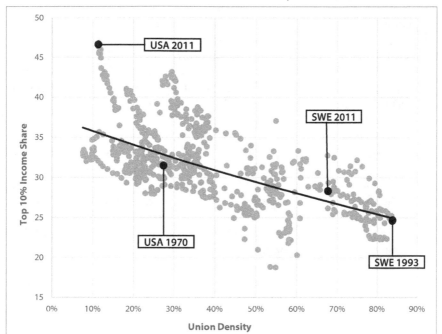

Note: Each point represents the combination of union density (horizontal axis) and top 10% income share (vertical axis) in a particular high-income country for a particular year between 1970 and 2011. The black line is fit, using standard statistical methods, through the middle of the cloud of points. It indicates the top 10% income share we would predict if we knew nothing but the union density in a particular country for a particular year. Its downward slope indicates that higher union density is associated with a lower income share for the top 10%; a lower union density, with a higher income share for the top 10%. As union density has declined in most high-income countries, income inequality has increased. In Sweden, for example, it has increased by about three percentage points from 1993 (the year of the country's union-density peak) to 2011. Its top 10% income share for both years is close to the predicted level for that union density. In the United States, union density has also declined over this time period (its highest union density came in 1970, the first year in the data series; its lowest came in 2011, the last year in the series). Over that time, the top 10% income share has increased dramatically, from a little below the predicted level to far above it. That is, the concentration of income at the top has increased far more than we would predict just from the decline in union density.

Source: Figure design by author; data courtesy of Florence Jaumotte and Carolina Osorio Buitron. Countries included: Australia, Canada, Denmark, Finland, France, Germany, Ireland, Italy, Japan, Netherlands, New Zealand, Norway, Portugal, Spain, Sweden, Switzerland, United Kingdom, United States. Years included: 1970-2011, with some exceptions due to unavailable data.

First, unions boost the incomes of workers in low-wage occupations relative to workers in other occupations. Workers in lower-wage occupations are more likely to become union members—and to get increased wages and employer-provided benefits—than workers in already higher-income occupations.

Second, unions tend to boost the incomes of their lowest-wage members to a greater degree than the incomes of higher-wage members. This reduces the income gaps (produces "wage compression") among unionized workers.

Third, unions tend to pull down the incomes of those at the top. While employers try to pass on cost increases (such as those resulting from higher wages and benefits) in the form of higher prices, they cannot normally do so fully. As a result, increases in worker compensation tend to "squeeze" profits and so reduce income inequalities between workers and employers. Since business owners and executives tend to have high incomes, this tends to reduce income the income share of those in, say, the top 10% or the top 1% of the income ranking.

Better-bargained outcomes for workers, while part of the income-distribution story, are not the whole story. In almost all high-income countries, taxes and transfers reduce the degree of income inequality to some degree—though in some countries much more than others.

Part 2: Time to Get Political

The income distribution in capitalist economies is determined to a great extent by "market incomes." Market incomes are those derived from the sale of something or another in a market. For business owners, market incomes are based on the amount and prices of the goods and services that they sell minus the amount and prices of the inputs that they buy. The difference is the "net income" (or profit) of the business. For workers, in turn, market incomes are largely based on the amount and price of what they sell—their labor power. Their market incomes depend on the hours per week they work, the number of weeks they are employed out of the year, and the rate of pay (including both wages and employer-provided benefits).

In the United States and other high-income countries, incomes "after taxes and transfers" are generally distributed at least somewhat more equally than market incomes. "Progressive" taxes—such as taxes on corporate income, individual income taxes with higher rates for higher income brackets, taxes on forms of income that go largely to high-income individuals (such as capital gains taxes), and taxes on wealth (such as estate taxes)—take income disproportionately from those at the top of the income ranking. Meanwhile, government programs benefiting low- and middle-income individuals redistribute some income to those closer to the bottom.

Economists Isabelle Joumard, Mauro Pisu, and Debbie Bloch have found that countries with more unequal market incomes, by and large, tend to do more to redistribute incomes via taxes and transfers. The United States, however, is both among the high-income countries with higher-than average inequality of market incomes and lower-than-average redistribution through taxes and transfers. It is no wonder, then, that the United States has such an unequal income distribution—after taxes and transfers—compared to other high-income countries.

In most high-income countries, labor-based political parties (usually referring to themselves as "labor," "social democratic," or "socialist" parties) have played a leading role historically in bringing about policies that reduce income inequality. While there is no generally agreed-upon way to define what is a labor-based party and what is not, some of the major factors are their historical origins in the workers' movement, formal institutional connections to labor unions and union federations, limitation of membership to ordinary workers (excluding employers and managers), and rejection of financing from business owners. Such parties tend

MARKET-INCOME INEQUALITY AND TAX-TRANSFER REDISTRIBUTION

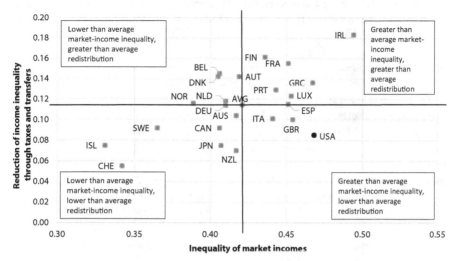

Sources: Figure design by author, based on a similar figure in Isabelle Joumard, Mauro Pisu, and Debbie Bloch, "Tackling Income Inequality: The Role of Taxes and Transfers," Organisation for Economic Co-operation and Development, *OECD Journal: Economic Studies*, Vol. 2012/1 (oecd.org). Inequality of market incomes measured as Gini coefficient (0 = perfect equality, 1= maximum inequality) for market incomes (before taxes and transfers), working-age population (18-65). Reduction of income inequality measured as Gini coefficient for market incomes, working-age population, minus Gini coefficient for disposable incomes (after taxes and transfers), working-age population (18-65). Data from OECD Income Distribution Database (IDD), Organisation for Economic Co-operation and Development (stats.oecd.org).

to influence the distribution of income through various different kinds of policies, including protections for unionization and other aspects of workplace organization, regulations on labor market outcomes like wages and hours, whole-economy policies emphasizing full employment, and taxes and transfers redistributing income downwards.

The high-income capitalist countries where labor-based parties have historically been strongest—such as the Nordic countries—are among those with the lowest income inequality. The United States, on the other hand, sticks out among high-income capitalist countries by the absence of a major labor-based political party. This is certainly among the main factors explaining the relative weakness of labor organization, labor-market regulation, and the welfare state in the United States, compared to other high-income countries. In almost all other such countries, there is at least one significant labor-based political party; in many, there are several with differing political programs.

The influence of reform-minded labor-based parties, however, is by no means a guarantee of declining inequality, and no country should be romanticized as some sort of workers' paradise. Tendencies towards declining economic inequality during the post-World War II period have been halted in almost all high-income countries, and dramatically reversed in many. Not all problems of capitalist economies can necessarily be solved by reforms that leave the basic structure of the economic system intact. If problems such as unacceptably large inequalities of wealth and power cannot be solved—or least cannot be solved in a lasting way—by reforms within the basic framework of a capitalist economy, this does not mean they cannot be solved at all. It does mean, however, that a lasting solution would require more fundamental systemic change. ❏

Sources: Florence Jaumotte and Carolina Osorio Buitron, "Inequality and Labor Market Institutions," International Monetary Fund, IMF Staff Discussion Note (SDN/15/14), July 2015 (imf.org); "Union Power and Inequality," Center for Economic Policy Research, Vox CEPR Policy Portal, October 22, 2015 (voxeu.org); Josh Bivens, *et al.*, "How Today's Unions Help Working People," Economic Policy Institute, August 24, 2017 (epinet.org); Isabelle Joumard, Mauro Pisu, and Debbie Bloch, "Tackling Income Inequality: The Role of Taxes and Transfers," Organisation for Economic Co-operation and Development, *OECD Journal: Economic Studies*, Vol. 2012/1 (oecd.org); Max Roser and Esteban Ortiz-Ospina, "Income Inequality," Our World in Data, University of Oxford (ourworldindata.org); Theda Skocpol and Edward Amenta, "States and Social Policies," *Annual Review of Sociology*, Vol. 12 (1986), pp. 131-157.

Note: The title of Part 1 of this piece alludes to the title of the book *Class Struggle is the Name of the Game*, by political scientist Bertell Ollman.

Article 8.3

"EQUAL PAY" IS NOT SO EQUAL

BY JOHN MILLER
September/October 2016

> The latest U.S. Department of Labor data show that women working full time make 81 percent of full-time men's wages. But this figure is both inaccurate and misleading. This statistic looks only at raw averages and does not take into account factors such as education, skills, and hours worked. After controlling for other factors, the gender pay gap practically disappears. Legislation to close the gender "wage gap" is misguided: in reality, there is no gap to close.
>
> —Diana Furchgott-Roth, "Sorry, Elizabeth Warren, Women Already Have Equal Pay," Economics21, The Manhattan Institute for Policy Research, July 27, 2016

"**W**e believe in equal pay for equal work." That was all Sen. Elizabeth Warren (D-Mass.) said about the gender pay gap during her keynote address to July's Democratic National Convention. But it was enough to provoke a response from economist Diana Furchgott-Roth, a senior fellow at the free-market Manhattan Institute.

That's hardly surprising. Furchgott-Roth has spent two decades issuing one version or another of one basic claim: "there is no gap to close between men's and women's wages."

Publishing article after article claiming that there is no gender pay gap, however, doesn't make it so. Here's why.

No Statistical Artifact

To begin with, the gender pay gap is no statistical artifact. The most common measure of the gender pay gap compares the median earnings (wages and salaries) of full-time working women over the year to the median earnings for men. That ratio does not compare the earnings of men and women doing the same job, but rather the earnings of all men and women who work full time.

In 2014, the latest year for which data are available, men's median earnings for the year were $50,383, while women's median earnings were $39,621, or 78.6% of men's. That's where the figure that women earn 79 cents for each dollar a man earns comes from. The National Committee on Pay Equity inaugurated the tradition of using this ratio to determine the date on which "Equal Pay Day" falls each year. This year, it fell on April 12, 2016, the date by which women would have earned enough to make up the $10,762 gap between their pay and men's in 2015. (Furchgott-Roth's figure for the gender pay gap, 81% in 2015, is calculated in the same way but compares the median weekly earnings of full-time wage and salary workers.)

Whether women earn 79 cents or 81 cents for every dollar a man earns, the gender pay gap is long-standing. In 1963, the year the Equal Pay Act became law, a full-time working woman (earning the median pay for women) got 59 cents for each dollar a full-time working man received (at the median pay for men). By the first Equal Pay Day in 1996, women earned 74 cents for a dollar of men's earnings; now the figure is up to 79 cents. The gender pay gap, however, is no longer narrowing as fast as it did earlier. During the 1980s, the gap declined by more than one-quarter (28.7%), as women's earnings improved from 60 cents for every dollar a man earned to 72 cents; during the 1990s, by just 6%, as women's earnings increased from 72 cents to 73 cents for every dollar of men's earnings; in the last 10 years (2004–2014), by 7.4%, as women's earnings increased from 77 cents to 79 cents for every dollar of men's earnings.

The gender pay gap is also pervasive. Regardless of her education, her occupation, her race, or her age, a full-time working woman (getting the median wage for women of that group) is paid less than a full-time working man (getting the median wage for men of that group).

Women earn less than men at every educational level. In 2015, the median weekly earnings of women without a high school diploma were 80% of their male counterparts' earnings, 77% for women with (only) a high school diploma, 75% for women with some college, 75% for women who were college graduates, and 74% for women with an advanced degree.

Women earn less than men in all but five of the 800 detailed occupations tracked by the Bureau of Labor Statistics (for which there is comparable data). Women in female-dominated occupations—from maids to secretaries to registered nurses—earn less than men do in those same jobs, as do women in male-dominated jobs—from truck drivers to retail supervisors to janitors. The same is true for women in elite jobs such as physicians, surgeons, and financial managers.

Women of all racial/ethnic groups are paid less than white men and less than men of the same race/ethnicity. In 2015, the median weekly earnings of white women working full time were 80.8% of those for white men. The weekly earnings of black women were 89% of the earnings of black men; the earnings of Hispanic women, 90% of the earnings of Hispanic men. Meanwhile, the weekly earnings of black and Hispanic women were just 62% and 67%, respectively, of the weekly earnings of white men.

Women workers of all ages are paid less than their male counterparts. Older women, however, face the largest pay gap as they are penalized for leaving the workforce more often than men for childbirth, childcare, and eldercare. In 2014, the annual median wage of women ages 18–24 who worked full time was 88% of the median wage of full-time male workers of the same age group, but 81% for women ages 35–44, and just 68% for women over 55.

Making the Unequal Look Equal

But those differences, no matter how widespread or long lasting, don't impress economist Furchgott-Roth. In her version of reality, those differences disappear once the pay gap is adjusted for gender differences in hours worked, education, experience, and choice of industry and occupation. But each of these adjustments is problematic or makes less of a difference than Furchgott-Roth and other pay gap deniers suggest.

The deniers complain that earnings differentials calculated for full-time workers, including anyone who works 35 or more hours a week, mask the fact that men work more hours (in the money economy) than women. In fact, men are almost twice as likely as women to work more than 40 hours a week. But that problem can be corrected by using hourly earnings to measure the gender pay gap. In 2014, hourly earnings of full- and part-time women wage-and-salary workers were 84.6% of men's. While smaller, that gap is still quite substantial and persists at all levels of education and for all racial/ethnic groups.

Nor will making adjustments for gender differences in education and experience, two traditional measures of labor-market skills, make the gender pay gap disappear. Adjustments for education explain much less of today's gender pay gap than they did in the early 1980s. Since then, more women have graduated from college than men, and by 1999 the average full-time working woman had more years of education than her male counterpart. Gender differences in years of experience are also far smaller than they were in the past. In 1981, men had, on average, 6.8 more years of full-time labor market experience than women, but the experience gap was just 1.4 years in 2011. In their detailed study of the sources of the gender pay gap, economists Francine Blau and Lawrence Kahn estimate that, taken together, differences in education (which favor women) and differences in experience (which favor men) explained 8.2% of the gender pay gap in 2011, or just 2 cents of the 23 cent gap.

There is little disagreement that differences between women and men in terms of the industries they work in and the jobs they hold have a profound effect on the gender pay gap. Blau and Kahn, for instance, estimate that industry and occupation accounted for fully one-half (49.5%) of the gender pay gap in 2010.

But just how women ended up in particular industries and occupations and not in others is a matter of sharp debate. For gender pay gap skeptics, this is a matter of individual choice. "Women gravitate toward jobs with fewer risks, more comfortable conditions, regular hours, more personal fulfillment, and greater flexibility," argues Carrie Lukas, executive director of the Independent Women's Forum. Women, she concludes, are "willing to trade higher pay for other desirable job characteristics." But the story Lukas tells is not the empirical reality faced by most women. To begin with, women's jobs do not possess the other desirable characteristics she says compensate women for accepting lower pay. In their study of the characteristics of men's and women's jobs in 27 countries including the United States, sociologists Haya Stier and Meir Yaish found that on average the jobs held by women offered less autonomy or time flexibility and that their working conditions were more stressful and exhausting than those of men, a condition that was surely exacerbated by women bearing an inordinate share of domestic labor. (Women's jobs did require less physical labor than men's jobs.)

If individual choices of women don't explain what crowds many women into lower paying jobs, then what is responsible for gender segregation by occupation and industry? Gender discrimination that disadvantages women in the labor market and devalues their work is the more plausible answer. If you doubt that women's work is undervalued, political scientist Ellen Frankel Paul would ask you to consider this example: zookeepers—a traditionally male job—earn more than workers caring for children—a traditionally female job. The evidence that the sorting of genders into industries and occupations is shaped "by discrimination, societal norms, and other forces beyond women's control," as economists Jessica Schieder and Elisa Gould argue, is compelling. For instance, it is well documented that women in better-paying male-dominated jobs have faced hostile work environments. A 2008 study found that "52% of highly qualified females working for SET (science, technology, and engineering) companies quit their jobs, driven out by hostile work environments and extreme job pressures." And gender discrimination plays a role in who gets hired in the first place. In two studies, when participants reviewed résumés that were identical except for the names, the ones with male names were more likely to be offered a job. According to another study, after five top U.S. symphony orchestras switched to blind auditions, women were 50% more likely to get past the first round. But gender norms already direct women and men toward different jobs long before they enter in the labor market. For instance, Schieder and Gould report that women arrive at college far less likely than men are to major in engineering, computer sciences, or physics, even though those fields promise lucrative job opportunities.

Most low-paying jobs, on the other hand, are female dominated. In their 2009 study, sociologists Asaf Levanon, Paula England, and Paul Allison reported that occupations with a higher percentage of women workers generally paid less than those with a lower percentage of women, even when correcting for education and skill demands. On top of that, they found evidence that when more women enter a job category, employers start paying less. For example, as jobs in parks and camps went from being male-dominated to female-dominated, between 1950 and 2000, the median hourly wages (corrected for inflation) fell by more than half.

Finally, the adjustments favored by Furchgott-Roth and other gender-gap skeptics are not enough to statistically eliminate the gender pay gap. For instance, one research study, commissioned by the Department of Labor during the George W. Bush administration, estimated a wage gap between 4.8 and 7.1 percentage points after making adjustments for other gender differences. In the Blau and Kahn study the remaining gender gap in 2010 was 8.4 percentage points when fully adjusting for differences in education, experience, region, race, unionization, industry and occupation. Those gender pay gaps, which assume that differences in occupation and industry are not evidence of ongoing gender discrimination, are much smaller than the unadjusted gap, but still substantial.

For Blau and Kahn, the unexplained portion of the gender pay gap, "suggests, though it does not prove, that labor market discrimination continues to contribute to the gender wage gap." The unexplained gender pay gap (the portion still left over after statistically adjusting for occupation, industry, or worker qualifications) has actually worsened since the late 1980s (from 7.6 cents for each dollar a man made in 1989 to 8.4 cents in 2010). In 2010, over one-third (38%) of the gender pay gap remained unexplained. If we include the portion of the gap due to gender differences in occupation and industry, a whopping 87.5%, or 18 cents of the 21 cents of the unadjusted gender gap in their study, can be interpreted as a product of continued discrimination.

Truly Equal Pay

One important step to reduce continued labor market gender discrimination would be to pass the Paycheck Fairness Act. The law would require employers to show that wage differentials are based on factors other than gender, and would strike a blow against pay secrecy by banning retaliation against employees who reveal their own wages to other employees.

But much more needs to be done to combat workplace gender discrimination. More family-friendly policies are needed. The United States is the only advanced country that does not guarantee paid maternity leave. Comparable-worth policies are needed to promote pay equity. Those policies would ensure that jobs having the same value to employers would be paid the same whether performed by women or men. Also, in order to short-circuit historical gender pay discrimination, newly passed comparable-worth legislation in Massachusetts bars employers from asking job applicants how much they earned in previous jobs. In addition, raising the minimum wage would boost the earnings of workers in low-income jobs, the vast majority of which are female-dominated. Unionization in female-dominated occupations would also reduce the gender pay gap, as it has done among public employees.

For Furchgott-Roth and the gender-pay-gap skeptics, the pay gap disappears by statistical manipulation. These policies, on the other hand, are ways to make it go away for real. ❏

Sources: Francine Blau and Lawrence Kahn, "The Gender Wage Gap: Extent, and Explanations," IZA Research Network, Discussion Paper No. 9656, Jan. 2016; Jessica Schleder and Elise Gould, "'Women's work' and the gender pay gap," Economic Policy Institute, July 20, 2016; Asaf Levanon, Paula England, and Paul Allison, "Occupational Feminization and Pay," *Social Forces*, December 2009; Hava Stier and Meir Yaish, "Occupational segregation and gender inequality in job quality," *Work, Employment, and Society*, 28(2), 2014; Marlene Kim, "Policies to End the Gender Wage Gap in the United States," *Review of Radical Political Economics*, 45(3), 2013; Emily Liner, "The Wage Gap Over Time," "A Dollar Short: What's Holding Women Back form Equal Pay?" *Third Way Report*, March 18, 2016; "An Analysis of Reasons for the Disparity in Wages Between Men and Women," A Report by CONSAD Research Corp. for the Department of Labor, 2009; Ellen Frankel, ed., *Equity and Gender: The Comparable Worth Debate* (Transactions Publishers, 1989); Corrine Moss-Racusin et al, "Science faculty's subtle gender biases favor male students," *Proceedings of the National Academy of Sciences*, Oct. 9, 2012; Claudia Goldin and Cecilia Rouse, "Orchestrating Impartiality," National Bureau of Economic Research, Working Paper 5903, January 1997; Sylvia Ann Hewlett, et al., "The Athena Factor," *Harvard Business Review*, 2008; National Committee on Pay Equity, accessed August 2016; "The Gender Wage Gap by Occupation 2015 and by Race and Ethnicity," Institute For Women's Policy Research, Fact Sheet WPR #C440; April, 2016; Janet Adamy and Paul Overberg, "Women in Elite Jobs Face Stubborn Pay Gap," *Wall Street Journal*, May 17, 2016; Stacy Cowley, "Illegal in Massachusetts: Asking Your Salary in a Job Interview," *New York Times*, Aug. 2, 2016; Kaitlin Holmes and Danielle Corley, "The Top 10 Facts About the Gender Wage Gap," Center for American Progress, April 12, 2016.

Article 8.4

UNDERVALUATION IS A CERTAINTY
Measuring Black Women's Wage Gap

AN INTERVIEW WITH MICHELLE HOLDER
May/June 2021

We're all probably aware of gender wage gaps and racial wage gaps in the U.S. labor market, but among economists there are disagreements about how to measure and how to explain the reasons for those gaps. Zoe Sherman spoke with Dr. Michelle Holder, associate professor of economics at John Jay College, part of the City University of New York, about her recent research, shared in her Roosevelt Institute report, The "Double Gap" and the Bottom Line: African-American Women's Wage Gap and Corporate Profits. She looks at the wage gap between African-American women and their white male colleagues from several different angles to show the scale of the annually reoccurring loss to the Black community.

Dollars & Sense: To start us off, can you explain your use of the term "double gap"? What gap are we looking at and what about it is double? Please give us your headline finding here about just how big the gap is, too!

Michelle Holder: The term "double gap" is speaking to the wage penalty or the earnings penalty borne by Black women given both their race and their gender. As I'm sure most of your readers know, existing economic research shows that there is indeed a gender wage gap and there's a racial wage gap. The double gap, however, does not simply mean that you either double the gender wage gap, or you double the racial wage gap, and you know, *voilà*, you have estimated the wage penalty that the average Black female worker encounters in the U.S. labor force. The term "double gap" is simply codifying what the average Black woman worker in the U.S. labor market faces in terms of earnings penalties, given their gender and race.

For an individual Black woman who's a worker, the gap ranges. It can be as low as $5,000 in certain low-wage occupations, or it can be as high as $50,000 to $75,000 in some high-wage occupations. More or less, on average, the gap is about $15,000 to $20,000 for your typical Black woman worker in in the U.S. workforce.

D&S: You also calculated the collective loss for Black women workers as a group, right? When you aggregated the data, what did you find for that total?

MH: I did aggregate it. I don't want to take complete credit for the work because I did enlist another researcher to compare my findings against his and to see how close they were, and they were pretty close. Using three different methodologies, when we aggregated [the estimates of] what I characterized as involuntarily forfeited wages, the aggregate loss to the Black community came to about $50 billion per year. This is an annually reoccurring loss. The analysis I did was for the year 2017. [See sidebar on methodologies. —*Eds.*]

Methodologies

(1) Within each occupation, Holder took the most educated half of the Black women working in that occupation, then took an equivalently-educated sample of white men in that occupation and compared the average wages of the two groups. (2) Within each occupation, she used a statistical technique called "linear regression" to explain wages as the sum of the effect of education plus the effect of job experience plus the effect of age, and so on. These are called the "control variables." Remaining differences in the data that aren't explained by the control variables can be interpreted as the effects of race and gender. (3) Holder's colleague Tom Masterson at the Levy Institute at Bard College used a technique called "statistical matching." He matched each Black female worker to a white male worker who closely resembled her in every dimension listed in method two and calculated the pairwise wage differences. For more details, search for "Double Gap Report" at rooseveltinstitute.org.

This estimate has actually been criticized as being a lowball estimate, which I don't disagree with. It's a conservative estimate, in part because when I undertook this research I decided that I would only look at Black women who were more highly educated. Typically, economists look at occupations when they're looking at wages and wage differentials. I decided that for every occupation that I was examining I would only look at Black women between the 50th and 99th percentile in educational attainment in that occupation, so just the more educated Black women in that occupation. By using that approach, my overall estimate is quite conservative.

D&S: If we go back to that individual lens on the gap, you compared Black women workers to white non-Latinx male workers, and when we express it as a ratio you write that the simplest look gives us a 61 cents to $1 ratio. Many of us have seen that ratio reported somewhere. It's commonly reported, and it is important. Still, and you started to get into this in what you were just saying, you warned us that trying to boil down the whole issue to a single ratio is losing a lot of information. What are some of the issues that make that ratio hard to interpret? Why did you have to break it down by occupation?

MH: Thank you for raising that. I don't want to take away from that working figure. The 61 cents to $1 ratio is a useful metric. But it does obscure a couple of important things. One of the most important things a metric like that doesn't really get to is that normally, in the economics discipline, one will explain that wages, while driven by productivity, are informed by human capital attributes. One of the most important human capital attributes that a worker can possess is their level of education. Currently in the American labor market when comparing—I'm even going to take away the gender lens for a second and just compare Black and white workers in the American workforce—there's still a considerable educational attainment gap between Black and white workers in this country. Meaning that, if we look at all white non-Hispanic individuals in the United States 25 years of age and older, about 35%

of them possess a bachelor's degree. But if you look at the African-American community, that number drops considerably to just over 20%, so there's a 14 to 15 percentage point differential there. That in and of itself explains some of the gap that we see between non-Latinx white male workers and Black female workers, given similar characteristics and similar jobs. It doesn't explain all of the gap, but it does explain some of the gap.

The other issue that just looking at that 61 cents to $1 metric doesn't really expose is that there is a difference, a not inconsiderable difference, between where men are situated in terms of their industrial and occupational distribution as workers and where women are situated ... and, by extension, where white male workers are situated and where Black female workers are situated. It is the case that women are over-represented in low-wage occupations and industries, and there are systemic and historical reasons for that. When you start to talk about a simple metric like how Black women earn 61 cents for every dollar white men earn—and you know we've also heard the metric that women overall earn about 79 to 80 cents on the dollar that men earn overall—those metrics don't make clear that women and African Americans tend to be over-represented in low-wage industries and occupations. Part of that wage gap is explicable by these differences in occupational concentration and industrial concentration between white male workers and Black female workers.

But even once you take those factors into account, what remains at the end of the day is still a gap between Black women workers and white male workers that cannot be explained by the educational attainment gap, that cannot be explained by each respective group's industrial and occupational concentration, or by their age, or whether they are married, or how many children they have, or how long they've been working. Even after you take all of the potential factors that you can think of that would contribute to this wage differential between non-Latinx white men and Black women, there's still this residual factor that cannot be explained by any other characteristic that we can capture in the data.

This is why I think it's important to do this research: because there's push-back. When I suggest as an economist that discrimination is occurring against Black women in the U.S. workforce, the pushback is well, no, it isn't discrimination; it is weaker networks that Black women tend to have, it is that Black women may not have the same work ethic, all of these other "it's the fault of Black women" [explanations]. [They claim that] the labor market is perfectly normal and competitive... and my research suggests that just isn't the case.

D&S: You are using the phrasing that this factor or that factor "explains," and my experience in trying to read this language is that often it feels like what that actually means is "explain away."

MH: Exactly, in a very nice way... and then let's just get back to business as usual. I think most Americans don't want to believe that there's a deliberate effort to under-value Black women workers. Whether or not the effort is deliberate, it is occurring and so we need to acknowledge that and not shy away from a very sensitive and difficult fact, as I see it, in the U.S. workforce.

D&S: Is it fair to say that your methods are isolating *wage* discrimination on the part of employers from all of these other things that you described?

MH: Yeah, it's pretty fair to say that. Three different methodologies were employed because I knew that there would be potential criticism about what this research was suggesting. Certainly, if you're using not one, not two, but three different method-ologies, each one of them being completely independent, it's hard to knock down the findings out of hand.

All three methodologies yielded a gap of around $50 billion, with the estimates ranging from $49 billion to $58 billion, so those three methodologies came very close to each other, and as a result it was hard to dismiss these findings.

D&S: You mentioned also that your calculations are relevant to the debates over reparations, because you have identified a specific loss for which there could and should be restitution. Can you help us understand the magnitude of this loss? Most of us find that our brains start getting a little fuzzy when we think about $50 billion. On the one hand it's huge and on the other hand, as a share of GDP it's tiny, so what would it mean for a typical worker's household if this gap were closed? And what would it mean for these households if there were also retroac-tive reparations?

MH: One caveat is that I'm nowhere near as qualified as someone like William "Sandy" Darrity to discuss the economics of reparations for the Black community, but the reason that I deliberately inserted the issue of reparations into my report is to bring up something that is occurring in the African-American community right now, which results in considerable monetary losses to our community, on the order of, minimally, $50 billion. That's in the aggregate, but by looking at it for individual Black women laborers and workers, that means roughly $15,000 to $20,000 per year that they should have been additionally compensated because their equal white male counterpart, that is ostensibly what he's receiving. But that's again for one year; over a lifetime that easily translates into a loss of over $1 million for Black women work-ers when compared to equally qualified, equally skilled, white male workers. You can imagine what could be done with resources like that on an individual basis, on a familial basis, and in terms of a community. I raised the issue of reparations partly because, as a community, we recognize that having been free labor for a few hun-dred years in this country resulted in riches for the country that we did not partici-pate in. Similarly, today, the fact that Black female workers are undervalued results in a benefit to someone, but not to the Black community, and so from my perspec-tive this seems quite similar to the situation that the current debate around repara-tions speaks to, which is not just the undervaluation but the outright confiscation of what should have been due to these workers: enslaved individuals were workers and today, Black women, we're still workers.

D&S: Picking up from there, because you're talking about how wealth is created and how it's not going to the workers who created it, I appreciated the way you framed your research. You're measuring the pay gap between demographic categories of workers, but you then directly connect that to the worker-owner divide. You talk about the bottom line in your title and in your subtitle about corporate profits. When you shared these findings with *Ms.* magazine, you argued that closing this gap should matter to all women. You noted in your paper that there has been long-term stagnation of wages for U.S. workers overall, while profits surge. This double gap that you calculated seems like it's just the tip of the maldistribution iceberg. I'm curious about how addressing this double gap then widens into other distributional issues and what kinds of opportunities for solidarity you see.

MH: First of all, thank you for raising the issue of the declining labor share. Other researchers have done a very good analysis of this declining labor share, which I cite in the paper. I'm going to probably pull a couple of things into my response to you on this one. The first one I'm going to reference is an economist by the name of Janelle Jones—she's now chief economist at the Department of Labor which is great, but she was the director of research at this organization called the Groundwork Collaborative in D.C.—and she put together a phrase called "Black women best." By that what she meant is if policymakers target and look at the condition and situation of Black women, particularly in the American workforce, and attempt to develop policies that would assist Black women workers in terms of fair wages and work conditions, these policies would help everyone. If we look at the American workforce simply through the lens of wages and we looked at it by gender, race, and ethnicity, what we would find is at the top of the hierarchy are non-Latinx white male workers, they are the best paid, and at the bottom of the hierarchy are women of color, African-American women, Latinas, and Native-American women. So according to Jones, if policymakers want to improve the conditions of all women workers, an easy way to do it is to target the least of these, which would be Black women workers. So, I draw from that. Any policy approach that would get at chipping away the double gap will help all women, there's no doubt about that.

But also, any policy approaches that would chip away at the double gap can only serve to strengthen the ties that bind all workers, because we are now in this post neoliberal, or still neoliberal, period where unionization has been on a steady decline in this country, both in the private and public sector, and workers are increasingly bargaining not as part of a union but as an individual with a corporation, with an agency, with an institution, and without the strength of other individuals to give that worker leverage. This double gap feeds into that because we have Black women workers who are singularly negotiating the terms and conditions of their employment both before they are hired and after they're hired. But we need to move away from this corporation versus individual worker approach and move back to the corporation versus the collective negotiating as the collective. Policies that would help alleviate this double gap that Black women workers face, I think, would go a long way in getting back to collective behaviors on the part of workers, rather than these individual [negotiations]. Not to say that workers prefer that, I don't think so, but this is where we're at today—this one-on-one bargaining with owners, rather than collective bargaining with owners. I'm not sure if that quite answered your question?

D&S: Yes, I think it does, because if we're bargaining one on one, maybe relatively privileged workers are going to think, "Well, maybe I can gain something at the expense of my coworker?" But if their fortunes are bound together, then they're going to have to do it together. Is there anything else that I forgot to ask about that you want to make sure we include?

MH: I've talked to other Black women about my research, some of whom are academics, some of whom aren't, and this surprised me: While I think most Black women who work in this country get at some level that they probably aren't making the same as an equally qualified, equally skilled, equally educated white male worker, they didn't quite understand how big this gap can be. And that's because in this country, there's a real climate where we don't talk about income because it gets to the issues of status and respectability and importance. So even amongst friends and family members, we tend not to talk about what we earn, because then it's, "Oh well, you're making more than me, then that must mean your work is more important than mine, or you're doing better work than I'm doing, or you're just a better worker and I'm a slacker," and all those things. That's the climate in this country and it contributes to this lack of awareness on the part of Black women workers of *how much* they are undervalued. They were surprised by how big this gap is and how it's not just about the gap on a weekly basis or an hourly basis, even a yearly basis, but it's about the gap over a lifetime, the impact of it, and also the aggregation of the gap for the community and what it means in terms of losses to the community. When I go on my tour of speaking about my research, I really get bombarded by Black women who are like, "Wow, thank you for identifying the degree to which Black women are undervalued in the American workplace."

Finally, I think the last thing I would say is, when you are, as a female worker, in the position where you are negotiating your compensation…after you do all of your due diligence, you do your research, you talk to your friends and family, you tap into your networks, and you hit upon a figure that you think is a fair ask, add 5% to 10% on top of that. If the wage in whatever job you have to take is really sticky you may not get it, but what I tell people when I speak about this research is whether they are women of any race or specifically Black women, at some point during your work life, you will be underpaid, you will be undervalued. That is pretty much a certainty. ❑

Article 8.5

THE UNDESERVING RICH

Collectively produced and inherited knowledge and the (re)distribution of income and wealth.

BY GAR ALPEROVITZ AND LEW DALY

March/April 2010

Warren Buffett, one of the wealthiest men in the nation, is worth nearly $50 billion. Does he "deserve" all this money? Why? Did he work so much harder than everyone else? Did he create something so extraordinary that no one else could have created it? Ask Buffett himself and he will tell you that he thinks "society is responsible for a very significant percentage of what I've earned." But if that's true, doesn't society deserve a very significant share of what he has earned?

When asked why he is so successful, Buffett commonly replies that this is the wrong question. The more important question, he stresses, is why he has *so much to work with* compared to other people in the world, or compared to previous generations of Americans. Buffett asks: how much money would he have if he had been born in Bangladesh, or in the United States in 1700?

Buffett may or may not deserve something more than another person working with what a given historical or collective context provides. As he observes, however, it is simply not possible to argue in any serious way that he deserves *all* of the benefits that are clearly attributable to living in a highly developed society.

Buffett has put his finger on one of the most explosive issues developing just beneath the surface of public awareness. Over the last several decades, economic research has done a great deal of solid work pinpointing much more precisely than in the past what share of what we call "wealth" society creates versus what share any individual can be said to have earned and thus deserved. This research raises profound moral—and ultimately political—questions.

Through No Effort of Our Own

Recent estimates suggest that U.S. economic output per capita has increased more than 20-fold since 1800. Output per hour worked has increased an estimated 15-fold since 1870 alone. Yet the average modern person likely works with no greater commitment, risk, or intelligence than his or her counterpart from the past. What is the primary cause of such vast gains if individuals do not really "improve"? Clearly, it is largely that the scientific, technical, and cultural knowledge available to us, and the efficiency of our means of storing and retrieving this knowledge, have grown at a scale and pace that far outstrip any other factor in the nation's economic development.

A half century ago, in 1957, economist Robert Solow calculated that nearly 90% of productivity growth in the first half of the 20th century (from 1909 to 1949) could only be attributed to "technical change in the broadest sense." The supply of labor and capital—what workers and employers contribute—appeared almost incidental to this massive technological "residual." Subsequent research inspired by

Solow and others continued to point to "advances in knowledge" as the main source of growth. Economist William Baumol calculates that "nearly 90 percent ... of current GDP was contributed by innovation carried out since 1870." Baumol judges that his estimate, in fact, understates the cumulative influence of past advances: Even "the steam engine, the railroad, and many other inventions of an earlier era, still add to today's GDP."

Related research on the sources of invention bolsters the new view, posing a powerful challenge to conventional, heroic views of technology that characterize progress as a sequence of extraordinary contributions by "Great Men" (occasionally "Great Women") and their "Great Inventions." In contrast to this popular view, historians of technology have carefully delineated the incremental and cumulative way most technologies actually develop. In general, a specific field of knowledge builds up slowly through diverse contributions over time until—at a particular moment when enough has been established—the next so-called "breakthrough" becomes all but inevitable.

Often many people reach the same point at virtually the same time, for the simple reason that they all are working from the same developing information and research base. The next step commonly becomes obvious (or if not obvious, very likely to be taken within a few months or years). We tend to give credit to the person who gets there first—or rather, who gets the first public attention, since often the real originator is not as good at public relations as the one who jumps to the front of the line and claims credit. Thus, we remember Alexander Graham Bell as the inventor of the telephone even though, among others, Elisha Gray and Antonio Meucci got there at the same time or even before him. Isaac Newton and Gottfried Wilhelm Leibniz hit upon the calculus at roughly the same time in the 1670s; Charles Darwin and Alfred Russel Wallace produced essentially the same theory of evolution at roughly the same time in the late 1850s.

Less important than who gets the credit is the simple fact that most breakthroughs occur not so much thanks to one "genius," but because of the longer historical unfolding of knowledge. All of this knowledge—the overwhelming source of all modern wealth—comes to us today *through no effort of our own*. It is the generous and unearned gift of the past. In the words of Northwestern economist Joel Mokyr, it is a "free lunch."

Collective knowledge is often created by formal public efforts as well, a point progressives often stress. Many of the advances which propelled our high-tech economy in the early 1990s grew directly out of research programs and technical systems financed and often collaboratively developed by the federal government. The internet, to take the most obvious example, began as a government defense project, the ARPANET, in the early 1960s. Up through the 1980s there was little private investment or interest in developing computer networks. Today's vast software industry also rests on a foundation of computer language and operating hardware developed in large part with public support. The Bill Gateses of the world—the heroes of the "New Economy"—might still be working with vacuum tubes and punch cards were it not for critical research and technology programs created or financed by the federal government after World War II. Other illustrations range from jet airplanes and radar to the basic life science research undergirding many pharmaceutical industry advances. Yet the truth is that the role of collectively inherited knowledge is far, far greater than just the contributions made by direct public support, important as they are.

Earned Income?

A straightforward but rarely confronted question arises from these facts: If most of what we have today is attributable to advances we inherit in common, then why should this gift of our collective history not more generously benefit all members of society?

The top 1% of U.S. households now receives more income than the bottom 120 million Americans combined. The richest 1% of households owns nearly half of all investment assets (stocks and mutual funds, financial securities, business equity, trusts, non-home real estate). The bottom 90% of the population owns less than 15%; the bottom half—150 million Americans—owns less than 1%. If America's vast wealth is mainly a gift of our common past, what justifies such disparities?

Robert Dahl, one of America's leading political scientists—and one of the few to have confronted these facts—put it this way after reading economist Edward Denison's pioneering work on growth accounting: "It is immediately obvious that little growth in the American economy can be attributed to the actions of particular individuals." He concluded straightforwardly that, accordingly, "the control and ownership of the economy rightfully belongs to 'society.'"

Contrast Dahl's view with that of Joe the Plumber, who famously inserted himself into the 2008 presidential campaign with his repeated claim that he has "earned" everything he gets and so any attempt to tax his earnings is totally unjustified. Likewise, "we didn't rely on somebody else to build what we built," banking titan Sanford Weill tells us in a *New York Times* front-page story on the "New Gilded Age." "I think there are people," another executive tells the *Times*, "who because of their uniqueness warrant whatever the market will bear."

A direct confrontation with the role of knowledge—and especially inherited knowledge—goes to the root of a profound challenge to such arguments. One way to think about all this is by focusing on the concept of "earned" versus "unearned" income. Today this distinction can be found in conservative attacks on welfare "cheats" who refuse to work to earn their keep, as well as in calls even by some Republican senators to tax the windfall oil-company profits occasioned by the Iraq War and Hurricane Katrina.

The concept of unearned income first came into clear focus during the era of rapidly rising land values caused by grain shortages in early 19th-century England. Wealth derived *simply* from owning land whose price was escalating appeared illegitimate because no individual truly "earned" such wealth. Land values—and especially explosively high values—were largely the product of factors such as fertility, location, and population pressures. The huge profits (unearned "rents," in the technical language of economics) landowners reaped when there were food shortages were viewed as particularly egregious. David Ricardo's influential theory of "differential rent"—i.e., that land values are determined by differences in fertility and location between different plots of land—along with religious perspectives reaching back to the Book of Genesis played a central role in sharpening this critical moral distinction.

John Stuart Mill, among others, developed the distinction between "earned" and "unearned" in the middle decades of the 19th century and applied it to other forms of "external wealth," or what he called "wealth created by circumstances." Mill's approach fed into a growing sense of the importance of societal inputs which produce economic gains beyond what can be ascribed to one person working alone in nature without benefit of civilization's many contributions. Here a second element of what appears, historically, as a slowly evolving understanding also becomes clear: If contribution is important in determining rewards, then, Mill and others urged, since society at large makes major contributions to economic achievement, it too has "earned" and deserves a share of what has been created. Mill believed strongly in personal contribution and individual reward, but he held that in principle wealth "created by circumstances" should be reclaimed for social purposes. Karl Marx, of course, tapped the distinction between earned and unearned in his much broader attack on capitalism and its exploitation of workers' labor.

The American republican writer Thomas Paine was among the first to articulate a societal theory of wealth based directly on the earned/unearned distinction. Paine argued that everything "beyond what a man's own hands produce" was a gift which came to him simply by living in society, and hence "he owes on every principle of justice, of gratitude, and of civilization, a part of that accumulation back again to society from whence the whole came." A later American reformer, Henry George, focused on urban land rather than the agricultural land at the heart of Ricardo's concern. George challenged what he called "the unearned increment" which is created when population growth and other societal factors increase land values. In Britain, J. A. Hobson argued that the unearned value created by the industrial system in general was much larger than just the part which accrued to landowners, and that it should be treated in a similar (if not more radical and comprehensive) fashion. In a similar vein, Hobson's early 20th-century contemporary Leonard Trelawny Hobhouse declared that the "prosperous business man" should consider "what single step he could have taken" without the "sum of intelligence which civilization has placed at his disposal." More recently, the famed American social scientist Herbert Simon judged that if "we are very generous with ourselves, I suppose we might claim that we 'earned' as much as one-fifth of [our income]."

The distinction between earned and unearned gains is central to most of these thinkers, as is the notion that societal contributions—including everything an industrial economy requires, from the creation of laws, police, and courts to the development of schools, trade restrictions, and patents—must be recognized and rewarded. The understanding that such societal contributions are both contemporary and have made a huge and cumulative contribution over all of history is also widely accepted. Much of the income they permit and confer now appears broadly analogous to the unearned rent a landlord claims. What is new and significant here is the further clarification that by far the most important element in all this is the accumulated *knowledge* which society contributes over time.

All of this, as sociologist Daniel Bell has suggested, requires a new "knowledge theory of value"—especially as we move deeper into the high-tech era through computerization, the internet, cybernetics, and cutting-edge fields such as gene therapy and nanotechnology. One way to grasp what is at stake is the following: A person today working the same number of hours as a similar person in 1870—working just as hard but no harder—will produce perhaps 15 times as much economic output. It is clear that the contemporary person can hardly be said to have "earned" his much greater productivity.

Consider further that if we project forward the past century's rate of growth, a person working a century from now would be able to produce—and potentially receive as "income"—up to seven times today's average income. By far the greatest part of this gain will also come to this person as a free gift of the past—the gift of the new knowledge created, passed on, and inherited from our own time forward.

She and her descendents, in fact, will inevitably contribute less, relative to the huge and now expanded contribution of the past, than we do today. The obvious question, again, is simply this: to what degree is it meaningful to say that this person will have "earned" all that may come her way? These and other realities suggest that the quiet revolution in our understanding of how wealth is created has ramifications for a much more profound and far-reaching challenge to today's untenable distribution of income and wealth. ❑

Article 8.6

DO PEOPLE CARE ABOUT EXTREME INEQUALITY?

BY ARTHUR MacEWAN
September/October 2021

> Dear Dr. Dollar:
>
> *The extreme inequality we have in this country is not fair. According to a report from the National Bureau of Economic Research (NBER), in 2016 the bottom 40% of households on average had a negative net worth (assets minus liabilities) of $9,000. In that same year, the richest 10% of households had an average positive net worth of $5.2 million. For the top 1%, the average was $26.4 million. Income is less unequally distributed than wealth, but the same NBER report shows that in 2015 the top 10% of households obtained 50% of income, while the bottom 40% obtained 9%. There is every reason to believe that in more recent years, especially with the pandemic experience, things have only gotten worse. This extreme inequality is having negative impacts throughout society, affecting everything from health to education to the environment to crime. How long can this situation last? Will public opinion ever reflect my disapproval?*
>
> —Ben Leet, by e-mail

Actually, polls indicate that public opinion tends to be consistent with your disapproval. A Pew Research Center poll from September 2019 found that 61% of adults believe "there's too much economic inequality in the country." In January 2020, Reuters reported that its poll found that "64% of those respondents strongly or somewhat agreed that 'the very rich should contribute an extra share of their total wealth each year to support public programs," a result that Reuters interpreted as support for a wealth tax.

Although in the Pew poll only 42% of respondents said inequality should be a top-priority issue for the federal government, at least two of the issues which more survey participants thought should be a top priority— "health care more affordable" and "addressing climate change"—are very much tied up with economic inequality.

I'll come back to the implications of the polls below, but whatever the polls say, one wonders why so many people do not see inequality as a top-priority issue, given how it has increased so greatly in recent decades and is so closely tied to many social problems. The increase is well known, but for now just one illustration: In 1965, the average compensation of CEOs in the top 350 companies (in terms of sales) was 20 times the average compensation of workers; in 2018, the CEO average was 278 times the worker average.

So Why Don't More People Care About Inequality?

Not surprisingly, the polls show that the higher peoples' incomes, the less they think inequality is a problem. Also, we can assume that the very rich, with few exceptions, oppose a wealth tax or higher income taxes on high incomes. But there are still many others who do not think inequality is a big problem, and even of those who think it is a problem, a good number do not view it as a high priority.

Many people seem to believe in two important and related myths. One of these is that markets are fair: If some people make a lot of money, they must deserve it; and if some people do not do well financially, it's their own fault. People who accept this myth do not deny that there are exceptions—some people are born rich, and some people just have bad luck. But these exceptions don't alter belief in the myth.

The second and related myth is that ours is the land of opportunity: No matter your origins, it is possible for you to rise to financial success. This myth was popularized and widely propagated during the 19th century in books by Horatio Alger, with their tales of people who (as stated in Dictionary. com) "begin life in poverty and achieve success and wealth through honesty, hard work, and virtuous behavior."

Yet these two myths are in fact myths, not descriptions of reality. Markets are not fair, and to a large extent are created in ways that favor certain groups. For example, the fossil fuel industry has received extensive government support over the decades, and pharmaceutical and high-tech firms are protected by sets of patent and copyright laws that allow them to obtain monopoly profits. A very unequal public education system yields a labor market that is also highly unequal, and the labor market is also affected by sets of rules that tend to favor firms' owners over workers and labor unions. Financial firms are allowed all sorts of manipulations that expand their profits. In addition to all this, markets are greatly shaped by racism and other forms of nefarious discrimination. (See Arthur MacEwan, "Are Taxes the Best Way of Dealing with Inequality?," *D&S*, November/December 2019, for more on how markets are constructed.)

As to the United States being the land of opportunity, several studies indicate that social mobility is less here than in many other high-income countries. Also, an authoritative study of recent years, reported in a 2014 article in the *American Economic Review*, showed no significant improvement in social mobility over the last several decades of the 20th century and concludes,

> Based on [several] measures, we find that children entering the labor market today have the same chances of moving up in the income distribution (relative to their parents) as children born in the 1970s. *However, because inequality has risen, the consequences of the "birth lottery"— the parents to whom a child is born—are larger today than in the past.* [Emphasis added.]

Widespread acceptance of the myths about fair markets and social mobility, and thus an aversion to the redistribution of income, go back a long way in the United States. James Madison, the principal author of the U.S. Constitution, in his famous *Federalist No. 10*, expressed the importance of a constitution that would protect against "...a rage for paper money, for abolition of debts, for an equal division of property, or any other improper and wicked project...." This view of redistribution as improper and wicked seems to have had a long life. (Madison, who became the fourth U.S. president, owned about 100 slaves and had been born into a wealthy plantation-owning family.)

Although higher taxes on the incomes and wealth of the very rich would be desirable in attenuating our severe inequality, this action would leave these myths in place. Improving income distribution through taxation implies that the basic operation of the system is okay, and that we just need some post hoc "fix up" to take care of the bad results of an "okay" system. More needs to be changed.

What Can Be Done?

Change is difficult and becomes more difficult as economic inequality rises. Regardless of democratic processes, the rich have great influence and power. Greater inequality increases their power, and thus it seems we are caught in a vicious circle—inequality increases the power of the rich, who then use that power to maintain the status quo, which generates more inequality, and so on.

Nonetheless, public opinion does matter, and through the spread of information and organizing, public opinion can be changed. Following from the points above, there are at least three things that could be useful in the effort to advance public opinion on economic inequality.

First, recognize and confront the myths that lead people to accept great economic inequalities. When people recognize that markets are not set in stone and that they are created in ways that are not fair, they are less likely to accept the inequalities generated in our markets.

Second, support higher taxes for the rich, but also support altering markets in ways that will lead to a reduction of inequality. Demand, for example, that the subsidies to fossil fuel industries be eliminated. As another example, work to change the regulations constraining the formation and activities of labor unions. And, as the other cases of unfair market structures listed above suggest, there are many opportunities for such efforts.

Third, demonstrate the connections between economic inequality and issues that are often of immediate practical concern to many people, such as the concerns given high priority by respondents in the Pew poll. Our excessively expensive health care system, with insurance companies and private hospitals playing a central role, both generates economic inequality and operates to serve the wealthy well while serving the poor badly. And climate change, education, housing, and many other social issues are also bound up with inequality.

Focusing on these points, along with other initiatives, could lead to some reductions in economic inequality. Moreover, reductions of inequality could move us in the direction of broader changes toward social justice. ❑

Sources: Juliana Menasce Horowitz, Ruth Iglielnik, and Rakesh Kochhar, "Most Americans Say There Is Too Much Economic Inequality in the U.S., but Fewer Than Half Call It a Top Priority," Pew Research Center, January 9, 2020 (pewresearch.org); Howard Schneider and Chris Kahn, "Majority of Americans favor wealth tax on very rich: Reuters/Ipsos poll," Reuters, January 10, 2020 (reuters.com); Lawrence Mishel and Julia Wolfe, "CEO compensation has grown 940% since 1978; Typical worker compensation has risen only 12% during that time," Economic Policy Institute, August 14, 2019 (epi.org); Arthur MacEwan, "An End in Itself and a Means to Good Ends: Why Income Equality is Important," ScholarWorks at UMass–Boston, January 1, 2009 (scholarworks.umb.edu); Raj Chetty et al., "Is the United States Still a Land of Opportunity? Recent Trends in Intergenerational Mobility," *American Economic Review*, May 2014 (aeaweb.org); E. N. Wolff, "Household Wealth Trends in the United States, 1962 to 2016: Has Middle Class Wealth Recovered?" National Bureau of Economic Research, Working Paper 24085, November 2017 (nber.org).

Article 8.7

CONCENTRATION OF STOCK OWNERSHIP

BY ED FORD

January/February 2022

Americans are treated to a daily stock market report on the nightly news. And for some (a small minority) this report will have considerable relevance. But for the vast majority of viewers, the numbers will seem unconnected to their daily struggle to make ends meet—because they are. Of course, the stock market and the economy are somewhat connected. The significant contraction in the broader economy in the first month or two of the Covid-19 pandemic led to a dramatic decline in stock prices. But the stock market soon parted ways with the rest of the economy—dramatic increases in stock prices began while the restoration of the economy was sluggish at best. The *New York Times* reports that each pandemic-related decline in the stock market since February 2020 has been shorter than the one before, and followed by a recovery to a new high.

So, are rising stock prices even relevant for the rest of us? Not very. While close to 50% of households hold some stock, if only indirectly (in pensions, mutual funds, and other retirement accounts), over 50% of households do not own any stock at all. What's more, ownership is highly concentrated, and because stocks are a significant portion of financial wealth in the United States, the result is great inequality of wealth. Over time, e.g., 2006 to 2021, despite the increased reliance on 401(k) and 403(b) savings plans, which are invested in the stock market, the proportion of shares owned by the top 10% has actually increased. And the dramatic increases in stocks prices over that period mean that the wealth of those at the top has increased dramatically.

FIG. 1: CONCENTRATION OF STOCK OWNERSHIP BY WEALTH CLASS, 2016.

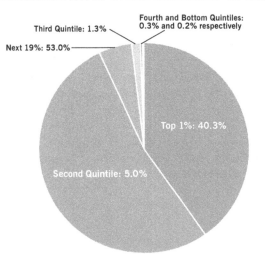

Third Quintile: 1.3%
Fourth and Bottom Quintiles: 0.3% and 0.2% respectively
Next 19%: 53.0%
Top 1%: 40.3%
Second Quintile: 5.0%

U.S. corporate stock ownership is highly concentrated, with over 93% owned by the top 20% of wealth holders, while the bottom 80% of households owned less than 7% of U.S. stocks, and the bottom 40% less than 1%. The proportion owned by the bottom 40% is so small, it is invisible in the diagram. While the proportions reported in Figure 1 are for 2016, change in ownership has been very slight over the last five years (see Figure 2).

FIGURE 2 DISTRIBUTION OF CORPORATE EQUITIES AND MUTUAL FUND SHARES BY WEALTH PERCENTILE GROUP, 2006–2021

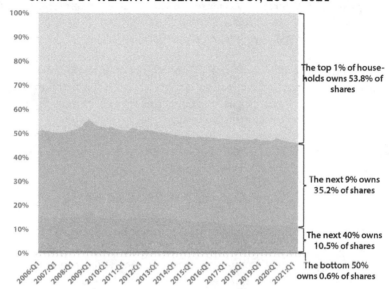

Shares of stock ownership remain highly concentrated over time, with the amount owned by the top 1% and 10% of households, measured by wealth, remaining consistently very high. In 2006 the top 1% held 48.6% of stocks and the top 10% held 84.3%. In 2021 the top 1% held 53.8% and the top 10% held 89%. Thus, the share owned by the top 1% rose slightly while the bottom 90% proportion decreased slightly.

Stocks owned are designated by the Fed as "corporate equities," while "mutual fund shares" refer to stocks owned by mutual funds. Thus Figure 2's underlying values differ slightly from those of Figure 1. But the proportion held by the top percentiles of households are comparable. And there is ample evidence that the very top of the distribution (i.e., billionaires) have increased their ownership dramatically during the pandemic. ❑

Sources: Figure 1: Edward N. Wolff, "Household Wealth Trends in the United States, 1962 TO 2016: Has Middle Class Wealth Recovered?" NBER Working Paper 24085 (nber.org). Figure 2: Federal Reserve Bank, Survey of Consumer Finances, "Distribution of Household Wealth in the U.S.: Corporate equities and mutual fund shares by wealth percentile group, 2006–2021" (federalreserve.gov); "Distribution of Household Wealth in the U.S. since 1989" (federalreserve. gov); "Updates: Billionaire Wealth, U.S. Job Loss and Pandemic Profiteers," Inequality.org, October, 2021 (inequality.org).

Article 8.8

FINANCIALIZATION AND INEQUALITY

BY ARTHUR MacEWAN
January/February 2022

> Dear Dr. Dollar:
> *Is financialization responsible for the great increase in economic inequality of*
> *recent decades in the United States?*
> —Anonymous, via e-mail

It is tempting to see the increasing role of big banks, other financial institutions, and the general rising role of financial activity as responsible for many evils, including rising economic inequality. In one sense, this view is accurate. Financialization has certainly had some detrimental impacts.

Yet, it is more accurate to see financialization as part of a complex of interconnected developments in the United States and the world economies—developments that together have generated rising inequality.

First of all, let's be clear about what we mean by "financialization." A widely used and useful definition, formulated by the UMass–Amherst economist Gerald Epstein, is that financialization is "the increasing role of financial motives, financial markets, financial actors and financial institutions in the operation of the domestic and international economies." In this definition "financial motives" should be contrasted with "productive motives." That is, when investments are increasingly motivated not by gain from productive activity but by gain from financial activity, this is financialization. Examples include speculating on the stock market, the purchase by corporations of their own stock, and predatory mortgage lending and the associated marketing of mortgage bundles. More on some of these examples shortly.

On the broadest level, financialization has meant an increasing reliance of nonfinancial firms on capital from the financial sector—banks, private equity firms, venture capital firms, hedge funds, and mortgage companies. This growing engagement of nonfinancial firms with financial firms has had two consequences affecting inequality. The financial firms have demanded quick (short-run) returns on their investments, requiring the nonfinancial firms to place short-run gains over long-term growth, which, in turn, has tended to weaken employment growth. Also, paying out a larger and larger share of their earnings to financial firms, the nonfinancial firms have squeezed labor to maintain their profits. The rising role of financial firms is reflected in the rising share of corporate profits of the financial sectors, as shown in the graph below.

Buybacks and Predatory Lending

Also, the nonfinancial firms themselves have engaged in financialization. A prime example has been firms' use of their earnings to buy back their own stock from investors. These buybacks became especially notable after the tax reductions of late 2017, as

FINANCIAL SECTOR PROFITS AS PERCENT OF TOTAL CORPORATE PROFITS, AVERAGES BY DECADE, 1970S TO 2010S

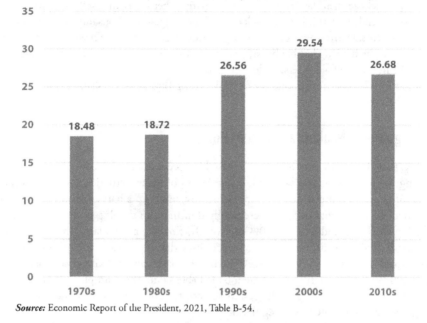

Source: Economic Report of the President, 2021, Table B-54.

firms tended to use the funds that they gained from the tax cuts for buybacks instead of investment in productive activity. This nonproductive action increased the price of the stock and raised the incomes of top executives, whose earnings were partially paid in their companies' stock and whose salaries were often tied to the stocks' value. Wages suffered relative to what they would have been had the companies' earnings been used for productive investment. (See "Stock Buybacks: Any Positive Outcomes?" *D&S*, Nov./Dec. 2016.)

One ironic inequality-generating effect of financialization was the predatory lending of financial firms (banks and mortgage companies) leading up to the housing bubble of the early 2000s that, when the bubble burst, led into the Great Recession of 2008–2009. Home-buying loans were pushed to low-income families who, the lenders knew, would often not be able to meet the payments. The impact was especially harsh with adjustable-rate mortgages—when the rates went up, the families could not meet the payments and lost their homes. African-American communities were especially hard hit by this practice. The irony exists because historically African-American communities had been denied loans, even when they were qualified for mortgages—the practice of "red-lining," where lenders and administrators of government programs drew red lines on maps around minority neighborhoods that were then defined as poor places to make loans. While there is irony in the switch from denying loans to African Americans to pushing loans on them, there is a clear consistency in the dishonest and exploitive manner in which banks, real estate firms, and the government have treated African Americans in the housing market.

But why would financial institutions make mortgage loans that they knew would not be paid back? The answer to this question lies in another aspect of financialization.

The makers of mortgage loans in recent decades do not continue to hold those loans, but, instead, package them (electronically) with many other loans, and sell those packages. Investors tended to think that packages of mortgages—a thousand or more mortgages—were safe investments because large numbers seemed to mean safety by diversity. Yet, when the housing bubble burst, the value of these mortgage packages fell sharply. But the many original lenders, no longer holding the mortgages, were not harmed. (See "What Role Did Securitization Play in the Housing Bubble and Collapse?" *D&S*, Nov./ Dec. 2013.)

Deregulation, Neoliberalism, and Power

Why, then, has this sort of activity increased in recent decades? A central factor facilitating financialization has been the deregulation of firms' activities. Deregulation of economic activity, in finance but more generally, has been a hallmark of the ideology of "neoliberalism" that became increasingly dominant in shaping government policy during the last decades of the 20th century. In finance, particularly, the removal of regulations allowed firms to engage in activities that increased their risk-taking but allowed them to raise their profits. And when the risk appeared and crises ensued (in the 2008–2009 crisis), the government bailed them out. The examples noted above of stock buybacks, predatory lending, and the creation of markets in bundles of mortgages were all facilitated by deregulation.

Neoliberal ideology did not appear out of nowhere. It reflected and enhanced the rising power of large businesses, especially in the financial sector, and wealthy individuals. It has been this power and the accompanying ideology that have shaped globalization, generated policies that have weakened labor unions, and brought about other government actions that have contributed to inequality—e.g., the privatization of prisons and health care and weak government support for education.

So, yes, financialization has been an important part of the story of inequality, but it is also part of a bundle of changes that have shaped the U.S. economy over several decades.

Sources: Gerald A. Epstein, editor, *Financialization and the World Economy* (Edward Elgar Publishing, 2006); B. M. Van Arnum & M. I. Naples, "Financialization and Income Inequality in the United States, 1967–2010," *The American Journal of Economics and Sociology*, October 2013; Donald Tomaskovic-Devey & Ken-Hou Lin, "Financialization: Causes, Inequality Consequences, and Policy Implications," University of North Carolina Banking Institute, 2013.

Chapter 9

TAXATION

INTRODUCTION

"Only the little people pay taxes." —*Leona Helmsley*
"Taxes are the price we pay for civilization." —*Oliver Wendell Holmes, Jr.*

Taxation is a fascinating subject. It is perhaps the clearest manifestation of class struggle one can find. How a modern government funds itself in order to provide services is an elaborate study in power. The contentious tango of taxes and their inverse, subsidies, plays out daily at all three levels of government—federal, state, and local. Who pays taxes and at what rates? What is taxed? Who bears the burden of taxation? And how are tax revenues collected? These are questions that this chapter addresses.

In the Reagan era, "supply-side" economist Arthur Laffer famously claimed that high marginal tax rates discourage work and saving, and that cutting tax rates on the rich would spur investment and economic growth. We start the chapter with two articles on the subject: In "Can Tax Cuts Really Increase Government Revenue?" (Article 9.1), economist Ellen Frank reviews the basic arguments made by Laffer and the other supply-siders, and why there is reason to be skeptical. Gerald Friedman puts these arguments to the test, and finds that cutting taxes on the very rich, as the U.S. government has been doing for decades, has not led to the promised investment or economic growth (Article 9.2).

In "Are Taxes the Best Way to Deal with Inequality?" (Article 9.3), Arthur MacEwan lays out some of the many ways in which markets are structured that lead to unequal distribution well before taxes are levied. From labor markets to intellectual property and the patent system to fossil-fuel markets, groups use their power and wealth to shape the rules of markets in their favor. The result is an economy in which the distribution of wealth and income is skewed to the top.

The remaining articles in the chapter are about different taxes on the wealthy and corporations. First, in "The Optimal Tax" (Article 9.4), Miller addresses recent proposals for a 70% top marginal tax rate on income over $10 million. Despite howls from the business press that such rates are soaking the rich and would inhibit investment, the economic literature on the "optimal" tax rate suggests it could be even higher, and that the top rate could start with much lower incomes.

Next, in "Corporate Taxes: Less, Less, and Less" (Article 9. 5), Arthur MacEwan answers a question as to the tax share of corporations "Corporate Taxes: Less, Less, and Less." It is not at all surprising that corporations have been highly successful in shifting the tax burden from themselves to working people. This is just "dropping the other shoe" as to the general financialization of the economy and Market Power.

Finally, in "Taxing Unrealized Capital Gains Is Key to Undoing Tax Injustice" (Article 9.6), John Miller covers the recent ProPublica report on tax evasion at the top of the income ladder, and how the unfairness of the tax code, shaped by the very wealthy, allows billionaires to shelter and increase their wealth.

Discussion Questions

1. (Article 9.1) What is the basis of supply-siders' claim that lowering the highest marginal tax rate will generate more tax revenue? What are the main arguments against this view?

2. (Article 9.2) In what way have tax policies contributed to growing inequality in the United States? How does U.S. tax policy compare to other developed countries, and how has that related to productivity growth?

3. (Article 9.3) Based on Arthur MacEwan's arguments about how the wealthy and powerful have shaped the rules of the game in multiple industries, why should we think that it is better to change those rules than to use taxes to redistribute income and wealth? What are the barriers to changing those rules?

4. (Article 9.4) What are the limits of how high an optimal top marginal tax rate should be? What reasons are there for thinking that the rate proposed by Congresswoman Alexandria Ocacio-Cortez is not too high? How does her proposal compare to the rates in the 1950s? (Compare both the rate and what incomes were in the top bracket.)

5. (Article 9.5) It is often said that if you want to understand who has power in a country, observe who does and does not pay taxes. Consider the table at the end of MacEwan's article on corporate taxation. Explain the difference between the statutory tax rate and the average effective tax rate. What does attending to that difference show about corporate tax rates?

6. (Article 9.6) The *Wall Street Journal* editors claim that ProPublica's "True Tax Rate" is a "phony concept" because it compares income tax payments to wealth holdings. Why did ProPublica use the True Tax Rate in analyzing American tax avoidance? In your view, is the True Tax Rate a valid tool for analyzing American tax burdens?

Article 9.1

CAN TAX CUTS REALLY INCREASE GOVERNMENT REVENUE?

BY ELLEN FRANK
November/December 2003

Dear Dr. Dollar:
A Republican friend tells me that the huge new tax cuts will actually produce more revenue than the government would have collected before the cut, because once rich beneficiaries invest the money, they will pay taxes on every transaction. He suggested that the increase could be as much as 50% more than the originally scheduled revenues. Is this possible?
—Judith Walker, New York, N.Y.

Back in the 1970s, conservative economist Arthur Laffer proposed that high marginal tax rates discouraged people from earning additional income. By cutting taxes, especially on those with the highest incomes, Laffer argued, governments would spur individuals to work harder and invest more, stoking economic growth. Though the government would get a smaller bite from every dollar the economy generated, there would be so many more dollars to tax that government revenues would actually rise. President Ronald Reagan invoked the "Laffer curve" in the 1980s, insisting he could cut taxes, hike defense spending, and still balance the budget.

President George W. Bush's 2001 and 2003 tax packages are eerily reminiscent of the Reagan cuts. They reduce rates levied on ordinary income, with the largest rate cut going to the wealthiest taxpayers. They extend business tax write-offs and increase the child tax credit (though only for two years and only for families who earn enough to pay federal income taxes). They cut the tax on capital gains from 28% to 15%; dividend income, previously taxed at the same rate as ordinary income, now faces a top rate of 15%.

Citizens for Tax Justice estimates that two-thirds of the 2003 tax cut will accrue to the richest 10% of taxpayers. By 2006, the increased child credit will be phased out and nine out of 10 taxpayers will find their taxes cut by less than $100. The top 1%, in contrast, will save an average $24,000 annually over the next four years, thanks to the 2003 cut alone.

Though inspired by the same "supply-side" vision that guided Reagan, Bush officials have not explicitly cited Laffer's arguments in defense of their tax packages. Probably, they wish to avoid ridicule. After the Reagan tax cut, the U.S. economy sank into recession and federal tax collections dropped nearly 10%. The deficit soared and economic growth was tepid through much of Reagan's presidency, despite sharp hikes in military spending. Some of the Republican faithful continue to argue that tax cuts will unleash enough growth to pay for themselves, but most are embarrassed to raise the now discredited Laffer curve.

The problem with your friend's assertion is fairly simple. If the government cuts projected taxes by $1.5 trillion over the next decade, those dollars will recirculate through the economy. The $1.5 trillion tax cut becomes $1.5 trillion in taxable income and is itself taxed, as your friend suggests. But this would be just as true if, instead of cutting taxes, the government spent $1.5 trillion on highways or national defense or schools or, for that matter, if it trimmed $1.5 trillion from the tax liability of low- and middle-income households. All tax cuts become income, are re-spent, and taxed. That reality is already factored into everyone's economic projections. But the new income, taxed at a lower rate, will generate lower overall tax collections.

To conclude that revenues will rise rather than fall following a tax cut, one must maintain that the tax cut causes the economy to grow faster than it would have otherwise—that cutting taxes on the upper crust stimulates enough additional growth to offset the lower tax rates, more growth than would be propelled by, say, building roads or reducing payroll taxes. Free-marketeers insist that this is indeed the case. Spend $1.5 trillion on highways and you get $1.5 trillion worth of highways. Give it to Wall Street and investors will develop new technologies, improve productivity, and spur the economy to new heights.

Critics of the Bush cuts contend, however, that faster growth arises from robust demand for goods and from solid, well-maintained public infrastructure. Give $1.5 to Wall Street and you get inflated stock prices and real estate bubbles. Give it to working families or state governments and you get crowded malls, ringing cash registers, and businesses busily investing to keep up with their customers.

Who is right? Die-hard supply-siders insist that the Reagan tax cuts worked as planned—the payoff just didn't arrive until the mid-1990s! But the Bush administration's own budget office is predicting sizable deficits for the next several years. Maybe, like your friend, they believe the tax cuts will pay for themselves—but they're not banking on it. ❑

Article 9.2

THE GREAT TAX-CUT EXPERIMENT

Has cutting tax rates for the rich helped the economy?

BY GERALD FRIEDMAN

January/February 2013

S ince the late 1970s, during the Carter Administration, conservative economists have been warning that high taxes retard economic growth by discouraging productive work and investment. These arguments have resonated with politicians, who have steadily cut income taxes, especially those borne by the richest Americans. The highest marginal tax rate, which stood at 70% by the end of the 1970s, was cut to less than 30% in less than a decade. (The "marginal" rate for a person is the one applied to his or her last dollar of income. A marginal rate that applies to, say, the bracket above $250,000, then, is paid only on that portion of income. The portion of a person's income below that threshold is taxed at the lower rates applying to lower tax brackets.) Despite increases in the early 1990s, the top marginal rate remained below 40%, when it was cut further during the administration of George W. Bush. These dramatic cuts in tax rates, however, have not led to an acceleration in economic growth, investment, or productivity.

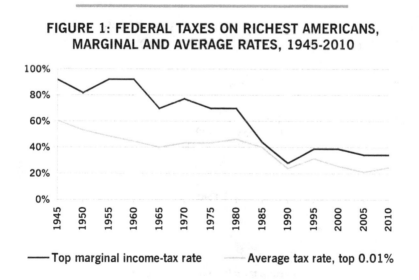

FIGURE 1: FEDERAL TAXES ON RICHEST AMERICANS, MARGINAL AND AVERAGE RATES, 1945-2010

—— Top marginal income-tax rate   —— Average tax rate, top 0.01%

The federal government has been cutting taxes on the richest Americans since the end of World War II. The average tax paid by the richest taxpayers, as a percentage of income, is typically less than the top marginal rate. Some of their income (the portion below the threshold for the top marginal rate, any capital-gains income, etc.) is taxed at lower rates. Some is not subject to federal income tax because of deductions for state and local taxes, healthcare costs, and other expenses. The decline in the average tax rate for the richest, however, does follow the cuts in the top marginal income-tax rate.

FIGURE 2: TAX REVENUE AS A PERCENTAGE OF GDP, 2008

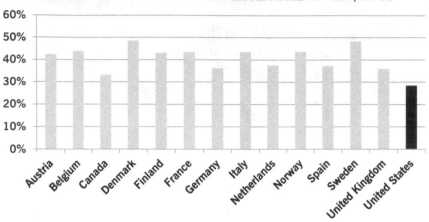

Americans pay a smaller proportion of total income in taxes than do people in any other advanced capitalist economy. As recently as the late 1960s, taxes accounted for as high a share of national income in the United States as in Western European countries. After decades of tax cuts, however, the United States now stands out for its low taxes and small government sector.

FIGURE 3: AVERAGE TAX RATES ON RICHEST AND REAL GDP GROWTH, BY PRESIDENT, 1947-2010

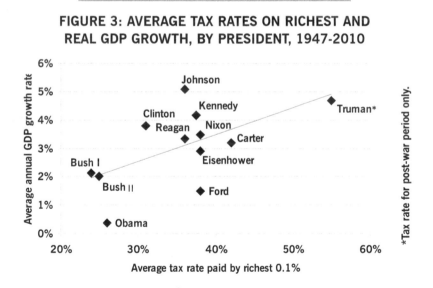

On average, the economy has grown faster during presidential administrations with higher tax rates on the richest Americans. Growth was unusually slow during President George W. Bush's two terms (Bush II) and during President Barack Obama's first term, when the Bush tax cuts remained in effect. On average, every 10 percentage-point rise in the average tax rate on the richest has been associated with an increase in annual GDP growth of almost one percentage point.

FIGURE 4: TOP MARGINAL TAX RATE AND INVESTMENT,1963-2011

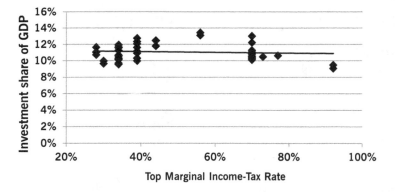

Cutting taxes on the richest Americans has not led them to invest more in plant and equipment. Over the past 50 years, as tax rates have declined, there has been no increase in investment spending as a percentage of GDP. (The flat trend line shows that changes in the highest marginal income-tax rate have not affected investment much, one way or the other.) Instead, the investment share of the economy has been determined by other factors, such as aggregate demand, rather than tax policy.

FIGURE 5: TAX SHARE OF GDP AND PRODUCTIVITY GROWTH

Despite lower and declining tax rates, especially on the rich, the United States has had slower productivity growth over the last several decades than other advanced economies. Overall, lower taxes are associated with slower growth in GDP per hour worked. A 10 percentage point increase in taxes as a share of GDP is associated with an increase in the productivity growth rate of 0.2 percentage points. ❏

Sources: Tom Petska and Mike Strudler, "Income, Taxes, and Tax Progressivity: An Examination of Recent Trends in the Distribution of Individual Income and Taxes" (Statistics of Income Division, Internal Revenue Service, 1997); Thomas Hungerford, "Taxes and the Economy: An Economic Analysis of the Top Tax Rates Since 1945" (Congressional Research Service, 2012); Economic Report of the President, 2012; Bureau of Economic Analysis (bea.gov); Organization of Economic Cooperation and Development, OECD STAT.

Article 9.3

ARE TAXES THE BEST WAY OF DEALING WITH INEQUALITY?

BY ARTHUR MacEWAN
November/December 2019

> Dear Dr. Dollar:
> *What steps can we take to reduce extreme economic inequality? Are taxes on the*
> *rich, on their income and their wealth, the best option?*
> —Anonymous, via e-mail

Higher taxes on the rich would be a good start. During the mid-20th century, we had much less inequality (though still too much), and this was partly due to higher taxes on the rich. Today, the very rich pay lower tax rates than any other group. (There is, by the way, no evidence that those higher tax rates of earlier years harmed economic growth.)

Yet, there is a problem with relying on taxes to reduce economic inequality. Taxes can redistribute income, but relying on taxes means we are accepting the way the system works—the way markets operate—to create inequality in the first place. So instead of only focusing on taxes to redistribute income, we should also focus on reconstructing markets to predistribute income. As the saying goes, "An ounce of prevention is worth a pound of cure."

Not Natural, Not God-Given

There is a pernicious myth that affects the way we think about markets. According to this myth, markets are natural phenomena, there for us to work within and carry out our economic lives. The rules of markets are viewed as though fixed in stone, as though God-given. This leads to the view that, as long as we play by the rules, there is a certain justice in the outcomes, however unequal. In fact, markets are created by people, sometimes through the long development of decisions and practices by many people, but often directly by legislative action.

A few examples make the point:

The labor market and the role of unions. Before the 1930s, laws greatly constrained the unified action of workers. The National Labor Relations Act of 1935 established a new set of rules, facilitating a burgeoning of unions. Even after things moved in the other direction with the Taft-Hartley Act of 1947, which restricted the activities and power of unions, the labor movement remained relatively powerful in the post-World War II years—and the period from World War II to the 1970s was an era of less economic inequality as compared to later and earlier periods.

From the 1980s to the present, government actions (particularly via the National Labor Relations Board) have restricted union formation by, for example, ignoring illegal actions by employers during workers' efforts to unionize. Other factors have also weakened unions, including the nature of international trade agreements, which give employers relatively unfettered opportunities to close shop at home and employ low-wage workers abroad. This reconstruction of the labor market has directly and indirectly weakened unions and contributed to rising inequality.

The market for intellectual property and the role of patent and copyright laws. The U.S. system of intellectual property rights contributes to inflated profit rates and outsized executive salaries, especially in pharmaceutical and software firms. Patent and copyright laws protect the monopoly positions of these firms. Supporters of these laws argue that they encourage innovation, but the laws can also be used to prevent innovation, as large firms can stifle the operations of small competitors by claiming patent or copyright infringement. Also, even if the protections provided by these laws were useful for innovation, there is no reason that the protections need to last as long as they do in the United States. (See box.)

There are, moreover, other ways to induce innovation. Indeed, much innovation is already based on research supported by the government through the National Institutes of Health, the National Science Foundation, the Defense Department, and other government agencies. In any case, regardless of whether one sees existing protections of intellectual property rights as good or bad, there is no disputing the point that the market in intellectual property is a constructed market, not "natural."

Free the Mouse!

In 1998, Congress passed the Sonny Bono Copyright Term Extension Act, extending existing copyright protections by an additional 20 years. Supporters claimed that passing the act was necessary to make sure that U.S. copyright holders had the same protection as those in the European Union, which were granted a 20-year extension in 1993. One of the prime beneficiaries of (and one of the strongest lobbyists for) this act was the Walt Disney Company; the act ensured that Disney's control over Mickey Mouse would not end in 2003, but would last until 2023—and Pluto, Goofy, and Donald Duck until 2025, 2027, and 2029, respectively.

Not surprisingly, the Copyright Extension Act aroused opposition, and critics campaigned under the banner of "Free the Mouse!" Along with popular efforts, the act was also challenged in the courts. While the challenge had particular legal nuances, it was based on the seemingly reasonable argument that the Copyright Extension Act, which protects creative activity retroactively, would do little to benefit the authors and composers who created their works in the first half of the 20th century, and would primarily enrich corporations and families that owned lucrative copyrights. The Supreme Court, apparently deciding that its view of the law trumped this reasonable argument, upheld the act.

Congress and the Court reconstructed the market for intellectual property in a way that provided a valuable handout to Disney and other firms, but it is hard to see how a 20-year extension of copyright protection will have any significant impact on creative efforts now or in the future.

Source: Arthur MacEwan, "Property: Who Has a Right to What and Why?" in *The Wealth Inequality Reader*, edited and published by *Dollars & Sense* and United for a Fair Economy (2004).

Financial markets. The operation of banks and other financial institutions doesn't simply "exist," but is organized with many regulations. Banks have to be chartered and follow various rules regarding reserves, reporting requirements, purchase and sale of assets, etc. Also, they operate under certain practices widely recognized and accepted by financial institutions, as well as the government. A particularly important example is the "too big to fail" principle, which gives investors confidence that the federal government will step in to support large firms if they run into serious trouble. This practice provides an implicit subsidy to big banks, because investors are willing to provide funds to them on favorable terms, knowing that if things go wrong the government will step in and save the banks.

Fossil-fuel markets. Current regulations and subsidies in the oil and gas industry (including policies to encourage fracking) inflate the profits of energy companies, keep fuel prices low, encourage the overuse of fossil fuels, and harm the environment. A May 2019 working paper from the International Monetary Fund estimates fossil fuel subsidies for 2015:

> This paper updates estimates of fossil fuel subsidies, defined as fuel consumption times the gap between existing and efficient prices (i.e., prices warranted by supply costs, environmental costs, and revenue considerations), for 191 countries. Globally, subsidies remained large at $4.7 trillion (6.3% of global GDP) in 2015 and are projected at $5.2 trillion (6.5% of GDP) in 2017. The largest subsidizers in 2015 were China ($1.4 trillion), United States ($649 billion), Russia ($551 billion), European Union ($289 billion), and India ($209 billion).

These subsidies are a fundamental part of the construction of the fossil-fuel market, having negative impacts on both economic equality and the climate.

Schooling and the labor market. Schooling, from pre-K through college, shapes the labor market. The U.S. school system is a multi-tiered system, preparing people for different levels in the workforce. Certain areas of education receive attention— which means funds—according to the needs of employers, as demonstrated by the emphasis in recent years on STEM (science, technology, engineering, and math) education. The structure of the school system, good or bad, is not a "natural" phenomenon, but it greatly affects the operation of the labor market and the distribution of income.

Playing by the Rules They Set

These examples involve conscious action by groups with direct interests in the structure of these markets. Financial institutions, fossil fuel firms, pharmaceutical companies, software giants, and many others use their wealth and power to see that markets are constructed in ways that work for them. (An extreme example: seats on the regional boards of the Federal Reserve Bank, which plays a major role in regulating banks, are reserved for bank representatives.) They get the rules made the way they want, play by the rules, and then claim they deserve what they get because they played by the rules. Nonsense, yes, but effective nonetheless.

Of course, it is difficult to fight these powerful firms and the individuals who reap their fortunes through these firms. They are quite powerful. But there is no reason to think it is more difficult than raising their taxes.

A first step is to establish a wide understanding of the fact that markets are social constructs and that they can be constructed differently. They have been structured differently in the past, and they can be structured differently in the future. For example, the medical care system could be removed from market relations by the creation of "Medicare for All." This would not only alter the provision of medical care, but would reconstruct various related markets (e.g., the market for pharmaceuticals). Even if little change comes in the short run, it is important to send the message that just because firms and rich people play by the rules of the markets, this does not lead to the conclusion that the results are just. (And, of course, they often don't play by the rules!) ❏

Sources: "The Social Construction of Markets," in Arthur MacEwan, *Neoliberalism or Democracy?* (1999); David Coady et al, "Global Fossil Fuel Subsidies Remain Large: An Update Based on Country-Level Estimates," IMF Working Paper, Fiscal Affairs Department, May 2019 (imf.org); Emmanuel Saez and Gabriel Zucman, *The Triumph of Injustice: How the Rich Dodge Taxes and How to Make Them Pay* (2019).

Article 9.4

THE OPTIMAL TAX
Mainstream economics supports a 70% top income tax rate.

BY JOHN MILLER
May/June 2019

> This week Paul Krugman leapt to the defense of Democratic freshman Rep. Alexandria Ocasio-Cortez's idea of paying for a "Green New Deal" with a 70% marginal tax rate on the incomes of top earners.
>
> Mr. Krugman cites a 2011 paper by Peter Diamond and Emmanuel Saez, based on a variety of extrapolations, [which] calculates that the "optimal" top tax rate is 73%.
>
> Case closed? Not even slightly. Messrs. Saez and Diamond are describing a world in which the wealthy have no opportunity to shield or hide their incomes.
>
> Politicians may find it politically handy to be seen dinging the rich. The net result isn't more revenue. It's more efficiency-inhibiting economic distortions.
>
> —Holman Jenkins, "High Tax Rates Aren't Optimal: Nobody Really Thinks a Top Rate of 70% or 80% is a Good Idea in the Real World," *Wall Street Journal*, Jan. 8, 2019.

We have been down this road before. In the 2016 presidential election Senator Bernie Sanders proposed a top income tax rate of 70% to reduce our ever-worsening levels of inequality and help to finance social programs that would support those left behind by today's economy. In response, a cavalcade of economic commentators lined up to denounce Sanders' proposal as socialist lunacy sure to bring on an economic disaster.

But that's not at all what the historical evidence shows. Sanders suggested as much when he quipped that he hadn't proposed a 90% top income tax because "I'm not that much of a socialist compared to Eisenhower." Economist Paul Krugman made the same point in his *New York Times* column that *Wall Street Journal* columnist Holman Jenkins found so objectionable: The top income tax bracket in the United States was higher than 70% "for 35 years after World War II—including the most successful period of economic growth in our history."

But Krugman's defense of Rep. Alexandria Ocasio-Cortez's (AOC's) proposed 70% top income tax rate to help finance a Green New Deal did not stop there. He invoked the "optimum" income tax rate—a concept firmly entrenched in the canon of economic tax literature. As I explain below, calculations of this optimum tax show that the U.S. income tax could be highly progressive with a top income tax rate of 73% or higher without reducing government tax revenues.

That's what really got Jenkins' goat. To see why the optimal top income tax rate is as high as 70%, and probably higher, despite Jenkins' objections, we'll need to unpack some of the economics tax literature.

The Optimal Tax Rate Literature

To begin with, the debate about the optimal tax rate is about the top income tax, or "marginal" income tax as economists call it, and not the average tax levied on all taxable income. A marginal tax rate is the tax rate levied against the next dollar of taxable income.

Currently, the graduated U.S. income tax has six tax brackets, or marginal tax rates, ranging from a low of 10% to a high of 37%. Individual taxpayers would pay 10% of their first $9,325 of taxable income (in 2018) in federal income taxes, whether that's all of their taxable income or just a small portion of it. As taxable income rises above that threshold, taxpayers pay a higher rate only on that additional income. For instance, a millionaire would pay 10% on their first $9,325, and 37% only on their taxable income above $500,000.

AOC's proposal would add an additional tax bracket, or a marginal tax rate of 70%, on taxable income above $10 million. So, like Sanders, she is not as much of a socialist as Eisenhower was. Actually, far from it. In the Eisenhower years, the top income tax rate of 91% was levied on individuals with taxable income of above $200,000—the equivalent of $1.14 million in 2019 when adjusted for inflation.

The economics literature on the "optimal" tax rate explores how high the top income tax rate could be raised without reducing government tax revenues. That tax rate is "optimal" in that it would reduce inequality and make society better off, because the value of an additional dollar of income is far greater to a poor person than to a rich person.

But there are limits to how high an optimal marginal tax should be. While a higher marginal tax rate would take a bigger bite out of the next dollar of taxable income, that higher marginal tax rate could discourage the rich from making more income, which would reduce the amount of income subject to that higher marginal tax rate.

In this way, the optimal tax rate relies on the cornerstone of liberal economics thinking that economist Arthur Okun popularized in his 1975 book *Equality and Efficiency: The Big Tradeoff*. Okun, who had been an economic advisor in the Johnson Administration, envisioned the government transferring income from the rich to the poor in a leaky bucket: the more income that went into the bucket to reduce inequality, the more leaked out in reduced economic efficiency by dulling the incentives of the well-to-do to work that would in turn slow economic growth in the private sector.

Just How High Is Optimal?

But just how full could liberal economists fill their bucket before all of the additional income leaks out in the form of lost efficiency? In their 2011 paper, Nobel prize winning economist Peter Diamond and his co-author economist Emmanuel Saez found that after taking into account the responsiveness of how much less the rich would work in response to a higher tax rate, the optimum tax rate was well above the average 42% tax rate that the rich paid in federal state and local taxes in 2005. Because their estimate of how many fewer hours the rich would work (what economists call "the elasticity of the labor supply of the rich") in response to higher taxes on adjusted gross income (income less income tax deductions) above $300,000 was "quite low," they recommended an optimal tax rate of 73%. After adjusting for inflation, this means that in today's dollars, an optimal tax rate of 73% would be levied on income above $383,000 of adjustable gross income.

As you can imagine, the Diamond and Saez estimates of the optimal tax rate did not go down very well with the "shrink the government down to the size it can be drowned in a bathtub" conservative crowd. Those conservatives objected that it was never their goal to make the income tax as progressive as possible without losing tax revenues to facilitate equity-enhancing redistribution. True enough. But that never stopped conservative economist Arthur Laffer from selling his proposal to cut what he called "prohibitively high" tax rates by promising that lower tax rates would increase government tax revenues, not lower them. Laffer's claim was predicated on lower tax rates boosting economic growth by so much that government tax revenues would rise despite lower tax rates—a claim which never held up in practice. Moreover, it flies in the face of the lack of responsiveness of the rich to higher taxes that Diamond and Saez report.

Jenkins, the *Wall Street Journal* op-ed writer, has yet other objections to the optimal tax literature. He is especially concerned that enacting a higher top income tax rate would push the rich to seek out yet more ways to avoid paying taxes. The net result would be, as he says, "more efficiency-inhibiting economic distortions"—not more revenues. Economists Diamond and Saez are concerned about this possible result as well. But they are convinced that "the natural policy response should be to close tax avoidance opportunities." Fewer tax loopholes would increase tax revenues, and make Diamond and Saez' estimate of a small reduction in the number of hours the rich would work in response to higher taxes (an estimate that holds even as incomes rise) "a reasonable benchmark."

Other conservative commentators, such as Matt Winesett from the American Enterprise Institute, a Washington, D.C.-based think tank dedicated to promoting free enterprise, worries that a high optimal tax would inhibit small business owners from expanding their business or push a medical student to decide to become a pediatrician instead of a heart surgeon "because a large share of the extra money she would earn being a surgeon would be taken away by the government." Diamond and Saez readily admit they have not taken these kinds of long-term effects into account because the economics literature does not have good estimates of them. Then again, neither does Winesett.

Plenty of Room to Do Good

Judged by Diamond and Saez's optimal tax calculations, AOC's tax proposal, which kicks in only on income above $10 million—a much higher threshold than was in effect during the Eisenhower administration—has left a considerable amount of money on the table. That money is much needed, whether it would go toward fighting climate change or making sure that everyone who wants a job can find one.

If Jenkins and his ilk need something to worry about, they should give up pondering immeasurable outcomes such as the likely effect an optimal tax might have on tax loopholes, capital formation, and the education of doctors, and try worrying about a warming planet. That threat is measurable and existential. Shouldn't that be enough for Jenkins, like Krugman, to leap to the defense of a Green New Deal that could measure up to counteracting global warming? ❑

Sources: Paul Krugman, "The Economics of Soaking the Rich: What does Alexandria Ocasio-Cortez know about tax policy? A lot," *New York Times*, Jan. 5, 2019; Peter Diamond and Emmanuel Saez, "The Case for a Progressive Tax: From Basic Research to Policy Recommendations," *Journal of Economic Perspectives*, vol. 25, no. 4, Fall 2011; Arthur Okun, *Equality and Efficiency: the Big Tradeoff* (Brookings Institution, 1975); Ryan Bourne, "No, Economists Don't Agree a 70 Percent Top Marginal Tax Rate Is a Good Idea," *Reason*, Jan. 9, 2019; Kimberly Amadeo, "Laffer Curve Explanation: Why Tax Cuts No Longer Work," *The Balance*, Jan. 6, 2019; Matt Winesett, "What is the optimal top marginal income tax rate? Probably far lower than 70 or 80 percent," AEIdeas, Jan. 9, 2019; Robert McClelland and Shannon Mok, "A Review of Recent Research on Labor Supply Elasticities," Congressional Budget Office Working Paper 2012-12, October 2012.

Article 9.5

CORPORATE TAXES: LESS, LESS, AND LESS

BY ARTHUR MacEWAN
March/April 2022

> Dear Dr. Dollar,
> *It seems that corporations say they need low taxes in order to do research, innovate,*
> *invest, and remain competitive. Why not take them at their word and offer them*
> *low taxes on specific terms? Say, a 10% tax on before-tax profits that are used for*
> *research, capital investment, workforce development, or the like, and something*
> *like 50%–70% on the rest of their profits?*
> —Katharine Rylaarsdam, Baltimore, Md.

The trouble is that corporations already have tax breaks of the sort you suggest. The Tax Foundation, which according to the organization's website, prides itself on being "the nation's leading independent tax policy nonprofit" summarizes the situation as follows:

> The tax treatment of different types of investments, such as those in research
> and development (R&D), physical capital, and human capital [worker training],
> varies. R&D expenses are immediately deductible and eligible for tax credits.
> Many physical capital investments are immediately deductible. Only certain
> categories of human capital investments are deductible for firms and individuals,
> and some credits are available for individuals.

CORPORATE PROFITS BEFORE TAXES, STATUTORY AND AVERAGE EFFECTIVE FEDERAL CORPORATE TAX RATES, AND FEDERAL CORPORATE TAX REVENUE AS A SHARE OF TOTAL FEDERAL REVENUE, 2015-2021

	Corporate Profits Before Taxes, in Trillions of Dollars	Statutory Tax Rate	Effective Rate	Share of Federal Revenue
2015	$2.128	35%	18.6%	10.5%
2016	$2.134	35%	17.6%	9.2%
2017	$2.195	35%	14.2%	9.0%
2018	$2.259	21%	12.5%	6.1%
2019	$2,255	21%	13.4%	6.6%
2020	$2.184	21%	12.6%	6.2%
2021	$2.965*	21%*	12.5%*	7.5%**

* Average of first three quarters of 2021

** Estimate of Office of Management and the Budget

Sources: St. Louis Federal Reserve Data on corporate profits; Office of Management and Budget, Historical Tables, Table 2.1.

So, in general, offering corporations a low tax rate on the income they use for these productivity-increasing activities would actually be presenting them with a higher tax rate than they pay now on expenditures for these activities. This "offer" would certainly not lead them to accept a higher rate on the rest of their income.

There is, however, a well-founded question implicit in the proposal, namely, how do we get corporations to pay more taxes? The experience of the last several decades, topped off by the corporate tax reduction enacted at the end of 2017, has long been one of declining corporate tax rates and a declining share of federal revenue coming from corporations.

In the 1950s and 1960s, the statutory federal corporate tax rate hovered around 50%, but today is only 21%. After slight declines in the 1970s and early 1980s, the rate fell to 34% in the late 1980s. It was then stable at 35% from 1992 through 2017, when the sharp reduction to 21% was enacted. The average effective rate, what corporations as a group actually pay, is substantially lower than the statutory rate, as corporations find many ways to lower their taxes—for example, the sorts of deductions and credits noted in the Tax Foundation quotation above. There are also "loopholes"; an especially large one is the opportunity for firms to locate profits abroad, often through book-keeping manipulations. (The "average effective rate" includes some firms that pay zero taxes and others that pay more; there may be some that actually pay the statutory rate!)

STATUTORY FEDERAL CORPORATE INCOME TAX RATE, AVERAGE EFFECTIVE FEDERAL CORPORATE INCOME TAX RATE, AND FEDERAL CORPORATE TAX REVENUE AS A SHARE OF TOTAL FEDERAL REVENUE, 1952–2021

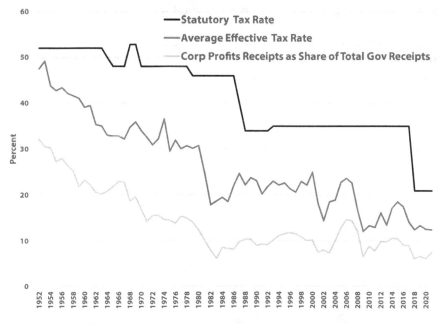

Sources: St. Louis Federal Reserve Data on corporate profits; Office of Management and Budget, Historical Tables, Table 2.1; Economic Policy Institute, "Corporate tax rates and economic growth since 1947." Note: The tax rate figures for 2021 are the average of data for the first three quarters of the year. For 2021, the government receipts from the corporate tax as a share of total government receipt is and estimate from the Office of Management and Budget.

The table above shows the statutory and average effective tax rates for 2015 through 2021, as well as the amount of corporate profits and the share of total government receipts accounted for by the corporate profits tax. (Don't miss that pre-tax corporate profits for the first three quarters of 2021 were 31% higher than in any previous year, far more than would be accounted for by inflation.) The graph above shows what has happened to the statutory rate, the average effective rate, and federal corporate tax revenue as a share of total federal revenue since 1952.

These data indicate the importance of finding an answer to the question of how to get corporations to pay more taxes. Corporate officials and their apologists will argue that low taxes help the economy grow. A glance at the graph on the next page, however, indicates that there is no connection between periods of strong growth and low corporate taxes. What the tax reductions have done, however, is contribute to the great rise of economic inequality.

The experience with corporate tax rates demonstrates the power of large corporations and wealthy individuals. But that power is exercised in many other ways, from tax breaks for fossil fuel firms to the deregulation of finance to undermining the strength of labor unions, all of which contribute to rising inequality. (See Arthur MacEwan, "Are Taxes the Best Way of Dealing with Inequality?" *D&S*, November/ December 2019.)

The answer to how to get corporations to pay more taxes is bound up with the broader question of how to reduce corporate power. I have no answer to this question other than the old answer of political organizing—through unions, community groups, student organizations, and other such groups—to overcome the great power that large firms exercise in our political system. ❏

Sources: Erica York, "Tax Treatment of Worker Training," Tax Foundation, March 21, 2019 (taxfoundation.org); Thomas L. Hungerford, "Corporate tax rates and economic growth since 1947," Economic Policy Institute, June 4, 2013 (epi.org).

Article 9.6

TAXING UNREALIZED CAPITAL GAINS IS KEY TO UNDOING TAX INJUSTICE.

BY JOHN MILLER
September/October 2021

> …ProPublica, a website whose journalism promotes progressive causes, published information from what it said are 15 years of the tax returns of Jeff Bezos, Warren Buffett and other rich Americans.
>
> The ProPublica story is a long argument that somehow the rich don't pay enough.
>
> There is no evidence of illegality in the ProPublica story. … ProPublica knows this, so its story tries to invent a scandal by calculating what it calls the "true tax rate" these fellows are paying. This is a phony construct that exists nowhere in the law and compares how much the "wealth" of these individuals increased from 2014 to 2018 compared to how much income tax they paid.
> —"Return of the IRS Scandal," The Editorial Board, *Wall Street Journal*, June 8, 2021

In some ways the June 2021 ProPublica report, "The Secret IRS Files," that exposed how nearly all the wealth gains of the 25 taxpayers who topped the Forbes list of the 400 richest Americans went untaxed was old news. "…Billionaires are very good at reducing their taxable income. Who knew?" was the ho-hum reaction of the *Wall Street Journal* editors.

Nonetheless, the ProPublica report was a bombshell that detonated just as the country's wealthiest had raked in immense profits during the pandemic. The scandalously low tax rates ProPublica reported for the superrich supercharged demands that the wealthy pay their fair share of taxes.

The real scandal, according to the *Wall Street Journal* editors, however, was that ProPublica had used stolen IRS data to carry out a political hit job that used a "phony construct," the true tax rate, to further the political agenda of taxing the ultra-wealthy.

ProPublica's true tax rate, which compares income tax payments to wealth gains, documents the failure of the U.S. income tax to make the super wealthy pay their fair share of taxes—and the need to tax wealth as well as income to make that happen.

More Money Than God and Just About the Same Tax Rate

Using 15 years of IRS tax data of the superrich that they received from an unnamed source, ProPublica, a nonprofit news organization, reported that the 25 wealthiest U.S. taxpayers paid astonishingly little of their wealth gains in income taxes.

From 2014 to 2018 these 25 billionaires added $401 billion (an average of $16 billion each) to their ever-expanding wealth, bringing their combined wealth to $1.1 trillion. They paid $13.6 billion in federal income taxes. But that amounted to just 3.4% of what they had gained in wealth, according to the "true tax rate" reported by ProPublica.

The ProPublica report looked closely at the tax records of four of the 25 wealthiest taxpayers: Warren Buffet (Berkshire Hathaway Inc.), Jeff Bezos (Amazon.com, Inc.), Michael Bloomberg (Bloomberg L.P.), and Elon Musk (Tesla, Inc.).

The results were stunning. From 2014 to 2018 they had accumulated more money than God, an average of $40 billion each. Nonetheless, their ProPublica average "true tax rates" on their wealth gains were 0.10% for Buffet, 0.98% for Bezos, 1.30% for Bloomberg, and 3.27% for Musk.

Since then, U.S. wealth inequality has continued to worsen. By the beginning of 2021, nearly one-third (32.1%) of the nation's wealth was held by the richest 1% of households, 16 times the 2.0% share of the wealth going to the bottom half of households, according to the latest Federal Reserve Board data. Three decades ago, in the beginning of 1991, just under one-quarter (23.1%) of the nation's wealth was held by the richest 1%, 6.4 times the wealth share of the bottom 50%.

The ProPublica report provoked outrage. How could the U.S. tax code treat the superrich and the taxpayers of the work-a-day world so differently at the very time U.S. inequality had reached its highest levels in nearly a century?

The Journal Editors Cry Foul

The *Wall Street Journal* editors were outraged as well—not by the tax injustice reported by ProPublica, but by the report itself. They dismissed the ProPublica story as a political hatchet job timed to support the call for higher taxes on the wealthy coming from the Biden administration and the advocates of a wealth tax. On top of that, the editors reminded their readers "that someone leaked confidential IRS information about individuals to serve a political agenda," and their opinion columnists chimed in attacking ProPublica's report for relying on "stolen tax records." Beyond leading these pen-and-ink cries for law and order, the editors assured their readers that, "there is no evidence of illegality in the ProPublica story"

Indeed, there was none. But that's precisely what's disturbing about the report. The massive tax inequality reported by ProPublica is so insidious because it is "baked into the core of the U.S.'s tax code," as Morris Pearl, former managing director at BlackRock (the giant asset management firm) and the chair of Patriotic Millionaires, put it in a recent *Financial Times* article. He explained, "It [the U.S. tax code] says that the way rich people make money, through investments increasing in value, shouldn't be taxed, while the way everyone else makes money, income, should be."

Buffett's tax returns provide a clear example of how the current tax code exempts the preponderance of wealth gains from taxation, letting the superrich pay rock-bottom tax rates. From 2014 to 2018, Buffet, as the chair and CEO of the Berkshire Hathaway holding company, accumulated $24.4 billion of wealth as the value of his stock portfolio increased. But almost all those gains went untaxed. This is because income tax collects taxes on gains from investment only when they are realized. More specifically, it taxes capital gains (the increase in the value of an asset), only when an appreciated asset is sold. Buffett's income, which came overwhelmingly from his realized capital gains, was $125 million, or about $5 of every $1,000 dollars his wealth increased. His income tax bill for those years totaled $23.7 million, but that was just 0.1% of his added wealth. The remaining $24.26 billion of unrealized gains went untaxed and added to his already outsized wealth holdings.

In addition, should the superrich hold assets that grow in value until they die, neither they nor their heirs ever pay taxes on the unrealized capital gains. Upon death, and even the superrich do die, the tax "basis" of assets becomes their value at the time of death, including untaxed, unrealized capital gains, instead of their value at the time when the assets were purchased. For example, say your Aunt Edith leaves you 10 shares of Apple stock worth $150 each that she originally purchased for $20 a share. You then sell the stock at a price of $200 a share. Only the capital gain of $50 a share after you inherited the stock would be taxed (and your aunt's $130-a-share capital gain would go untaxed). The death loophole makes more of a difference for the estate of the superrich than it does for the estate of your Aunt Edith. In 2013, most of the assets (55%) of large estates valued at over $100 million were unrealized capital gains that had never been taxed.

On top of that, capital gains on assets held a year or longer get taxed at preferential rates. Income tax rates on long-term capital gains income is capped at a 20% rate. That rate is lower than the 22% income rate levied against wage income above $39,476 and well below the 37% maximum income tax on wage income. The Tax Policy Center estimates that in 2019 three-quarters of long-term capital gains went to the richest 1% of taxpayers, and over half to the top 0.1%.

Is the True Tax Rate Wrong?

For the *Wall Street Journal* editors ProPublica's true tax rate is a "phony concept" because it compares income tax payments to wealth holdings. "Wealth and income are different," as the editors emphasize, "and what Americans pay is a tax on income, not wealth."

The true tax rate is not part of the U.S. tax code. But it's not a phony construct. It reveals just how out of line the U.S. income tax is with the usual notions of tax fairness. It also shows just how the U.S. tax code would need to change to make the ultra-wealthy pay their fair share of taxes.

Nor is it the case, as the *Wall Street Journal* editors suggest, that when tax rates are measured using income instead of wealth the superrich pay their fair share of taxes. In their recent book, *The Triumph of Injustice*, economists Emmanuel Saez and Gabriel Zucman report that in 1980 the average effective tax rate (the share of total income paid in all federal, state, and local taxes) of the richest 400 taxpayers was 47.2%. That was almost double the 25.7% average effective tax rate paid by the 50% of adults with the lowest incomes. By 2018, however, the average effective tax rate of the top 400 had fallen to 23%, while the poorer half of the population paid out 24.3% of their income in taxes. Now *that's* unfair.

While economists hold to different notions of tax fairness, they would all agree with the U.S. Department of the Treasury Resource Center that, "A basic principle underlying the income tax laws of the United States is that people should be taxed according to their 'ability to pay.'" The federal income tax, with its graduated rates (or tax brackets), was meant to adhere to the ability-to-pay principle that people with more income are able to and should pay more taxes. On its website, the Treasury Resource Center adds that, "Wealth, the total of assets less liabilities, is sometimes used as well as income as a measure of ability to pay."

Economists have long used the Haig-Simons definition of income, which takes wealth gains into account, to assess taxpayers' ability to pay. This comprehensive measure defines income as the sum of total consumption plus any increases in an individual's wealth during the year. The U.S. income tax falls far short of levying taxes based on the ability to pay as measured by the Haig-Simons definition in several ways. One of the most important is by not taxing unrealized capital gains. Economists Joel Slemrod and Jon Bakija found that during the years 1987 to 2013 realized capital gains (less deductible losses) included on personal income tax returns averaged 22% of the $1.947 trillion annual average of capital gains. The ProPublica "true tax rate" throws into sharp relief just how low the income tax rate of the super-rich is compared to their Haig-Simons ability to pay.

A Fair Tax Code Must Tax Unrealized Capital Gains

Taxing wealth gains, including unrealized as well as realized capital gains, is the key to creating a tax code that adheres to the ability to pay and requires the ultra-wealthy to pay their fair share of taxes. And unlike other measures needed to implement an income tax based on the comprehensive Haig-Simons definition, taxing unrealized capital gains yearly is administratively feasible.

In 2019 Senator Ron Wyden (D.-Ore.), the current chair of the Senate Finance Committee, introduced a bill that would take an important step in that direction. His plan would tax the unrealized capital gains of the richest taxpayers each year, and all capital gains would be taxed at the same rate as wages (with a top income tax of 37%). Wyden's tax on unrealized capital gains would be applied to taxpayers whose income exceeded $1 million or held $10 million of assets in each of the previous three years. (The asset threshold excludes personal residences of up to $2 million, pensions, 401(k) plans and similar plans, as well as $5 million of the value of family farms. The thresholds would be indexed for inflation and in practice the Wyden tax on unrealized capital gains would apply to the top 0.3% of taxpayers.)

While the Biden administration's "American Families Plan" has not proposed to tax unrealized capital gains directly, it too would increase the tax burden of the superrich. The Biden plan would restore the top income tax bracket to the 39.6% rate that existed prior to the Trump tax cuts. It would also tax realized capital gains at the same rate as other income, increasing the maximum tax rate on those gains from 20% to 39.6%. Finally, the Biden plan would close the loophole in the estate tax that allows inherited unrealized capital gains to go untaxed for estates worth more than $1 million (after exclusions).

The most direct way to require the wealthy to pay their fair share of taxes would be to tax their wealth. In the 2020 presidential campaign, Senators Bernie Sanders and Elizabeth Warren proposed wealth taxes that target the super wealthy. The

Sanders tax on "extreme wealth" would levy an annual tax on the wealth of households with a net worth of over $32 million and would begin at a 1% rate and reach an 8% rate on wealth over $10 billion. The Warren ultra-millionaire tax would apply to households with more than $50 million of net worth. Those households would pay an annual 2% tax on net worth above $50 million and a 3% tax on net worth above $1 billion. Economists Saez and Zucman estimate that the Sanders wealth tax would triple the taxes paid by the wealthiest 400, while the Warren wealth tax would more than double their taxes. (See John Miller, "The Wealth Tax Proposals," *D&S*, July/August 2019.)

Finally, in August Warren proposed to increase taxes on highly profitable corporations and to increase funding for the IRS to track down wealthy and corporate tax cheats. When combined with her wealth tax, her proposal would raise enough revenue to pay for the Democrats' $3.5 trillion reconciliation infrastructure plan.

The lesson here is clear: To create a fair tax code we need to tax wealth as it accumulates, and not "wait for billionaires to sell their stock," as Saez and Zucman put it. That requires taxing unrealized gains through a more comprehensive income tax or, better yet, taxing wealth directly.

Sources: Jessie Eisinger, Jeff Ernsthausen, and Paul Kiel, "The Secret IRS Files," ProPublica, June 8, 2021(propublica.org); Jeff Ernsthausen, Paul Kiel, and Jessie Eisinger, "How We Calculated the True Tax Rates of the Wealthiest," ProPublica, June 8, 2021 (propublica.org); "Distribution of Household Wealth in the U.S. since 1989," Distributional Financial Accounts, Federal Reserve Board (federalreserve.gov); Ari Paul, "Outrage at ProPublica Tax Leaks Underscores Their Importance," FAIR, June 17, 2021 (fair.org); Holman Jenkins, "Your Stolen Tax records Are News," *Wall Street Journal*, June 15, 2021 (wsj.com); Morris Pearl, "How the wealthiest Americans get away with paying no tax," *Financial Times*, June 14, 2001 (ft.com); "Policy Basics: The Federal Estate Tax," Center on Budget and Policy Priorities, November 7, 2018 (cbpp.org); Chuck Marr, Samantha Jacobs, Sam Washington, and George Fenton, "Asking Wealthiest Households to Pay Fairer Amount in Tax Would Help Fund a More Equitable Recovery," Center on Budget and Policy Priorities, April 22, 2021 (cbpp.org); Emmanuel Saez and Gabriel Zucman, *The Triumph of Injustice* (W.W. Norton & Company, 2019); "The Economics of Taxation: Taxes on Income," U.S. Department of the Treasury, Dec. 5, 2010 (treasury.gov); Jonathan Gruber, *Public Finance and Public Policy*, sixth edition, (Worth Publishers, 2019); Joel Slemrod and Jon Bakija, *Taxing Ourselves: A Citizen's Guide to the Debate over Taxes*, fifth edition, (MIT Press, 2017); "Treat Wealth Like Wages," Senate Finance Committee, Ranking Member Ron Wyden, April 4, 2019; "Fact Sheet: the American Family Plan," White House Briefing Room, April 28, 2021 (whitehouse.gov); Emmanuel Saez and Gabriel Zucman, "Don't wait for billionaires to sell their stock. Tax their riches now," *Washington Post*, April 14, 2021 (washingtonpost.com).

Chapter 10

TRADE AND DEVELOPMENT

INTRODUCTION

Given the economic turmoil of the last decade in high-income countries, it is ironic that the developing world is still being urged to adopt free markets and increased privatization as the keys to catching up with the West. These neoliberal policy prescriptions have been applied across the developing world over the last few decades as a one-size-fits-all solution to problems such as poverty, malnutrition, and political conflict. While spiking unemployment in the United States led to a (temporary) surge in government spending, developing countries with double-digit unemployment were routinely told that macroeconomic crises could only be dealt with by "tightening their belts." And while the West, having experienced a financial crisis, now embraced some new financial regulations, similar calls for more regulation from developing countries have been dismissed as misguided.

The first tenet of the neoliberal faith is the belief that openness to international trade is the key to growth and development. Ramaa Vasudevan, in her primer "Comparative Advantage" (Article 10.1), starts off this chapter with a critique of the Ricardian theory of comparative advantage that is central to the neoclassical argument for free trade.

Thomas Palley offers a concise and useful metaphor for the effects of globalization and outsourcing on productive industry in the United States. "The Globalization Clock" (Article 10.2) describes how globalization and outsourcing pick off domestic industries one by one, based on the relative exportability of the goods or services and the skill level of the workers. This metaphor also illustrates why, at any given period of time, there has not been a majority consensus against outsourcing: The majority of consumers benefit through lower prices from the outsourced industry; only those acutely affected through the loss of their jobs are against it. But as the clock ticks forward, more and more industries at higher and higher levels of skill become outsourced.

Next, Arthur MacEwan answers a reader's question, "Does U.S. Prosperity Depend on Exploitation?" (Article 10.3). Are trading relations between nations and exchanges within said nations "fair and equitable"? Or does history show us that the wealth of a nation does rely on "primitive accumulation" in the dispossession of others?

Next, Jawied Nawabi's "Whatever Happened to Development?" (Article 10.4) provides a primer on development economics. Nawabi begins with a simple observation: "…why have so few countries—out of about 120 newly independent countries that have emerged since World War II—achieved successful development?" To answer that question, he walks us through the history of development economics up through the present and introduces us to the "role of the state in economic development," or RSED, a school of thought which challenges the dominant neoliberal orthodoxy.

In "Ford Drives Away" (Article 10.5), Débora Nunes tells the story of Ford's departure from Brazil after more than a century of operation, and what it shows about the multi-sector deindustrialization that the country has undergone. Right-wing commentators want to blame capital flight on the so-called "Brazilian Cost"—the supposed burden of regulations, taxes, high wages, and overly generous benefits. Yet under the recent conservative governments that slashed taxes, regulations, wages, and benefits, deindustrialization accelerated. It seems that whatever its rhetoric about spurring growth, neoliberalism's main effects are destructive and redistributive— from the bottom to the top.

Finally, in "The Political Economy of Power vs. Policy in Gabriel Boric's Chile" (Article 10.6), James M. Cypher traces the history of the ideological alliance between Thatcher and Augusto Pinochet, who ruled Chile for 17 years, and dominance of Thatcher's dictum "There Is No Alternative" (TINA) in the neoliberal administrations that followed Pinochet's regime. The massive protests in 2019 and 2020 demanded an alternative; Boric is poised to deliver it—if the powers that be let him.

Discussion Questions

1. (Article 10.1) Under what conditions might the mainstream argument about the advantages of specialization based on comparative advantage break down?

2. (Article 10.2) Describe the different "times" on Palley's "globalization clock." What time is it in the United States today according to this clock?

3. (Article 10.3) In your main microeconomics textbook, can you find the term "exploitation"? If not, why not? What is "primitive accumulation"?

4. (Article 10.4) Nawabi presents the RSED school of thought as an emerging alternative to the current orthodox neoliberalism within development economics. Explain what the RSED school is and why it is critical of neoliberalism and the "Washington Consensus."

5. (Article 10.5) What is this "Brazilian Cost" that is blamed for Capital Flight from Brazil? Is there something missing from this list?

6. (Article 10.6) What is Margaret Thatcher's dictum "TINA," and could the arrival of Gabriel Boric to power in Chile also mark the end of TINA? What challenges does Boric face?

Article 10.1

COMPARATIVE ADVANTAGE

BY RAMAA VASUDEVAN
July/August 2007

Dear Dr. Dollar:
When economists argue that the outsourcing of jobs might be a plus for the U.S. economy, they often mention the idea of comparative advantage. So free trade would allow the United States to specialize in higher-end service-sector businesses, creating higher-paying jobs than the ones that would be outsourced. But is it really true that free trade leads to universal benefits?
—David Goodman, Boston, Mass.

You're right: The purveyors of the free trade gospel do invoke the doctrine of comparative advantage to dismiss widespread concerns about the export of jobs. Attributed to 19th-century British political-economist David Ricardo, the doctrine says that a nation always stands to gain if it exports the goods it produces *relatively* more cheaply in exchange for goods that it can get *comparatively* more cheaply from abroad. Free trade would lead to each country specializing in the products it can produce at *relatively* lower costs. Such specialization allows both trading partners to gain from trade, the theory goes, even if in one of the countries production of *both* goods costs more in absolute terms.

For instance, suppose that in the United States the cost to produce one car equals the cost to produce 10 bags of cotton, while in the Philippines the cost to produce one car equals the cost to produce 100 bags of cotton. The Philippines would then have a comparative advantage in the production of cotton, producing one bag at a cost equal to the production cost of 1/100 of a car, versus 1/10 of a car in the United States; likewise, the United States would hold a comparative advantage in the production of cars. Whatever the prices of cars and cotton in the global market, the theory goes, the Philippines would be better off producing only cotton and importing all its cars from the United States, and the United States would be better off producing only cars and importing all of its cotton from the Philippines. If the international terms of trade—the relative price—is one car for 50 bags, then the United States will take in 50 bags of cotton for each car it exports, 40 more than the 10 bags it forgoes by putting its productive resources into making the car rather than growing cotton. The Philippines is also better off: it can import a car in exchange for the export of 50 bags of cotton, whereas it would have had to forgo the production of 100 bags of cotton in order to produce that car domestically. If the price of cars goes up in the global marketplace, the Philippines will lose out in relative terms—but will still be better off than if it tried to produce its own cars.

The real world, unfortunately, does not always conform to the assumptions underlying comparative-advantage theory. One assumption is that trade is balanced. But many countries are running persistent deficits, notably the United States, whose trade deficit is now at nearly 7% of its GDP. A second premise, that there is full employment within the trading nations, is also patently unrealistic. As global trade intensifies, jobs created in the export sector do not necessarily compensate for the jobs lost in the sectors wiped out by foreign competition.

The comparative advantage story faces more direct empirical challenges as well. Nearly 70% of U.S. trade is trade in similar goods, known as *intra-industry trade*: for example, exporting Fords and importing BMWs. And about one-third of U.S. trade as of the late 1990s was trade between branches of a single corporation located in different countries (*intra-firm trade*). Comparative advantage cannot explain these patterns.

Comparative advantage is a static concept that identifies immediate gains from trade but is a poor guide to economic development, a process of structural change over time which is by definition dynamic. Thus the comparative advantage tale is particularly pernicious when preached to developing countries, consigning many to "specialize" in agricultural goods or be forced into a race to the bottom where cheap sweatshop labor is their sole source of competitiveness.

The irony, of course, is that none of the rich countries got that way by following the maxim that they now preach. These countries historically relied on tariff walls and other forms of protectionism to build their industrial base. And even now, they continue to protect sectors like agriculture with subsidies. The countries now touted as new models of the benefits of free trade—South Korea and the other "Asian tigers," for instance—actually flouted this economic wisdom, nurturing their technological capabilities in specific manufacturing sectors and taking advantage of their lower wage costs to *gradually* become effective competitors of the United States and Europe in manufacturing.

The fundamental point is this: Contrary to the comparative-advantage claim that trade is universally beneficial, nations as a whole do not prosper from free trade. Free trade creates winners and losers, both within and between countries. In today's context it is the global corporate giants that are propelling and profiting from "free trade": not only outsourcing white-collar jobs, but creating global commodity chains linking sweatshop labor in the developing countries of Latin America and Asia (Africa being largely left out of the game aside from the export of natural resources such as oil) with ever-more insecure consumers in the developed world. Promoting "free trade" as a political cause enables this process to continue.

It is a process with real human costs in terms of both wages and work. People in developing countries across the globe continue to face these costs as trade liberalization measures are enforced; and the working class in the United States is also being forced to bear the brunt of the relentless logic of competition. ❑

Sources: Arthur MacEwan, "The Gospel of Free Trade: The New Evangelists," *Dollars & Sense*, July/August 2002; Ha-Joon Chang, *Kicking away the Ladder: The Real History of Fair Trade*, Foreign Policy in Focus, 2003; Anwar Shaikh, "Globalization and the Myths of Free Trade," in *Globalization and the Myths of Free Trade: History, Theory, and Empirical Evidence*, ed. Anwar Shaikh, Routledge 2007.

Article 10.2

THE GLOBALIZATION CLOCK

BY THOMAS PALLEY
May/June 2006; revised November 2018

Over the past 40 years, real wages have stagnated in developed economies, and there has also been a massive increase in income and wealth inequality. Those developments are substantially attributable to the neoliberal economic policy paradigm which has dominated policymaking. Globalization is a critical element of that paradigm, and it has been a major contributing factor to wage stagnation and increased inequality.

The neoliberal policy era did not happen in a vacuum. Instead, it needs to be explained by political economy, which shows how particular economic interests triumphed in capturing political power and the world of economic ideas (i.e., economic theory), and how those ideas and policies were accepted by society. The Globalization Clock provides a metaphor for understanding that political process as it relates to globalization. It helps explain why globalization has been so politically difficult to turn back despite its injurious effects. A key reason is globalization's adverse impact on political solidarity, with globalization aggravating the pre-existing decline in solidarity caused by the rise of the consumer society.

Political economy has historically been constructed around the divide between capital and labor, with firms and workers at odds over the division of the economic pie. Within this construct, labor is usually represented as a monolithic interest, yet the reality is that labor has always suffered from internal divisions—by race, by occupational status, and along many other fault lines. Neoliberal globalization has in many ways sharpened these divisions, which helps to explain why corporations have been winning and workers losing.

One of these fault lines divides workers from themselves: since workers are also consumers, they face a divide between the desire for higher wages and the desire for lower prices. Historically, this identity split has been exploited to divide union from nonunion workers, with anti-labor advocates accusing union workers of causing higher prices. Today, globalization is amplifying the divide between people's interests as workers and their interests as consumers through its promise of ever-lower prices.

Consider the debate over Walmart's low-road labor policies. While Walmart's low wages and skimpy benefits have recently faced scrutiny, even some liberal commentators argue that Walmart is actually good for low-wage workers because they gain more as consumers from its "low, low prices" than they lose as workers from its low wages. But this static, snapshot analysis fails to capture the full impact of globalization, past and future.

Globalization affects the economy unevenly, hitting some sectors first and others later. The process can be understood in terms of the hands of a clock. At one o'clock is the apparel sector; at two o'clock, the textile sector; at three, the steel sector; at six, the auto sector. Workers in the apparel sector are the first to have their jobs shifted to lower-wage venues; at the same time, though, all other workers get price reductions. Next, the process picks off textile sector workers at two o'clock. Meanwhile, workers from three o'clock onward get price cuts, as do the apparel workers at one o'clock. Each time the hands of the clock move, the workers taking the hit are isolated. In this fashion, globalization moves around the clock, with labor perennially divided.

Manufacturing was first to experience this process, but technological innovations associated with the Internet are putting service and knowledge workers in the firing line as well. Online business models are making even retail workers vulnerable—consider Amazon.com, for example, which has opened a customer support center and two technology development centers in India. Public-sector wages are also in play, at least indirectly, since falling wages mean falling tax revenues. The problem is that each time the hands on the globalization clock move forward, workers are divided: the majority is made slightly better off while the few are made much worse off.

Globalization also alters the historical divisions within capital, creating a new split between bigger internationalized firms and smaller firms that remain nationally centered. This division has been brought into sharp focus with the debate over the trade deficit and the overvalued dollar. In previous decades, manufacturing as a whole opposed running trade deficits and maintaining an overvalued dollar because of the adverse impact of increased imports. The one major business sector with a different view was retailing, which benefited from cheap imports.

However, the spread of multinational production and outsourcing has divided manufacturing in wealthy countries into two camps. In one camp are larger multinational corporations that have gone global and benefit from cheap imports; in the other are smaller businesses that remain nationally centered in terms of sales, production and input sourcing. Multinational corporations tend to support an overvalued dollar since this makes imports produced in their foreign factories cheaper. Conversely, domestic manufacturers are hurt by an overvalued dollar, which advantages import competition.

This division opens the possibility of a new alliance between labor and those manufacturers and businesses that remain nationally based—potentially a potent one, since there are approximately 7 million enterprises with sales of less than $10 million in the United States, versus only 200,000 with sales greater than $10 million. However, such an alliance will always be unstable as the inherent labor-capital conflict over income distribution can always reassert itself. Indeed, this pattern is already evident in the internal politics of the National Association of Manufacturers (NAM), whose members have been significantly divided regarding the overvalued dollar. As one way to address this division, the group is promoting a domestic "competitiveness" agenda aimed at weakening regulation, reducing corporate legal liability, and lowering employee benefit costs—an agenda designed to appeal to both camps, but at the expense of workers.

Solidarity has always been key to the political and economic advancement of working families, and it is key to mastering the politics of globalization. Developing a coherent story about the economics of neoliberal globalization around which working families can coalesce is a key ingredient for solidarity. So, too, is understanding how globalization divides labor. These narratives and analyses can help counter deep cultural proclivities to individualism, as well as other historic divides such as racism. However, as if this were not difficult enough, globalization creates additional challenges. National political solutions that worked in the past are not adequate to the task of controlling international competition. That means the solidarity bar is further raised, calling for international solidarity that supports new forms of international economic regulation. ❑

Article 10.3

DOES U.S. PROSPERITY *DEPEND* ON EXPLOITATION?

BY ARTHUR MacEWAN
March/April 2019

> Dear Dr. Dollar:
> *I regularly hear the claim that U.S. prosperity* depends *on exploiting poorer countries, but I have never once seen an actual argument for it. What is the support for this claim?* —Ryan Cooper, via Twitter

Let's start with the two congenital blood stains on the cheek of U.S. economic development—slavery and the genocide/taking-of-lands of Native American peoples.

Certainly, the prosperity of the United States has depended to a substantial degree on the labor of slaves, based on stealing people from poor societies, disrupting the social order, and depleting the labor force of those societies. In the decade leading up to the Civil War, for example, the value of raw cotton exports accounted for over half of the value of all U.S. exports. Then there were the direct profits from the slave trade, which built the fortunes of several northern U.S. and European families. And the initial phase of U.S. industrialization, the cotton textile industry, was based on low-cost slave-produced cotton.

As to the economic role of lands taken from Native Americans, the value, though incalculable, was immense. Indeed, some historians have argued that a major pillar of U.S. economic success was the availability of "open land"—the so-called "frontier thesis." Not to mention that a large part of that "frontier" was the huge tract of land taken from Mexico after the Mexican-American War.

U.S. economic success—from slavery, "open land," and other aspects of exploiting people of low-income societies—meant different things for different groups. Clearly, for example, southern plantation owners, financiers of the slave trade, and owners of northern cotton mills reaped major gains. Yet, the economic growth that these activities generated seeped down to a broad spectrum of society, benefiting others less than the elites, but benefiting many nonetheless—of course, not including the slaves themselves. Likewise, while large-scale ranchers and land speculators gained disproportionately from stealing the lands of Native Americans, many homesteaders also benefited from "opening" the west. The Native Americans themselves, like the slaves, did not share in the prosperity.

Dependence on Government Support

As with slavery and the decimation of the Native American nations, economic activity beyond the current boundaries of the United States depended on government support, importantly including military support. This was especially evident in the "Gunboat Diplomacy" era in the early decades of the 20th century, when military action abroad was explicitly tied to economic interests, as was famously described and denounced by retired Marine Corps Major General Smedley Butler (see box).

U.S. Economic Interests and Military Action

Excerpt from a speech delivered in 1933 by retired Major General Smedley Butler, USMC.

"I spent 33 years and four months in active military service and during that period I spent most of my time as a high class muscle man for Big Business, for Wall Street and the bankers. In short, I was a racketeer, a gangster for capitalism. I helped make Mexico and especially Tampico safe for American oil interests in 1914. I helped make Haiti and Cuba a decent place for the National City Bank boys to collect revenues in. I helped in the raping of half a dozen Central American republics for the benefit of Wall Street. I helped purify Nicaragua for the International Banking House of Brown Brothers in 1902-1912. I brought light to the Dominican Republic for the American sugar interests in 1916. I helped make Honduras right for the American fruit companies in 1903. In China in 1927 I helped see to it that Standard Oil went on its way unmolested. Looking back on it, I might have given Al Capone a few hints. The best he could do was to operate his racket in three districts. I operated on three continents."

As Butler's statement makes clear, the activities being protected were often those of particular U.S. firms, not the prosperity of the U.S. economy in general. Indeed, in many cases, though the firms benefited, the military costs of the actions outweighed the direct benefits to the U.S. economy. Yet, by protecting the activities of particular firms, the U.S. government was protecting the access of U.S. firms to global markets and resources—that is, protecting the firms' ability to exploit the people and resources in many parts of the world. This access was driven by U.S. firms' search for profits and the firms' owners were the primary beneficiaries. Access, however, also provided low-cost goods—everything from bananas to oil—and markets for U.S. products to the benefit of the U.S. population generally.

At the outset of World War II in late 1939, working with the private, elite Council on Foreign Relations, the U.S. government began planning for the post-war era. According to Laurence H. Shoup and William Minter, in their 1977 book *Imperial Brain Trust*,

> The main issue for consideration [in this planning] was whether America could be self-sufficient and do without the markets and raw materials of the British Empire, Western hemisphere, and Asia. The Council thought that the answer was no and that, therefore, the United States had to enter the war and organize a new world order satisfactory to the United States.

For the United States, the outcome of the war was successful, of course, not only in its immediate military goal of defeating the Axis Powers, but also in establishing U.S. dominance and relatively unfettered access to the markets and raw materials of what the planning referred to as the "Grand Area."

Among the concerns of the planners' efforts to secure the "Grand Area" was Southeast Asia. In one of their memoranda, they wrote, "the Philippine Islands, the Dutch East Indies, and British Malaya are prime sources of raw materials very important to the United States in peace and war; control of these lands by a potentially hostile power would greatly limit our freedom of action." Vietnam would later become the focal point of securing this area from a "hostile power."

The Issue Is Access

The issue in all of this is not the value of some particular resource or raw material. The issue is always access—access that is unfettered by a hostile local government or by costly regulations designed to promote local economic expansion. Since early in the 20th century, access to oil has been a dominant factor in the foundation of U.S. prosperity, and access to oil has often meant political-military dominance of lower-income countries. Access to oil, however, has not meant simply that the United States would be able to purchase the oil produced in other countries, but that U.S. oil companies would be able to play the central role in controlling that oil and reaping the associated profits. Whatever other motivations were involved in the U.S. invasion of Iraq and the more recent actions against Venezuela, oil was certainly a major factor. (See Arthur MacEwan, "Is It Oil?" *D&S*, May/June 2003 and "Is It Oil?—The Issue Revisited," *D&S*, March/April 2017.)

The dominance by U.S. companies of the global oil industry certainly brought profits to the companies. Yet, as the economy became increasingly oil-dependent, oil was relatively inexpensive, providing a major element in the foundation of U.S. prosperity. And much of this oil came from low-income countries. The formation of the Organization of Petroleum Exporting Countries (OPEC) in 1960 did bring about some change, forcing up the price of oil.

Varied Impacts: Countries or Classes?

However, the major oil companies have been able to maintain a great deal of power through sharing more with the elites of some of the oil-source countries. This "sharing" experience with oil, which is common in much of the relation between U.S. firms and the low-income countries in which they operated, underscores the point that it is not quite accurate to say that *countries* are exploited by U.S. operations. Different social groups—different classes—in the countries are affected quite differently by these operations, some are thoroughly exploited while others benefit.

In the 21st century, the focus of U.S. economic connections to poor countries has shifted somewhat. Markets and raw materials remain important, but low-cost labor and lax (or lack of) environmental regulations have become important as well. All along, financial activity has played a role (see the Smedley Butler box). Access to low-cost labor and avoidance of environmental regulations have often been obtained indirectly, through reliance on local contractors supplying goods to U.S. firms (subcontracting). Walmart is a prime example, but many other firms that have been able to provide to U.S. consumers the inexpensive items produced by low-wage labor.

It is true that many of the workers supplying goods to the United States have better jobs than they had had prior to engagement with the U.S. market. And, on a broader level, some countries have attained economic growth (though its benefits often go disproportionally to elites) from the connection to the U.S. economy. Nonetheless, U.S. prosperity at least in part depends on those workers receiving low wages, often working in unsafe or unclean environments, and denied basic rights. (See John Miller, "After Horror, Apologetics: Sweatshop apologists cover for intransigent U.S. retail giants," *D&S*, September/October 2013.)

Moreover, in examining the impact of U.S. firms' operations in low-income countries, a distinction needs to be made between the immediate and direct impact and the longer-run more general impact. The former may carry benefits, as the trade and investment created by these operations can generate some economic expansion and much needed jobs in the low-income countries. Over the longer run, however, U.S. engagement tends to support unequal social structures and a weakening of an internal foundation for long-run prosperity in the countries. Furthermore, the U.S. government, in its role as supporter of U.S. firms' operations around the world, has often intervened to prevent social change that might have led to real improvements in the lives of people in low-income countries. (The list of interventions that Smedley Butler gives only begins to tell the story.)

Pillars of Prosperity

In addition to the international economic relations between the United States and low-low income countries, there are also extensive economic relations with other high-income countries. Indeed, the majority of U.S. global trade and the majority of foreign investment by U.S. firms is with other high-income countries. This activity does not generally have the same exploitive characteristics as does U.S. firms' penetration of low-income parts of the world. Both are pillars on which U.S. prosperity has depended.

There are other pillars as well. For example, the relative high degree of education of the U.S. population and the skills that many immigrants brought with them to this country are also pillars of prosperity. But, surely, the exploitation of people in low-income countries has been an important pillar. ❑

Sources: Smedley D. Butler, *War is a Racket: The Antiwar Classic by America's Most Decorated Soldier*; Walter Rodney, *How Europe Underdeveloped Africa*; Andre Gunder Frank, *The Development of Underdevelopment*; Arthur MacEwan, "Capitalist Expansion, Ideology and Intervention," *Review of Radical Political Economics*, Vol. 4, No. 1, Winter 1972.

Article 10.4

WHATEVER HAPPENED TO DEVELOPMENT?

BY JAWIED NAWABI
January/February 2018

Since World War II, if we count the number of countries that can be considered to have moved from being "Third World" (or "developing") countries to being developed countries, how many make the list? By my count it would be five: South Korea, Taiwan, Singapore, Hong Kong, and Qatar. China is on its way and certain regions of China are already fit to be termed "developed." In Africa, out of the 54 countries, we cannot confidently tally any to have attained developed status (South Africa is termed an "emerging market economy"). Latin America has had several more decades since independence to build an industrial base. (Most of Latin America, not including the Caribbean, nominally gained independence between the 1820s and 1880s, 80–150 years before most of Africa, the Caribbean (outside of Haiti), and most of Asia.) However, the region's industry has not reached globally competitive levels compared to the Asian "Tigers." Latin America and the Caribbean's share of world income grew from about 5.8% in 1985 to about 7.2% in 2010. Meanwhile, East Asia and Pacific's (excluding Japan) grew from 4.1% in 1985 to 11.6% in 2010.

An increasing share of total world income has been going to the developing part of the world. In 1995, about 17.5% of world income went to 83% of the world population (developing countries); by 2010, the figure had increased to about 30.3% (mostly because of East Asia). But that means that about 70% of the income still went to the richest 17% of the world population (the developed world) down from about 83%. This distribution is still starkly uneven: About 3 billion people, out of a world population of 7 billion, live on less than $2.50 a day, and about half of them (1.5 billion) live on less than $1.25, experiencing what international development agencies call "extreme poverty." Out of those living in extreme poverty, 800–900 million (depending on how we count) experience hunger or what the United Nations terms "chronic undernourishment." Out of these hundreds of millions of hungry people, one million children die yearly from malnourishment. So why have so few countries—out of about 120 newly independent countries that have emerged since World War II—achieved successful development?

The Optimism of Decolonization and Hope of Development

This question poses a challenge to mainstream economics, which has theorized that less-developed countries enjoy certain "advantages of backwardness" (like being able to copy technologies already developed elsewhere). If they simply have high rates of saving and investment in physical capital, within one to two generations they should be able to reach income parity with the developed world. So why haven't they?

After World War II, with the struggles of de-colonization movements, the concept of "growth and development" for Third World countries became an ideological battleground. The industrialized capitalist countries, engaged in postwar reconstruction, experienced an economic boom that is today considered "the Golden Age of Capitalism." Meanwhile, the Third World countries that had gained political independence remained mired in poverty and destitution. And because of the fear for the spread of the socialist system, the governments of the advanced capitalist West constantly pushed Third World governments, even to the point of using covert and overt physical force, to adopt to the laws of the "free market" and "free trade." The capitalist market system, they assured the Third World leaders, would surely move their countries out of poverty and towards prosperity and progress.

What had to happen, according to probably the most influential and famous modernist theorist, Walt Whitman Rostow, was for so-called backward countries to emulate Western ways. Rostow believed that development was a linear path through five stages along which all countries travel. The five stages were traditional society, the preconditions for takeoff, the takeoff, the drive to maturity, and the age of high consumption. Of course, the West had traveled these paths and reached the ultimate destination, which is the mature capitalist economic system and high-mass consumption. All that had to happen now was for the West to share its technology, capital, educational systems, forms of government, and most especially their value system, with those traditional countries. Then the latter, too, would be able to achieve the preconditions that would propel them into economic takeoff. This assumes the advantage to the newly independent countries of not having to "reinvent the wheel" of how to develop.

Keynesian policies—especially government management of total demand, with the aim of maintaining economic growth and high employment—were used in the West to help reconstruct their economies after World War II. So the core Western international institutions and mainstream economics field, between the 1950s and 1960s, tolerated or even encouraged a more central role for the state in the economic development for the newly independent countries. However, the modernist theories and the mainstream economic theories did not have a sophisticated understanding

---

What Is the "Third World"?

The term "Third World" refers to a wide array of countries which have wide living standard differences today but that share a common colonial historical background. They are predominately countries of Asia, Africa, and Latin America/Caribbean that have gained formal political independence since World War II and that were part of a non-aligned movement during the Cold War. The non-alignment movement originated with the intention to chart a third path of political and economic development for the newly independent countries, different from either the U.S. model of capitalism or the Soviet model of communism. (Since they were not part of the "Western World" or the "Eastern World" in the previous "two world" division of the globe, the term "Third World" was coined.) In that spirit, they struggled to protect their political sovereignty and formulate approaches to development which would not be dominated by the leading powers. Today, these same countries (about 125 of them) are struggling against the onslaught of neoliberalism. Thus, "Third World" is not just a geographic designation of countries of the Global South nor an economic category but rather a conceptual project of newly independent countries who have struggled to develop their own economic and political systems without being dominated by the big colonial/neocolonial powers.

of the legacies of colonialism and their role in the Third World countries' impoverished economies and lack of proper developmental institutions. Their equations assumed all states to be the same (just like the dominant model of economic growth assumed that all countries had access to the same level of technology). Thus, they did not differentiate between the newly independent countries and the developed Western states in terms of state effectiveness.

Unfortunately, colonialism had forcefully incorporated the Third World countries as subordinate economies, solely producing primary (raw materials) commodities for advanced capitalist markets. The diversity, scope, and technological sophistication of local industry was suppressed. In the years following independence, these asymmetric trade relations resulted in further disadvantages for Third World countries, in the form of deteriorating "terms of trade" of their primary commodities for the manufactured goods of the developed economies. Raul Prebisch and Hans Singer's empirical studies showed how the prices of the Third World countries' primary products steadily declined relative to those of the manufactured products they purchased from the advanced developed countries—a pattern that continued from the 1950s to the late 1990s.

It takes more and more cocoa, rubber, coffee, tea, bananas, tin, or copper to buy an automobile, a truck or a piece of heavy equipment. When an index of the prices of non-fuel primary commodities is divided by an index of the unit value of manufactured goods constructed so their ratio is 100 in 1960, this ratio is found to have fallen from 131 in 1900, and it continues falling to reach 67 in 1986.

By the early 1970s it had become clear that this was leading the developing countries into balance of payment problems: they were importing much more than exporting, which left little capital for investing into the advancement of their economies, kept them dependent on manufactured parts and goods from the developed world, and resulted in a major debt crisis. Data from the World Bank show the continuing falling prices of non-fuel commodities up to 1999.

On the political level, most of the new independent countries—mostly in Africa and Asia, the majority in Latin America and the Caribbean—lacked state institutions which were linked to and dependent on the population for the majority of their revenues. Instead, these countries were saddled with colonial state institutions which were designed by the colonizing powers to extract resources through despotic power. The term "despotic power," as used by sociologist Michael Mann, means having coercive power over society. In states with "despotic power" policing and military capabilities are emphasized, but administrative capacity for complex projects (like building rural roads, electrical power grids, public housing and transportation, public education, etc.) remains limited. Postcolonial states, with only very rare exceptions, did not have built-in professionalized bureaucracies which were accountable to the masses of the people. The postcolonial state was not open to the influence of civil society institutions—like labor unions that advocate for safer work conditions, rural farmers who want local rural roads, or a legal system independent from the coercive powers of the state. Since the postcolonial states were forcefully grafted onto indigenous societies, the governing elites were not challenged to build what Mann terms infrastructural power—power through society instead of over society.

The states which emerged from the post-World War II independence struggles exhibited the characteristics of either predatory or intermediate states. Governing elites were mainly from the landed class, part of the oligarchy which controlled the resources of the country. Alternately, if there emerged a political elite ideologically committed to the country's national development, it was not able to gain sufficient autonomy from the oligarchy to direct an independent course for the country's economy on behalf of the majority of its population. Instead, the states that emerged were dependent upon international sources for financial and military support and not sufficiently embedded with their own populations.

Neoliberalism: From State-Led to Market-Led Development

By the 1970s, the economies of the Third World had not shown significant results in converging towards the economies of the developed countries. Meanwhile, inside the United States and other developed economies, there was a counter-reaction to Keynesian policies, which business and government elites blamed for slow growth and high inflation (known as "stagflation"). This created the intellectual and political climate for a backlash against the role of the state in the economy. The argument was that "government is too big," stifling private entrepreneurship and investment—thus, there was a need to privatize state services and deregulate private industries. The state was viewed as creating opportunities for corruption and distorting the market's efficient allocation of resources. This was the start of so-called "free market" (or "neoliberal") policies, which were pushed on the Third World by international financial institutions like the World Bank and International Monetary Fund (IMF). Starting in the 1970s, they started placing policy conditions on loans and other forms of assistance for developing countries much more explicitly than previous decades.

Preventing states from intervening in the economy and unleashing the disciplining pressures of market competition, the argument went, would make the developing countries' economies perform more efficiently and productively. According to neoliberal theory (or the "Washington Consensus") the behavior of individuals in the market, due to self-interested motivations, was also capable of explaining public official malfeasance. As economist Ha-Joon Chang described the Washington Consensus in his article "The Economic Theory of the Developmental State," which was published in *The Developmental State*:

> Its contention was that the universally valid assumption of self-seeking motives by individuals should also be applied to politics as well as to economics and that it is therefore wrong to believe that the objective of the state, which is ultimately determined by certain individuals, will be commensurate with what is good for society. On this premise, various models of neo-liberal political economy characterized the state as an organization controlled by interest group, politicians or bureaucrats who utilize it for their own self-interest, producing socially undesirable outcomes. The possibility that at least some state may be run and influenced by groups whose objectives are not mere self-enrichment or personal aggrandizement but less personal things such as welfare statism or economic modernization was not even seriously contemplated on the grounds of the alleged self-seeking motives behind all human actions.

For the neoliberals, the solution was to deregulate private industries and privatize industries owned by Third World governments. Both government regulation and government ownership, it was believed, allowed officials to enrich themselves—demanding kickbacks and engaging in other "rent-seeking" behavior. Privatization would force these inefficient and subsidized industries to become disciplined, to adopt reforms and boost efficiency or else be punished by the competitive pressures of the market system. Competition would determine whether any particular industry or firm would swim or sink, depending on whether the proper reforms were made or not, and hence, indirectly benefit society with cheaper and higher-quality goods and services, and higher tax revenues.

The problem with the neoliberal theory of the state is that it does not distinguish between the various types of states that have existed in the capitalist world. Clearly, during the 1970s, the states of the developed world could not be considered to be as corrupt or inept as the newly independent states of the Third World. Neoliberal theory assumes that the minimalist state in an automatic evolution of state institutions in all capitalist societies. However, it is in these very basic bureaucratic functions that many developing nations have a critical shortage. It would have made sense to help the latter states become more institutionally effective, to build their infrastructural power so that they could perform at least the minimal state functions that neoliberalism delegated to the state. Instead, the World Bank/IMF complex, with their neoliberal policies, further weakened the already institutionally limited developmental aspects of these states, while helping to strengthen some of their policing powers. The developing countries were nudged, cajoled, even strong-armed to abandon the state-led model of development and adopt the market-led development model.

Listing the various roles of the state and the state's degree of involvement in the economy, moving from the most basic functions to the most extensive interventions:

- Legal protection of private property, contract enforcement, and regulation
- Defense of the state's sovereignty and territorial integrity (essentially policing the workers and the population at large)
- Provision of public goods and services (schools, infrastructure, health, clean water, sanitation, and rural and urban services)
- Counter-cyclical policies (monetary and fiscal) due to the instability of the market system
- Welfare services: unemployment, retirement, poverty programs
- Coordination of development projects (indicative planning through public-private cooperation)

The neoliberal advice to governments was and is basically to focus on the first two functions, while delegating the remaining functions as much as possible to a private sector exposed to the disciplinary pressures of competitive markets. The prediction was that private firms would do a much better job than the state in providing affordable private schools, clean water, health clinics, infrastructure like roads and bridges (with tolls), and private financial services for everyone from small farmers in the villages to large firms in the cities.

One would assume that, if the World Bank/IMF complex was advising the developing countries to downsize the state role in the economy, the total government expenditure (federal, state, and local) as the share of the economy would shrink in the advanced capitalist economies as well. In fact, as political economist Atilio Boron argues, the developed countries do not practice what they preach to the developing world. Between 1970 and 1995, Boron shows, the core capitalist countries' average government expenditures grew from about 35% to 49%. Furthermore, in the 1990s "the proportion of public employees over the total population was 7.2% in the United States, 8.3% in Germany, 8.5% in England, 9.7% in France." Comparatively, in Latin America, public employees represented 3.5% of the population in Brazil and 2.8% in Chile and Argentina. Despite these numbers, Boron observes, the "pundits at the World Bank or the IMF have successfully insisted that Latin American states are 'too big' and should be downsized."

Even when we look at the financial press, we don't find much evidence that the economies with the least state involvement are the best performing economies for businesses to invest in. On the contrary, *Forbes* magazine, today one of the foremost publications in defense of the "free market" and "free enterprise," in 2016 ranked Sweden number one on its list of the top countries in which to do business. If we scroll down the same list, the top 10 countries include Denmark, Holland, Finland, Norway, Ireland, England, and Canada. On average, their states account for 30–45% of GDP. Ironically, the very countries that are bastions of so-called welfare states (derogatorily called "nanny states") are considered by the pro-capitalist press to be the best places for business investors.

In almost all developing countries (in Latin America and the Caribbean, Africa, the Middle East, and South East Asia) the state contribution to GDP is much lower. For example, Mexico's is about 15% and Chile's is a little more than 20%. They are examples of the developing countries which arguably have insufficient government involvement as a percentage of their economies GDPs. Furthermore, these states rely overwhelmingly on indirect taxation like sales taxes and value added taxes (VAT), so their tax structures tend to be regressive (the poor and middle-class pay more). In contrast, the developed countries tend to rely on income and property taxes (direct taxes), and so have more progressive taxation (the higher income classes pay more).

While neoliberalism was able to push the developing world away from state-led development toward more market-oriented policies, these latter policies have not shown positive results either. Economists Mark Weisbrot and Rebecca Ray have surveyed the scorecard on development between 1960 and 2010: The developing countries had higher growth rates during the years of government-led development, from 1960 to 1980, averaging about 2.5% per year, compared to 1.1% between 1980 and 2000—the high years of neoliberal policy. Latin America's average annual real GDP per capita growth rate in the era of "too big" government, 1960–1980, was 3.3%; during the height of the neoliberal era, 1980–2000, just 0.3%.

Bringing the State Back into Economic Development

During the 1980s, while the majority of the developing world (and even the developed world) was experiencing declining growth rates, the East Asian countries were experiencing high growth. The institutions of the World Bank/IMF complex attempted to credit the East Asian economies' high growth rates to their adoptions of market policies. Scholars such as Chalmers Johnson, Alice Amsden, Robert Wade, Peter Evans, and others (together, I term them the Role of the State in Economic Development, or RSED, school) critically responded to the neoliberal assumptions of efficient markets and government malfeasance as too simplistic and without sufficient historical depth. They were able to empirically establish that state intervention in rapidly industrializing countries of East Asia was, "characterized by market-reinforcing behavior, understood in the sense of supporting profitability for private investors. ... The state-versus-market mind-set thus is simply not very helpful for understanding how the interaction of states and markets has served to produce a range of economic outcomes." So, instead of blanket generalizations—whether they come from the left, which views the state as nothing more than the executive committee of the bourgeoisie, or from the right, which argues that state intervention necessarily hinders economic growth and development—the real question is what kind of administrative structure do states need in order to enable growth and development within a market economy?

To the RSED school, this question required detailed study of each state. Why did some states perform as developmental states—guiding their economies to high living standards—while other states became predatory and impoverished their people? The fundamental characteristics of a developmental state are a determined elite which seeks their country's rapid development; relative autonomy of the state from powerful landed and industrial elites; a rational bureaucracy which is competent, powerful, and insulated from political swings; a somewhat authoritarian character which ensures that competing interests are subordinated to states' developmental goals of industrialization; and the capacity to manage effectively the economic sector through a broad range of policies. (The most important economic policies include tariffs, financial credit controls, technological promotion, human capital training, and competency in selecting which market signals to deliberately distort. Yes, states can promote development by deliberately altering market signals and incentives, for example, by using subsidies to help infant industries become competitive in the international market. The developmental state, in short, is the highest authority committed to economic development through growth, productivity, and competitiveness.

The relationship between the state and market need not be a zero-sum relationship, but rather can be one of synergy. The argument of the RSED school was that market society could not be what it is without the role of the state. The active role of the state has been clear at least as far back as economic historian Karl Polanyi's masterpiece, *The Great Transformation: The Political and Economic Origins of Our Time* (1944). In the words of economist and Noble laureate Joseph Stiglitz, Polanyi's analysis "exposes the myth of the free market: there never was a truly free, self-regulating market system. In their transformations, the governments of today's industrialized countries took an active role, not only in protecting their industries through tariffs, but also in promoting new technologies."

Theories of development have two axes around which they revolve: state-led development versus market-led development. Economic theories can be distinguished conceptually by the centrality of the state's role in "governing the market." Some theories envision a limited and passive role for the state because they view the market as an efficient mechanism for allocating resources to meet society's developmental needs. Government intervention, in this view, distorts prices and throws the market system into disequilibrium. In contrast, developmental economists like Ragnar Nurske, Paul Rosentein-Rodan, Albert Hirschman, Gunnar Myrdal, and Arthur Lewis—whose influence within academia and international institutions was at its height from the 1940s to late 1960s—viewed the state the one institution that could lead the "big-push" out of the poverty traps that ensnared the Third World. Unfortunately, by the 1970s, neoliberal/neoclassical economists rejected the theories of state-led development economists and excluded them from the policy calculations of the World Bank/IMF complex as well as the United Nations Development Program (UNDP). After about 20 years of neoliberal dominance in academia and international institutions (from 1980 to 2000), the RSED school and their state-led theories of development made a comeback. They undermined the intellectual hegemony of the neoliberal paradigm, demonstrating in their own original works the administrative and regulatory importance of the developmental state. They showed that economic development requires a state that is effective in managing the monetary system, protecting private property laws, setting taxes, funding public goods such as infrastructure and education, coordinating between industries, and promoting long-term investment—that is, in all six functions of the state listed above.

Return to the 1950s Spirit of Development

If we are serious about solving the problem of development, we must bring back mass development projects through the developmental state. In the last 30 or 40 years, parallel to the downsizing of the states in the Third World, there has been a shift towards micro-oriented development projects. Such projects give nongovernmental organizations (NGOs) and other charity aid organizations a central role, supported by the international institutions as well as mainstream economic theory. We have to make the case to returning international institutions to developmental policies—to what political scientist Eric Helleiner calls the "Forgotten Legacy of Bretton Woods"—infant industry tariffs protections, commodity price stabilization, international debt restructuring, short-term capital movement restrictions, and long-term development lending. In the spirit of the 1950s and 1960s, we must bring back the socially transforming aims of development policy—which include building the institutional capacity of states to collect taxes on a progressive basis, redistributing wealth through policies like radical land reforms, etc. Last but not least, the Third World needs to revive the planning and execution of their own regionally based and environmentally sustainable industrial policies. For these projects to be realized, we need to build the developmental capacity of the Third World states. ❑

Sources: Nina Bandelj and Elizabeth Sowers, *Economy and State: A Sociological Perspective* (Polity Press, 2010); Nancy Birdsall, Augusto De La Torre, and Rachel Menezes, *Fair Growth: Economic Policies for Latin America's Poor and Middle-Income Majority* (Center for Global Development and Inter-American Dialogue, 2008); A. Atilio Boron, "Latin American Thinking on the State and Development: From Statelessness to Statelessness," in Sam Moyo and Paris Yeros (eds.), *Reclaiming the Nation: The Return of the National Question in Africa, Asia and Latin America* (Pluto Press, 2011); Fred Block, "The Roles of the State in the Economy," in Neil J. Smelser and Richard Swedberg; Ana Corbacho, Vicente Fretes Cibils, and Eduardo Lora (eds.), *More Than Revenue: Taxation as a Developmental Tool* (Palgrave Macmillan, 2013); Ha-Joon Chang, "The Economic Theory of the Developmental State," in Meredith Woo-Cumings (ed.), *The Developmental State* (Cornell University Press, 1999); James Cypher, *The Process of Economic Development* (Routledge, 2014); Robert Chernomas and Ian Hudson, *Economics in the Twenty-First Century: A Critical Perspective* (University of Toronto Press, 2016); Peter Evans, *Embedded Autonomy: States & Industrial Transformation* (Princeton University Press, 1995); Stephan Haggard, *Pathways From the Periphery: The Politics of Growth in the Newly Industrializing Countries* (Cornell University Press, 1990); Eric Helleiner, "International Policy Coordination for Development: The Forgotten Legacy of Bretton Woods" United Nations Conference on Trade and Development (UNCTAD Discussion Papers, No. 221), May 2015; Chalmers Johnson, *MITI and The Japanese Miracle: The Growth of Industrial Policy, 1925-1975* (Stanford University Press, 1982); Atul Kohli, *State-Directed Development: Political Power and Industrialization in the Global Periphery* (Cambridge University Press, 2004); Jonathan Krieckahaus, *Dictating Development: How Europe Shaped the Global Periphery* (University of Pittsburgh Press, 2006); Matthew Lange and Dietrich Rueschemeyer, "States and Development," in Lange, Matthew and Dietrich Rueschemeyer, *States and Development: Historical Antecedents of Stagnation and Advance* (Palgrave Macmillan, 2005); Adrian Leftwich, *States of Development: On the Primacy of Politics in Development* (Polity Press, 2000); Michael Mann, *The Sources of Social Power: The Rise of Classes and Nation States, 1760-1914* (Vol.2) (Cambridge University Press, 1993); S.V.R. Nasr, "European Colonialism and The Emergence of Modern Muslim States," in John L. Esposito (ed.), *The Oxford History of Islam* (Oxford University Press, 1999); Ziya Onis, "The Logic of the Developmental State," *Comparative Politics*, Vol. 24, No. 1 (pp. 109-126), October 1991; James Petras, "Imperialism and NGOs in Latin America," *Monthly Review*, Vol. 49, Issue 7, December 1997; Prashant Prakash, "Property Taxes Across G20 Countries: Can India Get It Right?" Oxfam India Working Papers, January 2013; Vijay Prashad, *The Darker Nations: A People's History of the Third World* (New Press, 2007); Louis Putterman, *Dollars and Change: Economics in Context* (Yale University Press, 2001); Revenue Statistics 2016: Tax Revenue Trends in OECD (oecd.org); Joseph Stiglitz, "Foreword," in Karl Polanyi, *The Great Transformation: The Political and Economic Origins of Our Time* (Beacon Press, 2001); Bob Sutcliffe, *100 Ways of Seeing an Unequal World* (Zed Books, 2001); David Waldner, *State Building and Late Development* (Cornell University Press, 1999); Mark Weisbrot and Rebecca Ray, "The Scorecard on Development, 1960-2010: Closing the Gap?" United Nations Department of Economic and Social Affairs (UN DESA Working Paper No. 106), June 2011.

Article 10.5

FORD DRIVES AWAY
The neoliberal right oversees the deindustrialization of Brazil.

BY DÉBORA NUNES
September/October 2021

Since 2020, a growing number of companies have stopped manufacturing in Brazil, including Ford, Mercedes Benz, and Volkswagen. Since President Jair Bolsonaro's election, Brazil has also pursued a range of neoliberal policies, including radical cuts in social security coverage, a freeze in the minimum wage, and deep cuts in government investment. The departure of such companies seems to show that Bolsonaro's attempts to woo foreign corporations to Brazil are backfiring.

At the beginning of this year, Ford announced the permanent closure of all three of its factories in Brazil, ending more than 100 years of automobile production in the country. What is it about the Brazilian economy that made Ford stop producing vehicles in a country that represents more than 50% of automobile sales in South America? And why are industries from different sectors—ranging from electronics to pharmaceuticals—deciding to do the same?

To answer these questions, it's important to understand the economic context and the policies designed by the federal government that promoted a boom in the automobile sector during the previous decade. With the election of Luiz Inácio Lula da Silva, a former union leader from the left-wing Workers' Party (PT), in 2002, journalists at Brazil's two largest newspapers predicted that, under PT leadership, Brazil's investment environment was going to worsen. Then, when the party was ousted through a farcical coup in 2016 and Bolsonaro was elected in 2018, they claimed that the country would start to attract investment again. But it seems that the story is exactly the opposite: Many companies that arrived and/or expanded their businesses during the PT's government are now leaving. Exploring the reasons behind Ford's departure, as well as the government's response and what they are trying to do to prevent other companies from leaving, is key to understanding why all these efforts have failed.

Ford in Brazil: From Boom to Bust

Brazil's government has a long track record of supporting the automotive industry through federal programs, due to its unique job generation and technological development capacities. Facilitated by loans from the Brazilian Development Bank (BNDES)—a key state-owned entity at the epicenter of the PT's attempt to promote industrial development—the fiscal incentives and special withholding allowances provided through these programs were able to keep the industry thriving on Brazilian soil: The number of vehicles (including cars, buses, and trucks) produced monthly grew steadily from 2000 to 2013, jumping from 92,704 units in January 2000 to a peak of 352,328 units in May 2013 (thereby creating 84,917 new high-wage, high-benefit automotive jobs). (See James M. Cypher, "Brazil's Big Push," *D&S*, March/April 2013.)

Ford's decision to leave Brazil will result in 5,000 direct layoffs and the loss of more than 40,000 indirect jobs, according to the Inter-Union Department of Statistics and Socio-Economic Studies (DIEESE). However, the actual number of jobs that will be lost is much higher. Focusing on inter-industry relationships—derived from an input-output model of the economy showing how an output from one sector may become an input to another—and how this relationship impacts household incomes, the actual number of lost jobs was estimated to be 118,864. Not only will lost wages heavily impact Brazil's now fragile economy, but so too will lost tax revenues, which will mean further austerity cuts to public programs.

Before Ford ran for the exit, the average unemployment rate in the country for 2020 was 13.5%, which means 13.4 million Brazilians were unemployed. In addition, the number of discouraged workers—meaning working age people who have given up on finding a job—grew 16.1% from 2019 to 2020.

In the company's official statement, Ford mentioned the "continuity of the unfavorable economic environment" and the "additional pressure caused by the pandemic" as the main reasons for their decision to leave Brazil. The decreasing participation of Ford in the country's automobile sales was also a widely cited argument. Before its departure, Ford had dropped to the sixth position in national auto sales, while newer brands in the market, like Hyundai, saw their sales rankings increase (Hyundai is currently ranked fourth), and the impending arrival of giant Chinese firms such as Great Wall Motor, which took over Mercedes in July, would have put additional pressure on Ford. The pandemic was considered the final blow.

Mainstream economists were quick to back up Ford's explanation for pulling production out of Brazil. Industry groups and publications—including the National Confederation of Industry (CNI) and the economy experts of *Folha de São Paulo* and *O Estado de São Paulo* (two of the biggest newspapers nationwide)—were quick to blame the "unfavorable economic environment" together with the struggles of the traditional automobile industry worldwide (given the increasing demand for more energy efficient forms of transportation).

However, the problem with these arguments is that they don't explain why there are so many industries, from a diverse array of sectors, that are shutting down their Brazilian factories, nor why these closures began several years before the pandemic. If decreasing sales are driving Ford's decision to leave, why are Mercedes-Benz and Volkswagen also closing their factories in Brazil, despite their relatively stable market shares? And if the problem is the automobile industry, then why are Sony (electronics), Mitutoyo (measuring instruments and metrological technology), and Roche (pharmaceuticals)—just to name a few—leaving Brazil, too?

The only explanation left, as mainstream economists would have it, is the "Brazilian Cost," a term invented by the right wing to falsely allege that there are a number of investment-discouraging conditions endemic to the country, which include tax burdens, government corruption, high minimum wages, and generous employment benefits. Further, they insist that sweeping austerity measures must be taken to address these conditions. However, despite the insistence of Brazil's right wing, there is little evidence to support their claims.

This warped Brazilian Cost framework is the enemy of the "Confidence Fairy," a term coined by Paul Krugman a decade ago to capture that famous make-believe force that rewards well-behaved countries—meaning the ones that implement strict fiscal austerity measures, privatize industries, and obey the traditional policies that once upon a time were strongly advocated by the World Bank and mandatory for receiving International Monetary Fund loans—by stimulating spending that offsets the impact of such drastic funding cuts.

Since, in this fantasy, the Confidence Fairy allegedly brings investment, the Brazilian Cost is the main (and often, the only) justification for a spate of austerity measures in Brazil's recent history. But attempts to carry out these changes have backfired, causing the corporate interests that Brazil once attempted to woo to run toward the nearest exit instead.

Workers' Party Out, Businesspeople In

Though Brazil's corporate exodus kicked into high gear with the election of Bolsonaro, its origins can be traced back to the push for President Dilma Rousseff's impeachment, which started in December 2015. After her first term, which was successful enough to guarantee a (tight) reelection in 2014, a devastating two-year recession in 2015 and 2016 caused the country's economy to contract by almost 7%. This crisis divided the PT, to which Rousseff belonged, and their allies into two camps: the PT believed that continuing to rely on government spending to increase aggregate demand was the way to go (a strategy preferred by Rousseff); while others pushed for a strategic reduction of government expenditures and the promotion of more "market friendly" policies.

Led by a coalition of center and right-wing parties, together with powerful business owners who had benefited from massive federal loans that were made available during the Rousseff administration, the PT's opponents moved into high gear: The representatives of capital sought to destroy the PT's legitimacy, alleging widespread corruption emanating from BNDES, through the state-owned petroleum company Petrobras and beyond. Investigations of alleged PT corruption were wildly hyped by the media, inflaming protests by the (newly formed) Brazilian upper-middle classes and resulting in a weird mix of contradictory government actions that tried to please everyone. For instance, on the one hand, there were no immediate cuts to government spending, yet on the other hand, Joaquim Levy—a banker with a Ph.D. from the University of Chicago, famous for supporting fiscal austerity—was nominated to become the Minister of Finance. By March 2016, when Rousseff was still in charge, Eaton, Maxion, and Randon, all companies from the metallurgical sector, announced the closure of their production plants in São Paulo—warning, of course, that her attempts to remedy the crisis were not extensive enough.

After Rousseff's staged coup/impeachment in August 2016, Vice President Michel Temer, a member of a center-right party, became the acting president. By December 2016, he approved the most radical fiscal austerity plan in the country's history—a 20-year freeze on all primary federal expenses—which is particularly extreme for a country in which the government is the primary provider of health care and higher education. Just six months later, the most radical labor reforms (nicknamed "Labor Deform" by social movements) since the Consolidation of the Labor Laws—which laid the foundation for workplace protections and was approved in

1943—extinguished mandatory union tax contributions, increased the cap on daily working hours from eight to 12, decreased paid vacation days, and weakened workers' bargaining power overall. But these sweeping changes did little to generate the increased investment that austerity advocates claimed would follow. The national GDP showed a 3.5% decrease in 2016 and a timid 1% increase in 2017; unemployment kept to historically high levels, averaging 12% and 12.7%, respectively; and investments fell 13.3% between 2016 and 2017.

The 2018 Elections and Industrial Policy

By the end of 2017, the mainstream diagnosis was that these austerity policies had not been sufficient: The solution, therefore, was to elect someone like Bolsonaro, a politically conservative retired military officer who garnered broad political support by being openly racist and misogynistic. Bolsonaro was elected despite proudly declaring in every interview that he didn't have an economic plan. Mainstream economists' strong support for the nomination of Paulo Guedes as Bolsonaro's minister of the economy further strengthened the case for voting for Bolsonaro—after all, that seemingly meant that Guedes would have the necessary authority to carry out his neoliberal agenda. (See James M. Cypher, "Neoliberalism Unchained: Jair Bolsonaro and the Rise of the Extreme Right in Brazil," *D&S*, January/February 2019.)

Most of Bolsonaro's political platform relied on destroying (or rebranding) all that the PT had created, starting with discontinuing one of their most controversial industrial policies—the Inovar-Auto incentive program—which ran from 2012 to 2018 and offered heavy fiscal incentives for automakers to invest in research, engineering, and development, with a big focus on the creation of local value chains. For example, one of the requisites for participating in Inovar-Auto was to utilize a list of domestically produced auto parts in at least 80% of the vehicles assembled by the company. Through this incentive program, the automotive sector also received large amounts of facilitated loans through BNDES: between 2002 and 2018, Ford's Brazil operations alone received R$5.5 billion (equivalent to $2.4 billion in U.S. dollars) in credits. Bolsonaro made his lack of support for these kinds of initiatives clear when he publicly called Rota 2030, the program designed as a continuation of Inovar-Auto, "a waste of money," and his economic team declared that it was against continuing the program.

During the first year of Bolsonaro's administration in 2019, his clear intention to focus on commodity exports (Brazil's "natural endowment" as stressed by Guedes) and not incentivize the industrial sector was explicit in the numbers: According to the United Nation's Industrial Development Organization, in 2018, Brazil occupied the ninth position in the worldwide ranking of value added to GDP by manufacturing; in 2019, the country fell to the 16th position. From the start, Guedes was very explicit about his plan for reducing the state's promotion of industry through privatization, as well as social security and fiscal reforms. To increase investors' confidence, he also kept claiming that the Brazilian economy was going to take off at any moment—which contradicted Bolsonaro's statements in the press that "the country is financially broke" and his administration "can't do anything about it."

Presently, the government's privatization efforts are not going as fast as Guedes would wish, but he's very clear about the government's goal of privatizing the Brazilian Postal Office (*Correios*), Eletrobras (Latin America's biggest power utility company), and the Brazilian Bank. Petrobras, the state-owned Brazilian multinational corporation in the petroleum industry, is already seeing some of its operations become privatized. The administration's desired fiscal reforms are also proving difficult to implement and will require enticing Brazilian congress members to support the reforms by directing a few billion Reais to specific congressional districts via parliamentary amendments. So far, Guedes's only major win was the approval of social security reforms, which were signed in 2019, together with the stagnation of the minimum wage (per law, any increases in Brazil's minimum wage are determined by inflation rates and GDP growth), and the termination of the country's environmental protection agency.

So, after the ouster of Rousseff, the creation of a strict financial austerity program for the next 20 years, the approval of labor reforms, the election of President Bolsonaro (and Guedes' appointment), and the approval of social security reforms, one would expect that Brazil's economy would finally attract the investments it seeks. But that hasn't happened. Even after years of recession, Brazil's GDP grew a modest 1% in 2018, with an 11.6% unemployment rate by the end of the year; 2019 also showed no improvement, again with a 1% GDP increase and an unemployment rate of 11.9%. Instead of promoting investment and innovation within the country, 2019 registered the largest flow of foreign capital out of the country (essentially capital flight) since 2004 (when such variables were first measured). What *did* increase during this period, however, was Brazil's Gini coefficient (which measures the degree of inequality in the distribution of income). After almost two decades of constant decline the country's Gini coefficient started rising in 2015, the year that efforts to destroy Rousseff began. This increase poses a very serious problem for Brazil, as it is already the most unequal country in Latin America.

To believe that Ford—and all those other companies—left Brazil due to the crisis of the automobile sector and unfavorable economic conditions is to ignore that, long before the travel restrictions wrought by the Covid-19 pandemic, the mythical Confidence Fairy never had a ticket booked to the country to start with. The radical attempts to reduce the fictional Brazilian Cost were a resounding failure, and didn't generate a flow of capital, employment, or growth. Ironically, Ford moved its operations to Argentina, a country that elected Alberto Fernández, a long-time member of a left-leaning Peronist party who campaigned on reversing the austerity measures of the previous administration, as their president in 2019. When Guedes was informed about those elections results, he declared that it was "the final tragedy;" maybe he should have specified for whom it was a tragedy. ❑

Sources: UOL, "Ford's departure reinforces warning about cost for production in the country, says Anfavea," Nov. 1, 2021 (uol.com.br); Center for Economic Development Studies, "Deindustrialization in Brazil is real and structural," 2021 (www3.eco.unicamp.br); Robson Braga de Andrade, "De-industrialization can make Brazil the farm of the world," CNI News Agency, Jan. 27, 2021 (noticias.portaldaindustria.com.br); Bento Antunes de Andrade Maia, "Is there deindustrialization in Brazil? A study of the classical approach and alternative analyzes between 1998 and 2014," *Economia e Sociedade*, May/August 2020; "Methodological Note on Calculating the Impact of Closure of Ford's activities in Brazil," The Inter-Union Department of Statistics and Socioeconomic Studies (dieese.org.br); "A Very Difficult Choice," *Estadão*, October 8, 2018, (opiniao.estado.com.br); Alexandre Garcia, "Skaf declares support for Jair Bolsonaro in an eventual 2nd round against PT," R7, October 4, 2018 (noticias.r7.com); Tassia Kastner, "Dollar drops to R$ 3.94 and Stock market soars after Ibope research advantageous to Bolsonaro," UOL, Oct. 2, 2018 (uol.com.br); Daniel Gallas and Daniele Palumbo, "What's gone wrong with Brazil's economy?," BBC, May 27, 2019 (bbc.com); "Michel Temer: Brazil ex-president arrested in corruption probe," BBC, March 21, 2019 (bbc.com); OECD, "Purchasing Power Parities" (data.oecd.org); Renato Souza, "Social Security Reform: Government released R$4.3 billion in parliamentary amendments," *Estado de Minas*, July 11, 2019 (em.com.br); Maria Carolina Abe and André Jankavski, "Ford announces end of car production in Brazil and closing of three factories," CNN, November 1, 2021 (cnnbrasil.com.br); Luis Barrucho, "Ford: after all, why did the automaker decide to stop producing vehicles in Brazil?," BBC, January 31, 2021 (bbc.com); "'Brazil is broke. I can't do anything,' Bolsonaro tells supporters," *Globo*, January 5, 2021 (globo.com); Mariana Fonseca, "The flight of foreign investors from the Stock Exchange continues and reaches R$ 87.5 billion in 2020, according to BC," InfoMoney, Oct. 15, 2020 (infomoney.com.br); "Opposition's return to power in Argentina is "final tragedy", says Guedes," Reuters, September 23, 2019 (reuters.com); UOL, "Guedes team blames Brazil cost and Chinese probe to take over Ford factories," January 12, 2021 (uol.com.br).

Article 10.6

POWER VS. POLICY IN GABRIEL BORIC'S CHILE

BY JAMES M. CYPHER
March/April 2022

During the presidency of dictator Augusto Pinochet (1973–1990) Chile's economy was guided by the diktat of his close ideological ally, British Prime Minister Margaret Thatcher: "There Is No Alternative" (TINA) to allowing market forces to control any society. The supposition is that such unconstrained forces will bring about a result no one intended—the order-out-of-chaos argument often ascribed to Adam Smith. But economists have generally ignored the empirical record documenting how market forces actually function—particularly in a nation on the periphery like Chile, whose economy is dominated by agriculture and mineral extraction and was long conditioned by Spanish colonial domination. Since the onset of the neoliberal shock in 1973, the country's atrophied socioeconomic structure has been marked by ever-rising economic insecurity for the vast majority in tandem with an unceasing celebration of the abundance showered on a prosperous faction who endlessly trumpet the virtues of Chile's "miracle."

More recently, the Chilean electorate signaled its belief that there *is* an alternative, by handing a strong electoral victory to leftist Gabriel Boric in the December 2021 presidential elections. Boric's victory was a rebuke of far-right candidate José Kast, who was wedded to maintaining Pinochet's core program—neoliberalism by shock therapy resulting in grinding economic insecurity for the vast majority of citizens, as the export-based, resource-based economy generated high profits for transnational mining corporations and Chilean oligarchs. Boric now has a popular mandate behind his program—to create a national health care system, restructure the private-sector controlled national pension system, revert the privatized educational system to public control, achieve gender balance in the private and public sectors, and expand rights for indigenous peoples (which could help settle land restitution disputes). But, by a slim margin the neoliberal right controls the Senate, and the House of Deputies is split.

To achieve any of these goals Boric will have to face down and overpower Chile's miniscule arch-conservative elite (see sidebar, "Oligarchic Conglomerate Capitalism") and their legions of supporters who twice elected the billionaire, rightist, and former president Sebastián Piñera, who served two terms in 2010–2014 and 2018–2022. At this elite's core there are perhaps 45 families, adept at public relations, who set the tone of the discourse, preserving the myth that Chile is the great exception in Latin America, that markets work, and that neoliberalism has created a new nation of prosperity and opportunity. Abroad, the myth of Chile as a great success story has always resonated. Chile is, after all, the Saudi Arabia of copper production, with a 26.7% world market share in 2021. Lately, it has become popular to frame copper as the "new oil," undergirding the coming "sustainable" electric vehicle era which also hinges, in part, on Chile's 32% share of global lithium production (a key mineral for auto batteries, with 60% of the high value-added processing occurring in China).

Chile is clearly at a turning point, in more ways than one. The political trajectory has been jarred while the commodities-based economic structure, dominated by transnational corporations and a tiny elite of wealthy families, may face serious challenges, beginning with Boric's commitment to creating a state-run lithium mine. He proposes to increase taxes on copper mining transnationals, push up their limp royalty payments, institute a wealth tax on Chile's oligarchs, and overhaul the porous income tax regime that has coddled Chile's affluent strata. How and to what degree all this will materialize remains to be seen. To get a better idea of Chile's present prospects, it is necessary to contextualize the underlying edifice of economic and political power, which will set the parameters for Boric and his allies, who are now confronting a vigorous pushback from those who have until now happily absconded with the economic surplus.

Do Economists Matter?

Chile must be the only country in the world where a contingent of the highest dignitaries awaits the scheduled arrival of any prominent visiting neoliberal economist. After all, the "Chicago Boys" were spawned by University of Chicago economists Milton Friedman and, most of all, Arnold Harberger. A graduate program at the University of Chicago recruited and indoctrinated generations of ambitious economics students who, armed with Ph.D.'s, returned to Chile ready to implement Pinochet's anti-statist, anti-labor agenda, which was designed to erase the legacy of socialist president Salvador Allende. From 1973 to the present, the Chicago Boys have largely framed economic policy in Chile. When, on March 11, 2022, billionaire president Piñera steps down, his powerful Chicago Boy treasury secretary (and Harberger admirer) Rodrigo Cerda will be shown the door.

Boric was supportive when financial kingpin Piñera renewed the term of his central bank president, former World Bank economist Mario Marcel. More than once, progressive governments in Latin America have been deflected by central bank leaders who are beholden to the interests of the financial elite, as is Marcel, thereby undercutting programs instituted by progressive governments. Marcel raised interest rates in 2021 while decrying modest annual inflation of 4.3%; it appeared that

---

A Refresher on Chilean Political History Since the 1970s

Augusto Pinochet led a military assault on Chile's first, and only, democratically elected socialist Salvador Allende (1970–1973). Allende's policies of land reform (breaking up some neo-feudal estates including, first, a one-million-plus-acre hacienda, the largest in the world) enraged owners, while his pro-union and income redistribution policies and the expropriation of foreign-owned copper mines set the stage for the coup. Once Pinochet lost power in 1990, he left an anti-labor, market-centered neoliberal legacy that constrained a series of undirected—vaguely center-left—governments from 1990 to 2010. These coalitions, known as *Concertación*, confronted an unyielding, financially powerful, right-wing coalition that used legislative power and media control to block meaningful change. The resulting impasse created political disaffection and fatigue, particularly among youth who increasingly declined to vote. Under these conditions, the right regained power, by a small margin, in the 2009 election. Then *Concertación* resumed governance after a strong victory in 2013 but failed to address stagnation and growing economic inequality. In 2017 the right won, but 53% of the country did not vote.

the central bank could tighten the monetary straitjacket by further raising interest rates, undermining Boric's plans to expand public-sector programs. But in a surprise move championed by leading oligarch Andrónico Luksic (see the "Oligarchic Conglomerate Capitalism" sidebar), Boric bowed to the pressure of the business elites and designated Marcel as his Treasury secretary in January 2022. This move allowed lame-duck Piñera to appoint Rossana Costa, previously the assistant director at the Friedman-oriented think tank Libertad y Desarrollo ("Liberty and Development"), as central bank president. According to Chilean journalist and academic María Mönckeberg, this think tank is "the principal center for the diffusion of right-wing thinking and opinion."

Likely the central bank president most aligned with Chicago Boy ideas anywhere, Costa will have a five-year term, longer than Boric's. The new president's ambitious economic proposals initially received a cool reception from the 3,000-member Federation of Chilean Industry, until Piñera's man became the new Treasury secretary. Next, with the announcement of Piñera's central bank replacement, the president of the Association for Production and Commerce (CPC)—the official "peak business organization" representing all manufacturing, mining, banking, construction, and commercial capital—effusively praised Costa's appointment. UCLA-based Chicago Boy Sebastián Edwards (scion of Chile's aristocracy and student of Harberger) pronounced Costa as the tonic to "calm financial markets and … national and international investors."

Now, Piñera's neoliberal agenda, through Costa and Marcel, will define the limits of economic policy. At the outset, they will likely act on the pressure brought by the CPC to trim the federal government's unprecedented 2021 fiscal deficit (estimated at 8.3% of GDP) and slow the early 2022 annual inflation rate of 7.7%, thereby sabotaging Boric's aspirational agenda by tightening credit, slicing away at progressives' budget priorities, slowing the economy, and raising unemployment.

Days before insider Marcel was accepted as the next finance minister, Boric gave a widely reported speech to business elites to announce that he would govern through "gradualism and fiscal responsibility." As to the tax changes he championed in the campaign, he said that "they should not be seen as a confrontation of classes." Once pushing an array of edgy proposals, Boric's delivery dissolved into espousing "dialogue," "moderation," and "responsibility"—indicating to these imperious titans that Boric plans to govern within the rules and parameters that *they* set. His obeisance was designed to calm a business elite which, in early January 2022, registered its lowest level of business confidence since August 2020 (the worst moment of the pandemic) telegraphing a pullback in investment that would slow the economy in spite of soaring commodity prices. Capital flight accelerated before Boric's victory—reaching levels not seen since the 2008–2009 recession—while affluent households converted their accounts into U.S. dollars at breakneck speed.

Before bowing to the financial sector, Boric had aligned himself—at least to a degree—with a "developmentalist" project, thereby rejecting the libertarian/neoliberal market-led strategy, breaking with a Chilean taboo. For example, with progressive economist José Ahumada, in April 2021, he proposed a public development bank that would direct investment into alternative energy production. Crucially, it would promote high-wage employment in mining (well-paying jobs in mining are presently scarce since mineral concentrate is exported instead of pro-cessed locally) and other resource-based sectors (particularly timber) by providing credit to national supplier firms and/or imposing local content requirements to raise the industrial sector's meager 10% share of GDP. But, on this matter, would the inexperienced minister of economics, moderate neoclassical economist Nicolás Grau (with a Ph.D. from the University of Pennsylvania), confront the maximum pushback from the mining transnationals and the timber barons?

A Miracle or a Mirage?

The frequent claim that Chile is a success for neoliberalism has rarely been chal-lenged. (See James M. Cypher, "Is Chile a Neoliberal Success?" *D&S*, September/October 2004.) Chile's great claim has been fleetingly glimpsed—during the "golden age" of 1991–1997 and during the China-driven commodities boom from 2004–2012 (which stalled in 2008–2009, leaving Chile flat). For the rest of the neo-liberal era up to the present (excluding the Covid-19 period of 2020–2021), growth has been weak or nil, especially since 2012. Average per capita GDP, adjusted for inflation, increased a miniscule US$88 per year (24 cents per day) in the entire period from 2013 to 2019! All these meager increases went to the top, leaving 90% of Chileans with a mirage.

The stage was set in the 1980s for the 1991–1997 boom when, under Pinochet's constitution, vast unmined mineral lands previously reserved for Chileans were turned over to transnational corporations that were avid for new copper reserves and employing emerging technologies that made mining extremely profitable from pro-cessing massive amounts of low-yield concentrates. Hard data are difficult to find, but there is little doubt that Pinochet, and later the *Concertación* governments, facil-itated one of the largest natural resources giveaways in history: From 1974 to 1999, 80% of all new copper reserves discovered and developed in the world were Chilean. According to Senator Jorge Lavandero, when Codelco, a state-owned copper min-ing company, was forced to sell off Chile's tremendous mineral reserves, they were paid virtually nothing—perhaps as low as 1% of true market value. When pri-vate companies had the new mining concessions in hand, between 1989 and 1994 Chilean copper production in the private sector increased by 197%, while Codelco's production declined by 9%. From 1995 to 1999, private sector transnational cor-porate output increased by another 165%. But, by 1997, the runaway mining boom had created a global-level, industry-wide overproduction depression that lasted until 2003. Then the dance began again—with China admitted into the World Trade Organization (WTO) in 2001, U.S. capital soon flooded into China to access cheap manufacturing labor; China then drove round after round of investments in mas-sive industrial complexes and infrastructure, requiring copper; the price of copper boomed, and Chile's economy moved ahead from 2003 until 2012, when break-neck investments in mining surpassed global absorption capacity; inevitably, prices crashed—as did Chile's "miracle."

So it goes when a nation is nothing but a commodity exporter—economists have known this boom-bust cycle for hundreds of years. No nation with any state capac-ity would allow such an erratic pattern to dictate the well-being of its citizens. But this is the point: Neoliberalism stands for the annihilation of state capacity and the end of proactive policies—subscribing only passivity as a national "strategy," which facilitates recurrent phases of hyperactivity and bleak doldrums. Chile's outsized surge in forestry production in the 1980s—another important factor explaining the seven fat years—also experienced inevitable cycles of boom, global overproduction, and bust. The *Concertación* governments created the illusion of state capacity when they finally passed—nearly a century too late—a royalty (but termed a "mining profit tax") on the mining industry in 2005. It is now, depending on the year applied, a pitiful 4–6% rate on *declared* profits: But the near absence of state capacity has facilitated the use of massive tax-evasion schemes—including accelerated depreciation (the fast write-off of capital equipment to avoid taxation, thus raising profits) and other chimeras, such as "transfer pricing" schemes that surreptitiously move profits abroad through fake invoices on imports and exports—all designed to hide actual profits and move them offshore. Such subterfuges allowed 44 of the 47

Oligarchic Conglomerate Capitalism

The secret of great fortunes without apparent cause is a crime forgotten, for it was properly done. —Honoré de Balzac, Le Père Goriot (1835)

Chile has long been internationally recognized for its munificent treatment of large foreign corporations, first in the nitrate fields of the North from 1880 to 1930—which then provided the bulk of government revenues and constituted the leading export sector—and subsequently in the world's richest copper mines. But nationalist rejection of these giveaway practices forced the government in 1961 to buy controlling interest in the Chuquicamata mine—then the largest open-pit copper mine in the world. The company that controlled the mine—U.S. transnational Anaconda Corp., which was owned by Rockefeller interests (formerly Guggenheim)—was expropriated. The mine was fully nationalized in 1971 under President Salvador Allende and has operated as part of a publicly owned company, Codelco, now the world's largest copper company, from 1976 onward.

In late 2019 a secret arrangement under which the Chilean military received a certain portion of Codelco's mining profits was rescinded: This arrangement explains how a giant state-owned company could continue to exist even as Pinochet avidly sold underpriced, publicly held mining concessions to the transnationals. Such concessions have no time limit and allow mining corporations to extract and ship valuable minerals abroad as they see fit. As a result of the relinquishment of these resources, by 2019 Codelco produced only 26% of all copper: Antofagasta Minerals, a private Chilean company, now produces 12% of the country's annual copper output, with the remaining 62% operated by 11 foreign-dominated companies including Anglo-Australian (BHP with a 25% share and Rio Tinto), Japanese (Sumitomo, Mitsui), U.S. (Freeport McMoran), British (Anglo-American), Swiss (Glencore), Canadian (Lundin, Los Andes Copper, Teck), and Mexican (Southern Copper).

Looking beyond copper, Chile's oligarchic elite—the 0.01% that seizes 10.1% of national income through a select number of large family-owned conglomerates—sets the tone and calls the tune, economically, socially, and politically.

private mines in Chile to often avoid *any* tax payments during the 1980s and 1990s, according to Senator Jorge Lavandero's testimony before the Chilean Senate in July 2001. The La Disputa mine, owned by Exxon from 1978 to 2002, *never* paid taxes. From 1995 to 2003, only two of the 10 largest mines ever paid any corporate taxes. Until recently, mining companies were exempt from any charges to clean up environmental waste at abandoned mines.

However, Chile used a variety of state subsidy/promotion programs—all violating the premises of neoliberalism—in the 1980s and 1990s to diversify exports into producing avocados, vegetables (e.g., asparagus), berries, salmon, and, famously, wine. This relocated output to export markets that would grow strongly as foreigners' incomes rose. But when Chile's China-induced economic expansion hit in 2003, Chile essentially reverted to a mono-export rentier strategy, selling all the unprocessed mineral concentrates the world market could take.

Boric's Program, 2022–2026

In 2021, noted Chilean economist Gabriel Palma submitted to the Senate Mining Commission a proposal to put the royalty rate on a graduated scale, arguing that when prices are very high, as they were in 2021, the royalty should be set at 22% per pound; now the state would be able to receive a relatively higher share of windfall profits, instead of allowing the mining companies to take all the relative gain. Most of the resulting outsized funds would *not* be used to fund social programs but rather to provide the basis for strategic promotion of a reindustrialization strategy (manufacturing employment fell by 33% from 1974 to 1983, and never recovered thereafter). Centered on supplying mining operations at both the technical level (engineering, etc.) and in producing parts for machinery and equipment, the copper sector holds the potential to spearhead national industry. Boric has pledged to address the deeply entrenched pacts between the public and private sector in the mining industry, while bolstering Codelco's now minor role—pushing now to process and refine concentrates at home, a step opposed by China. Between an increase in royalty payments and other tax increases on the mining sector, he anticipates collecting a whopping 2% of GDP—about $7 billion dollars. But that is not all—Boric has projected additional state incomes of 3.5% of GDP by tightening the weak enforcement of income tax rules plus another 2.5% of GDP flowing into state coffers by raising taxes on the top 10% who receive, according to Palma, 60% of national income.

With a leap in state spending power fueled by an additional 8% of GDP—a shift of monumental proportions—Boric would make education publicly funded and free. This would particularly enrage a considerable cadre who are in the lucrative "education" business. Pre-university schooling is roughly two-thirds privatized, while higher education, technical, and professional schools are overwhelmingly private, for-profit operations. As a result, as the World Bank found by comparing 22 national educational systems from 1980 to 2015, Chile's qualitative decline was highest. Only 29% of universities are public with, until recently, roughly 80% of their funding from non-state sources—with tuition averaging about one-half of median family income in 2015–2016. Since then, state scholarships and aid programs designed to assist low- and middle-income students have become available.

Such students face entrance exams biased against their weak public school training. These rare scholarships are inadequate—poor students amass debt to pay living costs. The long fight over education injustice culminated in three weeks of massive, unprecedented protests in 2019. Chile fell to its knees and Boric was vaunted into the foreground, and then the presidency, due to his protest leadership. The attempts by *Concertación* to take the roughest edges off the privatized educational system proved totally inadequate.

In addition, the privatized pension system has become a lightning rod. It has worked well for a few professionals who are now alarmed over Boric's plan to abandon it. For the vast majority of the 11 million trapped in this system, mostly low- and middle-income workers, retirement means an average payout of $200 per month—leaving them indigent. The pension system is hated more than any of the changes imposed by the Chicago Boys—which came from a reading of the 11th chapter of Friedman's *Capitalism and Freedom* where he attacked the U.S. Social Security system. Most of the economists involved in creating the privatized system had ties to the few companies (all controlled by the then-reigning conglomerates) that were designated by Pinochet in 1981 to be the only financial intermediaries allowed to administer workers' accounts. In 2021 the pension administrator companies cleared roughly $500 million in profit. But now the question becomes one of putting something like the U.S. Social Security system into place—meaning that employers would pay a significant share of the Social Security tax, instead of zero now, and the lucrative administrator companies would be forced out of business—all of this will be fought tooth and nail.

And, finally, Boric's program to create the conditions for some reindustrialization—weaning the economy from the crazy gyrations of the commodities markets—will run straight into the power bloc of the peak business association—the CPC. The agribusiness, mining, and manufacturing associations that comprise the CPC know all the arguments against commodity dependence, which may be surprising. But, and this is the most important point of all, they will fight with all their considerable power—alongside their allies in transnational corporations who are totally unfazed by Boric—to block any shift toward reindustrialization because it means jobs for skilled workers and that means unions. The imperious business class is not about to share one iota of their power with unions, however meek. At its core, *this* is the struggle in Chile—for the oligarchy there is no alternative to commodity exports because the extractivist economy can operate without much direct labor (but instead with lots of imported machinery). High-paid jobs in mining employ only 3% of workers, leaving all others to compete for scarce jobs, condemning most to precarious, non-union, non-industrial, low-wage service work. Reindustrialization, more than any other issue, is the one that Boric needs to systematically address. ❑

Sources: José Miguel Ahumada, *The Political Economy of PoliPeripheral Growth: Chile in the Global Economy* (Palgrave Macmillan, 2019); Gabriel Boric and José Ahumada, "Propuestas para un nuevo modelo de desarrollo post crisis económica" ("Proposals for a new post-economic-development model"), 2021 (desarrollojustoysostenible.cl); James Cypher, "The Political Economy of the Chilean State," *Canadian Journal of Development Studies*, 2005; Jason Delisle and Andrés

Bernasconi, "Lessons from Chile's Transition to Free College," Brookings: Evidence Speaks Reports, March 15, 2018 (brookings.edu); Camille Erickson and Kip Keen, "Chile's mining industry unfazed by leftist Gabriel Boric's victory" S&P Global Market Intelligence, December 21, 2021 (spglobal.com); Tasha Fairfield, *Private Wealth and Public Revenue in Latin America* (Cambridge University Press, 2015); Intergovernmental Forum on Mining, Minerals, Metals and Sustainable Development, Chile: National Capacity, 2018 (iisd.org); Jorge Lavandero Illanes, *El cobre NO, es de Chile* (Ediciones Tierra Mía, 2001); Mariana Marusic, Julio Nahuelhual, and Olga Bustamante, "Chile Vamos y economistas celebran el nombramiento de Rosanna Costa en la presidencia del Banco Central" La Tercera, February 3, 2022 (latercera.com); Matías Menceyra, "Gobierno, Convención, Congreso: Las redes de LyD," *Interferencia*, April 25, 2021 (interferencia. cl); María Mönckeberg, *El Saqueo de los Grupos Económicos al Estado Chileno* (Ediciones B, 2001); Gabriel Palma, "El royalty como eje de una nueva estrategia productiva" *Ciper*, September 8, 2021 (ciphervhile.cl); David Sauvé, "Derogación de la Ley del Cobre: nuevas oportunidades," *El Mostrador*, September 22, 2021 (elmostrador.cl); Ignacio Schiappacasse and Carlos Tromben, "Más allá de José Piñera: Los verdaderos padres del actual sistema de pensiones chileno," *Interferencia*, May 8, 2020 (interferencia.cl).

CONTRIBUTORS

Frank Ackerman was the principal economist at Synapse Energy Economics and one of the founders of *Dollars & Sense*. He died in July 2019.

Francisco J. Aldape has a Ph.D. in economics from The New School and teaches at the Borough of Manhattan Community College and St. John's University.

Gar Alperovitz is a professor of political economy at the University of Maryland and co-author, with Lew Daly, of *Unjust Deserts: How the Rich Are Taking Our Common Inheritance and Why We Should Take It Back* (New Press, 2009).

Michael Ash is an associate professor of economics at the University of Massachusetts-Amherst.

Bill Barclay is a member of the Chicago Political Economy Group and a member of the Ventura County, Calif. chapter of Democratic Socialists of America (DSA). He worked for more than two decades in financial services.

Peter Barnes, co-founder of Working Assets, is a senior fellow at the Tomales Bay Institute.

Stephen Barton is on the board of the Bay Area Community Land Trust and was housing director for the City of Berkeley and deputy director of the Berkeley Rent Stabilization Program.

Martin J. Bennett is instructor emeritus of history at Santa Rosa Junior College and a research and policy associate for UNITE HERE Local 2850.

Sarah Blaskey is a reporter for the *Miami Herald* and co-author of *The Grifter's Club: Trump, Mar-a-Lago, and the Selling of the Presidency* (Public Affairs, 2020).

James K. Boyce is a professor of economics at the University of Massachusetts-Amherst and co-director of the Political Economy Research Institute (PERI) Program on Development, Peacebuilding, and the Environment.

Marc Breslow is co-chair of the Massachusetts Climate Action Network and a former *Dollars & Sense* collective member.

Sasha Breger Bush is a lecturer at the Josef Korbel School of International Studies at the University of Denver and author of *Derivatives and Development: A Political Economy of Global Finance, Farming, and Poverty* (Palgrave Macmillan, 2012).

Al Campbell is a professor emeritus of economics at the University of Utah.

Ying Chen is an assistant professor of economics at the New School for Social Research.

Mateo Crossa is a Ph.D. candidate in the doctoral program in Development Studies, Universidad Autónoma de Zacatecas, Mexico.

James M. Cypher is a professor of economics in the Doctoral Program in Development Studies, Universidad Autónoma de Zacatecas, Mexico.

Lew Daly is a senior fellow at Demos and co-author, with Gar Alperovitz, of *Unjust Deserts: How the Rich Are Taking Our Common Inheritance and Why We Should Take It Back* (New Press, 2009).

Ann Davis is a professor of economics at Marist College.

Cory Doctorow is a science fiction author, activist, journalist, and blogger.

Marie Christine Duggan holds a Ph.D. in economics and is professor of business management at Keene State College in New Hampshire.

David Fields teaches economics at the University of Utah.

Deborah M. Figart is a professor or education and economics at the Richard Stockton College of New Jersey.

Nancy Folbre is a professor emerita of economics at the University of Massachusetts-Amherst. She contributes regularly to the *New York Times* Economix blog.

Ellen Frank teaches economics at the University of Massachusetts-Boston and is a *Dollars & Sense* Associate.

Gerald Friedman is a professor of economics at the University of Massachusetts-Amherst.

Phil Gasper teaches at Madison College and wrote the "Critical Thinking" column for *International Socialist Review*.

Armağan Gezici (co-editor of this volume) is senior lecturer in economics at the University of the West of England, Bristol.

Lisa Heinzerling is a professor of law at Georgetown University Law School, specializing in environmental law.

Edward Herman was an economist and co-author of *The Global Media: The New Missionaries of Corporate Capitalism* (Cassell, 1998).

Eoin Higgins is a journalist based in New England. His work has appeared in publications around the country and around the world.

Michelle Holder is an associate professor of economics at John Jay College, part of the City University of New York.

Güney Işikara is a clinical assistant professor at New York University's Liberal Studies program.

Tim Koechlin, an economist, teaches International Studies and Urban Studies at Vassar College. He is director of Vassar's International Studies Program.

Rob Larson (co-editor of this volume) is a professor of economics at Tacoma Community College and author of *Bit Tyrants: The Political Economy of Silicon Valley*, which came out in February 2020 from Haymarket Books.

Arthur MacEwan, a *Dollars & Sense* Associate, is professor emeritus of economics at the University of Massachusetts-Boston.

John Miller, a *Dollars & Sense* collective member, teaches economics at Wheaton College.

Jawied Nawabi is a professor of economics and sociology at CUNY Bronx Community College and a member of the *Dollars & Sense* collective.

Jeff Nesbit is the author of Poison Tea, which exposed for the first time the close ties between the tobacco industry and Koch donor network front groups. He once helped lead efforts by the FDA to regulate cigarettes.

Débora Nunes is a graduate teaching instructor and Ph.D. student at Colorado State University. She received a bachelor's degree and a master's degree in economics from the Federal University of Rio Grande do Sul (UFRGS), Brazil.

Naomi Oreskes is a science historian at Harvard University, and the author of several books, including *Merchants of Doubt* and *Why Trust Science?*

Robert Ovetz is a senior lecturer in political science at San José State University, labor scholar, and organizer. He is the author of the forthcoming *We the Elite: How the U.S. Constitution Serves the Few* (Pluto, 2022).

Thomas Palley is an economist who has held positions at the AFL-CIO, Open Society Institute, and the U.S./China Economic and Security Review Commission.

Paddy Quick is a professor emerita of economics at St. Francis College.

Jared Ragusett teaches economics at Central Connecticut University.

Alejandro Reuss is an economist and historian and the former co-editor of *Dollars & Sense*.

Helen Scharber is an assistant professor of economics at Hampshire College.

Geoff Schneider is a professor of economics at Bucknell University.

Juliet Schor is a professor of sociology at Boston College and the author of *The Overworked American* (Basic Books, 1993), and *Plenitude* (Penguin Press, 2010).

Zoe Sherman is a member of the *Dollars & Sense* collective and is an associate professor of economics at Merrimack College.

Heidi Shierholz is a senior economist at the Economic Policy Institute.

Bryan Snyder (co-editor of this volume) is a senior lecturer in economics at Bentley University.

Chris Sturr (co-editor of this volume) is co-editor of *Dollars & Sense* and a lecturer in the Social Studies program at Harvard University.

Chris Tilly is a *Dollars & Sense* Associate and director of UCLA's Institute for Research on Labor and Employment and professor in the Urban Planning Department.

Marc Triller is a graduate student in economics at The New School and a member of the *Dollars & Sense* Writing Workshop.

Ramaa Vasudevan teaches economics at Colorado State University and is a *Dollars & Sense* Associate.

Klara Zwickl is a post-doctoral researcher at the Vienna University of Economics and Business.